HBase: The Definitive Guide

Lars George

Beijing · Cambridge · Farnham · Köln · Sebastopol · Tokyo

HBase: The Definitive Guide

by Lars George

Copyright © 2011 Lars George. All rights reserved.
Printed in the United States of America.

Published by O'Reilly Media, Inc., 1005 Gravenstein Highway North, Sebastopol, CA 95472.

O'Reilly books may be purchased for educational, business, or sales promotional use. Online editions are also available for most titles (*http://my.safaribooksonline.com*). For more information, contact our corporate/institutional sales department: (800) 998-9938 or *corporate@oreilly.com*.

Editors:	Mike Loukides and Julie Steele	**Indexer:**	Angela Howard
Production Editor:	Jasmine Perez	**Cover Designer:**	Karen Montgomery
Copyeditor:	Audrey Doyle	**Interior Designer:**	David Futato
Proofreader:	Jasmine Perez	**Illustrator:**	Robert Romano

Printing History:

September 2011:   First Edition.

ISBN: 978-1-449-39610-7

[LSI]

1314322884

For my wife Katja, my daughter Laura, and son Leon. I love you!

Table of Contents

Foreword

The HBase story begins in 2006, when the San Francisco-based startup Powerset was trying to build a natural language search engine for the Web. Their indexing pipeline was an involved multistep process that produced an index about two orders of magnitude larger, on average, than your standard term-based index. The datastore that they'd built on top of the then nascent Amazon Web Services to hold the index intermediaries and the webcrawl was buckling under the load (Ring. Ring. "Hello! This is AWS. Whatever you are running, please turn it off!"). They were looking for an alternative. The Google BigTable paper[*] had just been published.

Chad Walters, Powerset's head of engineering at the time, reflects back on the experience as follows:

> Building an open source system to run on top of Hadoop's Distributed Filesystem (HDFS) in much the same way that BigTable ran on top of the Google File System seemed like a good approach because: 1) it was a proven scalable architecture; 2) we could leverage existing work on Hadoop's HDFS; and 3) we could both contribute to and get additional leverage from the growing Hadoop ecosystem.

After the publication of the Google BigTable paper, there were on-again, off-again discussions around what a BigTable-like system on top of Hadoop might look. Then, in early 2007, out of the blue, Mike Cafarela dropped a tarball of thirty odd Java files into the Hadoop issue tracker: "I've written some code for HBase, a BigTable-like file store. It's not perfect, but it's ready for other people to play with and examine." Mike had been working with Doug Cutting on Nutch, an open source search engine. He'd done similar drive-by code dumps there to add features such as a Google File System clone so the Nutch indexing process was not bounded by the amount of disk you attach to a single machine. (This Nutch distributed filesystem would later grow up to be HDFS.)

Jim Kellerman of Powerset took Mike's dump and started filling in the gaps, adding tests and getting it into shape so that it could be committed as part of Hadoop. The first commit of the HBase code was made by Doug Cutting on April 3, 2007, under

---

[*] "BigTable: A Distributed Storage System for Structured Data" (*http://labs.google.com/papers/bigtable.html*) by Fay Chang et al.

the *contrib* subdirectory. The first HBase "working" release was bundled as part of Hadoop 0.15.0 in October 2007.

Not long after, Lars, the author of the book you are now reading, showed up on the #hbase IRC channel. He had a big-data problem of his own, and was game to try HBase. After some back and forth, Lars became one of the first users to run HBase in production outside of the Powerset home base. Through many ups and downs, Lars stuck around. I distinctly remember a directory listing Lars made for me a while back on his production cluster at WorldLingo, where he was employed as CTO, sysadmin, and grunt. The listing showed ten or so HBase releases from Hadoop 0.15.1 (November 2007) on up through HBase 0.20, each of which he'd run on his 40-node cluster at one time or another during production.

Of all those who have contributed to HBase over the years, it is poetic justice that Lars is the one to write this book. Lars was always dogging HBase contributors that the documentation needed to be better if we hoped to gain broader adoption. Everyone agreed, nodded their heads in ascent, amen'd, and went back to coding. So Lars started writing critical how-tos and architectural descriptions inbetween jobs and his intra-European travels as unofficial HBase European ambassador. His Lineland blogs on HBase (*http://www.larsgeorge.com*) gave the best description, outside of the source, of how HBase worked, and at a few critical junctures, carried the community across awkward transitions (e.g., an important blog explained the labyrinthian HBase build during the brief period we thought an Ivy-based build to be a "good idea"). His luscious diagrams were poached by one and all wherever an HBase presentation was given.

HBase has seen some interesting times, including a period of sponsorship by Microsoft, of all things. Powerset was acquired in July 2008, and after a couple of months during which Powerset employees were disallowed from contributing while Microsoft's legal department vetted the HBase codebase to see if it impinged on SQLServer patents, we were allowed to resume contributing (I was a Microsoft employee working near full time on an Apache open source project). The times ahead look promising, too, whether it's the variety of contortions HBase is being put through at Facebook—as the underpinnings for their massive Facebook mail app or fielding millions of of hits a second on their analytics clusters—or more deploys along the lines of Yahoo!'s 1k node HBase cluster used to host their snapshot of Microsoft's Bing crawl. Other developments include HBase running on filesystems other than Apache HDFS, such as MapR.

But plain to me though is that none of these developments would have been possible were it not for the hard work put in by our awesome HBase community driven by a core of HBase committers. Some members of the core have only been around a year or so—Todd Lipcon, Gary Helmling, and Nicolas Spiegelberg—and we would be lost without them, but a good portion have been there from close to project inception and have shaped HBase into the (scalable) general datastore that it is today. These include Jonathan Gray, who gambled his startup streamy.com on HBase; Andrew Purtell, who built an HBase team at Trend Micro long before such a thing was fashionable; Ryan Rawson, who got StumbleUpon—which became the main sponsor after HBase moved on from Powerset/Microsoft—on board, and who had the sense to hire John-Daniel Cryans, now a power contributor but just a bushy-tailed student at the time. And then there is Lars, who during the bug fixes, was always about documenting how it all worked. Of those of us who know HBase, there is no better man qualified to write this first, critical HBase book.

—Michael Stack, HBase Project Janitor

Preface

You may be reading this book for many reasons. It could be because you heard all about *Hadoop* and what it can do to crunch petabytes of data in a reasonable amount of time. While reading into Hadoop you found that, for random access to the accumulated data, there is something called *HBase*. Or it was the hype that is prevalent these days addressing a new kind of data storage architecture. It strives to solve large-scale data problems where traditional solutions may be either too involved or cost-prohibitive. A common term used in this area is *NoSQL*.

No matter how you have arrived here, I presume you want to know and learn—like I did not too long ago—how you can use HBase in your company or organization to store a virtually endless amount of data. You may have a background in relational database theory or you want to start fresh and this "column-oriented thing" is something that seems to fit your bill. You also heard that HBase can scale without much effort, and that alone is reason enough to look at it since you are building the next web-scale system.

I was at that point in late 2007 when I was facing the task of storing millions of documents in a system that needed to be fault-tolerant and scalable while still being maintainable by just me. I had decent skills in managing a MySQL database system, and was using the database to store data that would ultimately be served to our website users. This database was running on a single server, with another as a backup. The issue was that it would not be able to hold the amount of data I needed to store for this new project. I would have to either invest in serious RDBMS scalability skills, or find something else instead.

Obviously, I took the latter route, and since my mantra always was (and still is) "How does someone like Google do it?" I came across Hadoop. After a few attempts to use Hadoop directly, I was faced with implementing a random access layer on top of it—but that problem had been solved already: in 2006, Google had published a paper titled "Bigtable"* and the Hadoop developers had an open source implementation of it called HBase (the *Hadoop* Data*base*). That was the answer to all my problems. Or so it seemed...

---

* See *http://labs.google.com/papers/bigtable-osdi06.pdf* for reference.

These days, I try not to think about how difficult my first experience with Hadoop and HBase was. Looking back, I realize that I would have wished for this customer project to start today. HBase is now mature, nearing a 1.0 release, and is used by many high-profile companies, such as Facebook, Adobe, Twitter, Yahoo!, Trend Micro, and StumbleUpon (as per *http://wiki.apache.org/hadoop/Hbase/PoweredBy*). Mine was one of the very first clusters in production (and is still in use today!) and my use case triggered a few very interesting issues (let me refrain from saying more).

But that was to be expected, betting on a 0.1x version of a community project. And I had the opportunity over the years to contribute back and stay close to the development team so that eventually I was humbled by being asked to become a full-time committer as well.

I learned a lot over the past few years from my fellow HBase developers and am still learning more every day. My belief is that we are nowhere near the peak of this technology and it will evolve further over the years to come. Let me pay my respect to the entire HBase community with this book, which strives to cover not just the internal workings of HBase or how to get it going, but more specifically, how to apply it to your use case.

In fact, I strongly assume that this is why you are here right now. You want to learn how HBase can solve *your* problem. Let me help you try to figure this out.

General Information

Before we get started, here a few general notes.

HBase Version

While writing this book, I decided to cover what will eventually be released as 0.92.0, and what is currently developed in the trunk of the official repository (*http://svn.apache .org/viewvc/hbase/trunk/*) under the early access release 0.91.0-SNAPSHOT.

Since it was not possible to follow the frantic development pace of HBase, and because the book had a deadline before 0.92.0 was released, the book could not document anything after a specific revision: 1130916 (*http://svn.apache.org/viewvc/hbase/trunk/ ?pathrev=1130916*). When you find that something does not seem correct between what is written here and what HBase offers, you can use the aforementioned revision number to compare all changes that have been applied *after* this book went into print.

I have made every effort to update the *JDiff* (a tool to compare different revisions of a software project) documentation on the book's website at *http://www.hbasebook .com*. You can use it to quickly see what is different.

Building the Examples

The examples you will see throughout this book can be found in full detail in the publicly available GitHub repository at *http://github.com/larsgeorge/hbase-book*. For the sake of brevity, they are usually printed only in parts here, to focus on the important bits, and to avoid repeating the same boilerplate code over and over again.

The name of an example matches the filename in the repository, so it should be easy to find your way through. Each chapter has its own subdirectory to make the separation more intuitive. If you are reading, for instance, an example in Chapter 3, you can go to the matching directory in the source repository and find the full source code there.

Many examples use internal helpers for convenience, such as the `HBaseHelper` class, to set up a test environment for reproducible results. You can modify the code to create different scenarios, or introduce faulty data and see how the feature showcased in the example behaves. Consider the code a petri dish for your own experiments.

Building the code requires a few auxiliary command-line tools:

Java

> HBase is written in Java, so you do need to have Java set up for it to work. "Java" on page 46 has the details on how this affects the installation. For the examples, you also need Java on the workstation you are using to run them.

Git

> The repository is hosted by GitHub, an online service that supports *Git*—a distributed revision control system, created originally for the Linux kernel development.[†] There are many binary packages that can be used on all major operating systems to install the Git command-line tools required.

> Alternatively, you can download a static snapshot of the entire archive using the GitHub download (*https://github.com/larsgeorge/hbase-book/archives/master*) link.

Maven

> The build system for the book's repository is Apache Maven.[‡] It uses the so-called *Project Object Model* (POM) to describe what is needed to build a software project. You can download Maven from its website and also find installation instructions there.

Once you have gathered the basic tools required for the example code, you can build the project like so:

```
~$ cd /tmp
/tmp$ git clone git://github.com/larsgeorge/hbase-book.git
Initialized empty Git repository in /tmp/hbase-book/.git/
remote: Counting objects: 420, done.
```

---

† See the project's website (*http://git-scm.com/*) for details.

‡ See the project's website (*http://maven.apache.org/*) for details.

```
remote: Compressing objects: 100% (252/252), done.
remote: Total 420 (delta 159), reused 144 (delta 58)
Receiving objects: 100% (420/420), 70.87 KiB, done.
Resolving deltas: 100% (159/159), done.
/tmp$ cd hbase-book/
/tmp/hbase-book$ mvn package
[INFO] Scanning for projects...
[INFO] Reactor build order:
[INFO]   HBase Book
[INFO]   HBase Book Chapter 3
[INFO]   HBase Book Chapter 4
[INFO]   HBase Book Chapter 5
[INFO]   HBase Book Chapter 6
[INFO]   HBase Book Chapter 11
[INFO]   HBase URL Shortener
[INFO] ------------------------------------------------------------------------
[INFO] Building HBase Book
[INFO]    task-segment: [package]
[INFO] ------------------------------------------------------------------------
[INFO] [site:attach-descriptor {execution: default-attach-descriptor}]
[INFO] ------------------------------------------------------------------------
[INFO] Building HBase Book Chapter 3
[INFO]    task-segment: [package]
[INFO] ------------------------------------------------------------------------
[INFO] [resources:resources {execution: default-resources}]
...
[INFO] ------------------------------------------------------------------------
[INFO] Reactor Summary:
[INFO] ------------------------------------------------------------------------
[INFO] HBase Book ............................................. SUCCESS [1.601s]
[INFO] HBase Book Chapter 3 ................................... SUCCESS [3.233s]
[INFO] HBase Book Chapter 4 ................................... SUCCESS [0.589s]
[INFO] HBase Book Chapter 5 ................................... SUCCESS [0.162s]
[INFO] HBase Book Chapter 6 ................................... SUCCESS [1.354s]
[INFO] HBase Book Chapter 11 ................................. SUCCESS [0.271s]
[INFO] HBase URL Shortener ................................... SUCCESS [4.910s]
[INFO] ------------------------------------------------------------------------
[INFO] ------------------------------------------------------------------------
[INFO] BUILD SUCCESSFUL
[INFO] ------------------------------------------------------------------------
[INFO] Total time: 12 seconds
[INFO] Finished at: Mon Jun 20 17:08:30 CEST 2011
[INFO] Final Memory: 35M/81M
[INFO] ------------------------------------------------------------------------
```

This *clones*—which means it is downloading the repository to your local workstation—
the source code and subsequently *compiles* it. You are left with a *Java archive file* (also
called a *JAR* file) in the *target* directory in each of the subdirectories, that is, one for
each chapter of the book that has source code examples:

```
/tmp/hbase-book$ ls -l ch04/target/
total 152
drwxr-xr-x  48 larsgeorge  wheel   1632 Apr 15 10:31 classes
drwxr-xr-x   3 larsgeorge  wheel    102 Apr 15 10:31 generated-sources
```

```
-rw-r--r--   1 larsgeorge  wheel  75754 Apr 15 10:31 hbase-book-ch04-1.0.jar
drwxr-xr-x   3 larsgeorge  wheel    102 Apr 15 10:31 maven-archiver
```

In this case, the *hbase-book-ch04-1.0.jar* file contains the compiled examples for Chapter 4. Assuming you have a running installation of HBase, you can then run each of the included classes using the supplied command-line script:

```
/tmp/hbase-book$ cd ch04/
/tmp/hbase-book/ch04$ bin/run.sh client.PutExample
/tmp/hbase-book/ch04$ bin/run.sh client.GetExample
Value: val1
```

The supplied *bin/run.sh* helps to assemble the required Java *classpath*, adding the dependent JAR files to it.

Hush: The HBase URL Shortener

Looking at each feature HBase offers separately is a good way to understand what it does. The book uses code examples that set up a very specific set of tables, which contain an equally specific set of data. This makes it easy to understand what is given and how a certain operation changes the data from the before to the after state. You can execute every example yourself to replicate the outcome, and it should match exactly with what is described in the accompanying book section. You can also modify the examples to explore the discussed feature even further—and you can use the supplied helper classes to create your own set of proof-of-concept examples.

Yet, sometimes it is important to see all the features working in concert to make the final leap of understanding their full potential. For this, the book uses a single, real-world example to showcase most of the features HBase has to offer. The book also uses the example to explain advanced concepts that come with this different storage territory—compared to more traditional RDBMS-based systems.

The fully working application is called *Hush*—short for *HBase URL Shortener*. Many services on the Internet offer this kind of service. Simply put, you hand in a URL—for example, for a web page—and you get a much shorter link back. This link can then be used in places where real estate is at a premium: Twitter only allows you to send messages with a maximum length of 140 characters. URLs can be up to 4,096 bytes long; hence there is a need to reduce that length to something around 20 bytes instead, leaving you more space for the actual message.

For example, here is the Google Maps URL used to reference Sebastopol, California:

```
http://maps.google.com/maps?f=q&source=s_q&hl=en&geocode=&q=Sebastopol, \
+CA,+United+States&aq=0&sll=47.85931,10.85165&sspn=0.93616,1.345825&ie=UTF8& \
hq=&hnear=Sebastopol,+Sonoma,+California&z=14
```

Running this through a URL shortener like Hush results in the following URL:

```
http://hush.li/1337
```

Obviously, this is much shorter, and easier to copy into an email or send through a restricted medium, like Twitter or SMS.

But this service is not simply a large lookup table. Granted, popular services in this area have hundreds of millions of entries mapping short to long URLs. But there is more to it. Users want to shorten specific URLs and also track their usage: how often has a short URL been used? A shortener service should retain counters for every shortened URL to report how often they have been clicked.

More advanced features are vanity URLs that can use specific domain names, and/or custom short URL IDs, as opposed to auto-generated ones, as in the preceding example. Users must be able to log in to create their own short URLs, track their existing ones, and see reports for the daily, weekly, or monthly usage.

All of this is realized in Hush, and you can easily compile and run it on your own server. It uses a wide variety of HBase features, and it is mentioned, where appropriate, throughout this book, showing how a newly discussed topic is used in a production-type application.

While you could create your own user account and get started with Hush, it is also a great example of how to import legacy data from, for example, a previous system. To emulate this use case, the book makes use of a freely available data set on the Internet: the Delicious RSS feed. There are a few sets that were made available by individuals, and can be downloaded by anyone.

Use Case: Hush

Be on the lookout for boxes like this throughout the book. Whenever possible, such boxes support the explained features with examples from Hush. Many will also include example code, but often such code is kept very simple to showcase the feature at hand. The data is also set up so that you can repeatedly make sense of the functionality (even though the examples may be a bit academic). Using Hush as a use case more closely mimics what you would implement in a production system.

Hush is actually built to scale out of the box. It might not have the prettiest interface, but that is not what it should prove. You can run many Hush servers behind a load balancer and serve thousands of requests with no difficulties.

The snippets extracted from Hush show you how the feature is used in context, and since it is part of the publicly available repository accompanying the book, you have the full source available as well. Run it yourself, tweak it, and learn all about it!

Running Hush

Building and running Hush is as easy as building the example code. Once you have cloned—or downloaded—the book repository, and executed

```
$ mvn package
```

to build the entire project, you can start Hush with the included start script:

```
$ hush/bin/start-hush.sh
======================
 Starting Hush...
======================
 INFO [main] (HushMain.java:57) - Initializing HBase
 INFO [main] (HushMain.java:60) - Creating/updating HBase schema
 ...
 INFO [main] (HushMain.java:90) - Web server setup.
 INFO [main] (HushMain.java:111) - Configuring security.
 INFO [main] (Slf4jLog.java:55) - jetty-7.3.1.v20110307
 INFO [main] (Slf4jLog.java:55) - started ...
 INFO [main] (Slf4jLog.java:55) - Started SelectChannelConnector@0.0.0.0:8080
```

After the last log message is output on the console, you can navigate your browser to *http://localhost:8080* to access your local Hush server.

Stopping the server requires a Ctrl-C to abort the start script. As all data is saved on the HBase cluster accessed remotely by Hush, this is safe to do.

Conventions Used in This Book

The following typographical conventions are used in this book:

Italic
> Indicates new terms, URLs, email addresses, filenames, file extensions, and Unix commands

`Constant width`
> Used for program listings, as well as within paragraphs to refer to program elements such as variable or function names, databases, data types, environment variables, statements, and keywords

`Constant width bold`
> Shows commands or other text that should be typed literally by the user

`Constant width italic`
> Shows text that should be replaced with user-supplied values or by values determined by context

This icon signifies a tip, suggestion, or general note.

 This icon indicates a warning or caution.

Using Code Examples

This book is here to help you get your job done. In general, you may use the code in this book in your programs and documentation. You do not need to contact us for permission unless you're reproducing a significant portion of the code. For example, writing a program that uses several chunks of code from this book does not require permission. Selling or distributing a CD-ROM of examples from O'Reilly books does require permission. Answering a question by citing this book and quoting example code does not require permission. Incorporating a significant amount of example code from this book into your product's documentation does require permission.

We appreciate, but do not require, attribution. An attribution usually includes the title, author, publisher, and ISBN. For example: "*HBase: The Definitive Guide* by Lars George (O'Reilly). Copyright 2011 Lars George, 978-1-449-39610-7."

If you feel your use of code examples falls outside fair use or the permission given here, feel free to contact us at *permissions@oreilly.com*.

Safari® Books Online

 Safari Books Online is an on-demand digital library that lets you easily search over 7,500 technology and creative reference books and videos to find the answers you need quickly.

With a subscription, you can read any page and watch any video from our library online. Read books on your cell phone and mobile devices. Access new titles before they are available for print, and get exclusive access to manuscripts in development and post feedback for the authors. Copy and paste code samples, organize your favorites, download chapters, bookmark key sections, create notes, print out pages, and benefit from tons of other time-saving features.

O'Reilly Media has uploaded this book to the Safari Books Online service. To have full digital access to this book and others on similar topics from O'Reilly and other publishers, sign up for free at *http://my.safaribooksonline.com*.

How to Contact Us

Please address comments and questions concerning this book to the publisher:

O'Reilly Media, Inc.
1005 Gravenstein Highway North
Sebastopol, CA 95472
800-998-9938 (in the United States or Canada)
707-829-0515 (international or local)
707-829-0104 (fax)

We have a web page for this book, where we list errata, examples, and any additional information. You can access this page at:

http://www.oreilly.com/catalog/9781449396107

The author also has a site for this book at:

http://www.hbasebook.com/

To comment or ask technical questions about this book, send email to:

bookquestions@oreilly.com

For more information about our books, courses, conferences, and news, see our website at *http://www.oreilly.com.*

Find us on Facebook: *http://facebook.com/oreilly*

Follow us on Twitter: *http://twitter.com/oreillymedia*

Watch us on YouTube: *http://www.youtube.com/oreillymedia*

Acknowledgments

I first want to thank my late dad, Reiner, and my mother, Ingrid, who supported me and my aspirations all my life. You were the ones to make me a better person.

Writing this book was only possible with the support of the entire HBase community. Without that support, there would be no HBase, nor would it be as successful as it is today in production at companies all around the world. The relentless and seemingly tireless support given by the core committers as well as contributors and the community at large on IRC, the Mailing List, and in blog posts is the essence of what open source stands for. I stand tall on your shoulders!

Thank you to the committers, who included, as of this writing, Jean-Daniel Cryans, Jonathan Gray, Gary Helmling, Todd Lipcon, Andrew Purtell, Ryan Rawson, Nicolas Spiegelberg, Michael Stack, and Ted Yu; and to the emeriti, Mike Cafarella, Bryan Duxbury, and Jim Kellerman.

I would also like to thank the book's reviewers: Patrick Angeles, Doug Balog, Jeff Bean, Po Cheung, Jean-Daniel Cryans, Lars Francke, Gary Helmling, Michael Katzenellenbogen, Mingjie Lai, Todd Lipcon, Ming Ma, Doris Maassen, Cameron Martin, Matt Massie, Doug Meil, Manuel Meßner, Claudia Nielsen, Joseph Pallas, Josh Patterson, Andrew Purtell, Tim Robertson, Paul Rogalinski, Joep Rottinghuis, Stefan Rudnitzki, Eric Sammer, Michael Stack, and Suraj Varma.

I would like to extend a heartfelt thank you to all the contributors to HBase; you know who you are. Every single patch you have contributed brought us here. Please keep contributing!

Finally, I would like to thank Cloudera, my employer, which generously granted me time away from customers so that I could write this book.

## CHAPTER 1

Introduction

Before we start looking into all the moving parts of HBase, let us pause to think about why there was a need to come up with yet another storage architecture. Relational database management systems (RDBMSes) have been around since the early 1970s, and have helped countless companies and organizations to implement their solution to given problems. And they are equally helpful today. There are many use cases for which the relational model makes perfect sense. Yet there also seem to be specific problems that do not fit this model very well.[*]

The Dawn of Big Data

We live in an era in which we are all connected over the Internet and expect to find results instantaneously, whether the question concerns the best turkey recipe or what to buy mom for her birthday. We also expect the results to be useful and tailored to our needs.

Because of this, companies have become focused on delivering more targeted information, such as recommendations or online ads, and their ability to do so directly influences their success as a business. Systems like *Hadoop*[†] now enable them to gather and process petabytes of data, and the need to collect even more data continues to increase with, for example, the development of new machine learning algorithms.

Where previously companies had the liberty to ignore certain data sources because there was no cost-effective way to store all that information, they now are likely to lose out to the competition. There is an increasing need to store and analyze every data point

---

[*] See, for example, "'One Size Fits All': An Idea Whose Time Has Come and Gone" (*http://www.cs.brown.edu/~ugur/fits_all.pdf*) by Michael Stonebraker and Uğur Çetintemel.

[†] Information can be found on the project's website (*http://hadoop.apache.org/*). Please also see the excellent *Hadoop: The Definitive Guide (http://oreilly.com/catalog/9781449389734)* (Second Edition) by Tom White (O'Reilly) for everything you want to know about Hadoop.

they generate. The results then feed directly back into their e-commerce platforms and may generate even more data.

In the past, the only option to retain all the collected data was to prune it to, for example, retain the last N days. While this is a viable approach in the short term, it lacks the opportunities that having all the data, which may have been collected for months or years, offers: you can build mathematical models that span the entire time range, or amend an algorithm to perform better and rerun it with all the previous data.

Dr. Ralph Kimball, for example, states[‡] that

> Data assets are [a] major component of the balance sheet, replacing traditional physical assets of the 20th century

and that there is a

> Widespread recognition of the value of data even beyond traditional enterprise boundaries

Google and Amazon are prominent examples of companies that realized the value of data and started developing solutions to fit their needs. For instance, in a series of technical publications, Google described a scalable storage and processing system based on commodity hardware. These ideas were then implemented outside of Google as part of the open source Hadoop project: *HDFS* and *MapReduce*.

Hadoop excels at storing data of arbitrary, semi-, or even unstructured formats, since it lets you decide how to interpret the data at analysis time, allowing you to change the way you classify the data at any time: once you have updated the algorithms, you simply run the analysis again.

Hadoop also complements existing database systems of almost any kind. It offers a limitless pool into which one can sink data and still pull out what is needed when the time is right. It is optimized for large file storage and batch-oriented, streaming access. This makes analysis easy and fast, but users also need access to the final data, not in batch mode but using random access—this is akin to a full table scan versus using indexes in a database system.

We are used to querying databases when it comes to random access for structured data. RDBMSes are the most prominent, but there are also quite a few specialized variations and implementations, like object-oriented databases. Most RDBMSes strive to implement *Codd's 12 rules*,[§] which forces them to comply to very rigid requirements. The

---

[‡] The quotes are from a presentation titled "Rethinking EDW in the Era of Expansive Information Management" by Dr. Ralph Kimball, of the Kimball Group, available at *http://www.informatica.com/campaigns/rethink_edw_kimball.pdf*. It discusses the changing needs of an evolving *enterprise data warehouse* market.

[§] Edgar F. Codd defined 13 rules (numbered from 0 to 12), which define what is required from a *database management system* (DBMS) to be considered *relational*. While HBase does fulfill the more generic rules, it fails on others, most importantly, on rule 5: *the comprehensive data sublanguage rule*, defining the support for at least one *relational* language. See Codd's 12 rules (*http://en.wikipedia.org/wiki/Codd's_12_rules*) on Wikipedia.

architecture used underneath is well researched and has not changed significantly in quite some time. The recent advent of different approaches, like *column-oriented* or *massively parallel processing* (MPP) databases, has shown that we can rethink the technology to fit specific workloads, but most solutions still implement all or the majority of Codd's 12 rules in an attempt to not break with tradition.

Column-Oriented Databases

Column-oriented databases save their data grouped by columns. Subsequent column values are stored contiguously on disk. This differs from the usual row-oriented approach of traditional databases, which store entire rows contiguously—see Figure 1-1 for a visualization of the different physical layouts.

The reason to store values on a per-column basis instead is based on the assumption that, for specific queries, not all of the values are needed. This is often the case in analytical databases in particular, and therefore they are good candidates for this different storage schema.

Reduced I/O is one of the primary reasons for this new layout, but it offers additional advantages playing into the same category: since the values of one column are often very similar in nature or even vary only slightly between logical rows, they are often much better suited for compression than the heterogeneous values of a row-oriented record structure; most compression algorithms only look at a finite window.

Specialized algorithms—for example, delta and/or prefix compression—selected based on the type of the column (i.e., on the data stored) can yield huge improvements in compression ratios. Better ratios result in more efficient bandwidth usage.

Note, though, that HBase is *not* a column-oriented database in the typical RDBMS sense, but utilizes an on-disk column storage format. This is also where the majority of similarities end, because although HBase stores data on disk in a column-oriented format, it is distinctly different from traditional columnar databases: whereas columnar databases excel at providing real-time analytical access to data, HBase excels at providing key-based access to a specific cell of data, or a sequential range of cells.

The speed at which data is created today is already greatly increased, compared to only just a few years back. We can take for granted that this is only going to increase further, and with the rapid pace of globalization the problem is only exacerbated. Websites like Google, Amazon, eBay, and Facebook now reach the majority of people on this planet. The term *planet-size web application* comes to mind, and in this case it is fitting.

Facebook, for example, is adding more than 15 TB of data into its Hadoop cluster every day[‖] and is subsequently processing it all. One source of this data is click-stream logging, saving every step a user performs on its website, or on sites that use the social

---

‖ See this note (*http://www.facebook.com/note.php?note_id=89508453919*) published by Facebook.

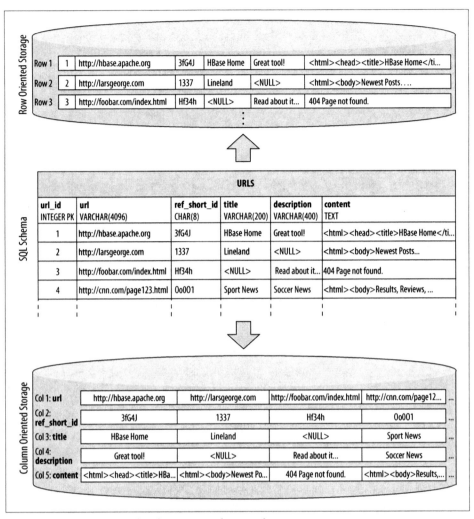

Figure 1-1. Column-oriented and row-oriented storage layouts

plug-ins offered by Facebook. This is an ideal case in which batch processing to build machine learning models for predictions and recommendations is appropriate.

Facebook also has a real-time component, which is its messaging system, including chat, wall posts, and email. This amounts to 135+ billion messages per month,# and storing this data over a certain number of months creates a huge tail that needs to be handled efficiently. Even though larger parts of emails—for example, attachments—

\# See this blog post (*http://www.facebook.com/note.php?note_id=454991608919*), as well as this one (*http://www.facebook.com/note.php?note_id=10150162742108920*), by the Facebook engineering team. Wall messages count for 15 billion and chat for 120 billion, totaling 135 billion messages a month. Then they also add SMS and others to create an even larger number.

are stored in a secondary system,* the amount of data generated by all these messages is mind-boggling. If we were to take 140 bytes per message, as used by Twitter, it would total more than 17 TB every month. Even before the transition to HBase, the existing system had to handle more than 25 TB a month.†

In addition, less web-oriented companies from across all major industries are collecting an ever-increasing amount of data. For example:

Financial
  Such as data generated by stock tickers

Bioinformatics
  Such as the *Global Biodiversity Information Facility* (*http://www.gbif.org/*)

Smart grid
  Such as the *OpenPDC* (*http://openpdc.codeplex.com/*) project

Sales
  Such as the data generated by *point-of-sale* (POS) or stock/inventory systems

Genomics
  Such as the *Crossbow* (*http://bowtie-bio.sourceforge.net/crossbow/index.shtml*) project

Cellular services, military, environmental
  Which all collect a tremendous amount of data as well

Storing petabytes of data efficiently so that updates and retrieval are still performed well is no easy feat. We will now look deeper into some of the challenges.

The Problem with Relational Database Systems

RDBMSes have typically played (and, for the foreseeable future at least, will play) an integral role when designing and implementing business applications. As soon as you have to retain information about your users, products, sessions, orders, and so on, you are typically going to use some storage backend providing a persistence layer for the frontend application server. This works well for a limited number of records, but with the dramatic increase of data being retained, some of the architectural implementation details of common database systems show signs of weakness.

Let us use *Hush*, the HBase URL Shortener mentioned earlier, as an example. Assume that you are building this system so that it initially handles a few thousand users, and that your task is to do so with a reasonable budget—in other words, use free software.

---

* Facebook uses Haystack (*http://www.facebook.com/note.php?note_id=76191543919*), which provides an optimized storage infrastructure for large binary objects, such as photos.

† See this presentation (*http://www.slideshare.net/brizzzdotcom/facebook-messages-hbase*), given by Facebook employee and HBase committer, Nicolas Spiegelberg.

The typical scenario here is to use the open source LAMP‡ stack to quickly build out a prototype for the business idea.

The relational database model normalizes the data into a user table, which is accompanied by a url, shorturl, and click table that link to the former by means of a foreign key. The tables also have indexes so that you can look up URLs by their short ID, or the users by their username. If you need to find all the shortened URLs for a particular list of customers, you could run an SQL JOIN over both tables to get a comprehensive list of URLs for each customer that contains not just the shortened URL but also the customer details you need.

In addition, you are making use of built-in features of the database: for example, *stored procedures*, which allow you to consistently update data from multiple clients while the database system guarantees that there is always coherent data stored in the various tables.

Transactions make it possible to update multiple tables in an atomic fashion so that either all modifications are visible or none are visible. The RDBMS gives you the so-called *ACID*§ properties, which means your data is *strongly consistent* (we will address this in greater detail in "Consistency Models" on page 9). *Referential integrity* takes care of enforcing relationships between various table schemas, and you get a domain-specific language, namely SQL, that lets you form complex queries over everything. Finally, you do not have to deal with how data is actually stored, but only with higher-level concepts such as table schemas, which define a fixed layout your application code can reference.

This usually works very well and will serve its purpose for quite some time. If you are lucky, you may be the next hot topic on the Internet, with more and more users joining your site every day. As your user numbers grow, you start to experience an increasing amount of pressure on your shared database server. Adding more application servers is relatively easy, as they share their state only with the central database. Your CPU and I/O load goes up and you start to wonder how long you can sustain this growth rate.

The first step to ease the pressure is to add slave database servers that are used to being read from in parallel. You still have a single master, but that is now only taking writes, and those are much fewer compared to the many reads your website users generate. But what if that starts to fail as well, or slows down as your user count steadily increases?

A common next step is to add a cache—for example, Memcached.‖ Now you can offload the reads to a very fast, in-memory system—however, you are losing consistency guarantees, as you will have to invalidate the cache on modifications of the original

---

‡ Short for Linux, Apache, MySQL, and PHP (or Perl and Python).

§ Short for Atomicity, Consistency, Isolation, and Durability. See "ACID" on Wikipedia (*http://en.wikipedia .org/wiki/ACID*).

‖ Memcached is an in-memory, nonpersistent, nondistributed key/value store. See the Memcached project home page (*http://memcached.org/*).

value in the database, and you have to do this fast enough to keep the time where the cache and the database views are inconsistent to a minimum.

While this may help you with the amount of reads, you have not yet addressed the writes. Once the master database server is hit too hard with writes, you may replace it with a beefed-up server—scaling up vertically—which simply has more cores, more memory, and faster disks... and costs a lot more money than the initial one. Also note that if you already opted for the master/slave setup mentioned earlier, you need to make the slaves as powerful as the master or the imbalance may mean the slaves fail to keep up with the master's update rate. This is going to double or triple the cost, if not more.

With more site popularity, you are asked to add more features to your application, which translates into more queries to your database. The SQL JOINs you were happy to run in the past are suddenly slowing down and are simply not performing well enough at scale. You will have to denormalize your schemas. If things get even worse, you will also have to cease your use of stored procedures, as they are also simply becoming too slow to complete. Essentially, you reduce the database to just storing your data in a way that is optimized for your access patterns.

Your load continues to increase as more and more users join your site, so another logical step is to prematerialize the most costly queries from time to time so that you can serve the data to your customers faster. Finally, you start dropping secondary indexes as their maintenance becomes too much of a burden and slows down the database too much. You end up with queries that can only use the primary key and nothing else.

Where do you go from here? What if your load is expected to increase by another order of magnitude or more over the next few months? You could start *sharding* (see the sidebar titled "Sharding") your data across many databases, but this turns into an operational nightmare, is very costly, and still does not give you a truly fitting solution. You essentially make do with the RDBMS for lack of an alternative.

Sharding

The term *sharding* describes the logical separation of records into horizontal partitions. The idea is to spread data across multiple storage files—or servers—as opposed to having each stored contiguously.

The separation of values into those partitions is performed on fixed boundaries: you have to set fixed rules ahead of time to route values to their appropriate store. With it comes the inherent difficulty of having to *reshard* the data when one of the horizontal partitions exceeds its capacity.

Resharding is a very costly operation, since the storage layout has to be rewritten. This entails defining new boundaries and then horizontally splitting the rows across them. Massive copy operations can take a huge toll on I/O performance as well as temporarily elevated storage requirements. And you may still take on updates from the client applications and need to negotiate updates during the resharding process.

This can be mitigated by using *virtual shards*, which define a much larger key partitioning range, with each server assigned an equal number of these shards. When you add more servers, you can reassign shards to the new server. This still requires that the data be moved over to the added server.

Sharding is often a simple afterthought or is completely left to the operator. Without proper support from the database system, this can wreak havoc on production systems.

Let us stop here, though, and, to be fair, mention that a lot of companies are using RDBMSes successfully as part of their technology stack. For example, Facebook—and also Google—has a very large MySQL setup, and for its purposes it works sufficiently. This database farm suits the given business goal and may not be replaced anytime soon. The question here is if you were to start working on implementing a new product and knew that it needed to scale very fast, wouldn't you want to have all the options available instead of using something you know has certain constraints?

Nonrelational Database Systems, Not-Only SQL or NoSQL?

Over the past four or five years, the pace of innovation to fill that exact problem space has gone from slow to insanely fast. It seems that every week another framework or project is announced to fit a related need. We saw the advent of the so-called *NoSQL* solutions, a term coined by Eric Evans in response to a question from Johan Oskarsson, who was trying to find a name for an event in that very emerging, new data storage system space.#

The term quickly rose to fame as there was simply no other name for this new class of products. It was (and is) discussed heavily, as it was also deemed the nemesis of "SQL"—or was meant to bring the plague to anyone still considering using traditional RDBMSes... just kidding!

 The actual idea of different data store architectures for specific problem sets is not new at all. Systems like Berkeley DB, Coherence, GT.M, and object-oriented database systems have been around for years, with some dating back to the early 1980s, and they fall into the NoSQL group by definition as well.

The tagword is actually a good fit: it is true that most new storage systems do not provide SQL as a means to query data, but rather a different, often simpler, API-like interface to the data.

On the other hand, tools are available that provide SQL dialects to NoSQL data stores, and they can be used to form the same complex queries you know from relational

---

#See "NoSQL" on Wikipedia (*http://en.wikipedia.org/wiki/NoSQL*).

databases. So, limitations in querying no longer differentiate RDBMSes from their nonrelational kin.

The difference is actually on a lower level, especially when it comes to schemas or ACID-like transactional features, but also regarding the actual storage architecture. A lot of these new kinds of systems do one thing first: throw out the limiting factors in truly scalable systems (a topic that is discussed in "Dimensions" on page 10). For example, they often have no support for transactions or secondary indexes. More importantly, they often have no fixed schemas so that the storage can evolve with the application using it.

Consistency Models

It seems fitting to talk about consistency a bit more since it is mentioned often throughout this book. On the outset, consistency is about guaranteeing that a database always appears *truthful* to its clients. Every operation on the database must carry its state from one consistent state to the next. How this is achieved or implemented is not specified explicitly so that a system has multiple choices. In the end, it has to get to the next consistent state, or return to the previous consistent state, to fulfill its obligation.

Consistency can be classified in, for example, decreasing order of its properties, or guarantees offered to clients. Here is an informal list:

Strict
> The changes to the data are atomic and appear to take effect instantaneously. This is the highest form of consistency.

Sequential
> Every client sees all changes in the same order they were applied.

Causal
> All changes that are causally related are observed in the same order by all clients.

Eventual
> When no updates occur for a period of time, eventually all updates will propagate through the system and all replicas will be consistent.

Weak
> No guarantee is made that all updates will propagate and changes may appear out of order to various clients.

The class of system adhering to eventual consistency can be even further divided into subtler sets, where those sets can also coexist. Werner Vogels, CTO of Amazon, lists them in his post titled "Eventually Consistent" (*http://www.allthingsdistributed.com/2007/12/eventually_consistent.html*). The article also picks up on the topic of the *CAP theorem*,* which states that a distributed system can only achieve two out of the

---

* See Eric Brewer's original paper (*http://www.cs.berkeley.edu/~brewer/cs262b-2004/PODC-keynote.pdf*) on this topic and the follow-up post (*http://codahale.com/you-cant-sacrifice-partition-tolerance/*) by Coda Hale, as well as this PDF (*http://lpd.epfl.ch/sgilbert/pubs/BrewersConjecture-SigAct.pdf*) by Gilbert and Lynch.

following three properties: consistency, availability, and partition tolerance. The CAP theorem is a highly discussed topic, and is certainly not the only way to classify, but it does point out that distributed systems are not easy to develop given certain requirements. Vogels, for example, mentions:

> An important observation is that in larger distributed scale systems, network partitions are a given and as such consistency and availability cannot be achieved at the same time. This means that one has two choices on what to drop; relaxing consistency will allow the system to remain highly available [...] and prioritizing consistency means that under certain conditions the system will not be available.

Relaxing consistency, while at the same time gaining availability, is a powerful proposition. However, it can force handling inconsistencies into the application layer and may increase complexity.

There are many overlapping features within the group of nonrelational databases, but some of these features also overlap with traditional storage solutions. So the new systems are not really revolutionary, but rather, from an engineering perspective, are more evolutionary.

Even projects like *memcached* are lumped into the NoSQL category, as if anything that is not an RDBMS is automatically NoSQL. This creates a kind of false dichotomy that obscures the exciting technical possibilities these systems have to offer. And there are many; within the NoSQL category, there are numerous dimensions you could use to classify where the strong points of a particular system lie.

Dimensions

Let us take a look at a handful of those dimensions here. Note that this is not a comprehensive list, or the only way to classify them.

Data model
There are many variations in how the data is stored, which include key/value stores (compare to a HashMap), semistructured, column-oriented stores, and document-oriented stores. How is your application accessing the data? Can the schema evolve over time?

Storage model
In-memory or persistent? This is fairly easy to decide since we are comparing with RDBMSes, which usually persist their data to permanent storage, such as physical disks. But you may explicitly need a purely in-memory solution, and there are choices for that too. As far as persistent storage is concerned, does this affect your access pattern in any way?

Consistency model
Strictly or eventually consistent? The question is, how does the storage system achieve its goals: does it have to weaken the consistency guarantees? While this seems like a cursory question, it can make all the difference in certain use cases. It

may especially affect latency, that is, how fast the system can respond to read and write requests. This is often measured in *harvest* and *yield*.†

Physical model

Distributed or single machine? What does the architecture look like—is it built from distributed machines or does it only run on single machines with the distribution handled client-side, that is, in your own code? Maybe the distribution is only an afterthought and could cause problems once you need to scale the system. And if it does offer scalability, does it imply specific steps to do so? The easiest solution would be to add one machine at a time, while sharded setups (especially those not supporting virtual shards) sometimes require for each shard to be increased simultaneously because each partition needs to be equally powerful.

Read/write performance

You have to understand what your application's access patterns look like. Are you designing something that is written to a few times, but is read much more often? Or are you expecting an equal load between reads and writes? Or are you taking in a lot of writes and just a few reads? Does it support range scans or is it better suited doing random reads? Some of the available systems are advantageous for only one of these operations, while others may do well in all of them.

Secondary indexes

Secondary indexes allow you to sort and access tables based on different fields and sorting orders. The options here range from systems that have absolutely no secondary indexes and no guaranteed sorting order (like a HashMap, i.e., you need to know the keys) to some that weakly support them, all the way to those that offer them out of the box. Can your application cope, or emulate, if this feature is missing?

Failure handling

It is a fact that machines crash, and you need to have a mitigation plan in place that addresses machine failures (also refer to the discussion of the CAP theorem in "Consistency Models" on page 9). How does each data store handle server failures? Is it able to continue operating? This is related to the "Consistency model" dimension discussed earlier, as losing a machine may cause *holes* in your data store, or even worse, make it completely unavailable. And if you are replacing the server, how easy will it be to get back to being 100% operational? Another scenario is decommissioning a server in a clustered setup, which would most likely be handled the same way.

Compression

When you have to store terabytes of data, especially of the kind that consists of prose or human-readable text, it is advantageous to be able to compress the data to gain substantial savings in required raw storage. Some compression algorithms

---

† See Brewer: "Lessons from giant-scale services." *Internet Computing*, IEEE (2001) vol. 5 (4) pp. 46–55 (*http: //ieeexplore.ieee.org/xpl/freeabs_all.jsp?arnumber=939450*).

can achieve a 10:1 reduction in storage space needed. Is the compression method pluggable? What types are available?

Load balancing

Given that you have a high read or write rate, you may want to invest in a storage system that transparently balances itself while the load shifts over time. It may not be the full answer to your problems, but it may help you to ease into a high-throughput application design.

Atomic read-modify-write

While RDBMSes offer you a lot of these operations directly (because you are talking to a central, single server), they can be more difficult to achieve in distributed systems. They allow you to prevent race conditions in multithreaded or shared-nothing application server design. Having these *compare and swap* (CAS) or *check and set* operations available can reduce client-side complexity.

Locking, waits, and deadlocks

It is a known fact that complex transactional processing, like two-phase commits, can increase the possibility of multiple clients waiting for a resource to become available. In a worst-case scenario, this can lead to deadlocks, which are hard to resolve. What kind of locking model does the system you are looking at support? Can it be free of waits, and therefore deadlocks?

 We will look back at these dimensions later on to see where HBase fits and where its strengths lie. For now, let us say that you need to carefully select the dimensions that are best suited to the issues at hand. Be pragmatic about the solution, and be aware that there is no hard and fast rule, in cases where an RDBMS is not working ideally, that a NoSQL system is the perfect match. Evaluate your options, choose wisely, and mix and match if needed.

An interesting term to describe this issue is *impedance match*, which describes the need to find the ideal solution for a given problem. Instead of using a "one-size-fits-all" approach, you should know what else is available. Try to use the system that solves your problem best.

Scalability

While the performance of RDBMSes is well suited for transactional processing, it is less so for very large-scale analytical processing. This refers to very large queries that scan wide ranges of records or entire tables. Analytical databases may contain hundreds or thousands of terabytes, causing queries to exceed what can be done on a single server in a reasonable amount of time. Scaling that server vertically—that is, adding more cores or disks—is simply not good enough.

What is even worse is that with RDBMSes, waits and deadlocks are increasing nonlinearly with the size of the transactions and concurrency—that is, the square of concurrency and the third or even fifth power of the transaction size.[‡] Sharding is often an impractical solution, as it has to be done within the application layer, and may involve complex and costly (re)partitioning procedures.

Commercial RDBMSes are available that solve many of these issues, but they are often specialized and only cover certain aspects. Above all, they are very, very expensive. Looking at open source alternatives in the RDBMS space, you will likely have to give up many or all relational features, such as secondary indexes, to gain some level of performance.

The question is, wouldn't it be good to trade relational features permanently for performance? You could denormalize (see the next section) the data model and avoid waits and deadlocks by minimizing necessary locking. How about built-in horizontal scalability without the need to repartition as your data grows? Finally, throw in fault tolerance and data availability, using the same mechanisms that allow scalability, and what you get is a NoSQL solution—more specifically, one that matches what HBase has to offer.

Database (De-)Normalization

At scale, it is often a requirement that we design schema differently, and a good term to describe this principle is *Denormalization, Duplication, and Intelligent Keys (DDI)*.[§] It is about rethinking how data is stored in Bigtable-like storage systems, and how to make use of it in an appropriate way.

Part of the principle is to denormalize schemas by, for example, duplicating data in more than one table so that, at read time, no further aggregation is required. Or the related prematerialization of required views, once again optimizing for fast reads without any further processing.

There is much more on this topic in Chapter 9, where you will find many ideas on how to design solutions that make the best use of the features HBase provides. Let us look at an example to understand the basic principles of converting a classic *relational* database model to one that fits the columnar nature of HBase much better.

Consider the HBase URL Shortener, Hush, which allows us to map long URLs to *short URLs*. The *entity relationship diagram* (ERD) can be seen in Figure 1-2. The full SQL schema can be found in Appendix E.[‖]

[‡] See "FT 101" (*http://research.microsoft.com/en-us/um/people/gray/talks/UCBerkeley_Gray_FT_Avialiability _talk.ppt*) by Jim Gray et al.

[§] The term *DDI* was coined in the paper "Cloud Data Structure Diagramming Techniques and Design Patterns" by D. Salmen et al. (2009).

[‖] Note, though, that this is provided purely for demonstration purposes, so the schema is deliberately kept simple.

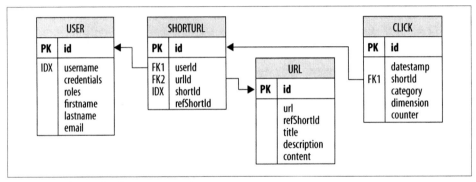

Figure 1-2. The Hush schema expressed as an ERD

The shortened URL, stored in the shorturl table, can then be given to others that subsequently click on it to open the linked full URL. Each click is tracked, recording the number of times it was used, and, for example, the country the click came from. This is stored in the click table, which aggregates the usage on a daily basis, similar to a counter.

Users, stored in the user table, can sign up with Hush to create their own list of shortened URLs, which can be edited to add a description. This links the user and short url tables with a foreign key relationship.

The system also downloads the linked page in the background, and extracts, for instance, the TITLE tag from the HTML, if present. The entire page is saved for later processing with asynchronous batch jobs, for analysis purposes. This is represented by the url table.

Every linked page is only stored once, but since many users may link to the same long URL, yet want to maintain their own details, such as the usage statistics, a separate entry in the shorturl is created. This links the url, shorturl, and click tables.

This also allows you to aggregate statistics to the original short ID, refShortId, so that you can see the overall usage of any short URL to map to the same long URL. The shortId and refShortId are the hashed IDs assigned uniquely to each shortened URL. For example, in

```
http://hush.li/a23eg
```

the ID is a23eg.

Figure 1-3 shows how the same schema could be represented in HBase. Every shortened URL is stored in a separate table, shorturl, which also contains the usage statistics, storing various time ranges in separate column families, with distinct *time-to-live* settings. The columns form the actual counters, and their name is a combination of the date, plus an optional dimensional postfix—for example, the country code.

Table: shorturl

Row Key:	shortId	
Family:	data:	Columns: url, refShortId, userId, clicks
	stats-daily: **[ttl: 7days]**	Columns: YYYYMMDD, YYYYMMDD\x00<country-code>
	stats-weekly: **[ttl: 4weeks]**	Columns: YYYYWW, YYYYWW\x00<country-code>
	stats-monthly: **[ttl: 12months]**	Columns: YYYYMM, YYYYMM\x00<country-code>

Table: url

Row Key:	MD5(url)	
Family:	data: **[compressed]**	Columns: refShortId, title, description
	content: **[compressed]**	Columns: raw

Table: user-shorturl

Row Key:	username\x00shortId	
Family:	data:	Columns: timestamp

Table: user

Row Key:	username	
Family:	data:	Columns: credentials, roles, firstname, lastname, email

Figure 1-3. The Hush schema in HBase

The downloaded page, and the extracted details, are stored in the url table. This table uses compression to minimize the storage requirements, because the pages are mostly HTML, which is inherently verbose and contains a lot of text.

The user-shorturl table acts as a lookup so that you can quickly find all short IDs for a given user. This is used on the user's home page, once she has logged in. The user table stores the actual user details.

We still have the same number of tables, but their meaning has changed: the clicks table has been absorbed by the shorturl table, while the statistics columns use the date as their key, formatted as YYYYMMDD—for instance, *20110502*—so that they can be accessed sequentially. The additional user-shorturl table is replacing the foreign key relationship, making user-related lookups faster.

There are various approaches to converting *one-to-one*, *one-to-many*, and *many-to-many* relationships to fit the underlying architecture of HBase. You could implement even this simple example in different ways. You need to understand the full potential of HBase storage design to make an educated decision regarding which approach to take.

The support for sparse, wide tables and column-oriented design often eliminates the need to normalize data and, in the process, the costly JOIN operations needed to aggregate the data at query time. Use of intelligent keys gives you fine-grained control over how—and where—data is stored. Partial key lookups are possible, and when combined with compound keys, they have the same properties as leading, left-edge indexes. Designing the schemas properly enables you to grow the data from 10 entries to 10 million entries, while still retaining the same write and read performance.

Building Blocks

This section provides you with an overview of the architecture behind HBase. After giving you some background information on its lineage, the section will introduce the general concepts of the data model and the available storage API, and presents a high-level overview on implementation.

Backdrop

In 2003, Google published a paper titled *"The Google File System"* (*http://labs.google.com/papers/gfs.html*). This scalable distributed file system, abbreviated as GFS, uses a cluster of commodity hardware to store huge amounts of data. The filesystem handled data replication between nodes so that losing a storage server would have no effect on data availability. It was also optimized for streaming reads so that data could be read for processing later on.

Shortly afterward, another paper by Google was published, titled *"MapReduce: Simplified Data Processing on Large Clusters"* (*http://labs.google.com/papers/mapreduce.html*). MapReduce was the missing piece to the GFS architecture, as it made use of the vast number of CPUs each commodity server in the GFS cluster provides. MapReduce plus GFS forms the backbone for processing massive amounts of data, including the entire search index Google owns.

What is missing, though, is the ability to access data randomly and in close to real-time (meaning good enough to drive a web service, for example). Another drawback of the GFS design is that it is good with a few very, very large files, but not as good with millions of tiny files, because the data retained in memory by the master node is ultimately bound to the number of files. The more files, the higher the pressure on the memory of the master.

So, Google was trying to find a solution that could drive interactive applications, such as Mail or Analytics, while making use of the same infrastructure and relying on GFS for replication and data availability. The data stored should be composed of much smaller entities, and the system would transparently take care of aggregating the small records into very large storage files and offer some sort of indexing that allows the user to retrieve data with a minimal number of disk seeks. Finally, it should be able to store the entire web crawl and work with MapReduce to build the entire search index in a timely manner.

Being aware of the shortcomings of RDBMSes at scale (see "Seek Versus Transfer" on page 315 for a discussion of one fundamental issue), the engineers approached this problem differently: forfeit relational features and use a simple API that has basic *create*, *read*, *update*, and *delete* (or CRUD) operations, plus a *scan* function to iterate over larger key ranges or entire tables. The culmination of these efforts was published in 2006 in a paper titled *"Bigtable: A Distributed Storage System for Structured Data"* (*http://labs.google.com/papers/bigtable.html*), two excerpts from which follow:

> Bigtable is a distributed storage system for managing structured data that is designed to scale to a very large size: petabytes of data across thousands of commodity servers.

> ...a sparse, distributed, persistent multi-dimensional sorted map.

It is highly recommended that everyone interested in HBase read that paper. It describes a lot of reasoning behind the design of Bigtable and, ultimately, HBase. We will, however, go through the basic concepts, since they apply directly to the rest of this book.

HBase is implementing the Bigtable storage architecture very faithfully so that we can explain everything using HBase. Appendix F provides an overview of where the two systems differ.

Tables, Rows, Columns, and Cells

First, a quick summary: the most basic unit is a *column*. One or more columns form a *row* that is addressed uniquely by a *row key*. A number of rows, in turn, form a *table*, and there can be many of them. Each column may have multiple versions, with each distinct value contained in a separate *cell*.

This sounds like a reasonable description for a typical database, but with the extra *dimension* of allowing multiple versions of each cells. But obviously there is a bit more to it.

All *rows* are always sorted lexicographically by their row key. Example 1-1 shows how this will look when adding a few rows with different keys.

Example 1-1. The sorting of rows done lexicographically by their key

```
hbase(main):001:0> scan 'table1'
ROW                     COLUMN+CELL
row-1                   column=cf1:, timestamp=1297073325971 ...
row-10                  column=cf1:, timestamp=1297073337383 ...
row-11                  column=cf1:, timestamp=1297073340493 ...
row-2                   column=cf1:, timestamp=1297073329851 ...
row-22                  column=cf1:, timestamp=1297073344482 ...
row-3                   column=cf1:, timestamp=1297073333504 ...
row-abc                 column=cf1:, timestamp=1297073349875 ...
7 row(s) in 0.1100 seconds
```

Note how the numbering is not in sequence as you may have expected it. You may have to pad keys to get a proper sorting order. In lexicographical sorting, each key is compared on a binary level, byte by byte, from left to right. Since `row-1...` is less than `row-2...`, no matter what follows, it is sorted first.

Having the row keys always sorted can give you something like a primary key index known from RDBMSes. It is also always unique, that is, you can have each row key only once, or you are updating the same row. While the original Bigtable paper only considers a single index, HBase adds support for secondary indexes (see "Secondary Indexes" on page 370). The row keys can be any *arbitrary array of bytes* and are not necessarily human-readable.

Rows are composed of *columns*, and those, in turn, are grouped into *column families*. This helps in building semantical or topical boundaries between the data, and also in applying certain features to them—for example, *compression*—or denoting them to stay in-memory. All columns in a column family are stored together in the same low-level storage file, called an *HFile*.

Column families need to be defined when the table is created and should not be changed too often, nor should there be too many of them. There are a few known shortcomings in the current implementation that force the count to be limited to the low tens, but in practice it is often a much smaller number (see Chapter 9 for details). The name of the column family must be composed of printable characters, a notable difference from all other names or values.

Columns are often referenced as *family:qualifier* with the `qualifier` being any arbitrary array of bytes.[#] As opposed to the limit on column families, there is no such thing for the number of columns: you could have millions of columns in a particular column family. There is also no type nor length boundary on the column values.

Figure 1-4 helps to visualize how different rows are in a normal database as opposed to the column-oriented design of HBase. You should think about rows and columns not being arranged like the classic spreadsheet model, but rather use a tag metaphor, that is, information is available under a specific tag.

[#]You will see in "Column Families" on page 212 that the qualifier also may be left unset.

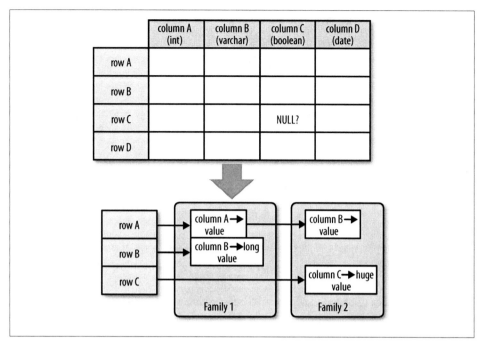

Figure 1-4. Rows and columns in HBase

 The "NULL?" in Figure 1-4 indicates that, for a database with a fixed schema, you have to store NULLs where there is no value, but for HBase's storage architectures, you simply omit the whole column; in other words, NULLs are free of any cost: they do not occupy any storage space.

All rows and columns are defined in the context of a *table*, adding a few more concepts across all included column families, which we will discuss shortly.

Every column value, or *cell*, either is timestamped implicitly by the system or can be set explicitly by the user. This can be used, for example, to save multiple *versions* of a value as it changes over time. Different versions of a cell are stored in decreasing time-stamp order, allowing you to read the newest value first. This is an optimization aimed at read patterns that favor more current values over historical ones.

The user can specify how many versions of a value should be kept. In addition, there is support for *predicate deletions* (see "Log-Structured Merge-Trees" on page 316 for the concepts behind them) allowing you to keep, for example, only values written in the past week. The values (or cells) are also just uninterpreted arrays of bytes, that the client needs to know how to handle.

If you recall from the quote earlier, the Bigtable model, as implemented by HBase, is a sparse, distributed, persistent, multidimensional map, which is indexed by row key, column key, and a timestamp. Putting this together, we can express the access to data like so:

```
(Table, RowKey, Family, Column, Timestamp) → Value
```

In a more programming language style, this may be expressed as:

```
SortedMap<
    RowKey, List<
        SortedMap<
            Column, List<
                Value, Timestamp
            >
        >
    >
>
```

or all in one line:

```
SortedMap<RowKey, List<SortedMap<Column, List<Value, Timestamp>>>>
```

The first `SortedMap` is the table, containing a `List` of column families. The families contain another `SortedMap`, which represents the columns, and their associated values. These values are in the final `List` that holds the value and the timestamp it was set.

An interesting feature of the model is that cells may exist in multiple versions, and different columns have been written at different times. The API, by default, provides you with a coherent view of all columns wherein it automatically picks the most current value of each cell. Figure 1-5 shows a piece of one specific row in an example table.

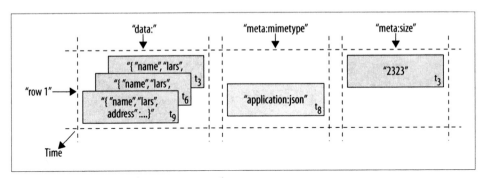

Figure 1-5. A time-oriented view into parts of a row

The diagram visualizes the time component using t_n as the timestamp when the cell was written. The ascending index shows that the values have been added at different times. Figure 1-6 is another way to look at the data, this time in a more spreadsheet-like layout wherein the timestamp was added to its own column.

Row Key	Time Stamp	Column "data:"	Column "meta:" "mimetype"	"size"	Column "counters:" "updates"
"row1"	t_3	"{ "name": "lars", "address": ...}"		"2323"	"1"
	t_6	"{ "name": "lars", "address": ...}"			"2"
	t_8		"application/json"		
	t_9	"{ "name": "lars", "address": ...}"			"3"

Figure 1-6. *The same parts of the row rendered as a spreadsheet*

Although they have been added at different times and exist in multiple versions, you would still see the row as the combination of all columns and their most current versions—in other words, the highest t_n from each column. There is a way to ask for values at (or before) a specific timestamp, or more than one version at a time, which we will see a little bit later in Chapter 3.

The Webtable

The *canonical* use case of Bigtable and HBase is the *webtable*, that is, the web pages stored while crawling the Internet.

The row key is the reversed URL of the page—for example, `org.hbase.www`. There is a column family storing the actual HTML code, the `contents` family, as well as others like `anchor`, which is used to store outgoing links, another one to store inbound links, and yet another for metadata like `language`.

Using multiple versions for the `contents` family allows you to store a few older copies of the HTML, and is helpful when you want to analyze how often a page changes, for example. The timestamps used are the actual times when they were fetched from the crawled website.

Access to row data is *atomic* and includes any number of columns being read or written to. There is no further guarantee or transactional feature that spans multiple rows or across tables. The atomic access is also a contributing factor to this architecture being *strictly consistent*, as each concurrent reader and writer can make safe assumptions about the state of a row.

Using multiversioning and timestamping can help with application layer consistency issues as well.

Auto-Sharding

The basic unit of scalability and load balancing in HBase is called a *region*. Regions are essentially contiguous ranges of rows stored together. They are dynamically split by the system when they become too large. Alternatively, they may also be merged to reduce their number and required storage files.*

 The HBase regions are equivalent to *range partitions* as used in database sharding. They can be spread across many physical servers, thus distributing the load, and therefore providing scalability.

Initially there is only one region for a table, and as you start adding data to it, the system is monitoring it to ensure that you do not exceed a configured maximum size. If you exceed the limit, the region is split into two at the *middle key*—the row key in the middle of the region—creating two roughly equal halves (more details in Chapter 8).

Each region is served by exactly one *region server*, and each of these servers can serve many regions at any time. Figure 1-7 shows how the logical view of a table is actually a set of regions hosted by many region servers.

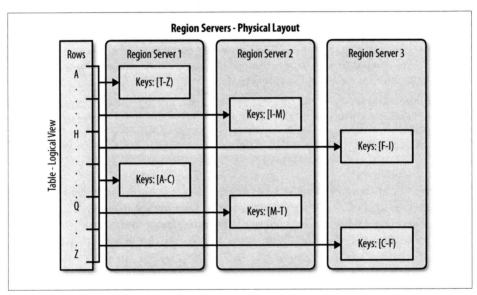

Figure 1-7. Rows grouped in regions and served by different servers

---

* Although HBase does not support online region merging, there are tools to do this offline. See "Merging Regions" on page 433.

The Bigtable paper notes that the aim is to keep the region count between 10 and 1,000 per server and each at roughly 100 MB to 200 MB in size. This refers to the hardware in use in 2006 (and earlier). For HBase and modern hardware, the number would be more like 10 to 1,000 regions per server, but each between 1 GB and 2 GB in size.

But, while the numbers have increased, the basic principle is the same: the number of regions per server, and their respective sizes, depend on what can be handled sufficiently by a single server.

Splitting and serving regions can be thought of as *autosharding*, as offered by other systems. The regions allow for fast recovery when a server fails, and fine-grained load balancing since they can be moved between servers when the load of the server currently serving the region is under pressure, or if that server becomes unavailable because of a failure or because it is being decommissioned.

Splitting is also very fast—close to instantaneous—because the split regions simply read from the original storage files until a compaction rewrites them into separate ones asynchronously. This is explained in detail in Chapter 8.

Storage API

> Bigtable does not support a full relational data model; instead, it provides clients with a simple data model that supports dynamic control over data layout and format [...]

The API offers operations to create and delete tables and column families. In addition, it has functions to change the table and column family metadata, such as compression or block sizes. Furthermore, there are the usual operations for clients to create or delete values as well as retrieving them with a given row key.

A *scan* API allows you to efficiently iterate over ranges of rows and be able to limit which columns are returned or the number of versions of each cell. You can match columns using filters and select versions using time ranges, specifying start and end times.

On top of this basic functionality are more advanced features. The system has support for single-row transactions, and with this support it implements atomic *read-modify-write* sequences on data stored under a single row key. Although there are no cross-row or cross-table transactions, the client can batch operations for performance reasons.

Cell values can be interpreted as counters and updated atomically. These counters can be read and modified in one operation so that, despite the distributed nature of the architecture, clients can use this mechanism to implement global, strictly consistent, sequential counters.

There is also the option to run client-supplied code in the address space of the server. The server-side framework to support this is called *coprocessors*. The code has access to the server local data and can be used to implement lightweight batch jobs, or use expressions to analyze or summarize data based on a variety of operators.

Coprocessors were added to HBase in version 0.91.0.

Finally, the system is integrated with the MapReduce framework by supplying wrappers that convert tables into input source and output targets for MapReduce jobs.

Unlike in the RDBMS landscape, there is no domain-specific language, such as SQL, to query data. Access is not done declaratively, but purely imperatively through the client-side API. For HBase, this is mostly Java code, but there are many other choices to access the data from other programming languages.

Implementation

> Bigtable [...] allows clients to reason about the locality properties of the data represented in the underlying storage.

The data is stored in *store files*, called *HFiles*, which are persistent and ordered immutable maps from keys to values. Internally, the files are sequences of blocks with a block index stored at the end. The index is loaded when the HFile is opened and kept in memory. The default block size is 64 KB but can be configured differently if required. The store files provide an API to access specific values as well as to scan ranges of values given a start and end key.

Implementation is discussed in great detail in Chapter 8. The text here is an introduction only, while the full details are discussed in the referenced chapter(s).

Since every HFile has a block index, lookups can be performed with a single disk seek. First, the block possibly containing the given key is determined by doing a binary search in the in-memory block index, followed by a block read from disk to find the actual key.

The store files are typically saved in the Hadoop Distributed File System (HDFS), which provides a scalable, persistent, replicated storage layer for HBase. It guarantees that data is never lost by writing the changes across a configurable number of physical servers.

When data is updated it is first written to a *commit log*, called a *write-ahead log* (WAL) in HBase, and then stored in the in-memory *memstore*. Once the data in memory has exceeded a given maximum value, it is flushed as an HFile to disk. After the flush, the commit logs can be discarded up to the last unflushed modification. While the system is flushing the memstore to disk, it can continue to serve readers and writers without having to block them. This is achieved by rolling the memstore in memory where the new/empty one is taking the updates, while the old/full one is converted into a file. Note that the data in the memstores is already sorted by keys matching exactly what HFiles represent on disk, so no sorting or other special processing has to be performed.

 We can now start to make sense of what the *locality properties* are, mentioned in the Bigtable quote at the beginning of this section. Since all files contain sorted key/value pairs, ordered by the key, and are optimized for block operations such as reading these pairs sequentially, you should specify keys to keep related data together. Referring back to the webtable example earlier, you may have noted that the key used is the reversed FQDN (the domain name part of the URL), such as org.hbase.www. The reason is to store all pages from hbase.org close to one another, and reversing the URL puts the most important part of the URL first, that is, the top-level domain (TLD). Pages under blog.hbase.org would then be sorted with those from www.hbase.org— or in the actual key format, org.hbase.blog sorts next to org.hbase.www.

Because store files are immutable, you cannot simply delete values by removing the key/value pair from them. Instead, a *delete marker* (also known as a tombstone marker) is written to indicate the fact that the given key has been deleted. During the retrieval process, these delete markers mask out the actual values and hide them from reading clients.

Reading data back involves a merge of what is stored in the memstores, that is, the data that has not been written to disk, and the on-disk store files. Note that the WAL is never used during data retrieval, but solely for recovery purposes when a server has crashed before writing the in-memory data to disk.

Since flushing memstores to disk causes more and more HFiles to be created, HBase has a housekeeping mechanism that merges the files into larger ones using *compaction*. There are two types of compaction: *minor compactions* and *major compactions*. The former reduce the number of storage files by rewriting smaller files into fewer but larger ones, performing an *n*-way merge. Since all the data is already sorted in each HFile, that merge is fast and bound only by disk I/O performance.

The *major compactions* rewrite all files within a column family for a region into a single new one. They also have another distinct feature compared to the minor compactions: based on the fact that they scan all key/value pairs, they can drop deleted entries including their deletion marker. Predicate deletes are handled here as well—for example, removing values that have expired according to the configured time-to-live or when there are too many versions.

This architecture is taken from LSM-trees (see "Log-Structured Merge-Trees" on page 316). The only difference is that LSM-trees are storing data in multipage blocks that are arranged in a B-tree-like structure on disk. They are updated, or merged, in a rotating fashion, while in Bigtable the update is more course-grained and the whole memstore is saved as a new store file and not merged right away. You could call HBase's architecture "Log-Structured Sort-and-Merge-Maps." The background compactions correspond to the merges in LSM-trees, but are occurring on a store file level instead of the partial tree updates, giving the LSM-trees their name.

There are three major components to HBase: the client library, one master server, and many region servers. The region servers can be added or removed while the system is up and running to accommodate changing workloads. The master is responsible for assigning regions to region servers and uses *Apache ZooKeeper*, a reliable, highly available, persistent and distributed coordination service, to facilitate that task.

Apache ZooKeeper

ZooKeeper[†] is a separate open source project, and is also part of the Apache Software Foundation. ZooKeeper is the comparable system to Google's use of Chubby for Bigtable. It offers filesystem-like access with directories and files (called *znodes*) that distributed systems can use to negotiate ownership, register services, or watch for updates.

Every region server creates its own ephemeral node in ZooKeeper, which the master, in turn, uses to discover available servers. They are also used to track server failures or network partitions.

Ephemeral nodes are bound to the session between ZooKeeper and the client which created it. The session has a heartbeat keepalive mechanism that, once it fails to report, is declared lost by ZooKeeper and the associated ephemeral nodes are deleted.

HBase uses ZooKeeper also to ensure that there is only one master running, to store the bootstrap location for region discovery, as a registry for region servers, as well as for other purposes. ZooKeeper is a critical component, and without it HBase is not operational. This is mitigated by ZooKeeper's distributed design using an assemble of servers and the *Zab* protocol to keep its state consistent.

---

† For more information on Apache ZooKeeper, please refer to the official project website (*http://hadoop .apache.org/zookeeper/*).

Figure 1-8 shows how the various components of HBase are orchestrated to make use of existing system, like HDFS and ZooKeeper, but also adding its own layers to form a complete platform.

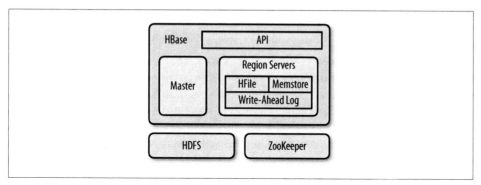

Figure 1-8. HBase using its own components while leveraging existing systems

The master server is also responsible for handling load balancing of regions across region servers, to unload busy servers and move regions to less occupied ones. The master is not part of the actual data storage or retrieval path. It negotiates load balancing and maintains the state of the cluster, but never provides any data services to either the region servers or the clients, and is therefore lightly loaded in practice. In addition, it takes care of schema changes and other metadata operations, such as creation of tables and column families.

Region servers are responsible for all read and write requests for all regions they serve, and also split regions that have exceeded the configured region size thresholds. Clients communicate directly with them to handle all data-related operations.

"Region Lookups" on page 345 has more details on how clients perform the region lookup.

Summary

> Billions of rows * millions of columns * thousands of versions = terabytes or petabytes of storage

We have seen how the Bigtable storage architecture is using many servers to distribute ranges of rows sorted by their key for load-balancing purposes, and can scale to peta-bytes of data on thousands of machines. The storage format used is ideal for reading adjacent key/value pairs and is optimized for block I/O operations that can saturate disk transfer channels.

Table scans run in linear time and row key lookups or mutations are performed in logarithmic order—or, in extreme cases, even constant order (using Bloom filters). Designing the schema in a way to completely avoid explicit locking, combined with row-level atomicity, gives you the ability to scale your system without any notable effect on read or write performance.

The column-oriented architecture allows for huge, wide, sparse tables as storing NULLs is free. Because each row is served by exactly one server, HBase is strongly consistent, and using its multiversioning can help you to avoid edit conflicts caused by concurrent decoupled processes or retain a history of changes.

The actual Bigtable has been in production at Google since at least 2005, and it has been in use for a variety of different use cases, from batch-oriented processing to real-time data-serving. The stored data varies from very small (like URLs) to quite large (e.g., web pages and satellite imagery) and yet successfully provides a flexible, high-performance solution for many well-known Google products, such as Google Earth, Google Reader, Google Finance, and Google Analytics.

HBase: The Hadoop Database

Having looked at the Bigtable architecture, we could simply state that HBase is a faithful, open source implementation of Google's Bigtable. But that would be a bit too simplistic, and there are a few (mostly subtle) differences worth addressing.

History

HBase was created in 2007 at Powerset‡ and was initially part of the contributions in Hadoop. Since then, it has become its own top-level project under the Apache Software Foundation umbrella. It is available under the Apache Software License, version 2.0.

The project home page is *http://hbase.apache.org/*, where you can find links to the documentation, wiki, and source repository, as well as download sites for the binary and source releases.

Here is a short overview of how HBase has evolved over time:

November 2006
    Google releases paper on BigTable

February 2007
    Initial HBase prototype created as Hadoop contrib§

October 2007
    First "usable" HBase (Hadoop 0.15.0)

---

‡ Powerset is a company based in San Francisco that was developing a natural language search engine for the Internet. On July 1, 2008, Microsoft acquired Powerset, and subsequent support for HBase development was abandoned.

§ For an interesting flash back in time, see HBASE-287 (*https://issues.apache.org/jira/browse/HBASE-287*) on the Apache JIRA, the issue tracking system. You can see how Mike Cafarella did a code drop that was then quickly picked up by Jim Kellerman, who was with Powerset back then.

January 2008
> Hadoop becomes an Apache top-level project, HBase becomes subproject

October 2008
> HBase 0.18.1 released

January 2009
> HBase 0.19.0 released

September 2009
> HBase 0.20.0 released, the *performance* release

May 2010
> HBase becomes an Apache top-level project

June 2010
> HBase 0.89.20100621, first developer release

January 2011
> HBase 0.90.0 released, the *durability and stability* release

Mid 2011
> HBase 0.92.0 released, tagged as *coprocessor and security* release

 Around May 2010, the developers decided to break with the version numbering that was used to be in *lockstep* with the Hadoop releases. The rationale was that HBase had a much faster release cycle and was also approaching a version 1.0 level sooner than what was expected from Hadoop.

To that effect, the jump was made quite obvious, going from 0.20.x to 0.89.x. In addition, a decision was made to title 0.89.x the *early access* version for developers and bleeding-edge integrators. Version 0.89 was eventually released as 0.90 for everyone as the next stable release.

Nomenclature

One of the biggest differences between HBase and Bigtable concerns naming, as you can see in Table 1-1, which lists the various terms and what they correspond to in each system.

Table 1-1. Differences in naming

HBase	Bigtable
Region	Tablet
RegionServer	Tablet server
Flush	Minor compaction
Minor compaction	Merging compaction
Major compaction	Major compaction

HBase	Bigtable
Write-ahead log	Commit log
HDFS	GFS
Hadoop MapReduce	MapReduce
MemStore	memtable
HFile	SSTable
ZooKeeper	Chubby

More differences are described in Appendix F.

Summary

Let us now circle back to "Dimensions" on page 10, and how dimensions can be used to classify HBase. HBase is a distributed, persistent, strictly consistent storage system with near-optimal write—in terms of I/O channel saturation—and excellent read performance, and it makes efficient use of disk space by supporting pluggable compression algorithms that can be selected based on the nature of the data in specific column families.

HBase extends the Bigtable model, which only considers a single index, similar to a primary key in the RDBMS world, offering the server-side hooks to implement flexible secondary index solutions. In addition, it provides push-down predicates, that is, filters, reducing data transferred over the network.

There is no declarative query language as part of the core implementation, and it has limited support for transactions. Row atomicity and read-modify-write operations make up for this in practice, as they cover most use cases and remove the wait or deadlock-related pauses experienced with other systems.

HBase handles shifting load and failures gracefully and transparently to the clients. Scalability is built in, and clusters can be grown or shrunk while the system is in production. Changing the cluster does not involve any complicated rebalancing or re-sharding procedure, but is completely automated.

## CHAPTER 2

Installation

In this chapter, we will look at how HBase is installed and initially configured. We will see how HBase can be used from the command line for basic operations, such as adding, retrieving, and deleting data.

 All of the following assumes you have the Java Runtime Environment (JRE) installed. Hadoop and also HBase require at least version 1.6 (also called Java 6), and the recommended choice is the one provided by Oracle (formerly by Sun), which can be found at *http://www.java.com/ download/*. If you do not have Java already or are running into issues using it, please see "Java" on page 46.

Quick-Start Guide

Let us get started with the "tl;dr" section of this book: you want to know how to run HBase and you want to know it now! Nothing is easier than that because all you have to do is download the most recent release of HBase from the Apache HBase release page (*http://www.apache.org/dyn/closer.cgi/hbase/*) and unpack the contents into a suitable directory, such as */usr/local* or */opt*, like so:

```
$ cd /usr/local
$ tar -zxvf hbase-x.y.z.tar.gz
```

Setting the Data Directory

At this point, you are ready to start HBase. But before you do so, it is advisable to set the data directory to a proper location. You need to edit the configuration file *conf/ hbase-site.xml* and set the directory you want HBase to write to by assigning a value to the property key named `hbase.rootdir`:

```
<?xml version="1.0"?>
<?xml-stylesheet type="text/xsl" href="configuration.xsl"?>
<configuration>
  <property>
    <name>hbase.rootdir</name>
```

```
        <value>file:///<PATH>/hbase</value>
    </property>
</configuration>
```

Replace <PATH> in the preceding example configuration file with a path to a directory
where you want HBase to store its data. By default, hbase.rootdir is set to /tmp/hbase-
${user.name}, which could mean you lose all your data whenever your server reboots
because a lot of operating systems (OSes) clear out /tmp during a restart.

With that in place, we can start HBase and try our first interaction with it. We will use
the interactive shell to enter the status command at the prompt (complete the command by pressing the Return key):

```
$ cd /usr/local/hbase-0.91.0-SNAPSHOT
$ bin/start-hbase.sh
starting master, logging to \
/usr/local/hbase-0.91.0-SNAPSHOT/bin/../logs/hbase-<username>-master-localhost.out
$ bin/hbase shell
HBase Shell; enter 'help<RETURN>' for list of supported commands.
Type "exit<RETURN>" to leave the HBase Shell
Version 0.91.0-SNAPSHOT, r1130916, Sat Jul 23 12:44:34 CEST 2011

hbase(main):001:0> status
1 servers, 0 dead, 2.0000 average load
```

This confirms that HBase is up and running, so we will now issue a few commands to
show that we can put data into it and retrieve the same data subsequently.

It may not be clear, but what we are doing right now is similar to sitting
in a car with its brakes engaged and in neutral while turning the ignition
key. There is much more that you need to configure and understand
before you can use HBase in a production-like environment. But it lets
you get started with some basic HBase commands and become familiar
with top-level concepts.

We are currently running in the so-called *Standalone Mode*. We will look
into the available modes later on (see "Run Modes" on page 58), but
for now it's important to know that in this mode everything is run in a
single Java process and all files are stored in /tmp by default—unless you
did heed the important advice given earlier to change it to something
different. Many people have lost their test data during a reboot, only to
learn that they kept the default path. Once it is deleted by the OS, there
is no going back!

Let us now create a simple table and add a few rows with some data:

```
hbase(main):002:0> create 'testtable', 'colfam1'
0 row(s) in 0.2930 seconds

        hbase(main):003:0> list 'testtable'
TABLE
testtable
1 row(s) in 0.0520 seconds

hbase(main):004:0> put 'testtable', 'myrow-1', 'colfam1:q1', 'value-1'
0 row(s) in 0.1020 seconds

hbase(main):005:0> put 'testtable', 'myrow-2', 'colfam1:q2', 'value-2'
0 row(s) in 0.0410 seconds

hbase(main):006:0> put 'testtable', 'myrow-2', 'colfam1:q3', 'value-3'
0 row(s) in 0.0380 seconds
```

After we create the table with one column family, we verify that it actually exists by issuing a list command. You can see how it outputs the testtable name as the only table currently known. Subsequently, we are putting data into a number of rows. If you read the example carefully, you can see that we are adding data to two different rows with the keys myrow-1 and myrow-2. As we discussed in Chapter 1, we have one column family named colfam1, and can add an arbitrary qualifier to form actual columns, here colfam1:q1, colfam1:q2, and colfam1:q3.

Next we want to check if the data we added can be retrieved. We are using a scan operation to do so:

```
hbase(main):007:0> scan 'testtable'
ROW                COLUMN+CELL
 myrow-1            column=colfam1:q1, timestamp=1297345476469, value=value-1
 myrow-2            column=colfam1:q2, timestamp=1297345495663, value=value-2
 myrow-2            column=colfam1:q3, timestamp=1297345508999, value=value-3

2 row(s) in 0.1100 seconds
```

You can observe how HBase is printing the data in a cell-oriented way by outputting each column separately. It prints out myrow-2 twice, as expected, and shows the actual value for each column next to it.

If we want to get exactly one row back, we can also use the get command. It has many more options, which we will look at later, but for now simply try the following:

```
hbase(main):008:0> get 'testtable', 'myrow-1'
COLUMN             CELL
colfam1:q1         timestamp=1297345476469, value=value-1

1 row(s) in 0.0480 seconds
```

What is missing in our basic set of operations is to delete a value. Again, delete offers many options, but for now we just delete one specific cell and check that it is gone:

```
hbase(main):009:0> delete 'testtable', 'myrow-2', 'colfam1:q2'
0 row(s) in 0.0390 seconds

hbase(main):010:0> scan 'testtable'
ROW                COLUMN+CELL
 myrow-1             column=colfam1:q1, timestamp=1297345476469, value=value-1
 myrow-2             column=colfam1:q3, timestamp=1297345508999, value=value-3

2 row(s) in 0.0620 seconds
```

Before we conclude this simple exercise, we have to clean up by first disabling and then dropping the test table:

```
hbase(main):011:0> disable 'testtable'
0 row(s) in 2.1250 seconds

 hbase(main):012:0> drop 'testtable'
0 row(s) in 1.2780 seconds
```

Finally, we close the shell by means of the exit command and return to our command-line prompt:

```
hbase(main):013:0> exit
$ _
```

The last thing to do is stop HBase on our local system. We do this by running the *stop-hbase.sh* script:

```
$ bin/stop-hbase.sh
stopping hbase.....
```

That is all there is to it. We have successfully created a table, added, retrieved, and deleted data, and eventually dropped the table using the HBase Shell.

Requirements

Not all of the following requirements are needed for specific run modes HBase supports. For purely local testing, you only need Java, as mentioned in "Quick-Start Guide" on page 31.

Hardware

It is difficult to specify a particular server type that is recommended for HBase. In fact, the opposite is more appropriate, as HBase runs on many, very different hardware configurations. The usual description is *commodity* hardware. But what does that mean?

For starters, we are not talking about desktop PCs, but server-grade machines. Given that HBase is written in Java, you at least need support for a current Java Runtime, and since the majority of the memory needed per region server is for internal structures—for example, the memstores and the block cache—you will have to install a 64-bit operating system to be able to address enough memory, that is, more than 4 GB.

In practice, a lot of HBase setups are collocated with Hadoop, to make use of locality using HDFS as well as MapReduce. This can significantly reduce the required network I/O and boost processing speeds. Running Hadoop and HBase on the same server results in at least three Java processes running (data node, task tracker, and region server) and may spike to much higher numbers when executing MapReduce jobs. All of these processes need a minimum amount of memory, disk, and CPU resources to run sufficiently.

 It is assumed that you have a reasonably good understanding of Ha-doop, since it is used as the backing store for HBase in all known pro-duction systems (as of this writing). If you are completely new to HBase *and* Hadoop, it is recommended that you get familiar with Hadoop first, even on a very basic level. For example, read the recommended *Hadoop: The Definitive Guide* (*http://oreilly.com/catalog/0636920010388*) (Second Edition) by Tom White (O'Reilly), and set up a working HDFS and MapReduce cluster.

Giving all the available memory to the Java processes is also not a good idea, as most operating systems need some spare resources to work more effectively—for example, disk I/O buffers maintained by Linux kernels. HBase indirectly takes advantage of this because the already local disk I/O, given that you collocate the systems on the same server, will perform even better when the OS can keep its own block cache.

We can separate the requirements into two categories: servers and networking. We will look at the server hardware first and then into the requirements for the networking setup subsequently.

Servers

In HBase and Hadoop there are two types of machines: masters (the HDFS NameNode, the MapReduce JobTracker, and the HBase Master) and slaves (the HDFS DataNodes, the MapReduce TaskTrackers, and the HBase RegionServers). They do benefit from slightly different hardware specifications when possible. It is also quite common to use exactly the same hardware for both (out of convenience), but the master does not need that much storage, so it makes sense to not add too many disks. And since the masters are also more important than the slaves, you could beef them up with redundant hard-ware components. We will address the differences between the two where necessary.

Since Java runs in *user land*, you can run it on top of every operating system that sup-ports a Java Runtime—though there are recommended ones, and those where it does *not* run without user intervention (more on this in "Operating system" on page 40).

It allows you to select from a wide variety of vendors, or even build your own hardware. It comes down to more generic requirements like the following:

CPU

It makes no sense to run three or more Java processes, plus the services provided by the operating system itself, on single-core CPU machines. For production use, it is typical that you use *multicore* processors.* Quad-core are state of the art and affordable, while hexa-core processors are also becoming more popular. Most server hardware supports more than one CPU so that you can use two quad-core CPUs for a total of eight cores. This allows for each basic Java process to run on its own core while the background tasks like Java garbage collection can be executed in parallel. In addition, there is *hyperthreading*, which adds to their overall performance.

As far as CPU is concerned, you should spec the master and slave machines the same.

Node type	Recommendation
Master	Dual quad-core CPUs, 2.0-2.5 GHz
Slave	Dual quad-core CPUs, 2.0-2.5 GHz

Memory

The question really is: is there too much memory? In theory, no, but in practice, it has been empirically determined that when using Java you should not set the amount of memory given to a single process too high. Memory (called *heap* in Java terms) can start to get fragmented, and in a worst-case scenario, the entire heap would need rewriting—this is similar to the well-known disk fragmentation, but it cannot run in the background. The Java Runtime pauses all processing to clean up the mess, which can lead to quite a few problems (more on this later). The larger you have set the heap, the longer this process will take. Processes that do not need a lot of memory should only be given their required amount to avoid this scenario, but with the region servers and their block cache there is, in theory, no upper limit. You need to find a sweet spot depending on your access pattern.

At the time of this writing, setting the heap of the region servers to larger than 16 GB is considered dangerous. Once a stop-the-world garbage collection is required, it simply takes too long to rewrite the fragmented heap. Your server could be considered dead by the master and be removed from the working set.

This may change sometime as this is ultimately bound to the Java Runtime Environment used, and there is development going on to implement JREs that do not stop the running Java processes when performing garbage collections.

---

* See "Multi-core processor" (*http://en.wikipedia.org/wiki/Multi-core*) on Wikipedia.

Table 2-1 shows a very basic distribution of memory to specific processes. Please note that this is an example only and highly depends on the size of your cluster and how much data you put in, but also on your access pattern, such as interactive access only or a combination of interactive and batch use (using MapReduce).

Table 2-1. Exemplary memory allocation per Java process for a cluster with 800 TB of raw disk storage space

Process	Heap	Description
NameNode	8 GB	About 1 GB of heap for every 100 TB of raw data stored, or per every million files/inodes
SecondaryNameNode	8 GB	Applies the edits in memory, and therefore needs about the same amount as the NameNode
JobTracker	2 GB	Moderate requirements
HBase Master	4 GB	Usually lightly loaded, moderate requirements only
DataNode	1 GB	Moderate requirements
TaskTracker	1 GB	Moderate requirements
HBase RegionServer	12 GB	Majority of available memory, while leaving enough room for the operating system (for the buffer cache), and for the Task Attempt processes
Task Attempts	1 GB (ea.)	Multiply by the maximum number you allow for each
ZooKeeper	1 GB	Moderate requirements

An exemplary setup could be as such: for the master machine, running the Name-Node, SecondaryNameNode, JobTracker, and HBase Master, 24 GB of memory; and for the slaves, running the DataNodes, TaskTrackers, and HBase RegionServers, 24 GB or more.

Node type	Recommendation
Master	24 GB
Slave	24 GB (and up)

It is recommended that you optimize your RAM for the memory channel width of your server. For example, when using dual-channel memory, each machine should be configured with pairs of DIMMs. With triple-channel memory, each server should have triplets of DIMMs. This could mean that a server has 18 GB (9 × 2GB) of RAM instead of 16 GB (4 × 4GB).

Also make sure that not just the server's motherboard supports this feature, but also your CPU: some CPUs only support dual-channel memory, and therefore, even if you put in triple-channel DIIMMs, they will only be used in dual-channel mode.

Disks

The data is stored on the slave machines, and therefore it is those servers that need plenty of capacity. Depending on whether you are more read/write- or processing-oriented, you need to balance the number of disks with the number of CPU cores available. Typically, you should have at least one core per disk, so in an eight-core server, adding six disks is good, but adding more might not be giving you optimal performance.

RAID or JBOD?

A common question concerns how to attach the disks to the server. Here is where we can draw a line between the master server and the slaves. For the slaves, you should *not* use RAID,[†] but rather what is called JBOD.[‡] RAID is slower than separate disks because of the administrative overhead and pipelined writes, and depending on the RAID level (usually RAID 0 to be able to use the entire raw capacity), entire data nodes can become unavailable when a single disk fails.

For the master nodes, on the other hand, it does make sense to use a RAID disk setup to protect the crucial filesystem data. A common configuration is RAID 1+0, or RAID 0+1.

For both servers, though, make sure to use disks with *RAID firmware*. The difference between these and consumer-grade disks is that the RAID firmware will fail fast if there is a hardware error, and therefore will not freeze the DataNode in disk wait for a long time.

Some consideration should be given regarding the type of drives—for example, 2.5" versus 3.5" drives or SATA versus SAS. In general, SATA drives are recommended over SAS since they are more cost-effective, and since the nodes are all redundantly storing replicas of the data across multiple servers, you can safely use the more affordable disks. On the other hand, 3.5" disks are more reliable compared to 2.5" disks, but depending on the server chassis you may need to go with the latter.

The disk capacity is usually 1 TB per disk, but you can also use 2 TB drives if necessary. Using from six to 12 high-density servers with 1 TB to 2 TB drives is good, as you get a lot of storage capacity and the JBOD setup with enough cores can saturate the disk bandwidth nicely.

Node type	Recommendation
Master	4 × 1 TB SATA, RAID 0+1 (2 TB usable)
Slave	6 × 1 TB SATA, JBOD

† See "RAID" (*http://en.wikipedia.org/wiki/RAID*) on Wikipedia.

‡ See "JBOD" (*http://en.wikipedia.org/wiki/JBOD#JBOD*) on Wikipedia.

IOPS

The size of the disks is also an important vector to determine the overall *I/O operations per second* (IOPS) you can achieve with your server setup. For example, 4 × 1 TB drives is good for a general recommendation, which means the node can sustain about 400 IOPS and 400 MB/second transfer throughput for cold data accesses.§

What if you need more? You could use 8 × 500 GB drives, for 800 IOPS/second and near GigE network line rate for the disk throughput per node. Depending on your requirements, you need to make sure to combine the right number of disks to achieve your goals.

Chassis

The actual server chassis is not that crucial, as most servers in a specific price bracket provide very similar features. It is often better to shy away from special hardware that offers proprietary functionality and opt for generic servers so that they can be easily combined over time as you extend the capacity of the cluster.

As far as networking is concerned, it is recommended that you use a two-port Gigabit Ethernet card—or two channel-bonded cards. If you already have support for 10 Gigabit Ethernet or InfiniBand, you should use it.

For the slave servers, a single power supply unit (PSU) is sufficient, but for the master node you should use redundant PSUs, such as the optional dual PSUs available for many servers.

In terms of density, it is advisable to select server hardware that fits into a low number of rack units (abbreviated as "U"). Typically, 1U or 2U servers are used in 19" racks or cabinets. A consideration while choosing the size is how many disks they can hold and their power consumption. Usually a 1U server is limited to a lower number of disks or forces you to use 2.5" disks to get the capacity you want.

Node type	Recommendation
Master	Gigabit Ethernet, dual PSU, 1U or 2U
Slave	Gigabit Ethernet, single PSU, 1U or 2U

Networking

In a data center, servers are typically mounted into 19" racks or cabinets with 40U or more in height. You could fit up to 40 machines (although with half-depth servers, some companies have up to 80 machines in a single rack, 40 machines on either side) and link them together with a *top-of-rack* (ToR) switch. Given the Gigabit speed per server, you need to ensure that the ToR switch is fast enough to handle the throughput these servers can create. Often the backplane of a switch cannot handle all ports at line

§ This assumes 100 IOPS per drive, and 100 MB/second per drive.

rate or is oversubscribed—in other words, promising you something in theory it cannot do in reality.

Switches often have 24 or 48 ports, and with the aforementioned channel-bonding or two-port cards, you need to size the networking large enough to provide enough bandwidth. Installing 40 1U servers would need 80 network ports; so, in practice, you may need a staggered setup where you use multiple rack switches and then aggregate to a much larger *core aggregation switch* (CaS). This results in a *two-tier* architecture, where the distribution is handled by the ToR switch and the aggregation by the CaS.

While we cannot address all the considerations for large-scale setups, we can still notice that this is a common design pattern. Given that the operations team is part of the planning, and it is known how much data is going to be stored and how many clients are expected to read and write concurrently, this involves basic math to compute the number of servers needed—which also drives the networking considerations.

When users have reported issues with HBase on the public mailing list or on other channels, especially regarding slower-than-expected I/O performance bulk inserting huge amounts of data, it became clear that networking was either the main or a contributing issue. This ranges from misconfigured or faulty network interface cards (NICs) to completely oversubscribed switches in the I/O path. Please make sure that you verify every component in the cluster to avoid sudden operational problems—the kind that could have been avoided by sizing the hardware appropriately.

Finally, given the current status of built-in security in Hadoop and HBase, it is common for the entire cluster to be located in its own network, possibly protected by a firewall to control access to the few required, client-facing ports.

Software

After considering the hardware and purchasing the server machines, it's time to consider software. This can range from the operating system itself to filesystem choices and configuration of various auxiliary services.

 Most of the requirements listed are independent of HBase and have to be applied on a very low, operational level. You may have to advise with your administrator to get everything applied and verified.

Operating system

Recommending an operating system (OS) is a tough call, especially in the open source realm. In terms of the past two to three years, it seems there is a preference for using Linux with HBase. In fact, Hadoop and HBase are inherently designed to work with Linux, or any other Unix-like system, or with Unix. While you are free to run either one on a different OS as long as it supports Java—for example, Windows—they have only been tested with Unix-like systems. The supplied start and stop scripts, for example, expect a command-line shell as provided by Linux or Unix.

Within the Unix and Unix-like group you can also differentiate between those that are free (as in they cost no money) and those you have to pay for. Again, both will work and your choice is often limited by company-wide regulations. Here is a short list of operating systems that are commonly found as a basis for HBase clusters:

CentOS

CentOS is a community-supported, free software operating system, based on Red Hat Enterprise Linux (as RHEL). It mirrors RHEL in terms of functionality, features, and package release levels as it is using the source code packages Red Hat provides for its own enterprise product to create CentOS-branded counterparts. Like RHEL, it provides the packages in *RPM* format.

It is also focused on enterprise usage, and therefore does not adopt new features or newer versions of existing packages too quickly. The goal is to provide an OS that can be rolled out across a large-scale infrastructure while not having to deal with short-term gains of small, incremental package updates.

Fedora

Fedora is also a community-supported, free and open source operating system, and is sponsored by Red Hat. But compared to RHEL and CentOS, it is more a playground for new technologies and strives to advance new ideas and features. Because of that, it has a much shorter life cycle compared to enterprise-oriented products. An average maintenance period for a Fedora release is around 13 months.

The fact that it is aimed at workstations and has been enhanced with many new features has made Fedora a quite popular choice, only beaten by more desktop-oriented operating systems.[||] For production use, you may want to take into account the reduced life cycle that counteracts the freshness of this distribution. You may also want to consider not using the latest Fedora release, but trailing by one version to be able to rely on some feedback from the community as far as stability and other issues are concerned.

Debian

Debian is another Linux-kernel-based OS that has software packages released as free and open source software. It can be used for desktop and server systems and has a conservative approach when it comes to package updates. Releases are only published after all included packages have been sufficiently tested and deemed stable.

As opposed to other distributions, Debian is not backed by a commercial entity, but rather is solely governed by its own project rules. It also uses its own packaging

---

[||] DistroWatch (*http://distrowatch.com/*) has a list of popular Linux and Unix-like operating systems and maintains a ranking by popularity.

system that supports *DEB* packages only. Debian is known to run on many hardware platforms as well as having a very large repository of packages.

Ubuntu

Ubuntu is a Linux distribution based on Debian. It is distributed as free and open source software, and backed by Canonical Ltd., which is not charging for the OS but is selling technical support for Ubuntu.

The life cycle is split into a longer- and a shorter-term release. The *long-term support* (LTS) releases are supported for three years on the desktop and five years on the server. The packages are also DEB format and are based on the *unstable* branch of Debian: Ubuntu, in a sense, is for Debian what Fedora is for Red Hat Linux. Using Ubuntu as a server operating system is made more difficult as the update cycle for critical components is very frequent.

Solaris

Solaris is offered by Oracle, and is available for a limited number of architecture platforms. It is a descendant of Unix System V Release 4, and therefore, the most different OS in this list. Some of the source code is available as open source while the rest is closed source. Solaris is a commercial product and needs to be purchased. The commercial support for each release is maintained for 10 to 12 years.

Red Hat Enterprise Linux

Abbreviated as RHEL, Red Hat's Linux distribution is aimed at commercial and enterprise-level customers. The OS is available as a server and a desktop version. The license comes with offerings for official support, training, and a certification program.

The package format for RHEL is called *RPM* (the Red Hat Package Manager), and it consists of the software packaged in the *.rpm* file format, and the package manager itself.

Being commercially supported and maintained, RHEL has a very long life cycle of 7 to 10 years.

You have a choice when it comes to the operating system you are going to use on your servers. A sensible approach is to choose one you feel comfortable with and that fits into your existing infrastructure.

As for a recommendation, many production systems running HBase are on top of CentOS, or RHEL.

Filesystem

With the operating system selected, you will have a few choices of filesystems to use with your disks. There is not a lot of publicly available empirical data in regard to comparing different filesystems and their effect on HBase, though. The common systems in use are ext3, ext4, and XFS, but you may be able to use others as well. For some there are HBase users reporting on their findings, while for more exotic ones you would need to run enough tests before using it on your production cluster.

> Note that the selection of filesystems is for the HDFS data nodes. HBase is directly impacted when using HDFS as its backing store.

Here are some notes on the more commonly used filesystems:

ext3

One of the most ubiquitous filesystems on the Linux operating system is *ext3* (see *http://en.wikipedia.org/wiki/Ext3* for details). It has been proven stable and reliable, meaning it is a safe bet in terms of setting up your cluster with it. Being part of Linux since 2001, it has been steadily improved over time and has been the default filesystem for years.

There are a few optimizations you should keep in mind when using ext3. First, you should set the `noatime` option when mounting the filesystem to reduce the administrative overhead required for the kernel to keep the *access time* for each file. It is not needed or even used by HBase, and disabling it speeds up the disk's read performance.

> Disabling the last access time gives you a performance boost and is a recommended optimization. Mount options are typically specified in a configuration file called */etc/fstab*. Here is a Linux example line where the `noatime` option is specified:
>
> ```
> /dev/sdd1  /data  ext3  defaults,noatime  0  0
> ```
>
> Note that this also implies the `nodiratime` option.

Another optimization is to make better use of the disk space provided by ext3. By default, it reserves a specific number of bytes in blocks for situations where a disk fills up but crucial system processes need this space to continue to function. This is really useful for critical disks—for example, the one hosting the operating system—but it is less useful for the storage drives, and in a large enough cluster it can have a significant impact on available storage capacities.

You can reduce the number of reserved blocks and gain more usable disk space by using the `tune2fs` command-line tool that comes with ext3 and Linux. By default, it is set to 5% but can safely be reduced to 1% (or even 0%) for the data drives. This is done with the following command:

```
tune2fs -m 1 <device-name>
```

Replace `<device-name>` with the disk you want to adjust—for example, `/dev/sdd1`. Do this for all disks on which you want to store data. The `-m 1` defines the percentage, so use `-m 0`, for example, to set the reserved block count to zero.

A final word of caution: only do this for your data disk, *NOT* for the disk hosting the OS nor for any drive on the master node!

Yahoo! has publicly stated that it is using ext3 as its filesystem of choice on its large Hadoop cluster farm. This shows that, although it is by far not the most current or modern filesystem, it does very well in large clusters. In fact, you are more likely to saturate your I/O on other levels of the stack before reaching the limits of ext3.

The biggest drawback of ext3 is that during the bootstrap process of the servers it requires the largest amount of time. Formatting a disk with ext3 can take minutes to complete and may become a nuisance when spinning up machines dynamically on a regular basis—although that is not a very common practice.

ext4

The successor to ext3 is called ext4 (see *http://en.wikipedia.org/wiki/Ext4* for details) and initially was based on the same code but was subsequently moved into its own project. It has been officially part of the Linux kernel since the end of 2008. To that extent, it has had only a few years to prove its stability and reliability. Nevertheless, Google has announced plans[#] to upgrade its storage infrastructure from ext2 to ext4. This can be considered a strong endorsement, but also shows the advantage of the *extended filesystem* (the *ext* in ext3, ext4, etc.) lineage to be upgradable in place. Choosing an entirely different filesystem like XFS would have made this impossible.

Performance-wise, ext4 does beat ext3 and allegedly comes close to the high-performance XFS. It also has many advanced features that allow it to store files up to 16 TB in size and support volumes up to 1 exabyte (i.e., 10^{18} bytes).

A more critical feature is the so-called *delayed allocation*, and it is recommended that you turn it off for Hadoop and HBase use. Delayed allocation keeps the data in memory and reserves the required number of blocks until the data is finally flushed to disk. It helps in keeping blocks for files together and can at times write

---

[#]See this post (*http://arstechnica.com/open-source/news/2010/01/google-upgrading-to-ext4-hires-former-linux-foundation-cto.ars*) on the Ars Technica website. Google hired the main developer of ext4, Theodore Ts'o, who announced plans to keep working on ext4 as well as other Linux kernel features.

the entire file into a contiguous set of blocks. This reduces fragmentation and improves performance when reading the file subsequently. On the other hand, it increases the possibility of data loss in case of a server crash.

XFS

XFS (see *http://en.wikipedia.org/wiki/Xfs* for details) became available on Linux at about the same time as ext3. It was originally developed by Silicon Graphics in 1993. Most Linux distributions today have XFS support included.

Its features are similar to those of ext4; for example, both have *extents* (grouping contiguous blocks together, reducing the number of blocks required to maintain per file) and the aforementioned delayed allocation.

A great advantage of XFS during bootstrapping a server is the fact that it formats the entire drive in virtually no time. This can significantly reduce the time required to provision new servers with many storage disks.

On the other hand, there are some drawbacks to using XFS. There is a known shortcoming in the design that impacts metadata operations, such as deleting a large number of files. The developers have picked up on the issue and applied various fixes to improve the situation. You will have to check how you use HBase to determine if this might affect you. For normal use, you should not have a problem with this limitation of XFS, as HBase operates on fewer but larger files.

ZFS

Introduced in 2005, ZFS (see *http://en.wikipedia.org/wiki/ZFS* for details) was developed by Sun Microsystems. The name is an abbreviation for *zettabyte filesystem*, as it has the ability to store 2^{58} zettabytes (which, in turn, is 10^{21} bytes).

ZFS is primarily supported on Solaris and has advanced features that may be useful in combination with HBase. It has built-in compression support that could be used as a replacement for the pluggable compression codecs in HBase.

It seems that choosing a filesystem is analogous to choosing an operating system: pick one that you feel comfortable with and that fits into your existing infrastructure. Simply picking one over the other based on plain numbers is difficult without proper testing and comparison. If you have a choice, it seems to make sense to opt for a more modern system like ext4 or XFS, as sooner or later they will replace ext3 and are already much more scalable and perform better than their older sibling.

 Installing different filesystems on a single server is not recommended. This can have adverse effects on performance as the kernel may have to split buffer caches to support the different filesystems. It has been reported that, for certain operating systems, this can have a devastating performance impact. Make sure you test this issue carefully if you have to mix filesystems.

Java

It was mentioned in the note on page 31 that you do need Java for HBase. Not just any version of Java, but version 6, a.k.a. 1.6, or later. The recommended choice is the one provided by Oracle (formerly by Sun), which can be found at *http://www.java.com/download/*.

You also should make sure the java binary is executable and can be found on your path. Try entering java -version on the command line and verify that it works and that it prints out the version number indicating it is version 1.6 or later—for example, java version "1.6.0_22". You usually want the latest update level, but sometimes you may find unexpected problems (version 1.6.0_18, for example, is known to cause random JVM crashes) and it may be worth trying an older release to verify.

If you do not have Java on the command-line path or if HBase fails to start with a warning that it was not able to find it (see Example 2-1), edit the *conf/hbase-env.sh* file by commenting out the JAVA_HOME line and changing its value to where your Java is installed.

Example 2-1. Error message printed by HBase when no Java executable was found

```
+========================================================================+
|      Error: JAVA_HOME is not set and Java could not be found           |
+------------------------------------------------------------------------+
| Please download the latest Sun JDK from the Sun Java web site          |
|         > http://java.sun.com/javase/downloads/ <                      |
|                                                                        |
| HBase requires Java 1.6 or later.                                      |
| NOTE: This script will find Sun Java whether you install using the     |
|        binary or the RPM based installer.                              |
+========================================================================+
```

 The supplied scripts try many default locations for Java, so there is a good chance HBase will find it automatically. If it does not, you most likely have no Java Runtime installed at all. Start with the download link provided at the beginning of this subsection and read the manuals of your operating system to find out how to install it.

Hadoop

Currently, HBase is bound to work only with the specific version of Hadoop it was built against. One of the reasons for this behavior concerns the *remote procedure call* (RPC) API between HBase and Hadoop. The wire protocol is versioned and needs to match up; even small differences can cause a broken communication between them.

The current version of HBase will only run on Hadoop 0.20.x (*http://hadoop.apache .org/common/releases.html*). It will not run on Hadoop 0.21.x (nor 0.22.x) as of this writing. HBase may lose data in a catastrophic event unless it is running on an HDFS that has durable *sync* support. Hadoop 0.20.2 and Hadoop 0.20.203.0 do *not* have this support. Currently, only the branch-0.20-append (*http://svn.apache.org/viewvc/ha doop/common/branches/branch-0.20-append/*) branch has this attribute.* No official re- leases have been made from this branch up to now, so you will have to build your own Hadoop from the tip of this branch. Scroll down in the Hadoop How To Release (*http: //wiki.apache.org/hadoop/HowToRelease*) to the "Build Requirements" section for in- structions on how to build Hadoop.[†]

Another option, if you do not want to build your own version of Hadoop, is to use a distribution that has the patches already applied. You could use Cloudera's CDH3 (*http://archive.cloudera.com/docs/*). CDH has the 0.20-append patches needed to add a durable *sync*. We will discuss this in more detail in "Cloudera's Distribution Including Apache Hadoop" on page 493.

Because HBase depends on Hadoop, it bundles an instance of the Hadoop JAR under its *lib* directory. The bundled Hadoop was made from the Apache branch-0.20-append branch at the time of HBase's release. It is *critical* that the version of Hadoop that is in use on your cluster matches what is used by HBase. Replace the Hadoop JAR found in the HBase *lib* directory with the *hadoop-xyz.jar* you are running on your cluster to avoid version mismatch issues. Make sure you replace the JAR on all servers in your cluster that run HBase. Version mismatch issues have various manifestations, but often the result is the same: HBase does not throw an error, but simply blocks indefinitely.

 The bundled JAR that ships with HBase is considered *only* for use in standalone mode.

A different approach is to install a vanilla Hadoop 0.20.2 and then replace the vanilla Hadoop JAR with the one supplied by HBase. This is not tested extensively but seems to work. Your mileage may vary.

---

* See CHANGES.txt (*http://svn.apache.org/viewvc/hadoop/common/branches/branch-0.20-append/CHANGES .txt*) in branch-0.20-append to see a list of patches involved in adding append on the Hadoop 0.20 branch.

† This is very likely to change after this book is printed. Consult with the online configuration guide (*http:// hbase.apache.org/book/configuration.html*) for the latest details; especially the section on Hadoop (*http:// hbase.apache.org/book/hadoop.html*).

HBase will run on any Hadoop 0.20.x that incorporates Hadoop security features—for example, CDH3—as long as you do as suggested in the preceding text and replace the Hadoop JAR that ships with HBase with the secure version.

SSH

Note that *ssh* must be installed and *sshd* must be running if you want to use the supplied scripts to manage remote Hadoop and HBase daemons. A commonly used software package providing these commands is OpenSSH, available from *http://www.openssh.com/*. Check with your operating system manuals first, as many OSes have mechanisms to install an already compiled binary release package as opposed to having to build it yourself. On a Ubuntu workstation, for example, you can use:

```
$ sudo apt-get install openssh-client
```

On the servers, you would install the matching server package:

```
$ sudo apt-get install openssh-server
```

You must be able to *ssh* to all nodes, including your local node, using *passwordless* login. You will need to have a public key pair—you can either use the one you already use (see the *.ssh* directory located in your home directory) or you will have to generate one—and add your public key on each server so that the scripts can access the remote servers without further intervention.

The supplied shell scripts make use of SSH to send commands to each server in the cluster. It is strongly advised that you not use simple *password* authentication. Instead, you should use public key authentication—only!

When you create your key pair, also add a *passphrase* to protect your private key. To avoid the hassle of being asked for the passphrase for every single command sent to a remote server, it is recommended that you use *ssh-agent*, a helper that comes with SSH. It lets you enter the passphrase only once and then takes care of all subsequent requests to provide it.

Ideally, you would also use the *agent forwarding* that is built in to log in to other remote servers from your cluster nodes.

Domain Name Service

HBase uses the local *hostname* to self-report its IP address. Both forward and reverse DNS resolving should work. You can verify if the setup is correct for forward DNS lookups by running the following command:

```
$ ping -c 1 $(hostname)
```

You need to make sure that it reports the public IP address of the server and *not* the *loopback* address `127.0.0.1`. A typical reason for this not to work concerns an incorrect */etc/hosts* file, containing a mapping of the machine name to the loopback address.

If your machine has multiple interfaces, HBase will use the interface that the primary hostname resolves to. If this is insufficient, you can set `hbase.regionserver.dns.interface` (see "Configuration" on page 63 for information on how to do this) to indicate the primary interface. This only works if your cluster configuration is consistent and every host has the same network interface configuration.

Another alternative is to set `hbase.regionserver.dns.nameserver` to choose a different name server than the system-wide default.

Synchronized time

The clocks on cluster nodes should be in basic alignment. Some skew is tolerable, but wild skew can generate odd behaviors. Even differences of only one minute can cause unexplainable behavior. Run NTP (*http://en.wikipedia.org/wiki/Network_Time_Proto col*) on your cluster, or an equivalent application, to synchronize the time on all servers.

If you are having problems querying data, or you are seeing *weird* behavior running cluster operations, check the system time!

File handles and process limits

HBase is a database, so it uses a lot of files at the same time. The default `ulimit -n` of 1024 on most Unix or other Unix-like systems is insufficient. Any significant amount of loading will lead to I/O errors stating the obvious: `java.io.IOException: Too many open files`. You may also notice errors such as the following:

```
2010-04-06 03:04:37,542 INFO org.apache.hadoop.hdfs.DFSClient: Exception
    in createBlockOutputStream java.io.EOFException
2010-04-06 03:04:37,542 INFO org.apache.hadoop.hdfs.DFSClient: Abandoning
    block blk_-6935524980745310745_1391901
```

 These errors are usually found in the logfiles. See "Analyzing the Logs" on page 469 for details on their location, and how to analyze their content.

You need to change the upper bound on the number of file descriptors. Set it to a number larger than 10,000. To be clear, upping the file descriptors for the user who is running the HBase process is an operating system configuration, not an HBase configuration. Also, a common mistake is that administrators will increase the file descriptors for a particular user but HBase is running with a different user account.

You can estimate the number of required file handles roughly as follows. Per column family, there is at least one storage file, and possibly up to five or six if a region is under load; on average, though, there are three storage files per column family. To determine the number of required file handles, you multiply the number of column families by the number of regions per region server. For example, say you have a schema of 3 column families per region and you have 100 regions per region server. The JVM will open 3 × 3 × 100 storage files = 900 file descriptors, not counting open JAR files, configuration files, CRC32 files, and so on. Run *lsof -p REGIONSERVER_PID* to see the accurate number.

As the first line in its logs, HBase prints the ulimit it is seeing. Ensure that it's correctly reporting the increased limit.[‡] See "Analyzing the Logs" on page 469 for details on how to find this information in the logs, as well as other details that can help you find—and solve—problems with an HBase setup.

You may also need to edit */etc/sysctl.conf* and adjust the `fs.file-max` value. See this post on Server Fault (*http://serverfault.com/questions/165316/how-to-configure-linux-file-descriptor-limit-with-fs-file-max-and-ulimit/*) for details.

Example: Setting File Handles on Ubuntu

If you are on Ubuntu, you will need to make the following changes.

In the file */etc/security/limits.conf* add this line:

```
hadoop  -       nofile  32768
```

Replace `hadoop` with whatever user is running Hadoop and HBase. If you have separate users, you will need two entries, one for each user.

In the file */etc/pam.d/common-session* add the following as the last line in the file:

```
session required  pam_limits.so
```

Otherwise, the changes in */etc/security/limits.conf* won't be applied.

Don't forget to log out and back in again for the changes to take effect!

[‡] A useful document on setting configuration values on your Hadoop cluster is Aaron Kimball's "Configuration Parameters: What can you just ignore?" (*http://www.cloudera.com/blog/2009/03/configuration-parameters-what-can-you-just-ignore/*).

You should also consider increasing the number of processes allowed by adjusting the nproc value in the same */etc/security/limits.conf* file referenced earlier. With a low limit and a server under duress, you could see `OutOfMemoryError` exceptions, which will eventually cause the entire Java process to end. As with the file handles, you need to make sure this value is set for the appropriate user account running the process.

Datanode handlers

A Hadoop HDFS data node has an upper bound on the number of files that it will serve at any one time. The upper bound parameter is called `xcievers` (yes, this is misspelled). Again, before doing any loading, make sure you have configured Hadoop's *conf/hdfs-site.xml* file, setting the `xcievers` value to at least the following:

```
<property>
  <name>dfs.datanode.max.xcievers</name>
  <value>4096</value>
</property>
```

 Be sure to restart your HDFS after making the preceding configuration changes.

Not having this configuration in place makes for strange-looking failures. Eventually, you will see a complaint in the datanode logs about the `xcievers` limit being exceeded, but on the run up to this one manifestation is a complaint about missing blocks. For example:

```
10/12/08 20:10:31 INFO hdfs.DFSClient: Could not obtain block
    blk_XXXXXXXXXXXXXXXXXXXXXX_YYYYYYYY from any node: java.io.IOException:
    No live nodes contain current block. Will get new block locations from
    namenode and retry...
```

Swappiness

You need to prevent your servers from running out of memory over time. We already discussed one way to do this: setting the heap sizes small enough that they give the operating system enough room for its own processes. Once you get close to the physically available memory, the OS starts to use the configured *swap* space. This is typically located on disk in its own partition and is used to page out processes and their allocated memory until it is needed again.

Swapping—while being a good thing on workstations—is something to be avoided at all costs on servers. Once the server starts swapping, performance is reduced significantly, up to a point where you may not even be able to log in to such a system because the remote access process (e.g., SSHD) is coming to a grinding halt.

HBase needs guaranteed CPU cycles and must obey certain freshness guarantees—for example, to renew the ZooKeeper sessions. It has been observed over and over again that swapping servers start to miss renewing their leases and are considered lost subsequently by the ZooKeeper ensemble. The regions on these servers are redeployed on other servers, which now take extra pressure and may fall into the same trap.

Even worse are scenarios where the swapping server wakes up and now needs to realize it is considered dead by the master node. It will report for duty as if nothing has happened and receive a YouAreDeadException in the process, telling it that it has missed its chance to continue, and therefore terminates itself. There are quite a few implicit issues with this scenario—for example, pending updates, which we will address later. Suffice it to say that this is *not good*.

You can tune down the *swappiness* of the server by adding this line to the */etc/sysctl.conf* configuration file on Linux and Unix-like systems:

```
vm.swappiness=5
```

You can try values like 0 or 5 to reduce the system's likelihood to use swap space.

Some more radical operators have turned off swapping completely (see *swappoff* on Linux), and would rather have their systems run "against the wall" than deal with swapping issues. Choose something you feel comfortable with, but make sure you keep an eye on this problem.

Finally, you may have to reboot the server for the changes to take effect, as a simple

```
sysctl -p
```

might not suffice. This obviously is for Unix-like systems and you will have to adjust this for your operating system.

Windows

HBase running on Windows has not been tested to a great extent. Running a production install of HBase on top of Windows is not recommended.

If you are running HBase on Windows, you must install Cygwin (*http://cygwin.com/*) to have a Unix-like environment for the shell scripts. The full details are explained in the Windows Installation guide (*http://hbase.apache.org/cygwin.html*) on the HBase website.

Filesystems for HBase

The most common filesystem used with HBase is HDFS. But you are not locked into HDFS because the FileSystem used by HBase has a pluggable architecture and can be used to replace HDFS with any other supported system. In fact, you could go as far as implementing your own filesystem—maybe even on top of another database. The possibilities are endless and waiting for the brave at heart.

In this section, we are not talking about the low-level filesystems used by the operating system (see "Filesystem" on page 43 for that), but the storage layer filesystems. These are abstractions that define higher-level features and APIs, which are then used by Hadoop to store the data. The data is eventually stored on a disk, at which point the OS filesystem is used.

HDFS is the most used and tested filesystem in production. Almost all production clusters use it as the underlying storage layer. It is proven stable and reliable, so deviating from it may impose its own risks and subsequent problems.

The primary reason HDFS is so popular is its built-in replication, fault tolerance, and scalability. Choosing a different filesystem should provide the same guarantees, as HBase implicitly assumes that data is stored in a reliable manner by the filesystem. It has no added means to replicate data or even maintain copies of its own storage files. This functionality *must* be provided by the lower-level system.

You can select a different filesystem implementation by using a URI[§] pattern, where the *scheme* (the part before the first ":", i.e., the colon) part of the URI identifies the driver to be used. Figure 2-1 shows how the Hadoop filesystem is different from the low-level OS filesystems for the actual disks.

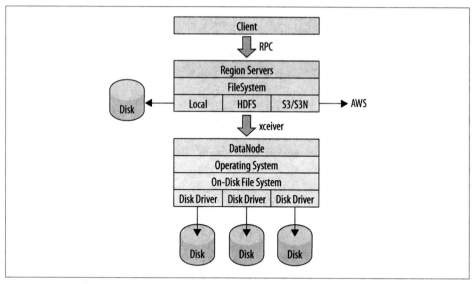

Figure 2-1. The filesystem negotiating transparently where data is stored

---

§ See "Uniform Resource Identifier" (*http://en.wikipedia.org/wiki/Uniform_Resource_Identifier*) on Wikipedia.

You can use a filesystem that is already supplied by Hadoop: it ships with a list of filesystems,‖ which you may want to try out first. As a last resort—or if you're an experienced developer—you can also write your own filesystem implementation.

Local

The *local* filesystem actually bypasses Hadoop entirely, that is, you do not need to have an HDFS or any other cluster at all. It is handled all in the `FileSystem` class used by HBase to connect to the filesystem implementation. The supplied `ChecksumFileSys tem` class is loaded by the client and uses local disk paths to store all the data.

The beauty of this approach is that HBase is unaware that it is not talking to a distributed filesystem on a remote or collocated cluster, but actually is using the local filesystem directly. The *standalone mode* of HBase uses this feature to run HBase only. You can select it by using the following scheme:

```
file:///<path>
```

Similar to the URIs used in a web browser, the `file:` scheme addresses local files.

HDFS

The *Hadoop Distributed File System* (HDFS) is the default filesystem when deploying a fully distributed cluster. For HBase, HDFS is the filesystem of choice, as it has all the required features. As we discussed earlier, HDFS is built to work with MapReduce, taking full advantage of its parallel, streaming access support. The scalability, fail safety, and automatic replication functionality is ideal for storing files reliably. HBase adds the random access layer missing from HDFS and ideally complements Hadoop. Using MapReduce, you can do bulk imports, creating the storage files at disk-transfer speeds.

The URI to access HDFS uses the following scheme:

```
hdfs://<namenode>:<port>/<path>
```

S3

Amazon's *Simple Storage Service* (S3)# is a storage system that is primarily used in combination with dynamic servers running on Amazon's complementary service named *Elastic Compute Cloud* (EC2).*

S3 can be used directly and without EC2, but the bandwidth used to transfer data in and out of S3 is going to be cost-prohibitive in practice. Transferring between EC2 and

---

‖ A full list was compiled by Tom White in his post "Get to Know Hadoop Filesystems" (*http://answers.oreilly .com/topic/456-get-to-know-hadoop-filesystems/*).

#See "Amazon S3" (*http://en.wikipedia.org/wiki/Amazon_S3*) for more background information.

* See "EC2" (*http://en.wikipedia.org/wiki/Amazon_EC2*) on Wikipedia.

S3 is free, and therefore a viable option. One way to start an EC2-based cluster is shown in "Apache Whirr" on page 69.

The S3 FileSystem implementation provided by Hadoop supports two different modes: the *raw* (or *native*) mode, and the *block-based* mode. The raw mode uses the `s3n:` URI scheme and writes the data directly into S3, similar to the local filesystem. You can see all the files in your bucket the same way as you would on your local disk.

The `s3:` scheme is the block-based mode and was used to overcome S3's former maximum file size limit of 5 GB. This has since been changed, and therefore the selection is now more difficult—or easy: opt for `s3n:` if you are not going to exceed 5 GB per file.

The block mode emulates the HDFS filesystem on top of S3. It makes browsing the bucket content more difficult as only the internal block files are visible, and the HBase storage files are stored arbitrarily inside these blocks and strewn across them. You can select the filesystem using these URIs:

```
s3://<bucket-name>
s3n://<bucket-name>
```

Other Filesystems

There are other filesystems, and one that deserves mention is *CloudStore* (formerly known as the *Kosmos filesystem*, abbreviated as KFS and the namesake of the URI scheme shown at the end of the next paragraph). It is an open source, distributed, high-performance filesystem written in C++, with similar features to HDFS. Find more information about it at the CloudStore website (*http://kosmosfs.sourceforge.net/*).

It is available for Solaris and Linux, originally developed by Kosmix and released as open source in 2007. To select CloudStore as the filesystem for HBase use the following URI format:

```
kfs:///<path>
```

Installation Choices

Once you have decided on the basic OS-related options, you must somehow get HBase onto your servers. You have a couple of choices, which we will look into next. Also see Appendix D for even more options.

Apache Binary Release

The canonical installation process of most Apache projects is to download a release, usually provided as an archive containing all the required files. Some projects have separate archives for a *binary* and *source* release—the former intended to have everything needed to run the release and the latter containing all files needed to build the project yourself. HBase comes as a single package, containing binary and source files together. For more information on HBase releases, you may also want to check out the *Release Notes*† page. Another interesting page is titled *Change Log*,‡ and it lists everything that was added, fixed, or changed in any form for each release version.

You can download the most recent release of HBase from the Apache HBase release page (*http://www.apache.org/dyn/closer.cgi/hbase/*) and unpack the contents into a suitable directory, such as */usr/local* or */opt*, like so:

```
$ cd /usr/local
$ tar -zxvf hbase-x.y.z.tar.gz
```

Once you have extracted all the files, you can make yourself familiar with what is in the project's directory. The content may look like this:

```
$ ls -lr
-rw-r--r--    1 larsgeorge  staff    192809 Feb 15 01:54 CHANGES.txt
-rw-r--r--    1 larsgeorge  staff     11358 Feb  9 01:23 LICENSE.txt
-rw-r--r--    1 larsgeorge  staff       293 Feb  9 01:23 NOTICE.txt
-rw-r--r--    1 larsgeorge  staff      1358 Feb  9 01:23 README.txt
drwxr-xr-x   23 larsgeorge  staff       782 Feb  9 01:23 bin
drwxr-xr-x    7 larsgeorge  staff       238 Feb  9 01:23 conf
drwxr-xr-x   64 larsgeorge  staff      2176 Feb 15 01:56 docs
-rwxr-xr-x    1 larsgeorge  staff    905762 Feb 15 01:56 hbase-0.90.1-tests.jar
-rwxr-xr-x    1 larsgeorge  staff   2242043 Feb 15 01:56 hbase-0.90.1.jar
drwxr-xr-x    5 larsgeorge  staff       170 Feb 15 01:55 hbase-webapps
drwxr-xr-x   32 larsgeorge  staff      1088 Mar  3 12:07 lib
-rw-r--r--    1 larsgeorge  staff     29669 Feb 15 01:28 pom.xml
drwxr-xr-x    9 larsgeorge  staff       306 Feb  9 01:23 src
```

The root of it only contains a few text files, stating the license terms (*LICENSE.txt* and *NOTICE.txt*) and some general information on how to find your way around (*README.txt*). The *CHANGES.txt* file is a static snapshot of the change log page mentioned earlier. It contains all the changes that went into the current release you downloaded.

You will also find the Java archive, or JAR files, that contain the compiled Java code plus all other necessary resources. There are two variations of the JAR file, one with just the name and version number and one with a postfix of *tests*. This file contains the code required to run the tests provided by HBase. These are functional unit tests that the developers use to verify a release is fully operational and that there are no regressions.

The last file found is named *pom.xml* and is the Maven project file needed to build HBase from the sources. See "Building from Source" on page 58.

---

† *https://issues.apache.org/jira/browse/HBASE?report=com.atlassian.jira.plugin.system.project:changelog-panel.*

‡ *https://issues.apache.org/jira/browse/HBASE?report=com.atlassian.jira.plugin.system.project:changelog-panel#selectedTab=com.atlassian.jira.plugin.system.project%3Achangelog-panel.*

The remainder of the content in the root directory consists of other directories, which are explained in the following list:

bin

> The *bin*—or *binaries*—directory contains the scripts supplied by HBase to start and stop HBase, run separate daemons,§ or start additional master nodes. See "Running and Confirming Your Installation" on page 71 for information on how to use them.

conf

> The configuration directory contains the files that define how HBase is set up. "Configuration" on page 63 explains the contained files in great detail.

docs

> This directory contains a copy of the HBase project website, including the documentation for all the tools, the API, and the project itself. Open your web browser of choice and open the *docs/index.html* file by either dragging it into the browser, double-clicking that file, or using the *File→Open* (or similarly named) menu.

hbase-webapps

> HBase has web-based user interfaces which are implemented as Java web applications, using the files located in this directory. Most likely you will never have to touch this directory when working with or deploying HBase into production.

lib

> Java-based applications are usually an assembly of many auxiliary libraries plus the JAR file containing the actual program. All of these libraries are located in the *lib* directory.

logs

> Since the HBase processes are started as daemons (i.e., they are running in the background of the operating system performing their duty), they use logfiles to report their state, progress, and optionally, errors that occur during their life cycle. "Analyzing the Logs" on page 469 explains how to make sense of their rather cryptic content.

> Initially, there may be no *logs* directory, as it is created when you start HBase for the first time. The logging framework used by HBase is creating the directory and logfiles dynamically.

src

> In case you plan to build your own binary package (see "Building from Source" on page 58 for information on how to do that), or you decide you would

---

§ Processes that are started and then run in the background to perform their task are often referred to as *daemons*.

like to join the international team of developers working on HBase, you will need this *source* directory, containing everything required to roll your own release.

Since you have unpacked a release archive, you can now move on to "Run Modes" on page 58 to decide how you want to run HBase.

Building from Source

HBase uses *Maven* to build the binary packages. You therefore need a working Maven installation, plus a full *Java Development Kit* (JDK)—not just a Java Runtime as used in "Quick-Start Guide" on page 31.

 This section is important only if you want to build HBase from its sources. This might be necessary if you want to apply patches, which can add new functionality you may be requiring.

Once you have confirmed that both are set up properly, you can build the binary packages using the following command:

```
$ mvn assembly:assembly
```

Note that the tests for HBase need more than one hour to complete. If you trust the code to be operational, or you are not willing to wait, you can also skip the test phase, adding a command-line switch like so:

```
$ mvn -DskipTests assembly:assembly
```

This process will take a few minutes to complete—and if you have not turned off the test phase, this goes into the tens of minutes—while creating a *target* directory in the HBase project home directory. Once the build completes with a `Build Successful` message, you can find the compiled and packaged *tarball* archive in the *target* directory. With that archive you can go back to "Apache Binary Release" on page 55 and follow the steps outlined there to install your own, private release on your servers.

Run Modes

HBase has two run modes: *standalone* and *distributed*. Out of the box, HBase runs in standalone mode, as seen in "Quick-Start Guide" on page 31. To set up HBase in distributed mode, you will need to edit files in the HBase *conf* directory.

Whatever your mode, you may need to edit *conf/hbase-env.sh* to tell HBase which *java* to use. In this file, you set HBase environment variables such as the heap size and other options for the JVM, the preferred location for logfiles, and so on. Set `JAVA_HOME` to point at the root of your *java* installation.

Standalone Mode

This is the default mode, as described and used in "Quick-Start Guide" on page 31. In standalone mode, HBase does not use HDFS—it uses the local filesystem instead—and it runs all HBase daemons and a local ZooKeeper in the same JVM process. ZooKeeper binds to a well-known port so that clients may talk to HBase.

Distributed Mode

The *distributed mode* can be further subdivided into *pseudodistributed*—all daemons run on a single node—and *fully distributed*—where the daemons are spread across multiple, physical servers in the cluster.‖

Distributed modes require an instance of the *Hadoop Distributed File System* (HDFS). See the Hadoop requirements and instructions (*http://hadoop.apache.org/common/ docs/current/api/overview-summary.html#overview_description*) for how to set up an HDFS. Before proceeding, ensure that you have an appropriate, working HDFS.

The following subsections describe the different distributed setups. Starting, verifying, and exploring of your install, whether a *pseudodistributed* or *fully distributed* configuration, is described in "Running and Confirming Your Installation" on page 71. The same verification script applies to both deploy types.

Pseudodistributed mode

A pseudodistributed mode is simply a distributed mode that is run on a single host. Use this configuration for testing and prototyping on HBase. Do *not* use this configuration for production or for evaluating HBase performance.

Once you have confirmed your HDFS setup, edit *conf/hbase-site.xml*. This is the file into which you add local customizations and overrides for the default HBase configuration values (see Appendix A for the full list, and "HDFS-Related Configuration" on page 64). Point HBase at the running Hadoop HDFS instance by setting the `hbase.rootdir` property. For example, adding the following properties to your *hbase-site.xml* file says that HBase should use the */hbase* directory in the HDFS whose name node is at port 9000 on your local machine, and that it should run with one replica only (recommended for pseudodistributed mode):

```
<configuration>
  ...
  <property>
    <name>hbase.rootdir</name>
    <value>hdfs://localhost:9000/hbase</value>
  </property>
  <property>
    <name>dfs.replication</name>
```

‖ The pseudodistributed versus fully distributed nomenclature comes from Hadoop.

```
        <value>1</value>
      </property>
      ...
    </configuration>
```

 In the example configuration, the server binds to localhost. This means that a remote client cannot connect. Amend accordingly, if you want to connect from a remote location.

If all you want to try for now is the pseudodistributed mode, you can skip to "Running and Confirming Your Installation" on page 71 for details on how to start and verify your setup. See Chapter 12 for information on how to start extra master and region servers when running in pseudodistributed mode.

Fully distributed mode

For running a fully distributed operation on more than one host, you need to use the following configurations. In *hbase-site.xml*, add the hbase.cluster.distributed property and set it to true, and point the HBase hbase.rootdir at the appropriate HDFS name node and location in HDFS where you would like HBase to write data. For example, if your name node is running at a server with the hostname namenode.foo.com on port 9000 and you want to home your HBase in HDFS at */hbase*, use the following configuration:

```
    <configuration>
      ...
      <property>
        <name>hbase.rootdir</name>
        <value>hdfs://namenode.foo.com:9000/hbase</value>
      </property>
      <property>
        <name>hbase.cluster.distributed</name>
        <value>true</value>
      </property>
      ...
    </configuration>
```

Specifying region servers. In addition, a fully distributed mode requires that you modify the *conf/regionservers* file. It lists all the hosts on which you want to run HRegionServer daemons. Specify one host per line (this file in HBase is like the Hadoop *slaves* file). All servers listed in this file will be started and stopped when the HBase cluster start or stop scripts are run.

ZooKeeper setup. A distributed HBase depends on a running ZooKeeper cluster. All participating nodes and clients need to be able to access the running ZooKeeper ensemble. HBase, by default, manages a ZooKeeper cluster (which can be as low as a single node) for you. It will start and stop the ZooKeeper ensemble as part of the HBase start and stop process. You can also manage the ZooKeeper ensemble independent of HBase and just point HBase at the cluster it should use. To toggle HBase management of Zoo-Keeper, use the `HBASE_MANAGES_ZK` variable in *conf/hbase-env.sh*. This variable, which defaults to `true`, tells HBase whether to start and stop the ZooKeeper ensemble servers as part of the start and stop commands supplied by HBase.

When HBase manages the ZooKeeper ensemble, you can specify the ZooKeeper configuration using its native *zoo.cfg* file, or just specify the ZooKeeper options directly in *conf/hbase-site.xml*. You can set a ZooKeeper configuration option as a property in the HBase *hbase-site.xml* XML configuration file by prefixing the ZooKeeper option name with `hbase.zookeeper.property`. For example, you can change the `clientPort` setting in ZooKeeper by setting the `hbase.zookeeper.property.clientPort` property. For all default values used by HBase, including ZooKeeper configuration, see Appendix A. Look for the `hbase.zookeeper.property` prefix.#

---

zoo.cfg Versus hbase-site.xml

There is some confusion concerning the usage of *zoo.cfg* and *hbase-site.xml* in combination with ZooKeeper settings. For starters, if there is a *zoo.cfg* on the classpath (meaning it can be found by the Java process), it takes precedence over all settings in *hbase-site.xml*—but only those starting with the `hbase.zookeeper.property` prefix, plus a few others.

There are some ZooKeeper client settings that are not read from *zoo.cfg* but *must* be set in *hbase-site.xml*. This includes, for example, the important client session timeout value set with `zookeeper.session.timeout`. The following table describes the dependencies in more detail.

Property	zoo.cfg + hbase-site.xml	hbase-site.xml only
hbase.zookeeper.quorum	Constructed from `server.n` lines as specified in *zoo.cfg*. Overrides any setting in *hbase-site.xml*.	Used as specified.
hbase.zookeeper.property.*	All values from *zoo.cfg* override any value specified in *hbase-site.xml*.	Used as specified.
zookeeper.*	Only taken from *hbase-site.xml*.	Only taken from *hbase-site.xml*.

To avoid any confusion during deployment, it is highly recommended that you *not* use a *zoo.cfg* file with HBase, and instead use only the *hbase-site.xml* file. Especially in a fully distributed setup where you have your own ZooKeeper servers, it is not practical to copy the configuration from the ZooKeeper nodes to the HBase servers.

If you are using the *hbase-site.xml* approach to specify all ZooKeeper settings, you must at least set the ensemble servers with the `hbase.zookeeper.quorum` property. It otherwise

---

#For the full list of ZooKeeper configurations, see ZooKeeper's *zoo.cfg*. HBase does not ship with that file, so you will need to browse the *conf* directory in an appropriate ZooKeeper download.

defaults to a single ensemble member at localhost, which is not suitable for a fully distributed HBase (it binds to the local machine only and remote clients will not be able to connect).

How Many ZooKeepers Should I Run?

You can run a ZooKeeper ensemble that comprises one node only, but in production it is recommended that you run a ZooKeeper ensemble of three, five, or seven machines; the more members an ensemble has, the more tolerant the ensemble is of host failures. Also, run an odd number of machines, since running an even count does not make for an extra server building consensus—you need a majority vote, and if you have three or four servers, for example, both would have a majority with three nodes. Using an odd number allows you to have two servers fail, as opposed to only one with even numbers.

Give each ZooKeeper server around 1 GB of RAM, and if possible, its own dedicated disk (a dedicated disk is the best thing you can do to ensure a performant ZooKeeper ensemble). For very heavily loaded clusters, run ZooKeeper servers on separate machines from RegionServers, DataNodes, and TaskTrackers.

For example, in order to have HBase manage a ZooKeeper quorum on nodes *rs{1,2,3,4,5}.foo.com*, bound to port 2222 (the default is 2181), you must ensure that HBASE_MANAGE_ZK is commented out or set to true in *conf/hbase-env.sh* and then edit *conf/hbase-site.xml* and set hbase.zookeeper.property.clientPort and hbase.zookeeper.quorum. You should also set hbase.zookeeper.property.dataDir to something other than the default, as the default has ZooKeeper persist data under */tmp*, which is often cleared on system restart. In the following example, we have ZooKeeper persist to */var/zookeeper*:

```
<configuration>
  ...
  <property>
    <name>hbase.zookeeper.property.clientPort</name>
    <value>2222</value>
  </property>
  <property>
    <name>hbase.zookeeper.quorum</name>
    <value>rs1.foo.com,rs2.foo.com,rs3.foo.com,rs4.foo.com,rs5.foo.com</value>
  </property>
  <property>
    <name>hbase.zookeeper.property.dataDir</name>
    <value>/var/zookeeper</value>
  </property>
  ...
</configuration>
```

Using the existing ZooKeeper ensemble. To point HBase at an existing ZooKeeper cluster, one that is not managed by HBase, set HBASE_MANAGES_ZK in *conf/hbase-env.sh* to false:

```
...
# Tell HBase whether it should manage it's own instance of Zookeeper or not.
export HBASE_MANAGES_ZK=false
```

Next, set the ensemble locations and client port, if nonstandard, in *hbase-site.xml*, or add a suitably configured *zoo.cfg* to HBase's *CLASSPATH*. HBase will prefer the configuration found in *zoo.cfg* over any settings in *hbase-site.xml*.

When HBase manages ZooKeeper, it will start/stop the ZooKeeper servers as a part of the regular start/stop scripts. If you would like to run ZooKeeper yourself, independent of HBase start/stop, do the following:

```
${HBASE_HOME}/bin/hbase-daemons.sh {start,stop} zookeeper
```

Note that you can use HBase in this manner to spin up a ZooKeeper cluster, unrelated to HBase. Just make sure to set `HBASE_MANAGES_ZK` to `false` if you want it to stay up across HBase restarts so that when HBase shuts down, it doesn't take ZooKeeper down with it.

For more information about running a distinct ZooKeeper cluster, see the ZooKeeper Getting Started Guide (*http://hadoop.apache.org/zookeeper/docs/current/zookeeperStar ted.html*). Additionally, see the ZooKeeper wiki (*http://wiki.apache.org/hadoop/Zoo Keeper/FAQ#A7*), or the ZooKeeper documentation (*http://zookeeper.apache.org/doc/ r3.3.3/zookeeperAdmin.html#sc_zkMulitServerSetup*) for more information on Zoo-Keeper sizing.

Configuration

Now that the basics are out of the way (we've looked at all the choices when it comes to selecting the filesystem, discussed the run modes, and fine-tuned the operating system parameters), we can look at how to configure HBase itself. Similar to Hadoop, all configuration parameters are stored in files located in the *conf* directory. These are simple text files either in XML format arranged as a set of *properties*, or in simple flat files listing one option per line.

> For more details on how to modify your configuration files for specific workloads refer to "Configuration" on page 436.

Configuring an HBase setup entails editing a file with environment variables, named *conf/hbase-env.sh*, which is used mostly by the shell scripts (see "Operating a Cluster" on page 71) to start or stop a cluster. You also need to add configuration properties to an XML file[*] named *conf/hbase-site.xml* to, for example, override HBase defaults, tell HBase what filesystem to use, and tell HBase the location of the ZooKeeper ensemble.

---

[*] Be careful when editing XML. Make sure you close all elements. Check your file using a tool like *xmlint*, or something similar, to ensure well-formedness of your document after an edit session.

When running in distributed mode, after you make an edit to an HBase configuration file, make sure you copy the content of the *conf* directory to all nodes of the cluster. HBase will *not* do this for you.

 There are many ways to synchronize your configuration files across your cluster. The easiest is to use a tool like *rsync*. There are many more elaborate ways, and you will see a selection in "Deployment" on page 68.

hbase-site.xml and hbase-default.xml

Just as in Hadoop where you add site-specific HDFS configurations to the *hdfs-site.xml* file, for HBase, site-specific customizations go into the file *conf/hbase-site.xml*. For the list of configurable properties, see Appendix A, or view the raw *hbase-default.xml* source file in the HBase source code at *src/main/resources*. The *doc* directory also has a static HTML page that lists the configuration options.

 Not all configuration options make it out to *hbase-default.xml*. Configurations that users would rarely change can exist only in code; the only way to turn up such configurations is to read the source code itself.

The servers always read the *hbase-default.xml* file first and subsequently merge it with the *hbase-site.xml* file content—if present. The properties set in *hbase-site.xml* always take precedence over the default values loaded from *hbase-default.xml*.

Any modifications in your site file require a cluster restart for HBase to notice the changes.

HDFS-Related Configuration

If you have made *HDFS*-related configuration changes on your Hadoop cluster—in other words, properties you want the HDFS clients to use as opposed to the server-side configuration—HBase will not see these properties unless you do one of the following:

- Add a pointer to your HADOOP_CONF_DIR to the HBASE_CLASSPATH environment variable in *hbase-env.sh*.
- Add a copy of *hdfs-site.xml* (or *hadoop-site.xml*) or, better, symbolic links, under ${HBASE_HOME}/conf.
- Add them to *hbase-site.xml* directly.

An example of such an HDFS client property is dfs.replication. If, for example, you want to run with a replication factor of 5, HBase will create files with the default of 3 unless you do one of the above to make the configuration available to HBase.

When you add Hadoop configuration files to HBase, they will always take the lowest priority. In other words, the properties contained in any of the HBase-related

---

configuration files, that is, the default and site files, take precedence over any Hadoop configuration file containing a property with the same name. This allows you to override Hadoop properties in your HBase configuration file.

hbase-env.sh

You set HBase environment variables in this file. Examples include options to pass to the JVM when an HBase daemon starts, such as Java heap size and garbage collector configurations. You also set options for HBase configuration, log directories, niceness, SSH options, where to locate process *pid* files, and so on. Open the file at *conf/hbase-env.sh* and peruse its content. Each option is fairly well documented. Add your own environment variables here if you want them read when an HBase daemon is started.

Changes here will require a cluster restart for HBase to notice the change.[†]

regionserver

This file lists all the known region server names. It is a flat text file that has one hostname per line. The list is used by the HBase maintenance script to be able to iterate over all the servers to start the region server process.

 If you used previous versions of HBase, you may miss the *masters* file, available in the 0.20.x line. It has been removed as it is no longer needed. The list of masters is now dynamically maintained in ZooKeeper and each master registers itself when started.

log4j.properties

Edit this file to change the rate at which HBase files are rolled and to change the level at which HBase logs messages. Changes here will require a cluster restart for HBase to notice the change, though log levels can be changed for particular daemons via the HBase UI. See "Changing Logging Levels" on page 466 for information on this topic, and "Analyzing the Logs" on page 469 for details on how to use the logfiles to find and solve problems.

Example Configuration

Here is an example configuration for a distributed 10-node cluster. The nodes are named master.foo.com, host1.foo.com, and so on, through node host9.foo.com. The HBase Master and the HDFS name node are running on the node master.foo.com.

---

† As of this writing, you have to restart the server. However, work is being done to enable online schema and configuration changes, so this will change over time.

Region servers run on nodes host1.foo.com to host9.foo.com. A three-node ZooKeeper ensemble runs on zk1.foo.com, zk2.foo.com, and zk3.foo.com on the default ports. ZooKeeper data is persisted to the directory */var/zookeeper*. The following subsections show what the main configuration files—*hbase-site.xml*, *regionservers*, and *hbase-env.sh*—found in the HBase *conf* directory might look like.

hbase-site.xml

The *hbase-site.xml* file contains the essential configuration properties, defining the HBase cluster setup.

```
<?xml version="1.0"?>
<?xml-stylesheet type="text/xsl" href="configuration.xsl"?>
<configuration>
  <property>
    <name>hbase.zookeeper.quorum</name>
    <value>zk1.foo.com,zk2.foo.com,zk3.foo.com</value>
  </property>
  <property>
    <name>hbase.zookeeper.property.dataDir</name>
    <value>/var/zookeeper</value>
  </property>
  <property>
    <name>hbase.rootdir</name>
    <value>hdfs://master.foo.com:9000/hbase</value>
  </property>
  <property>
    <name>hbase.cluster.distributed</name>
    <value>true</value>
  </property>
</configuration>
```

regionservers

In this file, you list the nodes that will run region servers. In our example, we run region servers on all but the head node master.foo.com, which is carrying the HBase Master and the HDFS name node.

```
host1.foo.com
host2.foo.com
host3.foo.com
host4.foo.com
host5.foo.com
host6.foo.com
host7.foo.com
host8.foo.com
host9.foo.com
```

hbase-env.sh

Here are the lines that were changed from the default in the supplied *hbase-env.sh* file. Here we are setting the HBase heap to be 4 GB instead of the default 1 GB:

```
...
# export HBASE_HEAPSIZE=1000
export HBASE_HEAPSIZE=4096
...
```

Once you have edited the configuration files, you need to distribute them across all servers in the cluster. One option to copy the content of the *conf* directory to all servers in the cluster is to use the *rsync* command on Unix and Unix-like platforms. This approach and others are explained in "Deployment" on page 68.

 "Configuration" on page 436 discusses the settings you are most likely to change first when you start scaling your cluster.

Client Configuration

Since the HBase Master may move around between physical machines (see "Adding a backup master" on page 450 for details), clients start by requesting the vital information from ZooKeeper—something visualized in "Region Lookups" on page 345. For that reason, clients require the ZooKeeper quorum information in an *hbase-site.xml* file that is on their Java CLASSPATH.

 You can also set the hbase.zookeeper.quorum configuration key in your code. Doing so would lead to clients that need no external configuration files. This is explained in "Put Method" on page 76.

If you are configuring an IDE to run an HBase client, you could include the *conf/* directory on your classpath. That would make the configuration files discoverable by the client code.

Minimally, a Java client needs the following JAR files specified in its CLASSPATH, when connecting to HBase: *hbase, hadoop-core, zookeeper, log4j, commons-logging,* and *commons-lang*. All of these JAR files come with HBase and are usually postfixed with the a version number of the required release. Ideally, you use the supplied JARs and do not acquire them somewhere else because even minor release changes could cause problems when running the client against a remote HBase cluster.

A basic example *hbase-site.xml* file for client applications might contain the following properties:

```
<?xml version="1.0"?>
<?xml-stylesheet type="text/xsl" href="configuration.xsl"?>
<configuration>
  <property>
    <name>hbase.zookeeper.quorum</name>
    <value>zk1.foo.com,zk2.foo.com,zk3.foo.com</value>
```

```
    </property>
  </configuration>
```

Deployment

After you have configured HBase, the next thing you need to do is to think about deploying it on your cluster. There are many ways to do that, and since Hadoop and HBase are written in Java, there are only a few necessary requirements to look out for. You can simply copy all the files from server to server, since they usually share the same configuration. Here are some ideas on how to do that. Please note that you would need to make sure that all the suggested selections and adjustments discussed in "Requirements" on page 34 have been applied—or are applied at the same time when provisioning new servers.

Script-Based

Using a script-based approach seems archaic compared to the more advanced approaches listed shortly. But they serve their purpose and do a good job for small to even medium-size clusters. It is not so much the size of the cluster but the number of people maintaining it. In a larger operations group, you want to have repeatable deployment procedures, and not deal with someone having to run scripts to update the cluster.

The scripts make use of the fact that the *regionservers* configuration file has a list of all servers in the cluster. Example 2-2 shows a very simple script that could be used to copy a new release of HBase from the master node to all slave nodes.

Example 2-2. Example Script to copy the HBase files across a cluster

```
#!/bin/bash
# Rsyncs HBase files across all slaves. Must run on master. Assumes
# all files are located in /usr/local

if [ "$#" != "2" ]; then
  echo "usage: $(basename $0) <dir-name> <ln-name>"
  echo "    example: $(basename $0) hbase-0.1 hbase"
  exit 1
fi

SRC_PATH="/usr/local/$1/conf/regionservers"
for srv in $(cat $SRC_PATH); do
  echo "Sending command to $srv...";
  rsync -vaz --exclude='logs/*' /usr/local/$1 $srv:/usr/local/
  ssh $srv "rm -fR /usr/local/$2 ; ln -s /usr/local/$1 /usr/local/$2"
done

echo "done."
```

Another simple script is shown in Example 2-3; it can be used to copy the configuration files of HBase from the master node to all slave nodes. It assumes you are editing the configuration files on the master in such a way that the master can be copied across to all region servers.

Example 2-3. Example Script to copy configurations across a cluster

```
#!/bin/bash
# Rsync's HBase config files across all region servers. Must run on master.

for srv in $(cat /usr/local/hbase/conf/regionservers); do
  echo "Sending command to $srv...";
  rsync -vaz --delete --exclude='logs/*' /usr/local/hadoop/ $srv:/usr/local/hadoop/
  rsync -vaz --delete --exclude='logs/*' /usr/local/hbase/ $srv:/usr/local/hbase/
done

echo "done."
```

The second script uses *rsync* just like the first script, but adds the *--delete* option to make sure the region servers do not have any older files remaining but have an exact copy of what is on the originating server.

There are obviously many ways to do this, and the preceding examples are simply for your perusal and to get you started. Ask your administrator to help you set up mechanisms to synchronize the configuration files appropriately. Many beginners in HBase have run into a problem that was ultimately caused by inconsistent configurations among the cluster nodes. Also, do not forget to restart the servers when making changes. If you want to update settings while the cluster is in production, please refer to "Rolling Restarts" on page 447.

Apache Whirr

Recently, we have seen an increase in the number of users who want to run their cluster in dynamic environments, such as the public cloud offerings by Amazon's EC2, or Rackspace Cloud Servers, as well as in private server farms, using open source tools like Eucalyptus.

The advantage is to be able to quickly provision servers and run analytical workloads and, once the result has been retrieved, to simply shut down the entire cluster, or reuse the servers for other dynamic loads. Since it is not trivial to program against each of the APIs providing dynamic cluster infrastructures, it would be useful to abstract the provisioning part and, once the cluster is operational, simply launch the MapReduce jobs the same way you would on a local, static cluster. This is where Apache Whirr comes in.

Whirr—available at *http://incubator.apache.org/whirr/*‡—has support for a variety of public and private cloud APIs and allows you to provision clusters running a range of services. One of those is HBase, giving you the ability to quickly deploy a fully operational HBase cluster on dynamic setups.

You can download the latest Whirr release from the aforementioned site and find preconfigured configuration files in the *recipes* directory. Use it as a starting point to deploy your own dynamic clusters.

The basic concept of Whirr is to use very simple machine images that already provide the operating system (see "Operating system" on page 40) and SSH access. The rest is handled by Whirr using *services* that represent, for example, Hadoop or HBase. Each service executes every required step on each remote server to set up the user accounts, download and install the required software packages, write out configuration files for them, and so on. This is all highly customizable and you can add extra steps as needed.

Puppet and Chef

Similar to Whirr, there are other deployment frameworks for dedicated machines. *Puppet* by Puppet Labs (*http://www.puppetlabs.com/*) and *Chef* by Opscode (*http://www.opscode.com/chef/*) are two such offerings.

Both work similar to Whirr in that they have a central provisioning server that stores all the configurations, combined with client software, executed on each server, which communicates with the central server to receive updates and apply them locally.

Also similar to Whirr, both have the notion of *recipes*, which essentially translate to scripts or commands executed on each node.§ In fact, it is quite possible to replace the scripting employed by Whirr with a Puppet- or Chef-based process.

While Whirr solely handles the bootstrapping, Puppet and Chef have further support for changing running clusters. Their master process monitors the configuration repository and, upon updates, triggers the appropriate remote action. This can be used to reconfigure clusters on-the-fly or push out new releases, do rolling restarts, and so on. It can be summarized as configuration management, rather than just provisioning.

---

‡ Please note that Whirr is still part of the incubator program of the Apache Software Foundation. Once it is accepted and promoted to a full member, its URL is going to change to a permanent place.

§ Some of the available recipe packages are an adaption of early EC2 scripts, used to deploy HBase to dynamic, cloud-based server. For Chef, you can find HBase-related examples at *http://cookbooks.opscode.com/cookbooks/hbase*. For Puppet, please refer to *http://hstack.org/hstack-automated-deployment-using-puppet/* and the repository with the recipes at *http://github.com/hstack/puppet*.

You heard it before: select an approach you like and maybe even are familiar with already. In the end, they achieve the same goal: installing everything you need on your cluster nodes. If you need a full configuration management solution with live updates, a Puppet- or Chef-based approach—maybe in combination with Whirr for the server provisioning—is the right choice.

Operating a Cluster

Now that you have set up the servers, configured the operating system and filesystem, and edited the configuration files, you are ready to start your HBase cluster for the first time.

Running and Confirming Your Installation

Make sure HDFS is running first. Start and stop the Hadoop HDFS daemons by running *bin/start-dfs.sh* over in the *HADOOP_HOME* directory. You can ensure that it started properly by testing the *put* and *get* of files into the Hadoop filesystem. HBase does not normally use the MapReduce daemons. You only need to start them for actual MapReduce jobs, something we will look into in detail in Chapter 7.

If you are managing your own ZooKeeper, start it and confirm that it is running: otherwise, HBase will start up ZooKeeper for you as part of its start process.

Just as you started the standalone mode in "Quick-Start Guide" on page 31, you start a fully distributed HBase with the following command:

```
bin/start-hbase.sh
```

Run the preceding command from the *HBASE_HOME* directory. You should now have a running HBase instance. The HBase logfiles can be found in the *logs* subdirectory. If you find that HBase is not working as expected, please refer to "Analyzing the Logs" on page 469 for help finding the problem.

Once HBase has started, see "Quick-Start Guide" for information on how to create tables, add data, scan your insertions, and finally, disable and drop your tables.

Web-based UI Introduction

HBase also starts a web-based user interface (UI) listing vital attributes. By default, it is deployed on the master host at port 60010 (HBase region servers use 60030 by default). If the master is running on a host named `master.foo.com` on the default port, to see the master's home page you can point your browser at `http://master.foo.com:60010`. Figure 2-2 is an example of how the resultant page should look. You can find a more detailed explanation in "Web-based UI" on page 277.

Figure 2-2. The HBase Master user interface

From this page you can access a variety of status information about your HBase cluster. The page is separated into multiple sections. The top part has the attributes pertaining to the cluster setup. You can see the *currently running tasks*—if there are any. The *catalog* and *user* tables list details about the available tables. For the user table you also see the table schema.

The lower part of the page has the *region servers* table, giving you access to all the currently registered servers. Finally, the *region in transition* list informs you about regions that are currently being maintained by the system.

After you have started the cluster, you should verify that all the region servers have registered themselves with the master and appear in the appropriate table with the expected hostnames (that a client can connect to). Also verify that you are indeed running the correct version of HBase and Hadoop.

Shell Introduction

You already used the command-line shell that comes with HBase when you went through "Quick-Start Guide" on page 31. You saw how to create a table, add and retrieve data, and eventually drop the table.

The HBase Shell is (J)Ruby (*http://jruby.org*)'s IRB with some HBase-related commands added. Anything you can do in IRB, you should be able to do in the HBase Shell. You can start the shell with the following command:

```
$ $HBASE_HOME/bin/hbase shell
HBase Shell; enter 'help<RETURN>' for list of supported commands.
Type "exit<RETURN>" to leave the HBase Shell
Version 0.91.0-SNAPSHOT, r1130916, Sat Jul 23 12:44:34 CEST 2011

hbase(main):001:0>
```

Type help and then press Return to see a listing of shell commands and options. Browse at least the paragraphs at the end of the help text for the gist of how variables and command arguments are entered into the HBase Shell; in particular, note how table names, rows, and columns, must be quoted. Find the full description of the shell in "Shell" on page 268.

Since the shell is JRuby-based, you can mix Ruby with HBase commands, which enables you to do things like this:

```
hbase(main):001:0> create 'testtable', 'colfam1'
hbase(main):002:0> for i in 'a'..'z' do for j in 'a'..'z' do \
put 'testtable', "row-#{i}#{j}", "colfam1:#{j}", "#{j}" end end
```

The first command is creating a new table named testtable, with one column family called colfam1, using default values (see "Column Families" on page 212 for what that means). The second command uses a Ruby loop to create rows with columns in the newly created tables. It creates row keys starting with row-aa, row-ab, all the way to row-zz.

Stopping the Cluster

To stop HBase, enter the following command. Once you have started the script, you will see a message stating that the cluster is being stopped, followed by "." (period) characters printed in regular intervals (just to indicate that the process is still running, not to give you any percentage feedback, or some other hidden meaning):

```
$ ./bin/stop-hbase.sh
stopping hbase..............
```

Shutdown can take several minutes to complete. It can take longer if your cluster is composed of many machines. If you are running a distributed operation, be sure to wait until HBase has shut down completely before stopping the Hadoop daemons.

Chapter 12 has more on advanced administration tasks—for example, how to do a rolling restart, add extra master nodes, and more. It also has information on how to analyze and fix problems when the cluster does not start, or shut down.

## CHAPTER 3

Client API: The Basics

This chapter will discuss the client APIs provided by HBase. As noted earlier, HBase is written in Java and so is its native API. This does not mean, though, that you *must* use Java to access HBase. In fact, Chapter 6 will show how you can use other programming languages.

General Notes

The primary client interface to HBase is the `HTable` class in the `org.apache.hadoop.hbase.client` package. It provides the user with all the functionality needed to store and retrieve data from HBase as well as delete obsolete values and so on. Before looking at the various methods this class provides, let us address some general aspects of its usage.

All operations that mutate data are guaranteed to be *atomic* on a per-row basis. This affects all other concurrent readers and writers of that same row. In other words, it does not matter if another client or thread is reading from or writing to the same row: they either read a consistent last mutation, or may have to wait before being able to apply their change.* More on this in Chapter 8.

Suffice it to say for now that during normal operations and load, a reading client will not be affected by another updating a particular row since their contention is nearly negligible. There is, however, an issue with many clients trying to update the same row at the same time. Try to batch updates together to reduce the number of separate operations on the same row as much as possible.

It also does not matter how many columns are written for the particular row; all of them are covered by this guarantee of atomicity.

---

* The region servers use a *multiversion concurrency control* mechanism, implemented internally by the `ReadWriteConsistencyControl` (RWCC) class, to guarantee that readers can read without having to wait for writers. Writers do need to wait for other writers to complete, though, before they can continue.

Finally, creating HTable instances is not without cost. Each instantiation involves scanning the .META. table to check if the table actually exists and if it is enabled, as well as a few other operations that make this call quite costly. Therefore, it is recommended that you create HTable instances only once—and one per thread—and reuse that instance for the rest of the lifetime of your client application.

As soon as you need multiple instances of HTable, consider using the HTablePool class (see "HTablePool" on page 199), which provides you with a convenient way to reuse multiple instances.

Here is a summary of the points we just discussed:

- Create HTable instances only once, usually when your application starts.
- Create a separate HTable instance for every thread you execute (or use HTablePool).
- Updates are atomic on a per-row basis.

CRUD Operations

The initial set of basic operations are often referred to as *CRUD*, which stands for create, read, update, and delete. HBase has a set of those and we will look into each of them subsequently. They are provided by the HTable class, and the remainder of this chapter will refer directly to the methods without specifically mentioning the containing class again.

Most of the following operations are often seemingly self-explanatory, but the subtle details warrant a close look. However, this means you will start to see a pattern of repeating functionality so that we do not have to explain them again and again.

The examples you will see in partial source code can be found in full detail in the publicly available GitHub repository at *https://github.com/larsgeorge/hbase-book*. For details on how to compile them, see "Building the Examples" on page xxi.

Initially you will see the import statements, but they will be subsequently omitted for the sake of brevity. Also, specific parts of the code are not listed if they do not immediately help with the topic explained. Refer to the full source if in doubt.

Put Method

This group of operations can be split into separate types: those that work on single rows and those that work on lists of rows. Since the latter involves some more complexity, we will look at each group separately. Along the way, you will also be introduced to accompanying client API features.

Single Puts

The very first method you may want to know about is one that lets you store data in HBase. Here is the call that lets you do that:

```
void put(Put put) throws IOException
```

It expects one or a list of Put objects that, in turn, are created with one of these constructors:

```
Put(byte[] row)
Put(byte[] row, RowLock rowLock)
Put(byte[] row, long ts)
Put(byte[] row, long ts, RowLock rowLock)
```

You need to supply a row to create a Put instance. A row in HBase is identified by a unique *row key* and—as is the case with most values in HBase—this is a Java byte[] array. You are free to choose any row key you like, but please also note that Chapter 9 provides a whole section on row key design (see "Key Design" on page 357). For now, we assume this can be anything, and often it represents a fact from the physical world—for example, a *username* or an *order ID*. These can be simple numbers but also *UUIDs*[†] and so on.

HBase is kind enough to provide us with a helper class that has many static methods to convert Java types into byte[] arrays. Example 3-1 provides a short list of what it offers.

Example 3-1. Methods provided by the Bytes class

```
static byte[] toBytes(ByteBuffer bb)
static byte[] toBytes(String s)
static byte[] toBytes(boolean b)
static byte[] toBytes(long val)
static byte[] toBytes(float f)
static byte[] toBytes(int val)
...
```

Once you have created the Put instance you can add data to it. This is done using these methods:

```
Put add(byte[] family, byte[] qualifier, byte[] value)
Put add(byte[] family, byte[] qualifier, long ts, byte[] value)
Put add(KeyValue kv) throws IOException
```

Each call to add() specifies exactly one column, or, in combination with an optional timestamp, one single cell. Note that if you do *not* specify the timestamp with the

---

[†] Universally Unique Identifier; see *http://en.wikipedia.org/wiki/Universally_unique_identifier* for details.

add() call, the Put instance will use the optional timestamp parameter from the constructor (also called ts) and you should leave it to the region server to set it.

The variant that takes an existing KeyValue instance is for advanced users that have learned how to retrieve, or create, this internal class. It represents a single, unique cell; like a coordination system used with maps it is addressed by the row key, column family, column qualifier, and timestamp, pointing to one value in a three-dimensional, cube-like system—where time is the third dimension.

One way to come across the internal KeyValue type is by using the reverse methods to add(), aptly named get():

```
List<KeyValue> get(byte[] family, byte[] qualifier)
Map<byte[], List<KeyValue>> getFamilyMap()
```

These two calls retrieve what you have added earlier, while having converted the unique cells into KeyValue instances. You can retrieve all cells for either an entire column family, a specific column within a family, or everything. The latter is the getFamilyMap() call, which you can then iterate over to check the details contained in each available Key Value.

> Every KeyValue instance contains its full address—the row key, column family, qualifier, timestamp, and so on—as well as the actual data. It is *the* lowest-level class in HBase with respect to the storage architecture. "Storage" on page 319 explains this in great detail. As for the available functionality in regard to the KeyValue class from the client API, see "The KeyValue class" on page 83.

Instead of having to iterate to check for the existence of specific cells, you can use the following set of methods:

```
boolean has(byte[] family, byte[] qualifier)
boolean has(byte[] family, byte[] qualifier, long ts)
boolean has(byte[] family, byte[] qualifier, byte[] value)
boolean has(byte[] family, byte[] qualifier, long ts, byte[] value)
```

They increasingly ask for more specific details and return true if a match can be found. The first method simply checks for the presence of a column. The others add the option to check for a timestamp, a given value, or both.

There are more methods provided by the Put class, summarized in Table 3-1.

> Note that the getters listed in Table 3-1 for the Put class only retrieve what you have set beforehand. They are rarely used, and make sense only when you, for example, prepare a Put instance in a private method in your code, and inspect the values in another place.

Table 3-1. Quick overview of additional methods provided by the Put class

Method	Description
getRow()	Returns the row key as specified when creating the Put instance.
getRowLock()	Returns the row RowLock instance for the current Put instance.
getLockId()	Returns the optional lock ID handed into the constructor using the rowLock parameter. Will be -1L if not set.
setWriteToWAL()	Allows you to disable the default functionality of writing the data to the server-side write-ahead log.
getWriteToWAL()	Indicates if the data will be written to the write-ahead log.
getTimeStamp()	Retrieves the associated timestamp of the Put instance. Can be optionally set using the constructor's ts parameter. If not set, may return Long.MAX_VALUE.
heapSize()	Computes the heap space required for the current Put instance. This includes all contained data and space needed for internal structures.
isEmpty()	Checks if the family map contains any KeyValue instances.
numFamilies()	Convenience method to retrieve the size of the family map, containing all KeyValue instances.
size()	Returns the number of KeyValue instances that will be added with this Put.

Example 3-2 shows how all this is put together (no pun intended) into a basic application.

 The examples in this chapter use a very limited, but exact, set of data. When you look at the full source code you will notice that it uses an internal class named HBaseHelper. It is used to create a test table with a very specific number of rows and columns. This makes it much easier to compare the before and after.

Feel free to run the code as-is against a standalone HBase instance on your local machine for testing—or against a fully deployed cluster. "Building the Examples" on page xxi explains how to compile the examples. Also, be adventurous and modify them to get a good feel for the functionality they demonstrate.

The example code usually first removes all data from a previous execution by dropping the table it has created. If you run the examples against a production cluster, please make sure that you have no name collisions. Usually the table is testtable to indicate its purpose.

Example 3-2. Application inserting data into HBase

```
import org.apache.hadoop.conf.Configuration;
import org.apache.hadoop.hbase.HBaseConfiguration;
import org.apache.hadoop.hbase.client.HTable;
import org.apache.hadoop.hbase.client.Put;
import org.apache.hadoop.hbase.util.Bytes;
```

```
import java.io.IOException;

public class PutExample {

  public static void main(String[] args) throws IOException {
    Configuration conf = HBaseConfiguration.create(); ❶

    HTable table = new HTable(conf, "testtable"); ❷

    Put put = new Put(Bytes.toBytes("row1")); ❸

    put.add(Bytes.toBytes("colfam1"), Bytes.toBytes("qual1"),
      Bytes.toBytes("val1")); ❹
    put.add(Bytes.toBytes("colfam1"), Bytes.toBytes("qual2"),
      Bytes.toBytes("val2")); ❺

    table.put(put); ❻
  }
}
```

❶ Create the required configuration.

❷ Instantiate a new client.

❸ Create Put with specific row.

❹ Add a column, whose name is "colfam1:qual1", to the Put.

❺ Add another column, whose name is "colfam1:qual2", to the Put.

❻ Store the row with the column into the HBase table.

This is a (nearly) full representation of the code used and every line is explained. The following examples will omit more and more of the boilerplate code so that you can focus on the important parts.

Accessing Configuration Files from Client Code

"Client Configuration" on page 67 introduced the configuration files used by HBase client applications. They need access to the *hbase-site.xml* file to learn where the cluster resides—or you need to specify this location in your code.

Either way, you need to use an `HBaseConfiguration` class within your code to handle the configuration properties. This is done using one of the following static methods, provided by that class:

```
static Configuration create()
static Configuration create(Configuration that)
```

Example 3-2 is using `create()` to retrieve a `Configuration` instance. The second method allows you to hand in an existing configuration to merge with the HBase-specific one.

When you call any of the static `create()` methods, the code behind it will attempt to load two configuration files, *hbase-default.xml* and *hbase-site.xml*, using the current Java *classpath*.

If you specify an existing configuration, using `create(Configuration that)`, it will take the highest precedence over the configuration files loaded from the classpath.

The `HBaseConfiguration` class actually extends the Hadoop `Configuration` class, but is still compatible with it: you could hand in a Hadoop configuration instance and it would be merged just fine.

After you have retrieved an `HBaseConfiguration` instance, you will have a merged configuration composed of the default values and anything that was overridden in the *hbase-site.xml* configuration file—and optionally the existing configuration you have handed in. You are then free to modify this configuration in any way you like, before you use it with your `HTable` instances. For example, you could override the ZooKeeper *quorum* address, to point to a different cluster:

```
Configuration config = HBaseConfiguration.create();
config.set("hbase.zookeeper.quorum", "zk1.foo.com,zk2.foo.com");
```

In other words, you could simply omit any external, client-side configuration file by setting the quorum property in code. That way, you create a client that needs no extra configuration.

You should share the configuration instance for the reasons explained in "Connection Handling" on page 203.

You can, once again, make use of the command-line shell (see "Quick-Start Guide" on page 31) to verify that our insert has succeeded:

```
hbase(main):001:0> list
TABLE
testtable
1 row(s) in 0.0400 seconds

hbase(main):002:0> scan 'testtable'
ROW                COLUMN+CELL
row1               column=colfam1:qual1, timestamp=1294065304642, value=val1
1 row(s) in 0.2050 seconds
```

Another optional parameter while creating a `Put` instance is called `ts`, or *timestamp*. It allows you to store a value at a particular *version* in the HBase table.

Versioning of Data

A special feature of HBase is the possibility to store multiple *versions* of each cell (the value of a particular column). This is achieved by using timestamps for each of the versions and storing them in descending order. Each timestamp is a long integer value measured in milliseconds. It records the time that has passed since midnight, January 1, 1970 UTC—also known as *Unix time*‡ or *Unix epoch*. Most operating systems provide a timer that can be read from programming languages. In Java, for example, you could use the `System.currentTimeMillis()` function.

‡ See "Unix time" (*http://en.wikipedia.org/wiki/Unix_epoch*) on Wikipedia.

When you put a value into HBase, you have the choice of either explicitly providing a timestamp or omitting that value, which in turn is then filled in by the RegionServer when the put operation is performed.

As noted in "Requirements" on page 34, you *must* make sure your servers have the proper time and are synchronized with one another. Clients might be outside your control, and therefore have a different time, possibly different by hours or sometimes even years.

As long as you do not specify the time in the client API calls, the server time will prevail. But once you allow or have to deal with explicit timestamps, you need to make sure you are not in for unpleasant surprises. Clients could insert values at unexpected time-stamps and cause seemingly unordered version histories.

While most applications never worry about versioning and rely on the built-in handling of the timestamps by HBase, you should be aware of a few peculiarities when using them explicitly.

Here is a larger example of inserting multiple versions of a cell and how to retrieve them:

```
hbase(main):001:0> create 'test', 'cf1'
0 row(s) in 0.9810 seconds

hbase(main):002:0> put 'test', 'row1', 'cf1', 'val1'
0 row(s) in 0.0720 seconds

hbase(main):003:0> put 'test', 'row1', 'cf1', 'val2'
0 row(s) in 0.0520 seconds

hbase(main):004:0> scan 'test'
ROW               COLUMN+CELL
 row1             column=cf1:, timestamp=1297853125623, value=val2
1 row(s) in 0.0790 seconds

hbase(main):005:0> scan 'test', { VERSIONS => 3 }
ROW               COLUMN+CELL
 row1             column=cf1:, timestamp=1297853125623, value=val2
 row1             column=cf1:, timestamp=1297853122412, value=val1
1 row(s) in 0.0640 seconds
```

The example creates a table named test with one column family named cf1. Then two put commands are issued with the same row and column key, but two different values: val1 and val2, respectively. Then a scan operation is used to see the full content of the table. You may not be surprised to see only val2, as you could assume you have simply replaced val1 with the second put call.

But that is not the case in HBase. By default, it keeps three versions of a value and you can use this fact to slightly modify the scan operation to get all available values (i.e., versions) instead. The last call in the example lists both versions you have saved. Note how the row key stays the same in the output; you get all cells as separate lines in the shell's output.

For both operations, scan and get, you only get the *latest* (also referred to as the *newest*) version, because HBase saves versions in time descending order and is set to return only one version by default. Adding the *maximum version* parameter to the calls allows you to retrieve more than one. Set it to the aforementioned `Integer.MAX_VALUE` and you get all available versions.

The term *maximum versions* stems from the fact that you may have fewer versions in a particular cell. The example sets `VERSIONS` (a shortcut for `MAX_VERSIONS`) to "3", but since only two are stored, that is all that is shown.

Another option to retrieve more versions is to use the *time range* parameter these calls expose. They let you specify a start and end time and will retrieve all versions matching the time range. More on this in "Get Method" on page 95 and "Scans" on page 122.

There are many more subtle (and not so subtle) issues with versioning and we will discuss them in "Read Path" on page 342, as well as revisit the advanced concepts and nonstandard behavior in "Versioning" on page 381.

When you do not specify that parameter, it is implicitly set to the current time of the RegionServer responsible for the given row at the moment it is added to the underlying storage.

The constructors of the `Put` class have another optional parameter, called `rowLock`. It gives you the ability to hand in an external *row lock*, something discussed in "Row Locks" on page 118. Suffice it to say for now that you can create your own `RowLock` instance that can be used to prevent other clients from accessing specific rows while you are modifying it repeatedly.

The KeyValue class

From your code you may have to deal with `KeyValue` instances directly. As you may recall from our discussion earlier in this book, these instances contain the data as well as the *coordinates* of one specific cell. The coordinates are the row key, name of the column family, column qualifier, and timestamp. The class provides a plethora of constructors that allow you to combine all of these in many variations. The fully specified constructor looks like this:

```
KeyValue(byte[] row, int roffset, int rlength,
  byte[] family, int foffset, int flength, byte[] qualifier, int qoffset,
  int qlength, long timestamp, Type type, byte[] value, int voffset,
  int vlength)
```

 Be advised that the `KeyValue` class, and its accompanying comparators, are designed for internal use. They are available in a few places in the client API to give you access to the raw data so that extra copy operations can be avoided. They also allow byte-level comparisons, rather than having to rely on a slower, class-level comparison.

The data as well as the coordinates are stored as a Java `byte[]`, that is, as a byte array. The design behind this type of low-level storage is to allow for arbitrary data, but also to be able to efficiently store only the required bytes, keeping the overhead of internal data structures to a minimum. This is also the reason that there is an `offset` and `length` parameter for each byte array paremeter. They allow you to pass in existing byte arrays while doing very fast byte-level operations.

For every member of the coordinates, there is a getter that can retrieve the byte arrays and their given offset and length. This also can be accessed at the topmost level, that is, the underlying byte buffer:

```
byte[] getBuffer()
int getOffset()
int getLength()
```

They return the full byte array details backing the current `KeyValue` instance. There will be few occasions where you will ever have to go that far. But it is available and you can make use of it—if need be.

Two very interesting methods to know are:

```
byte [] getRow()
byte [] getKey()
```

The question you may ask yourself is: what is the difference between a *row* and a *key*? While you will learn about the difference in "Storage" on page 319, for now just remember that the row is what we have been referring to alternatively as the *row key*, that is, the `row` parameter of the `Put` constructor, and the key is what was previously introduced as the *coordinates of a cell*—in their raw, byte array format. In practice, you hardly ever have to use `getKey()` but will be more likely to use `getRow()`.

The `KeyValue` class also provides a large list of internal classes implementing the `Compa rator` interface. They can be used in your own code to do the same comparisons as done inside HBase. This is useful when retrieving `KeyValue` instances using the API and further sorting or processing them in order. They are listed in Table 3-2.

Table 3-2. Brief overview of comparators provided by the KeyValue class

Comparator	Description
KeyComparator	Compares two KeyValue keys, i.e., what is returned by the getKey() method, in their raw, byte array format.
KVComparator	Wraps the raw KeyComparator, providing the same functionality based on two given Key Value instances.
RowComparator	Compares the row key (returned by getRow()) of two KeyValue instances.
MetaKeyComparator	Compares two keys of .META. entries in their raw, byte array format.
MetaComparator	Special version of the KVComparator class for the entries in the .META. catalog table. Wraps the MetaKeyComparator.
RootKeyComparator	Compares two keys of -ROOT- entries in their raw, byte array format.
RootComparator	Special version of the KVComparator class for the entries in the -ROOT- catalog table. Wraps the RootKeyComparator.

The KeyValue class exports most of these comparators as a static instance for each class. For example, there is a public field named KEY_COMPARATOR, giving access to a KeyCompa rator instance. The COMPARATOR field is pointing to an instance of the more frequently used KVComparator class. So instead of creating your own instances, you could use a provided one—for example, when creating a set holding KeyValue instances that should be sorted in the same order that HBase is using internally:

```
TreeSet<KeyValue> set =
  new TreeSet<KeyValue>(KeyValue.COMPARATOR)
```

There is one more field per KeyValue instance that is representing an additional dimension for its unique coordinates: the *type*. Table 3-3 lists the possible values.

Table 3-3. The possible type values for a given KeyValue instance

Type	Description
Put	The KeyValue instance represents a normal Put operation.
Delete	This instance of KeyValue represents a Delete operation, also known as a *tombstone* marker.
DeleteColumn	This is the same as Delete, but more broadly deletes an entire column.
DeleteFamily	This is the same as Delete, but more broadly deletes an entire column family, including all contained columns.

You can see the type of an existing KeyValue instance by, for example, using another provided call:

```
String toString()
```

This prints out the meta information of the current KeyValue instance, and has the following format:

```
<row-key>/<family>:<qualifier>/<version>/<type>/<value-length>
```

This is used by some of the example code for this book to check if data has been set or retrieved, and what the meta information is.

The class has many more convenience methods that allow you to compare parts of the stored data, as well as check what type it is, get its computed heap size, clone or copy it, and more. There are static methods to create special instances of KeyValue that can be used for comparisons, or when manipulating data on that low of a level within HBase. You should consult the provided Java documentation to learn more about them.[§] Also see "Storage" on page 319 for a detailed explanation of the raw, binary format.

[§] See the API documentation for the KeyValue class (*http://hbase.apache.org/apidocs/org/apache/hadoop/hbase/ KeyValue.html*) for a complete description.

Client-side write buffer

Each put operation is effectively an RPC[||] that is transferring data from the client to the server and back. This is OK for a low number of operations, but not for applications that need to store thousands of values per second into a table.

 The importance of reducing the number of separate RPC calls is tied to the *round-trip time*, which is the time it takes for a client to send a request and the server to send a response over the network. This does not include the time required for the data transfer. It simply is the overhead of sending packages over the wire. On average, these take about 1ms on a LAN, which means you can handle 1,000 round-trips per second only.

The other important factor is the message size: if you send large requests over the network, you already need a much lower number of round-trips, as most of the time is spent transferring data. But when doing, for example, counter increments, which are small in size, you will see better performance when batching updates into fewer requests.

The HBase API comes with a built-in client-side *write buffer* that collects put operations so that they are sent in one RPC call to the server(s). The global switch to control if it is used or not is represented by the following methods:

```
void setAutoFlush(boolean autoFlush)
boolean isAutoFlush()
```

By default, the client-side buffer is not enabled. You activate the buffer by setting *auto-flush* to `false`, by invoking:

```
table.setAutoFlush(false)
```

This will enable the client-side buffering mechanism, and you can check the state of the flag respectively with the `isAutoFlush()` method. It will return `true` when you initially create the `HTable` instance. Otherwise, it will obviously return the current state as set by your code.

Once you have activated the buffer, you can store data into HBase as shown in "Single Puts" on page 77. You do not cause any RPCs to occur, though, because the `Put` instances you stored are kept in memory in your client process. When you want to force the data to be written, you can call another API function:

```
void flushCommits() throws IOException
```

The `flushCommits()` method ships all the modifications to the remote server(s). The buffered `Put` instances can span many different rows. The client is smart enough to batch these updates accordingly and send them to the appropriate region server(s). Just as with the single `put()` call, you do not have to worry about where data resides, as this

---

[||] See "Remote procedure call" (*http://en.wikipedia.org/wiki/Remote_procedure_call*) on Wikipedia.

is handled transparently for you by the HBase client. Figure 3-1 shows how the operations are sorted and grouped before they are shipped over the network, with one single RPC per region server.

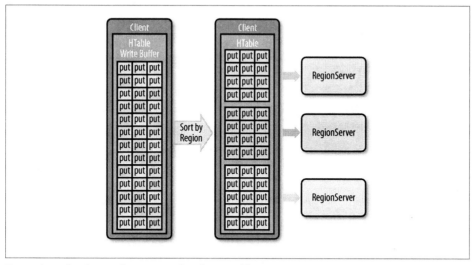

Figure 3-1. *The client-side puts sorted and grouped by region server*

While you can force a flush of the buffer, this is usually not necessary, as the API tracks how much data you are buffering by counting the required heap size of every instance you have added. This tracks the entire overhead of your data, also including necessary internal data structures. Once you go over a specific limit, the client will call the flush command for you implicitly. You can control the configured maximum allowed client-side write buffer size with these calls:

```
long getWriteBufferSize()
void setWriteBufferSize(long writeBufferSize) throws IOException
```

The default size is a moderate 2 MB (or 2,097,152 bytes) and assumes you are inserting reasonably small records into HBase, that is, each a fraction of that buffer size. If you were to store larger data, you may want to consider increasing this value to allow your client to efficiently group together a certain number of records per RPC.

 Setting this value for every HTable instance you create may seem cumbersome and can be avoided by adding a higher value to your local *hbase-site.xml* configuration file—for example, adding:

```
<property>
  <name>hbase.client.write.buffer</name>
  <value>20971520</value>
</property>
```

This will increase the limit to 20 MB.

The buffer is only ever flushed on two occasions:

Explicit flush

Use the flushCommits() call to send the data to the servers for permanent storage.

Implicit flush

This is triggered when you call put() or setWriteBufferSize(). Both calls compare the currently used buffer size with the configured limit and optionally invoke the flushCommits() method. In case the entire buffer is disabled, setting setAuto Flush(true) will force the client to call the flush method for every invocation of put().

Another call triggering the flush implicitly and unconditionally is the close() method of HTable.

Example 3-3 shows how the write buffer is controlled from the client API.

Example 3-3. Using the client-side write buffer

```
HTable table = new HTable(conf, "testtable");
System.out.println("Auto flush: " + table.isAutoFlush());   ❶

table.setAutoFlush(false);   ❷

Put put1 = new Put(Bytes.toBytes("row1"));
put1.add(Bytes.toBytes("colfam1"), Bytes.toBytes("qual1"),
  Bytes.toBytes("val1"));
table.put(put1);   ❸

Put put2 = new Put(Bytes.toBytes("row2"));
put2.add(Bytes.toBytes("colfam1"), Bytes.toBytes("qual1"),
  Bytes.toBytes("val2"));
table.put(put2);

Put put3 = new Put(Bytes.toBytes("row3"));
put3.add(Bytes.toBytes("colfam1"), Bytes.toBytes("qual1"),
  Bytes.toBytes("val3"));
table.put(put3);

Get get = new Get(Bytes.toBytes("row1"));
Result res1 = table.get(get);
System.out.println("Result: " + res1);   ❹

table.flushCommits();   ❺

Result res2 = table.get(get);
System.out.println("Result: " + res2);   ❻
```

❶ Check what the auto flush flag is set to; should print "Auto flush: true".

❷ Set the auto flush to false to enable the client-side write buffer.

❸ Store some rows with columns into HBase.

❹ Try to load previously stored row. This will print "Result: keyvalues=NONE".

❺ Force a flush. This causes an RPC to occur.

❻ Now the row is persisted and can be loaded.

This example also shows a specific behavior of the buffer that you may not anticipate. Let's see what it prints out when executed:

```
Auto flush: true
Result: keyvalues=NONE
Result: keyvalues={row1/colfam1:qual1/1300267114099/Put/vlen=4}
```

While you have not seen the get() operation yet, you should still be able to correctly infer what it does, that is, reading data back from the servers. But for the first get() in the example, the API returns a NONE value—what does that mean? It is caused by the fact that the client write buffer is an in-memory structure that is literally holding back any unflushed records. Nothing was sent to the servers yet, and therefore you cannot access it.

If you were ever required to access the write buffer content, you would find that ArrayList<Put> getWriteBuffer() can be used to get the internal list of buffered Put instances you have added so far calling table.put(put).

I mentioned earlier that it is exactly that list that makes HTable not safe for multithreaded use. Be very careful with what you do to that list when accessing it directly. You are bypassing the heap size checks, or you might modify it while a flush is in progress!

Since the client buffer is a simple list retained in the local process memory, you need to be careful not to run into a problem that terminates the process mid-flight. If that were to happen, any data that has not yet been flushed will be lost! The servers will have never received that data, and therefore there will be no copy of it that can be used to recover from this situation.

Also note that a bigger buffer takes more memory—on both the client and server side since the server instantiates the passed write buffer to process it. On the other hand, a larger buffer size reduces the number of RPCs made. For an estimate of server-side memory-used, evaluate hbase.client.write.buffer * hbase.regionserver.handler.count * number of region server.

Referring to the *round-trip time* again, if you only store large cells, the local buffer is less useful, since the transfer is then dominated by the transfer time. In this case, you are better advised to not increase the client buffer size.

List of Puts

The client API has the ability to insert single Put instances as shown earlier, but it also has the advanced feature of batching operations together. This comes in the form of the following call:

```
void put(List<Put> puts) throws IOException
```

You will have to create a list of Put instances and hand it to this call. Example 3-4 updates the previous example by creating a list to hold the mutations and eventually calling the list-based put() method.

Example 3-4. Inserting data into HBase using a list

```
List<Put> puts = new ArrayList<Put>(); ❶

Put put1 = new Put(Bytes.toBytes("row1"));
put1.add(Bytes.toBytes("colfam1"), Bytes.toBytes("qual1"),
  Bytes.toBytes("val1"));
puts.add(put1); ❷

Put put2 = new Put(Bytes.toBytes("row2"));
put2.add(Bytes.toBytes("colfam1"), Bytes.toBytes("qual1"),
  Bytes.toBytes("val2"));
puts.add(put2); ❸

Put put3 = new Put(Bytes.toBytes("row2"));
put3.add(Bytes.toBytes("colfam1"), Bytes.toBytes("qual2"),
  Bytes.toBytes("val3"));
puts.add(put3); ❹

table.put(puts); ❺
```

❶ Create a list that holds the Put instances.

❷ Add a Put to the list.

❸ Add another Put to the list.

❹ Add a third Put to the list.

❺ Store multiple rows with columns into HBase.

A quick check with the HBase Shell reveals that the rows were stored as expected. Note that the example actually modified three columns, but in two rows only. It added two columns into the row with the key row2, using two separate qualifiers, qual1 and qual2, creating two uniquely named columns in the same row.

```
hbase(main):001:0> scan 'testtable'
ROW                COLUMN+CELL
 row1              column=colfam1:qual1, timestamp=1300108258094, value=val1
 row2              column=colfam1:qual1, timestamp=1300108258094, value=val2
 row2              column=colfam1:qual2, timestamp=1300108258098, value=val3
2 row(s) in 0.1590 seconds
```

Since you are issuing a list of row mutations to possibly many different rows, there is a chance that not all of them will succeed. This could be due to a few reasons—for example, when there is an issue with one of the region servers and the client-side retry mechanism needs to give up because the number of retries has exceeded the configured maximum. If there is problem with any of the put calls on the remote servers, the error is reported back to you subsequently in the form of an IOException.

Example 3-5 uses a *bogus* column family name to insert a column. Since the client is not aware of the structure of the remote table—it could have been altered since it was created—this check is done on the server side.

Example 3-5. Inserting a faulty column family into HBase

```
Put put1 = new Put(Bytes.toBytes("row1"));
put1.add(Bytes.toBytes("colfam1"), Bytes.toBytes("qual1"),
  Bytes.toBytes("val1"));
puts.add(put1);
Put put2 = new Put(Bytes.toBytes("row2"));
put2.add(Bytes.toBytes("BOGUS"), Bytes.toBytes("qual1"),
  Bytes.toBytes("val2")); ❶
puts.add(put2);
Put put3 = new Put(Bytes.toBytes("row2"));
put3.add(Bytes.toBytes("colfam1"), Bytes.toBytes("qual2"),
  Bytes.toBytes("val3"));
puts.add(put3);

table.put(puts); ❷
```

❶ Add a Put with a nonexistent family to the list.

❷ Store multiple rows with columns into HBase.

The call to put() fails with the following (or similar) error message:

```
org.apache.hadoop.hbase.client.RetriesExhaustedWithDetailsException:
  Failed 1 action: NoSuchColumnFamilyException: 1 time,
  servers with issues: 10.0.0.57:51640,
```

You may wonder what happened to the other, nonfaulty puts in the list. Using the shell again you should see that the two correct puts have been applied:

```
hbase(main):001:0> scan 'testtable'
ROW                COLUMN+CELL
 row1              column=colfam1:qual1, timestamp=1300108925848, value=val1
 row2              column=colfam1:qual2, timestamp=1300108925848, value=val3
2 row(s) in 0.0640 seconds
```

The servers iterate over all operations and try to apply them. The failed ones are returned and the client reports the remote error using the RetriesExhausted WithDetailsException, giving you insight into how many operations have failed, with what error, and how many times it has retried to apply the erroneous modification. It is interesting to note that, for the bogus column family, the retry is automatically set to 1 (see the `NoSuchColumnFamilyException: 1 time`), as this is an error from which HBase cannot recover.

Those `Put` instances that have failed on the server side are kept in the local write buffer. They will be retried the next time the buffer is flushed. You can also access them using the `getWriteBuffer()` method of `HTable` and take, for example, evasive actions.

Some checks are done on the *client side*, though—for example, to ensure that the put has a column specified or that it is completely empty. In that event, the client is throwing an exception that leaves the operations preceding the faulty one in the client buffer.

 The list-based `put()` call uses the client-side write buffer to insert all puts into the local buffer and then to call `flushCache()` implicitly. While inserting each instance of `Put`, the client API performs the mentioned check. If it fails, for example, at the third put out of five—the first two are added to the buffer while the last two are not. It also then does not trigger the flush command at all.

You could catch the exception and flush the write buffer manually to apply those modifications. Example 3-6 shows one approach to handle this.

Example 3-6. Inserting an empty Put instance into HBase

```
Put put1 = new Put(Bytes.toBytes("row1"));
put1.add(Bytes.toBytes("colfam1"), Bytes.toBytes("qual1"),
  Bytes.toBytes("val1"));
puts.add(put1);
Put put2 = new Put(Bytes.toBytes("row2"));
put2.add(Bytes.toBytes("BOGUS"), Bytes.toBytes("qual1"),
  Bytes.toBytes("val2"));
puts.add(put2);
Put put3 = new Put(Bytes.toBytes("row2"));
put3.add(Bytes.toBytes("colfam1"), Bytes.toBytes("qual2"),
  Bytes.toBytes("val3"));
puts.add(put3);
Put put4 = new Put(Bytes.toBytes("row2"));
puts.add(put4); ❶

try {
  table.put(puts);
} catch (Exception e) {
  System.err.println("Error: " + e);
  table.flushCommits(); ❷
}
```

❶ Add a put with no content at all to the list.

❷ Catch a local exception and commit queued updates.

The example code this time should give you two errors, similar to:

```
Error: java.lang.IllegalArgumentException: No columns to insert
Exception in thread "main"
```

```
org.apache.hadoop.hbase.client.RetriesExhaustedWithDetailsException:
Failed 1 action: NoSuchColumnFamilyException: 1 time,
servers with issues: 10.0.0.57:51640,
```

The first Error is the client-side check, while the second is the remote exception that now is caused by calling

```
table.flushCommits()
```

in the try/catch block.

 Since you possibly have the client-side write buffer enabled—refer to "Client-side write buffer" on page 86—you will find that the exception is not reported right away, but is delayed until the buffer is flushed.

You need to watch out for a peculiarity using the list-based put call: you cannot control the *order* in which the puts are applied on the server side, which implies that the order in which the servers are called is also not under your control. Use this call with caution if you have to guarantee a specific order—in the worst case, you need to create smaller batches and explicitly flush the client-side write cache to enforce that they are sent to the remote servers.

Atomic compare-and-set

There is a special variation of the put calls that warrants its own section: *check and put*. The method signature is:

```
boolean checkAndPut(byte[] row, byte[] family, byte[] qualifier,
    byte[] value, Put put) throws IOException
```

This call allows you to issue atomic, server-side mutations that are guarded by an accompanying check. If the check passes successfully, the put operation is executed; otherwise, it aborts the operation completely. It can be used to update data based on current, possibly related, values.

Such guarded operations are often used in systems that handle, for example, account balances, state transitions, or data processing. The basic principle is that you read data at one point in time and process it. Once you are ready to write back the result, you want to make sure that no other client has done the same already. You use the atomic check to compare that the value is not modified and therefore apply your value.

 A special type of check can be performed using the checkAndPut() call: only update if another value is not already present. This is achieved by setting the value parameter to null. In that case, the operation would succeed when the specified column is nonexistent.

The call returns a boolean result value, indicating whether the Put has been applied or not, returning true or false, respectively. Example 3-7 shows the interactions between the client and the server, returning the expected results.

Example 3-7. Application using the atomic compare-and-set operations

```
Put put1 = new Put(Bytes.toBytes("row1"));
put1.add(Bytes.toBytes("colfam1"), Bytes.toBytes("qual1"),
  Bytes.toBytes("val1")); ❶

boolean res1 = table.checkAndPut(Bytes.toBytes("row1"),
  Bytes.toBytes("colfam1"), Bytes.toBytes("qual1"), null, put1); ❷
System.out.println("Put applied: " + res1); ❸

boolean res2 = table.checkAndPut(Bytes.toBytes("row1"),
  Bytes.toBytes("colfam1"), Bytes.toBytes("qual1"), null, put1); ❹
System.out.println("Put applied: " + res2); ❺

Put put2 = new Put(Bytes.toBytes("row1"));
put2.add(Bytes.toBytes("colfam1"), Bytes.toBytes("qual2"),
  Bytes.toBytes("val2")); ❻

boolean res3 = table.checkAndPut(Bytes.toBytes("row1"),
  Bytes.toBytes("colfam1"), Bytes.toBytes("qual1"), ❼
  Bytes.toBytes("val1"), put2);
System.out.println("Put applied: " + res3); ❽

Put put3 = new Put(Bytes.toBytes("row2"));
put3.add(Bytes.toBytes("colfam1"), Bytes.toBytes("qual1"),
  Bytes.toBytes("val3")); ❾

boolean res4 = table.checkAndPut(Bytes.toBytes("row1"),
  Bytes.toBytes("colfam1"), Bytes.toBytes("qual1"), ❿
  Bytes.toBytes("val1"), put3);
System.out.println("Put applied: " + res4); ⓫
```

❶ Create a new Put instance.

❷ Check if the column does not exist and perform an optional put operation.

❸ Print out the result; it should be "Put applied: true."

❹ Attempt to store the same cell again.

❺ Print out the result; it should be "Put applied: false", as the column now already exists.

❻ Create another Put instance, but using a different column qualifier.

❼ Store new data only if the previous data has been saved.

❽ Print out the result; it should be "Put applied: true", as the checked column already exists.

❾ Create yet another Put instance, but using a different row.

❿ Store new data while checking a different row.

⓫ We will not get here, as an exception is thrown beforehand!

The last call in the example will throw the following error:

```
Exception in thread "main" org.apache.hadoop.hbase.DoNotRetryIOException:
Action's getRow must match the passed row
```

> The compare-and-set operations provided by HBase rely on checking
> and modifying the *same* row! As with other operations only providing
> atomicity guarantees on single rows, this also applies for this call. Trying
> to check and modify two different rows will return an exception.

Compare-and-set (CAS) operations are very powerful, especially in distributed systems, with even more decoupled client processes. In providing these calls, HBase sets itself apart from other architectures that give no means to reason about concurrent updates performed by multiple, independent clients.

Get Method

The next step in a client API is to retrieve what was just saved. For that the HTable is providing you with the Get call and matching classes. The operations are split into those that operate on a single row and those that retrieve multiple rows in one call.

Single Gets

First, the method that is used to retrieve specific values from an HBase table:

```
Result get(Get get) throws IOException
```

Similar to the Put class for the put() call, there is a matching Get class used by the aforementioned get() function. As another similarity, you will have to provide a row key when creating an instance of Get, using one of these constructors:

```
Get(byte[] row)
Get(byte[] row, RowLock rowLock)
```

> A get() operation is bound to one specific row, but can retrieve any
> number of columns and/or cells contained therein.

Each constructor takes a row parameter specifying the row you want to access, while the second constructor adds an optional rowLock parameter, allowing you to hand in your own locks. And, similar to the put operations, you have methods to specify rather broad criteria to find what you are looking for—or to specify everything down to exact coordinates for a single cell:

```
Get addFamily(byte[] family)
Get addColumn(byte[] family, byte[] qualifier)
Get setTimeRange(long minStamp, long maxStamp) throws IOException
Get setTimeStamp(long timestamp)
Get setMaxVersions()
Get setMaxVersions(int maxVersions) throws IOException
```

The addFamily() call narrows the request down to the given column family. It can be called multiple times to add more than one family. The same is true for the addColumn() call. Here you can add an even narrower address space: the specific column. Then there are methods that let you set the exact timestamp you are looking for—or a time range to match those cells that fall inside it.

Lastly, there are methods that allow you to specify how many versions you want to retrieve, given that you have not set an exact timestamp. By default, this is set to 1, meaning that the get() call returns the most current match only. If you are in doubt, use getMaxVersions() to check what it is set to. The setMaxVersions() *without* a parameter sets the number of versions to return to Integer.MAX_VALUE—which is also the maximum number of versions you can configure in the column family descriptor, and therefore tells the API to return every available version of all matching cells (in other words, up to what is set at the column family level).

The Get class provides additional calls, which are listed in Table 3-4 for your perusal.

Table 3-4. Quick overview of additional methods provided by the Get class

Method	Description
getRow()	Returns the row key as specified when creating the Get instance.
getRowLock()	Returns the row RowLock instance for the current Get instance.
getLockId()	Returns the optional lock ID handed into the constructor using the rowLock parameter. Will be -1L if not set.
getTimeRange()	Retrieves the associated timestamp or time range of the Get instance. Note that there is no getTimeStamp() since the API converts a value assigned with set TimeStamp() into a TimeRange instance internally, setting the minimum and maximum values to the given timestamp.
setFilter()/getFilter()	Special filter instances can be used to select certain columns or cells, based on a wide variety of conditions. You can get and set them with these methods. See "Filters" on page 137 for details.
setCacheBlocks()/ getCacheBlocks()	Each HBase region server has a block cache that efficiently retains recently accessed data for subsequent reads of contiguous information. In some events it is better to not engage the cache to avoid too much churn when doing completely random gets. These methods give you control over this feature.
numFamilies()	Convenience method to retrieve the size of the family map, containing the families added using the addFamily() or addColumn() calls.
hasFamilies()	Another helper to check if a family—or column—has been added to the current instance of the Get class.

Method	Description
familySet()/getFamilyMap()	These methods give you access to the column families and specific columns, as added by the addFamily() and/or addColumn() calls. The family map is a map where the key is the family name and the value a list of added column qualifiers for this particular family. The familySet() returns the Set of all stored families, i.e., a set containing only the family names.

 The getters listed in Table 3-4 for the Get class only retrieve what you have set beforehand. They are rarely used, and make sense only when you, for example, prepare a Get instance in a private method in your code, and inspect the values in another place.

As mentioned earlier, HBase provides us with a helper class named **Bytes** that has many static methods to convert Java types into **byte[]** arrays. It also can do the same in reverse: as you are retrieving data from HBase—for example, one of the rows stored previously—you can make use of these helper functions to convert the **byte[]** data back into Java types. Here is a short list of what it offers, continued from the earlier discussion:

```
static String toString(byte[] b)
static boolean toBoolean(byte[] b)
static long toLong(byte[] bytes)
static float toFloat(byte[] bytes)
static int toInt(byte[] bytes)
...
```

Example 3-8 shows how this is all put together.

Example 3-8. Application retrieving data from HBase

```
Configuration conf = HBaseConfiguration.create(); ❶
HTable table = new HTable(conf, "testtable"); ❷
Get get = new Get(Bytes.toBytes("row1")); ❸
get.addColumn(Bytes.toBytes("colfam1"), Bytes.toBytes("qual1")); ❹
Result result = table.get(get); ❺
byte[] val = result.getValue(Bytes.toBytes("colfam1"),
  Bytes.toBytes("qual1")); ❻
System.out.println("Value: " + Bytes.toString(val)); ❼
```

❶ Create the configuration.

❷ Instantiate a new table reference.

❸ Create a Get with a specific row.

❹ Add a column to the Get.

❺ Retrieve a row with selected columns from HBase.

❻ Get a specific value for the given column.

❼ Print out the value while converting it back.

If you are running this example after, say Example 3-2, you should get this as the output:

```
Value: val1
```

The output is not very spectacular, but it shows that the basic operation works. The example also only adds the specific column to retrieve, relying on the default for maximum versions being returned set to 1. The call to get() returns an instance of the Result class, which you will learn about next.

The Result class

When you retrieve data using the get() calls, you receive an instance of the Result class that contains all the matching cells. It provides you with the means to access everything that was returned from the server for the given row and matching the specified query, such as column family, column qualifier, timestamp, and so on.

There are utility methods you can use to ask for specific results—just as Example 3-8 used earlier—using more concrete dimensions. If you have, for example, asked the server to return all columns of one specific column family, you can now ask for specific columns within that family. In other words, you need to call get() with just enough concrete information to be able to process the matching data on the client side. The functions provided are:

```
byte[] getValue(byte[] family, byte[] qualifier)
byte[] value()
byte[] getRow()
int size()
boolean isEmpty()
KeyValue[] raw()
List<KeyValue> list()
```

The getValue() call allows you to get the data for a specific cell stored in HBase. As you cannot specify what timestamp—in other words, version—you want, you get the newest one. The value() call makes this even easier by returning the data for the newest cell in the first column found. Since columns are also sorted lexicographically on the server, this would return the value of the column with the column name (including family and qualifier) sorted first.

You saw getRow() before: it returns the row key, as specified when creating the current instance of the Get class. size() is returning the number of KeyValue instances the server has returned. You may use this call—or isEmpty(), which checks if size() returns a number greater than zero—to check in your own client code if the retrieval call returned any matches.

Access to the raw, low-level KeyValue instances is provided by the raw() method, returning the array of KeyValue instances backing the current Result instance. The list() call simply converts the array returned by raw() into a List instance, giving you convenience by providing iterator access, for example. The created list is backed by the original array of KeyValue instances.

The array returned by `raw()` is already lexicographically sorted, taking the full coordinates of the `KeyValue` instances into account. So it is sorted first by column family, then within each family by qualifier, then by timestamp, and finally by type.

Another set of accessors is provided which are more column-oriented:

```
List<KeyValue> getColumn(byte[] family, byte[] qualifier)
KeyValue getColumnLatest(byte[] family, byte[] qualifier)
boolean containsColumn(byte[] family, byte[] qualifier)
```

Here you ask for multiple values of a specific column, which solves the issue pointed out earlier, that is, how to get multiple versions of a given column. The number returned obviously is bound to the maximum number of versions you have specified when configuring the `Get` instance, before the call to `get()`, with the default being set to 1. In other words, the returned list contains zero (in case the column has no value for the given row) or one entry, which is the newest version of the value. If you have specified a value greater than the default of 1 version to be returned, it could be any number, up to the specified maximum.

The `getColumnLatest()` method is returning the newest cell of the specified column, but in contrast to `getValue()`, it does not return the raw byte array of the value but the full `KeyValue` instance instead. This may be useful when you need more than just the data. The `containsColumn()` is a convenience method to check if there was any cell returned in the specified column.

These methods all support the fact that the qualifier can be left unspecified—setting it to `null`—and therefore matching the special column with no name.

Using no qualifier means that there is no label to the column. When looking at the table from, for example, the HBase Shell, you need to know what it contains. A rare case where you might want to consider using the empty qualifier is in column families that only ever contain a single column. Then the family name might indicate its purpose.

There is a third set of methods that provide access to the returned data from the get request. These are map-oriented and look like this:

```
NavigableMap<byte[], NavigableMap<byte[],
  NavigableMap<Long, byte[]>>> getMap()
NavigableMap<byte[],
  NavigableMap<byte[], byte[]>> getNoVersionMap()
NavigableMap<byte[], byte[]> getFamilyMap(byte[] family)
```

The most generic call, named `getMap()`, returns the entire result set in a Java `Map` class instance that you can iterate over to access all the values. The `getNoVersionMap()` does the same while only including the latest cell for each column. Finally, the `getFamily`

Map() lets you select the KeyValue instances for a specific column family only—but including all versions, if specified.

Use whichever access method of Result matches your access pattern; the data has already been moved across the network from the server to your client process, so it is not incurring any other performance or resource penalties.

Dump the Contents

All Java objects have a toString() method, which, when overridden by a class, can be used to convert the data of an instance into a text representation. This is not for serialization purposes, but is most often used for debugging.

The Result class has such an implementation of toString(), dumping the result of a read call as a string. The output looks like this:

```
keyvalues={row-2/colfam1:col-5/1300802024293/Put/vlen=7,
           row-2/colfam2:col-33/1300802024325/Put/vlen=8}
```

It simply prints all contained KeyValue instances, that is, calling KeyValue.toString() respectively. If the Result instance is empty, the output will be:

```
keyvalues=NONE
```

This indicates that there were *no* KeyValue instances returned. The code examples in this book make use of the toString() method to quickly print the results of previous read operations.

List of Gets

Another similarity to the put() calls is that you can ask for more than one row using a single request. This allows you to quickly and efficiently retrieve related—but also completely random, if required—data from the remote servers.

 As shown in Figure 3-1, the request may actually go to more than one server, but for all intents and purposes, it looks like a single call from the client code.

The method provided by the API has the following signature:

```
Result[] get(List<Get> gets) throws IOException
```

Using this call is straightforward, with the same approach as seen earlier: you need to create a list that holds all instances of the Get class you have prepared. This list is handed into the call and you will be returned an array of equal size holding the matching Result instances. Example 3-9 brings this together, showing two different approaches to accessing the data.

Example 3-9. Retrieving data from HBase using lists of Get instances

```java
byte[] cf1 = Bytes.toBytes("colfam1");
byte[] qf1 = Bytes.toBytes("qual1");
byte[] qf2 = Bytes.toBytes("qual2"); ❶
byte[] row1 = Bytes.toBytes("row1");
byte[] row2 = Bytes.toBytes("row2");

List<Get> gets = new ArrayList<Get>(); ❷

Get get1 = new Get(row1);
get1.addColumn(cf1, qf1);
gets.add(get1);

Get get2 = new Get(row2);
get2.addColumn(cf1, qf1); ❸
gets.add(get2);

Get get3 = new Get(row2);
get3.addColumn(cf1, qf2);
gets.add(get3);

Result[] results = table.get(gets); ❹

System.out.println("First iteration...");
for (Result result : results) {
  String row = Bytes.toString(result.getRow());
  System.out.print("Row: " + row + " ");
  byte[] val = null;
  if (result.containsColumn(cf1, qf1)) { ❺
    val = result.getValue(cf1, qf1);
    System.out.println("Value: " + Bytes.toString(val));
  }
  if (result.containsColumn(cf1, qf2)) {
    val = result.getValue(cf1, qf2);
    System.out.println("Value: " + Bytes.toString(val));
  }
}

System.out.println("Second iteration...");
for (Result result : results) {
  for (KeyValue kv : result.raw()) {
    System.out.println("Row: " + Bytes.toString(kv.getRow()) + ❻
      " Value: " + Bytes.toString(kv.getValue()));
  }
}
```

❶ Prepare commonly used byte arrays.

❷ Create a list that holds the Get instances.

❸ Add the Get instances to the list.

❹ Retrieve rows with selected columns from HBase.

❺ Iterate over the results and check what values are available.

❻ Iterate over the results again, printing out all values.

Assuming that you execute Example 3-4 just before you run Example 3-9, you should see something like this on the command line:

```
First iteration...
Row: row1 Value: val1
Row: row2 Value: val2
Row: row2 Value: val3
Second iteration...
Row: row1 Value: val1
Row: row2 Value: val2
Row: row2 Value: val3
```

Both iterations return the same values, showing that you have a number of choices on how to access them, once you have received the results. What you have not yet seen is how errors are reported back to you. This differs from what you learned in "List of Puts" on page 90. The get() call either returns the said array, matching the same size as the given list by the gets parameter, or throws an exception. Example 3-10 showcases this behavior.

Example 3-10. Trying to read an erroneous column family

```
List<Get> gets = new ArrayList<Get>();

Get get1 = new Get(row1);
get1.addColumn(cf1, qf1);
gets.add(get1);

Get get2 = new Get(row2);
get2.addColumn(cf1, qf1); ❶
gets.add(get2);

Get get3 = new Get(row2);
get3.addColumn(cf1, qf2);
gets.add(get3);

Get get4 = new Get(row2);
get4.addColumn(Bytes.toBytes("BOGUS"), qf2);
gets.add(get4); ❷

Result[] results = table.get(gets); ❸

System.out.println("Result count: " + results.length); ❹
```

❶ Add the Get instances to the list.

❷ Add the bogus column family Get.

❸ An exception is thrown and the process is aborted.

❹ This line will never be reached!

Executing this example will abort the entire get() operation, throwing the following (or similar) error, and not returning a result at all:

```
org.apache.hadoop.hbase.client.RetriesExhaustedWithDetailsException:
  Failed 1 action: NoSuchColumnFamilyException: 1 time,
  servers with issues: 10.0.0.57:51640,
```

One way to have more control over how the API handles partial faults is to use the batch() operations discussed in "Batch Operations" on page 114.

Related retrieval methods

There are a few more calls that you can use from your code to retrieve or check your stored data. The first is:

```
boolean exists(Get get) throws IOException
```

You can set up a Get instance, just like you do when using the get() calls of HTable. Instead of having to retrieve the data from the remote servers, using an RPC, to verify that it actually exists, you can employ this call because it only returns a boolean flag indicating that same fact.

 Using exists() involves the same lookup semantics on the region servers, including loading file blocks to check if a row or column actually exists. You only avoid shipping the data over the network—but that is very useful if you are checking very large columns, or do so very frequently.

Sometimes it might be necessary to find a specific row, or the one just before the requested row, when retrieving data. The following call can help you find a row using these semantics:

```
Result getRowOrBefore(byte[] row, byte[] family) throws IOException
```

You need to specify the row you are looking for, and a column family. The latter is required because, in HBase, which is a column-oriented database, there is no row if there are no columns. Specifying a family name tells the servers to check if the row searched for has any values in a column contained in the given family.

 Be careful to specify an existing column family name when using the getRowOrBefore() method, or you will get a Java NullPointerException back from the server. This is caused by the server trying to access a nonexistent storage file.

The returned instance of the Result class can be used to retrieve the found row key. This should be either the exact row you were asking for, or the one preceding it. If there is no match at all, the call returns null. Example 3-11 uses the call to find the rows you created using the put examples earlier.

Example 3-11. Using a special retrieval method

```
Result result1 = table.getRowOrBefore(Bytes.toBytes("row1"), ❶
  Bytes.toBytes("colfam1"));
System.out.println("Found: " + Bytes.toString(result1.getRow())); ❷

Result result2 = table.getRowOrBefore(Bytes.toBytes("row99"), ❸
  Bytes.toBytes("colfam1"));
System.out.println("Found: " + Bytes.toString(result2.getRow())); ❹

for (KeyValue kv : result2.raw()) {
  System.out.println("  Col: " + Bytes.toString(kv.getFamily()) + ❺
    "/" + Bytes.toString(kv.getQualifier()) +
    ", Value: " + Bytes.toString(kv.getValue()));
}

Result result3 = table.getRowOrBefore(Bytes.toBytes("abc"), ❻
  Bytes.toBytes("colfam1"));
System.out.println("Found: " + result3); ❼
```

❶ Attempt to find an existing row.

❷ Print what was found.

❸ Attempt to find a nonexistent row.

❹ Returns the row that was sorted at the end of the table.

❺ Print the returned values.

❻ Attempt to find a row before the test rows.

❼ Should return "null" since there is no match.

Assuming you ran Example 3-4 just before this code, you should see output similar or equal to the following:

```
Found: row1
Found: row2
  Col: colfam1/qual1, Value: val2
  Col: colfam1/qual2, Value: val3
Found: null
```

The first call tries to find a matching row and succeeds. The second call uses a large number postfix to find the last stored row, starting with the prefix row-. It did find row-2 accordingly. Lastly, the example tries to find row abc, which sorts before the rows the put example added, using the row- prefix, and therefore does not exist, nor matches any previous row keys. The returned result is then null and indicates the missed lookup.

What is interesting is the loop to print out the data that was returned along with the matching row. You can see from the preceding code that all columns of the specified column family were returned, including their *latest* values. You could use this call to quickly retrieve all the latest values from an entire column family—in other words, all columns contained in the given column family—based on a specific sorting pattern. For example, assume our put() example, which is using row- as the prefix for all keys.

Calling getRowOrBefore() with a row set to row-999999999 will always return the row that is, based on the lexicographical sorting, placed at the end of the table.

Delete Method

You are now able to create, read, and update data in HBase tables. What is left is the ability to delete from it. And surely you may have guessed by now that the HTable provides you with a method of exactly that name, along with a matching class aptly named Delete.

Single Deletes

The variant of the delete() call that takes a single Delete instance is:

```
void delete(Delete delete) throws IOException
```

Just as with the get() and put() calls you saw already, you will have to create a Delete instance and then add details about the data you want to remove. The constructors are:

```
Delete(byte[] row)
Delete(byte[] row, long timestamp, RowLock rowLock)
```

You need to provide the row you want to modify, and optionally provide a rowLock, an instance of RowLock to specify your own lock details, in case you want to modify the same row more than once subsequently. Otherwise, you would be wise to narrow down what you want to remove from the given row, using one of the following methods:

```
Delete deleteFamily(byte[] family)
Delete deleteFamily(byte[] family, long timestamp)
Delete deleteColumns(byte[] family, byte[] qualifier)
Delete deleteColumns(byte[] family, byte[] qualifier, long timestamp)
Delete deleteColumn(byte[] family, byte[] qualifier)
Delete deleteColumn(byte[] family, byte[] qualifier, long timestamp)
void setTimestamp(long timestamp)
```

You do have a choice to narrow in on what to remove using four types of calls. First you can use the deleteFamily() methods to remove an entire column family, including all contained columns. You have the option to specify a timestamp that triggers more specific filtering of cell versions. If specified, the timestamp matches the same and all older versions of all columns.

The next type is deleteColumns(), which operates on exactly one column and deletes either all versions of that cell when no timestamp is given, or all matching and older versions when a timestamp is specified.

The third type is similar, using deleteColumn(). It also operates on a specific, given column only, but deletes either the most current or the specified version, that is, the one with the matching timestamp.

Finally, there is setTimestamp(), which is not considered when using any of the other three types of calls. But if you do not specify either a family or a column, this call can make the difference between deleting the entire row or just all contained columns, in all column families, that match or have an older timestamp compared to the given one. Table 3-5 shows the functionality in a matrix to make the semantics more readable.

Table 3-5. Functionality matrix of the delete() calls

Method	Deletes without timestamp	Deletes with timestamp
none	Entire row, i.e., all columns, all versions.	All versions of all columns in all column families, whose timestamp is equal to or older than the given timestamp.
deleteColumn()	Only the latest version of the given column; older versions are kept.	Only exactly the specified version of the given column, with the matching timestamp. If nonexistent, nothing is deleted.
deleteColumns()	All versions of the given column.	Versions equal to or older than the given timestamp of the given column.
deleteFamily()	All columns (including all versions) of the given family.	Versions equal to or older than the given timestamp of all columns of the given family.

The Delete class provides additional calls, which are listed in Table 3-6 for your reference.

Table 3-6. Quick overview of additional methods provided by the Delete class

Method	Description
getRow()	Returns the row key as specified when creating the Delete instance.
getRowLock()	Returns the row RowLock instance for the current Delete instance.
getLockId()	Returns the optional lock ID handed into the constructor using the rowLock parameter. Will be -1L if not set.
getTimeStamp()	Retrieves the associated timestamp of the Delete instance.
isEmpty()	Checks if the family map contains any entries. In other words, if you specified any column family, or column qualifier, that should be deleted.
getFamilyMap()	Gives you access to the added column families and specific columns, as added by the delete Family() and/or deleteColumn()/deleteColumns() calls. The returned map uses the family name as the key, and the value it points to is a list of added column qualifiers for this particular family.

Example 3-12 shows how to use the single delete() call from client code.

Example 3-12. Application deleting data from HBase

```
Delete delete = new Delete(Bytes.toBytes("row1")); ❶

delete.setTimestamp(1); ❷
```

```
delete.deleteColumn(Bytes.toBytes("colfam1"), Bytes.toBytes("qual1"), 1); ❸

delete.deleteColumns(Bytes.toBytes("colfam2"), Bytes.toBytes("qual1")); ❹
delete.deleteColumns(Bytes.toBytes("colfam2"), Bytes.toBytes("qual3"), 15); ❺

delete.deleteFamily(Bytes.toBytes("colfam3")); ❻
delete.deleteFamily(Bytes.toBytes("colfam3"), 3); ❼

table.delete(delete); ❽

table.close();
```

❶ Create a `Delete` with a specific row.

❷ Set a timestamp for row deletes.

❸ Delete a specific version in one column.

❹ Delete all versions in one column.

❺ Delete the given and all older versions in one column.

❻ Delete the entire family, all columns and versions.

❼ Delete the given and all older versions in the entire column family, that is, from all columns therein.

❽ Delete the data from the HBase table.

The example lists all the different calls you can use to parameterize the `delete()` operation. It does not make too much sense to call them all one after another like this. Feel free to comment out the various delete calls to see what is printed on the console.

Setting the timestamp for the deletes has the effect of *only* matching the exact cell, that is, the matching column and value with the exact timestamp. On the other hand, not setting the timestamp forces the server to retrieve the latest timestamp on the server side on your behalf. This is slower than performing a delete with an explicit timestamp.

If you attempt to delete a cell with a timestamp that does *not* exist, nothing happens. For example, given that you have two versions of a column, one at version 10 and one at version 20, deleting from this column with version 15 will not affect either existing version.

Another note to be made about the example is that it showcases custom versioning. Instead of relying on timestamps, implicit or explicit ones, it uses sequential numbers, starting with 1. This is perfectly valid, although you are forced to always set the version yourself, since the servers do not know about your schema and would use epoch-based timestamps instead.

As of this writing, using custom versioning is not recommended. It will very likely work, but is not tested very well. Make sure you carefully evaluate your options before using this technique.

Another example of using custom versioning can be found in "Search Integration" on page 374.

List of Deletes

The list-based `delete()` call works very similarly to the list-based `put()`. You need to create a list of `Delete` instances, configure them, and call the following method:

```
void delete(List<Delete> deletes) throws IOException
```

Example 3-13 shows where three different rows are affected during the operation, deleting various details they contain. When you run this example, you will see a printout of the *before* and *after* states of the delete. The output is printing the raw `KeyValue` instances, using `KeyValue.toString()`.

 Just as with the other list-based operation, you cannot make any assumption regarding the order in which the deletes are applied on the remote servers. The API is free to reorder them to make efficient use of the single RPC per affected region server. If you need to enforce specific orders of how operations are applied, you would need to batch those calls into smaller groups and ensure that they contain the operations in the desired order across the batches. In a worst-case scenario, you would need to send separate `delete` calls altogether.

Example 3-13. Application deleting a list of values

```
List<Delete> deletes = new ArrayList<Delete>(); ❶

Delete delete1 = new Delete(Bytes.toBytes("row1"));
delete1.setTimestamp(4); ❷
deletes.add(delete1);

Delete delete2 = new Delete(Bytes.toBytes("row2"));
delete2.deleteColumn(Bytes.toBytes("colfam1"), Bytes.toBytes("qual1")); ❸
delete2.deleteColumns(Bytes.toBytes("colfam2"), Bytes.toBytes("qual3"), 5); ❹
deletes.add(delete2);

Delete delete3 = new Delete(Bytes.toBytes("row3"));
delete3.deleteFamily(Bytes.toBytes("colfam1")); ❺
delete3.deleteFamily(Bytes.toBytes("colfam2"), 3); ❻
deletes.add(delete3);

table.delete(deletes); ❼

table.close();
```

❶ Create a list that holds the `Delete` instances.

❷ Set a timestamp for row deletes.

❸ Delete the latest version only in one column.

❹ Delete the given and all older versions in another column.

❺ Delete the entire family, all columns and versions.

❻ Delete the given and all older versions in the entire column family, that is, from all columns therein.

❼ Delete the data from multiple rows in the HBase table.

The output you should see is:#

```
Before delete call...
KV: row1/colfam1:qual1/2/Put/vlen=4, Value: val2
KV: row1/colfam1:qual1/1/Put/vlen=4, Value: val1
KV: row1/colfam1:qual2/4/Put/vlen=4, Value: val4
KV: row1/colfam1:qual2/3/Put/vlen=4, Value: val3
KV: row1/colfam1:qual3/6/Put/vlen=4, Value: val6
KV: row1/colfam1:qual3/5/Put/vlen=4, Value: val5

KV: row1/colfam2:qual1/2/Put/vlen=4, Value: val2
KV: row1/colfam2:qual1/1/Put/vlen=4, Value: val1
KV: row1/colfam2:qual2/4/Put/vlen=4, Value: val4
KV: row1/colfam2:qual2/3/Put/vlen=4, Value: val3
KV: row1/colfam2:qual3/6/Put/vlen=4, Value: val6
KV: row1/colfam2:qual3/5/Put/vlen=4, Value: val5

KV: row2/colfam1:qual1/2/Put/vlen=4, Value: val2
KV: row2/colfam1:qual1/1/Put/vlen=4, Value: val1
KV: row2/colfam1:qual2/4/Put/vlen=4, Value: val4
KV: row2/colfam1:qual2/3/Put/vlen=4, Value: val3
KV: row2/colfam1:qual3/6/Put/vlen=4, Value: val6
KV: row2/colfam1:qual3/5/Put/vlen=4, Value: val5

KV: row2/colfam2:qual1/2/Put/vlen=4, Value: val2
KV: row2/colfam2:qual1/1/Put/vlen=4, Value: val1
KV: row2/colfam2:qual2/4/Put/vlen=4, Value: val4
KV: row2/colfam2:qual2/3/Put/vlen=4, Value: val3
KV: row2/colfam2:qual3/6/Put/vlen=4, Value: val6
KV: row2/colfam2:qual3/5/Put/vlen=4, Value: val5

KV: row3/colfam1:qual1/2/Put/vlen=4, Value: val2
KV: row3/colfam1:qual1/1/Put/vlen=4, Value: val1
KV: row3/colfam1:qual2/4/Put/vlen=4, Value: val4
KV: row3/colfam1:qual2/3/Put/vlen=4, Value: val3
KV: row3/colfam1:qual3/6/Put/vlen=4, Value: val6
KV: row3/colfam1:qual3/5/Put/vlen=4, Value: val5

KV: row3/colfam2:qual1/2/Put/vlen=4, Value: val2
KV: row3/colfam2:qual1/1/Put/vlen=4, Value: val1
KV: row3/colfam2:qual2/4/Put/vlen=4, Value: val4
KV: row3/colfam2:qual2/3/Put/vlen=4, Value: val3
KV: row3/colfam2:qual3/6/Put/vlen=4, Value: val6
KV: row3/colfam2:qual3/5/Put/vlen=4, Value: val5
```

#For easier readability, the related details were broken up into groups using blank lines.

```
After delete call...
KV: row1/colfam1:qual3/6/Put/vlen=4, Value: val6
KV: row1/colfam1:qual3/5/Put/vlen=4, Value: val5

KV: row1/colfam2:qual3/6/Put/vlen=4, Value: val6
KV: row1/colfam2:qual3/5/Put/vlen=4, Value: val5

KV: row2/colfam1:qual1/1/Put/vlen=4, Value: val1
KV: row2/colfam1:qual2/4/Put/vlen=4, Value: val4
KV: row2/colfam1:qual2/3/Put/vlen=4, Value: val3
KV: row2/colfam1:qual3/6/Put/vlen=4, Value: val6
KV: row2/colfam1:qual3/5/Put/vlen=4, Value: val5

KV: row2/colfam2:qual1/2/Put/vlen=4, Value: val2
KV: row2/colfam2:qual1/1/Put/vlen=4, Value: val1
KV: row2/colfam2:qual2/4/Put/vlen=4, Value: val4
KV: row2/colfam2:qual2/3/Put/vlen=4, Value: val3
KV: row2/colfam2:qual3/6/Put/vlen=4, Value: val6

KV: row3/colfam2:qual2/4/Put/vlen=4, Value: val4
KV: row3/colfam2:qual3/6/Put/vlen=4, Value: val6
KV: row3/colfam2:qual3/5/Put/vlen=4, Value: val5
```

The deleted original data is highlighted in the *Before delete call...* block. All three rows contain the same data, composed of two column families, three columns in each family, and two versions for each column.

The example code first deletes, from the entire row, everything up to version 4. This leaves the columns with versions 5 and 6 as the remainder of the row content.

It then goes about and uses the two different column-related delete calls on row2 to remove the newest cell in the column named colfam1:qual1, and subsequently every cell with a version of 5 and older—in other words, those with a lower version number— from colfam1:qual3. Here you have only one matching cell, which is removed as expected in due course.

Lastly, operating on row-3, the code removes the entire column family colfam1, and then everything with a version of 3 or less from colfam2. During the execution of the example code, you will see the printed KeyValue details, using something like this:

```
System.out.println("KV: " + kv.toString() +
        ", Value: " + Bytes.toString(kv.getValue()))
```

By now you are familiar with the usage of the Bytes class, which is used to print out the value of the KeyValue instance, as returned by the getValue() method. This is necessary because the KeyValue.toString() output (as explained in "The KeyValue class" on page 83) is not printing out the actual value, but rather the key part only. The toString() does not print the value since it could be very large.

Here, the example code inserts the column values, and therefore knows that these are short and human-readable; hence it is safe to print them out on the console as shown. You could use the same mechanism in your own code for debugging purposes.

Please refer to the entire example code in the accompanying source code repository for this book. You will see how the data is inserted and retrieved to generate the discussed output.

What is left to talk about is the error handling of the list-based `delete()` call. The handed-in `deletes` parameter, that is, the list of `Delete` instances, is modified to only contain the failed delete instances when the call returns. In other words, when everything has succeeded, the list will be empty. The call also throws the exception—if there was one—reported from the remote servers. You will have to guard the call using a `try/catch`, for example, and react accordingly. Example 3-14 may serve as a starting point.

Example 3-14. Deleting faulty data from HBase

```
Delete delete4 = new Delete(Bytes.toBytes("row2"));
delete4.deleteColumn(Bytes.toBytes("BOGUS"), Bytes.toBytes("qual1")); ❶
deletes.add(delete4);

try {
  table.delete(deletes); ❷
} catch (Exception e) {
  System.err.println("Error: " + e); ❸
}
table.close();

System.out.println("Deletes length: " + deletes.size()); ❹
for (Delete delete : deletes) {
  System.out.println(delete); ❺
}
```

❶ Add the bogus column family to trigger an error.

❷ Delete the data from multiple rows in the HBase table.

❸ Guard against remote exceptions.

❹ Check the length of the list after the call.

❺ Print out the failed delete for debugging purposes.

Example 3-14 modifies Example 3-13 but adds an erroneous delete detail: it inserts a *BOGUS* column family name. The output is the same as that for Example 3-13, but has some additional details printed out in the middle part:

```
Before delete call...
KV: row1/colfam1:qual1/2/Put/vlen=4, Value: val2
KV: row1/colfam1:qual1/1/Put/vlen=4, Value: val1
...
KV: row3/colfam2:qual3/6/Put/vlen=4, Value: val6
KV: row3/colfam2:qual3/5/Put/vlen=4, Value: val5

Error: org.apache.hadoop.hbase.client.RetriesExhaustedWithDetailsException:
  Failed 1 action: NoSuchColumnFamilyException: 1 time,
  servers with issues: 10.0.0.43:59057,
```

```
Deletes length: 1
row=row2, ts=9223372036854775807, families={(family=BOGUS, keyvalues= \
  (row2/BOGUS:qual1/9223372036854775807/Delete/vlen=0)}

After delete call...
KV: row1/colfam1:qual3/6/Put/vlen=4, Value: val6
KV: row1/colfam1:qual3/5/Put/vlen=4, Value: val5
...
KV: row3/colfam2:qual3/6/Put/vlen=4, Value: val6
KV: row3/colfam2:qual3/5/Put/vlen=4, Value: val5
```

As expected, the list contains one remaining Delete instance: the one with the bogus column family. Printing out the instance—Java uses the implicit toString() method when *printing* an object—reveals the internal details of the failed delete. The important part is the family name being the obvious reason for the failure. You can use this technique in your own code to check why an operation has failed. Often the reasons are rather obvious indeed.

Finally, note the exception that was caught and printed out in the catch statement of the example. It is the same RetriesExhaustedWithDetailsException you saw twice already. It reports the number of failed actions plus how often it did retry to apply them, and on which server. An advanced task that you will learn about in later chapters is how to verify and monitor servers so that the given server address could be useful to find the root cause of the failure.

Atomic compare-and-delete

You saw in "Atomic compare-and-set" on page 93 how to use an atomic, conditional operation to insert data into a table. There is an equivalent call for deletes that gives you access to server-side, *read-and-modify* functionality:

```
boolean checkAndDelete(byte[] row, byte[] family, byte[] qualifier,
    byte[] value, Delete delete) throws IOException
```

You need to specify the row key, column family, qualifier, and value to check before the actual delete operation is performed. Should the test fail, nothing is deleted and the call returns a false. If the check is successful, the delete is applied and true is returned. Example 3-15 shows this in context.

Example 3-15. Application deleting values using the atomic compare-and-set operations

```
Delete delete1 = new Delete(Bytes.toBytes("row1"));
delete1.deleteColumns(Bytes.toBytes("colfam1"), Bytes.toBytes("qual3")); ❶

boolean res1 = table.checkAndDelete(Bytes.toBytes("row1"),
    Bytes.toBytes("colfam2"), Bytes.toBytes("qual3"), null, delete1); ❷
System.out.println("Delete successful: " + res1); ❸

Delete delete2 = new Delete(Bytes.toBytes("row1"));
delete2.deleteColumns(Bytes.toBytes("colfam2"), Bytes.toBytes("qual3")); ❹
table.delete(delete2);
```

```
boolean res2 = table.checkAndDelete(Bytes.toBytes("row1"),
  Bytes.toBytes("colfam2"), Bytes.toBytes("qual3"), null, delete1); ❺
System.out.println("Delete successful: " + res2); ❻

Delete delete3 = new Delete(Bytes.toBytes("row2"));
delete3.deleteFamily(Bytes.toBytes("colfam1")); ❼

try{
  boolean res4 = table.checkAndDelete(Bytes.toBytes("row1"),
    Bytes.toBytes("colfam1"), Bytes.toBytes("qual1"), ❽
    Bytes.toBytes("val1"), delete3);
  System.out.println("Delete successful: " + res4); ❾
} catch (Exception e) {
  System.err.println("Error: " + e);
}
```

❶ Create a new `Delete` instance.

❷ Check if the column does not exist and perform an optional delete operation.

❸ Print out the result; it should be "Delete successful: false."

❹ Delete the checked column manually.

❺ Attempt to delete the same cell again.

❻ Print out the result; it should be "Delete successful: true," as the column now already exists.

❼ Create yet another `Delete` instance, but using a different row.

❽ Try to delete it while checking a different row.

❾ We will not get here, as an exception is thrown beforehand!

The entire output of the example should look like this:

```
Before delete call...
KV: row1/colfam1:qual1/2/Put/vlen=4, Value: val2
KV: row1/colfam1:qual1/1/Put/vlen=4, Value: val1
KV: row1/colfam1:qual2/4/Put/vlen=4, Value: val4
KV: row1/colfam1:qual2/3/Put/vlen=4, Value: val3
KV: row1/colfam1:qual3/6/Put/vlen=4, Value: val6
KV: row1/colfam1:qual3/5/Put/vlen=4, Value: val5
KV: row1/colfam2:qual1/2/Put/vlen=4, Value: val2
KV: row1/colfam2:qual1/1/Put/vlen=4, Value: val1
KV: row1/colfam2:qual2/4/Put/vlen=4, Value: val4
KV: row1/colfam2:qual2/3/Put/vlen=4, Value: val3
KV: row1/colfam2:qual3/6/Put/vlen=4, Value: val6
KV: row1/colfam2:qual3/5/Put/vlen=4, Value: val5
Delete successful: false
Delete successful: true
After delete call...
KV: row1/colfam1:qual1/2/Put/vlen=4, Value: val2
KV: row1/colfam1:qual1/1/Put/vlen=4, Value: val1
KV: row1/colfam1:qual2/4/Put/vlen=4, Value: val4
KV: row1/colfam1:qual2/3/Put/vlen=4, Value: val3
```

```
KV: row1/colfam2:qual1/2/Put/vlen=4, Value: val2
KV: row1/colfam2:qual1/1/Put/vlen=4, Value: val1
KV: row1/colfam2:qual2/4/Put/vlen=4, Value: val4
KV: row1/colfam2:qual2/3/Put/vlen=4, Value: val3
Error: org.apache.hadoop.hbase.DoNotRetryIOException:
  org.apache.hadoop.hbase.DoNotRetryIOException:
    Action's getRow must match the passed row
...
```

Using null as the value parameter triggers the *nonexistence* test, that is, the check is successful if the column specified does *not* exist. Since the example code inserts the checked column before the check is performed, the test will initially fail, returning false and aborting the delete operation.

The column is then deleted by hand and the check-and-modify call is run again. This time the check succeeds and the delete is applied, returning true as the overall result.

Just as with the put-related CAS call, you can only perform the check-and-modify on the same row. The example attempts to check on one row key while the supplied instance of Delete points to another. An exception is thrown accordingly, once the check is performed. It is allowed, though, to check across column families—for example, to have one set of columns control how the filtering is done for another set of columns.

This example cannot justify the importance of the check-and-delete operation. In distributed systems, it is inherently difficult to perform such operations reliably, and without incurring performance penalties caused by external locking approaches, that is, where the atomicity is guaranteed by the client taking out exclusive locks on the entire row. When the client goes away during the locked phase the server has to rely on lease recovery mechanisms ensuring that these rows are eventually unlocked again. They also cause additional RPCs to occur, which will be slower than a single, server-side operation.

Batch Operations

You have seen how you can add, retrieve, and remove data from a table using single or list-based operations. In this section, we will look at API calls to batch different operations across multiple rows.

 In fact, a lot of the internal functionality of the list-based calls, such as delete(List<Delete> deletes) or get(List<Get> gets), is based on the batch() call. They are more or less legacy calls and kept for convenience. If you start fresh, it is recommended that you use the batch() calls for all your operations.

The following methods of the client API represent the available batch operations. You may note the introduction of a new class type named Row, which is the ancestor, or parent class, for Put, Get, and Delete.

```
void batch(List<Row> actions, Object[] results)
  throws IOException, InterruptedException
Object[] batch(List<Row> actions)
  throws IOException, InterruptedException
```

Using the same parent class allows for polymorphic list items, representing any of these three operations. It is equally easy to use these calls, just like the list-based methods you saw earlier. Example 3-16 shows how you can mix the operations and then send them off as one server call.

Be aware that you should *not* mix a Delete and Put operation for the same row in one batch call. The operations will be applied in a different order that guarantees the best performance, but also causes unpredictable results. In some cases, you may see fluctuating results due to race conditions.

Example 3-16. Application using batch operations
```
private final static byte[] ROW1 = Bytes.toBytes("row1");
private final static byte[] ROW2 = Bytes.toBytes("row2");
private final static byte[] COLFAM1 = Bytes.toBytes("colfam1"); ❶
private final static byte[] COLFAM2 = Bytes.toBytes("colfam2");
private final static byte[] QUAL1 = Bytes.toBytes("qual1");
private final static byte[] QUAL2 = Bytes.toBytes("qual2");

List<Row> batch = new ArrayList<Row>(); ❷

Put put = new Put(ROW2);
put.add(COLFAM2, QUAL1, Bytes.toBytes("val5")); ❸
batch.add(put);

Get get1 = new Get(ROW1);
get1.addColumn(COLFAM1, QUAL1); ❹
batch.add(get1);

Delete delete = new Delete(ROW1);
delete.deleteColumns(COLFAM1, QUAL2); ❺
batch.add(delete);

Get get2 = new Get(ROW2);
get2.addFamily(Bytes.toBytes("BOGUS")); ❻
batch.add(get2);

Object[] results = new Object[batch.size()]; ❼
try {
  table.batch(batch, results);
} catch (Exception e) {
  System.err.println("Error: " + e); ❽
}

for (int i = 0; i < results.length; i++) {
  System.out.println("Result[" + i + "]: " + results[i]); ❾
}
```

❶ Use constants for easy reuse.

❷ Create a list to hold all values.

❸ Add a `Put` instance.

❹ Add a `Get` instance for a different row.

❺ Add a `Delete` instance.

❻ Add a `Get` instance that will fail.

❼ Create a result array.

❽ Print an error that was caught.

❾ Print all results.

You should see the following output on the console:

```
Before batch call...
KV: row1/colfam1:qual1/1/Put/vlen=4, Value: val1
KV: row1/colfam1:qual2/2/Put/vlen=4, Value: val2
KV: row1/colfam1:qual3/3/Put/vlen=4, Value: val3

Result[0]: keyvalues=NONE
Result[1]: keyvalues={row1/colfam1:qual1/1/Put/vlen=4}
Result[2]: keyvalues=NONE
Result[3]: org.apache.hadoop.hbase.regionserver.NoSuchColumnFamilyException:
  org.apache.hadoop.hbase.regionserver.NoSuchColumnFamilyException:
    Column family BOGUS does not exist in ...

After batch call...
KV: row1/colfam1:qual1/1/Put/vlen=4, Value: val1
KV: row1/colfam1:qual3/3/Put/vlen=4, Value: val3
KV: row2/colfam2:qual1/1308836506340/Put/vlen=4, Value: val5

Error: org.apache.hadoop.hbase.client.RetriesExhaustedWithDetailsException:
  Failed 1 action: NoSuchColumnFamilyException: 1 time,
    servers with issues: 10.0.0.43:60020,
```

As with the previous examples, there is some wiring behind the printed lines of code that inserts a test row before executing the batch calls. The content is printed first, then you will see the output from the example code, and finally the dump of the rows *after* everything else. The deleted column was indeed removed, and the new column was added to the row as expected.

Finding the result of the `Get` operation requires you to investigate the middle part of the output, that is, the lines printed by the example code. The lines starting with `Result[n]`—with n ranging from zero to 3—is where you see the outcome of the corresponding operation in the `actions` parameter. The first operation in the example is a `Put`, and the result is an empty `Result` instance, containing no `KeyValue` instances. This is the general contract of the batch calls; they return a best match result per input action, and the possible types are listed in Table 3-7.

Table 3-7. Possible result values returned by the batch() calls

Result	Description
null	The operation has failed to communicate with the remote server.
Empty Result	Returned for successful Put and Delete operations.
Result	Returned for successful Get operations, but may also be empty when there was no matching row or column.
Throwable	In case the servers return an exception for the operation it is returned to the client as-is. You can use it to check what went wrong and maybe handle the problem automatically in your code.

Looking further through the returned result array in the console output you can see the empty Result instances printing keyvalues=NONE. The Get call succeeded and found a match, returning the KeyValue instances accordingly. Finally, the operation with the BOGUS column family has the exception for your perusal.

 When you use the *batch()* functionality, the included Put instances will not be buffered using the client-side write buffer. The batch() calls are synchronous and send the operations directly to the servers; no delay or other intermediate processing is used. This is obviously different compared to the put() calls, so choose which one you want to use carefully.

There are two different batch calls that look very similar. The difference is that one needs to have the array handed into the call, while the other creates it for you. So why do you need both, and what—if any—semantical differences do they expose? Both throw the RetriesExhaustedWithDetailsException that you saw already, so the crucial difference is that

```
void batch(List<Row> actions, Object[] results)
    throws IOException, InterruptedException
```

gives you access to the partial results, while

```
Object[] batch(List<Row> actions)
    throws IOException, InterruptedException
```

does not! The latter throws the exception and nothing is returned to you since the control flow of the code is interrupted *before* the new result array is returned.

The former function fills your given array and *then* throws the exception. The code in Example 3-16 makes use of that fact and hands in the results array. Summarizing the features, you can say the following about the batch() functions:

Both calls

Supports gets, puts, and deletes. If there is a problem executing any of them, a client-side exception is thrown, reporting the issues. The client-side write buffer is not used.

```
void batch(actions, results)
```
Gives access to the results of all succeeded operations, and the remote exceptions for those that failed.

```
Object[] batch(actions)
```
Only returns the client-side exception; no access to partial results is possible.

 All batch operations are executed before the results are checked: even if you receive an error for one of the actions, all the other ones have been applied. In a worst-case scenario, all actions might return faults, though.

On the other hand, the batch code is aware of transient errors, such as the `NotServingRegionException` (indicating, for instance, that a region has been moved), and is trying to apply the action multiple times. The `hbase.client.retries.number` configuration property (by default set to 10) can be adjusted to increase, or reduce, the number of retries.

Row Locks

Mutating operations—like `put()`, `delete()`, `checkAndPut()`, and so on—are executed exclusively, which means in a serial fashion, for each row, to guarantee row-level atomicity. The region servers provide a *row lock* feature ensuring that only a client holding the matching lock can modify a row. In practice, though, most client applications do *not* provide an explicit lock, but rather rely on the mechanism in place that guards each operation separately.

 You should *avoid* using row locks whenever possible. Just as with RDBMSes, you can end up in a situation where two clients create a deadlock by waiting on a locked row, with the lock held by the other client.

While the locks wait to time out, these two blocked clients are holding on to a handler, which is a scarce resource. If this happens on a heavily used row, many other clients will lock the remaining few handlers and block access to the complete server for all other clients: the server will not be able to serve any row of any region it hosts.

To reiterate: do *not* use row locks if you do not have to. And if you do, use them sparingly!

When you send, for example, a `put()` call to the server with an instance of Put, created with the following constructor:

```
Put(byte[] row)
```

which is *not* providing a `RowLock` instance parameter, the servers will create a lock on your behalf, just for the duration of the call. In fact, from the client API you cannot even retrieve this short-lived, server-side lock instance.

Instead of relying on the implicit, server-side locking to occur, clients can also acquire explicit locks and use them across multiple operations on the same row. This is done using the following calls:

```
RowLock lockRow(byte[] row) throws IOException
void unlockRow(RowLock rl) throws IOException
```

The first call, lockRow(), takes a row key and returns an instance of RowLock, which you can hand in to the constructors of Put or Delete subsequently. Once you no longer require the lock, you *must* release it with the accompanying unlockRow() call.

Each unique lock, provided by the server for you, or handed in by you through the client API, guards the row it pertains to against any other lock that attempts to access the same row. In other words, locks *must* be taken out against an entire row, specifying its row key, and—once it has been acquired—will protect it against any other concurrent modification.

While a lock on a row is held by someone—whether by the server briefly or a client explicitly—all other clients trying to acquire another lock on that very same row will *stall*, until either the current lock has been released, or the lease on the lock has expired. The latter case is a safeguard against faulty processes holding a lock for too long—or possibly indefinitely.

> The default timeout on locks is one minute, but can be configured system-wide by adding the following property key to the *hbase-site.xml* file and setting the value to a different, millisecond-based timeout:
>
> ```
> <property>
>   <name>hbase.regionserver.lease.period</name>
>   <value>120000</value>
> </property>
> ```
>
> Adding the preceding code would double the timeout to 120 seconds, or two minutes, instead. Be careful not to set this value too high, since every client trying to acquire an already locked row will have to block for up to that timeout for the lock in limbo to be recovered.

Example 3-17 shows how a user-generated lock on a row will block all concurrent readers.

Example 3-17. Using row locks explicitly

```
static class UnlockedPut implements Runnable { ❶
  @Override
  public void run() {
    try {
      HTable table = new HTable(conf, "testtable");
      Put put = new Put(ROW1);
      put.add(COLFAM1, QUAL1, VAL3);
      long time = System.currentTimeMillis();
```

```
        System.out.println("Thread trying to put same row now...");
        table.put(put); ❷
        System.out.println("Wait time: " +
          (System.currentTimeMillis() - time) + "ms");
      } catch (IOException e) {
        System.err.println("Thread error: " + e);
      }
    }
  }
}

System.out.println("Taking out lock...");
RowLock lock = table.lockRow(ROW1); ❸
System.out.println("Lock ID: " + lock.getLockId());

Thread thread = new Thread(new UnlockedPut()); ❹
thread.start();

try {
  System.out.println("Sleeping 5secs in main()..."); ❺
  Thread.sleep(5000);
} catch (InterruptedException e) {
  // ignore
}

try {
  Put put1 = new Put(ROW1, lock); ❻
  put1.add(COLFAM1, QUAL1, VAL1);
  table.put(put1);

  Put put2 = new Put(ROW1, lock); ❼
  put2.add(COLFAM1, QUAL1, VAL2);
  table.put(put2);
} catch (Exception e) {
  System.err.println("Error: " + e);
} finally {
  System.out.println("Releasing lock..."); ❽
  table.unlockRow(lock);
}
```

❶ Use an asynchronous thread to update the same row, but without a lock.

❷ The put() call will block until the lock is released.

❸ Lock the entire row.

❹ Start the asynchronous thread, which will block.

❺ Sleep for some time to block other writers.

❻ Create a Put using its own lock.

❼ Create another Put using its own lock.

❽ Release the lock, which will make the thread continue.

When you run the example code, you should see the following output on the console:

```
Taking out lock...
Lock ID: 4751274798057238718
Sleeping 5secs in main()...
Thread trying to put same row now...
Releasing lock...
Wait time: 5007ms
After thread ended...
KV: row1/colfam1:qual1/1300775520118/Put/vlen=4, Value: val2
KV: row1/colfam1:qual1/1300775520113/Put/vlen=4, Value: val1
KV: row1/colfam1:qual1/1300775515116/Put/vlen=4, Value: val3
```

You can see how the explicit lock blocks the thread using a different, implicit lock. The main thread sleeps for five seconds, and once it wakes up, it calls put() twice, setting the same column to two different values, respectively.

Once the main thread releases the lock, the thread's run() method continues to execute and applies the third put call. An interesting observation is how the puts are applied on the server side. Notice that the timestamps of the KeyValue instances show the third put having the lowest timestamp, even though the put was seemingly applied last. This is caused by the fact that the put() call in the thread was executed *before* the two puts in the main thread, after it had slept for five seconds. Once a put is sent to the servers, it is assigned a timestamp—assuming you have not provided your own—and then tries to acquire the implicit lock. But the example code has already taken out the lock on that row, and therefore the server-side processing stalls until the lock is released, five seconds and a tad more later. In the preceding output, you can also see that it took seven milliseconds to execute the two put calls in the main thread and to unlock the row.

Do Gets Require a Lock?

It makes sense to lock rows for any row mutation, but what about retrieving data? The Get class has a constructor that lets you specify an explicit lock:

```
Get(byte[] row, RowLock rowLock)
```

This is actually legacy and *not* used at all on the server side. In fact, the servers do *not* take out any locks during the get operation. They instead apply a *multiversion concurrency control-style*[*] mechanism ensuring that row-level read operations, such as get() calls, never return half-written data—for example, what is written by another thread or client.

Think of this like a small-scale transactional system: only after a mutation has been applied to the entire row can clients read the changes. While a mutation is in progress, all reading clients will be seeing the previous state of all columns.

When you try to use an explicit row lock that you have acquired earlier but failed to use within the lease recovery time range, you will receive an error from the servers, in the form of an UnknownRowLockException. It tells you that the server has already

[*] See "MVCC" (*http://en.wikipedia.org/wiki/Multiversion_concurrency_control*) on Wikipedia.

discarded the lock you are trying to use. Drop it in your code and acquire a new one to recover from this state.

Scans

Now that we have discussed the basic CRUD-type operations, it is time to take a look at *scans*, a technique akin to *cursors*† in database systems, which make use of the underlying sequential, sorted storage layout HBase is providing.

Introduction

Use of the scan operations is very similar to the `get()` methods. And again, similar to all the other functions, there is also a supporting class, named Scan. But since scans are similar to iterators, you do not have a `scan()` call, but rather a `getScanner()`, which returns the actual scanner instance you need to iterate over. The available methods are:

```
ResultScanner getScanner(Scan scan) throws IOException
ResultScanner getScanner(byte[] family) throws IOException
ResultScanner getScanner(byte[] family, byte[] qualifier)
  throws IOException
```

The latter two are for your convenience, implicitly creating an instance of Scan on your behalf, and subsequently calling the getScanner(Scan scan) method.

The Scan class has the following constructors:

```
Scan()
Scan(byte[] startRow, Filter filter)
Scan(byte[] startRow)
Scan(byte[] startRow, byte[] stopRow)
```

The difference between this and the Get class is immediately obvious: instead of specifying a single row key, you now can optionally provide a startRow parameter—defining the row key where the scan begins to read from the HBase table. The optional stopRow parameter can be used to limit the scan to a specific row key where it should conclude the reading.

 The start row is always inclusive, while the end row is exclusive. This is often expressed as [startRow, stopRow) in the interval notation.

A special feature that scans offer is that you do *not* need to have an exact match for either of these rows. Instead, the scan will match the first row key that is *equal to or*

---

† Scans are similar to *nonscrollable* cursors. You need to *declare*, *open*, *fetch*, and eventually *close* a database cursor. While scans do not need the declaration step, they are otherwise used in the same way. See "Cursors" (*http://en.wikipedia.org/wiki/Database_cursor*) on Wikipedia.

larger than the given start row. If no start row was specified, it will start at the beginning of the table.

It will also end its work when the current row key is *equal to or greater* than the optional stop row. If no stop row was specified, the scan will run to the end of the table.

There is another optional parameter, named `filter`, referring to a `Filter` instance. Often, though, the `Scan` instance is simply created using the empty constructor, as all of the optional parameters also have matching getter and setter methods that can be used instead.

Once you have created the `Scan` instance, you may want to add more limiting details to it—but you are also allowed to use the empty scan, which would read the entire table, including all column families and their columns. You can narrow down the read data using various methods:

```
Scan addFamily(byte [] family)
Scan addColumn(byte[] family, byte[] qualifier)
```

There is a lot of similar functionality compared to the `Get` class: you may limit the data returned by the scan in setting the column families to specific ones using `addFamily()`, or, even more constraining, to only include certain columns with the `addColumn()` call.

 If you only need subsets of the data, narrowing the scan's scope is playing into the strengths of HBase, since data is stored in column families and omitting entire families from the scan results in those storage files not being read at all. This is the power of column-oriented architecture at its best.

```
Scan setTimeRange(long minStamp, long maxStamp) throws IOException
Scan setTimeStamp(long timestamp)
Scan setMaxVersions()
Scan setMaxVersions(int maxVersions)
```

A further limiting detail you can add is to set the specific timestamp you want, using `setTimestamp()`, or a wider time range with `setTimeRange()`. The same applies to `set MaxVersions()`, allowing you to have the scan only return a specific number of versions per column, or return them all.

```
Scan setStartRow(byte[] startRow)
Scan setStopRow(byte[] stopRow)
Scan setFilter(Filter filter)
boolean hasFilter()
```

Using `setStartRow()`, `setStopRow()`, and `setFilter()`, you can define the same parameters the constructors exposed, all of them limiting the returned data even further, as explained earlier. The additional `hasFilter()` can be used to check that a filter has been assigned.

There are a few more related methods, listed in Table 3-8.

Table 3-8. *Quick overview of additional methods provided by the Scan class*

Method	Description
getStartRow()/getStopRow()	Can be used to retrieve the currently assigned values.
getTimeRange()	Retrieves the associated timestamp or time range of the Get instance. Note that there is no getTimeStamp() since the API converts a value assigned with setTimeStamp() into a TimeRange instance internally, setting the minimum and maximum values to the given timestamp.
getMaxVersions()	Returns the currently configured number of versions that should be retrieved from the table for every column.
getFilter()	Special filter instances can be used to select certain columns or cells, based on a wide variety of conditions. You can get the currently assigned filter using this method. It may return null if none was previously set. See "Filters" on page 137 for details.
setCacheBlocks()/getCache Blocks()	Each HBase region server has a block cache that efficiently retains recently accessed data for subsequent reads of contiguous information. In some events it is better to not engage the cache to avoid too much churn when doing full table scans. These methods give you control over this feature.
numFamilies()	Convenience method to retrieve the size of the family map, containing the families added using the addFamily() or addColumn() calls.
hasFamilies()	Another helper to check if a family—or column—has been added to the current instance of the Scan class.
getFamilies()/setFamilyMap()/ getFamilyMap()	These methods give you access to the column families and specific columns, as added by the addFamily() and/or addColumn() calls. The family map is a map where the key is the family name and the value is a list of added column qualifiers for this particular family. The getFamilies() returns an array of all stored families, i.e., containing only the family names (as byte[] arrays).

Once you have configured the Scan instance, you can call the HTable method, named getScanner(), to retrieve the ResultScanner instance. We will discuss this class in more detail in the next section.

The ResultScanner Class

Scans do not ship all the matching rows in one RPC to the client, but instead do this on a row basis. This obviously makes sense as rows could be very large and sending thousands, and most likely more, of them in one call would use up too many resources, and take a long time.

The ResultScanner converts the scan into a get-like operation, wrapping the Result instance for each row into an iterator functionality. It has a few methods of its own:

```
Result next() throws IOException
Result[] next(int nbRows) throws IOException
void close()
```

You have two types of next() calls at your disposal. The close() call is required to release all the resources a scan may hold explicitly.

Scanner Leases

Make sure you release a scanner instance as quickly as possible. An open scanner holds quite a few resources on the server side, which could accumulate to a large amount of heap space being occupied. When you are done with the current scan call close(), and consider adding this into a try/finally construct to ensure it is called, even if there are exceptions or errors during the iterations.

The example code does not follow this advice for the sake of brevity only.

Like row locks, scanners are protected against stray clients blocking resources for too long, using the same lease-based mechanisms. You need to set the same configuration property to modify the timeout threshold (in milliseconds):

```
<property>
  <name>hbase.regionserver.lease.period</name>
  <value>120000</value>
</property>
```

You need to make sure that the property is set to an appropriate value that makes sense for locks and the scanner leases.

The next() calls return a single instance of Result representing the next available row. Alternatively, you can fetch a larger number of rows using the next(int nbRows) call, which returns an array of up to nbRows items, each an instance of Result, representing a unique row. The resultant array may be shorter if there were not enough rows left. This obviously can happen just before you reach the end of the table, or the stop row. Otherwise, refer to "The Result class" on page 98 for details on how to make use of the Result instances. This works exactly like you saw in "Get Method" on page 95.

Example 3-18 brings together the explained functionality to scan a table, while accessing the column data stored in a row.

Example 3-18. Using a scanner to access data in a table

```
Scan scan1 = new Scan(); ❶
ResultScanner scanner1 = table.getScanner(scan1); ❷
for (Result res : scanner1) {
  System.out.println(res); ❸
}
scanner1.close(); ❹

Scan scan2 = new Scan();
scan2.addFamily(Bytes.toBytes("colfam1")); ❺
ResultScanner scanner2 = table.getScanner(scan2);
```

```
for (Result res : scanner2) {
  System.out.println(res);
}
scanner2.close();

Scan scan3 = new Scan();
scan3.addColumn(Bytes.toBytes("colfam1"), Bytes.toBytes("col-5")).
  addColumn(Bytes.toBytes("colfam2"), Bytes.toBytes("col-33")). ❻
  setStartRow(Bytes.toBytes("row-10")).
  setStopRow(Bytes.toBytes("row-20"));
ResultScanner scanner3 = table.getScanner(scan3);
for (Result res : scanner3) {
  System.out.println(res);
}
scanner3.close();
```

❶ Create an empty Scan instance.

❷ Get a scanner to iterate over the rows.

❸ Print the row's content.

❹ Close the scanner to free remote resources.

❺ Add one column family only; this will suppress the retrieval of "colfam2".

❻ Use a builder pattern to add very specific details to the Scan.

The code inserts 100 rows with two column families, each containing 100 columns. The scans performed vary from the full table scan, to one that only scans one column family, and finally to a very restrictive scan, limiting the row range, and only asking for two very specific columns. The output should look like this:

```
Scanning table #3...
keyvalues={row-10/colfam1:col-5/1300803775078/Put/vlen=8,
           row-10/colfam2:col-33/1300803775099/Put/vlen=9}
keyvalues={row-100/colfam1:col-5/1300803780079/Put/vlen=9,
           row-100/colfam2:col-33/1300803780095/Put/vlen=10}
keyvalues={row-11/colfam1:col-5/1300803775152/Put/vlen=8,
           row-11/colfam2:col-33/1300803775170/Put/vlen=9}
keyvalues={row-12/colfam1:col-5/1300803775212/Put/vlen=8,
           row-12/colfam2:col-33/1300803775246/Put/vlen=9}
keyvalues={row-13/colfam1:col-5/1300803775345/Put/vlen=8,
           row-13/colfam2:col-33/1300803775376/Put/vlen=9}
keyvalues={row-14/colfam1:col-5/1300803775479/Put/vlen=8,
           row-14/colfam2:col-33/1300803775498/Put/vlen=9}
keyvalues={row-15/colfam1:col-5/1300803775554/Put/vlen=8,
           row-15/colfam2:col-33/1300803775582/Put/vlen=9}
keyvalues={row-16/colfam1:col-5/1300803775665/Put/vlen=8,
           row-16/colfam2:col-33/1300803775687/Put/vlen=9}
keyvalues={row-17/colfam1:col-5/1300803775734/Put/vlen=8,
           row-17/colfam2:col-33/1300803775748/Put/vlen=9}
keyvalues={row-18/colfam1:col-5/1300803775791/Put/vlen=8,
           row-18/colfam2:col-33/1300803775805/Put/vlen=9}
keyvalues={row-19/colfam1:col-5/1300803775843/Put/vlen=8,
           row-19/colfam2:col-33/1300803775859/Put/vlen=9}
```

```
keyvalues={row-2/colfam1:col-5/1300803774463/Put/vlen=7,
            row-2/colfam2:col-33/1300803774485/Put/vlen=8}
```

Once again, note the actual rows that have been matched. The lexicographical sorting of the keys makes for interesting results. You could simply pad the numbers with zeros, which would result in a more human-readable sort order. This is completely under your control, so choose carefully what you need.

Caching Versus Batching

So far, each call to next() will be a separate RPC for each row—even when you use the next(int nbRows) method, because it is nothing else but a client-side loop over next() calls. Obviously, this is not very good for performance when dealing with small cells (see "Client-side write buffer" on page 86 for a discussion). Thus it would make sense to fetch more than one row per RPC if possible. This is called *scanner caching* and is disabled by default.

You can enable it at two different levels: on the table level, to be effective for all scan instances, or at the scan level, only affecting the current scan. You can set the table-wide scanner caching using these HTable calls:

```
void setScannerCaching(int scannerCaching)
int getScannerCaching()
```

> You can also change the default value of 1 for the entire HBase setup. You do this by adding the following configuration key to the *hbase-site.xml* configuration file:
>
> ```
> <property>
>   <name>hbase.client.scanner.caching</name>
>   <value>10</value>
> </property>
> ```
>
> This would set the scanner caching to 10 for all instances of Scan. You can still override the value at the table and scan levels, but you would need to do so explicitly.

The setScannerCaching() call sets the value, while getScannerCaching() retrieves the current value. Every time you call getScanner(scan) thereafter, the API will assign the set value to the scan instance—unless you use the scan-level settings, which take highest precedence. This is done with the following methods of the Scan class:

```
void setCaching(int caching)
int getCaching()
```

They work the same way as the table-wide settings, giving you control over how many rows are retrieved with every RPC. Both types of next() calls take these settings into account.

You may need to find a sweet spot between a low number of RPCs and the memory used on the client and server. Setting the scanner caching higher will improve scanning performance most of the time, but setting it too high can have adverse effects as well: each call to next() will take longer as more data is fetched and needs to be transported to the client, and once you exceed the maximum heap the client process has available it may terminate with an OutOfMemoryException.

 When the time taken to transfer the rows to the client, or to process the data on the client, exceeds the configured scanner lease threshold, you will end up receiving a *lease expired* error, in the form of a Scan nerTimeoutException being thrown.

Example 3-19 showcases the issue with the scanner leases.

Example 3-19. Timeout while using a scanner

```
Scan scan = new Scan();
ResultScanner scanner = table.getScanner(scan);

int scannerTimeout = (int) conf.getLong(
  HConstants.HBASE_REGIONSERVER_LEASE_PERIOD_KEY, -1); ❶
try {
  Thread.sleep(scannerTimeout + 5000); ❷
} catch (InterruptedException e) {
  // ignore
}
while (true){
  try {
    Result result = scanner.next();
    if (result == null) break;
    System.out.println(result); ❸
  } catch (Exception e) {
    e.printStackTrace();
    break;
  }
}
scanner.close();
```

❶ Get the currently configured lease timeout.

❷ Sleep a little longer than the lease allows.

❸ Print the row's content.

The code gets the currently configured lease period value and sleeps a little longer to trigger the lease recovery on the server side. The console output (abbreviated for the sake of readability) should look similar to this:

```
Adding rows to table...
Current (local) lease period: 60000
Sleeping now for 65000ms...
Attempting to iterate over scanner...
Exception in thread "main" java.lang.RuntimeException:
```

```
    org.apache.hadoop.hbase.client.ScannerTimeoutException: 65094ms passed
        since the last invocation, timeout is currently set to 60000
        at org.apache.hadoop.hbase.client.HTable$ClientScanner$1.hasNext
        at ScanTimeoutExample.main
    Caused by: org.apache.hadoop.hbase.client.ScannerTimeoutException: 65094ms
        passed since the last invocation, timeout is currently set to 60000
        at org.apache.hadoop.hbase.client.HTable$ClientScanner.next
        at org.apache.hadoop.hbase.client.HTable$ClientScanner$1.hasNext
        ... 1 more
    Caused by: org.apache.hadoop.hbase.UnknownScannerException:
        org.apache.hadoop.hbase.UnknownScannerException: Name: -315058406354472427
        at org.apache.hadoop.hbase.regionserver.HRegionServer.next
    ...
```

The example code prints its progress and, after sleeping for the specified time, attempts to iterate over the rows the scanner should provide. This triggers the said timeout exception, while reporting the configured values.

 You might be tempted to add the following into your code:

```
Configuration conf = HBaseConfiguration.create()
conf.setLong(HConstants.HBASE_REGIONSERVER_LEASE_PERIOD_KEY, 120000)
```

assuming this increases the lease threshold (in this example, to two minutes). But that is not going to work as the value is configured on the remote region servers, not your client application. Your value is not being sent to the servers, and therefore will have no effect.

If you want to change the lease period setting you need to add the appropriate configuration key to the *hbase-site.xml* file on the region servers—while not forgetting to restart them for the changes to take effect!

The stack trace in the console output also shows how the ScannerTimeoutException is a wrapper around an UnknownScannerException. It means that the next() call is using a scanner ID that has since expired and been removed in due course. In other words, the ID your client has memorized is now *unknown* to the region servers—which is the name of the exception.

So far you have learned to use client-side scanner caching to make better use of bulk transfers between your client application and the remote region's servers. There is an issue, though, that was mentioned in passing earlier: very *large rows*. Those—potentially—do not fit into the memory of the client process. HBase and its client API have an answer for that: *batching*. You can control batching using these calls:

```
void setBatch(int batch)
int getBatch()
```

As opposed to caching, which operates on a row level, batching works on the column level instead. It controls how many columns are retrieved for every call to any of the next() functions provided by the ResultScanner instance. For example, setting the scan to use setBatch(5) would return five columns per Result instance.

When a row contains more columns than the value you used for the batch, you will get the entire row piece by piece, with each next Result returned by the scanner.

The last Result may include fewer columns, when the total number of columns in that row is not divisible by whatever batch it is set to. For example, if your row has 17 columns and you set the batch to 5, you get four Result instances, with 5, 5, 5, and the remaining two columns within.

The combination of scanner caching and batch size can be used to control the number of RPCs required to scan the row key range selected. Example 3-20 uses the two parameters to fine-tune the size of each Result instance in relation to the number of requests needed.

Example 3-20. Using caching and batch parameters for scans

```java
private static void scan(int caching, int batch) throws IOException {
  Logger log = Logger.getLogger("org.apache.hadoop");
  final int[] counters = {0, 0};
  Appender appender = new AppenderSkeleton() {
    @Override
    protected void append(LoggingEvent event) {
      String msg = event.getMessage().toString();
      if (msg != null && msg.contains("Call: next")) {
        counters[0]++;
      }
    }
    @Override
    public void close() {}
    @Override
    public boolean requiresLayout() {
      return false;
    }
  };
  log.removeAllAppenders();
  log.setAdditivity(false);
  log.addAppender(appender);
  log.setLevel(Level.DEBUG);


  Scan scan = new Scan();
  scan.setCaching(caching);   ❶
  scan.setBatch(batch);
  ResultScanner scanner = table.getScanner(scan);
  for (Result result : scanner) {
    counters[1]++; ❷
  }
  scanner.close();
  System.out.println("Caching: " + caching + ", Batch: " + batch +
    ", Results: " + counters[1] + ", RPCs: " + counters[0]);
}
```

```
public static void main(String[] args) throws IOException {
    scan(1, 1);
    scan(200, 1);
    scan(2000, 100);  ❸
    scan(2, 100);
    scan(2, 10);
    scan(5, 100);
    scan(5, 20);
    scan(10, 10);
}
```

❶ Set caching and batch parameters.

❷ Count the number of Results available.

❸ Test various combinations.

The code prints out the values used for caching and batching, the number of results returned by the servers, and how many RPCs were needed to get them. For example:

```
Caching: 1, Batch: 1, Results: 200, RPCs: 201
Caching: 200, Batch: 1, Results: 200, RPCs: 2
Caching: 2000, Batch: 100, Results: 10, RPCs: 1
Caching: 2, Batch: 100, Results: 10, RPCs: 6
Caching: 2, Batch: 10, Results: 20, RPCs: 11
Caching: 5, Batch: 100, Results: 10, RPCs: 3
Caching: 5, Batch: 20, Results: 10, RPCs: 3
Caching: 10, Batch: 10, Results: 20, RPCs: 3
```

You can tweak the two numbers to see how they affect the outcome. Table 3-9 lists a few selected combinations. The numbers relate to Example 3-20, which creates a table with two column families, adds 10 rows, with 10 columns per family in each row. This means there are a total of 200 columns—or cells, as there is only one version for each column—with 20 columns per row.

Table 3-9. Example settings and their effects

Caching	Batch	Results	RPCs	Notes
1	1	200	201	Each column is returned as a separate Result instance. One more RPC is needed to realize the scan is complete.
200	1	200	2	Each column is a separate Result, but they are all transferred in one RPC (plus the extra check).
2	10	20	11	The batch is half the row width, so 200 divided by 10 is 20 Results needed. 10 RPCs (plus the check) to transfer them.
5	100	10	3	The batch is too large for each row, so all 20 columns are batched. This requires 10 Result instances. Caching brings the number of RPCs down to two (plus the check).
5	20	10	3	This is the same as above, but this time the batch matches the columns available. The outcome is the same.
10	10	20	3	This divides the table into smaller Result instances, but larger caching also means only two RPCs are needed.

To compute the number of RPCs required for a scan, you need to first multiply the number of rows with the number of columns per row (at least some approximation). Then you divide that number by the smaller value of either the batch size or the columns per row. Finally, divide that number by the scanner caching value. In mathematical terms this could be expressed like so:

```
RPCs = (Rows * Cols per Row) / Min(Cols per Row, Batch Size) /
Scanner Caching
```

In addition, RPCs are also required to open and close the scanner. You would need to add these two calls to get the overall total of remote calls when dealing with scanners.

Figure 3-2 shows how the caching and batching works in tandem. It has a table with nine rows, each containing a number of columns. Using a scanner caching of six, and a batch set to three, you can see that three RPCs are necessary to ship the data across the network (the dashed, rounded-corner boxes).

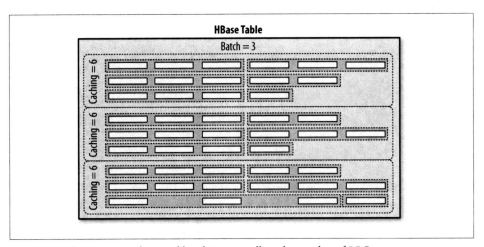

Figure 3-2. The scanner caching and batching controlling the number of RPCs

The small batch value causes the servers to group three columns into one Result, while the scanner caching of six causes one RPC to transfer six rows—or, more precisely, *results*—sent in the batch. When the batch size is not specified but scanner caching is specified, the result of the call will contain complete rows, because each row will be contained in one Result instance. Only when you start to use the batch mode are you getting access to the *intra-row* scanning functionality.

You may not have to worry about the consequences of using scanner caching and batch mode initially, but once you try to squeeze the optimal performance out of your setup, you should keep all of this in mind and find the sweet spot for both values.

Miscellaneous Features

Before looking into more involved features that clients can use, let us first wrap up a handful of miscellaneous features and functionality provided by HBase and its client API.

The HTable Utility Methods

The client API is represented by an instance of the `HTable` class and gives you access to an existing HBase table. Apart from the major features we already discussed, there are a few more notable methods of this class that you should be aware of:

`void close()`
> This method was mentioned before, but for the sake of completeness, and its importance, it warrants repeating. Call `close()` once you have completed your work with a table. It will flush any buffered write operations: the `close()` call implicitly invokes the `flushCache()` method.

`byte[] getTableName()`
> This is a convenience method to retrieve the table name.

`Configuration getConfiguration()`
> This allows you to access the configuration in use by the `HTable` instance. Since this is handed out *by reference*, you can make changes that are effective immediately.

`HTableDescriptor getTableDescriptor()`
> As explained in "Tables" on page 207, each table is defined using an instance of the `HTableDescriptor` class. You gain access to the underlying definition using `getTableDescriptor()`.

`static boolean isTableEnabled(table)`
> There are four variants of this static helper method. They all need either an explicit configuration—if one is not provided, it will create one implicitly using the default values, and the configuration found on your application's classpath—and a table name. It checks if the table in question is marked as enabled in ZooKeeper.

`byte[][] getStartKeys()`
`byte[][] getEndKeys()`
`Pair<byte[][],byte[][]> getStartEndKeys()`
> These calls give you access to the current physical layout of the table—this is likely to change when you are adding more data to it. The calls give you the start and/or end keys of all the regions of the table. They are returned as arrays of byte arrays. You can use `Bytes.toStringBinary()`, for example, to print out the keys.

```
void clearRegionCache()
HRegionLocation getRegionLocation(row)
Map<HRegionInfo, HServerAddress> getRegionsInfo()
```
> This set of methods lets you retrieve more details regarding where a row lives, that is, in what region, and the entire map of the region information. You can also clear out the cache if you wish to do so. These calls are only for advanced users that wish to make use of this information to, for example, route traffic or perform work close to where the data resides.

```
void prewarmRegionCache(Map<HRegionInfo, HServerAddress> regionMap)
static void setRegionCachePrefetch(table, enable)
static boolean getRegionCachePrefetch(table)
```
> Again, this is a group of methods for advanced usage. In "Implementation" on page 24 it was mentioned that it would make sense to prefetch region information on the client to avoid more costly lookups for every row—until the local cache is stable. Using these calls, you can either warm up the region cache while providing a list of regions—you could, for example, use getRegionsInfo() to gain access to the list, and then process it—or switch on region prefetching for the entire table.

The Bytes Class

You saw how this class was used to convert native Java types, such as String, or long, into the raw, byte array format HBase supports natively. There are a few more notes that are worth mentioning about the class and its functionality.

Most methods come in three variations, for example:

```
static long toLong(byte[] bytes)
static long toLong(byte[] bytes, int offset)
static long toLong(byte[] bytes, int offset, int length)
```

You hand in just a byte array, or an array and an offset, or an array, an offset, and a length value. The usage depends on the originating byte array you have. If it was created by toBytes() beforehand, you can safely use the first variant, and simply hand in the array and nothing else. All the array contains is the converted value.

The API, and HBase internally, store data in larger arrays, though, using, for example, the following call:

```
static int putLong(byte[] bytes, int offset, long val)
```

This call allows you to write the long value into a given byte array, at a specific offset. If you want to access the data in that larger byte array you can make use of the latter two toLong() calls instead.

The Bytes class has support to convert from and to the following native Java types: String, boolean, short, int, long, double, and float. Apart from that, there are some noteworthy methods, which are listed in Table 3-10.

Table 3-10. Overview of additional methods provided by the Bytes class

Method	Description
toStringBinary()	While working very similar to toString(), this variant has an extra safeguard to convert nonprintable data into their human-readable hexadecimal numbers. Whenever you are not sure what a byte array contains you should use this method to print its content, for example, to the console, or into a logfile.
compareTo()/equals()	These methods allow you to compare two byte[], that is, byte arrays. The former gives you a comparison result and the latter a boolean value, indicating whether the given arrays are equal to each other.
add()/head()/tail()	You can use these to add two byte arrays to each other, resulting in a new, concatenated array, or to get the first, or last, few bytes of the given byte array.
binarySearch()	This performs a binary search in the given array of values. It operates on byte arrays for the values and the key you are searching for.
incrementBytes()	This increments a long value in its byte array representation, as if you had used toBytes(long) to create it. You can decrement using a negative amount parameter.

There is some overlap of the Bytes class to the Java-provided ByteBuffer. The difference is that the former does all operations without creating new class instances. In a way it is an optimization, because the provided methods are called many times within HBase, while avoiding possibly costly garbage collection issues.

For the full documentation, please consult the JavaDoc-based API documentation.[‡]

[‡] See the Bytes documentation online (*http://hbase.apache.org/apidocs/org/apache/hadoop/hbase/util/Bytes .html*).

## CHAPTER 4

Client API: Advanced Features

Now that you understand the basic client API, we will discuss the advanced features that HBase offers to clients.

Filters

HBase filters are a powerful feature that can greatly enhance your effectiveness when working with data stored in tables. You will find predefined filters, already provided by HBase for your use, as well as a framework you can use to implement your own. You will now be introduced to both.

Introduction to Filters

The two prominent read functions for HBase are get() and scan(), both supporting either direct access to data or the use of a start and end key, respectively. You can limit the data retrieved by progressively adding more limiting selectors to the query. These include column families, column qualifiers, timestamps or ranges, as well as version number.

While this gives you control over what is included, it is missing more fine-grained features, such as selection of keys, or values, based on regular expressions. Both classes support *filters* for exactly these reasons: what cannot be solved with the provided API functionality to filter row or column keys, or values, can be achieved with filters. The base interface is aptly named Filter, and there is a list of concrete classes supplied by HBase that you can use without doing any programming.

You can, on the other hand, extend the Filter classes to implement your own requirements. All the filters are actually applied on the server side, also called *predicate pushdown*. This ensures the most efficient selection of the data that needs to be transported back to the client. You could implement most of the filter functionality in your client code as well, but you would have to transfer much more data—something you need to avoid at scale.

Figure 4-1 shows how the filters are configured on the client, then serialized over the network, and then applied on the server.

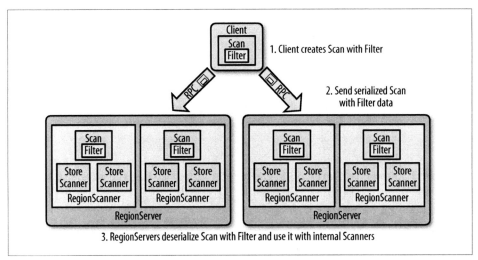

Figure 4-1. The filters created on the client side, sent through the RPC, and executed on the server side

The filter hierarchy

The lowest level in the filter hierarchy is the `Filter` interface, and the abstract `Filter Base` class that implements an empty shell, or skeleton, that is used by the actual filter classes to avoid having the same boilerplate code in each of them.

Most concrete filter classes are direct descendants of `FilterBase`, but a few use another, intermediate ancestor class. They all work the same way: you define a new instance of the filter you want to apply and hand it to the `Get` or `Scan` instances, using:

```
setFilter(filter)
```

While you initialize the filter instance itself, you often have to supply parameters for whatever the filter is designed for. There is a special subset of filters, based on `CompareFilter`, that ask you for at least two specific parameters, since they are used by the base class to perform its task. You will learn about the two parameter types next so that you can use them in context.

 Filters have access to the entire row they are applied to. This means that they can decide the fate of a row based on any available information. This includes the row key, column qualifiers, actual value of a column, timestamps, and so on.

When referring to *values*, or *comparisons*, as we will discuss shortly, this can be applied to any of these details. Specific filter implementations are available that consider only one of those criteria each.

Comparison operators

As `CompareFilter`-based filters add one more feature to the base `FilterBase` class, namely the `compare()` operation, it has to have a user-supplied operator type that defines how the result of the comparison is interpreted. The values are listed in Table 4-1.

Table 4-1. The possible comparison operators for CompareFilter-based filters

Operator	Description
LESS	Match values less than the provided one.
LESS_OR_EQUAL	Match values less than or equal to the provided one.
EQUAL	Do an exact match on the value and the provided one.
NOT_EQUAL	Include everything that does not match the provided value.
GREATER_OR_EQUAL	Match values that are equal to or greater than the provided one.
GREATER	Only include values greater than the provided one.
NO_OP	Exclude everything.

The comparison operators define what is included, or excluded, when the filter is applied. This allows you to select the data that you want as either a range, subset, or exact and single match.

Comparators

The second type that you need to provide to `CompareFilter`-related classes is a *comparator*, which is needed to compare various values and keys in different ways. They are derived from `WritableByteArrayComparable`, which implements `Writable`, and `Comparable`. You do not have to go into the details if you just want to use an implementation provided by HBase and listed in Table 4-2. The constructors usually take the control value, that is, the one to compare each table value against.

Table 4-2. The HBase-supplied comparators, used with CompareFilter-based filters

Comparator	Description
BinaryComparator	Uses `Bytes.compareTo()` to compare the current with the provided value.
BinaryPrefixComparator	Similar to the above, but does a lefthand, prefix-based match using `Bytes.compareTo()`.
NullComparator	Does not compare against an actual value but whether a given one is `null`, or not `null`.
BitComparator	Performs a bitwise comparison, providing a `BitwiseOp` class with AND, OR, and XOR operators.
RegexStringComparator	Given a regular expression at instantiation this comparator does a pattern match on the table data.
SubstringComparator	Treats the value and table data as `String` instances and performs a `contains()` check.

The last three comparators listed in Table 4-2—the BitComparator, RegexStringComparator, and SubstringComparator—*only* work with the EQUAL and NOT_EQUAL operators, as the compareTo() of these comparators returns 0 for a match or 1 when there is no match. Using them in a LESS or GREATER comparison will yield erroneous results.

Each of the comparators usually has a constructor that takes the comparison value. In other words, you need to define a value you compare each cell against. Some of these constructors take a byte[], a byte array, to do the binary comparison, for example, while others take a String parameter—since the data point compared against is assumed to be some sort of readable text. Example 4-1 shows some of these in action.

 The string-based comparators, RegexStringComparator and Substring Comparator, are more expensive in comparison to the purely byte-based version, as they need to convert a given value into a String first. The subsequent string or regular expression operation also adds to the overall cost.

Comparison Filters

The first type of supplied filter implementations are the comparison filters. They take the comparison operator and comparator instance as described earlier. The constructor of each of them has the same signature, inherited from CompareFilter:

```
CompareFilter(CompareOp valueCompareOp,
  WritableByteArrayComparable valueComparator)
```

You need to supply this comparison operator and comparison class for the filters to do their work. Next you will see the actual filters implementing a specific comparison.

 Please keep in mind that the general contract of the HBase filter API means you are filtering *out* information—filtered data is *omitted* from the results returned to the client. The filter is not specifying what you want to have, but rather what you do *not* want to have returned when reading data.

In contrast, all filters based on CompareFilter are doing the *opposite*, in that they include the matching values. In other words, be careful when choosing the comparison operator, as it makes the difference in regard to what the server returns. For example, instead of using LESS to skip some information, you may need to use GREATER_OR_EQUAL to include the desired data points.

RowFilter

This filter gives you the ability to filter data based on row keys.

Example 4-1 shows how the filter can use different comparator instances to get the desired results. It also uses various operators to include the row keys, while omitting others. Feel free to modify the code, changing the operators to see the possible results.

Example 4-1. Using a filter to select specific rows

```
Scan scan = new Scan();
scan.addColumn(Bytes.toBytes("colfam1"), Bytes.toBytes("col-0"));

Filter filter1 = new RowFilter(CompareFilter.CompareOp.LESS_OR_EQUAL, ❶
  new BinaryComparator(Bytes.toBytes("row-22")));
scan.setFilter(filter1);
ResultScanner scanner1 = table.getScanner(scan);
for (Result res : scanner1) {
  System.out.println(res);
}
scanner1.close();

Filter filter2 = new RowFilter(CompareFilter.CompareOp.EQUAL, ❷
  new RegexStringComparator(".*-.5"));
scan.setFilter(filter2);
ResultScanner scanner2 = table.getScanner(scan);
for (Result res : scanner2) {
  System.out.println(res);
}
scanner2.close();

Filter filter3 = new RowFilter(CompareFilter.CompareOp.EQUAL, ❸
  new SubstringComparator("-5"));
scan.setFilter(filter3);
ResultScanner scanner3 = table.getScanner(scan);
for (Result res : scanner3) {
  System.out.println(res);
}
scanner3.close();
```

❶ Create a filter, while specifying the comparison operator and comparator. Here an exact match is needed.

❷ Another filter is created, this time using a regular expression to match the row keys.

❸ The third filter uses a substring match approach.

Here is the full printout of the example on the console:

```
Adding rows to table...
Scanning table #1...
keyvalues={row-1/colfam1:col-0/1301043190260/Put/vlen=7}
keyvalues={row-10/colfam1:col-0/1301043190908/Put/vlen=8}
keyvalues={row-100/colfam1:col-0/1301043195275/Put/vlen=9}
keyvalues={row-11/colfam1:col-0/1301043190982/Put/vlen=8}
keyvalues={row-12/colfam1:col-0/1301043191040/Put/vlen=8}
```

```
keyvalues={row-13/colfam1:col-0/1301043191172/Put/vlen=8}
keyvalues={row-14/colfam1:col-0/1301043191318/Put/vlen=8}
keyvalues={row-15/colfam1:col-0/1301043191429/Put/vlen=8}
keyvalues={row-16/colfam1:col-0/1301043191509/Put/vlen=8}
keyvalues={row-17/colfam1:col-0/1301043191593/Put/vlen=8}
keyvalues={row-18/colfam1:col-0/1301043191673/Put/vlen=8}
keyvalues={row-19/colfam1:col-0/1301043191771/Put/vlen=8}
keyvalues={row-2/colfam1:col-0/1301043190346/Put/vlen=7}
keyvalues={row-20/colfam1:col-0/1301043191841/Put/vlen=8}
keyvalues={row-21/colfam1:col-0/1301043191933/Put/vlen=8}
keyvalues={row-22/colfam1:col-0/1301043191998/Put/vlen=8}
Scanning table #2...
keyvalues={row-15/colfam1:col-0/1301043191429/Put/vlen=8}
keyvalues={row-25/colfam1:col-0/1301043192140/Put/vlen=8}
keyvalues={row-35/colfam1:col-0/1301043192665/Put/vlen=8}
keyvalues={row-45/colfam1:col-0/1301043193138/Put/vlen=8}
keyvalues={row-55/colfam1:col-0/1301043193729/Put/vlen=8}
keyvalues={row-65/colfam1:col-0/1301043194092/Put/vlen=8}
keyvalues={row-75/colfam1:col-0/1301043194457/Put/vlen=8}
keyvalues={row-85/colfam1:col-0/1301043194806/Put/vlen=8}
keyvalues={row-95/colfam1:col-0/1301043195121/Put/vlen=8}
Scanning table #3...
keyvalues={row-5/colfam1:col-0/1301043190562/Put/vlen=7}
keyvalues={row-50/colfam1:col-0/1301043193332/Put/vlen=8}
keyvalues={row-51/colfam1:col-0/1301043193514/Put/vlen=8}
keyvalues={row-52/colfam1:col-0/1301043193603/Put/vlen=8}
keyvalues={row-53/colfam1:col-0/1301043193654/Put/vlen=8}
keyvalues={row-54/colfam1:col-0/1301043193696/Put/vlen=8}
keyvalues={row-55/colfam1:col-0/1301043193729/Put/vlen=8}
keyvalues={row-56/colfam1:col-0/1301043193766/Put/vlen=8}
keyvalues={row-57/colfam1:col-0/1301043193802/Put/vlen=8}
keyvalues={row-58/colfam1:col-0/1301043193842/Put/vlen=8}
keyvalues={row-59/colfam1:col-0/1301043193889/Put/vlen=8}
```

You can see how the first filter did an exact match on the row key, including all of those rows that have a key, equal to or less than the given one. Note once again the lexicographical sorting and comparison, and how it filters the row keys.

The second filter does a regular expression match, while the third uses a substring match approach. The results show that the filters work as advertised.

FamilyFilter

This filter works very similar to the `RowFilter`, but applies the comparison to the column families available in a row—as opposed to the row key. Using the available combinations of operators and comparators you can filter what is included in the retrieved data on a column family level. Example 4-2 shows how to use this.

Example 4-2. Using a filter to include only specific column families

```
Filter filter1 = new FamilyFilter(CompareFilter.CompareOp.LESS, ❶
  new BinaryComparator(Bytes.toBytes("colfam3")));

Scan scan = new Scan();
```

```
scan.setFilter(filter1);
ResultScanner scanner = table.getScanner(scan); ❷
for (Result result : scanner) {
  System.out.println(result);
}
scanner.close();

Get get1 = new Get(Bytes.toBytes("row-5"));
get1.setFilter(filter1);
Result result1 = table.get(get1); ❸
System.out.println("Result of get(): " + result1);

Filter filter2 = new FamilyFilter(CompareFilter.CompareOp.EQUAL,
  new BinaryComparator(Bytes.toBytes("colfam3")));
Get get2 = new Get(Bytes.toBytes("row-5")); ❹
get2.addFamily(Bytes.toBytes("colfam1"));
get2.setFilter(filter2);
Result result2 = table.get(get2); ❺
System.out.println("Result of get(): " + result2);
```

❶ Create a filter, while specifying the comparison operator and comparator.

❷ Scan over the table while applying the filter.

❸ Get a row while applying the same filter.

❹ Create a filter on one column family while trying to retrieve another.

❺ Get the same row while applying the new filter; this will return "NONE".

The output—reformatted and abbreviated for the sake of readability—shows the filter in action. The input data has four column families, with two columns each, and 10 rows in total.

```
Adding rows to table...
Scanning table...
keyvalues={row-1/colfam1:col-0/1303721790522/Put/vlen=7,
          row-1/colfam1:col-1/1303721790574/Put/vlen=7,
          row-1/colfam2:col-0/1303721790522/Put/vlen=7,
          row-1/colfam2:col-1/1303721790574/Put/vlen=7}
keyvalues={row-10/colfam1:col-0/1303721790785/Put/vlen=8,
          row-10/colfam1:col-1/1303721790792/Put/vlen=8,
          row-10/colfam2:col-0/1303721790785/Put/vlen=8,
          row-10/colfam2:col-1/1303721790792/Put/vlen=8}
...
keyvalues={row-9/colfam1:col-0/1303721790778/Put/vlen=7,
          row-9/colfam1:col-1/1303721790781/Put/vlen=7,
          row-9/colfam2:col-0/1303721790778/Put/vlen=7,
          row-9/colfam2:col-1/1303721790781/Put/vlen=7}

Result of get(): keyvalues={row-5/colfam1:col-0/1303721790652/Put/vlen=7,
          row-5/colfam1:col-1/1303721790664/Put/vlen=7,
          row-5/colfam2:col-0/1303721790652/Put/vlen=7,
          row-5/colfam2:col-1/1303721790664/Put/vlen=7}

Result of get(): keyvalues=NONE
```

The last get() shows that you can (inadvertently) create an empty set by applying a filter for exactly one column family, while specifying a different column family selector using addFamily().

QualifierFilter

Example 4-3 shows how the same logic is applied on the column qualifier level. This allows you to filter specific columns from the table.

Example 4-3. Using a filter to include only specific column qualifiers

```
Filter filter = new QualifierFilter(CompareFilter.CompareOp.LESS_OR_EQUAL,
  new BinaryComparator(Bytes.toBytes("col-2")));

Scan scan = new Scan();
scan.setFilter(filter);
ResultScanner scanner = table.getScanner(scan);
for (Result result : scanner) {
  System.out.println(result);
}
scanner.close();

Get get = new Get(Bytes.toBytes("row-5"));
get.setFilter(filter);
Result result = table.get(get);
System.out.println("Result of get(): " + result);
```

ValueFilter

This filter makes it possible to include only columns that have a specific value. Combined with the RegexStringComparator, for example, this can filter using powerful expression syntax. Example 4-4 showcases this feature. Note, though, that with certain comparators—as explained earlier—you can only employ a subset of the operators. Here a substring match is performed and this *must* be combined with an EQUAL, or NOT_EQUAL, operator.

Example 4-4. Using the value-based filter

```
Filter filter = new ValueFilter(CompareFilter.CompareOp.EQUAL,  ❶
  new SubstringComparator(".4"));

Scan scan = new Scan();
scan.setFilter(filter);  ❷
ResultScanner scanner = table.getScanner(scan);
for (Result result : scanner) {
  for (KeyValue kv : result.raw()) {
    System.out.println("KV: " + kv + ", Value: " + ❸
      Bytes.toString(kv.getValue()));
  }
}
scanner.close();

Get get = new Get(Bytes.toBytes("row-5"));
```

```
      get.setFilter(filter); ❹
      Result result = table.get(get);
      for (KeyValue kv : result.raw()) {
        System.out.println("KV: " + kv + ", Value: " +
          Bytes.toString(kv.getValue()));
      }
```

❶ Create a filter, while specifying the comparison operator and comparator.

❷ Set the filter for the scan.

❸ Print out the value to check that the filter works.

❹ Assign the same filter to the Get instance.

DependentColumnFilter

Here you have a more complex filter that does not simply filter out data based on directly available information. Rather, it lets you specify a *dependent* column—or *reference* column—that controls how other columns are filtered. It uses the timestamp of the reference column and includes all other columns that have the same timestamp. Here are the constructors provided:

```
      DependentColumnFilter(byte[] family, byte[] qualifier)
      DependentColumnFilter(byte[] family, byte[] qualifier,
        boolean dropDependentColumn)
      DependentColumnFilter(byte[] family, byte[] qualifier,
        boolean dropDependentColumn, CompareOp valueCompareOp,
        WritableByteArrayComparable valueComparator)
```

Since it is based on CompareFilter, it also offers you to further select columns, but for this filter it does so based on their values. Think of it as a combination of a ValueFilter and a filter selecting on a reference timestamp. You can optionally hand in your own operator and comparator pair to enable this feature. The class provides constructors, though, that let you omit the operator and comparator and disable the value filtering, including all columns by default, that is, performing the timestamp filter based on the reference column only.

Example 4-5 shows the filter in use. You can see how the optional values can be handed in as well. The dropDependentColumn parameter is giving you additional control over how the reference column is handled: it is either included or dropped by the filter, setting this parameter to false or true, respectively.

Example 4-5. Using a filter to include only specific column families

```
      private static void filter(boolean drop,
          CompareFilter.CompareOp operator,
          WritableByteArrayComparable comparator)
      throws IOException {
        Filter filter;
        if (comparator != null) {
          filter = new DependentColumnFilter(Bytes.toBytes("colfam1"), ❶
            Bytes.toBytes("col-5"), drop, operator, comparator);
```

```
    } else {
      filter = new DependentColumnFilter(Bytes.toBytes("colfam1"),
        Bytes.toBytes("col-5"), drop);
    }

    Scan scan = new Scan();
    scan.setFilter(filter);
    ResultScanner scanner = table.getScanner(scan);
    for (Result result : scanner) {
      for (KeyValue kv : result.raw()) {
        System.out.println("KV: " + kv + ", Value: " +
          Bytes.toString(kv.getValue()));
      }
    }
    scanner.close();

    Get get = new Get(Bytes.toBytes("row-5"));
    get.setFilter(filter);
    Result result = table.get(get);
    for (KeyValue kv : result.raw()) {
      System.out.println("KV: " + kv + ", Value: " +
        Bytes.toString(kv.getValue()));
    }
  }

  public static void main(String[] args) throws IOException {
    filter(true, CompareFilter.CompareOp.NO_OP, null);
    filter(false, CompareFilter.CompareOp.NO_OP, null); ❷
    filter(true, CompareFilter.CompareOp.EQUAL,
      new BinaryPrefixComparator(Bytes.toBytes("val-5")));
    filter(false, CompareFilter.CompareOp.EQUAL,
      new BinaryPrefixComparator(Bytes.toBytes("val-5")));
    filter(true, CompareFilter.CompareOp.EQUAL,
      new RegexStringComparator(".*\\.5"));
    filter(false, CompareFilter.CompareOp.EQUAL,
      new RegexStringComparator(".*\\.5"));
  }
```

❶ Create the filter with various options.

❷ Call the filter method with various options.

 This filter is *not* compatible with the batch feature of the scan operations, that is, setting Scan.setBatch() to a number larger than zero. The filter needs to see the entire row to do its work, and using batching will not carry the reference column timestamp over and would result in erroneous results.

If you try to enable the batch mode nevertheless, you will get an error:

```
Exception org.apache.hadoop.hbase.filter.IncompatibleFilterException:
Cannot set batch on a scan using a filter that returns true for
filter.hasFilterRow
```

The example also proceeds slightly differently compared to the earlier filters, as it sets the version to the column number for a more reproducible result. The implicit time-stamps that the servers use as the version could result in fluctuating results as you cannot guarantee them using the exact time, down to the millisecond.

The `filter()` method used is called with different parameter combinations, showing how using the built-in value filter and the drop flag is affecting the returned data set.

Dedicated Filters

The second type of supplied filters are based directly on `FilterBase` and implement more specific use cases. Many of these filters are only really applicable when performing scan operations, since they filter out entire rows. For `get()` calls, this is often too restrictive and would result in a very harsh filter approach: include the whole row or nothing at all.

SingleColumnValueFilter

You can use this filter when you have exactly one column that decides if an entire row should be returned or not. You need to first specify the column you want to track, and then some value to check against. The constructors offered are:

```
SingleColumnValueFilter(byte[] family, byte[] qualifier,
  CompareOp compareOp, byte[] value)
SingleColumnValueFilter(byte[] family, byte[] qualifier,
  CompareOp compareOp, WritableByteArrayComparable comparator)
```

The first one is a convenience function as it simply creates a `BinaryComparator` instance internally on your behalf. The second takes the same parameters we used for the `CompareFilter`-based classes. Although the `SingleColumnValueFilter` does not inherit from the `CompareFilter` directly, it still uses the same parameter types.

The filter class also exposes a few auxiliary methods you can use to fine-tune its behavior:

```
boolean getFilterIfMissing()
void setFilterIfMissing(boolean filterIfMissing)
boolean getLatestVersionOnly()
void setLatestVersionOnly(boolean latestVersionOnly)
```

The former controls what happens to rows that do not have the column at all. By default, they are included in the result, but you can use `setFilterIfMissing(true)` to reverse that behavior, that is, all rows that do not have the reference column are dropped from the result.

You must include the column you want to filter by, in other words, the reference column, into the families you query for—using addColumn(), for example. If you fail to do so, the column is considered missing and the result is either empty, or contains all rows, based on the getFilter IfMissing() result.

By using setLatestVersionOnly(false)—the default is true—you can change the default behavior of the filter, which is only to check the newest version of the reference column, to instead include previous versions in the check as well. Example 4-6 combines these features to select a specific set of rows only.

Example 4-6. Using a filter to return only rows with a given value in a given column

```
SingleColumnValueFilter filter = new SingleColumnValueFilter(
  Bytes.toBytes("colfam1"),
  Bytes.toBytes("col-5"),
  CompareFilter.CompareOp.NOT_EQUAL,
  new SubstringComparator("val-5"));
filter.setFilterIfMissing(true);

Scan scan = new Scan();
scan.setFilter(filter);
ResultScanner scanner = table.getScanner(scan);
for (Result result : scanner) {
  for (KeyValue kv : result.raw()) {
    System.out.println("KV: " + kv + ", Value: " +
      Bytes.toString(kv.getValue()));
  }
}
scanner.close();

Get get = new Get(Bytes.toBytes("row-6"));
get.setFilter(filter);
Result result = table.get(get);
System.out.println("Result of get: ");
for (KeyValue kv : result.raw()) {
  System.out.println("KV: " + kv + ", Value: " +
    Bytes.toString(kv.getValue()));
}
```

SingleColumnValueExcludeFilter

The SingleColumnValueFilter we just discussed is extended in this class to provide slightly different semantics: the reference column, as handed into the constructor, is omitted from the result. In other words, you have the same features, constructors, and methods to control how this filter works. The only difference is that you will never get the column you are checking against as part of the Result instance(s) on the client side.

PrefixFilter

Given a *prefix*, specified when you instantiate the filter instance, all rows that *match* this prefix are returned to the client. The constructor is:

```
public PrefixFilter(byte[] prefix)
```

Example 4-7 has this applied to the usual test data set.

Example 4-7. Using the prefix-based filter

```
Filter filter = new PrefixFilter(Bytes.toBytes("row-1"));

Scan scan = new Scan();
scan.setFilter(filter);
ResultScanner scanner = table.getScanner(scan);
for (Result result : scanner) {
  for (KeyValue kv : result.raw()) {
    System.out.println("KV: " + kv + ", Value: " +
      Bytes.toString(kv.getValue()));
  }
}
scanner.close();

Get get = new Get(Bytes.toBytes("row-5"));
get.setFilter(filter);
Result result = table.get(get);
for (KeyValue kv : result.raw()) {
  System.out.println("KV: " + kv + ", Value: " +
    Bytes.toString(kv.getValue()));
}
```

It is interesting to see how the get() call fails to return anything, because it is asking for a row that does *not* match the filter prefix. This filter does not make much sense when doing get() calls but is highly useful for scan operations.

The scan also is actively ended when the filter encounters a row key that is larger than the prefix. In this way, and combining this with a start row, for example, the filter is improving the overall performance of the scan as it has knowledge of when to skip the rest of the rows altogether.

PageFilter

You paginate through rows by employing this filter. When you create the instance, you specify a `pageSize` parameter, which controls how many rows per page should be returned.

There is a fundamental issue with filtering on physically separate servers. Filters run on different region servers in parallel and cannot retain or communicate their current state across those boundaries. Thus, each filter is required to scan at least up to pageCount rows before ending the scan. This means a slight inefficiency is given for the PageFilter as more rows are reported to the client than necessary. The final consolidation on the client obviously has visibility into all results and can reduce what is accessible through the API accordingly.

The client code would need to remember the last row that was returned, and then, when another iteration is about to start, set the *start row* of the scan accordingly, while retaining the same filter properties.

Because pagination is setting a strict limit on the number of rows to be returned, it is possible for the filter to *early out* the entire scan, once the limit is reached or exceeded. Filters have a facility to indicate that fact and the region servers make use of this hint to stop any further processing.

Example 4-8 puts this together, showing how a client can reset the scan to a new start row on the subsequent iterations.

Example 4-8. Using a filter to paginate through rows

```
Filter filter = new PageFilter(15);

int totalRows = 0;
byte[] lastRow = null;
while (true) {
  Scan scan = new Scan();
  scan.setFilter(filter);
  if (lastRow != null) {
    byte[] startRow = Bytes.add(lastRow, POSTFIX);
    System.out.println("start row: " +
      Bytes.toStringBinary(startRow));
    scan.setStartRow(startRow);
  }
  ResultScanner scanner = table.getScanner(scan);
  int localRows = 0;
  Result result;
  while ((result = scanner.next()) != null) {
    System.out.println(localRows++ + ": " + result);
    totalRows++;
    lastRow = result.getRow();
  }
  scanner.close();
  if (localRows == 0) break;
}
System.out.println("total rows: " + totalRows);
```

Because of the lexicographical sorting of the row keys by HBase and the comparison taking care of finding the row keys in order, and the fact that the start key on a scan is always inclusive, you need to add an extra zero byte to the previous key. This will ensure that the last seen row key is skipped and the next, in sorting order, is found. The zero byte is the smallest increment, and therefore is safe to use when resetting the scan boundaries. Even if there were a row that would match the previous plus the extra zero byte, the scan would be correctly doing the next iteration—this is because the start key is inclusive.

KeyOnlyFilter

Some applications need to access just the keys of each `KeyValue`, while omitting the actual data. The `KeyOnlyFilter` provides this functionality by applying the filter's ability to modify the processed columns and cells, as they pass through. It does so by applying the `KeyValue.convertToKeyOnly(boolean)` call that strips out the data part.

The constructor of this filter has a `boolean` parameter, named `lenAsVal`. It is handed to the `convertToKeyOnly()` call as-is, controlling what happens to the value part of each `KeyValue` instance processed. The default `false` simply sets the value to zero length, while the opposite `true` sets the value to the number representing the length of the original value.

The latter may be useful to your application when quickly iterating over columns, where the keys already convey meaning and the length can be used to perform a secondary sort, for example. "Client API: Best Practices" on page 434 has an example.

FirstKeyOnlyFilter

If you need to access the first column—as sorted implicitly by HBase—in each row, this filter will provide this feature. Typically this is used by *row counter* type applications that only need to check if a row exists. Recall that in column-oriented databases a row really is composed of columns, and if there are none, the row ceases to exist.

Another possible use case is relying on the column sorting in lexicographical order, and setting the column qualifier to an epoch value. This would sort the column with the oldest timestamp name as the first to be retrieved. Combined with this filter, it is possible to retrieve the oldest column from every row using a single scan.

This class makes use of another optimization feature provided by the filter framework: it indicates to the region server applying the filter that the current row is done and that it should skip to the next one. This improves the overall performance of the scan, compared to a full table scan.

InclusiveStopFilter

The row boundaries of a scan are inclusive for the start row, yet exclusive for the stop row. You can overcome the stop row semantics using this filter, which *includes* the specified stop row. Example 4-9 uses the filter to start at `row-3`, and stop at `row-5` *inclusively*.

Example 4-9. Using a filter to include a stop row

```
Filter filter = new InclusiveStopFilter(Bytes.toBytes("row-5"));

Scan scan = new Scan();
scan.setStartRow(Bytes.toBytes("row-3"));
scan.setFilter(filter);
ResultScanner scanner = table.getScanner(scan);
for (Result result : scanner) {
  System.out.println(result);
}
scanner.close();
```

The output on the console, when running the example code, confirms that the filter works as advertised:

```
Adding rows to table...
Results of scan:
keyvalues={row-3/colfam1:col-0/1301337961569/Put/vlen=7}
keyvalues={row-30/colfam1:col-0/1301337961610/Put/vlen=8}
keyvalues={row-31/colfam1:col-0/1301337961612/Put/vlen=8}
keyvalues={row-32/colfam1:col-0/1301337961613/Put/vlen=8}
keyvalues={row-33/colfam1:col-0/1301337961614/Put/vlen=8}
keyvalues={row-34/colfam1:col-0/1301337961615/Put/vlen=8}
keyvalues={row-35/colfam1:col-0/1301337961616/Put/vlen=8}
keyvalues={row-36/colfam1:col-0/1301337961617/Put/vlen=8}
keyvalues={row-37/colfam1:col-0/1301337961618/Put/vlen=8}
keyvalues={row-38/colfam1:col-0/1301337961619/Put/vlen=8}
keyvalues={row-39/colfam1:col-0/1301337961620/Put/vlen=8}
keyvalues={row-4/colfam1:col-0/1301337961571/Put/vlen=7}
keyvalues={row-40/colfam1:col-0/1301337961621/Put/vlen=8}
keyvalues={row-41/colfam1:col-0/1301337961622/Put/vlen=8}
keyvalues={row-42/colfam1:col-0/1301337961623/Put/vlen=8}
keyvalues={row-43/colfam1:col-0/1301337961624/Put/vlen=8}
keyvalues={row-44/colfam1:col-0/1301337961625/Put/vlen=8}
keyvalues={row-45/colfam1:col-0/1301337961626/Put/vlen=8}
keyvalues={row-46/colfam1:col-0/1301337961627/Put/vlen=8}
keyvalues={row-47/colfam1:col-0/1301337961628/Put/vlen=8}
keyvalues={row-48/colfam1:col-0/1301337961629/Put/vlen=8}
keyvalues={row-49/colfam1:col-0/1301337961630/Put/vlen=8}
keyvalues={row-5/colfam1:col-0/1301337961573/Put/vlen=7}
```

TimestampsFilter

When you need fine-grained control over what versions are included in the scan result, this filter provides the means. You have to hand in a List of timestamps:

```
TimestampsFilter(List<Long> timestamps)
```

 As you have seen throughout the book so far, a *version* is a specific value of a column at a unique point in time, denoted with a *timestamp*. When the filter is asking for a list of timestamps, it will attempt to retrieve the column versions with the matching timestamps.

Example 4-10 sets up a filter with three timestamps and adds a time range to the second scan.

Example 4-10. Filtering data by timestamps

```
List<Long> ts = new ArrayList<Long>();
ts.add(new Long(5));
ts.add(new Long(10)); ❶
ts.add(new Long(15));
Filter filter = new TimestampsFilter(ts);

Scan scan1 = new Scan();
scan1.setFilter(filter); ❷
ResultScanner scanner1 = table.getScanner(scan1);
for (Result result : scanner1) {
  System.out.println(result);
}
scanner1.close();

Scan scan2 = new Scan();
scan2.setFilter(filter);
scan2.setTimeRange(8, 12); ❸
ResultScanner scanner2 = table.getScanner(scan2);
for (Result result : scanner2) {
  System.out.println(result);
}
scanner2.close();
```

❶ Add timestamps to the list.

❷ Add the filter to an otherwise default Scan instance.

❸ Also add a time range to verify how it affects the filter.

Here is the output on the console in an abbreviated form:

```
Adding rows to table...
Results of scan #1:
keyvalues={row-1/colfam1:col-10/10/Put/vlen=8,
           row-1/colfam1:col-15/15/Put/vlen=8,
           row-1/colfam1:col-5/5/Put/vlen=7}
keyvalues={row-10/colfam1:col-10/10/Put/vlen=9,
           row-10/colfam1:col-15/15/Put/vlen=9,
           row-10/colfam1:col-5/5/Put/vlen=8}
keyvalues={row-100/colfam1:col-10/10/Put/vlen=10,
           row-100/colfam1:col-15/15/Put/vlen=10,
           row-100/colfam1:col-5/5/Put/vlen=9}
...
Results of scan #2:
keyvalues={row-1/colfam1:col-10/10/Put/vlen=8}
keyvalues={row-10/colfam1:col-10/10/Put/vlen=9}
keyvalues={row-100/colfam1:col-10/10/Put/vlen=10}
keyvalues={row-11/colfam1:col-10/10/Put/vlen=9}
...
```

The first scan, only using the filter, is outputting the column values for all three specified timestamps as expected. The second scan only returns the timestamp that fell into the time range specified when the scan was set up. Both time-based restrictions, the filter and the scanner time range, are doing their job and the result is a combination of both.

ColumnCountGetFilter

You can use this filter to only retrieve a specific maximum number of columns per row. You can set the number using the constructor of the filter:

```
ColumnCountGetFilter(int n)
```

Since this filter stops the entire scan once a row has been found that matches the maximum number of columns configured, it is not useful for scan operations, and in fact, it was written to test filters in get() calls.

ColumnPaginationFilter

Similar to the PageFilter, this one can be used to page through columns in a row. Its constructor has two parameters:

```
ColumnPaginationFilter(int limit, int offset)
```

It skips all columns up to the number given as offset, and then includes limit columns afterward. Example 4-11 has this applied to a normal scan.

Example 4-11. Paginating through columns in a row

```
Filter filter = new ColumnPaginationFilter(5, 15);

Scan scan = new Scan();
scan.setFilter(filter);
ResultScanner scanner = table.getScanner(scan);
for (Result result : scanner) {
  System.out.println(result);
}
scanner.close();
```

Running this example should render the following output:

```
Adding rows to table...
Results of scan:
keyvalues={row-01/colfam1:col-15/15/Put/vlen=9,
           row-01/colfam1:col-16/16/Put/vlen=9,
           row-01/colfam1:col-17/17/Put/vlen=9,
           row-01/colfam1:col-18/18/Put/vlen=9,
           row-01/colfam1:col-19/19/Put/vlen=9}
keyvalues={row-02/colfam1:col-15/15/Put/vlen=9,
           row-02/colfam1:col-16/16/Put/vlen=9,
           row-02/colfam1:col-17/17/Put/vlen=9,
           row-02/colfam1:col-18/18/Put/vlen=9,
           row-02/colfam1:col-19/19/Put/vlen=9}
    ...
```

This example slightly changes the way the rows and columns are numbered by adding a padding to the numeric counters. For example, the first row is padded to be `row-01`. This also shows how padding can be used to get a more *human-readable* style of sorting, for example—as known from a dictionary or telephone book.

The result includes all 10 rows, starting each row at column (`offset` = 15) and printing five columns (`limit` = 5).

ColumnPrefixFilter

Analog to the `PrefixFilter`, which worked by filtering on row key prefixes, this filter does the same for columns. You specify a prefix when creating the filter:

```
ColumnPrefixFilter(byte[] prefix)
```

All columns that have the given prefix are then included in the result.

RandomRowFilter

Finally, there is a filter that shows what is also possible using the API: including random rows into the result. The constructor is given a parameter named `chance`, which represents a value between `0.0` and `1.0`:

```
RandomRowFilter(float chance)
```

Internally, this class is using a Java `Random.nextFloat()` call to randomize the row inclusion, and then compares the value with the `chance` given. Giving it a negative chance value will make the filter exclude all rows, while a value larger than `1.0` will make it include all rows.

Decorating Filters

While the provided filters are already very powerful, sometimes it can be useful to modify, or extend, the behavior of a filter to gain additional control over the returned data. Some of this additional control is not dependent on the filter itself, but can be applied to any of them. This is what the *decorating filter* group of classes is about.

SkipFilter

This filter wraps a given filter and extends it to exclude an entire row, when the wrapped filter hints for a `KeyValue` to be skipped. In other words, as soon as a filter indicates that a column in a row is omitted, the entire row is omitted.

The wrapped filter *must* implement the `filterKeyValue()` method, or the `SkipFilter` will not work as expected.* This is because the `SkipFilter` is only checking the results of that method to decide how to handle the current row. See Table 4-5 on page 167 for an overview of compatible filters.

Example 4-12 combines the `SkipFilter` with a `ValueFilter` to first select all columns that have no zero-valued column, and subsequently drops all other partial rows that do not have a matching value.

Example 4-12. Using a filter to skip entire rows based on another filter's results

```
Filter filter1 = new ValueFilter(CompareFilter.CompareOp.NOT_EQUAL,
  new BinaryComparator(Bytes.toBytes("val-0")));

Scan scan = new Scan();
scan.setFilter(filter1); ❶
ResultScanner scanner1 = table.getScanner(scan);
for (Result result : scanner1) {
  for (KeyValue kv : result.raw()) {
    System.out.println("KV: " + kv + ", Value: " +
      Bytes.toString(kv.getValue()));
  }
}
scanner1.close();

Filter filter2 = new SkipFilter(filter1);

scan.setFilter(filter2); ❷
ResultScanner scanner2 = table.getScanner(scan);
for (Result result : scanner2) {
  for (KeyValue kv : result.raw()) {
    System.out.println("KV: " + kv + ", Value: " +
      Bytes.toString(kv.getValue()));
  }
}
scanner2.close();
```

❶ Only add the `ValueFilter` to the first scan.

❷ Add the decorating skip filter for the second scan.

The example code should print roughly the following results when you execute it—note, though, that the values are randomized, so you should get a slightly different result for every invocation:

```
Adding rows to table...
Results of scan #1:
KV: row-01/colfam1:col-00/0/Put/vlen=5, Value: val-4
KV: row-01/colfam1:col-01/1/Put/vlen=5, Value: val-2
```

---

* The various filter methods are discussed in "Custom Filters" on page 160.

```
KV: row-01/colfam1:col-02/2/Put/vlen=5, Value: val-4
KV: row-01/colfam1:col-03/3/Put/vlen=5, Value: val-3
KV: row-01/colfam1:col-04/4/Put/vlen=5, Value: val-1
KV: row-02/colfam1:col-00/0/Put/vlen=5, Value: val-3
KV: row-02/colfam1:col-01/1/Put/vlen=5, Value: val-1
KV: row-02/colfam1:col-03/3/Put/vlen=5, Value: val-4
KV: row-02/colfam1:col-04/4/Put/vlen=5, Value: val-1
...
Total KeyValue count for scan #1: 122

Results of scan #2:
KV: row-01/colfam1:col-00/0/Put/vlen=5, Value: val-4
KV: row-01/colfam1:col-01/1/Put/vlen=5, Value: val-2
KV: row-01/colfam1:col-02/2/Put/vlen=5, Value: val-4
KV: row-01/colfam1:col-03/3/Put/vlen=5, Value: val-3
KV: row-01/colfam1:col-04/4/Put/vlen=5, Value: val-1
KV: row-07/colfam1:col-00/0/Put/vlen=5, Value: val-4
KV: row-07/colfam1:col-01/1/Put/vlen=5, Value: val-1
KV: row-07/colfam1:col-02/2/Put/vlen=5, Value: val-1
KV: row-07/colfam1:col-03/3/Put/vlen=5, Value: val-2
KV: row-07/colfam1:col-04/4/Put/vlen=5, Value: val-4
...
Total KeyValue count for scan #2: 50
```

The first scan returns *all* columns that are *not* zero valued. Since the value is assigned at random, there is a high probability that you will get at least one or more columns of each possible row. Some rows will miss a column—these are the omitted zero-valued ones.

The second scan, on the other hand, wraps the first filter and forces all partial rows to be dropped. You can see from the console output how only complete rows are emitted, that is, those with all five columns the example code creates initially. The total Key Value count for each scan confirms the more restrictive behavior of the SkipFilter variant.

WhileMatchFilter

This second decorating filter type works somewhat similarly to the previous one, but aborts the entire scan once a piece of information is filtered. This works by checking the wrapped filter and seeing if it skips a row by its key, or a column of a row because of a KeyValue check.[†]

Example 4-13 is a slight variation of the previous example, using different filters to show how the decorating class works.

Example 4-13. Using a filter to skip entire rows based on another filter's results

```
Filter filter1 = new RowFilter(CompareFilter.CompareOp.NOT_EQUAL,
  new BinaryComparator(Bytes.toBytes("row-05")));
```

---

† See Table 4-5 for an overview of compatible filters.

```
Scan scan = new Scan();
scan.setFilter(filter1);
ResultScanner scanner1 = table.getScanner(scan);
for (Result result : scanner1) {
  for (KeyValue kv : result.raw()) {
    System.out.println("KV: " + kv + ", Value: " +
      Bytes.toString(kv.getValue()));
  }
}
scanner1.close();

Filter filter2 = new WhileMatchFilter(filter1);

scan.setFilter(filter2);
ResultScanner scanner2 = table.getScanner(scan);
for (Result result : scanner2) {
  for (KeyValue kv : result.raw()) {
    System.out.println("KV: " + kv + ", Value: " +
      Bytes.toString(kv.getValue()));
  }
}
scanner2.close();
```

Once you run the example code, you should get this output on the console:

```
Adding rows to table...
Results of scan #1:
KV: row-01/colfam1:col-00/0/Put/vlen=9, Value: val-01.00
KV: row-02/colfam1:col-00/0/Put/vlen=9, Value: val-02.00
KV: row-03/colfam1:col-00/0/Put/vlen=9, Value: val-03.00
KV: row-04/colfam1:col-00/0/Put/vlen=9, Value: val-04.00
KV: row-06/colfam1:col-00/0/Put/vlen=9, Value: val-06.00
KV: row-07/colfam1:col-00/0/Put/vlen=9, Value: val-07.00
KV: row-08/colfam1:col-00/0/Put/vlen=9, Value: val-08.00
KV: row-09/colfam1:col-00/0/Put/vlen=9, Value: val-09.00
KV: row-10/colfam1:col-00/0/Put/vlen=9, Value: val-10.00
Total KeyValue count for scan #1: 9
Results of scan #2:
KV: row-01/colfam1:col-00/0/Put/vlen=9, Value: val-01.00
KV: row-02/colfam1:col-00/0/Put/vlen=9, Value: val-02.00
KV: row-03/colfam1:col-00/0/Put/vlen=9, Value: val-03.00
KV: row-04/colfam1:col-00/0/Put/vlen=9, Value: val-04.00
Total KeyValue count for scan #2: 4
```

The first scan used just the RowFilter to skip one out of 10 rows; the rest is returned to the client. Adding the WhileMatchFilter for the second scan shows its behavior to stop the entire scan operation, once the wrapped filter omits a row or column. In the example this is row-05, triggering the end of the scan.

 Decorating filters implement the same Filter interface, just like any other single-purpose filter. In doing so, they can be used as a drop-in replacement for those filters, while combining their behavior with the wrapped filter instance.

FilterList

So far you have seen how filters—on their own, or decorated—are doing the work of filtering out various dimensions of a table, ranging from rows, to columns, and all the way to versions of values within a column. In practice, though, you may want to have more than one filter being applied to reduce the data returned to your client application. This is what the `FilterList` is for.

 The `FilterList` class implements the same `Filter` interface, just like any other single-purpose filter. In doing so, it can be used as a drop-in replacement for those filters, while combining the effects of each included instance.

You can create an instance of `FilterList` while providing various parameters at instantiation time, using one of these constructors:

```
FilterList(List<Filter> rowFilters)
FilterList(Operator operator)
FilterList(Operator operator, List<Filter> rowFilters)
```

The `rowFilters` parameter specifies the list of filters that are assessed together, using an `operator` to combine their results. Table 4-3 lists the possible choices of operators. The default is `MUST_PASS_ALL`, and can therefore be omitted from the constructor when you do not need a different one.

Table 4-3. Possible values for the FilterList.Operator enumeration

Operator	Description
MUST_PASS_ALL	A value is only included in the result when *all* filters agree to do so, i.e., no filter is omitting the value.
MUST_PASS_ONE	As soon as a value was allowed to pass one of the filters, it is included in the overall result.

Adding filters, *after* the `FilterList` instance has been created, can be done with:

```
void addFilter(Filter filter)
```

You can only specify *one* operator per `FilterList`, but you are free to add other `Filter List` instances to an existing `FilterList`, thus creating a hierarchy of filters, combined with the operators you need.

You can further control the execution order of the included filters by carefully choosing the `List` implementation you require. For example, using `ArrayList` would guarantee that the filters are applied in the order they were added to the list. This is shown in Example 4-14.

Example 4-14. Using a filter list to combine single-purpose filters

```
List<Filter> filters = new ArrayList<Filter>();

Filter filter1 = new RowFilter(CompareFilter.CompareOp.GREATER_OR_EQUAL,
```

```
      new BinaryComparator(Bytes.toBytes("row-03")));
    filters.add(filter1);

    Filter filter2 = new RowFilter(CompareFilter.CompareOp.LESS_OR_EQUAL,
      new BinaryComparator(Bytes.toBytes("row-06")));
    filters.add(filter2);

    Filter filter3 = new QualifierFilter(CompareFilter.CompareOp.EQUAL,
      new RegexStringComparator("col-0[03]"));
    filters.add(filter3);

    FilterList filterList1 = new FilterList(filters);

    Scan scan = new Scan();
    scan.setFilter(filterList1);
    ResultScanner scanner1 = table.getScanner(scan);
    for (Result result : scanner1) {
      for (KeyValue kv : result.raw()) {
        System.out.println("KV: " + kv + ", Value: " +
          Bytes.toString(kv.getValue()));
      }
    }
    scanner1.close();

    FilterList filterList2 = new FilterList(
      FilterList.Operator.MUST_PASS_ONE, filters);

    scan.setFilter(filterList2);
    ResultScanner scanner2 = table.getScanner(scan);
    for (Result result : scanner2) {
      for (KeyValue kv : result.raw()) {
        System.out.println("KV: " + kv + ", Value: " +
          Bytes.toString(kv.getValue()));
      }
    }
    scanner2.close();
```

The first scan filters out a lot of details, as at least one of the filters in the list excludes some information. Only where they all let the information pass is it returned to the client.

In contrast, the second scan includes *all* rows and columns in the result. This is caused by setting the FilterList operator to MUST_PASS_ONE, which includes all the information as soon as a single filter lets it pass. And in this scenario, all values are passed by at least one of them, including everything.

Custom Filters

Eventually, you may exhaust the list of supplied filter types and need to implement your own. This can be done by either implementing the Filter interface, or extending the provided FilterBase class. The latter provides default implementations for all methods that are members of the interface.

The `Filter` interface has the following structure:

```
public interface Filter extends Writable {
  public enum ReturnCode {
    INCLUDE, SKIP, NEXT_COL, NEXT_ROW, SEEK_NEXT_USING_HINT
  }
  public void reset()
  public boolean filterRowKey(byte[] buffer, int offset, int length)
  public boolean filterAllRemaining()
  public ReturnCode filterKeyValue(KeyValue v)
  public void filterRow(List<KeyValue> kvs)
  public boolean hasFilterRow()
  public boolean filterRow()
  public KeyValue getNextKeyHint(KeyValue currentKV)
```

The interface provides a public enumeration type, named `ReturnCode`, that is used by the `filterKeyValue()` method to indicate what the execution framework should do next. Instead of blindly iterating over all values, the filter has the ability to skip a value, the remainder of a column, or the rest of the entire row. This helps tremendously in terms of improving performance while retrieving data.

 The servers may still need to scan the entire row to find matching data, but the optimizations provided by the `filterKeyValue()` return code can reduce the work required to do so.

Table 4-4 lists the possible values and their meaning.

Table 4-4. Possible values for the Filter.ReturnCode enumeration

Return code	Description
INCLUDE	Include the given KeyValue instance in the result.
SKIP	Skip the current KeyValue and proceed to the next.
NEXT_COL	Skip the remainder of the current column, proceeding to the next. This is used by the TimestampsFilter, for example.
NEXT_ROW	Similar to the previous, but skips the remainder of the current row, moving to the next. The RowFilter makes use of this return code, for example.
SEEK_NEXT_USING_HINT	Some filters want to skip a variable number of values and use this return code to indicate that the framework should use the getNextKeyHint() method to determine where to skip to. The ColumnPrefixFilter, for example, uses this feature.

Most of the provided methods are called at various stages in the process of retrieving a row for a client—for example, during a scan operation. Putting them in call order, you can expect them to be executed in the following sequence:

`filterRowKey(byte[] buffer, int offset, int length)`

The next check is against the *row key*, using this method of the `Filter` implementation. You can use it to skip an entire row from being further processed. The `RowFilter` uses it to suppress entire rows being returned to the client.

`filterKeyValue(KeyValue v)`

When a row is not filtered (yet), the framework proceeds to invoke this method for every `KeyValue` that is part of the current row. The `ReturnCode` indicates what should happen with the current value.

`filterRow(List<KeyValue> kvs)`

Once all row and value checks have been performed, this method of the filter is called, giving you access to the list of `KeyValue` instances that have been included by the previous filter methods. The `DependentColumnFilter` uses it to drop those columns that do not match the reference column.

`filterRow()`

After everything else was checked and invoked, the final inspection is performed using `filterRow()`. A filter that uses this functionality is the `PageFilter`, checking if the number of rows to be returned for one iteration in the pagination process is reached, returning `true` afterward. The default `false` would include the current row in the result.

`reset()`

This resets the filter for every new row the scan is iterating over. It is called by the server, *after* a row is read, implicitly. This applies to *get* and *scan* operations, although obviously it has no effect for the former, as `get`s only read a single row.

`filterAllRemaining()`

This method can be used to stop the scan, by returning `true`. It is used by filters to provide the *early out* optimizations mentioned earlier. If a filter returns `false`, the scan is continued, and the aforementioned methods are called.

Obviously, this also implies that for `get` operations this call is not useful.

---

filterRow() and Batch Mode

A filter using `filterRow()` to filter out an entire row, or `filterRow(List)` to modify the final list of included values, *must* also override the `hasRowFilter()` function to return `true`.

The framework is using this flag to ensure that a given filter is compatible with the selected scan parameters. In particular, these filter methods collide with the scanner's batch mode: when the scanner is using batches to ship partial rows to the client, the previous methods are *not* called for every batch, but only at the actual end of the current row.

Figure 4-2 shows the logical flow of the filter methods for a single row. There is a more fine-grained process to apply the filters on a column level, which is not relevant in this context.

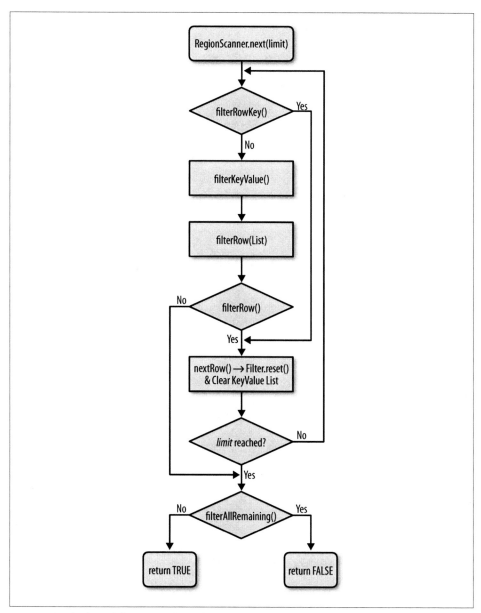

Figure 4-2. The logical flow through the filter methods for a single row

Example 4-15 implements a custom filter, using the methods provided by `FilterBase`, overriding only those methods that need to be changed.

The filter first assumes all rows should be filtered, that is, removed from the result. Only when there is a value in any column that matches the given reference does it include the row, so that it is sent back to the client.

Example 4-15. Implementing a filter that lets certain rows pass

```java
public class CustomFilter extends FilterBase{

  private byte[] value = null;
  private boolean filterRow = true;

  public CustomFilter() {
    super();
  }

  public CustomFilter(byte[] value) {
    this.value = value; ❶
  }

  @Override
  public void reset() {
    this.filterRow = true; ❷
  }

  @Override
  public ReturnCode filterKeyValue(KeyValue kv) {
    if (Bytes.compareTo(value, kv.getValue()) == 0) {
      filterRow = false; ❸
    }
    return ReturnCode.INCLUDE; ❹
  }

  @Override
  public boolean filterRow() {
    return filterRow; ❺
  }

  @Override
  public void write(DataOutput dataOutput) throws IOException {
    Bytes.writeByteArray(dataOutput, this.value); ❻
  }

  @Override
  public void readFields(DataInput dataInput) throws IOException {
    this.value = Bytes.readByteArray(dataInput); ❼
  }
}
```

❶ Set the value to compare against.

❷ Reset the filter flag for each new row being tested.

❸ When there is a matching value, let the row pass.

❹ Always include this, since the final decision is made later.

❺ Here the actual decision is taking place, based on the flag status.

❻ Write the given value out so that it can be sent to the servers.

❼ Used by the servers to establish the filter instance with the correct values.

Deployment of Custom Filters

Once you have written your filter, you need to deploy it to your HBase setup. You need to compile the class, pack it into a Java Archive (JAR) file, and make it available to the region servers.

You can use the build system of your choice to prepare the JAR file for deployment, and a configuration management system to actually provision the file to all servers. Once you have uploaded the JAR file, you need to add it to the *hbase-env.sh* configuration file, for example:

```
# Extra Java CLASSPATH elements.  Optional.
# export HBASE_CLASSPATH=
export HBASE_CLASSPATH="/hbase-book/ch04/target/hbase-book-ch04-1.0.jar"
```

This is using the JAR file created by the Maven build as supplied by the source code repository accompanying this book. It uses an absolute, local path since testing is done on a standalone setup, in other words, with the development environment and HBase running on the same physical machine.

Note that you *must* restart the HBase daemons so that the changes in the configuration file are taking effect. Once this is done you can proceed to test the new filter.

Example 4-16 uses the new custom filter to find rows with specific values in it, also using a `FilterList`.

Example 4-16. Using a custom filter

```
List<Filter> filters = new ArrayList<Filter>();

Filter filter1 = new CustomFilter(Bytes.toBytes("val-05.05"));
filters.add(filter1);

Filter filter2 = new CustomFilter(Bytes.toBytes("val-02.07"));
filters.add(filter2);

Filter filter3 = new CustomFilter(Bytes.toBytes("val-09.00"));
filters.add(filter3);

FilterList filterList = new FilterList(
  FilterList.Operator.MUST_PASS_ONE, filters);

Scan scan = new Scan();
scan.setFilter(filterList);
```

```
ResultScanner scanner = table.getScanner(scan);
for (Result result : scanner) {
  for (KeyValue kv : result.raw()) {
    System.out.println("KV: " + kv + ", Value: " +
      Bytes.toString(kv.getValue()));
  }
}
scanner.close();
```

Just as with the earlier examples, here is what should appear as output on the console when executing this example:

```
Adding rows to table...
Results of scan:
KV: row-02/colfam1:col-00/1301507323088/Put/vlen=9, Value: val-02.00
KV: row-02/colfam1:col-01/1301507323090/Put/vlen=9, Value: val-02.01
KV: row-02/colfam1:col-02/1301507323092/Put/vlen=9, Value: val-02.02
KV: row-02/colfam1:col-03/1301507323093/Put/vlen=9, Value: val-02.03
KV: row-02/colfam1:col-04/1301507323096/Put/vlen=9, Value: val-02.04
KV: row-02/colfam1:col-05/1301507323104/Put/vlen=9, Value: val-02.05
KV: row-02/colfam1:col-06/1301507323108/Put/vlen=9, Value: val-02.06
KV: row-02/colfam1:col-07/1301507323110/Put/vlen=9, Value: val-02.07
KV: row-02/colfam1:col-08/1301507323112/Put/vlen=9, Value: val-02.08
KV: row-02/colfam1:col-09/1301507323113/Put/vlen=9, Value: val-02.09
KV: row-05/colfam1:col-00/1301507323148/Put/vlen=9, Value: val-05.00
KV: row-05/colfam1:col-01/1301507323150/Put/vlen=9, Value: val-05.01
KV: row-05/colfam1:col-02/1301507323152/Put/vlen=9, Value: val-05.02
KV: row-05/colfam1:col-03/1301507323153/Put/vlen=9, Value: val-05.03
KV: row-05/colfam1:col-04/1301507323154/Put/vlen=9, Value: val-05.04
KV: row-05/colfam1:col-05/1301507323155/Put/vlen=9, Value: val-05.05
KV: row-05/colfam1:col-06/1301507323157/Put/vlen=9, Value: val-05.06
KV: row-05/colfam1:col-07/1301507323158/Put/vlen=9, Value: val-05.07
KV: row-05/colfam1:col-08/1301507323158/Put/vlen=9, Value: val-05.08
KV: row-05/colfam1:col-09/1301507323159/Put/vlen=9, Value: val-05.09
KV: row-09/colfam1:col-00/1301507323192/Put/vlen=9, Value: val-09.00
KV: row-09/colfam1:col-01/1301507323194/Put/vlen=9, Value: val-09.01
KV: row-09/colfam1:col-02/1301507323196/Put/vlen=9, Value: val-09.02
KV: row-09/colfam1:col-03/1301507323199/Put/vlen=9, Value: val-09.03
KV: row-09/colfam1:col-04/1301507323201/Put/vlen=9, Value: val-09.04
KV: row-09/colfam1:col-05/1301507323202/Put/vlen=9, Value: val-09.05
KV: row-09/colfam1:col-06/1301507323203/Put/vlen=9, Value: val-09.06
KV: row-09/colfam1:col-07/1301507323204/Put/vlen=9, Value: val-09.07
KV: row-09/colfam1:col-08/1301507323205/Put/vlen=9, Value: val-09.08
KV: row-09/colfam1:col-09/1301507323206/Put/vlen=9, Value: val-09.09
```

As expected, the entire row that has a column with the value matching one of the references is included in the result.

Filters Summary

Table 4-5 summarizes some of the features and compatibilities related to the provided filter implementations. The ✓ symbol means the feature is available, while ✗ indicates it is missing.

Table 4-5. Summary of filter features and compatibilities between them

Filter	Batch[a]	Skip[b]	While-Match[c]	List[d]	Early Out[e]	Gets[f]	Scans[g]
RowFilter	✓	✓	✓	✓	✓	✗	✓
FamilyFilter	✓	✓	✓	✓	✗	✓	✓
QualifierFilter	✓	✓	✓	✓	✗	✓	✓
ValueFilter	✓	✓	✓	✓	✗	✓	✓
DependentColumnFilter	✗	✓	✓	✓	✗	✓	✓
SingleColumnValueFilter	✓	✓	✓	✓	✗	✗	✓
SingleColumnValueExcludeFilter	✓	✓	✓	✓	✗	✗	✓
PrefixFilter	✓	✗	✓	✓	✓	✗	✓
PageFilter	✓	✗	✓	✓	✓	✗	✓
KeyOnlyFilter	✓	✓	✓	✓	✗	✓	✓
FirstKeyOnlyFilter	✓	✓	✓	✓	✗	✓	✓
InclusiveStopFilter	✓	✗	✓	✓	✓	✗	✓
TimestampsFilter	✓	✓	✓	✓	✗	✓	✓
ColumnCountGetFilter	✓	✓	✓	✓	✗	✓	✗
ColumnPaginationFilter	✓	✓	✓	✓	✗	✓	✓
ColumnPrefixFilter	✓	✓	✓	✓	✗	✓	✓
RandomRowFilter	✓	✓	✓	✓	✗	✗	✓
SkipFilter	✓	✓/✗[h]	✓/✗[h]	✓	✗	✗	✓
WhileMatchFilter	✓	✓/✗[h]	✓/✗[h]	✓	✓	✗	✓
FilterList	✓/✗[h]	✓/✗[h]	✓/✗[h]	✓	✓/✗[h]	✓	✓

[a] Filter supports Scan.setBatch(), i.e., the scanner batch mode.

[b] Filter can be used with the decorating SkipFilter class.

[c] Filter can be used with the decorating WhileMatchFilter class.

[d] Filter can be used with the combining FilterList class.

[e] Filter has optimizations to stop a scan early, once there are no more matching rows ahead.

[f] Filter can be usefully applied to Get instances.

[g] Filter can be usefully applied to Scan instances.

[h] Depends on the included filters.

Counters

In addition to the functionality we already discussed, HBase offers another advanced feature: *counters*. Many applications that collect statistics—such as clicks or views in online advertising—were used to collect the data in logfiles that would subsequently be analyzed. Using counters offers the potential of switching to live accounting, foregoing the delayed batch processing step completely.

Introduction to Counters

In addition to the check-and-modify operations you saw earlier, HBase also has a mechanism to treat columns as counters. Otherwise, you would have to lock a row, read the value, increment it, write it back, and eventually unlock the row for other writers to be able to access it subsequently. This can cause a lot of contention, and in the event of a client process, crashing it could leave the row locked until the lease recovery kicks in—which could be disastrous in a heavily loaded system.

The client API provides specialized methods to do the *read-and-modify* operation atomically in a single client-side call. Earlier versions of HBase only had calls that would involve an RPC for every counter update, while newer versions started to add the same mechanisms used by the *CRUD* operations—as explained in "CRUD Operations" on page 76—which can bundle multiple counter updates in a single RPC.

 While you can update multiple counters, you are still limited to single rows. Updating counters in multiple rows would require separate API—and therefore RPC—calls. The batch() calls currently do not support the Increment instance, though this should change in the near future.

Before we discuss each type separately, you need to have a few more details regarding how counters work on the column level. Here is an example using the shell that creates a table, increments a counter twice, and then queries the current value:

```
hbase(main):001:0> create 'counters', 'daily', 'weekly', 'monthly'
0 row(s) in 1.1930 seconds

hbase(main):002:0> incr 'counters', '20110101', 'daily:hits', 1
COUNTER VALUE = 1

hbase(main):003:0> incr 'counters', '20110101', 'daily:hits', 1
COUNTER VALUE = 2

hbase(main):04:0> get_counter 'counters', '20110101', 'daily:hits'
COUNTER VALUE = 2
```

Every call to incr returns the new value of the counter. The final check using get_coun ter shows the current value as expected.

The format of the shell's incr command is as follows:

```
incr '<table>', '<row>', '<column>', [<increment-value>]
```

Initializing Counters

You should *not* initialize counters, as they are automatically assumed to be zero when you first use a new counter, that is, a column qualifier that does not yet exist. The first increment call to a new counter will return 1—or the increment value, if you have specified one—as its result.

You can read and write to a counter directly, but you must use

```
Bytes.toLong()
```

to decode the value and

```
Bytes.toBytes(long)
```

for the encoding of the stored value. The latter, in particular, can be tricky, as you need to make sure you are using a **long** number when using the **toBytes()** method. You might want to consider typecasting the variable or number you are using to a **long** explicitly, like so:

```
byte[] b1 = Bytes.toBytes(1L)
byte[] b2 = Bytes.toBytes((long) var)
```

If you were to try to *erroneously* initialize a counter using the **put** method in the HBase Shell, you might be tempted to do this:

```
hbase(main):001:0> put 'counters', '20110101', 'daily:clicks', '1'
0 row(s) in 0.0540 seconds
```

But when you are going to use the increment method, you would get this result instead:

```
hbase(main):013:0> incr 'counters', '20110101', 'daily:clicks', 1
COUNTER VALUE = 3530822107858468865
```

That is not the expected value of 2! This is caused by the **put** call storing the counter in the wrong format: the value is the character 1, a single **byte**, not the **byte** array representation of a Java **long** value—which is composed of eight **bytes**.

As a side note: the single **byte** the shell did store is interpreted as a **byte** array, with the highest byte set to **49**—which is the ASCII code for the character 1 that the Ruby-based shell received from your input. Incrementing this value in the lowest **byte** and converting it to **long** gives the very large—and unexpected—number, shown as the COUNTER VALUE in the preceding code:

```
hbase(main):001:0> include_class org.apache.hadoop.hbase.util.Bytes
=> Java::OrgApacheHadoopHbaseUtil::Bytes
hbase(main):002:0> Bytes::toLong([49,0,0,0,0,0,0,1].to_java :byte)
=> 3530822107858468865
```

You can also access the counter with a get call, giving you this result:

```
hbase(main):005:0> get 'counters', '20110101'
COLUMN         CELL
 daily:hits  timestamp=1301570823471, value=\x00\x00\x00\x00\x00\x00\x00\x02
1 row(s) in 0.0600 seconds
```

This is obviously not very readable, but it shows that a counter is simply a column, like any other. You can also specify a larger increment value:

```
hbase(main):006:0> incr 'counters',
'20110101', 'daily:hits', 20
COUNTER VALUE = 22

hbase(main):007:0> get 'counters', '20110101'
COLUMN         CELL
 daily:hits  timestamp=1301574412848, value=\x00\x00\x00\x00\x00\x00\x00\x16
1 row(s) in 0.0400 seconds

hbase(main):008:0> get_counter 'counters',
'20110101', 'daily:hits'
COUNTER VALUE = 22
```

Accessing the counter directly gives you the byte array representation, with the shell printing the separate bytes as hexadecimal values. Using the get_counter once again shows the current value in a more human-readable format, and confirms that variable increments are possible and work as expected.

Finally, you can use the increment value of the incr call to not only increase the counter, but also retrieve the current value, and decrease it as well. In fact, you can omit it completely and the default of 1 is assumed:

```
hbase(main):004:0> incr 'counters', '20110101',
'daily:hits'
COUNTER VALUE = 3

hbase(main):005:0> incr 'counters', '20110101', 'daily:hits'
COUNTER VALUE = 4

hbase(main):006:0> incr 'counters', '20110101', 'daily:hits', 0
COUNTER VALUE = 4

hbase(main):007:0> incr 'counters', '20110101', 'daily:hits', -1
COUNTER VALUE = 3

hbase(main):008:0> incr 'counters', '20110101', 'daily:hits', -1
COUNTER VALUE = 2
```

Using the increment value—the last parameter of the incr command—you can achieve the behavior shown in Table 4-6.

Table 4-6. The increment value and its effect on counter increments

Value	Effect
greater than zero	*Increase* the counter by the given value.
zero	Retrieve the *current value* of the counter. Same as using the get_counter shell command.
less than zero	*Decrease* the counter by the given value.

Obviously, using the shell's incr command only allows you to increase a single counter. You can do the same using the client API, described next.

Single Counters

The first type of increment call is for single counters only: you need to specify the exact column you want to use. The methods, provided by HTable, are as such:

```
long incrementColumnValue(byte[] row, byte[] family, byte[] qualifier,
    long amount) throws IOException
long incrementColumnValue(byte[] row, byte[] family, byte[] qualifier,
    long amount, boolean writeToWAL) throws IOException
```

Given the *coordinates* of a column, and the increment account, these methods only differ by the optional writeToWAL parameter—which works the same way as the Put.set WriteToWAL() method.

Omitting writeToWAL uses the default value of true, meaning the write-ahead log is active.

Apart from that, you can use them easily, as shown in Example 4-17.

Example 4-17. Using the single counter increment methods

```
HTable table = new HTable(conf, "counters");

long cnt1 = table.incrementColumnValue(Bytes.toBytes("20110101"), ❶
    Bytes.toBytes("daily"), Bytes.toBytes("hits"), 1);
long cnt2 = table.incrementColumnValue(Bytes.toBytes("20110101"), ❷
    Bytes.toBytes("daily"), Bytes.toBytes("hits"), 1);

long current = table.incrementColumnValue(Bytes.toBytes("20110101"), ❸
    Bytes.toBytes("daily"), Bytes.toBytes("hits"), 0);

long cnt3 = table.incrementColumnValue(Bytes.toBytes("20110101"), ❹
    Bytes.toBytes("daily"), Bytes.toBytes("hits"), -1);
```

❶ Increase the counter by one.

❷ Increase the counter by one a second time.

❸ Get the current value of the counter without increasing it.

❹ Decrease the counter by one.

The output on the console is:

```
cnt1: 1, cnt2: 2, current: 2, cnt3: 1
```

Just as with the shell commands used earlier, the API calls have the same effect: they increment the counter when using a positive increment value, retrieve the current value when using zero for the increment, and eventually decrease the counter by using a negative increment value.

Multiple Counters

Another way to increment counters is provided by the `increment()` call of `HTable`. It works similarly to the CRUD-type operations discussed earlier, using the following method to do the increment:

```
Result increment(Increment increment) throws IOException
```

You must create an instance of the `Increment` class and fill it with the appropriate details—for example, the counter coordinates. The constructors provided by this class are:

```
Increment() {}
Increment(byte[] row)
Increment(byte[] row, RowLock rowLock)
```

You must provide a row key when instantiating an `Increment`, which sets the row containing all the counters that the subsequent call to `increment()` should modify.

The optional parameter `rowLock` specifies a custom row lock instance, allowing you to run the entire operation under your exclusive control—for example, when you want to modify the same row a few times while protecting it against updates from other writers.

While you can guard the increment operation against other writers, you currently cannot do this for readers. In fact, there is *no* atomicity guarantee made for readers.

Since readers are not taking out locks on rows that are incremented, it may happen that they have access to some counters—within one row—that are already updated, and some that are not! This applies to scan and get operations equally.

Once you have decided which row to update and created the `Increment` instance, you need to add the actual counters—meaning columns—you want to increment, using this method:

```
Increment addColumn(byte[] family, byte[] qualifier, long amount)
```

The difference here, as compared to the Put methods, is that there is no option to specify a version—or timestamp—when dealing with increments: versions are handled implicitly. Furthermore, there is no `addFamily()` equivalent, because counters are specific columns, and they need to be specified as such. It therefore makes no sense to add a column family alone.

A special feature of the Increment class is the ability to take an optional time range:

```
Increment setTimeRange(long minStamp, long maxStamp)
    throws IOException
```

Setting a time range for a set of counter increments seems odd in light of the fact that versions are handled implicitly. The time range is actually passed on to the servers to restrict the internal get operation from retrieving the current counter values. You can use it to *expire* counters, for example, to partition them by time: when you set the time range to be restrictive enough, you can mask out older counters from the internal get, making them look like they are nonexistent. An increment would assume they are unset and start at 1 again.

The Increment class provides additional methods, which are summarized in Table 4-7.

Table 4-7. Quick overview of additional methods provided by the Increment class

Method	Description
getRow()	Returns the row key as specified when creating the Increment instance.
getRowLock()	Returns the row RowLock instance for the current Increment instance.
getLockId()	Returns the optional lock ID handed into the constructor using the rowLock parameter. Will be -1L if not set.
setWriteToWAL()	Allows you to disable the default functionality of writing the data to the server-side write-ahead log.
getWriteToWAL()	Indicates if the data will be written to the write-ahead log.
getTimeRange()	Retrieves the associated time range of the Increment instance—as assigned using the setTimeStamp() method.
numFamilies()	Convenience method to retrieve the size of the family map, containing all column families of the added columns.
numColumns()	Returns the number of columns that will be incremented.
hasFamilies()	Another helper to check if a family—or column—has been added to the current instance of the Increment class.
familySet()/ getFamilyMap()	Give you access to the specific columns, as added by the addColumn() call. The family map is a map where the key is the family name and the value a list of added column qualifiers for this particular family. The familySet() returns the Set of all stored families, i.e., a set containing only the family names.

Similar to the shell example shown earlier, Example 4-18 uses various increment values to increment, retrieve, and decrement the given counters.

Example 4-18. Incrementing multiple counters in one row

```
Increment increment1 = new Increment(Bytes.toBytes("20110101"));

increment1.addColumn(Bytes.toBytes("daily"), Bytes.toBytes("clicks"), 1);
```

```
increment1.addColumn(Bytes.toBytes("daily"), Bytes.toBytes("hits"), 1);  ❶
increment1.addColumn(Bytes.toBytes("weekly"), Bytes.toBytes("clicks"), 10);
increment1.addColumn(Bytes.toBytes("weekly"), Bytes.toBytes("hits"), 10);

Result result1 = table.increment(increment1);  ❷

for (KeyValue kv : result1.raw()) {
  System.out.println("KV: " + kv +
    " Value: " + Bytes.toLong(kv.getValue()));  ❸
}

Increment increment2 = new Increment(Bytes.toBytes("20110101"));

increment2.addColumn(Bytes.toBytes("daily"), Bytes.toBytes("clicks"), 5);
increment2.addColumn(Bytes.toBytes("daily"), Bytes.toBytes("hits"), 1);  ❹
increment2.addColumn(Bytes.toBytes("weekly"), Bytes.toBytes("clicks"), 0);
increment2.addColumn(Bytes.toBytes("weekly"), Bytes.toBytes("hits"), -5);

Result result2 = table.increment(increment2);

for (KeyValue kv : result2.raw()) {
  System.out.println("KV: " + kv +
    " Value: " + Bytes.toLong(kv.getValue()));
}
```

❶ Increment the counters with various values.

❷ Call the actual increment method with the earlier counter updates and receive the results.

❸ Print the KeyValue and returned the counter value.

❹ Use positive, negative, and zero increment values to achieve the desired counter changes.

When you run the example, the following is output on the console:

```
KV: 20110101/daily:clicks/1301948275827/Put/vlen=8 Value: 1
KV: 20110101/daily:hits/1301948275827/Put/vlen=8 Value: 1
KV: 20110101/weekly:clicks/1301948275827/Put/vlen=8 Value: 10
KV: 20110101/weekly:hits/1301948275827/Put/vlen=8 Value: 10

KV: 20110101/daily:clicks/1301948275829/Put/vlen=8 Value: 6
KV: 20110101/daily:hits/1301948275829/Put/vlen=8 Value: 2
KV: 20110101/weekly:clicks/1301948275829/Put/vlen=8 Value: 10
KV: 20110101/weekly:hits/1301948275829/Put/vlen=8 Value: 5
```

When you compare the two sets of increment results, you will notice that this works as expected.

Coprocessors

Earlier we discussed how you can use filters to reduce the amount of data being sent over the network from the servers to the client. With the coprocessor feature in HBase, you can even move part of the computation to where the data lives.

Introduction to Coprocessors

Using the client API, combined with specific selector mechanisms, such as filters, or column family scoping, it is possible to limit what data is transferred to the client. It would be good, though, to take this further and, for example, perform certain operations directly on the server side while only returning a small result set. Think of this as a small *MapReduce* framework that distributes work across the entire cluster.

A coprocessor enables you to run arbitrary code directly on each region server. More precisely, it executes the code on a per-region basis, giving you *trigger*-like functionality—similar to stored procedures in the RDBMS world. From the client side, you do not have to take specific actions, as the framework handles the distributed nature transparently.

There is a set of implicit events that you can use to hook into, performing auxiliary tasks. If this is not enough, you can also extend the RPC protocol to introduce your own set of calls, which are invoked from your client and executed on the server on your behalf.

Just as with the custom filters (see "Custom Filters" on page 160), you need to create special Java classes that implement specific interfaces. Once they are compiled, you make these classes available to the servers in the form of a JAR file. The region server process can instantiate these classes and execute them in the correct environment. In contrast to the filters, though, coprocessors can be loaded dynamically as well. This allows you to extend the functionality of a running HBase cluster.

Use cases for coprocessors are, for instance, using hooks into row mutation operations to maintain secondary indexes, or implementing some kind of referential integrity. Filters could be enhanced to become stateful, and therefore make decisions across row boundaries. Aggregate functions, such as *sum()*, or *avg()*, known from RDBMSes and SQL, could be moved to the servers to scan the data locally and only returning the single number result across the network.

 Another good use case for coprocessors is access control. The *authentication, authorization, and auditing* features added in HBase version 0.92 are based on coprocessors. They are loaded at system startup and use the provided trigger-like hooks to check if a user is authenticated, and authorized to access specific values stored in tables.

The framework already provides classes, based on the coprocessor framework, which you can use to extend from when implementing your own functionality. They fall into two main groups: *observer* and *endpoint*. Here is a brief overview of their purpose:

Observer

This type of coprocessor is comparable to *triggers*: callback functions (also referred to here as *hooks*) are executed when certain events occur. This includes user-generated, but also server-internal, automated events.

The interfaces provided by the coprocessor framework are:

RegionObserver

You can handle data manipulation events with this kind of observer. They are closely bound to the regions of a table.

MasterObserver

This can be used to react to administrative or DDL-type operations. These are cluster-wide events.

WALObserver

This provides hooks into the write-ahead log processing.

Observers provide you with well-defined event callbacks, for every operation a cluster server may handle.

Endpoint

Next to event handling there is also a need to add custom operations to a cluster. User code can be deployed to the servers hosting the data to, for example, perform server-local computations.

Endpoints are dynamic extensions to the RPC protocol, adding callable remote procedures. Think of them as stored procedures, as known from RDBMSes. They may be combined with observer implementations to directly interact with the server-side state.

All of these interfaces are based on the Coprocessor interface to gain common features, but then implement their own specific functionality.

Finally, coprocessors can be chained, very similar to what the Java Servlet API does with request filters. The following section discusses the various types available in the coprocessor framework.

The Coprocessor Class

All coprocessor classes *must* be based on this interface. It defines the basic contract of a coprocessor and facilitates the management by the framework itself. The interface provides two enumerations, which are used throughout the framework: Priority and State. Table 4-8 explains the priority values.

Table 4-8. Priorities as defined by the Coprocessor.Priority enumeration

Value	Description
SYSTEM	Highest priority, defines coprocessors that are executed first
USER	Defines all other coprocessors, which are executed subsequently

The priority of a coprocessor defines in what order the coprocessors are executed: *system*-level instances are called *before* the *user*-level coprocessors are executed.

 Within each priority level, there is also the notion of a *sequence number*, which keeps track of the order in which the coprocessors were loaded. The number starts with zero, and is increased by one thereafter.

The number itself is not very helpful, but you can rely on the framework to order the coprocessors—in each priority group—ascending by sequence number. This defines their execution order.

Coprocessors are managed by the framework in their own life cycle. To that effect, the Coprocessor interface offers two calls:

```
void start(CoprocessorEnvironment env) throws IOException;
void stop(CoprocessorEnvironment env) throws IOException;
```

These two methods are called when the coprocessor class is started, and eventually when it is decommissioned. The provided CoprocessorEnvironment instance is used to retain the state across the lifespan of the coprocessor instance. A coprocessor instance is always contained in a provided environment. Table 4-9 lists the methods available from it.

Table 4-9. Methods provided by the CoprocessorEnvironment class

Method	Description
String getHBaseVersion()	Returns the HBase version identification string.
int getVersion()	Returns the version of the Coprocessor interface.
Coprocessor getInstance()	Returns the loaded coprocessor instance.
Coprocessor.Priority getPriority()	Provides the priority level of the coprocessor.
int getLoadSequence()	The sequence number of the coprocessor. This is set when the instance is loaded and reflects the execution order.
HTableInterface getTable(byte[] tableName)	Returns an HTable instance for the given table name. This allows the coprocessor to access the actual table data.

Coprocessors should only deal with what they have been given by their environment. There is a good reason for that, mainly to guarantee that there is no back door for malicious code to harm your data.

Coprocessor implementations should be using the getTable() method to access tables. Note that this class adds certain safety measures to the default HTable class. For example, coprocessors are *not* allowed to lock a row.

While there is currently nothing that can stop you from creating your own HTable instances inside your coprocessor code, this is likely to be checked against in the future and possibly denied.

The start() and stop() methods of the Coprocessor interface are invoked implicitly by the framework as the instance is going through its life cycle. Each step in the process has a well-known state. Table 4-10 lists the life-cycle state values as provided by the coprocessor interface.

Table 4-10. The states as defined by the Coprocessor.State enumeration

Value	Description
UNINSTALLED	The coprocessor is in its initial state. It has no environment yet, nor is it initialized.
INSTALLED	The instance is installed into its environment.
STARTING	This state indicates that the coprocessor is about to be started, i.e., its start() method is about to be invoked.
ACTIVE	Once the start() call returns, the state is set to active.
STOPPING	The state set just before the stop() method is called.
STOPPED	Once stop() returns control to the framework, the state of the coprocessor is set to stopped.

The final piece of the puzzle is the CoprocessorHost class that maintains all the coprocessor instances and their dedicated environments. There are specific subclasses, depending on where the host is used, in other words, on the master, region server, and so on.

The trinity of Coprocessor, CoprocessorEnvironment, and CoprocessorHost forms the basis for the classes that implement the advanced functionality of HBase, depending on where they are used. They provide the life-cycle support for the coprocessors, manage their state, and offer the environment for them to execute as expected. In addition, these classes provide an abstraction layer that developers can use to easily build their own custom implementation.

Figure 4-3 shows how the calls from a client are flowing through the list of coprocessors. Note how the order is the same on the incoming and outgoing sides: first are the system-level ones, and then the user ones in the order they were loaded.

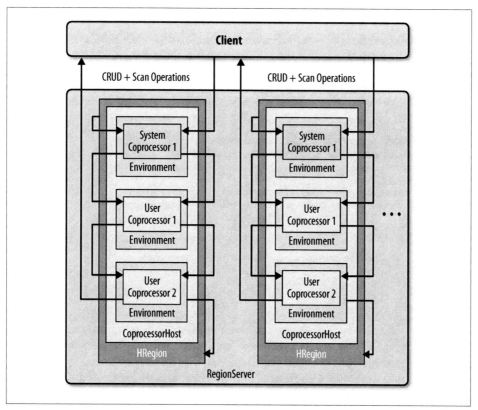

Figure 4-3. Coprocessors executed sequentially, in their environment, and per region

Coprocessor Loading

Coprocessors are loaded in a variety of ways. Before we discuss the actual coprocessor types and how to implement your own, we will talk about how to deploy them so that you can try the provided examples.

You can either configure coprocessors to be loaded in a static way, or load them dynamically while the cluster is running. The static method uses the configuration files and table schemas—and is discussed next. Unfortunately, there is not yet an exposed API to load them dynamically.[‡]

---

‡ Coprocessors are a fairly recent addition to HBase, and are therefore still in flux. Check with the online documentation and issue tracking system to see what is not yet implemented, or planned to be added.

Loading from the configuration

You can configure globally which coprocessors are loaded when HBase starts. This is done by adding one, or more, of the following to the *hbase-site.xml* configuration file:

```
<property>
  <name>hbase.coprocessor.region.classes</name>
  <value>coprocessor.RegionObserverExample, coprocessor.AnotherCoprocessor</value>
</property>
<property>
  <name>hbase.coprocessor.master.classes</name>
  <value>coprocessor.MasterObserverExample</value>
</property>
<property>
  <name>hbase.coprocessor.wal.classes</name>
  <value>coprocessor.WALObserverExample, bar.foo.MyWALObserver</value>
</property>
```

 Replace the example class names with your own ones!

The order of the classes in each configuration property is important, as it defines the execution order. All of these coprocessors are loaded with the *system* priority. You should configure all globally active classes here so that they are executed first and have a chance to take authoritative actions. Security coprocessors are loaded this way, for example.

 The configuration file is the first to be examined as HBase starts. Although you can define additional system-level coprocessors in other places, the ones here are executed first.

Only one of the three possible configuration keys is read by the matching `CoprocessorHost` implementation. For example, the coprocessors defined in `hbase.coprocessor.master.classes` are loaded by the `MasterCoprocessorHost` class.

Table 4-11 shows where each configuration property is used.

Table 4-11. Possible configuration properties and where they are used

Property	Coprocessor host	Server type
hbase.coprocessor.master.classes	MasterCoprocessorHost	Master server
hbase.coprocessor.region.classes	RegionCoprocessorHost	Region server
hbase.coprocessor.wal.classes	WALCoprocessorHost	Region server

The coprocessors defined with hbase.coprocessor.region.classes are loaded as defaults when a region is opened for a table. Note that you *cannot* specify for which table, or region, they are loaded: the default coprocessors are loaded for *every* table and region. You need to keep this in mind when designing your own coprocessors.

Loading from the table descriptor

The other option to define what coprocessors to load is the table descriptor. As this is per table, the coprocessors defined here are *only* loaded for regions of that table—and only by the region servers. In other words, you can only use this approach for region-related coprocessors, not for master or WAL-related ones.

Since they are loaded in the context of a table, they are more targeted compared to the configuration loaded ones, which apply to all tables.

You need to add their definition to the table descriptor using the HTableDescriptor.set Value() method. The key *must* start with COPROCESSOR, and the value has to conform to the following format:

```
<path-to-jar>|<classname>|<priority>
```

Here is an example that defines two coprocessors, one with system-level priority, the other with user-level priority:

```
'COPROCESSOR$1' => \
  'hdfs://localhost:8020/users/leon/test.jar|coprocessor.Test|SYSTEM'
'COPROCESSOR$2' => \
  '/Users/laura/test2.jar|coprocessor.AnotherTest|USER'
```

The path-to-jar can either be a fully specified HDFS location, or any other path supported by the Hadoop FileSystem class. The second coprocessor definition, for example, uses a local path instead.

The classname defines the actual implementation class. While the JAR may contain many coprocessor classes, only one can be specified per table attribute. Use the standard Java package name conventions to specify the class.

The priority must be either SYSTEM or USER. This is case-sensitive and must be specified exactly this way.

> Avoid using extra whitespace characters in the coprocessor definition. The parsing is quite strict, and adding leading, trailing, or spacing characters will render the entire entry invalid.

Using the $<number> postfix for the key enforces the order in which the definitions, and therefore the coprocessors, are loaded. Although only the prefix of COPROCESSOR is checked, using the numbered postfix is the advised way to define them. Example 4-19 shows how this can be done using the administrative API for HBase.

Example 4-19. Region observer checking for special get requests

```
public class LoadWithTableDescriptorExample {

  public static void main(String[] args) throws IOException {
    Configuration conf = HBaseConfiguration.create();

    FileSystem fs = FileSystem.get(conf);
    Path path = new Path(fs.getUri() + Path.SEPARATOR + "test.jar");  ❶

    HTableDescriptor htd = new HTableDescriptor("testtable");  ❷
    htd.addFamily(new HColumnDescriptor("colfam1"));
    htd.setValue("COPROCESSOR$1", path.toString() +
      "|" + RegionObserverExample.class.getCanonicalName() +  ❸
      "|" + Coprocessor.Priority.USER);

    HBaseAdmin admin = new HBaseAdmin(conf);  ❹
    admin.createTable(htd);

    System.out.println(admin.getTableDescriptor(Bytes.toBytes("testtable")));  ❺
  }
}
```

❶ Get the location of the JAR file containing the coprocessor implementation.

❷ Define a table descriptor.

❸ Add the coprocessor definition to the descriptor.

❹ Instantiate an administrative API to the cluster and add the table.

❺ Verify if the definition has been applied as expected.

The final check should show you the following result when running this example against a local, standalone HBase cluster:

```
{NAME => 'testtable', COPROCESSOR$1 => \
  'file:/test.jar|coprocessor.RegionObserverExample|USER', FAMILIES => \
  [{NAME => 'colfam1', BLOOMFILTER => 'NONE', REPLICATION_SCOPE => '0', \
  COMPRESSION => 'NONE', VERSIONS => '3', TTL => '2147483647', BLOCKSIZE \
  => '65536', IN_MEMORY => 'false', BLOCKCACHE => 'true'}]}
```

The coprocessor definition has been successfully applied to the table schema. Once the table is enabled and the regions are opened, the framework will first load the configuration coprocessors and then the ones defined in the table descriptor.

The RegionObserver Class

The first subclass of Coprocessor we will look into is the one used at the region level: the RegionObserver class. You can learn from its name that it belongs to the group of *observer* coprocessors: they have hooks that trigger when a specific region-level operation occurs.

These operations can be divided into two groups as well: region *life-cycle* changes and `client API` calls. We will look into both in that order.

Handling region life-cycle events

While "The Region Life Cycle" on page 348 explains the region life-cycle, Figure 4-4 shows a simplified form.

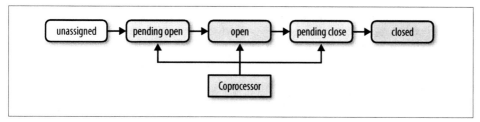

Figure 4-4. The coprocessor reacting to life-cycle state changes of a region

The observers have the opportunity to hook into the *pending open*, *open*, and *pending close* state changes. For each of them there is a set of hooks that are called implicitly by the framework.

> For the sake of brevity, all parameters and exceptions are omitted when referring to the observer calls. Read the online documentation for the full specification.§ Note, though, that all calls have a special first parameter:
>
>   ObserverContext<RegionCoprocessorEnvironment> c
>
> This special `CoprocessorEnvironment` wrapper gives you additional control over what should happen after the hook execution. See "The RegionCoprocessorEnvironment class" on page 185 and "The ObserverContext class" on page 186 for the details.

State: pending open. A region is in this state when it is about to be opened. Observing coprocessors can either *piggyback* or *fail* this process. To do so, the following calls are available:

    void preOpen(...) / void postOpen(...)

These methods are called just before the region is opened, and just after it was opened. Your coprocessor implementation can use them, for instance, to indicate to the framework—in the preOpen() call—that it should abort the opening process. Or hook into the postOpen() call to trigger a cache warm up, and so on.

---

§ See *http://hbase.apache.org/apidocs/org/apache/hadoop/hbase/coprocessor/RegionObserver.html*.

After the *pending open*, but just before the *open* state, the region server may have to apply records from the write-ahead log (WAL). This, in turn, invokes the following methods of the observer:

```
void preWALRestore(...) / void postWALRestore(...)
```

Hooking into these calls gives you fine-grained control over what mutation is applied during the log replay process. You get access to the edit record, which you can use to inspect what is being applied.

State: open. A region is considered open when it is deployed to a region server and fully operational. At this point, all the operations discussed throughout the book can take place; for example, the region's in-memory store could be flushed to disk, or the region could be split when it has grown too large. The possible hooks are:

```
void preFlush(...) / void postFlush(...)
void preCompact(...) / void postCompact(...)
void preSplit(...) / void postSplit(...)
```

This should be quite intuitive by now: the *pre* calls are executed *before*, while the *post* calls are executed *after* the respective operation. For example, using the pre Split() hook, you could effectively disable the built-in region splitting process and perform these operations manually.

State: pending close. The last group of hooks for the observers is for regions that go into the pending close state. This occurs when the region transitions from *open* to *closed*. Just before, and after, the region is closed the following hooks are executed:

```
void preClose(..., boolean abortRequested) /
void postClose(..., boolean abortRequested)
```

The abortRequested parameter indicates why a region was closed. Usually regions are closed during normal operation, when, for example, the region is moved to a different region server for load-balancing reasons. But there also is the possibility for a region server to have gone rogue and be *aborted* to avoid any side effects. When this happens, all hosted regions are also aborted, and you can see from the given parameter if that was the case.

Handling client API events

As opposed to the life-cycle events, all client API calls are explicitly sent from a client application to the region server. You have the opportunity to hook into these calls just before they are applied, and just thereafter. Here is the list of the available calls:

void preGet(...) / void postGet(...)
    Called before and after a client makes an HTable.get() request

void prePut(...) / void postPut(...)
    Called before and after a client makes an HTable.put() request

void preDelete(...) / void postDelete(...)
    Called before and after a client makes an HTable.delete() request

```
boolean preCheckAndPut(...) / boolean postCheckAndPut(...)
```
Called before and after a client invokes an `HTable.checkAndPut()` call

```
boolean preCheckAndDelete(...) / boolean postCheckAndDelete(...)
```
Called before and after a client invokes an `HTable.checkAndDelete()` call

```
void preGetClosestRowBefore(...) / void postGetClosestRowBefore(...)
```
Called before and after a client invokes an `HTable.getClosestRowBefore()` call

```
boolean preExists(...) / boolean postExists(...)
```
Called before and after a client invokes an `HTable.exists()` call

```
long preIncrementColumnValue(...) / long postIncrementColumnValue(...)
```
Called before and after a client invokes an `HTable.incrementColumnValue()` call

```
void preIncrement(...) / void postIncrement(...)
```
Called before and after a client invokes an `HTable.increment()` call

```
InternalScanner preScannerOpen(...) / InternalScanner postScannerOpen(...)
```
Called before and after a client invokes an `HTable.getScanner()` call

```
boolean preScannerNext(...) / boolean postScannerNext(...)
```
Called before and after a client invokes a `ResultScanner.next()` call

```
void preScannerClose(...) / void postScannerClose(...)
```
Called before and after a client invokes a `ResultScanner.close()` call

The RegionCoprocessorEnvironment class

The environment instances provided to a coprocessor that is implementing the `RegionObserver` interface are based on the `RegionCoprocessorEnvironment` class—which in turn is implementing the `CoprocessorEnvironment` interface. The latter was discussed in "The Coprocessor Class" on page 176.

On top of the provided methods, the more specific, region-oriented subclass is adding the methods described in Table 4-12.

Table 4-12. Methods provided by the RegionCoprocessorEnvironment class, in addition to the inherited one

Method	Description
HRegion getRegion()	Returns a reference to the region the current observer is associated with
RegionServerServices getRegionServerServices()	Provides access to the shared RegionServerServices instance

The `getRegion()` call can be used to get a reference to the hosting `HRegion` instance, and to invoke calls this class provides. In addition, your code can access the shared region server services instance, which is explained in Table 4-13.

Table 4-13. Methods provided by the RegionServerServices class

Method	Description
boolean isStopping()	Returns true when the region server is stopping.
HLog getWAL()	Provides access to the write-ahead log instance.
CompactionRequestor getCompactionRequester()	Provides access to the shared CompactionRequestor instance. This can be used to initiate compactions from within the coprocessor.
FlushRequester getFlushRequester()	Provides access to the shared FlushRequester instance. This can be used to initiate memstore flushes.
RegionServerAccounting getRegionServerAccounting()	Provides access to the shared RegionServerAccounting instance. It allows you to check on what the server currently has allocated—for example, the global memstore size.
postOpenDeployTasks(HRegion r, CatalogTracker ct, final boolean daughter)	An internal call, invoked inside the region server.
HBaseRpcMetrics getRpcMetrics()	Provides access to the shared HBaseRpcMetrics instance. It has details on the RPC statistics for the current server.

I will not be discussing all the details on the provided functionality, and instead refer you to the Java API documentation.‖

The ObserverContext class

For the callbacks provided by the RegionObserver class, there is a special context handed in as the first parameter to all calls: the ObserverContext class. It provides access to the current environment, but also adds the crucial ability to indicate to the coprocessor framework what it should do after a callback is completed.

The context instance is the same for all coprocessors in the execution chain, but with the environment swapped out for each coprocessor.

Table 4-14 lists the methods as provided by the context class.

‖ The Java HBase classes are documented online at *http://hbase.apache.org/apidocs/*.

Table 4-14. Methods provided by the ObserverContext class

Method	Description
`E getEnvironment()`	Returns the reference to the current coprocessor environment.
`void bypass()`	When your code invokes this method, the framework is going to use your provided value, as opposed to what usually is returned.
`void complete()`	Indicates to the framework that any further processing can be skipped, skipping the remaining coprocessors in the execution chain. It implies that this coprocessor's response is definitive.
`boolean shouldBypass()`	Used internally by the framework to check on the flag.
`boolean shouldComplete()`	Used internally by the framework to check on the flag.
`void prepare(E env)`	Prepares the context with the specified environment. This is used internally only. It is used by the static `createAndPrepare()` method.
`static <T extends Coprocessor Environment> ObserverCon text<T> createAndPrepare( T env, ObserverContext<T> con text)`	Static function to initialize a context. When the provided `context` is `null`, it will create a new instance.

The important context functions are `bypass()` and `complete()`. These functions give your coprocessor implementation the option to control the subsequent behavior of the framework. The `complete()` call influences the execution chain of the coprocessors, while the `bypass()` call stops any further default processing on the server. Use it with the earlier example of avoiding automated region splits like so:

```
@Override
public void preSplit(ObserverContext<RegionCoprocessorEnvironment> e) {
    e.bypass();
}
```

Instead of having to implement your own `RegionObserver`, based on the interface, you can use the following base class to only implement what is needed.

The BaseRegionObserver class

This class can be used as the basis for all your observer-type coprocessors. It has placeholders for all methods required by the `RegionObserver` interface. They are all left blank, so by default nothing is done when extending this class. You must override all the callbacks that you are interested in to add the required functionality.

Example 4-20 is an observer that handles specific row key requests.

Example 4-20. Region observer checking for special get requests

```
public class RegionObserverExample extends BaseRegionObserver {
  public static final byte[] FIXED_ROW = Bytes.toBytes("@@@GETTIME@@@");

  @Override
  public void preGet(final ObserverContext<RegionCoprocessorEnvironment> e,
      final Get get, final List<KeyValue> results) throws IOException {
    if (Bytes.equals(get.getRow(), FIXED_ROW)) { ❶
      KeyValue kv = new KeyValue(get.getRow(), FIXED_ROW, FIXED_ROW,
        Bytes.toBytes(System.currentTimeMillis()));
      results.add(kv); ❷
    }
  }
}
```

❶ Check if the request row key matches a well-known one.

❷ Create a special `KeyValue` instance containing just the current time on the server.

 The following was added to the *hbase-site.xml* file to enable the coprocessor:

```
<property>
  <name>hbase.coprocessor.region.classes</name>
  <value>coprocessor.RegionObserverExample</value>
</property>
```

The class is available to the region server's Java Runtime Environment because we have already added the JAR of the compiled repository to the `HBASE_CLASSPATH` variable in *hbase-env.sh*—see "Deployment of Custom Filters" on page 165 for reference.

Do not forget to *restart* HBase, though, to make the changes to the static configuration files active.

The row key `@@@GETTIME@@@` is handled by the observer's `preGet()` hook, inserting the current time of the server. Using the HBase Shell—after deploying the code to servers— you can see this in action:

```
hbase(main):001:0> get 'testtable', '@@@GETTIME@@@'
COLUMN                        CELL
 @@@GETTIME@@@:@@@GETTIME@@@  timestamp=9223372036854775807, \
                              value=\x00\x00\x01/s@3\xD8

1 row(s) in 0.0410 seconds

hbase(main):002:0> Time.at(Bytes.toLong( \
  "\x00\x00\x01/s@3\xD8".to_java_bytes) / 1000)
=> Wed Apr 20 16:11:18 +0200 2011
```

This requires an existing table, because trying to issue a get call to a nonexistent table will raise an error, before the actual get operation is executed. Also, the example does not set the *bypass* flag, in which case something like the following could happen:

```
hbase(main):003:0> create 'testtable2', 'colfam1'
0 row(s) in 1.3070 seconds

hbase(main):004:0> put 'testtable2', '@@@GETTIME@@@', \
  'colfam1:qual1', 'Hello there!'
0 row(s) in 0.1360 seconds

hbase(main):005:0> get 'testtable2', '@@@GETTIME@@@'
COLUMN                            CELL
  @@@GETTIME@@@:@@@GETTIME@@@       timestamp=9223372036854775807, \
                                    value=\x00\x00\x01/sJ\xBC\xEC
  colfam1:qual1                     timestamp=1303309353184, value=Hello there!
2 row(s) in 0.0450 seconds
```

A new table is created and a row with the special row key is inserted. Subsequently, the row is retrieved. You can see how the artificial column is mixed with the actual one stored earlier. To avoid this issue, Example 4-21 adds the necessary e.bypass() call.

Example 4-21. Region observer checking for special get requests and bypassing further processing

```
if (Bytes.equals(get.getRow(), FIXED_ROW)) {
  KeyValue kv = new KeyValue(get.getRow(), FIXED_ROW, FIXED_ROW,
    Bytes.toBytes(System.currentTimeMillis()));
  results.add(kv);
  e.bypass(); ❶
}
```

❶ Once the special KeyValue is inserted, all further processing is skipped.

> You need to adjust the *hbase-site.xml* file to point to the new example:
>
> ```
> <property>
>   <name>hbase.coprocessor.region.classes</name>
>   <value>coprocessor.RegionObserverWithBypassExample</value>
> </property>
> ```
>
> Just as before, please restart HBase after making these adjustments.

As expected, and using the shell once more, the result is now different:

```
hbase(main):069:0> get 'testtable2', '@@@GETTIME@@@'
COLUMN                            CELL
  @@@GETTIME@@@:@@@GETTIME@@@       timestamp=9223372036854775807, \
                                    value=\x00\x00\x01/s]\x1D4
1 row(s) in 0.0470 seconds
```

Only the artificial column is returned, and since the default get operation is bypassed, it is the only column retrieved. Also note how the timestamp of this column is 9223372036854775807—which is Long.MAX_VALUE on purpose. Since the example creates the KeyValue instance without specifying a timestamp, it is set to HConstants.LATEST_TIMESTAMP by default, and that is, in turn, set to Long.MAX_VALUE. You can amend the example by adding a timestamp and see how that would be printed when using the shell (an exercise left to you).

The MasterObserver Class

The second subclass of `Coprocessor` discussed handles all possible callbacks the master server may initiate. The operations and API calls are explained in Chapter 5, though they can be classified as data-manipulation operations, similar to DDL used in relational database systems. For that reason, the `MasterObserver` class provides the following hooks:

`void preCreateTable(...) / void postCreateTable(...)`
> Called before and after a table is created.

`void preDeleteTable(...) / void postDeleteTable(...)`
> Called before and after a table is deleted.

`void preModifyTable(...) / void postModifyTable(...)`
> Called before and after a table is altered.

`void preAddColumn(...) / void postAddColumn(...)`
> Called before and after a column is added to a table.

`void preModifyColumn(...) / void postModifyColumn(...)`
> Called before and after a column is altered.

`void preDeleteColumn(...) / void postDeleteColumn(...)`
> Called before and after a column is deleted from a table.

`void preEnableTable(...) / void postEnableTable(...)`
> Called before and after a table is enabled.

`void preDisableTable(...) / void postDisableTable(...)`
> Called before and after a table is disabled.

`void preMove(...) / void postMove(...)`
> Called before and after a region is moved.

`void preAssign(...) / void postAssign(...)`
> Called before and after a region is assigned.

`void preUnassign(...) / void postUnassign(...)`
> Called before and after a region is unassigned.

`void preBalance(...) / void postBalance(...)`
> Called before and after the regions are balanced.

`boolean preBalanceSwitch(...) / void postBalanceSwitch(...)`
> Called before and after the flag for the balancer is changed.

`void preShutdown(...)`
> Called before the cluster shutdown is initiated. There is no *post* hook, because after the shutdown, there is no longer a cluster to invoke the callback.

`void preStopMaster(...)`
> Called before the master process is stopped. There is no *post* hook, because after the master has stopped, there is no longer a process to invoke the callback.

The MasterCoprocessorEnvironment class

Similar to how the `RegionCoprocessorEnvironment` is enclosing a single `RegionObserver` coprocessor, the `MasterCoprocessorEnvironment` is wrapping `MasterOb server` instances. It also implements the `CoprocessorEnvironment` interface, thus giving you, for instance, access to the `getTable()` call to access data from within your own implementation.

On top of the provided methods, the more specific, master-oriented subclass adds the one method described in Table 4-15.

Table 4-15. The method provided by the MasterCoprocessorEnvironment class, in addition to the inherited one

Method	Description
`MasterServices getMasterServices()`	Provides access to the shared `MasterServices` instance

Your code can access the shared master services instance, the methods of which are listed and described in Table 4-16.

Table 4-16. Methods provided by the MasterServices class

Method	Description
`AssignmentManager getAssignmentManager()`	Gives you access to the assignment manager instance. It is responsible for all region assignment operations, such as assign, unassign, balance, and so on.
`MasterFileSystem getMasterFileSystem()`	Provides you with an abstraction layer for all filesystem-related operations the master is involved in—for example, creating directories for table files and logfiles.
`ServerManager getServerManager()`	Returns the server manager instance. With it you have access to the list of servers, live or considered dead, and more.
`ExecutorService getExecutorService()`	Used by the master to schedule system-wide events.
`void checkTableModifiable(byte[] tableName)`	Convenient to check if a table exists and is offline so that it can be altered.

I will not be discussing all the details on the provided functionality, and instead refer you to the Java API documentation once more.[#]

[#]The Java HBase classes are documented online at *http://hbase.apache.org/apidocs/*.

The BaseMasterObserver class

Either you can base your efforts to implement a `MasterObserver` on the interface directly, or you can extend the `BaseMasterObserver` class instead. It implements the interface while leaving all callback functions empty. If you were to use this class unchanged, it would not yield any kind of reaction.

Adding functionality is achieved by overriding the appropriate event methods. You have the choice of hooking your code into the *pre* and/or *post* calls.

Example 4-22 uses the post hook after a table was created to perform additional tasks.

Example 4-22. Master observer that creates a separate directory on the filesystem when a table is created

```java
public class MasterObserverExample extends BaseMasterObserver {

  @Override
  public void postCreateTable(
    ObserverContext<MasterCoprocessorEnvironment> env,
    HRegionInfo[] regions, boolean sync)
  throws IOException {
    String tableName = regions[0].getTableDesc().getNameAsString(); ❶

    MasterServices services = env.getEnvironment().getMasterServices();
    MasterFileSystem masterFileSystem = services.getMasterFileSystem(); ❷
    FileSystem fileSystem = masterFileSystem.getFileSystem();

    Path blobPath = new Path(tableName + "-blobs"); ❸
    fileSystem.mkdirs(blobPath);

  }
}
```

❶ Get the new table's name from the table descriptor.

❷ Get the available services and retrieve a reference to the actual filesystem.

❸ Create a new directory that will store binary data from the client application.

> You need to add the following to the *hbase-site.xml* file for the coprocessor to be loaded by the master process:
>
> ```xml
> <property>
>   <name>hbase.coprocessor.master.classes</name>
>   <value>coprocessor.MasterObserverExample</value>
> </property>
> ```
>
> Just as before, restart HBase after making these adjustments.

Once you have activated the coprocessor, it is listening to the said events and will trigger your code automatically. The example is using the supplied services to create a directory on the filesystem. A fictitious application, for instance, could use it to store very large binary objects (known as *blobs*) outside of HBase.

To trigger the event, you can use the shell like so:

```
hbase(main):001:0> create 'testtable', 'colfam1'
0 row(s) in 0.4300 seconds
```

This creates the table and afterward calls the coprocessor's `postCreateTable()` method. The Hadoop command-line tool can be used to verify the results:

```
$ bin/hadoop dfs -ls
Found 1 items
drwxr-xr-x  - larsgeorge supergroup  0 ... /user/larsgeorge/testtable-blobs
```

There are many things you can implement with the `MasterObserver` coprocessor. Since you have access to most of the shared master resources through the `MasterServices` instance, you should be careful what you do, as it can potentially wreak havoc.

Finally, because the environment is wrapped in an `ObserverContext`, you have the same extra flow controls, exposed by the `bypass()` and `complete()` methods. You can use them to explicitly disable certain operations or skip subsequent coprocessor execution, respectively.

Endpoints

The earlier `RegionObserver` example used a well-known row key to add a computed column during a get request. It seems that this could suffice to implement other functionality as well—for example, aggregation functions that return the sum of all values in a specific column.

Unfortunately, this does not work, as the row key defines which region is handling the request, therefore only sending the computation request to a single server. What we want, though, is a mechanism to send such a request to *all* regions, and therefore all region servers, so that they can build the sum of the columns they have access to locally. Once each region has returned its partial result, we can aggregate the total on the client side much more easily. If you were to have 1,000 regions and 1 million columns, you would receive 1,000 decimal numbers on the client side—one for each region. This is fast to aggregate for the final result.

If you were to scan the entire table using a purely client API approach, in a worst-case scenario you would transfer all 1 million numbers to build the sum. Moving such computation to the servers where the data resides is a much better option. HBase, though, does not know what you may need, so to overcome this limitation, the coprocessor framework provides you with a dynamic call implementation, represented by the *endpoint* concept.

The CoprocessorProtocol interface

In order to provide a custom RPC protocol to clients, a coprocessor implementation defines an interface that extends `CoprocessorProtocol`. The interface can define any methods that the coprocessor wishes to expose. Using this protocol, you can communicate with the coprocessor instances via the following calls, provided by `HTable`:

```
<T extends CoprocessorProtocol> T coprocessorProxy(
  Class<T> protocol, byte[] row)
<T extends CoprocessorProtocol, R> Map<byte[],R> coprocessorExec(
  Class<T> protocol, byte[] startKey, byte[] endKey,
  Batch.Call<T,R> callable)
<T extends CoprocessorProtocol, R> void coprocessorExec(
  Class<T> protocol, byte[] startKey, byte[] endKey,
  Batch.Call<T,R> callable, Batch.Callback<R> callback)
```

Since `CoprocessorProtocol` instances are associated with individual regions within the table, the client RPC calls must ultimately identify which regions should be used in the `CoprocessorProtocol` method invocations. Though regions are seldom handled directly in client code and the region names may change over time, the coprocessor RPC calls use row keys to identify which regions should be used for the method invocations. Clients can call `CoprocessorProtocol` methods against one of the following:

Single region
> This is done by calling `coprocessorProxy()` with a single row key. This returns a dynamic proxy of the `CoprocessorProtocol` interface, which uses the region containing the given row key—even if the row does not exist—as the RPC endpoint.

Range of regions
> You can call `coprocessorExec()` with a start row key and an end row key. All regions in the table from the one containing the start row key to the one containing the end row key (inclusive) will be used as the RPC endpoints.

 The row keys passed as parameters to the `HTable` methods are not passed to the `CoprocessorProtocol` implementations. They are only used to identify the regions for endpoints of the remote calls.

The `Batch` class defines two interfaces used for `CoprocessorProtocol` invocations against multiple regions: clients implement `Batch.Call` to call methods of the actual `CoprocessorProtocol` instance. The interface's `call()` method will be called once per selected region, passing the `CoprocessorProtocol` instance for the region as a parameter.

Clients can optionally implement `Batch.Callback` to be notified of the results from each region invocation as they complete. The instance's

```
void update(byte[] region, byte[] row, R result)
```

method will be called with the value returned by `R call(T instance)` from each region.

The BaseEndpointCoprocessor class

Implementing an endpoint involves the following two steps:

1. Extend the `CoprocessorProtocol` interface.

   This specifies the communication details for the new endpoint: it defines the RPC protocol between the client and the servers.

2. Extend the `BaseEndpointCoprocessor` class.

   You need to provide the actual implementation of the endpoint by extending both the abstract `BaseEndpointCoprocessor` class and the protocol interface provided in step 1, defining your endpoint protocol.

Example 4-23 implements the `CoprocessorProtocol` to add custom functions to HBase. A client can invoke these remote calls to retrieve the number of rows and `KeyValues` in each region where it is running.

Example 4-23. Endpoint protocol, adding a row and KeyValue count method

```
public interface RowCountProtocol extends CoprocessorProtocol {
  long getRowCount() throws IOException;

  long getRowCount(Filter filter) throws IOException;

  long getKeyValueCount() throws IOException;
}
```

Step 2 is to combine this new protocol interface with a class that also extends `BaseEnd pointCoprocessor`. Example 4-24 uses the environment provided to access the data using an `InternalScanner` instance.

Example 4-24. Endpoint implementation, adding a row and KeyValue count method

```
public class RowCountEndpoint extends BaseEndpointCoprocessor
  implements RowCountProtocol {

  private long getCount(Filter filter, boolean countKeyValues)
    throws IOException {
    Scan scan = new Scan();
    scan.setMaxVersions(1);
    if (filter != null) {
      scan.setFilter(filter);
    }
    RegionCoprocessorEnvironment environment =
      (RegionCoprocessorEnvironment) getEnvironment();
    // use an internal scanner to perform scanning.
    InternalScanner scanner = environment.getRegion().getScanner(scan);
    int result = 0;
    try {
      List<KeyValue> curVals = new ArrayList<KeyValue>();
      boolean done = false;
      do {
        curVals.clear();
```

```
      done = scanner.next(curVals);
      result += countKeyValues ? curVals.size() : 1;
    } while (done);
  } finally {
    scanner.close();
  }
  return result;
}

@Override
public long getRowCount() throws IOException {
  return getRowCount(new FirstKeyOnlyFilter());
}

@Override
public long getRowCount(Filter filter) throws IOException {
  return getCount(filter, false);
}

@Override
public long getKeyValueCount() throws IOException {
  return getCount(null, true);
}
}
```

Note how the FirstKeyOnlyFilter is used to reduce the number of columns being
scanned.

 You need to add (or amend from the previous examples) the following
to the *hbase-site.xml* file for the endpoint coprocessor to be loaded by
the region server process:

```
<property>
  <name>hbase.coprocessor.region.classes</name>
  <value>coprocessor.RowCountEndpoint</value>
</property>
```

Just as before, restart HBase after making these adjustments.

Example 4-25 showcases how a client can use the provided calls of HTable to execute
the deployed coprocessor endpoint functions. Since the calls are sent to each region
separately, there is a need to summarize the total number at the end.

Example 4-25. Using the custom row-count endpoint

```
public class EndpointExample {

  public static void main(String[] args) throws IOException {
    Configuration conf = HBaseConfiguration.create();
    HTable table = new HTable(conf, "testtable");
    try {
      Map<byte[], Long> results = table.coprocessorExec(
        RowCountProtocol.class, ❶
```

```
        null, null, ❷
        new Batch.Call<RowCountProtocol, Long>() { ❸

          @Override
          public Long call(RowCountProtocol counter) throws IOException {
            return counter.getRowCount(); ❹
          }
        });

      long total = 0;
      for (Map.Entry<byte[], Long> entry : results.entrySet()) { ❺
        total += entry.getValue().longValue();
        System.out.println("Region: " + Bytes.toString(entry.getKey()) +
          ", Count: " + entry.getValue());
      }
      System.out.println("Total Count: " + total);
    } catch (Throwable throwable) {
      throwable.printStackTrace();
    }
  }
}
```

❶ Define the protocol interface being invoked.

❷ Set start and end row keys to "null" to count all rows.

❸ Create an anonymous class to be sent to all region servers.

❹ The call() method is executing the endpoint functions.

❺ Iterate over the returned map, containing the result for each region separately.

The code emits the region names, the count for each of them, and eventually the grand total:

```
Region: testtable,,1303417572005.51f9e2251c29ccb2...cbcb0c66858f., Count: 2
Region: testtable,row3,1303417572005.7f3df4dcba3f...dbc99fce5d87., Count: 3
Total Count: 5
```

The Batch class also offers a more convenient way to access the remote endpoint: using Batch.forMethod(), you can retrieve a fully configured Batch.Call instance, ready to be sent to the region servers. Example 4-26 amends the previous example to make use of this shortcut.

Example 4-26. One way in which Batch.forMethod() can reduce the client code size

```
Batch.Call call = Batch.forMethod(RowCountProtocol.class,
  "getKeyValueCount");
Map<byte[], Long> results = table.coprocessorExec(
  RowCountProtocol.class, null, null, call);
```

The forMethod() call uses the Java reflection API to retrieve the named method. The returned Batch.Call instance will execute the endpoint function and return the same data types as defined by the protocol for this method.

However, if you want to perform additional processing on the results, implementing `Batch.Call` directly will provide more power and flexibility. This can be seen in Example 4-27, which combines the row and key-value count for each region.

Example 4-27. Extending the batch call to execute multiple endpoint calls

```
Map<byte[], Pair<Long, Long>> results = table.coprocessorExec(
  RowCountProtocol.class,
  null, null,
  new Batch.Call<RowCountProtocol, Pair<Long, Long>>() {
    public Pair<Long, Long> call(RowCountProtocol counter)
      throws IOException {
      return new Pair(counter.getRowCount(),
        counter.getKeyValueCount());
    }
  });

long totalRows = 0;
long totalKeyValues = 0;
for (Map.Entry<byte[], Pair<Long, Long>> entry : results.entrySet()) {
  totalRows += entry.getValue().getFirst().longValue();
  totalKeyValues += entry.getValue().getSecond().longValue();
  System.out.println("Region: " + Bytes.toString(entry.getKey()) +
    ", Count: " + entry.getValue());
}
System.out.println("Total Row Count: " + totalRows);
System.out.println("Total KeyValue Count: " + totalKeyValues);
```

Running the code will yield the following output:

```
Region: testtable,,1303420252525.9c336bd2b294a...0647a1f2d13b., Count: {2,4}
Region: testtable,row3,1303420252525.6d7c95de8a7...386cfec7f2., Count: {3,6}
Total Row Count: 5
Total KeyValue Count: 10
```

The examples so far all used the `coprocessorExec()` calls to batch the requests across all regions, matching the given start and end row keys. Example 4-28 uses the `coprocessorProxy()` call to get a local, client-side proxy of the endpoint. Since a row key is specified, the client API will route the proxy calls to the region—and to the server currently hosting it—that contains the given key, regardless of whether it actually exists: regions are specified with a start and end key only, so the match is done by range only.

Example 4-28. Using the proxy call of HTable to invoke an endpoint on a single region

```
RowCountProtocol protocol = table.coprocessorProxy(
  RowCountProtocol.class, Bytes.toBytes("row4"));
long rowsInRegion = protocol.getRowCount();
System.out.println("Region Row Count: " + rowsInRegion);
```

With the proxy reference, you can invoke any remote function defined in your `CoprocessorProtocol` implementation from within client code, and it returns the result for the region that served the request. Figure 4-5 shows the difference between the two approaches.

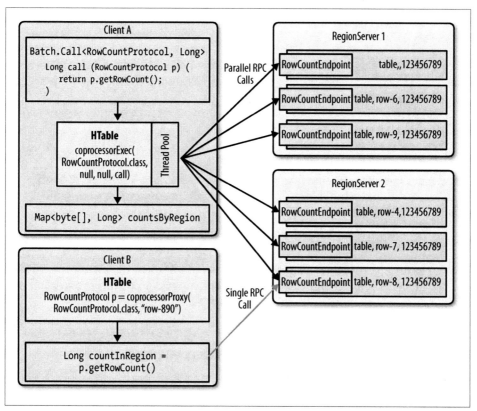

Figure 4-5. Coprocessor calls batched and executed in parallel, and addressing a single region only

HTablePool

Instead of creating an HTable instance for every request from your client application, it makes much more sense to create one initially and subsequently reuse them.

The primary reason for doing so is that creating an HTable instance is a fairly expensive operation that takes a few seconds to complete. In a highly contended environment with thousands of requests per second, you would not be able to use this approach at all—creating the HTable instance would be too slow. You need to create the instance at startup and use it for the duration of your client's life cycle.

There is an additional issue with the HTable being reused by multiple threads within the same process.

The HTable class is *not* thread-safe, that is, the local write buffer is not guarded against concurrent modifications. Even if you were to use setAutoFlush(true) (which is the default currently; see "Client-side write buffer" on page 86) this is not advisable. Instead, you should use one instance of HTable for each thread you are running in your client application.

Clients can solve this problem using the HTablePool class. It only serves one purpose, namely to pool client API instances to the HBase cluster. Creating the pool is accomplished using one of these constructors:

```
HTablePool()
HTablePool(Configuration config, int maxSize)
HTablePool(Configuration config, int maxSize,
  HTableInterfaceFactory tableFactory)
```

The default constructor—the one without any parameters—creates a pool with the configuration found in the classpath, while setting the maximum size to unlimited. This equals calling the second constructor like so:

```
Configuration conf = HBaseConfiguration.create()
HTablePool pool = new HTablePool(conf, Integer.MAX_VALUE)
```

Setting the maxSize parameter gives you control over how many HTable instances a pool is allowed to contain. The optional tableFactory parameter can be used to hand in a custom factory class that creates the actual HTable instances.

The HTableInterfaceFactory Interface

You can create your own factory class to, for example, prepare the HTable instances with specific settings. Or you could use the instance to perform some initial operations, such as adding some rows, or updating counters. If you want to implement your own HTableInterfaceFactory you need to implement two methods:

```
HTableInterface createHTableInterface(Configuration config,
  byte[] tableName)
void releaseHTableInterface(HTableInterface table)
```

The first creates the HTable instance, while the second releases it. Take any actions you require in these calls to prepare an instance, or clean up afterward. The client-side write buffer, in particular, is a concern when sharing the table references. The **releaseHTableInterface()** is the ideal place to handle implicit actions, such as flushing the write buffer, calling flushCommits() in the process.

There is a default implementation of the factory class, called HTableFactory, which does exactly that: it creates HTable instances, when the *create* method of the factory is called—while calling HTable.close(), when the client invokes the *release* method.

If you do *not* specify your own HTableInterfaceFactory, the default HTableFactory is created and assigned implicitly.

Using the pool is a matter of employing the following calls:

```
HTableInterface getTable(String tableName)
HTableInterface getTable(byte[] tableName)
void putTable(HTableInterface table)
```

The getTable() calls retrieve an HTable instance from the pool, while the putTable() returns it after you are done using it. Both internally defer some of the work to the mentioned HTableInterfaceFactory instance the pool is configured with.

 Setting the maxSize parameter during the construction of a pool does *not* impose an upper limit on the number of HTableInterface instances the pool is allowing you to retrieve. You can call getTable() as much as you like to get a valid table reference.

The maximum size of the pool only sets the number of HTableInter face instances retained within the pool, for a given table name. For example, when you set the size to 5, but then call getTable() 10 times, you have created 10 HTable instances (assuming you use the default). Upon returning them using the putTable() method, five are kept for subsequent use, while the additional five you requested are simply ignored. More importantly, the *release* mechanisms of the factory are *not* invoked.

Finally, there are calls to close the pool for specific tables:

```
void closeTablePool(String tableName)
void closeTablePool(byte[] tableName)
```

Obviously, both do the same thing, with one allowing you to specify a String, and the other a byte array—use whatever is more convenient for you.

The close call of the pool iterates over the list of retained references for a specific table, invoking the release mechanism provided by the factory. This is useful for freeing all resources for a named table, and starting all over again. Keep in mind that for *all* resources to be released, you would need to call these methods for every table name you have used so far.

Example 4-29 uses these methods to create and use a pool.

Example 4-29. Using the HTablePool class to share HTable instances

```
Configuration conf = HBaseConfiguration.create();
HTablePool pool = new HTablePool(conf, 5); ❶

HTableInterface[] tables = new HTableInterface[10];
for (int n = 0; n < 10; n++) {
  tables[n] = pool.getTable("testtable"); ❷
  System.out.println(Bytes.toString(tables[n].getTableName()));
}

for (int n = 0; n < 5; n++) {
```

```
      pool.putTable(tables[n]); ❸
    }

    pool.closeTablePool("testtable"); ❹
```

❶ Create the pool, allowing five `HTables` to be retained.

❷ Get 10 `HTable` references, which is more than the pool is retaining.

❸ Return `HTable` instances to the pool. Five will be kept, while the additional five will be dropped.

❹ Close the entire pool, releasing all retained table references.

You should receive the following output on the console:

```
Acquiring tables...
testtable
testtable
testtable
testtable
testtable
testtable
testtable
testtable
testtable
testtable
Releasing tables...
Closing pool...
```

Note that using more than the configured maximum size of the pool works as we discussed earlier: we receive more references than were configured. Returning the tables to the pool is not yielding any logging or printout, though, doing its work behind the scenes.

Use Case: Hush

All of the tables in Hush are acquired through a shared table pool. The code below provides the pool to calling classes:

```
private ResourceManager(Configuration conf) throws IOException {
  this.conf = conf;
  this.pool = new HTablePool(conf, 10);
  /* ... */
}

public HTable getTable(byte[] tableName) throws IOException {
  return (HTable) pool.getTable(tableName);
}

public void putTable(HTable table) throws IOException {
  if (table != null) {
    pool.putTable(table);
  }
}
```

The next code block shows how these methods are called in context. The table is retrieved from the pool and used. Once the operations are concluded, the table is returned to the pool subsequently.

```
public void createUser(String username, String firstName, String lastName,
  String email, String password, String roles) throws IOException {
  HTable table = rm.getTable(UserTable.NAME);
  Put put = new Put(Bytes.toBytes(username));
  put.add(UserTable.DATA_FAMILY, UserTable.FIRSTNAME,
    Bytes.toBytes(firstName));
  put.add(UserTable.DATA_FAMILY, UserTable.LASTNAME, Bytes.toBytes(lastName));
  put.add(UserTable.DATA_FAMILY, UserTable.EMAIL, Bytes.toBytes(email));
  put.add(UserTable.DATA_FAMILY, UserTable.CREDENTIALS,
    Bytes.toBytes(password));
  put.add(UserTable.DATA_FAMILY, UserTable.ROLES, Bytes.toBytes(roles));
  table.put(put);
  table.flushCommits();
  rm.putTable(table);
}
```

Connection Handling

Every instance of HTable requires a connection to the remote servers. This is internally represented by the HConnection class, and more importantly managed process-wide by the shared HConnectionManager class. From a user perspective, there is usually no immediate need to deal with either of these two classes; instead, you simply create a new Configuration instance, and use that with your client API calls.

Internally, the connections are keyed in a map, where the key is the Configuration instance you are using. In other words, if you create a number of HTable instances while providing the same configuration reference, they all share the same underlying HConnection instance. There are good reasons for this to happen:

Share ZooKeeper connections

As each client eventually needs a connection to the ZooKeeper ensemble to perform the initial lookup of where user table regions are located, it makes sense to share this connection once it is established, with all subsequent client instances.

Cache common resources

Every lookup performed through ZooKeeper, or the -ROOT-, or .META. table, of where user table regions are located requires network round-trips. The location is then cached on the client side to reduce the amount of network traffic, and to speed up the lookup process.

Since this list is the same for every local client connecting to a remote cluster, it is equally useful to share it among multiple clients running in the same process. This is accomplished by the shared HConnection instance.

In addition, when a lookup fails—for instance, when a region was split—the connection has the built-in retry mechanism to refresh the stale cache information.

This is then immediately available to all other clients sharing the same connection reference, thus further reducing the number of network round-trips initiated by a client.

Another class that benefits from the same advantages is the HTablePool: all of the pooled HTable instances automatically share the provided configuration instances, and therefore also the shared connection it references to. This also means you should always create your own configuration, whenever you plan to instantiate more than one HTable instance. For example:

```
HTable table1 = new HTable("table1");
//...
HTable table2 = new HTable("table2");
```

is less efficient than the following code:

```
Configuration conf = HBaseConfiguration.create();
HTable table1 = new HTable(conf, "table1");
//...
HTable table2 = new HTable(conf, "table2");
```

The latter implicitly uses the connection sharing, as provided by the HBase client-side API classes.

 There are no known performance implications for sharing a connection, even for heavily multithreaded applications.

The drawback of sharing a connection is the cleanup: when you do not explicitly close a connection, it is kept open until the client process exits. This can result in many connections that remain open to ZooKeeper, especially for heavily distributed applications, such as MapReduce jobs talking to HBase. In a worst-case scenario, you can run out of available connections, and receive an IOException instead.

You can avoid this problem by explicitly closing the shared connection, when you are done using it. This is accomplished with the close() method provided by HTable. The call decreases an internal reference count and eventually closes all shared resources, such as the connection to the ZooKeeper ensemble, and removes the connection reference from the internal list.

Every time you reuse a Configuration instance, the connection manager internally increases the reference count, so you only have to make sure you call the close() method to trigger the cleanup. There is also an explicit call to clear out a connection, or all open connections:

```
static void deleteConnection(Configuration conf, boolean stopProxy)
static void deleteAllConnections(boolean stopProxy)
```

Since all shared connections are internally keyed by the configuration instance, you need to provide that instance to close the associated connection. The boolean stop Proxy parameter lets you further enforce the cleanup of the entire RPC stack of the client—which is its umbilical cord to the remote servers. Only use true when you do not need any further communication with the server to take place.

The deleteAllConnections() call only requires the boolean stopProxy flag; it simply iterates over the entire list of shared connections known to the connection manager and closes them.

If you are ever in need of using a connection explicitly, you can make use of the get Connection() call like so:

```
Configuration newConfig = new Configuration(originalConf);
HConnection connection = HConnectionManager.getConnection(newConfig);
// Use the connection to your hearts' delight and then when done...
HConnectionManager.deleteConnection(newConfig, true);
```

The advantage is that you are the sole user of that connection, but you must make sure you close it out properly as well.

Client API: Administrative Features

Apart from the client API used to deal with data manipulation features, HBase also exposes a *data definition*-like API. This is similar to the separation into DDL and DML found in RDBMSes. First we will look at the classes required to define the data schemas and subsequently see the API that makes use of it to, for example, create a new HBase table.

Schema Definition

Creating a table in HBase implicitly involves the definition of a table schema, as well as the schemas for all contained column families. They define the pertinent characteristics of how—and when—the data inside the table and columns is ultimately stored.

Tables

Everything stored in HBase is ultimately grouped into one or more *tables*. The primary reason to have tables is to be able to control certain features that all columns in this table share. The typical things you will want to define for a table are *column families*. The constructor of the *table descriptor* in Java looks like the following:

```
HTableDescriptor();
HTableDescriptor(String name);
HTableDescriptor(byte[] name);
HTableDescriptor(HTableDescriptor desc);
```

Writable and the Parameterless Constructor

You will find that most classes provided by the API and discussed throughout this chapter do possess a special constructor, one that does not take any parameters. This is attributed to these classes implementing the Hadoop `Writable` interface.

Every communication between remote disjoint systems—for example, the client talking to the servers, but also the servers talking with one another—is done using the

Hadoop RPC framework. It employs the `Writable` class to denote objects that can be sent over the network. Those objects implement the two `Writable` methods required:

```
void write(DataOutput out) throws IOException;
void readFields(DataInput in) throws IOException;
```

They are invoked by the framework to *write* the object's data into the output stream, and subsequently *read* it back on the receiving system. For that the framework calls `write()` on the sending side, serializing the object's fields—while the framework is taking care of noting the class name and other details on their behalf.

On the receiving server the framework reads the metadata, and will create an *empty* instance of the class, then call `readFields()` of the newly created instance. This will read back the field data and leave you with a fully working and initialized copy of the sending object.

Since the receiver needs to create the class using reflection, it is implied that it must have access to the matching, compiled class. Usually that is the case, as both the servers and clients are using the same HBase Java archive file, or JAR.

But if you develop your own extensions to HBase—for example, filters and coprocessors, as we discussed in Chapter 4—you must ensure that your custom class follows these rules:

- It is available on both sides of the RPC communication channel, that is, the sending and receiving processes.
- It implements the `Writable` interface, along with its `write()` and `readFields()` methods.
- It has the *parameterless* constructor, that is, one without any parameters.

Failing to provide the special constructor will result in a runtime error. And calling the constructor explicitly from your code is also a futile exercise, since it leaves you with an uninitialized instance that most definitely does not behave as expected.

As a client API developer, you should simply acknowledge the underlying dependency on RPC, and how it manifests itself. As an advanced developer extending HBase, you need to implement and deploy your custom code appropriately. "Custom Filters" on page 160 has an example and further notes.

You either create a table with a name or an existing descriptor. The constructor without any parameters is only for deserialization purposes and should not be used directly. You can specify the name of the table as a Java `String` or `byte[]`, a byte array. Many functions in the HBase Java API have these two choices. The string version is plainly for convenience and converts the string internally into the usual byte array representation as HBase treats everything as such. You can achieve the same using the supplied `Bytes` class:

```
byte[] name = Bytes.toBytes("test");
HTableDescriptor desc = new HTableDescriptor(name);
```

There are certain restrictions on the characters you can use to create a table name. The name is used as part of the path to the actual storage files, and therefore complies with filename rules. You can later browse the low-level storage system—for example, HDFS—to see the tables as separate directories—in case you ever need to.

The column-oriented storage format of HBase allows you to store many details into the same table, which, under relational database modeling, would be divided into many separate tables. The usual *database normalization*[*] rules do not apply directly to HBase, and therefore the number of tables is usually very low. More on this is discussed in "Database (De-)Normalization" on page 13.

Although conceptually a table is a collection of rows with columns in HBase, physically they are stored in separate partitions called *regions*. Figure 5-1 shows the difference between the logical and physical layout of the stored data. Every region is served by exactly one region server, which in turn serve the stored values directly to clients.

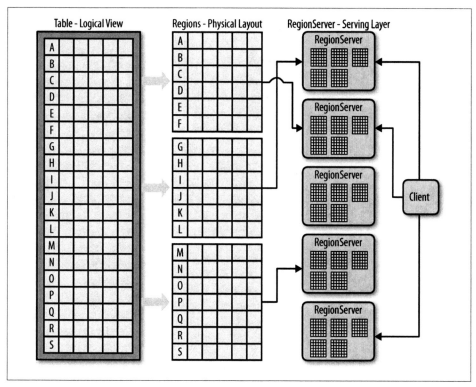

Figure 5-1. Logical and physical layout of rows within regions

---

[*] See "Database normalization" (*http://en.wikipedia.org/wiki/Database_normalization*) on Wikipedia.

Table Properties

The table descriptor offers *getters* and *setters*† to set other options of the table. In practice, a lot are not used very often, but it is important to know them all, as they can be used to fine-tune the table's performance.

Name

The constructor already had the parameter to specify the table name. The Java API has additional methods to access the name or change it.

```
byte[] getName();
String getNameAsString();
void setName(byte[] name);
```

 The name of a table must not start with a "." (period) or a "-" (hyphen). Furthermore, it can only contain Latin letters or numbers, as well as "_" (underscore), "-" (hyphen), or "." (period). In regular expression syntax, this could be expressed as [a-zA-Z_0-9-.].

For example, .testtable is wrong, but test.table is allowed.

Refer to "Column Families" on page 212 for more details, and Figure 5-2 for an example of how the table name is used to form a filesystem path.

Column families

This is the most important part of defining a table. You need to specify the *column families* you want to use with the table you are creating.

```
void addFamily(HColumnDescriptor family);
boolean hasFamily(byte[] c);
HColumnDescriptor[] getColumnFamilies();
HColumnDescriptor getFamily(byte[]column);
HColumnDescriptor removeFamily(byte[] column);
```

You have the option of adding a family, checking if it exists based on its name, getting a list of all known families, and getting or removing a specific one. More on how to define the required `HColumnDescriptor` is explained in "Column Families" on page 212.

Maximum file size

This parameter is specifying the maximum size a region within the table can grow to. The size is specified in bytes and is read and set using the following methods:

```
long getMaxFileSize();
void setMaxFileSize(long maxFileSize);
```

---

† Getters and setters in Java are methods of a class that expose internal fields in a controlled manner. They are usually named like the field, prefixed with **get** and **set**, respectively—for example, **getName()** and **setName()**.

Maximum file size is actually a misnomer, as it really is about the maximum size of each store, that is, all the files belonging to each column family. If one single column family exceeds this maximum size, the region is split. Since in practice, this involves multiple files, the better name would be *maxStoreSize*.

The maximum size is helping the system to split regions when they reach this configured size. As discussed in "Building Blocks" on page 16, the unit of scalability and load balancing in HBase is the region. You need to determine what a good number for the size is, though. By default, it is set to *256 MB*, which is good for many use cases, but a larger value may be required when you have a lot of data.

Please note that this is more or less a *desired* maximum size and that, given certain conditions, this size can be exceeded and actually be completely rendered without effect. As an example, you could set the maximum file size to 10 MB and insert a 20 MB cell in one row. Since a row cannot be split across regions, you end up with a region of at least 20 MB in size, and the system cannot do anything about it.

Read-only

By default, all tables are *writable*, but it may make sense to specify the *read-only* option for specific tables. If the flag is set to true, you can only read from the table and not modify it at all. The flag is set and read by these methods:

```
boolean isReadOnly();
void setReadOnly(boolean readOnly);
```

Memstore flush size

We discussed the storage model earlier and identified how HBase uses an in-memory store to buffer values before writing them to disk as a new storage file in an operation called *flush*. This parameter of the table controls when this is going to happen and is specified in bytes. It is controlled by the following calls:

```
long getMemStoreFlushSize();
void setMemStoreFlushSize(long memstoreFlushSize);
```

As you do with the aforementioned maximum file size, you need to check your requirements before setting this value to something other than the default *64 MB*. A larger size means you are generating larger store files, which is good. On the other hand, you might run into the problem of longer blocking periods, if the region server cannot keep up with flushing the added data. Also, it increases the time needed to replay the write-ahead log (the WAL) if the server crashes and all in-memory updates are lost.

Deferred log flush

We will look into log flushing in great detail in "Write-Ahead Log" on page 333, where this option is explained. For now, note that HBase uses one of two different approaches to save write-ahead-log entries to disk. You either use *deferred log flushing* or not. This is a boolean option and is, by default, set to `false`. Here is how to access this parameter through the Java API:

```
synchronized boolean isDeferredLogFlush();
void setDeferredLogFlush(boolean isDeferredLogFlush);
```

Miscellaneous options

In addition to those already mentioned, there are methods that let you set arbitrary key/value pairs:

```
byte[] getValue(byte[] key) {
String getValue(String key)
Map<ImmutableBytesWritable, ImmutableBytesWritable> getValues()
void setValue(byte[] key, byte[] value)
void setValue(String key, String value)
void remove(byte[] key)
```

They are stored with the table definition and can be retrieved if necessary. One actual use case within HBase is the loading of coprocessors, as detailed in "Coprocessor Loading" on page 179. You have a few choices in terms of how to specify the key and value, either as a `String`, or as a `byte` array. Internally, they are stored as `ImmutableBytesWritable`, which is needed for serialization purposes (see "Writable and the Parameterless Constructor" on page 207).

Column Families

We just saw how the `HTableDescriptor` exposes methods to add column families to a table. Similar to this is a class called `HColumnDescriptor` that wraps each column family's settings into a dedicated Java class. In other programming languages, you may find the same concept or some other means of specifying the column family properties.

 The class in Java is somewhat of a misnomer. A more appropriate name would be `HColumnFamilyDescriptor`, which would indicate its purpose to define column family parameters as opposed to actual columns.

Column families define shared features that apply to all columns that are created within them. The client can create an arbitrary number of columns by simply using new *column qualifiers* on the fly. Columns are addressed as a combination of the column family name and the column qualifier (or sometimes also called the *column key*), divided by a colon:

```
family:qualifier
```

The column family name *must* be composed of printable characters: the qualifier can be composed of any arbitrary binary characters. Recall the `Bytes` class mentioned earlier, which you can use to convert your chosen names to byte arrays. The reason why the family name must be printable is that because the name is used as part of the directory name by the lower-level storage layer. Figure 5-2 visualizes how the families are mapped to storage files. The family name is added to the path and must comply with filename standards. The advantage is that you can easily access families on the filesystem level as you have the name in a human-readable format.

> You should also be aware of the *empty* column qualifier. You can simply omit the *qualifier* and specify just the column family name. HBase then creates a column with the special empty qualifier. You can write and read that column like any other, but obviously there is only one of those, and you will have to name the other columns to distinguish them.
>
> For simple applications, using no qualifier is an option, but it also carries no meaning when looking at the data—for example, using the HBase Shell. You should get used to naming your columns and do this from the start, because you cannot simply rename them later.

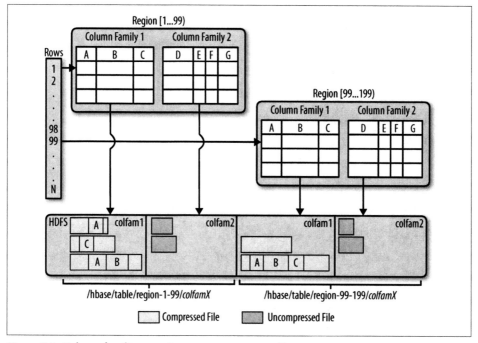

Figure 5-2. Column families mapping to separate storage files

When you create a column family, you can specify a variety of parameters that control all of its features. The Java class has many constructors that allow you to specify most parameters while creating an instance. Here are the choices:

```
HColumnDescriptor();
HColumnDescriptor(String familyName),
HColumnDescriptor(byte[] familyName);
```

```
HColumnDescriptor(HColumnDescriptor desc);
HColumnDescriptor(byte[] familyName, int maxVersions, String compression,
  boolean inMemory, boolean blockCacheEnabled, int timeToLive,
String bloomFilter);
HColumnDescriptor(byte [] familyName, int maxVersions, String compression,
  boolean inMemory, boolean blockCacheEnabled, int blocksize,
  int timeToLive, String bloomFilter, int scope);
```

The first one is only used internally for deserialization again. The next two simply take a name as a String or byte[], the usual byte array we have seen many times now. There is another one that takes an existing HColumnDescriptor and then two more that list all available parameters.

Instead of using the constructor, you can also use the getters and setters to specify the various details. We will now discuss each of them.

Name

Each column family has a name, and you can use the following methods to retrieve it from an existing HColumnDescriptor instance:

```
byte[] getName();
String getNameAsString();
```

A column family cannot be renamed. The common approach to rename a family is to create a new family with the desired name and copy the data over, using the API.

You cannot set the name, but you have to use these constructors to hand it in. Keep in mind the requirement for the name to be *printable* characters.

The name of a column family must not start with a "." (period) and not contain ":" (colon), "/" (slash), or ISO control characters, in other words, if its code is in the range \u0000 through \u001F or in the range \u007F through \u009F.

Maximum versions

Per family, you can specify how many versions of each value you want to keep. Recall the *predicate deletion* mentioned earlier where the housekeeping of HBase removes values that exceed the set maximum. Getting and setting the value is done using the following API calls:

```
int getMaxVersions();
void setMaxVersions(int maxVersions);
```

The default value is 3, but you may reduce it to 1, for example, in case you know for sure that you will never want to look at older values.

Compression

HBase has pluggable compression algorithm support (you can find more on this topic in "Compression" on page 424) that allows you to choose the best compression—or none—for the data stored in a particular column family. The possible algorithms are listed in Table 5-1.

Table 5-1. Supported compression algorithms

Value	Description
NONE	Disables compression (default)
GZ	Uses the Java-supplied or native GZip compression
LZO	Enables LZO compression; must be installed separately
SNAPPY	Enables Snappy compression; binaries must be installed separately

The default value is NONE—in other words, no compression is enabled when you create a column family. Once you deal with the Java API and a column descriptor, you can use these methods to change the value:

```
Compression.Algorithm getCompression();
Compression.Algorithm getCompressionType();
void setCompressionType(Compression.Algorithm type);
Compression.Algorithm getCompactionCompression();
Compression.Algorithm getCompactionCompressionType();
void setCompactionCompressionType(Compression.Algorithm type);
```

Note how the value is not a String, but rather a Compression.Algorithm enumeration that exposes the same values as listed in Table 5-1. The constructor of HColumnDescriptor takes the same values as a string, though.

Another observation is that there are two sets of methods, one for the general compression setting and another for the *compaction* compression setting. Also, each group has a getCompression() and getCompressionType() (or getCompactionCompression() and getCompactionCompressionType(), respectively) returning the same type of value. They are indeed redundant, and you can use either to retrieve the current compression algorithm type.[‡]

We will look into this topic in much greater detail in "Compression" on page 424.

Block size

All stored files in HBase are divided into smaller blocks that are loaded during a get or scan operation, analogous to pages in RDBMSes. The default is set to *64 KB* and can be adjusted with these methods:

```
synchronized int getBlocksize();
void setBlocksize(int s);
```

[‡] After all, this is open source and a redundancy like this is often caused by legacy code being carried forward. Please feel free to help clean this up and to contribute back to the HBase project.

The value is specified in bytes and can be used to control how much data HBase is required to read from the storage files during retrieval as well as what is cached in memory for subsequent accesses. How this can be used to fine-tune your setup can be found in "Configuration" on page 436.

> There is an important distinction between the column family block size, or HFile block size, and the block size specified on the HDFS level. Hadoop, and HDFS specifically, is using a block size of—by default—64 MB to split up large files for distributed, parallel processing using the MapReduce framework. For HBase the HFile block size is—again by default—64 KB, or one 1024th of the HDFS block size. The storage files used by HBase are using this much more fine-grained size to efficiently load and cache data in block operations. It is independent from the HDFS block size and only used internally. See "Storage" on page 319 for more details, especially Figure 8-3, which shows the two different block types.

Block cache

As HBase reads entire blocks of data for efficient I/O usage, it retains these blocks in an in-memory cache so that subsequent reads do not need any disk operation. The default of `true` enables the block cache for every read operation. But if your use case only ever has sequential reads on a particular column family, it is advisable that you disable it from polluting the block cache by setting the block cache-enabled flag to `false`. Here is how the API can be used to change this flag:

```
boolean isBlockCacheEnabled();
void setBlockCacheEnabled(boolean blockCacheEnabled);
```

There are other options you can use to influence how the block cache is used, for example, during a `scan` operation. This is useful during full table scans so that you do not cause a major churn on the cache. See "Configuration" for more information about this feature.

Time-to-live

HBase supports predicate deletions on the number of versions kept for each value, but also on specific times. The time-to-live (or TTL) sets a threshold based on the timestamp of a value and the internal housekeeping is checking automatically if a value exceeds its TTL. If that is the case, it is dropped during major compactions.

The API provides the following getter and setter to read and write the TTL:

```
int getTimeToLive();
void setTimeToLive(int timeToLive);
```

The value is specified in seconds and is, by default, set to `Integer.MAX_VALUE` or 2,147,483,647 seconds. The default value also is treated as the special case of keeping the values *forever*, that is, any positive value less than the default enables this feature.

In-memory

We mentioned the block cache and how HBase is using it to keep entire blocks of data in memory for efficient sequential access to values. The *in-memory* flag defaults to `false` but can be modified with these methods:

```
boolean isInMemory();
void setInMemory(boolean inMemory);
```

Setting it to `true` is not a guarantee that all blocks of a family are loaded into memory nor that they stay there. Think of it as a promise, or elevated priority, to keep them in memory as soon as they are loaded during a normal retrieval operation, and until the pressure on the heap (the memory available to the Java-based server processes) is too high, at which time they need to be discarded by force.

In general, this setting is good for small column families with few values, such as the passwords of a user table, so that logins can be processed very fast.

Bloom filter

An advanced feature available in HBase is Bloom filters,[§] allowing you to improve lookup times given you have a specific access pattern (see "Bloom Filters" on page 377 for details). Since they add overhead in terms of storage and memory, they are turned off by default. Table 5-2 shows the possible options.

Table 5-2. Supported Bloom filter types

Type	Description
NONE	Disables the filter (default)
ROW	Use the row key for the filter
ROWCOL	Use the row key and column key (family+qualifier) for the filter

Because there are many more columns than rows (unless you only have a single column in each row), the last option, ROWCOL, requires the largest amount of space. It is more fine-grained, though, since it knows about each row/column combination, as opposed to just rows.

The Bloom filter can be changed and retrieved with these calls:

```
StoreFile.BloomType getBloomFilterType();
void setBloomFilterType(StoreFile.BloomType bt);
```

As with the compression value, these methods take a `StoreFile.BloomType` type, while the constructor for the column descriptor lets you specify the aforementioned types as a string. The letter casing is not important, so you can, for example, use *"row"*. "Bloom Filters" has more on the Bloom filters and how to use them best.

---

§ See "Bloom filter" (*http://en.wikipedia.org/wiki/Bloom_filter*) on Wikipedia.

Replication scope

Another more advanced feature coming with HBase is *replication*. It enables you to have multiple clusters that ship local updates across the network so that they are applied to the remote copies.

By default, replication is disabled and the *replication scope* is set to 0, meaning it is disabled. You can change the scope with these functions:

```
int getScope();
void setScope(int scope);
```

The only other supported value (as of this writing) is 1, which enables replication to a remote cluster. There may be more scope values in the future. See Table 5-3 for a list of supported values.

Table 5-3. Supported replication scopes

Scope	Description
0	Local scope, i.e., no replication for this family (default)
1	Global scope, i.e., replicate family to a remote cluster

The full details can be found in "Replication" on page 462.

Finally, the Java class has a helper method to check if a family name is valid:

```
static byte[] isLegalFamilyName(byte[] b);
```

Use it in your program to verify user-provided input conforming to the specifications that are required for the name. It does not return a boolean flag, but throws an IllegalArgumentException when the name is malformed. Otherwise, it returns the given parameter value unchanged. The fully specified constructors shown earlier use this method internally to verify the given name; in this case, you do not need to call the method beforehand.

HBaseAdmin

Just as with the client API, you also have an API for administrative tasks at your disposal. Compare this to the *Data Definition Language* (DDL) found in RDBMSes—while the client API is more an analog to the *Data Manipulation Language* (DML).

It provides operations to create tables with specific column families, check for table existence, alter table and column family definitions, drop tables, and much more. The provided functions can be grouped into related operations; they're discussed separately on the following pages.

Basic Operations

Before you can use the administrative API, you will have to create an instance of the HBaseAdmin class. The constructor is straightforward:

```
HBaseAdmin(Configuration conf)
    throws MasterNotRunningException, ZooKeeperConnectionException
```

This section omits the fact that most methods may throw either an IOException (or an exception that inherits from it), or an InterruptedException. The former is usually a result of a communication error between your client application and the remote servers. The latter is caused by an event that interrupts a running operation, for example, when the region server executing the command is shut down before being able to complete it.

Handing in an existing configuration instance gives enough details to the API to find the cluster using the ZooKeeper quorum, just like the client API does. Use the administrative API instance for the operation required and discard it afterward. In other words, you should not hold on to the instance for too long.

The HBaseAdmin instances should be short-lived as they do not, for example, handle master failover gracefully right now.

The class implements the Abortable interface, adding the following call to it:

```
void abort(String why, Throwable e)
```

This method is called by the framework implicitly—for example, when there is a fatal connectivity issue and the API should be stopped. You should not call it directly, but rely on the system taking care of invoking it, in case of dire emergencies, that require a complete shutdown—and possible restart—of the API instance.

You can get access to the remote master using:

```
HMasterInterface getMaster()
    throws MasterNotRunningException, ZooKeeperConnectionException
```

This will return an RPC proxy instance of HMasterInterface, allowing you to communicate directly with the master server. This is not required because the HBaseAdmin class provides a convenient wrapper to *all* calls exposed by the master interface.

Do *not* use the `HMasterInterface` returned by `getMaster()` directly, unless you are sure what you are doing. The wrapper functions in `HBaseAdmin` perform additional work—for example, checking that the input parameters are valid, converting remote exceptions to client exceptions, or adding the ability to run inherently asynchronous operations as if they were synchronous.

In addition, the `HBaseAdmin` class also exports these basic calls:

`boolean isMasterRunning()`
Checks if the master server is running. You may use it from your client application to verify that you can communicate with the master, before instantiating the `HBaseAdmin` class.

`HConnection getConnection()`
Returns a connection instance. See "Connection Handling" on page 203 for details on the returned class type.

`Configuration getConfiguration()`
Gives you access to the configuration that was used to create the current `HBaseAdmin` instance. You can use it to modify the configuration for a running administrative API instance.

`close()`
Closes all resources kept by the current `HBaseAdmin` instance. This includes the connection to the remote servers.

Table Operations

After the first set of basic operations, there is a group of calls related to HBase tables. These calls help when working with the tables themselves, not the actual schemas inside. The commands addressing this are in "Schema Operations" on page 228.

Before you can do anything with HBase, you need to create tables. Here is the set of functions to do so:

```
void createTable(HTableDescriptor desc)
void createTable(HTableDescriptor desc, byte[] startKey,
   byte[] endKey, int numRegions)
void createTable(HTableDescriptor desc, byte[][] splitKeys)

void createTableAsync(HTableDescriptor desc, byte[][] splitKeys)
```

All of these calls must be given an instance of `HTableDescriptor`, as described in detail in "Tables" on page 207. It holds the details of the table to be created, including the column families. Example 5-1 uses the simple variant of `createTable()` that just takes a table name.

Example 5-1. Using the administrative API to create a table

```
Configuration conf = HBaseConfiguration.create();

HBaseAdmin admin = new HBaseAdmin(conf); ❶

HTableDescriptor desc = new HTableDescriptor( ❷
  Bytes.toBytes("testtable"));

HColumnDescriptor coldef = new HColumnDescriptor( ❸
  Bytes.toBytes("colfam1"));
desc.addFamily(coldef);

admin.createTable(desc); ❹

boolean avail = admin.isTableAvailable(Bytes.toBytes("testtable")); ❺
System.out.println("Table available: " + avail);
```

❶ Create an administrative API instance.

❷ Create the table descriptor instance.

❸ Create a column family descriptor and add it to the table descriptor.

❹ Call the createTable() method to do the actual work.

❺ Check if the table is available.

The other createTable() versions have an additional—yet more advanced—feature set: they allow you to create tables that are already populated with specific regions. The code in Example 5-2 uses both possible ways to specify your own set of region boundaries.

Example 5-2. Using the administrative API to create a table with predefined regions

```
private static void printTableRegions(String tableName) throws IOException { ❶
  System.out.println("Printing regions of table: " + tableName);
  HTable table = new HTable(Bytes.toBytes(tableName));
  Pair<byte[][], byte[][]> pair = table.getStartEndKeys(); ❷
  for (int n = 0; n < pair.getFirst().length; n++) {
    byte[] sk = pair.getFirst()[n];
    byte[] ek = pair.getSecond()[n];
    System.out.println("[" + (n + 1) + "]" +
      " start key: " +
      (sk.length == 8 ? Bytes.toLong(sk) : Bytes.toStringBinary(sk)) + ❸
      ", end key: " +
      (ek.length == 8 ? Bytes.toLong(ek) : Bytes.toStringBinary(ek)));
  }
}
public static void main(String[] args) throws IOException, InterruptedException {
  Configuration conf = HBaseConfiguration.create();
  HBaseAdmin admin = new HBaseAdmin(conf);

  HTableDescriptor desc = new HTableDescriptor(
    Bytes.toBytes("testtable1"));
  HColumnDescriptor coldef = new HColumnDescriptor(
```

```
    Bytes.toBytes("colfam1"));
desc.addFamily(coldef);

admin.createTable(desc, Bytes.toBytes(1L), Bytes.toBytes(100L), 10); ❹
printTableRegions("testtable1");

byte[][] regions = new byte[][] { ❺
  Bytes.toBytes("A"),
  Bytes.toBytes("D"),
  Bytes.toBytes("G"),
  Bytes.toBytes("K"),
  Bytes.toBytes("O"),
  Bytes.toBytes("T")
};
desc.setName(Bytes.toBytes("testtable2"));
admin.createTable(desc, regions); ❻
printTableRegions("testtable2");
  }
```

❶ Helper method to print the regions of a table.

❷ Retrieve the start and end keys from the newly created table.

❸ Print the key, but guarding against the empty start (and end) key.

❹ Call the createTable() method while also specifying the region boundaries.

❺ Manually create region split keys.

❻ Call the createTable() method again, with a new table name and the list of region split keys.

Running the example should yield the following output on the console:

```
Printing regions of table: testtable1
[1] start key: , end key: 1
[2] start key: 1, end key: 13
[3] start key: 13, end key: 25
[4] start key: 25, end key: 37
[5] start key: 37, end key: 49
[6] start key: 49, end key: 61
[7] start key: 61, end key: 73
[8] start key: 73, end key: 85
[9] start key: 85, end key: 100
[10] start key: 100, end key:
Printing regions of table: testtable2
[1] start key: , end key: A
[2] start key: A, end key: D
[3] start key: D, end key: G
[4] start key: G, end key: K
[5] start key: K, end key: O
[6] start key: O, end key: T
[7] start key: T, end key:
```

The example uses a method of the HTable class that you saw earlier, getStartEnd Keys(), to retrieve the region boundaries. The first *start* and the last *end* keys are empty, as is customary with HBase regions. In between the keys are either the computed, or the provided split keys. Note how the end key of a region is also the start key of the subsequent one—just that it is exclusive for the former, and inclusive for the latter, respectively.

The createTable(HTableDescriptor desc, byte[] startKey, byte[] endKey, int num Regions) call takes a start and end key, which is interpreted as numbers. You *must* provide a start value that is less than the end value, and a numRegions that is at least 3: otherwise, the call will return with an exception. This is to ensure that you end up with at least a minimum set of regions.

The start and end key values are subtracted and divided by the given number of regions to compute the region boundaries. In the example, you can see how we end up with the correct number of regions, while the computed keys are filling in the range.

The createTable(HTableDescriptor desc, byte[][] splitKeys) method used in the second part of the example, on the other hand, is expecting an already set array of split keys: they form the start and end keys of the regions created. The output of the example demonstrates this as expected.

The createTable() calls are, in fact, related. The createTable(HTable Descriptor desc, byte[] startKey, byte[] endKey, int numRegions) method is calculating the region keys implicitly for you, using the Bytes.split() method to use your given parameters to compute the boundaries. It then proceeds to call the createTable(HTableDescriptor desc, byte[][] splitKeys), doing the actual table creation.

Finally, there is the createTableAsync(HTableDescriptor desc, byte[][] splitKeys) method that is taking the table descriptor, and region keys, to asynchronously perform the same task as the createTable() call.

Most of the table-related administrative API functions are asynchronous in nature, which is useful, as you can send off a command and not have to deal with waiting for a result. For a client application, though, it is often necessary to know if a command has succeeded before moving on with other operations. For that, the calls are provided in asynchronous—using the Async postfix—and synchronous versions.

In fact, the synchronous commands are simply a wrapper around the asynchronous ones, adding a loop at the end of the call to repeatedly check for the command to have done its task. The createTable() method, for example, wraps the createTableAsync() method, while adding a loop that waits for the table to be created on the remote servers before yielding control back to the caller.

Once you have created a table, you can use the following helper functions to retrieve the list of tables, retrieve the descriptor for an existing table, or check if a table exists:

```
boolean tableExists(String tableName)
boolean tableExists(byte[] tableName)
HTableDescriptor[] listTables()
HTableDescriptor getTableDescriptor(byte[] tableName)
```

Example 5-1 uses the tableExists() method to check if the previous command to create the table has succeeded. The listTables() returns a list of HTableDescriptor instances for every table that HBase knows about, while the getTableDescriptor() method is returning it for a specific one. Example 5-3 uses both to show what is returned by the administrative API.

Example 5-3. Listing the existing tables and their descriptors

```
HBaseAdmin admin = new HBaseAdmin(conf);

HTableDescriptor[] htds = admin.listTables();
for (HTableDescriptor htd : htds) {
  System.out.println(htd);
}

HTableDescriptor htd1 = admin.getTableDescriptor(
  Bytes.toBytes("testtable1"));
System.out.println(htd1);

HTableDescriptor htd2 = admin.getTableDescriptor(
  Bytes.toBytes("testtable10"));
System.out.println(htd2);
```

The console output is quite long, since every table descriptor is printed, including every possible property. Here is an abbreviated version:

```
Printing all tables...
{NAME => 'testtable1', FAMILIES => [{NAME => 'colfam1', BLOOMFILTER =>
'NONE', REPLICATION_SCOPE => '0', COMPRESSION => 'NONE', VERSIONS => '3',
TTL => '2147483647', BLOCKSIZE => '65536', IN_MEMORY => 'false', BLOCKCACHE
=> 'true'}, {NAME => 'colfam2', BLOOMFILTER => 'NONE', REPLICATION_SCOPE
=> '0', COMPRESSION => 'NONE', VERSIONS => '3', TTL => '2147483647',
BLOCKSIZE => '65536', IN_MEMORY => 'false', BLOCKCACHE => 'true'}, {NAME =>
'colfam3', BLOOMFILTER => 'NONE', REPLICATION_SCOPE => '0', COMPRESSION =>
'NONE', VERSIONS => '3', TTL => '2147483647', BLOCKSIZE => '65536',
IN_MEMORY => 'false', BLOCKCACHE => 'true'}]}
...
Exception org.apache.hadoop.hbase.TableNotFoundException: testtable10
  ...
    at ListTablesExample.main(ListTablesExample.java)
```

The interesting part is the exception you should see being printed as well. The example uses a nonexistent table name to showcase the fact that you *must* be using existing table names—or wrap the call into a try/catch guard, handling the exception more gracefully.

After creating a table, it is time to also be able to delete them. The `HBaseAdmin` calls to do so are:

```
void deleteTable(String tableName)
void deleteTable(byte[] tableName)
```

Hand in a table name as a `String`, or a `byte` array, and the rest is taken care of: the table is removed from the servers, and all data deleted.

But before you can delete a table, you need to ensure that it is first `disabled`, using the following methods:

```
void disableTable(String tableName)
void disableTable(byte[] tableName)
void disableTableAsync(String tableName)
void disableTableAsync(byte[] tableName)
```

Disabling the table first tells every region server to flush any uncommitted changes to disk, close all the regions, and update the `.META.` table to reflect that no region of this table is not deployed to any servers.

The choices are again between doing this asynchronously, or synchronously, and supplying the table name in various formats for convenience.

 Disabling a table can potentially take a very long time, up to several minutes. This depends on how much data is residual in the server's memory and not yet persisted to disk. Undeploying a region requires all the data to be written to disk first, and if you have a large heap value set for the servers this may result in megabytes, if not even gigabytes, of data being saved. In a heavily loaded system this could contend with other processes writing to disk, and therefore require time to complete.

Once a table has been disabled, but not deleted, you can enable it again:

```
void enableTable(String tableName)
void enableTable(byte[] tableName)
void enableTableAsync(String tableName)
void enableTableAsync(byte[] tableName)
```

This call—again available in the usual flavors—reverses the disable operation by deploying the regions of the given table to the active region servers. Finally, there is a set of calls to check on the status of a table:

```
boolean isTableEnabled(String tableName)
boolean isTableEnabled(byte[] tableName)
boolean isTableDisabled(String tableName)
boolean isTableDisabled(byte[] tableName)
boolean isTableAvailable(byte[] tableName)
boolean isTableAvailable(String tableName)
```

Example 5-4 uses various combinations of the preceding calls to create, delete, disable, and check the state of a table.

Example 5-4. Using the various calls to disable, enable, and check the status of a table

```
HBaseAdmin admin = new HBaseAdmin(conf);

HTableDescriptor desc = new HTableDescriptor(
  Bytes.toBytes("testtable"));
HColumnDescriptor coldef = new HColumnDescriptor(
  Bytes.toBytes("colfam1"));
desc.addFamily(coldef);
admin.createTable(desc);

try {
  admin.deleteTable(Bytes.toBytes("testtable"));
} catch (IOException e) {
  System.err.println("Error deleting table: " + e.getMessage());
}

admin.disableTable(Bytes.toBytes("testtable"));
boolean isDisabled = admin.isTableDisabled(Bytes.toBytes("testtable"));
System.out.println("Table is disabled: " + isDisabled);

boolean avail1 = admin.isTableAvailable(Bytes.toBytes("testtable"));
System.out.println("Table available: " + avail1);

admin.deleteTable(Bytes.toBytes("testtable"));

boolean avail2 = admin.isTableAvailable(Bytes.toBytes("testtable"));
System.out.println("Table available: " + avail2);

admin.createTable(desc);
boolean isEnabled = admin.isTableEnabled(Bytes.toBytes("testtable"));
System.out.println("Table is enabled: " + isEnabled);
```

The output on the console should look like this (the exception printout was abbreviated, for the sake of brevity):

```
Creating table...
Deleting enabled table...
Error deleting table:
  org.apache.hadoop.hbase.TableNotDisabledException: testtable
  ...
Disabling table...
Table is disabled: true
Table available: true
Deleting disabled table...
Table available: false
Creating table again...
Table is enabled: true
```

The error thrown when trying to delete an enabled table shows that you either disable it first, or handle the exception gracefully in case that is what your client application requires. You could prompt the user to disable the table explicitly and retry the operation.

Also note how the `isTableAvailable()` is returning `true`, even when the table is disabled. In other words, this method checks if the table is physically present, no matter what its state is. Use the other two functions, `isTableEnabled()` and `isTableDisabled()`, to check for the state of the table.

After creating your tables with the specified schema, you must either delete the newly created table to change the details, or use the following method to *alter* its structure:

```
void modifyTable(byte[] tableName, HTableDescriptor htd)
```

As with the aforementioned `deleteTable()` commands, you must first disable the table to be able to modify it. Example 5-5 does create a table, and subsequently modifies it.

Example 5-5. Modifying the structure of an existing table

```
byte[] name = Bytes.toBytes("testtable");
HBaseAdmin admin = new HBaseAdmin(conf);
HTableDescriptor desc = new HTableDescriptor(name);
HColumnDescriptor coldef1 = new HColumnDescriptor(
  Bytes.toBytes("colfam1"));
desc.addFamily(coldef1);

admin.createTable(desc); ❶

HTableDescriptor htd1 = admin.getTableDescriptor(name); ❷
HColumnDescriptor coldef2 = new HColumnDescriptor(
  Bytes.toBytes("colfam2"));
htd1.addFamily(coldef2);
htd1.setMaxFileSize(1024 * 1024 * 1024L);

admin.disableTable(name);
admin.modifyTable(name, htd1); ❸
admin.enableTable(name);

HTableDescriptor htd2 = admin.getTableDescriptor(name);
System.out.println("Equals: " + htd1.equals(htd2)); ❹
System.out.println("New schema: " + htd2);
```

❶ Create the table with the original structure.

❷ Get the schema, and update by adding a new family and changing the maximum file size property.

❸ Disable, modify, and enable the table.

❹ Check if the table schema matches the new one created locally.

The output shows that both the schema modified in the client code and the final schema retrieved from the server *after* the modification are consistent:

```
Equals: true
New schema: {NAME => 'testtable', MAX_FILESIZE => '1073741824', FAMILIES =>
[{NAME => 'colfam1', BLOOMFILTER => 'NONE', REPLICATION_SCOPE => '0',
COMPRESSION => 'NONE', VERSIONS => '3', TTL => '2147483647', BLOCKSIZE =>
'65536', IN_MEMORY => 'false', BLOCKCACHE => 'true'}, {NAME => 'colfam2',
```

```
BLOOMFILTER => 'NONE', REPLICATION_SCOPE => '0', COMPRESSION => 'NONE',
VERSIONS => '3', TTL => '2147483647', BLOCKSIZE => '65536', IN_MEMORY =>
'false', BLOCKCACHE => 'true'}]}
```

Calling the equals() method on the HTableDescriptor class compares the current with the specified instance and returns true if they match in all properties, also including the contained column families and their respective settings.

 The modifyTable() call is asynchronous, and there is no synchronous variant. If you want to make sure that changes have been propagated to all the servers and applied accordingly, you should use the getTableDescriptor() call and loop over it in your client code until the schema you sent matches up with the remote schema.

Schema Operations

Besides using the modifyTable() call, there are dedicated methods provided by the HBaseAdmin class to modify specific aspects of the current table schema. As usual, you need to make sure the table to be modified is disabled first.

The whole set of column-related methods is as follows:

```
void addColumn(String tableName, HColumnDescriptor column)
void addColumn(byte[] tableName, HColumnDescriptor column)
void deleteColumn(String tableName, String columnName)
void deleteColumn(byte[] tableName, byte[] columnName)
void modifyColumn(String tableName, HColumnDescriptor descriptor)
void modifyColumn(byte[] tableName, HColumnDescriptor descriptor)
```

You can add, delete, and modify columns. Adding or modifying a column requires that you first prepare an HColumnDescriptor instance, as described in detail in "Column Families" on page 212. Alternatively, you could use the getTableDescriptor() call to retrieve the current table schema, and subsequently invoke getColumnFamilies() on the returned HTableDescriptor instance to retrieve the existing columns.

Otherwise, you supply the table name—and optionally the column name for the delete calls—in one of the common format variations to eventually invoke the method of choice. All of these calls are asynchronous, so as mentioned before, caveat emptor.

Use Case: Hush

An interesting use case for the administrative API is to create and alter tables and their schemas based on an external configuration file. Hush is making use of this idea and defines the table and column descriptors in an XML file, which is read and the contained schema compared with the current table definitions. If there are any differences they are applied accordingly. The following example has the core of the code that does this task:

```
private void createOrChangeTable(final TableSchema schema)
  throws IOException {
```

```
        HTableDescriptor desc = null;
        if (tableExists(schema.getName(), false)) {
          desc = getTable(schema.getName(), false);
          LOG.info("Checking table " + desc.getNameAsString() + "...");
          final HTableDescriptor d = convertSchemaToDescriptor(schema);

          final List<HColumnDescriptor> modCols =
            new ArrayList<HColumnDescriptor>();
          for (final HColumnDescriptor cd : desc.getFamilies()) {
            final HColumnDescriptor cd2 = d.getFamily(cd.getName());
            if (cd2 != null && !cd.equals(cd2)) { ❶
              modCols.add(cd2);
            }
          }
          final List<HColumnDescriptor> delCols =
            new ArrayList<HColumnDescriptor>(desc.getFamilies());
          delCols.removeAll(d.getFamilies());
          final List<HColumnDescriptor> addCols =
            new ArrayList<HColumnDescriptor>(d.getFamilies());
          addCols.removeAll(desc.getFamilies());

          if (modCols.size() > 0 || addCols.size() > 0 || delCols.size() > 0 || ❷
              !hasSameProperties(desc, d)) {
            LOG.info("Disabling table...");
            hbaseAdmin.disableTable(schema.getName());
            if (modCols.size() > 0 || addCols.size() > 0 || delCols.size() > 0) {
              for (final HColumnDescriptor col : modCols) {
                LOG.info("Found different column -> " + col);
                hbaseAdmin.modifyColumn(schema.getName(), col.getNameAsString(), ❸
                  col);
              }
              for (final HColumnDescriptor col : addCols) {
                LOG.info("Found new column -> " + col);
                hbaseAdmin.addColumn(schema.getName(), col); ❹
              }
              for (final HColumnDescriptor col : delCols) {
                LOG.info("Found removed column -> " + col);
                hbaseAdmin.deleteColumn(schema.getName(), col.getNameAsString()); ❺
              }
            } else if (!hasSameProperties(desc, d)) {
              LOG.info("Found different table properties...");
              hbaseAdmin.modifyTable(Bytes.toBytes(schema.getName()), d); ❻
            }
            LOG.info("Enabling table...");
            hbaseAdmin.enableTable(schema.getName());
            LOG.info("Table enabled");
            desc = getTable(schema.getName(), false);
            LOG.info("Table changed");
          } else {
            LOG.info("No changes detected!");
          }
        } else {
          desc = convertSchemaToDescriptor(schema);
          LOG.info("Creating table " + desc.getNameAsString() + "...");
          hbaseAdmin.createTable(desc); ❼
          LOG.info("Table created");
        }
      }
    }
```

● Compute the differences between the XML-based schema and what is currently in HBase.

❷ See if there are any differences in the column and table definitions.

❸ Alter the columns that have changed. The table was properly disabled first.

❹ Add newly defined columns.

❺ Delete removed columns.

❻ Alter the table itself, if there are any differences found.

❼ If the table did not exist yet, create it now.

Cluster Operations

The last group of operations the HBaseAdmin class exposes is related to *cluster operations*. They allow you to check the status of the cluster, and perform tasks on tables and/or regions. "The Region Life Cycle" on page 348 has the details on regions and their life cycle.

 Many of the following operations are for advanced users, so please handle with care.

```
static void checkHBaseAvailable(Configuration conf)
ClusterStatus getClusterStatus()
```
You can use checkHBaseAvailable() to verify that your client application can communicate with the remote HBase cluster, as specified in the given configuration file. If it fails to do so, an exception is thrown—in other words, this method does *not* return a boolean flag, but either silently succeeds, or throws said error.

The getClusterStatus() call allows you to retrieve an instance of the ClusterStatus class, containing detailed information about the cluster status. See "Cluster Status Information" on page 233 for what you are provided with.

```
void closeRegion(String regionname, String hostAndPort)
void closeRegion(byte[] regionname, String hostAndPort)
```
Use these calls to close regions that have previously been deployed to region servers. Any enabled table has all regions enabled, so you could actively close and undeploy a region.

You need to supply the exact regionname as stored in the .META. table. Further, you may optionally supply the hostAndPort parameter, that overrides the server assignment as found in the .META. as well.

Using this close call does bypass any master notification, that is, the region is directly closed by the region server, unseen by the master node.

```
void flush(String tableNameOrRegionName)
void flush(byte[] tableNameOrRegionName)
```
As updates to a region (and the table in general) accumulate the MemStore instances of the region, servers fill with unflushed modifications. A client application can use these synchronous methods to flush such pending records to disk, before they are implicitly written by hitting the *memstore flush size* (see "Table Properties" on page 210) at a later time.

The method takes either a region name, or a table name. The value provided by your code is tested to see if it matches an existing table; if it does, it is assumed to be a table, otherwise it is treated as a region name. If you specify neither a proper table nor a region name, an UnknownRegionException is thrown.

```
void compact(String tableNameOrRegionName)
void compact(byte[] tableNameOrRegionName)
```
Similar to the preceding operations, you must give either a table or a region name. The call itself is asynchronous, as compactions can potentially take a long time to complete. Invoking this method queues the table, or region, for compaction, which is executed in the background by the server hosting the named region, or by all servers hosting any region of the given table (see "Auto-Sharding" on page 22 for details on compactions).

```
void majorCompact(String tableNameOrRegionName)
void majorCompact(byte[] tableNameOrRegionName)
```
These are the same as the compact() calls, but they queue the region, or table, for a major compaction instead. In case a table name is given, the administrative API iterates over all regions of the table and invokes the compaction call implicitly for each of them.

```
void split(String tableNameOrRegionName)
void split(byte[] tableNameOrRegionName)
void split(String tableNameOrRegionName, String splitPoint)
void split(byte[] tableNameOrRegionName, byte[] splitPoint)
```
Using these calls allows you to split a specific region, or table. In case a table name is given, it iterates over all regions of that table and implicitly invokes the split command on each of them.

A noted exception to this rule is when the splitPoint parameter is given. In that case, the split() command will try to split the given region at the provided row key. In the case of specifying a table name, all regions are checked and the one containing the splitPoint is split at the given key.

The splitPoint must be a valid row key, and—in case you specify a region name—be part of the region to be split. It also *must* be greater than the region's start key, since splitting a region at its start key would make no sense. If you fail to give the correct row key, the split request is ignored without reporting back to the client. The region server currently hosting the region will log this locally with the following message:

```
Split row is not inside region key range or is equal to startkey:
<split row>
```

void assign(byte[] regionName, boolean force)
void unassign(byte[] regionName, boolean force)

When a client requires a region to be deployed or undeployed from the region servers, it can invoke these calls. The first would assign a region, based on the overall assignment plan, while the second would unassign the given region.

The force parameter set to true has different meanings for each of the calls: first, for assign(), it forces the region to be marked as *unassigned* in ZooKeeper before continuing in its attempt to assign the region to a new region server. Be careful when using this on already-assigned regions.

Second, for unassign(), it means that a region already marked to be unassigned—for example, from a previous call to unassign()—is forced to be unassigned again. If force were set to false, this would have no effect.

void move(byte[] encodedRegionName, byte[] destServerName)

Using the move() call enables a client to actively control which server is hosting what regions. You can move a region from its current region server to a new one. The destServerName parameter can be set to null to pick a new server at random; otherwise, it must be a valid server name, running a region server process. If the server name is wrong, or currently not responding, the region is deployed to a different server instead. In a worst-case scenario, the move could fail and leave the region unassigned.

boolean balanceSwitch(boolean b)
boolean balancer()

The first method allows you to switch the region balancer on or off. When the balancer is enabled, a call to balancer() will start the process of moving regions from the servers, with more deployed to those with less deployed regions. "Load Balancing" on page 432 explains how this works in detail.

void shutdown()
void stopMaster() {
void stopRegionServer(String hostnamePort)

These calls either shut down the entire cluster, stop the master server, or stop a particular region server only. Once invoked, the affected servers will be stopped, that is, there is no delay nor a way to revert the process.

Chapters 8 and 11 have more information on these advanced—yet very powerful—features. Use with utmost care!

Cluster Status Information

When you query the cluster status using the `HBaseAdmin.getClusterStatus()` call, you will be given a `ClusterStatus` instance, containing all the information the master server has about the current state of the cluster. Note that this class also has setters—methods starting with `set`, allowing you to modify the information they contain—but since you will be given a copy of the current state, it is impractical to call the setters, unless you want to modify your local-only copy.

Table 5-4 lists the methods of the `ClusterStatus` class.

Table 5-4. Quick overview of the information provided by the ClusterStatus class

Method	Description
`int getServersSize()`	The number of region servers currently live as known to the master server. The number does not include the number of dead servers.
`Collection<ServerName> getServers()`	The list of live servers. The names in the collection are `ServerName` instances, which contain the hostname, RPC port, and start code.
`int getDeadServers()`	The number of servers listed as dead. This does not contain the live servers.
`Collection<ServerName> getDeadServerNames()`	A list of all server names currently considered dead. The names in the collection are `ServerName` instances, which contain the hostname, RPC port, and start code.
`double getAverageLoad()`	The total average number of regions per region server. This is the same currently as `getRegionsCount()/getServers()`.
`int getRegionsCount()`	The total number of regions in the cluster.
`int getRequestsCount()`	The current number of requests across all regions' servers in the cluster.
`String getHBaseVersion()`	Returns the HBase version identification string.
`byte getVersion()`	Returns the version of the `ClusterStatus` instance. This is used during the serialization process of sending an instance over RPC.
`String getClusterId()`	Returns the unique identifier for the cluster. This is a UUID generated when HBase starts with an empty storage directory. It is stored in *hbase.id* under the root directory.
`Map<String, RegionState> getRegionsInTransition()`	Gives you access to a map of all regions currently in transition, e.g., being moved, assigned, or unassigned. The key of the map is the encoded region name (as returned by `HRegionInfo.getEncodedName()`, for example), while the value is an instance of `RegionState`.[a]
`HServerLoad get Load(ServerName sn)`	Retrieves the status information available for the given server name.

[a] See "The Region Life Cycle" on page 348 for the details.

Accessing the overall cluster status gives you a high-level view of what is going on with your servers—as a whole. Using the `getServers()` array, and the returned `ServerName` instances, lets you drill further into each actual live server, and see what it is doing currently. Table 5-5 lists the available methods.

Table 5-5. Quick overview of the information provided by the ServerName class

Method	Description
`String getHostname()`	Returns the *hostname* of the server. This might resolve to the IP address, when the hostname cannot be looked up.
`String getHostAndPort()`	Concatenates the *hostname* and *RPC port*, divided by a colon: `<hostname>:<rpc-port>`.
`long getStartcode()`	The start code is the epoch time in milliseconds of when the server was started, as returned by `System.currentTimeMillis()`.
`String getServerName()`	The *server name*, consisting of `<hostname>`,`<rpc-port>`,`<start-code>`.
`int getPort()`	Specifies the port used by the server for the RPCs.

Each server also exposes details about its load, by offering an `HServerLoad` instance, returned by the `getLoad()` method of the `ClusterStatus` instance. Using the aforementioned `ServerName`, as returned by the `getServers()` call, you can iterate over all live servers and retrieve their current details. The `HServerLoad` class gives you access to not just the load of the server itself, but also for each hosted region. Table 5-6 lists the provided methods.

Table 5-6. Quick overview of the information provided by the HServerLoad class

Method	Description
`byte getVersion()`	Returns the version of the HServerLoad instance. This is used during the serialization process of sending an instance over RPC.
`int getLoad()`	Currently returns the same value as getNumberOfRegions().
`int getNumberOfRegions()`	The number of regions on the current server.
`int getNumberOfRequests()`	Returns the number of requests accumulated within the last `hbase.regionserver.msginterval` time frame. It is reset at the end of this time frame, and counts all API requests, such as gets, puts, increments, deletes, and so on.
`int getUsedHeapMB()`	The currently used Java Runtime heap size in megabytes.
`int getMaxHeapMB()`	The configured maximum Java Runtime heap size in megabytes.
`int getStorefiles()`	The number of store files in use by the server. This is across all regions it hosts.
`int getStorefileSizeInMB()`	The total size in megabytes of the used store files.
`int getStorefileIndexSizeInMB()`	The total size in megabytes of the indexes—the block and meta index, to be precise—across all store files in use by this server.
`int getMemStoreSizeInMB()`	The total size of the in-memory stores, across all regions hosted by this server.
`Map<byte[], RegionLoad> getRegions Load()`	Returns a map containing the load details for each hosted region of the current server. The key is the region name and the value an instance of the RegionsLoad class, discussed next.

Finally, there is a dedicated class for the region load, aptly named `RegionLoad`. See Table 5-7 for the list of provided information.

Table 5-7. Quick overview of the information provided by the RegionLoad class

Method	Description
`byte[] getName()`	The region name in its raw, `byte[]` byte array form.
`String getNameAsString()`	Converts the raw region name into a `String` for convenience.
`int getStores()`	The number of stores in this region.
`int getStorefiles()`	The number of store files, across all stores of this region.
`int getStorefileSizeMB()`	The size in megabytes of the store files for this region.
`int getStorefileIndexSizeMB()`	The size of the indexes for all store files, in megabytes, for this region.
`int getMemStoreSizeMB()`	The heap size in megabytes as used by the `MemStore` of the current region.
`long getRequestsCount()`	The number of requests for the current region.
`long getReadRequestsCount()`	The number of read requests for this region, since it was deployed to the region server. This counter is not reset.
`long getWriteRequestsCount()`	The number of write requests for this region, since it was deployed to the region server. This counter is not reset.

Example 5-6 shows all of the getters in action.

Example 5-6. Reporting the status of a cluster

```
HBaseAdmin admin = new HBaseAdmin(conf);

ClusterStatus status = admin.getClusterStatus(); ❶

System.out.println("Cluster Status:\n--------------");
System.out.println("HBase Version: " + status.getHBaseVersion());
System.out.println("Version: " + status.getVersion());
System.out.println("No. Live Servers: " + status.getServersSize());
System.out.println("Cluster ID: " + status.getClusterId());
System.out.println("Servers: " + status.getServers());
System.out.println("No. Dead Servers: " + status.getDeadServers());
System.out.println("Dead Servers: " + status.getDeadServerNames());
System.out.println("No. Regions: " + status.getRegionsCount());
System.out.println("Regions in Transition: " +
  status.getRegionsInTransition());
System.out.println("No. Requests: " + status.getRequestsCount());
System.out.println("Avg Load: " + status.getAverageLoad());

System.out.println("\nServer Info:\n--------------");
for (ServerName server : status.getServers()) { ❷
  System.out.println("Hostname: " + server.getHostname());
  System.out.println("Host and Port: " + server.getHostAndPort());
  System.out.println("Server Name: " + server.getServerName());
  System.out.println("RPC Port: " + server.getPort());
  System.out.println("Start Code: " + server.getStartcode());
```

```
HServerLoad load = status.getLoad(server); ❸

System.out.println("\nServer Load:\n--------------");
System.out.println("Load: " + load.getLoad());
System.out.println("Max Heap (MB): " + load.getMaxHeapMB());
System.out.println("Memstore Size (MB): " + load.getMemStoreSizeInMB());
System.out.println("No. Regions: " + load.getNumberOfRegions());
System.out.println("No. Requests: " + load.getNumberOfRequests());
System.out.println("Storefile Index Size (MB): " +
  load.getStorefileIndexSizeInMB());
System.out.println("No. Storefiles: " + load.getStorefiles());
System.out.println("Storefile Size (MB): " + load.getStorefileSizeInMB());
System.out.println("Used Heap (MB): " + load.getUsedHeapMB());

System.out.println("\nRegion Load:\n--------------");
for (Map.Entry<byte[], HServerLoad.RegionLoad> entry : ❹
  load.getRegionsLoad().entrySet()) {
  System.out.println("Region: " + Bytes.toStringBinary(entry.getKey()));

  HServerLoad.RegionLoad regionLoad = entry.getValue(); ❺

  System.out.println("Name: " + Bytes.toStringBinary(
    regionLoad.getName()));
  System.out.println("No. Stores: " + regionLoad.getStores());
  System.out.println("No. Storefiles: " + regionLoad.getStorefiles());
  System.out.println("Storefile Size (MB): " +
    regionLoad.getStorefileSizeMB());
  System.out.println("Storefile Index Size (MB): " +
    regionLoad.getStorefileIndexSizeMB());
  System.out.println("Memstore Size (MB): " +
    regionLoad.getMemStoreSizeMB());
  System.out.println("No. Requests: " + regionLoad.getRequestsCount());
  System.out.println("No. Read Requests: " +
    regionLoad.getReadRequestsCount());
  System.out.println("No. Write Requests: " +
    regionLoad.getWriteRequestsCount());
  System.out.println();
  }
}
```

❶ Get the cluster status.

❷ Iterate over the included server instances.

❸ Retrieve the load details for the current server.

❹ Iterate over the region details of the current server.

❺ Get the load details for the current region.

On a standalone setup, and having run the earlier examples in the book, you should see something like this:

```
Cluster Status:
--------------
Avg Load: 12.0
```

```
HBase Version: 0.91.0-SNAPSHOT
Version: 2
No. Servers: [10.0.0.64,60020,1304929650573]
No. Dead Servers: 0
Dead Servers: []
No. Regions: 12
No. Requests: 0

Server Info:
--------------
Hostname: 10.0.0.64
Host and Port: 10.0.0.64:60020
Server Name: 10.0.0.64,60020,1304929650573
RPC Port: 60020
Start Code: 1304929650573

Server Load:
--------------
Load: 12
Max Heap (MB): 987
Memstore Size (MB): 0
No. Regions: 12
No. Requests: 0
Storefile Index Size (MB): 0
No. Storefiles: 3
Storefile Size (MB): 0
Used Heap (MB): 62

Region Load:
--------------
Region: -ROOT-,,0
Name: -ROOT-,,0
No. Stores: 1
No. Storefiles: 1
Storefile Size (MB): 0
Storefile Index Size (MB): 0
Memstore Size (MB): 0
No. Requests: 52
No. Read Requests: 51
No. Write Requests: 1

Region: .META.,,1
Name: .META.,,1
No. Stores: 1
No. Storefiles: 0
Storefile Size (MB): 0
Storefile Index Size (MB): 0
Memstore Size (MB): 0
No. Requests: 4764
No. Read Requests: 4734
No. Write Requests: 30

Region: hush,,1304930393059.1ae3ea168c42fa9c855051c888ed36d4.
Name: hush,,1304930393059.1ae3ea168c42fa9c855051c888ed36d4.
No. Stores: 1
```

```
No. Storefiles: 0
Storefile Size (MB): 0
Storefile Index Size (MB): 0
Memstore Size (MB): 0
No. Requests: 20
No. Read Requests: 14
No. Write Requests: 6

Region: ldom,,1304930390882.520fc727a3ce79749bcbbad51e138fff.
Name: ldom,,1304930390882.520fc727a3ce79749bcbbad51e138fff.
No. Stores: 1
No. Storefiles: 0
Storefile Size (MB): 0
Storefile Index Size (MB): 0
Memstore Size (MB): 0
No. Requests: 14
No. Read Requests: 6
No. Write Requests: 8

Region: sdom,,1304930389795.4a49f5ba47e4466d284cea27629c26cc.
Name: sdom,,1304930389795.4a49f5ba47e4466d284cea27629c26cc.
No. Stores: 1
No. Storefiles: 0
Storefile Size (MB): 0
Storefile Index Size (MB): 0
Memstore Size (MB): 0
No. Requests: 8
No. Read Requests: 0
No. Write Requests: 8

Region: surl,,1304930386482.c965c89368951cf97d2339a05bc4bad5.
Name: surl,,1304930386482.c965c89368951cf97d2339a05bc4bad5.
No. Stores: 4
No. Storefiles: 0
Storefile Size (MB): 0
Storefile Index Size (MB): 0
Memstore Size (MB): 0
No. Requests: 1329
No. Read Requests: 1226
No. Write Requests: 103

Region: testtable,,1304930621191.962abda0515c910ed91f7520e71ba101.
Name: testtable,,1304930621191.962abda0515c910ed91f7520e71ba101.
No. Stores: 2
No. Storefiles: 0
Storefile Size (MB): 0
Storefile Index Size (MB): 0
Memstore Size (MB): 0
No. Requests: 29
No. Read Requests: 0
No. Write Requests: 29

Region: testtable,row-030,1304930621191.0535bb40b407321d499d65bab9d3b2d7.
Name: testtable,row-030,1304930621191.0535bb40b407321d499d65bab9d3b2d7.
No. Stores: 2
```

```
No. Storefiles: 2
Storefile Size (MB): 0
Storefile Index Size (MB): 0
Memstore Size (MB): 0
No. Requests: 6
No. Read Requests: 6
No. Write Requests: 0

Region: testtable,row-060,1304930621191.81b04004d72bd28cc877cb1514dbab35.
Name: testtable,row-060,1304930621191.81b04004d72bd28cc877cb1514dbab35.
No. Stores: 2
No. Storefiles: 0
Storefile Size (MB): 0
Storefile Index Size (MB): 0
Memstore Size (MB): 0
No. Requests: 41
No. Read Requests: 0
No. Write Requests: 41

Region: url,,1304930387617.a39d16967d51b020bb4dad13a80a1a02.
Name: url,,1304930387617.a39d16967d51b020bb4dad13a80a1a02.
No. Stores: 1
No. Storefiles: 0
Storefile Size (MB): 0
Storefile Index Size (MB): 0
Memstore Size (MB): 0
No. Requests: 11
No. Read Requests: 8
No. Write Requests: 3

Region: user,,1304930388702.60bae27e577a620ae4b59bc830486233.
Name: user,,1304930388702.60bae27e577a620ae4b59bc830486233.
No. Stores: 1
No. Storefiles: 0
Storefile Size (MB): 0
Storefile Index Size (MB): 0
Memstore Size (MB): 0
No. Requests: 11
No. Read Requests: 9
No. Write Requests: 2

Region: user-surl,,1304930391974.71b9cecc9c111a5217bd1a81bde60418.
Name: user-surl,,1304930391974.71b9cecc9c111a5217bd1a81bde60418.
No. Stores: 1
No. Storefiles: 0
Storefile Size (MB): 0
Storefile Index Size (MB): 0
Memstore Size (MB): 0
No. Requests: 24
No. Read Requests: 21
No. Write Requests: 3
```

Available Clients

HBase comes with a variety of clients that can be used from various programming languages. This chapter will give you an overview of what is available.

Introduction to REST, Thrift, and Avro

Access to HBase is possible from virtually every popular programming language and environment. You either use the client API directly, or access it through some sort of proxy that translates your request into an API call. These proxies wrap the native Java API into other protocol APIs so that clients can be written in any language the external API provides. Typically, the external API is implemented in a dedicated Java-based server that can internally use the provided HTable client API. This simplifies the implementation and maintenance of these gateway servers.

The protocol between the gateways and the clients is then driven by the available choices and requirements of the remote client. An obvious choice is *Representational State Transfer* (REST),* which is based on existing web-based technologies. The actual transport is typically HTTP—which is *the* standard protocol for web applications. This makes REST ideal for communicating between heterogeneous systems: the protocol layer takes care of transporting the data in an interoperable format.

REST defines the semantics so that the protocol can be used in a generic way to address remote resources. By not changing the protocol, REST is compatible with existing technologies, such as web servers, and proxies. Resources are uniquely specified as part of the request URI—which is the opposite of, for example, SOAP-based† services, which define a new protocol that conforms to a standard.

---

* See "Architectural Styles and the Design of Network-based Software Architectures" (*http://www.ics.uci.edu/ ~fielding/pubs/dissertation/top.htm*) by Roy T. Fielding, 2000.

† See the official SOAP specification online (*http://www.w3.org/TR/soap/*). SOAP—or *Simple Object Access Protocol*—also uses HTTP as the underlying transport protocol, but exposes a different API for every service.

However, both REST and SOAP suffer from the verbosity level of the protocol. Human-readable text, be it plain or XML-based, is used to communicate between client and server. Transparent compression of the data sent over the network can mitigate this problem to a certain extent.

As a result, companies with very large server farms, extensive bandwidth usage, and many disjoint services felt the need to reduce the overhead and implemented their own RPC layers. One of them was Google, which implemented *Protocol Buffers*.[‡] Since the implementation was initially not published, Facebook developed its own version, named *Thrift*.[§] The Hadoop project founders started a third project, *Apache Avro*,[||] providing an alternative implementation.

All of them have similar feature sets, vary in the number of languages they support, and have (arguably) slightly better or worse levels of encoding efficiencies. The key difference with Protocol Buffers when compared to Thrift and Avro is that it has no RPC stack of its own; rather, it generates the RPC definitions, which have to be used with other RPC libraries subsequently.

HBase ships with auxiliary servers for REST, Thrift, and Avro. They are implemented as standalone gateway servers, which can run on shared or dedicated machines. Since Thrift and Avro have their own RPC implementation, the gateway servers simply provide a wrapper around them. For REST, HBase has its own implementation, offering access to the stored data.

 The supplied *RESTServer* actually supports Protocol Buffers. Instead of implementing a separate RPC server, it leverages the `Accept` header of HTTP to send and receive the data encoded in Protocol Buffers. See "REST" on page 244 for details.

Figure 6-1 shows how dedicated gateway servers are used to provide endpoints for various remote clients.

Internally, these servers use the common `HTable`-based client API to access the tables. You can see how they are started on top of the region server processes, sharing the same physical machine. There is no one true recommendation for how to place the gateway servers. You may want to collocate them, or have them on dedicated machines.

Another approach is to run them directly on the client nodes. For example, when you have web servers constructing the resultant HTML pages using PHP, it is advantageous to run the gateway process on the same server. That way, the communication between

---

‡ See the official Protocol Buffer project website (*http://code.google.com/p/protobuf/*).

§ See the Thrift project website (*http://thrift.apache.org/*).

|| See the Apache Avro project website (*http://avro.apache.org/*).

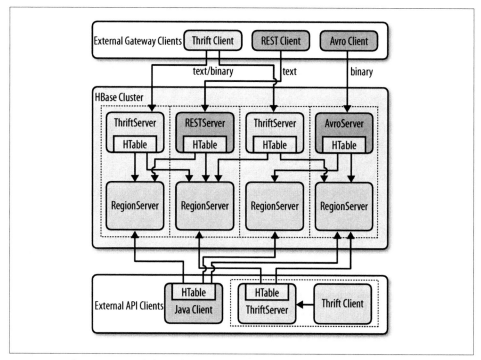

Figure 6-1. Clients connected through gateway servers

the client and gateway is local, while the RPC between the gateway and HBase is using the native protocol.

 Check carefully how you access HBase from your client, to place the gateway servers on the appropriate physical machine. This is influenced by the load on each machine, as well as the amount of data being transferred: make sure you are not starving either process for resources, such as CPU cycles, or network bandwidth.

The advantage of using a server as opposed to creating a new connection for every request goes back to when we discussed "HTablePool" on page 199—you need to reuse connections to gain maximum performance. Short-lived processes would spend more time setting up the connection and preparing the metadata than in the actual operation itself. The caching of region information in the server, in particular, makes the reuse important; otherwise, every client would have to perform a full row-to-region lookup for every bit of data they want to access.

Selecting one server type over the others is a nontrivial task, as it depends on your use case. The initial argument over REST in comparison to the more efficient Thrift, or similar serialization formats, shows that for high-throughput scenarios it is advantageous to use a purely binary format. However, if you have few requests, but they are large in size, REST is interesting. A rough separation could look like this:

REST use case
> Since REST supports existing web-based infrastructure, it will fit nicely into setups with reverse proxies and other caching technologies. Plan to run many REST servers in parallel, to distribute the load across them. For example, run a server on every application server you have, building a *single-app-to-server* relationship.

Thrift/Avro use case
> Use the compact binary protocols when you need the best performance in terms of throughput. You can run fewer servers—for example, one per region server—with a *many-apps-to-server* cardinality.

Interactive Clients

The first group of clients consists of the *interactive* ones, those that send client API calls on demand, such as get, put, or delete, to servers. Based on your choice of protocol, you can use the supplied gateway servers to gain access from your applications.

Native Java

The native Java API was discussed in Chapters 3 and 4. There is no need to start any gateway server, as your client using `HTable` is directly communicating with the HBase servers, via the native RPC calls. Refer to the aforementioned chapters to implement a native Java client.

REST

HBase ships with a powerful REST server, which supports the complete client and administrative API. It also provides support for different message formats, offering many choices for a client application to communicate with the server.

Operation

For REST-based clients to be able to connect to HBase, you need to start the appropriate gateway server. This is done using the supplied scripts. The following commands show you how to get the command-line help, and then start the REST server in a non-daemonized mode:

```
$ bin/hbase rest
usage: bin/hbase rest start [-p <arg>] [-ro]
 -p,--port <arg>    Port to bind to [default: 8080]
 -ro,--readonly     Respond only to GET HTTP method requests [default:
                    false]

To run the REST server as a daemon, execute bin/hbase-daemon.sh start|stop
```

```
rest [-p <port>] [-ro]
```

```
$ bin/hbase rest start
^C
```

You need to press Ctrl-C to quit the process. The help stated that you need to run the server using a different script to start it as a background process:

```
$ bin/hbase-daemon.sh start rest
starting rest, logging to /var/lib/hbase/logs/hbase-larsgeorge-rest-<servername>.out
```

Once the server is started you can use *curl#* on the command line to verify that it is operational:

```
$ curl http://<servername>:8080/
testtable
```

```
$ curl http://<servername>:8080/version
rest 0.0.2 [JVM: Apple Inc. 1.6.0_24-19.1-b02-334] [OS: Mac OS X 10.6.7 \
    x86_64] [Server: jetty/6.1.26] [Jersey: 1.4]
```

Retrieving the root URL, that is "/" (slash), returns the list of available tables, here testtable. Using "/version" retrieves the REST server version, along with details about the machine it is running on.

Stopping the REST server, and running as a daemon, involves the same script, just replacing start with stop:

```
$ bin/hbase-daemon.sh stop rest
stopping rest..
```

The REST server gives you all the operations required to work with HBase tables.

> The current documentation for the REST server is online at *http://hbase .apache.org/apidocs/org/apache/hadoop/hbase/rest/package-summary .html*. Please refer to it for all the provided operations. Also, be sure to carefully read the XML schemas documentation on that page (*http:// hbase.apache.org/apidocs/org/apache/hadoop/hbase/rest/package-sum mary.html#xmlschema*). It explains the schemas you need to use when requesting information, as well as those returned by the server.

You can start as many REST servers as you like, and, for example, use a load balancer to route the traffic between them. Since they are stateless—any state required is carried as part of the request—you can use a round-robin (or similar) approach to distribute the load.

Finally, use the -p, or --port, parameter to specify a different port for the server to listen on. The default is 8080.

#curl is a command-line tool for transferring data with URL syntax, supporting a large variety of protocols. See the project's website (*http://curl.haxx.se/*) for details.

Supported formats

Using the HTTP `Content-Type` and `Accept` headers, you can switch between different formats being sent or returned to the caller. As an example, you can create a table and row in HBase using the shell like so:

```
hbase(main):001:0> create 'testtable', 'colfam1'
0 row(s) in 1.1790 seconds

hbase(main):002:0> put 'testtable', "\x01\x02\x03", 'colfam1:col1', 'value1'
0 row(s) in 0.0990 seconds

hbase(main):003:0> scan 'testtable'
ROW                COLUMN+CELL
 \x01\x02\x03      column=colfam1:col1, timestamp=1306140523371, value=value1
1 row(s) in 0.0730 seconds
```

This inserts a row with the binary row key 0x01 0x02 0x03 (in hexadecimal numbers), with one column, in one column family, that contains the value `value1`.

Plain (text/plain). For some operations it is permissible to have the data returned as plain text. One example is the aforementioned `/version` operation:

```
$ curl -H "Accept: text/plain" http://<servername>:8080/version
rest 0.0.2 [JVM: Apple Inc. 1.6.0_24-19.1-b02-334] [OS: Mac OS X 10.6.7 \
  x86_64] [Server: jetty/6.1.26] [Jersey: 1.4]
```

On the other hand, using plain text with more complex return values is not going to work as expected:

```
$ curl -H "Accept: text/plain" \
  http://<servername>:8080/testtable/%01%02%03/colfam1:col1
<html> http://<servername>:8080/testtable/%01%02%03/colfam1:col1
<head>
<meta http-equiv="Content-Type" content="text/html; charset=ISO-8859-1"/>
<title>Error 406 Not Acceptable</title>
</head>
<body><h2>HTTP ERROR 406</h2>
<p>Problem accessing /testtable/%01%02%03/colfam1:col1. Reason:
<pre>    Not Acceptable</pre></p><hr /><i><small>Powered by Jetty://</small></i><br/>
<br/>
...
</body>
</html>
```

This is caused by the fact that the server cannot make any assumptions regarding how to format a complex result value in plain text. You need to use a format that allows you to express nested information natively.

As per the example table created in the previous text, the row key is a binary one, consisting of three bytes. You can use REST to access those bytes by encoding the key using *URL encoding,** which in this case results in %01%02%03. The entire URL to retrieve a cell is then:

```
http://<servername>:8080/testtable/%01%02%03/colfam1:col1
```

See the online documentation referred to earlier for the entire syntax.

XML (text/xml). When storing or retrieving data, XML is considered the default format. For example, when retrieving the example row with no particular `Accept` header, you receive:

```
$ curl http://<servername>:8080/testtable/%01%02%03/colfam1:col1
<?xml version="1.0" encoding="UTF-8" standalone="yes"?>
  <CellSet>
    <Row key="AQID">
      <Cell timestamp="1306140523371" \
            column="Y29sZmFtMTpjb2wx">dmFsdWUx</Cell>
    </Row>
  </CellSet>
```

The returned format defaults to XML. The column name and the actual value are encoded in *Base64,*† as explained in the online schema documentation. Here is the excerpt:

```
<complexType name="Row">
  <sequence>
    <element name="key" type="base64Binary"></element>
    <element name="cell" type="tns:Cell" maxOccurs="unbounded" \
            minOccurs="1"></element>
  </sequence>
</complexType>

<element name="Cell" type="tns:Cell"></element>

<complexType name="Cell">
  <sequence>
    <element name="value" maxOccurs="1" minOccurs="1">
      <simpleType><restriction base="base64Binary">
      </simpleType>
    </element>
  </sequence>
  <attribute name="column" type="base64Binary" />
  <attribute name="timestamp" type="int" />
</complexType>
```

---

* The basic idea is to encode any unsafe or unprintable character code as *"%"* + *ASCII Code.* Because it uses the percent sign as the prefix, it is also called *percent encoding.* See the Wikipedia page on percent encoding (*http://en.wikipedia.org/wiki/Percent-encoding*) for details.

† See the Wikipedia page on Base64 (*http://en.wikipedia.org/wiki/Base64*) for details.

All occurrences of `base64Binary` are where the REST server returns the encoded data. This is done to safely transport the binary data that can be contained in the keys, or the value.

This is also true for data that is sent to the REST server. Make sure to read the schema documentation to encode the data appropriately, including the payload, in other words, the actual data, but also the column name, row key, and so on.

A quick test on the console using the `base64` command reveals the proper content:

```
$ echo AQID | base64 -d | hexdump
0000000 01 02 03

$ echo Y29sZmFtMTpjb2wx | base64 -d
colfam1:col1

$ echo dmFsdWUx | base64 -d
value11
```

This is obviously useful only to verify the details on the command line. From within your code you can use any available Base64 implementation to decode the returned values.

JSON (application/json). Similar to XML, requesting (or setting) the data in JSON simply requires setting the `Accept` header:

```
$ curl -H "Accept: application/json" \
  http://<servername>:8080/testtable/%01%02%03/colfam1:col1

{
  "Row": [{
    "key": "AQID",
    "Cell": [{
      "timestamp": 1306140523371,
      "column": "Y29sZmFtMTpjb2wx",
      "$": "dmFsdWUx"
    }]
  }]
}
```

The preceding JSON result was reformatted to be easier to read. Usually the result on the console is returned as a single line, for example:

```
{"Row":[{"key":"AQID","Cell":[{"timestamp":1306140523371,"column": \
"Y29sZmFtMTpjb2wx","$":"dmFsdWUx"}]}]}
```

The encoding of the values is the same as for XML, that is, Base64 is used to encode any value that potentially contains binary data. An important distinction to XML is that JSON does not have nameless data fields. In XML the cell data is returned between

Cell tags, but JSON *must* specify *key/value* pairs, so there is no immediate counterpart available. For that reason, JSON has a special field called "*$*" (the dollar sign). The value of the *dollar* field is the cell data. In the preceding example, you can see it being used:

```
...
"$":"dmFsdWUx"
...
```

You need to query the dollar field to get the Base64-encoded data.

Protocol Buffer (application/x-protobuf). An interesting application of REST is to be able to switch encodings. Since Protocol Buffers have no native RPC stack, the HBase REST server offers support for its encoding. The schemas are documented online (*hbase .apache.org*) for your perusal.

Getting the results returned in Protocol Buffer encoding requires the matching Accept header:

```
$ curl -H "Accept: application/x-protobuf" \
  http://<servername>:8080/testtable/%01%02%03/colfam1:col1 | hexdump -C
00000000  0a 24 0a 03 01 02 03 12  1d 12 0c 63 6f 6c 66 61  |.$.........colfa|
00000010  6d 31 3a 63 6f 6c 31 18  eb f6 aa e0 81 26 22 06  |m1:col1......&".|
00000020  76 61 6c 75 65 31                                 |value1|
```

The use of *hexdump* allows you to print out the encoded message in its binary format. You need a Protocol Buffer decoder to actually access the data in a structured way. The ASCII printout on the righthand side of the output shows the column name and cell value for the example row.

Raw binary (application/octet-stream). Finally, you can dump the data in its raw form, while omitting structural data. In the following console command, only the data is returned, as stored in the cell.

```
$ curl -H "Accept: application/octet-stream" \
  http://<servername>:8080/testtable/%01%02%03/colfam1:col1 | hexdump -C
00000000  76 61 6c 75 65 31                                 |value1|
```

 Depending on the format request, the REST server puts structural data into a custom header. For example, for the raw get request in the preceding paragraph, the headers look like this (adding -D- to the *curl* command):

```
HTTP/1.1 200 OK
Content-Length: 6
X-Timestamp: 1306140523371
Content-Type: application/octet-stream
```

The timestamp of the cell has been moved to the header as X-Time stamp. Since the row and column keys are part of the request URI, they are omitted from the response to prevent unnecessary data from being transferred.

REST Java client

The REST server also comes with a comprehensive Java client API. It is located in the org.apache.hadoop.hbase.rest.client package. The central classes are RemoteHTable and RemoteAdmin. Example 6-1 shows the use of the RemoteHTable class.

Example 6-1. Using the REST client classes

```
Cluster cluster = new Cluster();
cluster.add("localhost", 8080); ❶

Client client = new Client(cluster); ❷

RemoteHTable table = new RemoteHTable(client, "testtable"); ❸

Get get = new Get(Bytes.toBytes("row-30")); ❹
get.addColumn(Bytes.toBytes("colfam1"), Bytes.toBytes("col-3"));
Result result1 = table.get(get);

System.out.println("Get result1: " + result1);

Scan scan = new Scan();
scan.setStartRow(Bytes.toBytes("row-10"));
scan.setStopRow(Bytes.toBytes("row-15"));
scan.addColumn(Bytes.toBytes("colfam1"), Bytes.toBytes("col-5"));
ResultScanner scanner = table.getScanner(scan); ❺

for (Result result2 : scanner) {
  System.out.println("Scan row[" + Bytes.toString(result2.getRow()) +
    "]: " + result2);
}
```

❶ Set up a cluster list adding all known REST server hosts.

❷ Create the client handling the HTTP communication.

❸ Create a remote table instance, wrapping the REST access into a familiar interface.

❹ Perform a get() operation as if it were a direct HBase connection.

❺ Scan the table; again, this is the same approach as if using the native Java API.

Running the example requires that the REST server has been started and is listening on the specified port. If you are running the server on a different machine and/or port, you need to first adjust the value added to the Cluster instance.

Here is what is printed on the console when running the example:

```
Adding rows to table...
Get result1: keyvalues={row-30/colfam1:col-3/1306157569144/Put/vlen=8}
Scan row[row-10]: keyvalues={row-10/colfam1:col-5/1306157568822/Put/vlen=8}
Scan row[row-100]: keyvalues={row-100/colfam1:col-5/1306157570225/Put/vlen=9}
Scan row[row-11]: keyvalues={row-11/colfam1:col-5/1306157568841/Put/vlen=8}
Scan row[row-12]: keyvalues={row-12/colfam1:col-5/1306157568857/Put/vlen=8}
Scan row[row-13]: keyvalues={row-13/colfam1:col-5/1306157568875/Put/vlen=8}
Scan row[row-14]: keyvalues={row-14/colfam1:col-5/1306157568890/Put/vlen=8}
```

Due to the lexicographical sorting of row keys, you will receive the preceding rows. The selected columns have been included as expected.

The `RemoteHTable` is a convenient way to talk to a number of REST servers, while being able to use the normal Java client API classes, such as `Get` or `Scan`.

 The current implementation of the Java REST client is using the Protocol Buffer encoding internally to communicate with the remote REST server. It is the most compact protocol the server supports, and therefore provides the best bandwidth efficiency.

Thrift

Apache Thrift is written in C++, but provides schema compilers for many programming languages, including Java, C++, Perl, PHP, Python, Ruby, and more. Once you have compiled a schema, you can exchange messages transparently between systems implemented in one or more of those languages.

Installation

Before you can use Thrift, you need to install it, which is preferably done using a binary distribution package for your operating system. If that is not an option, you need to compile it from its sources.

Download the source tarball from the website, and unpack it into a common location:

```
$ wget http://www.apache.org/dist/thrift/0.6.0/thrift-0.6.0.tar.gz
$ tar -xzvf thrift-0.6.0.tar.gz -C /opt
$ rm thrift-0.6.0.tar.gz
```

Install the dependencies, which are `Automake`, `LibTool`, `Flex`, `Bison`, and the `Boost` libraries:

```
$ sudo apt-get install build-essential automake libtool flex bison libboost
```

Now you can build and install the Thrift binaries like so:

```
$ cd /opt/thrift-0.6.0
$ ./configure
$ make
$ sudo make install
```

You can verify that everything succeeded by calling the main thrift executable:

```
$ thrift -version
Thrift version 0.6.0
```

Once you have Thrift installed, you need to compile a schema into the programming language of your choice. HBase comes with a schema file for its client and administrative API. You need to use the Thrift binary to create the wrappers for your development environment.

The supplied schema file exposes the majority of the API functionality, but is lacking in a few areas. It was created when HBase had a different API and that is noticeable when using it. Newer implementations of features—for example, filters—are not supported at all.

An example of the differences in API calls is the mutateRow() call the Thrift schema is using, while the new API has the appropriate get() call.

Work is being done in HBASE-1744 (*https://issues.apache.org/jira/browse/HBASE-1744*) to port the Thrift schema file to the current API, while adding all missing features. Once this is complete, it will be added as the *thrift2* package so that you can maintain your existing code using the older schema, while working on porting it over to the new schema.

Before you can access HBase using Thrift, though, you also have to start the supplied ThriftServer.

Operation

Starting the Thrift server is accomplished by using the supplied scripts. You can get the command-line help by adding the -h switch, or omitting all options:

```
$ bin/hbase thrift
usage: Thrift [-b <arg>] [-c] [-f] [-h] [-hsha | -nonblocking |
       -threadpool] [-p <arg>]
 -b,--bind <arg>   Address to bind the Thrift server to. Not supported by
                   the Nonblocking and HsHa server [default: 0.0.0.0]
 -c,--compact      Use the compact protocol
 -f,--framed       Use framed transport
 -h,--help         Print help information
 -hsha             Use the THsHaServer. This implies the framed transport.
 -nonblocking      Use the TNonblockingServer. This implies the framed
                   transport.
 -p,--port <arg>   Port to bind to [default: 9090]
 -threadpool       Use the TThreadPoolServer. This is the default.
To start the Thrift server run 'bin/hbase-daemon.sh start thrift'
To shutdown the thrift server run 'bin/hbase-daemon.sh stop thrift' or
send a kill signal to the thrift server pid
```

There are many options to choose from. The type of server, protocol, and transport used is usually enforced by the client, since not all language implementations have support for them. From the command-line help you can see that, for example, using the *nonblocking* server implies the *framed transport*.

Using the defaults, you can start the Thrift server in nondaemonized mode:

```
$ bin/hbase thrift start
^C
```

You need to press Ctrl-C to quit the process. The help stated that you need to run the server using a different script to start it as a background process:

```
$ bin/hbase-daemon.sh start thrift
starting thrift, logging to /var/lib/hbase/logs/ \
hbase-larsgeorge-thrift-<servername>.out
```

Stopping the Thrift server, running as a daemon, involves the same script, just replacing start with stop:

```
$ bin/hbase-daemon.sh stop thrift
stopping thrift..
```

The Thrift server gives you all the operations required to work with HBase tables.

> The current documentation for the Thrift server is online at *http://wiki .apache.org/hadoop/Hbase/ThriftApi*. You should refer to it for all the provided operations. It is also advisable to read the provided *$HBASE_HOME/src/main/resources/org/apache/hadoop/hbase/thrift/ Hbase.thrift* schema definition file for the full documentation of the available functionality.

You can start as many Thrift servers as you like, and, for example, use a load balancer to route the traffic between them. Since they are stateless, you can use a round-robin (or similar) approach to distribute the load.

Finally, use the -p, or --port, parameter to specify a different port for the server to listen on. The default is 9090.

Example: PHP

HBase not only ships with the required Thrift schema file, but also with an example client for many programming languages. Here we will enable the PHP implementation to demonstrate the required steps.

> You need to enable PHP support for your web server! Follow your server documentation to do so.

The first step is to copy the supplied schema file and compile the necessary PHP source files for it:

```
$ cp -r $HBASE_HOME/src/main/resources/org/apache/hadoop/hbase/thrift ~/thrift_src
$ cd thrift_src/
$ thrift -gen php Hbase.thrift
```

The call to *thrift* should complete with no error or other output on the command line. Inside the *thrift_src* directory you will now find a directory named *gen-php* containing the two generated PHP files required to access HBase:

```
$ ls -l gen-php/Hbase/
total 616
```

```
-rw-r--r--  1 larsgeorge  staff  285433 May 24 10:08 Hbase.php
-rw-r--r--  1 larsgeorge  staff   27426 May 24 10:08 Hbase_types.php
```

These generated files require the Thrift-supplied PHP harness to be available as well. They need to be copied into your web server's *document root* directory, along with the generated files:

```
$ cd /opt/thrift-0.6.0
$ sudo cp lib/php/src $DOCUMENT_ROOT/thrift
$ sudo mkdir $DOCUMENT_ROOT/thrift/packages
$ sudo cp -r ~/thrift_src/gen-php/Hbase $DOCUMENT_ROOT/thrift/packages/
```

The generated PHP files are copied into a *packages* subdirectory, as per the Thrift documentation, which needs to be created if it does not exist yet.

 The $DOCUMENT_ROOT in the preceding code could be */var/www*, for example, on a Linux system using Apache, or */Library/WebServer/ Documents/* on an Apple Mac OS 10.6 machine. Check your web server configuration for the appropriate location.

HBase ships with a *DemoClient.php* file that uses the generated files to communicate with the servers. This file is copied into the same document root directory of the web server:

```
$ sudo cp $HBASE_HOME/src/examples/thrift/DemoClient.php $DOCUMENT_ROOT/
```

You need to edit the *DemoClient.php* file and adjust the following fields at the beginning of the file:

```
# Change this to match your thrift root
$GLOBALS['THRIFT_ROOT'] = 'thrift';
...
# According to the thrift documentation, compiled PHP thrift libraries should
# reside under the THRIFT_ROOT/packages directory.  If these compiled libraries
# are not present in this directory, move them there from gen-php/.
require_once( $GLOBALS['THRIFT_ROOT'].'/packages/Hbase/Hbase.php' );
...
$socket = new TSocket( 'localhost', 9090 );
...
```

Usually, editing the first line is enough to set the THRIFT_ROOT path. Since the *Demo-Client.php* file is also located in the document root directory, it is sufficient to set the variable to *thrift*, that is, the directory copied from the Thrift sources earlier.

The last line in the preceding excerpt has a hardcoded server name and port. If you set up the example in a distributed environment, you need to adjust this line to match your environment as well.

After everything has been put into place and adjusted appropriately, you can open a browser and point it to the demo page. For example:

```
http://<webserver-address>/DemoClient.php
```

This should load the page and output the following details (abbreviated here for the sake of brevity):

```
scanning tables...
   found: testtable
creating table: demo_table
column families in demo_table:
   column: entry:, maxVer: 10
   column: unused:, maxVer: 3
Starting scanner...
...
```

The same client is also available in C++, Java, Perl, Python, and Ruby. Follow the same steps to start the Thrift server, compile the schema definition into the necessary language, and start the client. Depending on the language, you will need to put the generated code into the appropriate location first.

HBase already ships with the generated Java classes to communicate with the Thrift server. You can always regenerate them again from the schema file, but for convenience they are already included.

Avro

Apache Avro, like Thrift, provides schema compilers for many programming languages, including Java, C++, PHP, Python, Ruby, and more. Once you have compiled a schema, you can exchange messages transparently between systems implemented in one or more of those languages.

Installation

Before you can use Avro, you need to install it, which is preferably done using a binary distribution package for your operating system. If that is not an option, you need to compile it from its sources.

Once you have Avro installed, you need to compile a schema into the programming language of your choice. HBase comes with a schema file for its client and administrative API. You need to use the Avro tools to create the wrappers for your development environment.

Before you can access HBase using Avro, though, you also have to start the supplied AvroServer.

Operation

Starting the Avro server is accomplished by using the supplied scripts. You can get the command-line help by adding the -h switch, or omitting all options:

```
$ bin/hbase avro
Usage: java org.apache.hadoop.hbase.avro.AvroServer --help | [--port=PORT] start
Arguments:
  start Start Avro server
```

```
     stop  Stop Avro server
   Options:
     port  Port to listen on. Default: 9090
     help  Print this message and exit
```

You can start the Avro server in nondaemonized mode using the following command:

```
$ bin/hbase avro start
^C
```

You need to press Ctrl-C to quit the process. You need to run the server using a different script to start it as a background process:

```
$ bin/hbase-daemon.sh start avro
starting avro, logging to /var/lib/hbase/logs/hbase-larsgeorge-avro-<servername>.out
```

Stopping the Avro server, running as a daemon, involves the same script, just replacing start with stop:

```
$ bin/hbase-daemon.sh stop avro
stopping avro..
```

The Avro server gives you all the operations required to work with HBase tables.

 The current documentation for the Avro server is available online at *http://hbase.apache.org/apidocs/org/apache/hadoop/hbase/avro/package -summary.html.* Please refer to it for all the provided operations. You are also advised to read the provided *$HBASE_HOME/src/main/java/ org/apache/hadoop/hbase/avro/hbase.avpr* schema definition file for the full documentation of the available functionality.

You can start as many Avro servers as you like, and, for example, use a load balancer to route the traffic between them. Since they are stateless, you can use a round-robin (or similar) approach to distribute the load.

Finally, use the -p, or --port, parameter to specify a different port for the server to listen on. The default is 9090.

Other Clients

There are other client libraries that allow you to access an HBase cluster. They can roughly be divided into those that run directly on the Java Virtual Machine, and those that use the gateway servers to communicate with an HBase cluster. Here are some examples:

JRuby

The HBase Shell is an example of using a JVM-based language to access the Java-based API. It comes with the full source code, so you can use it to add the same features to your own JRuby code.

HBql

> HBql adds an SQL-like syntax on top of HBase, while adding the extensions needed where HBase has unique features. See the project's website (*http://www.hbql .com/*) for details.

HBase-DSL

> This project gives you dedicated classes that help when formulating queries against an HBase cluster. Using a builder-like style, you can quickly assemble all the options and parameters necessary. See its wiki (*https://github.com/nearinfinity/hbase -dsl/wiki*) online for more information.

JPA/JPO

> You can use, for example, DataNucleus (*http://www.datanucleus.org/*) to put a JPA/ JPO access layer on top of HBase.

PyHBase

> The PyHBase project (*https://github.com/hammer/pyhbase/*) offers an HBase client through the Avro gateway server.

AsyncHBase

> AsyncHBase offers a completely asynchronous, nonblocking, and thread-safe client to access HBase clusters. It uses the native RPC protocol to talk directly to the various servers. See the project's website (*https://github.com/stumbleupon/asyn chbase*) for details.

 Note that some of these projects have not seen any activity for quite some time. They usually were created to fill a need of the authors, and since then have been made public. You can use them as a starting point for your own projects.

Batch Clients

The opposite use case of interactive clients is *batch* access to data. The difference is that these clients usually run asynchronously in the background, scanning large amounts of data to build, for example, search indexes, machine-learning-based mathematical models, or statistics needed for reporting.

Access is less user-driven, and therefore, SLAs are geared more toward overall runtime, as opposed to per-request latencies. The majority of the batch frameworks reading and writing from and to HBase are MapReduce-based.

MapReduce

The Hadoop MapReduce framework is built to process petabytes of data, in a reliable, deterministic, yet easy-to-program way. There are a variety of ways to include HBase as a source and target for MapReduce jobs.

Native Java

The Java-based MapReduce API for HBase is discussed in Chapter 7.

Clojure

The HBase-Runner project (*https://github.com/mudphone/hbase-runner/*) offers support for HBase from the functional programming language Clojure. You can write MapReduce jobs in Clojure while accessing HBase tables.

Hive

The *Apache Hive* project[‡] offers a data warehouse infrastructure atop Hadoop. It was initially developed at Facebook, but is now part of the open source Hadoop ecosystem.

Hive offers an SQL-like query language, called *HiveQL*, which allows you to query the semistructured data stored in Hadoop. The query is eventually turned into a MapReduce job, executed either locally or on a distributed MapReduce cluster. The data is parsed at job execution time and Hive employs a *storage handler*[§] abstraction layer that allows for data not to just reside in HDFS, but other data sources as well. A storage handler transparently makes arbitrarily stored information available to the HiveQL-based user queries.

Since version 0.6.0, Hive also comes with a handler for HBase.[ǁ] You can define Hive tables that are backed by HBase tables, mapping columns as required. The row key can be exposed as another column when needed.

HBase Version Support

As of this writing, version 0.7.0 of Hive includes support for HBase `0.89.0-SNAPSHOT` only, though this is likely to change soon. The implication is that you cannot run the HBase integration against a more current version, since the RPC is very sensitive to version changes and will bail out at even minor differences.

The only way currently is to replace the HBase JARs with the newer ones and recompile Hive from source. You either need to update the Ivy settings to include the version of HBase (and probably Hadoop) you need, or try to build Hive, then copy the newer JARs into the *$HIVE_HOME/src/build/dist/lib* directory and compile again (YMMV).

The better approach is to let Ivy load the appropriate version from the remote repositories, and then compile Hive normally. To get started, download the source tarball from the website and unpack it into a common location:

---

‡ *http://hive.apache.org/*

§ See the Hive wiki (*http://wiki.apache.org/hadoop/Hive/StorageHandlers*) for more details on storage handlers.

ǁ The Hive wiki (*http://wiki.apache.org/hadoop/Hive/HBaseIntegration*) has a full explanation of the HBase integration into Hive.

```
$ wget http://www.apache.org/dist//hive/hive-0.7.0/hive-0.7.0.tar.gz
$ tar -xzvf hive-0.7.0.tar.gz -C /opt
```

Then edit the Ivy library configuration file:

```
$ cd /opt/hive-0.7.0/src
$ vim ivy/libraries.properties
...
#hbase.version=0.89.0-SNAPSHOT
#hbase-test.version=0.89.0-SNAPSHOT
hbase.version=0.91.0-SNAPSHOT
hbase-test.version=0.91.0-SNAPSHOT
...
```

You can now build Hive from the sources using *ant*, but not before you have set the environment variable for the Hadoop version you are building against:

```
$ export HADOOP_HOME="/<your-path>/hadoop-0.20.2"
$ ant package
Buildfile: /opt/hive-0.7.0/src/build.xml

jar:

create-dirs:

compile-ant-tasks:

...

package:
    [echo] Deploying Hive jars to /opt/hive-0.7.0/src/build/dist

BUILD SUCCESSFUL
```

The build process will take awhile, since Ivy needs to download all required libraries, and that depends on your Internet connection speed. Once the build is complete, you can start using the HBase handler with the new version of HBase.

In some cases, you need to slightly edit all files in *src/hbase-handler/src/java/org/apache/hadoop/hive/hbase/* and replace the way the configuration is created, from:

```
HBaseConfiguration hbaseConf = new HBaseConfiguration(hiveConf);
```

to the newer style, using a static factory method:

```
Configuration hbaseConf = HBaseConfiguration.create(hiveConf);
```

After you have installed Hive itself, you have to edit its configuration files so that it has access to the HBase JAR file, and the accompanying configuration. Modify *$HIVE_HOME/conf/hive-env.sh* to contain these lines:

```
# Set HADOOP_HOME to point to a specific hadoop install directory
HADOOP_HOME=/usr/local/hadoop
HBASE_HOME=/usr/local/hbase

# Hive Configuration Directory can be controlled by:
# export HIVE_CONF_DIR=
export HIVE_CLASSPATH=/etc/hbase/conf
```

```
# Folder containing extra libraries required for hive compilation/execution
# can be controlled by:
export HIVE_AUX_JARS_PATH=/usr/local/hbase/hbase-0.91.0-SNAPSHOT.jar
```

 You may have to copy the supplied *$HIVE_HOME/conf/hive-env.sh.template* file, and save it in the same directory, but without the *.template* extension. Once you have copied the file, you can edit it as described.

Once Hive is installed and operational, you can start using the new handler. First start the Hive command-line interface, create a native Hive table, and insert data from the supplied example files:

```
$ build/dist/bin/hive
Hive history file=/tmp/larsgeorge/hive_job_log_larsgeorge_201105251455_2009910117.txt
hive> CREATE TABLE pokes (foo INT, bar STRING);
OK
Time taken: 3.381 seconds

hive> LOAD DATA LOCAL INPATH '/opt/hive-0.7.0/examples/files/kv1.txt'
  OVERWRITE INTO TABLE pokes;
Copying data from file:/opt/hive-0.7.0/examples/files/kv1.txt
Copying file: file:/opt/hive-0.7.0/examples/files/kv1.txt
Loading data to table default.pokes
Deleted file:/user/hive/warehouse/pokes
OK
Time taken: 0.266 seconds
```

This is using the pokes table, as described in the Hive guide at *http://wiki.apache.org/hadoop/Hive/GettingStarted*. Next you create an HBase-backed table like so:

```
hive> CREATE TABLE hbase_table_1(key int, value string)
STORED BY 'org.apache.hadoop.hive.hbase.HBaseStorageHandler'
WITH SERDEPROPERTIES ("hbase.columns.mapping" = ":key,cf1:val")
TBLPROPERTIES ("hbase.table.name" = "hbase_table_1");
OK
Time taken: 0.144 seconds
```

This DDL statement maps the HBase table, defined using the TBLPROPERTIES, and SERDEPROPERTIES, using the new HBase handler, to a Hive table named hbase_table_1. The hbase.columns.mapping has a special feature, which is mapping the column with the name ":key" to the HBase row key. You can place this special column to perform row key mapping anywhere in your definition. Here it is placed as the first column, thus mapping the values in the key column of the Hive table to be the row key in the HBase table.

The `hbase.table.name` in the table properties is optional and only needed when you want to use different names for the tables in Hive and HBase. Here it is set to the same value, and therefore could be omitted.

Loading the table from the previously filled `pokes` Hive table is done next. According to the mapping, this will save the `pokes.foo` values in the row key, and the `pokes.bar` in the column `cf1:val`:

```
hive> INSERT OVERWRITE TABLE hbase_table_1 SELECT * FROM pokes;
Total MapReduce jobs = 1
Launching Job 1 out of 1
Number of reduce tasks is set to 0 since there's no reduce operator
Execution log at: /tmp/larsgeorge/larsgeorge_20110525152020_de5f67d1-9411- \
446f-99bb-35621e1b259d.log
Job running in-process (local Hadoop)
2011-05-25 15:20:31,031 null map = 100%,  reduce = 0%
Ended Job = job_local_0001
OK
Time taken: 3.925 seconds
```

This starts the first MapReduce job in this example. You can see how the Hive command line prints out the values it is using. The job copies the values from the internal Hive table into the HBase-backed one.

 In certain setups, especially in the local, pseudodistributed mode, the Hive job may fail with an obscure error message. Before trying to figure out the details, try running the job in Hive *local* MapReduce mode. In the Hive CLI enter:

```
hive> SET mapred.job.tracker=local;
```

Then execute the job again. This mode was added in Hive 0.7.0, and may not be available to you. If it is, try to use it, since it avoids using the Hadoop MapReduce framework—which means you have one less part to worry about when debugging a failed Hive job.

The following counts the rows in the `pokes` and `hbase_table_1` tables (the CLI output of the job details are omitted for the second and all subsequent queries):

```
hive> select count(*) from pokes;
Total MapReduce jobs = 1
Launching Job 1 out of 1
Number of reduce tasks determined at compile time: 1
In order to change the average load for a reducer (in bytes):
  set hive.exec.reducers.bytes.per.reducer=<number>
In order to limit the maximum number of reducers:
  set hive.exec.reducers.max=<number>
In order to set a constant number of reducers:
  set mapred.reduce.tasks=<number>
Execution log at: /tmp/larsgeorge/larsgeorge_20110525152323_418769e6-1716- \
48ee-a0ab-dacd59e55da8.log
Job running in-process (local Hadoop)
```

```
2011-05-25 15:23:07,058 null map = 100%,  reduce = 100%
Ended Job = job_local_0001
OK
500
Time taken: 3.627 seconds

hive> select count(*) from hbase_table_1;
...
OK
309
Time taken: 4.542 seconds
```

What is interesting to note is the difference in the actual count for each table. They differ by more than 100 rows, where the HBase-backed table is the shorter one. What could be the reason for this? In HBase, you cannot have duplicate row keys, so every row that was copied over, and which had the same value in the originating pokes.foo column, is saved as the same row. This is the same as performing a SELECT DISTINCT on the source table:

```
hive> select count(distinct foo) from pokes;
...
OK
309
Time taken: 3.525 seconds
```

This is now the same outcome and proves that the previous results are correct. Finally, drop both tables, which also removes the underlying HBase table:

```
hive> drop table pokes;
OK
Time taken: 0.741 seconds

hive> drop table hbase_table_1;
OK
Time taken: 3.132 seconds

hive> exit;
```

You can also map an existing HBase table into Hive, or even map the table into multiple Hive tables. This is useful when you have very distinct column families, and querying them is done separately. This will improve the performance of the query significantly, since it uses a Scan internally, selecting only the mapped column families. If you have a sparsely set family, this will only scan the much smaller files on disk, as opposed to running a job that has to scan everything just to filter out the sparse data.

Mapping an existing table requires the Hive EXTERNAL keyword, which is also used in other places to access data stored in *unmanaged* Hive tables, that is, those that are not under Hive's control:

```
hive> CREATE EXTERNAL TABLE hbase_table_2(key int, value string)
STORED BY 'org.apache.hadoop.hive.hbase.HBaseStorageHandler'
WITH SERDEPROPERTIES ("hbase.columns.mapping" = ":key,cf1:val")
TBLPROPERTIES("hbase.table.name" = "<existing-table-name>");
```

External tables are *not* deleted when the table is dropped within Hive. This simply removes the metadata information about the table.

You have the option to map any HBase column directly to a Hive column, or you can map an entire column family to a Hive `MAP` type. This is useful when you do not know the column qualifiers ahead of time: map the family and iterate over the columns from within the Hive query instead.

 HBase columns you do not map into Hive are not accessible for Hive queries.

Since storage handlers work transparently for the higher-level layers in Hive, you can also use any *user-defined function* (UDF) supplied with Hive—or your own custom functions.

There are a few shortcomings in the current version, though:

No custom serialization
HBase only stores `byte[]` arrays, so Hive is simply converting every column value to `String`, and serializes it from there. For example, an `INT` column set to `12` in Hive would be stored as if using `Bytes.toBytes("12")`.

No version support
There is currently no way to specify any version details when handling HBase tables. Hive always returns the most recent version.

Check with the Hive project site to see if these features have since been added.

Pig

The *Apache Pig* project[#] provides a platform to analyze large amounts of data. It has its own high-level query language, called *Pig Latin*, which uses an imperative programming style to formulate the steps involved in transforming the input data to the final output. This is the opposite of Hive's declarative approach to emulate SQL.

The nature of Pig Latin, in comparison to HiveQL, appeals to everyone with a procedural programming background, but also lends itself to significant parallelization. When it is combined with the power of Hadoop and the MapReduce framework, you can process massive amounts of data in reasonable time frames.

Version 0.7.0 of Pig introduced the `LoadFunc`/`StoreFunc` classes and functionality, which allows you to load and store data from sources other than the usual HDFS. One of those sources is HBase, implemented in the `HBaseStorage` class.

[#] *http://pig.apache.org/*

Pigs' support for HBase includes reading and writing to existing tables. You can map table columns as Pig *tuples*, which optionally include the row key as the first field for read operations. For writes, the first field is always used as the row key.

The storage also supports basic filtering, working on the row level, and providing the comparison operators explained in "Comparison operators" on page 139.[*]

Pig Installation

You should try to install the prebuilt binary packages for the operating system distribution of your choice. If this is not possible, you can download the source from the project website and build it locally. For example, on a Linux-based system you could perform the following steps.[†]

Download the source tarball from the website, and unpack it into a common location:

```
$ wget http://www.apache.org/dist//pig/pig-0.8.1/pig-0.8.1.tar.gz
$ tar -xzvf pig-0.8.1.tar.gz -C /opt
$ rm pig-0.8.1.tar.gz
```

Add the *pig* script to the shell's search path, and set the `PIG_HOME` environment variable like so:

```
$ export PATH=/opt/pig-0.8.1/bin:$PATH
$ export PIG_HOME=/opt/pig-0.8.1
```

After that, you can try to see if the installation is working:

```
$ pig -version
Apache Pig version 0.8.1
compiled May 27 2011, 14:58:51
```

You can use the supplied tutorial code and data to experiment with Pig and HBase. You do have to create the table in the HBase Shell first to work with it from within Pig:

```
hbase(main):001:0> create 'excite', 'colfam1'
```

Starting the Pig Shell, aptly called *Grunt*, requires the *pig* script. For local testing add the -x local switch:

```
$ pig -x local
grunt>
```

Local mode implies that Pig is not using a separate MapReduce installation, but uses the `LocalJobRunner` that comes as part of Hadoop. It runs the resultant MapReduce jobs within the same process. This is useful for testing and prototyping, but should not be used for larger data sets.

---

[*] Internally it uses the `RowFilter` class; see "RowFilter" on page 141.

[†] The full details can be found on the Pig setup page (*http://pig.apache.org/docs/r0.8.0/setup.html*).

You have the option to write the script beforehand in an editor of your choice, and subsequently specify it when you invoke the *pig* script. Or you can use Grunt, the Pig Shell, to enter the Pig Latin statements interactively. Ultimately, the statements are translated into one or more MapReduce jobs, but not all statements trigger the execution. Instead, you first define the steps line by line, and a call to DUMP or STORE will eventually set the job in motion.

> The Pig Latin functions are case-insensitive, though commonly they are written in uppercase. Names and fields you define are case-sensitive, and so are the Pig Latin functions.

The Pig tutorial comes with a small data set that was published by Excite, and contains an anonymous user ID, a timestamp, and the search terms used on its site. The first step is to load the data into HBase using a slight transformation to generate a compound key. This is needed to enforce uniqueness for each entry:

```
grunt> raw = LOAD 'tutorial/data/excite-small.log' \
USING PigStorage('\t') AS (user, time, query);
T = FOREACH raw GENERATE CONCAT(CONCAT(user, '\u0000'), time), query;
grunt> STORE T INTO 'excite' USING \
org.apache.pig.backend.hadoop.hbase.HBaseStorage('colfam1:query');
...
2011-05-27 22:55:29,717 [main] INFO  org.apache.pig.backend.hadoop. \
executionengine.mapReduceLayer.MapReduceLauncher - 100% complete
2011-05-27 22:55:29,717 [main] INFO  org.apache.pig.tools.pigstats.PigStats \
- Detected Local mode. Stats reported below may be incomplete
2011-05-27 22:55:29,718 [main] INFO  org.apache.pig.tools.pigstats.PigStats \
- Script Statistics:

HadoopVersion PigVersion     UserId StartedAt        FinishedAt Features
0.20.2  0.8.1  larsgeorge  2011-05-27 22:55:22 2011-05-27 22:55:29  UNKNOWN

Success!

Job Stats (time in seconds):
JobId    Alias    Feature Outputs
job_local_0002  T,raw   MAP_ONLY      excite,

Input(s):
Successfully read records from: "file:///opt/pig-0.8.1/tutorial/data/excite-small.log"

Output(s):
Successfully stored records in: "excite"

Job DAG:
job_local_0002
```

You can use the DEFINE statement to abbreviate the long Java package reference for the HBaseStorage class. For example:

```
grunt> DEFINE LoadHBaseUser org.apache.pig.backend.hadoop.hbase.HBaseStorage( \
'data:roles', '-loadKey');
grunt> U = LOAD 'user' USING LoadHBaseUser;
grunt> DUMP U;
...
```

This is useful if you are going to reuse the specific load or store function.

The STORE statement started a MapReduce job that read the data from the given logfile and copied it into the HBase table. The statement in between is changing the *relation* to generate a compound row key—which is the first field specified in the STORE statement afterward—which is the user and time fields, separated by a zero byte.

Accessing the data involves another LOAD statement, this time using the HBaseStorage class:

```
grunt> R = LOAD 'excite' USING \
org.apache.pig.backend.hadoop.hbase.HBaseStorage('colfam1:query', '-loadKey') \
AS (key: chararray, query: chararray);
```

The parameters in the brackets define the column to field mapping, as well as the extra option to load the row key as the first field in relation R. The AS part explicitly defines that the row key and the colfam1:query column are converted to chararray, which is Pig's string type. By default, they are returned as bytearray, matching the way they are stored in the HBase table. Converting the data type allows you, for example, to subsequently split the row key.

You can test the statements entered so far by dumping the content of R, which is the result of the previous statement.

```
grunt> DUMP R;
...
Success!
...
(002BB5A52580A8ED970916150445,margaret laurence the stone angel)
(002BB5A52580A8ED970916150505,margaret laurence the stone angel)
...
```

The row key, placed as the first field in the tuple, is the concatenated representation created during the initial copying of the data from the file into HBase. It can now be split back into two fields so that the original layout of the text file is re-created:

```
grunt> S = foreach R generate FLATTEN(STRSPLIT(key, '\u0000', 2)) AS \
(user: chararray, time: long), query;
grunt> DESCRIBE S;
S: {user: chararray,time: long,query: chararray}
```

Using DUMP once more, this time using relation S, shows the final result:

```
grunt> DUMP S;
(002BB5A52580A8ED,970916150445,margaret laurence the stone angel)
(002BB5A52580A8ED,970916150505,margaret laurence the stone angel)
...
```

With this in place, you can proceed to the remainder of the Pig tutorial, while replacing the LOAD and STORE statements with the preceding code. Concluding this example, type in QUIT to finally exit the Grunt shell:

```
grunt> QUIT;
$
```

Pig's support for HBase has a few shortcomings in the current version, though:

No version support
>   There is currently no way to specify any version details when handling HBase cells. Pig always returns the most recent version.

Fixed column mapping
>   The row key must be the first field and cannot be placed anywhere else. This can be overcome, though, with a subsequent FOREACH...GENERATE statement, reordering the relation layout.

Check with the Pig project site to see if these features have since been added.

Cascading

Cascading is an alternative API to MapReduce. Under the covers, it uses MapReduce during execution, but during development, users don't have to think in MapReduce to create solutions for execution on Hadoop.

The model used is similar to a real-world *pipe assembly*, where data sources are *taps*, and outputs are *sinks*. These are *piped* together to form the processing flow, where data passes through the pipe and is transformed in the process. Pipes can be connected to larger *pipe assemblies* to form more complex processing pipelines from existing pipes.

Data then *streams* through the pipeline and can be split, merged, grouped, or joined. The data is represented as *tuples*, forming a *tuple stream* through the assembly. This very visually oriented model makes building MapReduce jobs more like construction work, while abstracting the complexity of the actual work involved.

Cascading (as of version 1.0.1) has support for reading and writing data to and from an HBase cluster. Detailed information and access to the source code can be found on the Cascading Modules page (*http://www.cascading.org/modules.html*).

Example 6-2 shows how to *sink* data into an HBase cluster. See the GitHub repository, linked from the modules page, for more up-to-date API information.

Example 6-2. Using Cascading to insert data into HBase

```
// read data from the default filesystem
// emits two fields: "offset" and "line"
Tap source = new Hfs(new TextLine(), inputFileLhs);

// store data in an HBase cluster, accepts fields "num", "lower", and "upper"
// will automatically scope incoming fields to their proper familyname,
// "left" or "right"
Fields keyFields = new Fields("num");
String[] familyNames = {"left", "right"};
Fields[] valueFields = new Fields[] {new Fields("lower"),
  new Fields("upper") };
Tap hBaseTap = new HBaseTap("multitable", new HBaseScheme(keyFields,
  familyNames, valueFields), SinkMode.REPLACE);

// a simple pipe assembly to parse the input into fields
// a real app would likely chain multiple Pipes together for more complex
// processing
Pipe parsePipe = new Each("insert", new Fields("line"),
  new RegexSplitter(new Fields("num", "lower", "upper"), " "));

// "plan" a cluster executable Flow
// this connects the source Tap and hBaseTap (the sink Tap) to the parsePipe
Flow parseFlow = new FlowConnector(properties).connect(source, hBaseTap,
  parsePipe);

// start the flow, and block until complete
parseFlow.complete();

// open an iterator on the HBase table we stuffed data into
TupleEntryIterator iterator = parseFlow.openSink();

while(iterator.hasNext()) {
  // print out each tuple from HBase
  System.out.println( "iterator.next() = " + iterator.next() );
}

iterator.close();
```

Cascading to Hive and Pig offers a Java API, as opposed to the domain-specific languages (DSLs) provided by the others. There are add-on projects that provide DSLs on top of Cascading.

Shell

The *HBase Shell* is the command-line interface to your HBase cluster(s). You can use it to connect to local or remote servers and interact with them. The shell provides both client and administrative operations, mirroring the APIs discussed in the earlier chapters of this book.

Basics

The first step to experience the shell is to start it:

```
$ $HBASE_HOME/bin/hbase shell
HBase Shell; enter 'help<RETURN>' for list of supported commands.
Type "exit<RETURN>" to leave the HBase Shell
Version 0.91.0-SNAPSHOT, r1130916, Sat Jul 23 12:44:34 CEST 2011

hbase(main):001:0>
```

The shell is based on *JRuby*, the Java Virtual Machine-based implementation of Ruby.‡ More specifically, it uses the *Interactive Ruby Shell* (IRB), which is used to enter Ruby commands and get an immediate response. HBase ships with Ruby scripts that extend the IRB with specific commands, related to the Java-based APIs. It inherits the built-in support for command history and completion, as well as all Ruby commands.

 There is no need to install Ruby on your machines, as HBase ships with the required JAR files to execute the JRuby shell. You use the supplied script to start the shell on top of Java, which is already a necessary requirement.

Once started, you can type in *help*, and then press Return, to get the help text (abbreviated in the following code sample):

```
hbase(main):001:0> help
HBase Shell, version 0.91.0-SNAPSHOT, r1130916, Sat Jul 23 12:44:34 CEST 2011
Type 'help "COMMAND"', (e.g. 'help "get"' -- the quotes are necessary) for
help on a specific command. Commands are grouped. Type 'help "COMMAND_GROUP"',
(e.g. 'help "general"') for help on a command group.

COMMAND GROUPS:
  Group name: general
  Commands: status, version

  Group name: ddl
  Commands: alter, create, describe, disable, drop, enable, exists,
            is_disabled, is_enabled, list

...

SHELL USAGE:
Quote all names in HBase Shell such as table and column names.  Commas delimit
command parameters.  Type <RETURN> after entering a command to run it.
Dictionaries of configuration used in the creation and alteration of tables are
Ruby Hashes. They look like this:
...
```

---

‡ Visit the Ruby website (*http://www.ruby-lang.org/*) for details.

As stated, you can request help for a specific command by adding the command when invoking help, or print out the help of all commands for a specific group when using the group name with the *help* command. The *command* or *group name* has the enclosed in quotes.

You can leave the shell by entering *exit*, or *quit*:

```
hbase(main):002:0> exit
$
```

The shell also has specific command-line options, which you can see when adding the -h, or --help, switch to the command:

```
$ $HBASE_HOME/bin.hbase shell -h
HBase Shell command-line options:
 format        Formatter for outputting results: console | html. Default: console
 -d | --debug  Set DEBUG log levels.
```

Debugging

Adding the -d, or --debug switch, to the shell's start command enables the *debug* mode, which switches the logging levels to DEBUG, and lets the shell print out any *backtrace* information—which is similar to *stacktraces* in Java.

Once you are inside the shell, you can use the *debug* command to toggle the debug mode:

```
hbase(main):001:0> debug
Debug mode is ON

hbase(main):002:0> debug
Debug mode is OFF
```

You can check the status with the *debug?* command:

```
hbase(main):003:0> debug?
Debug mode is OFF
```

Without the debug mode, the shell is set to print only ERROR-level messages, and no backtrace details at all, on the console.

There is an option to switch the formatting being used by the shell. As of this writing, only console is available, though.

The shell start script automatically uses the configuration directory located in the same $HBASE_HOME directory. You can override the location to use other settings, but most importantly to connect to different clusters. Set up a separate directory that contains an *hbase-site.xml* file, with an hbase.zookeeper.quorum property pointing to another cluster, and start the shell like so:

```
$ HBASE_CONF_DIR="/<your-other-config-dir>/" bin/hbase shell
```

Note that you have to specify an entire directory, *not* just the *hbase-site.xml* file.

Commands

The commands are grouped into five different categories, representing their semantic relationships. When entering commands, you have to follow a few guidelines:

Quote names

Commands that require a table or column name expect the name to be quoted in either single or double quotes.

Quote values

The shell supports the output and input of binary values using a hexadecimal—or octal—representation. You *must* use double quotes or the shell will interpret them as literals.

```
hbase> get 't1', "key\x00\x6c\x65\x6f\x6e"
hbase> get 't1', "key\000\154\141\165\162\141"
hbase> put 't1', "test\xef\xff", 'f1:', "\x01\x33\x70"
```

Note the mixture of quotes: you need to make sure you use the correct ones, or the result might not be what you had expected. Text in single quotes is treated as a literal, whereas double-quoted text is *interpolated*, that is, it transforms the octal, or hexadecimal, values into bytes.

Comma delimiters for parameters

Separate command parameters using commas. For example:

```
hbase(main):001:0> get 'testtable', 'row-1',
'colfam1:qual1'
```

Ruby hashes for properties

For some commands, you need to hand in a map with *key/value* properties. This is done using Ruby hashes:

```
{'key1' => 'value1', 'key2' => 'value2', ...}
```

The keys/values are wrapped in curly braces, and in turn are separated by "=>". Usually keys are predefined constants such as NAME, VERSIONS, or COMPRESSION, and do not need to be quoted. For example:

```
hbase(main):001:0> create 'testtable', {NAME =>
'colfam1', VERSIONS => 1, \
TTL => 2592000, BLOCKCACHE => true}
```

Restricting Output

The *get* command has an optional parameter that you can use to restrict the printed values by length. This is useful if you have many columns with values of varying length. To get a quick overview of the actual columns, you could suppress any longer value being printed in full—which on the console can get unwieldy very quickly otherwise.

In the following example, a very long value is inserted and subsequently retrieved with a restricted length, using the MAXLENGTH parameter:

```
hbase(main):001:0> put
'testtable','rowlong','colfam1:qual1','abcdefghijklmnopqrstuvwxyzabcdefghi \
jklmnopqrstuvwxyzabcdefghijklmnopqrstuvwxyzabcdefghijklmnopqrstuvwxyzabcde \
...
xyzabcdefghijklmnopqrstuvwxyzabcdefghijklmnopqrstuvwxyz'

hbase(main):018:0> get 'testtable', 'rowlong', MAXLENGTH => 60
COLUMN              CELL
colfam1:qual1   timestamp=1306424577316, value=abcdefghijklmnopqrstuvwxyzabc
```

The MAXLENGTH is counted from the start of the row (i.e., it includes the column name).
Set it to the width (or slightly less) of your console to fit each column into one line.

For any command, you can get detailed help by typing in help '*<command>*'. Here's an
example:

```
hbase(main):001:0> help 'status'
Show cluster status. Can be 'summary', 'simple', or 'detailed'. The
default is 'summary'. Examples:

  hbase> status
  hbase> status 'simple'
  hbase> status 'summary'
  hbase> status 'detailed'
```

The majority of commands have a direct match with a method provided by either the
client or administrative API. Next is a brief overview of each command and the matching API functionality.

General

The general commands are listed in Table 6-1. They allow you to retrieve details about
the status of the cluster itself, and the version of HBase it is running. See the Cluster
Status class in "Cluster Status Information" on page 233 for details.

Table 6-1. General shell commands

Command	Description
status	Returns various levels of information contained in the ClusterStatus class. See the help to get the *simple*, *summary*, and *detailed* status information.
version	Returns the current version, repository revision, and compilation date of your HBase cluster. See ClusterStatus.getHBaseVersion() in Table 5-4.

Data definition

The data definition commands are listed in Table 6-2. Most of them stem from the administrative API, as described in Chapter 5.

Table 6-2. Data definition shell commands

Command	Description
alter	Modifies an existing table schema using modifyTable(). See "Schema Operations" on page 228 for details.
create	Creates a new table. See the createTable() call in "Table Operations" on page 220 for details.
describe	Prints the HTableDescriptor. See "Tables" on page 207 for details.
disable	Disables a table. See "Table Operations" and the disableTable() method.
drop	Drops a table. See the deleteTable() method in "Table Operations".
enable	Enables a table. See the enableTable() call in "Table Operations" for details.
exists	Checks if a table exists. It uses the tableExists() call; see "Table Operations".
is_disabled	Checks if a table is disabled. See the isTableDisabled() method in "Table Operations".
is_enabled	Checks if a table is enabled. See the isTableEnabled() method in "Table Operations".
list	Returns a list of all user tables. Uses the listTables() method, described in "Table Operations".

Data manipulation

The data manipulation commands are listed in Table 6-3. Most of them are provided by the client API, as described in Chapters 3 and 4.

Table 6-3. Data manipulation shell commands

Command	Description
count	Counts the rows in a table. Uses a Scan internally, as described in "Scans" on page 122.
delete	Deletes a cell. See "Delete Method" on page 105 and the Delete class.
deleteall	Similar to *delete* but does not require a column. Deletes an entire family or row. See "Delete Method" and the Delete class.
get	Retrieves a cell. See the Get class in "Get Method" on page 95.
get_counter	Retrieves a counter value. Same as the *get* command but converts the raw counter value into a readable number. See the Get class in "Get Method".
incr	Increments a counter. Uses the Increment class; see "Counters" on page 168 for details.
put	Stores a cell. Uses the Put class, as described in "Put Method" on page 76.
scan	Scans a range of rows. Relies on the Scan class. See "Scans" on page 122 for details.
truncate	Truncates a table, which is the same as executing the disable and drop commands, followed by a create, using the same schema.

Tools

The tools commands are listed in Table 6-4. These commands are provided by the administrative API; see "Cluster Operations" on page 230 for details.

Table 6-4. Tools shell commands

Command	Description
assign	Assigns a region to a server. See "Cluster Operations" on page 230 and the assign() method.
balance_switch	Toggles the balancer switch. See "Cluster Operations" and the balanceSwitch() method.
balancer	Starts the balancer. See "Cluster Operations" and the balancer() method.
close_region	Closes a region. Uses the closeRegion() method, as described in "Cluster Operations".
compact	Starts the asynchronous compaction of a region or table. Uses compact(), as described in "Cluster Operations".
flush	Starts the asynchronous flush of a region or table. Uses flush(), as described in "Cluster Operations".
major_compact	Starts the asynchronous major compaction of a region or table. Uses majorCompact(), as described in "Cluster Operations".
move	Moves a region to a different server. See the move() call, and "Cluster Operations" for details.
split	Splits a region or table. See the split() call, and "Cluster Operations" for details.
unassign	Unassigns a region. See the unassign() call, and "Cluster Operations" for details.
zk_dump	Dumps the ZooKeeper details pertaining to HBase. This is a special function offered by an internal class. The web-based UI of the HBase Master exposes the same information.

Replication

The replication commands are listed in Table 6-5.

Table 6-5. Replication shell commands

Command	Description
add_peer	Adds a replication peer
disable_peer	Disables a replication peer
enable_peer	Enables a replication peer
remove_peer	Removes a replication peer
start_replication	Starts the replication process
stop_replication	Stops the replications process

Scripting

Inside the shell, you can execute the provided commands interactively, getting immediate feedback. Sometimes, though, you just want to send one command, and possibly script this call from the scheduled maintenance system (e.g., *cron* or *at*). Or you want to send a command in response to a check run in Nagios, or another monitoring tool. You can do this by *piping* the command into the shell:

```
$ echo "status" | bin/hbase shell
HBase Shell; enter 'help<RETURN>' for list of supported commands.
Type "exit<RETURN>" to leave the HBase Shell
Version 0.91.0-SNAPSHOT, r1130916, Sat Jul 23 12:44:34 CEST 2011

status
1 servers, 0 dead, 44.0000 average load
```

Once the command is complete, the shell is closed and control is given back to the caller. Finally, you can hand in an entire script to be executed by the shell at startup:

```
$ cat ~/hbase-shell-status.rb
status
$ bin/hbase shell ~/hbase-shell-status.rb
1 servers, 0 dead, 44.0000 average load

HBase Shell; enter 'help<RETURN>' for list of supported commands.
Type "exit<RETURN>" to leave the HBase Shell
Version 0.91.0-SNAPSHOT, r1130916, Sat Jul 23 12:44:34 CEST 2011

hbase(main):001:0> exit
```

Once the script has completed, you can continue to work in the shell or exit it as usual. There is also an option to execute a script using the raw JRuby interpreter, which involves running it directly as a Java application. Using the *hbase* script sets up the classpath to be able to use any Java class necessary. The following example simply retrieves the list of tables from the remote cluster:

```
$ cat ~/hbase-shell-status-2.rb
include Java
import org.apache.hadoop.hbase.HBaseConfiguration
import org.apache.hadoop.hbase.client.HBaseAdmin

conf = HBaseConfiguration.new
admin = HBaseAdmin.new(conf)
tables = admin.listTables
tables.each { |table| puts table.getNameAsString()  }

$ bin/hbase org.jruby.Main ~/hbase-shell-status-2.rb
testtable
```

Since the shell is based on JRuby's IRB, you can use its built-in features, such as command completion and history. Enabling them is a matter of creating an *.irbrc* in your home directory, which is read when the shell starts:

```
$ cat ~/.irbrc
require 'irb/ext/save-history'
IRB.conf[:SAVE_HISTORY] = 100
IRB.conf[:HISTORY_FILE] = "#{ENV['HOME']}/.irb-save-history"
```

This enables the command history to save across shell starts. The command completion is already enabled by the HBase scripts.

Another advantage of the interactive interpreter is that you can use the HBase classes and functions to perform, for example, something that would otherwise require you to write a Java application. Here is an example of binary output received from a `Bytes.toBytes()` call that is converted into an integer value:

```
hbase(main):001:0>
org.apache.hadoop.hbase.util.Bytes.toInt( \
  "\x00\x01\x06[".to_java_bytes)
=> 67163
```

 Note how the shell encoded the first three unprintable characters as hexadecimal values, while the fourth, the "[", was printed as a character.

Another example is to convert a date into a Linux epoch number, and back into a human-readable date:

```
hbase(main):002:0> java.text.SimpleDateFormat.new("yyyy/MM/dd HH:mm:ss").parse( \
  "2011/05/30 20:56:29").getTime()
=> 1306781789000

hbase(main):002:0> java.util.Date.new(1306781789000).toString()
=> "Mon May 30 20:56:29 CEST 2011"
```

Finally, you can also add many cells in a loop—for example, to populate a table with test data:

```
hbase(main):003:0> for i in 'a'..'z' do for j in
'a'..'z' do put 'testtable', \
"row-#{i}#{j}", "colfam1:#{j}", "#{j}" end end
```

A more elaborate loop to populate counters could look like this:

```
hbase(main):004:0> require 'date';
import java.lang.Long
import org.apache.hadoop.hbase.util.Bytes
(Date.new(2011, 01, 01)..Date.today).each { |x| put "testtable", "daily", \
"colfam1:" + x.strftime("%Y%m%d"), Bytes.toBytes(Long.new(rand * \
4000).longValue).to_a.pack("CCCCCCCC") }
```

Obviously, this is getting very much into Ruby itself. But even with a little bit of programming skills in another language, you might be able to use the features of the IRB-based shell to your advantage. Start easy and progress from there.

Web-based UI

The HBase processes expose a web-based *user interface* (UI), which you can use to gain insight into the cluster's state, as well as the tables it hosts. The majority of the functionality is read-only, but a few selected operations can be triggered through the UI.

Master UI

HBase also starts a web-based listing of vital attributes. By default, it is deployed on the master host at port 60010, while region servers use 60030. If the master is running on a host named `master.foo.com` on the default port, to see the master's home page, you can point your browser at *http://master.foo.com:60010*.

 The ports used by the servers can be set in the *hbase-site.xml* configuration file. The properties to change are:

    hbase.master.info.port
    hbase.regionserver.info.port

Main page

The first page you will see when opening the master's web UI is shown in Figure 6-2. It consists of multiple sections that give you insight into the cluster status itself, the tables it serves, what the region servers are, and so on.

The details can be broken up into the following groups:

Master attributes
> You will find cluster-wide details in a table at the top of the page. It has information on the version of HBase and Hadoop that you are using, where the root directory is located,[§] the overall load average, and the ZooKeeper quorum used.
>
> There is also a link in the description for the ZooKeeper quorum allowing you to see the information for your current HBase cluster stored in ZooKeeper. "ZooKeeper page" on page 282 discusses its content.

Running tasks
> The next group of details on the master's main page is the list of *currently running tasks*. Every internal operation performed by the master is listed here while it is running, and for another minute after its completion. Entries with a white background are currently running, a green background indicates successful completion of the task, and a yellow background means the task was aborted. The latter can happen when an operation failed due to an inconsistent state. Figure 6-3 shows a completed, a running, and a failed task.

---

§ Recall that this should better not be starting with */tmp*, or you may lose your data during a machine restart. Refer to "Quick-Start Guide" on page 31 for details.

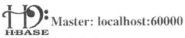Master: localhost:60000

H·BASE

Local logs, Thread Dump, Log Level

Master Attributes

Attribute Name	Value	Description
HBase Version	0.91.0-SNAPSHOT, r1127782	HBase version and svn revision
HBase Compiled	Thu May 26 10:28:47 CEST 2011, larsgeorge	When HBase version was compiled and by whom
Hadoop Version	0.20-append-r1057313, r1057313	Hadoop version and svn revision
Hadoop Compiled	Wed Feb 9 22:25:52 PST 2011, Stack	When Hadoop version was compiled and by whom
HBase Root Directory	hdfs://localhost:8020/hbase	Location of HBase home directory
HBase Cluster ID	698e057d-78ac-4d01-8db9-3cec937bc619	Unique identifier generated for each HBase cluster
Load average	4	Average number of regions per regionserver. Naive computation.
Zookeeper Quorum	localhost:2181	Addresses of all registered ZK servers. For more, see zk dump.

Currently running tasks

No tasks currently running on this node.

Catalog Tables

Table	Description
-ROOT-	The -ROOT- table holds references to all .META. regions.
.META.	The .META. table holds references to all User Table regions

User Tables

3 table(s) in set.

Table	Description
testtable	{NAME => 'testtable', FAMILIES => [{NAME => 'colfam1', BLOOMFILTER => 'NONE', REPLICATION_SCOPE => '0', COMPRESSION => 'NONE', VERSIONS => '3', TTL => '2147483647', BLOCKSIZE => '65536', IN_MEMORY => 'false', BLOCKCACHE => 'true'}]}
user	{NAME => 'user', DEFERRED_LOG_FLUSH => 'false', READONLY => 'false', MEMSTORE_FLUSHSIZE => '67108864', MAX_FILESIZE => '268435456', FAMILIES => [{NAME => 'data', BLOOMFILTER => 'NONE', REPLICATION_SCOPE => '0', COMPRESSION => 'NONE', VERSIONS => '3', TTL => '2147483647', BLOCKSIZE => '65536', IN_MEMORY => 'false', BLOCKCACHE => 'true'}]}
usertable	{NAME => 'usertable', FAMILIES => [{NAME => 'family', BLOOMFILTER => 'NONE', REPLICATION_SCOPE => '0', VERSIONS => '3', COMPRESSION => 'NONE', TTL => '2147483647', BLOCKSIZE => '65536', IN_MEMORY => 'false', BLOCKCACHE => 'true'}]}

Region Servers

Address	Start Code	Load
localhost:60030	1306411472676localhost,60020,1306411472676	requests=0, regions=4, usedHeap=53, maxHeap=987
Total: servers: 1		requests=0, regions=4

Load is requests per second and count of regions loaded

Regions in Transition

No regions in transition.

Figure 6-2. The HBase Master user interface

Currently running tasks

Description	Status	Age
Doing distributed log split in hdfs://localhost:8020/hbase/.logs/42.1.3.74,60020,1306849761977	finished splitting (more than or equal to) 120291 bytes in 2 log files in hdfs://localhost:8020/hbase/.logs/42.1.3.74,60020,1306849761977 in 2370ms	45s (Completed 43s ago)
Doing distributed log split in hdfs://localhost:8020/hbase/.logs/10.132.225.53,60020,1306687635971	Checking directory contents...	45s (Completed 2s ago)
Master startup	Assigning META region	52s

Figure 6-3. The list of currently running tasks on the master

Catalog tables

This section list the two catalog tables, `.META.` and `-ROOT-`. You can click on the name of the table to see more details on the table regions—for example, on what server they are currently hosted.

User tables

Here you will see the list of all tables known to your HBase cluster. These are the ones you—or your users—have created using the API, or the HBase Shell. The description column in the list gives you a printout of the current table descriptor, including all column descriptors; see "Schema Definition" on page 207 for an explanation of how to read them.

The table names are links to another page with details on the selected table. See "User Table page" on page 279 for an explanation of the contained information.

Region servers

The next section lists the actual region servers the master knows about. The table lists the *address*, which you can click on to see more details. It also states the server *start code*, a timestamp representing an ID for each server, and finally, the *load* of the server. For information on the values listed refer to "Cluster Status Information" on page 233, and especially the `HServerLoad` class.

Regions in transition

As regions are managed by the master and region servers to, for example, balance the load across servers, they go through short phases of transition. This applies to opening, closing, and splitting a region. Before the operation is performed, the region is added to the list, and once the operation is complete, it is removed. "The Region Life Cycle" on page 348 describes the possible states a region can be in. Figure 6-4 shows a region that is currently split.

Figure 6-4. The Regions in Transitions table provided by the master web UI

User Table page

When you click on the name of a user table in the master's web-based user interface, you have access to the information pertaining to the selected table. Figure 6-5 shows an abbreviated version of a User Table page (it has a shortened list of regions for the sake of space).

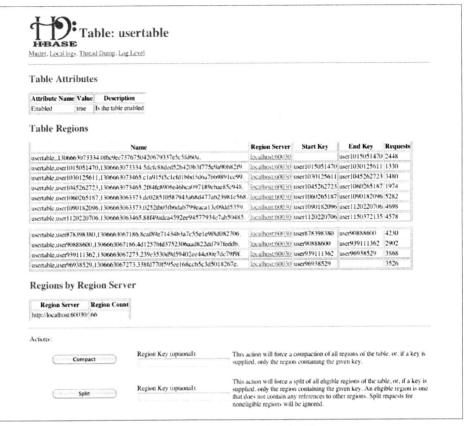

Figure 6-5. *The User Table page with details about the selected table*

The following groups of information are available in the User Table page:

Table attributes

Here you can find details about the table itself. As of this writing, this section only lists the *table status* (i.e., it indicates if it is enabled or not). See "Table Operations" on page 220, and the `disableTable()` call especially.

The boolean value states whether the table is enabled, so when you see a `true` in the *Value* column, this is the case. On the other hand, a value of `false` would mean the table is currently disabled.

Table regions

This list can be rather large and shows all regions of a table. The *Name* column has the region name itself, and the *Region Server* column has a link to the server hosting the region. Clicking on the link takes you to the page explained in "Region Server UI" on page 283.

Sometimes you may see the words *not deployed* where the server name should be. This happens when a user table region is not currently served by any region server. Figure 6-6 shows an example of this situation.

The *Start Key* and *End Key* columns show the region's start and end keys as expected. Finally, the *Requests* column shows the total number of requests, including all read (e.g., get or scan) and write (e.g., put or delete) operations, since the region was deployed to the server.

usertable,user1002506221,1505724105705.uay19u10100544z9u100aue5050154T.	uu.aiiub.00050	user1002506221	user1722720758	16
usertable,user1722720758,1305724102196.dbbc63057028b09ef74f7d7e3d079c58.	localhost:60030	user1722720758	user1782933999	16
usertable,user1782933999,1305724102196.d47e20439a72381465940c7e42add3d8.	not deployed	user1782933999	user184325569	0
usertable,user184325569,1305724060793.8728710ab629d5266bce7d56643f3469.	localhost:60030	user184325569	user1903293836	16
usertable,user1903293836,1305724060793.fa89ab10c48a73d60773da384a670300.	localhost:60030	user1903293836	user1964024582	16

Figure 6-6. Example of a region that has not been assigned to a server and is listed as not deployed

Regions by region server

The last group on the User Table page lists which region server is hosting how many regions of the selected table. This number is usually distributed evenly across all available servers. If not, you can use the HBase Shell or administrative API to initiate the balancer, or use the move command to manually balance the table regions (see "Cluster Operations" on page 230).

The User Table page also offers a form that can be used to trigger administrative operations on a specific region, or the entire table. See "Cluster Operations" again for details, and "Optimizing Splits and Compactions" on page 429 for information on when you want to use them. The available operations are:

Compact

This triggers the compact functionality, which is asynchronously running in the background. Specify the optional name of a region to run the operation more selectively. The name of the region can be taken from the table above, that is, the entries in the *Name* column of the *Table Regions* table.

 Make sure to copy the entire region name *as-is*. This includes the trailing "." (the dot)!

If you do *not* specify a region name, the operation is performed on all regions of the table instead.

Split

Similar to the compact action, the *split* form action triggers the split command, operating on a table or region scope. Not all regions may be splittable—for example, those that contain no, or very few, cells, or one that has already been split, but which has not been compacted to complete the process.

Once you trigger one of the operations, you will receive a confirmation page; for example, for a split invocation, you will see:

```
Split request accepted.

Reload.
```

Use the Back button of your web browser to go back to the previous page, showing the user table details.

ZooKeeper page

There is also a link in the description column that lets you dump the content of all the nodes stored in ZooKeeper by HBase. This is useful when trying to solve problems with the cluster setup (see "Troubleshooting" on page 467).

The page shows the same information as invoking the *zk_dump* command of the HBase Shell. It shows you the root directory HBase is using inside the configured filesystem. You also can see the currently assigned master, which region server is hosting the -ROOT- catalog table, the list of region servers that have registered with the master, as well as ZooKeeper internal details. Figure 6-7 shows an exemplary output available on the ZooKeeper page.

```
HBase is rooted at /hbase
Master address: localhost,60000,1306663023371
Region server holding ROOT: localhost,60020,1306663024434
Region servers:
 localhost,60020,1306663024434
Quorum Server Statistics:
 localhost:2181
  Zookeeper version: 3.3.2-1031432, built on 11/05/2010 05:32 GMT
  Clients:
   /fe80:0:0:0:0:0:0:1%1:54451[1](queued=0,recved=298,sent=300)
   /fe80:0:0:0:0:0:0:1%1:55217[1](queued=0,recved=283,sent=283)
   /fe80:0:0:0:0:0:0:1%1:52307[1](queued=0,recved=634,sent=638)
   /0:0:0:0:0:0:0:1%0:59324[1](queued=0,recved=6897,sent=6901)
   /0:0:0:0:0:0:0:1%0:54449[1](queued=0,recved=870,sent=877)
   /127.0.0.1:60703[0](queued=0,recved=1,sent=0)
   /0:0:0:0:0:0:0:1%0:64611[1](queued=0,recved=12815,sent=12824)
   /127.0.0.1:54442[1](queued=0,recved=316,sent=318)
   /fe80:0:0:0:0:0:0:1%1:54433[1](queued=0,recved=1141,sent=1549)

  Latency min/avg/max: 0/0/780
  Received: 274270
  Sent: 276689
  Outstanding: 0
  Zxid: 0x90a4a
  Mode: standalone
  Node count: 19
```

Figure 6-7. The ZooKeeper page, listing HBase and ZooKeeper details, which is useful when debugging HBase installations

Region Server UI

The region servers have their own web-based UI, which you usually access through the master UI, by clicking on the server name links provided. You can access the page directly by entering

```
http://<region-server-address>:60030
```

into your browser (while making sure to use the configured port, here using the default of 60030).

Main page

The main page of the region servers has details about the server, the tasks, and regions it is hosting. Figure 6-8 shows an abbreviated example of this page (the list of tasks and regions is shortened for the sake of space).

The page can be broken up into the following groups of distinct information:

Region server attributes
> This group of information contains the version of HBase you are running, when it was compiled, a printout of the server metrics, and the ZooKeeper quorum used. The metrics are explained in "Region Server Metrics" on page 394.

Running tasks
> The table lists all currently running tasks, using a white background for running tasks, a yellow one for failed tasks, and a green one for completed tasks. Failed or completed tasks are removed after one minute.

Online regions
> Here you can see all the regions hosted by the currently selected region server. The table has the region name, the start and end keys, as well as the region metrics.

Shared Pages

On the top of the master, region server, and table pages there are also a few generic links that lead to subsequent pages, displaying or controlling additional details of your setup:

Local logs
> This link provides a quick way to access the logfiles without requiring access to the server itself. It firsts list the contents of the *log* directory where you can select the logfile you want to see. Click on a log to reveal its content. "Analyzing the Logs" on page 469 helps you to make sense of what you may see. Figure 6-9 shows an example page.

Region Server: localhost:60020

Local logs, Thread Dump, Log Level

Region Server Attributes

Attribute Name	Value	Description
HBase Version	0.91.0-SNAPSHOT, r1127782	HBase version and svn revision
HBase Compiled	Thu May 26 10:28:47 CEST 2011, larsgeorge	When HBase version was compiled and by whom
Metrics	request=70.333336, regions=70, stores=70, storefiles=73, storefileIndexSize=5, memstoreSize=0, readRequestsCount=357385, writeRequestsCount=239, compactionQueueSize=40, flushQueueSize=0, usedHeap=139, maxHeap=987, blockCacheSize=100321464, blockCacheFree=106772296, blockCacheCount=1510, blockCacheHitCount=189520, blockCacheMissCount=104532, blockCacheEvictedCount=553, blockCacheHitRatio=64, blockCacheHitCachingRatio=98	RegionServer Metrics; file and heap sizes are in megabytes
Zookeeper Quorum	localhost:2181	Addresses of all registered ZK servers

Currently running tasks

Description	Status	Age
Compacting family in usertable,user1994048399,1306663065728.f886662627e8ba1e2a9a3e935d900e8d.	Compacting store family	3s
Compacting family in usertable,user1964024582,1306663065728.5a90de794798b504c3d840ad55280f55.	Compaction complete	8s (Completed 3s ago)
Compacting family in usertable,user1933568427,1306663065637.232fed5409e36654d5ca5312944691c6.	Compaction complete	14s (Completed 8s ago)
Compacting family in usertable,user1632175403,1306663064560.f14d1d74d780e3357abe7a4105975f6.	Compaction complete	60s (Completed 55s ago)

Online Regions

Region Name	Start Key	End Key	Metrics
-ROOT-,,0.70236052			stores=1, storefiles=2, storefileSizeMB=0, memstoreSizeMB=0, storefileIndexSizeMB=0, readRequestsCount=132, writeRequestsCount=1
.META.,,1.1028785192			stores=1, storefiles=2, storefileSizeMB=0, memstoreSizeMB=0, storefileIndexSizeMB=0, readRequestsCount=8099, writeRequestsCount=238
testtable,,1306157568418.ce2b0fc91fi9dd40ed498d1c8edb75bc.			stores=1, storefiles=2, storefileSizeMB=0, memstoreSizeMB=0, storefileIndexSizeMB=0, readRequestsCount=0, writeRequestsCount=0
user,,1305633635075.fc7c2af59dd58ec4d7d20edc5efa8905.			stores=1, storefiles=1, storefileSizeMB=0, memstoreSizeMB=0, storefileIndexSizeMB=0, readRequestsCount=0, writeRequestsCount=0
usertable,,1306663073334.0f6c9ee7376750420679337e5c5td60a.		user1015051470	stores=1, storefiles=1, storefileSizeMB=32, memstoreSizeMB=0, storefileIndexSizeMB=0, readRequestsCount=2504, writeRequestsCount=0
			stores=1, storefiles=1, writeRequestsCount=0
usertable,user96938529,1306663067273.338fd770f595ee168ccb5c3d5018267e.	user96938529		stores=1, storefiles=1, storefileSizeMB=65, memstoreSizeMB=0, storefileIndexSizeMB=0, readRequestsCount=3600, writeRequestsCount=0

Region names are made of the containing table's name, a comma, the start key, a comma, and a randomly generated region id. To illustrate, the region named *domains,apache.org,5464829424211263407* is party to the table *domains*, has an id of *5464829424211263407* and the first key in the region is *apache.org*. The -ROOT- and .META. 'tables' are internal sytem tables (or 'catalog' tables in db-speak). The -ROOT- keeps a list of all regions in the .META. table. The .META. table keeps a list of all regions in the system. The empty key is used to denote table start and table end. A region with an empty start key is the first region in a table. If region has both an empty start and an empty end key, its the only region in the table. See HBase Home for further explication.

Figure 6-8. The Region Server main page

Directory: /logs/

hbase-larsgeorge-master-de1-app-mbp-2.log	581480 bytes	May 29, 2011 12:58:08 PM
hbase-larsgeorge-master-de1-app-mbp-2.log.2011-05-16	985818 bytes	May 16, 2011 11:58:11 PM
hbase-larsgeorge-master-de1-app-mbp-2.log.2011-05-17	99460809 bytes	May 17, 2011 11:59:49 PM
hbase-larsgeorge-master-de1-app-mbp-2.log.2011-05-18	1495814 bytes	May 18, 2011 11:56:54 PM
hbase-larsgeorge-master-de1-app-mbp-2.log.2011-05-23	1254398 bytes	May 23, 2011 11:57:47 PM
hbase-larsgeorge-master-de1-app-mbp-2.log.2011-05-24	169627 bytes	May 24, 2011 11:57:37 PM
hbase-larsgeorge-master-de1-app-mbp-2.log.2011-05-25	112382 bytes	May 25, 2011 11:57:47 PM
hbase-larsgeorge-master-de1-app-mbp-2.log.2011-05-26	418021 bytes	May 26, 2011 11:59:47 PM
hbase-larsgeorge-master-de1-app-mbp-2.log.2011-05-27	114861 bytes	May 27, 2011 11:59:55 PM
hbase-larsgeorge-master-de1-app-mbp-2.log.2011-05-28	103291 bytes	May 28, 2011 11:59:59 PM
hbase-larsgeorge-master-de1-app-mbp-2.out	0 bytes	May 29, 2011 11:57:01 AM
hbase-larsgeorge-master-de1-app-mbp-2.out.1	8927 bytes	May 29, 2011 11:56:28 AM
hbase-larsgeorge-master-de1-app-mbp-2.out.2	8927 bytes	May 26, 2011 2:04:21 PM
hbase-larsgeorge-master-de1-app-mbp-2.out.3	10684 bytes	May 26, 2011 8:52:55 AM
hbase-larsgeorge-master-de1-app-mbp-2.out.4	8942 bytes	May 23, 2011 3:25:19 PM
hbase-larsgeorge-master-de1-app-mbp-2.out.5	0 bytes	May 23, 2011 9:21:35 AM
hbase-larsgeorge-regionserver-de1-app-mbp-2.log	993370 bytes	May 29, 2011 12:58:54 PM
hbase-larsgeorge-regionserver-de1-app-mbp-2.log.2011-05-16	59611624 bytes	May 17, 2011 12:00:00 AM
hbase-larsgeorge-regionserver-de1-app-mbp-2.log.2011-05-17	24931009 bytes	May 18, 2011 12:00:10 AM
hbase-larsgeorge-regionserver-de1-app-mbp-2.log.2011-05-18	8655825 bytes	May 18, 2011 11:56:24 PM
hbase-larsgeorge-regionserver-de1-app-mbp-2.log.2011-05-23	3417214 bytes	May 23, 2011 11:57:17 PM

Figure 6-9. The Local Logs page

Thread dumps

For debugging purposes, you can use this link to dump the Java stacktraces of the running HBase processes. You can find more details in "Troubleshooting" on page 467. Figure 6-10 shows example output.

Log level

This link leads you to a small form that allows you to retrieve and set the logging levels used by the HBase processes. More on this is provided in "Changing Logging Levels" on page 466. Figure 6-11 shows the form when it is loaded afresh.

When you enter, for example, `org.apache.hadoop.hbase` into the first input field, and click on the Get Log Level button, you should see a result similar to that shown in Figure 6-12.

The web-based UI provided by the HBase servers is a good way to quickly gain insight into the cluster, the hosted tables, the status of regions and tables, and so on. The majority of the information can also be accessed using the HBase Shell, but that requires console access to the cluster.

You can use the UI to trigger selected administrative operations; therefore, it might not be advisable to give everyone access to it: similar to the shell, the UI should be used by the operators and administrators of the cluster.

If you want your users to create, delete, and display their own tables, you will need an additional layer on top of HBase, possibly using Thrift or REST as the gateway server, to offer this functionality to end users.

```
Process Thread Dump:
55 active threads
Thread 265 (409754308@qtp-873128399-22):
  State: RUNNABLE
  Blocked count: 11
  Waited count: 11
  Stack:
    sun.management.ThreadImpl.getThreadInfo0(Native Method)
    sun.management.ThreadImpl.getThreadInfo(ThreadImpl.java:147)
    sun.management.ThreadImpl.getThreadInfo(ThreadImpl.java:123)
    org.apache.hadoop.util.ReflectionUtils.printThreadInfo(ReflectionUtils.java:149)
    org.apache.hadoop.http.HttpServer$StackServlet.doGet(HttpServer.java:513)
    javax.servlet.http.HttpServlet.service(HttpServlet.java:707)
    javax.servlet.http.HttpServlet.service(HttpServlet.java:820)
    org.mortbay.jetty.servlet.ServletHolder.handle(ServletHolder.java:511)
    org.mortbay.jetty.servlet.ServletHandler.handle(ServletHandler.java:401)
    org.mortbay.jetty.security.SecurityHandler.handle(SecurityHandler.java:216)
    org.mortbay.jetty.servlet.SessionHandler.handle(SessionHandler.java:182)
    org.mortbay.jetty.handler.ContextHandler.handle(ContextHandler.java:766)
    org.mortbay.jetty.webapp.WebAppContext.handle(WebAppContext.java:450)
    org.mortbay.jetty.handler.ContextHandlerCollection.handle(ContextHandlerCollection.java:230)
    org.mortbay.jetty.handler.HandlerWrapper.handle(HandlerWrapper.java:152)
    org.mortbay.jetty.Server.handle(Server.java:326)
    org.mortbay.jetty.HttpConnection.handleRequest(HttpConnection.java:542)
    org.mortbay.jetty.HttpConnection$RequestHandler.headerComplete(HttpConnection.java:928)
    org.mortbay.jetty.HttpParser.parseNext(HttpParser.java:549)
    org.mortbay.jetty.HttpParser.parseAvailable(HttpParser.java:212)
Thread 254 (210958960@qtp-873128399-20):
  State: TIMED_WAITING
  Blocked count: 159
  Waited count: 157
  Stack:
    java.lang.Object.wait(Native Method)
    org.mortbay.thread.QueuedThreadPool$PoolThread.run(QueuedThreadPool.java:626)
Thread 76 (MASTER_SERVER_OPERATIONS-localhost,60000,1306663023371-2):
  State: WAITING
  Blocked count: 108
  Waited count: 99
  Waiting on java.util.concurrent.locks.AbstractQueuedSynchronizer$ConditionObject@6063f5af
  Stack:
    sun.misc.Unsafe.park(Native Method)
    java.util.concurrent.locks.LockSupport.park(LockSupport.java:158)
    java.util.concurrent.locks.AbstractQueuedSynchronizer$ConditionObject.await(AbstractQueuedSynchronizer.java:1987)
    java.util.concurrent.LinkedBlockingQueue.take(LinkedBlockingQueue.java:399)
    java.util.concurrent.ThreadPoolExecutor.getTask(ThreadPoolExecutor.java:947)
    java.util.concurrent.ThreadPoolExecutor$Worker.run(ThreadPoolExecutor.java:907)
    java.lang.Thread.run(Thread.java:680)
```

Figure 6-10. The Thread Dump page

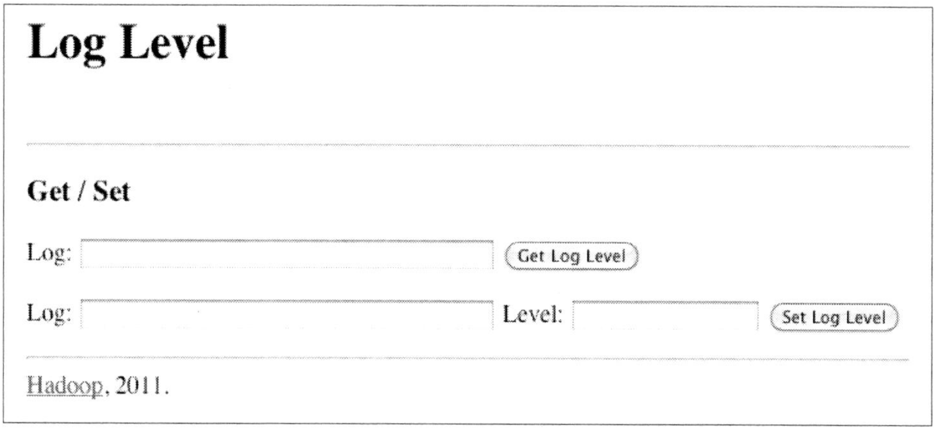

Log Level

Get / Set

Log: [   ] (Get Log Level)

Log: [   ] Level: [   ] (Set Log Level)

Hadoop, 2011.

Figure 6-11. The Log Level page

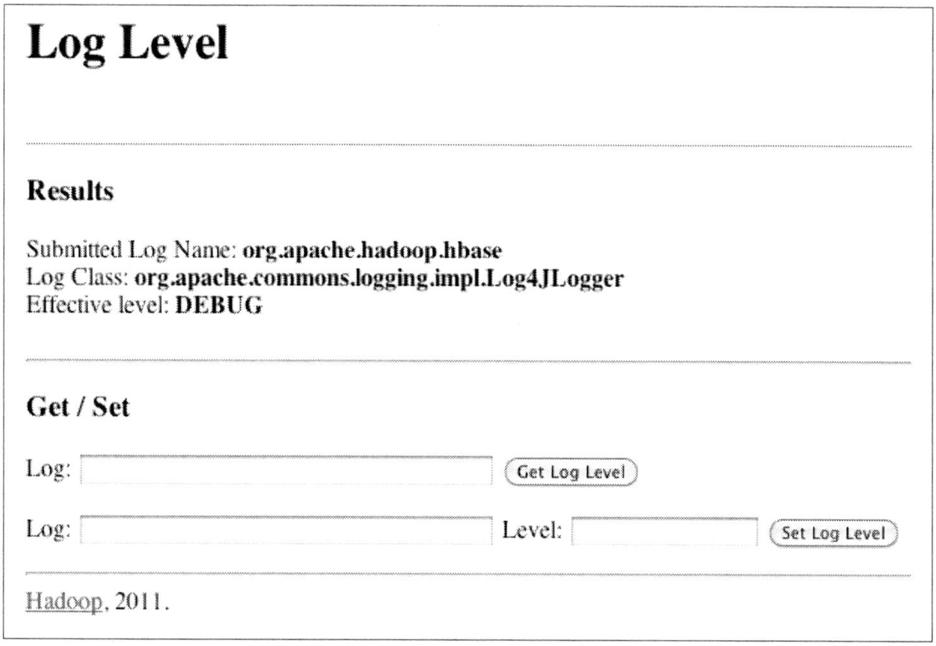

Log Level

Results

Submitted Log Name: **org.apache.hadoop.hbase**
Log Class: **org.apache.commons.logging.impl.Log4JLogger**
Effective level: **DEBUG**

Get / Set

Log: [   ] (Get Log Level)

Log: [   ] Level: [   ] (Set Log Level)

Hadoop, 2011.

Figure 6-12. The Log Level Result page

MapReduce Integration

One of the great features of HBase is its tight integration with Hadoop's MapReduce framework. Here you will see how this can be leveraged and how unique traits of HBase can be used advantageously in the process.

Framework

Before going into the application of HBase with MapReduce, we will first have a look at the building blocks.

MapReduce Introduction

MapReduce as a process was designed to solve the problem of processing in excess of terabytes of data in a scalable way. There should be a way to build such a system that increases in performance linearly with the number of physical machines added. That is what MapReduce strives to do. It follows a divide-and-conquer approach by splitting the data located on a distributed filesystem so that the servers (or rather CPUs, or more modern "cores") available can access these chunks of data and process them as fast as they can. The problem with this approach is that you will have to consolidate the data at the end. Again, MapReduce has this built right into it. Figure 7-1 gives a high-level overview of the process.

This (rather simplified) figure of the MapReduce process shows you how the data is processed. The first thing that happens is the *split*, which is responsible for dividing the input data into reasonably sized chunks that are then processed by one server at a time. This splitting has to be done in a somewhat smart way to make best use of available servers and the infrastructure in general. In this example, the data may be a very large logfile that is divided into pieces of equal size. This is good, for example, for Apache logfiles. Input data may also be binary, though, in which case you may have to write your own getSplits() method—but more on that shortly.

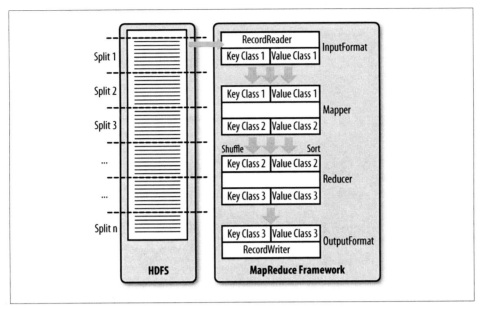

Figure 7-1. The MapReduce process

Classes

Figure 7-1 also shows you the classes that are involved in the Hadoop implementation of MapReduce. Let us look at them and also at the specific implementations that HBase provides on top of them.

 Hadoop version 0.20.0 introduced a new MapReduce API. Its classes are located in the package named mapreduce, while the existing classes for the previous API are located in mapred. The older API was deprecated and should have been dropped in version 0.21.0—but that did not happen. In fact, the old API was undeprecated since the adoption of the new one was hindered by its incompleteness.

HBase also has these two packages, which only differ slightly. The new API has more support by the community, and writing jobs against it is not impacted by the Hadoop changes. This chapter will only refer to the new API.

InputFormat

The first class to deal with is the InputFormat class (Figure 7-2). It is responsible for two things. First it splits the input data, and then it returns a RecordReader instance that defines the classes of the *key* and *value* objects, and provides a next() method that is used to iterate over each input record.

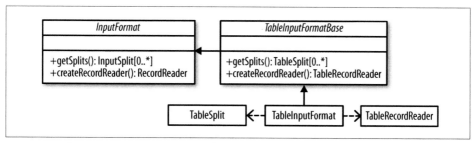

Figure 7-2. The InputFormat hierarchy

As far as HBase is concerned, there is a special implementation called `TableInput FormatBase` whose subclass is `TableInputFormat`. The former implements the majority of the functionality but remains abstract. The subclass is a lightweight concrete version of `TableInputFormat` and is used by many supplied samples and real MapReduce classes.

These classes implement the full turnkey solution to scan an HBase table. You have to provide a `Scan` instance that you can prepare in any way you want: specify start and stop keys, add filters, specify the number of versions, and so on. The `TableInputFormat` splits the table into proper blocks for you and hands them over to the subsequent classes in the MapReduce process. See "Table Splits" on page 294 for details on how the table is split.

Mapper

The `Mapper` class(es) is for the next stage of the MapReduce process and one of its namesakes (Figure 7-3). In this step, each record read using the `RecordReader` is processed using the `map()` method. Figure 7-1 also shows that the `Mapper` reads a specific type of key/value pair, but emits possibly another type. This is handy for converting the raw data into something more useful for further processing.

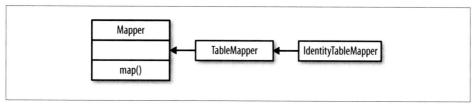

Figure 7-3. The Mapper hierarchy

HBase provides the `TableMapper` class that enforces *key class 1* to be an `ImmutableBytes Writable`, and *value class 1* to be a `Result` type—since that is what the `TableRecordReader` is returning.

One specific implementation of the `TableMapper` is the `IdentityTableMapper`, which is also a good example of how to add your own functionality to the supplied classes. The `TableMapper` class itself does not implement anything but only adds the signatures of the actual key/value pair classes. The IdentityTableMapper is simply passing on the keys/values to the next stage of processing.

Reducer

The Reducer stage and class hierarchy (Figure 7-4) is very similar to the Mapper stage. This time we get the output of a Mapper class and process it after the data has been *shuffled* and *sorted*.

In the implicit shuffle between the Mapper and Reducer stages, the intermediate data is copied from different Map servers to the Reduce servers and the sort combines the shuffled (copied) data so that the Reducer sees the intermediate data as a nicely sorted set where each unique key is now associated with all of the possible values it was found with.

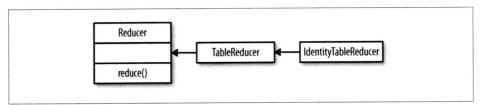

Figure 7-4. The Reducer hierarchy

OutputFormat

The final stage is the OutputFormat class (Figure 7-5), and its job is to persist the data in various locations. There are specific implementations that allow output to files, or to HBase tables in the case of the TableOutputFormat class. It uses a TableRecord Writer to write the data into the specific HBase output table.

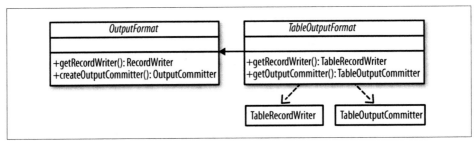

Figure 7-5. The OutputFormat hierarchy

It is important to note the cardinality as well. Although many Mappers are handing records to many Reducers, only one OutputFormat takes each output record from its Reducer subsequently. It is the final class that handles the key/value pairs and writes them to their final destination, this being a file or a table.

The `TableOutputCommitter` class is required for the Hadoop classes to do their job. For HBase integration, this class is not needed. In fact, it is a dummy and does not do anything. Other implementations of `OutputFormat` do require it.

The name of the output table is specified when the job is created. Otherwise, the `TableOutputFormat` does not add much more complexity. One rather significant thing it does do is to set the table's *autoflush* to `false` and handle the buffer flushing implicitly. This helps a lot in terms of speeding up the import of large data sets. Also see "Client API: Best Practices" on page 434 for information on how to optimize your scan performance.

Supporting Classes

The MapReduce support comes with the `TableMapReduceUtil` class that helps in setting up MapReduce jobs over HBase. It has static methods that configure a job so that you can run it with HBase as the source and/or the target.

MapReduce Locality

One of the more ambiguous things in Hadoop is block replication: it happens automatically and you should not have to worry about it. HBase relies on it to provide durability as it stores its files into the distributed filesystem. Although block replication works completely transparently, users sometimes ask how it affects performance.

This question usually arises when the user starts writing MapReduce jobs against either HBase or Hadoop directly. Especially when larger amounts of data are being stored in HBase, how does the system take care of placing the data close to where it is needed? This concept is referred to as data locality, and in the case of HBase using the Hadoop filesystem (HDFS), users may have doubts as to whether it is working.

First let us see how Hadoop handles this: the MapReduce documentation states that tasks run close to the data they process. This is achieved by breaking up large files in HDFS into smaller chunks, or blocks, with a default setting of 64 MB (128 MB and larger is very common in practice).

Each block is assigned to a map task to process the contained data. This means larger block sizes equal fewer map tasks to run as the number of mappers is driven by the number of blocks that need processing. Hadoop knows where blocks are located, and runs the map tasks directly on the node that hosts the block. Since block replication ensures that we have (by default) three copies on three different physical servers, the framework has the choice of executing the code on any of those three, which it uses to balance workloads. This is how it guarantees data locality during the MapReduce process.

Back to HBase. Once you understand that Hadoop can process data locally, you may start to question how this may work with HBase. As discussed in

"Storage" on page 319, HBase transparently stores files in HDFS. It does so for the actual data files (HFile) as well as the log (WAL). And if you look into the code, it uses the Hadoop API call `FileSystem.create(Path path)` to create these files.

 If you do not co-share your cluster with Hadoop and HBase, but instead employ a separate Hadoop as well as a standalone HBase cluster, there is *no* data locality—there can't be. This is the same as running a separate MapReduce cluster that would not be able to execute tasks directly on the data node. It is imperative for data locality to have the Hadoop and HBase processes running on the same cluster—*end of line*.

How does Hadoop figure out where data is located as HBase accesses it? The most important factor is that HBase servers are not restarted frequently and that they perform housekeeping on a regular basis. These so-called compactions rewrite files as new data is added over time. All files in HDFS, once written, are immutable (for all sorts of reasons). Because of that, data is written into new files, and as their number grows, HBase compacts them into another set of new, consolidated files.

And here is the kicker: HDFS is smart enough to put the data where it is needed! It has a block placement policy in place that enforces all blocks to be written first on a co-located server. The receiving data node compares the server name of the writer with its own, and if they match, the block is written to the local filesystem. Then a replica is sent to a server within the same rack, and another to a remote rack—assuming you are using rack awareness in HDFS. If not, the additional copies get placed on the least loaded data node in the cluster.

If you have configured a higher replication factor, more replicas are stored on distinct machines. The important factor here, though, is that you now have a local copy of the block available. For HBase, this means that if the region server stays up for long enough (which is what you want), after a major compaction on all tables—which can be invoked manually or is triggered by a configuration setting—it has the files stored locally on the same host. The data node that shares the same physical host has a copy of all data the region server requires. If you are running a scan or get or any other use case, you can be sure to get the best performance.

An issue to be aware of is region movements during load balancing, or server failures. In that case, the data is no longer local, but over time it will be once again. The master also takes this into consideration when a cluster is restarted: it assigns all regions to the original region servers. If one of them is missing, it has to fall back to the random region assignment approach.

Table Splits

When running a MapReduce job in which you read from a table, you are typically using the `TableInputFormat`. It fits into the framework by overriding the required public methods `getSplits()` and `createRecordReader()`. Before a job is executed, the framework calls `getSplit()` to determine how the data is to be separated into chunks, because it sets the number of map tasks the job requires.

For HBase, the `TableInputFormat` uses the information about the table it represents—based on the `Scan` instance you provided—to divide the table at region boundaries. Since it has no direct knowledge of the effect of the optional filter, it uses the start and stop keys to narrow down the number of regions. The number of splits, therefore, is equal to all regions between the start and stop keys. If you do not set the start and/or stop key, all are included.

When the job starts, the framework is calling `createRecordReader()` as many times as it has splits. It iterates over the splits and creates a new `TableRecordReader` by calling `createRecordReader()` with the current split. In other words, each `TableRecordReader` handles exactly one region, reading and mapping every row between the region's start and end keys.

The split also contains the server name hosting the region. This is what drives locality for MapReduce jobs over HBase: the framework checks the server name, and if a task tracker is running on the same machine, it will preferably run it on that server. Because the region server is also collocated with the data node on that same node, the scan of the region will be able to retrieve all data from the local disk.

 When running MapReduce over HBase, it is strongly advised that you turn *off speculative execution* mode. It will only create more load on the same region and server, and also works against locality: the speculative task is executed on a different machine, and therefore will not have the region server local, which is hosting the region. This results in all data being sent over the network, adding to the overall I/O load.

MapReduce over HBase

The following sections will introduce you to using HBase in combination with MapReduce. Before you can use HBase as a source or sink, or both, for data processing jobs, you have to first decide how you want to prepare the support by Hadoop.

Preparation

To run a MapReduce job that needs classes from libraries not shipped with Hadoop or the MapReduce framework, you'll need to make those libraries available before the job is executed. You have two choices: static preparation of all task nodes, or supplying everything needed with the job.

Static Provisioning

For a library that is used often, it is useful to permanently install its JAR file(s) locally on the task tracker machines, that is, those machines that run the MapReduce tasks. This is done by doing the following:

1. Copy the JAR files into a common location on all nodes.
2. Add the JAR files with full location into the *hadoop-env.sh* configuration file, into the HADOOP_CLASSPATH variable:

   ```
   # Extra Java CLASSPATH elements.  Optional.
   # export HADOOP_CLASSPATH="<extra_entries>:$HADOOP_CLASSPATH"
   ```
3. Restart all task trackers for the changes to be effective.

Obviously this technique is quite static, and every update (e.g., to add new libraries) requires a restart of the task tracker daemons. Adding HBase support requires at least the HBase and ZooKeeper JARs. Edit the *hadoop-env.sh* to contain the following:

```
export HADOOP_CLASSPATH="$HBASE_HOME/hbase-0.91.0-SNAPSHOT.jar: \
$ZK_HOME/zookeeper-3.3.2.jar:$HADOOP_CLASSPATH"
```

This assumes you have defined the two $*XYZ*_HOME environment variables to point to the location of where you have installed the respective packages.[*]

 Note that this fixes the versions of these globally provided libraries to whatever is specified on the servers and in their configuration files.

The issue of locking into specific versions of required libraries can be circumvented with the dynamic provisioning approach, explained next.

Dynamic Provisioning

In case you need to provide different libraries to each job you want to run, or you want to update the library versions along with your job classes, then using the dynamic provisioning approach is more useful.

For this, Hadoop has a special feature: it reads all libraries from an optional */lib* directory contained in the job JAR. You can use this feature to generate so-called *fat* JAR files, as they ship not just with the actual job code, but also with all libraries needed. This results in considerably larger job JAR files, but on the other hand, represents a complete, self-contained processing job.

---

[*] You can use an absolute path as well.

Using Maven

The example code for this book uses Maven to build the JAR files (see "Building the Examples" on page xxi). Maven allows you to create the JAR files not just with the example code, but also to build the enhanced fat JAR file that can be deployed to the MapReduce framework as-is. This avoids editing the server-side configuration files.

Maven has support for so-called *profiles*, which can be used to customize the build process. The *pom.xml* for this chapter makes use of this feature to add a `fatjar` profile that creates the required */lib* directory inside the final job JAR, and copies all required libraries into it. For this to work properly, some of the dependencies need to be defined with a *scope* of `provided` so that they are not included in the copy operation. This is done by adding the appropriate tag to all libraries that are already available on the server, for instance, the Hadoop JARs:

```
<dependency>
  <groupId>org.apache.hadoop</groupId>
  <artifactId>hadoop-core</artifactId>
  <version>0.20-append-r1044525</version>
  <scope>provided</scope>
  ...
</dependency>
```

This is done in the parent POM file, located in the root directory of the book repository, as well as inside the POM for the chapter, depending on where a dependency is added. One example is the Apache Commons CLI library, which is also part of Hadoop.

The `fatjar` profile uses the Maven Assembly plug-in with an accompanying *src/main/assembly/job.xml* file that specifies what should, and what should not, be included in the generated target JAR (e.g., it skips the provided libraries). With the profile in place, you can compile a *lean* JAR—one that only contains the job classes and would need an updated server configuration to include the HBase and ZooKeeper JARs—like so:

```
<ch07>$ mvn package
```

This will build a JAR that can be used to execute any of the included MapReduce, using the *hadoop jar* command:

```
<ch07>$ hadoop jar target/hbase-book-ch07-1.0.jar
An example program must be given as the first argument.
Valid program names are:
  AnalyzeData: Analyze imported JSON
  ImportFromFile: Import from file
  ParseJson: Parse JSON into columns
  ParseJson2: Parse JSON into columns (map only)
  ...
```

The command will list all possible job names. It makes use of the Hadoop `Program Driver` class, which is prepared with all known job classes and their names. The Maven build takes care of adding the `Driver` class—which is the one wrapping the `Program Driver` instance—as the main class of the JAR file; hence, it is automatically executed by the *hadoop jar* command.

Building a *fat* JAR only requires the addition of the profile name:

```
<ch07>$ mvn package -Dfatjar
```

The generated JAR file has an added postfix to distinguish it, but that is just a matter of taste (you can simply override the lean JAR if you prefer, although I refrain from explaining it here):

```
<ch07>$ hadoop jar target/hbase-book-ch07-1.0-job.jar
```

It behaves exactly like the lean JAR, and you can launch the same jobs with the same parameters. The difference is that it includes the required libraries, avoiding the configuration change on the servers:

```
$ unzip -l target/hbase-book-ch07-1.0-job.jar
Archive:  target/hbase-book-ch07-1.0-job.jar
 Length     Date   Time    Name
--------    ----   ----    ----
       0  07-14-11 12:01   META-INF/
     159  07-14-11 12:01   META-INF/MANIFEST.MF
       0  07-13-11 15:01   mapreduce/
       0  07-13-11 10:06   util/
     740  07-13-11 10:06   mapreduce/Driver.class
    3547  07-14-11 12:01   mapreduce/ImportFromFile$ImportMapper.class
    5326  07-14-11 12:01   mapreduce/ImportFromFile.class
    ...
    8739  07-13-11 10:06   util/HBaseHelper.class
       0  07-14-11 12:01   lib/
   16046  05-06-10 16:08   lib/json-simple-1.1.jar
   58160  05-06-10 16:06   lib/commons-codec-1.4.jar
  598364  11-22-10 21:43   lib/zookeeper-3.3.2.jar
 2731371  07-02-11 15:20   lib/hbase-0.91.0-SNAPSHOT.jar
   14837  07-14-11 12:01   lib/hbase-book-ch07-1.0.jar
--------                   -------
 3445231                   16 files
```

Maven is not the only way to generate different job JARs; you can also use Apache Ant, for example. What matters is not how you build the JARs, but that they contain the necessary information (either just the code, or the code and its required libraries).

Another option to dynamically provide the necessary libraries is the *libjars* feature of Hadoop's MapReduce framework. When you create a MapReduce job using the supplied GenericOptionsParser harness, you get support for the libjar parameter for free. Here is the documentation of the parser class:

```
GenericOptionsParser is a utility to parse command line arguments generic to
the Hadoop framework. GenericOptionsParser recognizes several standarad
command line arguments, enabling applications to easily specify a namenode,
a jobtracker, additional configuration resources etc.

Generic Options
The supported generic options are:

    -conf <configuration file>     specify a configuration file
    -D <property=value>            use value for given property
    -fs <local|namenode:port>      specify a namenode
    -jt <local|jobtracker:port>    specify a job tracker
    -files <comma separated list of files>    specify comma separated
```

```
                    files to be copied to the map reduce cluster
    -libjars <comma separated list of jars>   specify comma separated
                    jar files to include in the classpath.
    -archives <comma separated list of archives>   specify comma
            separated archives to be unarchived on the compute machines.
```

The general command line syntax is:

```
    bin/hadoop command [genericOptions] [commandOptions]
```

The reason to carefully read the documentation is that it not only states the `libjars` parameter, but also how and where to specify it on the command line. Failing to add the `libjars` parameter properly will result in the MapReduce job to fail. This can be seen from the job's logfiles, for every task attempt. The errors are also reported when starting the job on the command line, for example:

```
$ HADOOP_CLASSPATH=$HBASE_HOME/target/hbase-0.91.0-SNAPSHOT.jar: \
$ZK_HOME/zookeeper-3.3.2.jar hadoop jar target/hbase-book-ch07-1.0.jar \
ImportFromFile -t testtable -i test-data.txt -c data:json
...
11/08/08 11:13:17 INFO mapred.JobClient: Running job: job_201108081021_0003
11/08/08 11:13:18 INFO mapred.JobClient:  map 0% reduce 0%
11/08/08 11:13:29 INFO mapred.JobClient: Task Id : \
 attempt_201108081021_0003_m_000002_0, Status : FAILED
java.lang.RuntimeException: java.lang.ClassNotFoundException: \
 org.apache.hadoop.hbase.mapreduce.TableOutputFormat
 at org.apache.hadoop.conf.Configuration.getClass(Configuration.java:809)
 at org.apache.hadoop.mapreduce.JobContext.getOutputFormatClass(JobContext.java:197)
 at org.apache.hadoop.mapred.Task.initialize(Task.java:413)
 at org.apache.hadoop.mapred.MapTask.run(MapTask.java:288)
 at org.apache.hadoop.mapred.Child.main(Child.java:170)
```

The leading `HADOOP_CLASSPATH` assignment is also required to be able to launch the job from the command line. The `Driver` class setting up the job needs to have access to the HBase and ZooKeeper classes. Fixing the above error requires the `libjars` parameter to be added, like so:

```
$ HADOOP_CLASSPATH=$HBASE_HOME/target/hbase-0.91.0-SNAPSHOT.jar: \
$ZK_HOME/zookeeper-3.3.2.jar hadoop jar target/hbase-bk-ch07-1.0.jar \
ImportFromFile -libjars $HBASE_HOME/target/hbase-0.91.0-SNAPSHOT.jar, \
$ZK_HOME/zookeeper-3.3.2.jar -t testtable -i test-data.txt -c data:json
...
11/08/08 11:19:38 INFO mapred.JobClient: Running job: job_201108081021_0006
11/08/08 11:19:39 INFO mapred.JobClient:  map 0% reduce 0%
11/08/08 11:19:48 INFO mapred.JobClient:  map 100% reduce 0%
11/08/08 11:19:50 INFO mapred.JobClient: Job complete: job_201108081021_0006
```

Finally, the HBase helper class `TableMapReduceUtil` comes with a method that you can use from your own code to dynamically provision additional JAR and configuration files with your job:

```
static void addDependencyJars(Job job) throws IOException;
static void addDependencyJars(Configuration conf, Class... classes)
  throws IOException;
```

The former uses the latter function to add all the necessary HBase, ZooKeeper, and job classes:

```
addDependencyJars(job.getConfiguration(),
    org.apache.zookeeper.ZooKeeper.class,
    job.getMapOutputKeyClass(),
    job.getMapOutputValueClass(),
    job.getInputFormatClass(),
    job.getOutputKeyClass(),
    job.getOutputValueClass(),
    job.getOutputFormatClass(),
    job.getPartitionerClass(),
    job.getCombinerClass());
```

You can see in the source code of the ImportTsv class how this is used:

```
public static Job createSubmittableJob(Configuration conf, String[] args)
throws IOException, ClassNotFoundException {
    ...
    Job job = new Job(conf, NAME + "_" + tableName);
    ...
    TableMapReduceUtil.addDependencyJars(job);
    TableMapReduceUtil.addDependencyJars(job.getConfiguration(),
        com.google.common.base.Function.class /* Guava used by TsvParser */);
    return job;
}
```

The first call to addDependencyJars() adds the job and its necessary classes, including the input and output format, the various key and value types, and so on. The second call adds the Google *Guava* JAR, which is needed on top of the others already added. Note how this method does not require you to specify the actual JAR file. It uses the Java ClassLoader API to determine the name of the JAR containing the class in question. This might resolve to the same JAR, but that is irrelevant in this context. It is important that you have access to these classes in your Java CLASSPATH; otherwise, these calls will fail with a ClassNotFoundException error, similar to what you have seen already. You are still required to at least add the HADOOP_CLASSPATH to the command line for an unprepared Hadoop setup, or else you will not be able to run the job.

 Which approach you take is your choice. The fat JAR has the advantage of containing everything that is needed for the job to run on a generic Hadoop setup. The other approaches require at least a prepared classpath.

As far as this book is concerned, we will be using the fat JAR to build and launch MapReduce jobs.

Data Sink

Subsequently, we will go through various MapReduce jobs that use HBase to read from, or write to, as part of the process. The first use case explained is using HBase as a *data sink*. This is facilitated by the TableOutputFormat class and demonstrated in Example 7-1.

 The example data used is based on the public RSS feed offered by Delicious (*http://delicious.com*). Arvind Narayanan used the feed to collect a sample data set, which he published on his blog (*http://arvindn.live journal.com/116137.html*).

There is no inherent need to acquire the data set, or capture the RSS feed (*http://feeds.delicious.com/v2/rss/recent*); if you prefer, you can use any other source, including JSON records. On the other hand, the Delicious data set provides records that can be used nicely with Hush: every entry has a link, user name, date, categories, and so on.

The *test-data.txt* included in the book's repository is a small subset of the public data set. For testing, this subset is sufficient, but you can obviously execute the jobs with the full data set just as well.

The code, shown here in nearly complete form, includes some sort of standard template, and the subsequent examples will not show these *boilerplate* parts. This includes, for example, the command line parameter parsing.

Example 7-1. MapReduce job that reads from a file and writes into a table

```java
public class ImportFromFile {
  public static final String NAME = "ImportFromFile"; ❶
  public enum Counters { LINES }

  static class ImportMapper
  extends Mapper<LongWritable, Text, ImmutableBytesWritable, Writable> { ❷

    private byte[] family = null;
    private byte[] qualifier = null;

    @Override
    protected void setup(Context context)
      throws IOException, InterruptedException {
      String column = context.getConfiguration().get("conf.column");
      byte[][] colkey = KeyValue.parseColumn(Bytes.toBytes(column));
      family = colkey[0];
      if (colkey.length > 1) {
        qualifier = colkey[1];
      }
    }

    @Override
    public void map(LongWritable offset, Text line, Context context) ❸
```

```
  throws IOException {
    try {
      String lineString = line.toString();
      byte[] rowkey = DigestUtils.md5(lineString); ❹
      Put put = new Put(rowkey);
      put.add(family, qualifier, Bytes.toBytes(lineString)); ❺
      context.write(new ImmutableBytesWritable(rowkey), put);
      context.getCounter(Counters.LINES).increment(1);
    } catch (Exception e) {
      e.printStackTrace();
    }
  }
}

private static CommandLine parseArgs(String[] args) throws ParseException { ❻
  Options options = new Options();
  Option o = new Option("t", "table", true,
    "table to import into (must exist)");
  o.setArgName("table-name");
  o.setRequired(true);
  options.addOption(o);
  o = new Option("c", "column", true,
    "column to store row data into (must exist)");
  o.setArgName("family:qualifier");
  o.setRequired(true);
  options.addOption(o);
  o = new Option("i", "input", true,
    "the directory or file to read from");
  o.setArgName("path-in-HDFS");
  o.setRequired(true);
  options.addOption(o);
  options.addOption("d", "debug", false, "switch on DEBUG log level");
  CommandLineParser parser = new PosixParser();
  CommandLine cmd = null;
  try {
    cmd = parser.parse(options, args);
  } catch (Exception e) {
    System.err.println("ERROR: " + e.getMessage() + "\n");
    HelpFormatter formatter = new HelpFormatter();
    formatter.printHelp(NAME + " ", options, true);
    System.exit(-1);
  }
  return cmd;
}

public static void main(String[] args) throws Exception {
  Configuration conf = HBaseConfiguration.create();
  String[] otherArgs =
    new GenericOptionsParser(conf, args).getRemainingArgs(); ❼
  CommandLine cmd = parseArgs(otherArgs);
  String table = cmd.getOptionValue("t");
  String input = cmd.getOptionValue("i");
  String column = cmd.getOptionValue("c");
  conf.set("conf.column", column);
```

```
    Job job = new Job(conf, "Import from file " + input + " into table " + table); ❽
    job.setJarByClass(ImportFromFile.class);
    job.setMapperClass(ImportMapper.class);
    job.setOutputFormatClass(TableOutputFormat.class);
    job.getConfiguration().set(TableOutputFormat.OUTPUT_TABLE, table);
    job.setOutputKeyClass(ImmutableBytesWritable.class);
    job.setOutputValueClass(Writable.class);
    job.setNumReduceTasks(0); ❾
    FileInputFormat.addInputPath(job, new Path(input));

    System.exit(job.waitForCompletion(true) ? 0 : 1);
  }
}
```

❶ Define a job name for later use.

❷ Define the mapper class, extending the provided Hadoop class.

❸ The map() function transforms the key/value provided by the InputFormat to what is needed by the OutputFormat.

❹ The row key is the MD5 hash of the line to generate a random key.

❺ Store the original data in a column in the given table.

❻ Parse the command line parameters using the Apache Commons CLI classes. These are already part of HBase and therefore are handy to process the job specific parameters.

❼ Give the command line arguments to the generic parser first to handle "-Dxyz" properties.

❽ Define the job with the required classes.

❾ This is a map only job; therefore, tell the framework to bypass the reduce step.

The code sets up the MapReduce job in its main() class by first parsing the command line, which determines the target table name and column, as well as the name of the input file. This could be hardcoded here as well, but it is good practice to write your code in a configurable way.

The next step is setting up the job instance, assigning the variable details from the command line, as well as all fixed parameters, such as class names. One of those is the mapper class, set to ImportMapper. This class is defined in the same source code file, defining what should be done during the map phase of the job.

The main() code also assigns the output format class, which is the aforementioned TableOutputFormat class. It is provided by HBase and allows the job to easily write data into a table. The key and value types needed by this class is implicitly fixed to ImmutableBytesWritable for the key, and Writable for the value.

Before you can execute the job, you first have to create a target table, for example, using the HBase Shell:

```
hbase(main):001:0> create 'testtable', 'data'
0 row(s) in 0.5330 seconds
```

Once the table is ready you can launch the job:

```
$ hadoop dfs -put /projects/private/hbase-book-code/ch07/test-data.txt .
$ hadoop jar target/hbase-book-ch07-1.0-job.jar ImportFromFile \
-t testtable -i test-data.txt -c data:json
...
11/08/08 12:35:01 INFO mapreduce.TableOutputFormat: \
 Created table instance for testtable
11/08/08 12:35:01 INFO input.FileInputFormat: Total input paths to process : 1
11/08/08 12:35:02 INFO mapred.JobClient: Running job: job_201108081021_0007
11/08/08 12:35:03 INFO mapred.JobClient:  map 0% reduce 0%
11/08/08 12:35:10 INFO mapred.JobClient:  map 100% reduce 0%
11/08/08 12:35:12 INFO mapred.JobClient: Job complete: job_201108081021_0007
```

The first command, *hadoop dfs -put*, stores the sample data in the user's home directory in HDFS. The second command launches the job itself, which completes in a short amount of time. The data is read using the default `TextInputFormat`, as provided by Hadoop and its MapReduce framework. This input format can read text files that have *newline* characters at the end of each line. For every line read, it calls the `map()` function of the defined mapper class. This triggers our `ImportMapper.map()` function.

As shown in Example 7-1, the `ImportMapper` defines two methods, overriding the ones with the same name from the parent `Mapper` class.

Override Woes

It is *highly* recommended to add `@Override` annotations to your methods, so that wrong signatures can be detected at compile time. Otherwise, the implicit `map()` or `reduce()` methods might be called and do an identity function. For example, consider this `reduce()` method:

```
public void reduce(Writable key, Iterator<Writable> values,
  Context context) throws IOException, InterruptedException {
...
}
```

While this looks correct, it does *not*, in fact, override the `reduce()` method of the `Reducer` class, but instead defines a new version of the method. The MapReduce framework will silently ignore this method and execute the default implementation as provided by the `Reducer` class.

The reason is that the actual signature of the method is this:

```
protected void reduce(KEYIN key, Iterable<VALUEIN> values, \
    Context context) throws IOException, InterruptedException
```

This is a common mistake; the `Iterable` was erroneously replaced by an `Iterator` class. This is all it takes to make for a new signature. Adding the `@Override` annotation to an

---

overridden method in your code will make the compiler (and hopefully your background compilation check of your IDE) throw an error—before you run into what you might perceive as *strange* behavior during the job execution. Adding the annotation to the previous example:

```
@Override
public void reduce(Writable key, Iterator<Writable> values,
  Context context) throws IOException, InterruptedException {
...
}
```

The IDE you are using should already display an error, but at a minimum the compiler will report the mistake:

```
...
[INFO] -------------------------------------------------------------------
[ERROR] BUILD FAILURE
[INFO] -------------------------------------------------------------------
[INFO] Compilation failure
ch07/src/main/java/mapreduce/InvalidReducerOverride.java:[18,4] method does
not override or implement a method from a supertype
```

The `setup()` method of `ImportMapper` overrides the method called once when the class is instantiated by the framework. Here it is used to parse the given column into a column family and qualifier.

The `map()` of that same class is doing the actual work. As noted, it is called for every row in the input text file, each containing a JSON record. The code creates an HBase row key by using an MD5 hash of the line content. It then stores the line content as-is in the provided column, titled `data:json`.

The example makes use of the implicit write buffer set up by the `TableOutputFormat` class. The call to `context.write()` issues an internal `table.put()` with the given instance of `Put`. The `TableOutputFormat` takes care of calling `flushCommits()` when the job is complete—saving the remaining data in the write buffer.

> The `map()` method *writes* `Put` instances to store the input data. You can also write `Delete` instances to delete data from the target table. This is also the reason why the output key format of the job is set to `Writable`, instead of the explicit `Put` class.
>
> The `TableOutputFormat` can (currently) only handle `Put` and `Delete` instances. Passing anything else will raise an `IOException` with the message set to `Pass a Delete or a Put`.

Finally, note how the job is just using the map phase, and no reduce is needed. This is fairly typical with MapReduce jobs in combination with HBase: since data is already stored in sorted tables, or the raw data already has unique keys, you can avoid the more costly *sort, shuffle,* and *reduce* phases in the process.

Data Source

After importing the raw data into the table, we can use the contained data to parse the JSON records and extract information from it. This is accomplished using the TableInputFormat class, the counterpart to TableOutputFormat. It sets up a table as an input to the MapReduce process. Example 7-2 makes use of the provided InputFor mat class.

Example 7-2. MapReduce job that reads the imported data and analyzes it

```
static class AnalyzeMapper extends TableMapper<Text, IntWritable> { ❶

  private JSONParser parser = new JSONParser();
  private IntWritable ONE = new IntWritable(1);

  @Override
  public void map(ImmutableBytesWritable row, Result columns, Context context)
  throws IOException {
    context.getCounter(Counters.ROWS).increment(1);
    String value = null;
    try {
      for (KeyValue kv : columns.list()) {
        context.getCounter(Counters.COLS).increment(1);
        value = Bytes.toStringBinary(kv.getValue());
        JSONObject json = (JSONObject) parser.parse(value);
        String author = (String) json.get("author"); ❷
        context.write(new Text(author), ONE);
        context.getCounter(Counters.VALID).increment(1);
      }
    } catch (Exception e) {
      e.printStackTrace();
      System.err.println("Row: " + Bytes.toStringBinary(row.get()) +
        ", JSON: " + value);
      context.getCounter(Counters.ERROR).increment(1);
    }
  }
}

static class AnalyzeReducer
extends Reducer<Text, IntWritable, Text, IntWritable> { ❸

  @Override
  protected void reduce(Text key, Iterable<IntWritable> values,
    Context context) throws IOException, InterruptedException {
    int count = 0;
    for (IntWritable one : values) count++; ❹
    context.write(key, new IntWritable(count));
  }
}

public static void main(String[] args) throws Exception {
  ...
  Scan scan = new Scan(); ❺
  if (column != null) {
```

```
    byte[][] colkey = KeyValue.parseColumn(Bytes.toBytes(column));
    if (colkey.length > 1) {
      scan.addColumn(colkey[0], colkey[1]);
    } else {
      scan.addFamily(colkey[0]);
    }
  }

  Job job = new Job(conf, "Analyze data in " + table);
  job.setJarByClass(AnalyzeData.class);
  TableMapReduceUtil.initTableMapperJob(table, scan, AnalyzeMapper.class,
    Text.class, IntWritable.class, job); ❻
  job.setReducerClass(AnalyzeReducer.class);
  job.setOutputKeyClass(Text.class); ❼
  job.setOutputValueClass(IntWritable.class);
  job.setNumReduceTasks(1);
  FileOutputFormat.setOutputPath(job, new Path(output));

  System.exit(job.waitForCompletion(true) ? 0 : 1);
}
```

❶ Extend the supplied `TableMapper` class, setting your own output key and value types.

❷ Parse the JSON data, extract the author, and count the occurrence.

❸ Extend a Hadoop `Reducer` class, assigning the proper types.

❹ Count the occurrences and emit a sum.

❺ Create and configure a `Scan` instance.

❻ Set up the table mapper phase using the supplied utility.

❼ Configure the reduce phase using the normal Hadoop syntax.

This job runs as a full MapReduce process, where the map phase is reading the JSON data from the input table, and the reduce phase is aggregating the counts for every user. This is very similar to the `WordCount` example[†] that ships with Hadoop: the mapper emits counts of `ONE`, while the reducer counts those up to the sum per key (which in Example 7-2 is the *Author*). Executing the job on the command line is done like so:

```
$ hadoop jar target/hbase-book-ch07-1.0-job.jar AnalyzeData \
-t testtable -c data:json -o analyze1
11/08/08 15:36:37 INFO mapred.JobClient: Running job: job_201108081021_0021
11/08/08 15:36:38 INFO mapred.JobClient:  map 0% reduce 0%
11/08/08 15:36:45 INFO mapred.JobClient:  map 100% reduce 0%
11/08/08 15:36:57 INFO mapred.JobClient:  map 100% reduce 100%
11/08/08 15:36:59 INFO mapred.JobClient: Job complete: job_201108081021_0021
11/08/08 15:36:59 INFO mapred.JobClient: Counters: 19
...
11/08/08 15:36:59 INFO mapred.JobClient:   mapreduce.AnalyzeData$Counters
11/08/08 15:36:59 INFO mapred.JobClient:     ROWS=993
11/08/08 15:36:59 INFO mapred.JobClient:     COLS=993
```

[†] See the Hadoop wiki page (*http://wiki.apache.org/hadoop/WordCount*) for details.

```
11/08/08 15:36:59 INFO mapred.JobClient:      VALID=993
...
```

The end result is a list of counts per author, and can be accessed from the command line using, for example, the *hadoop dfs -text* command:

```
$ hadoop dfs -text analyze1/part-r-00000
10sr    1
13tohl    1
14bcps    1
21721725    1
2centime    1
33rpm    1
...
```

The example also shows how to use the `TableMapReduceUtil` class, with its static methods, to quickly configure a job with all the required classes. Since the job also needs a reduce phase, the `main()` code adds the `Reducer` classes as required, once again making implicit use of the default value when no other is specified (in this case, the `TextOut` `putFormat` class).

Obviously, this is a simple example, and in practice you will have to perform more involved analytical processing. But even so, the template shown in the example stays the same: you read from a table, extract the required information, and eventually output the results to a specific target.

Data Source and Sink

As already shown, the source or target of a MapReduce job can be a HBase table, but it is also possible for a job to use HBase as both input and output. In other words, a third kind of MapReduce template uses a table for the input and output types. This involves setting the `TableInputFormat` and `TableOutputFormat` classes into the respective fields of the job configuration. This also implies the various key and value types, as shown before. Example 7-3 shows this in context.

Example 7-3. MapReduce job that parses the raw data into separate columns

```
static class ParseMapper
extends TableMapper<ImmutableBytesWritable, Writable> {

  private JSONParser parser = new JSONParser();
  private byte[] columnFamily = null;

  @Override
  protected void setup(Context context)
  throws IOException, InterruptedException {
    columnFamily = Bytes.toBytes(
      context.getConfiguration().get("conf.columnfamily"));
  }

  @Override
  public void map(ImmutableBytesWritable row, Result columns, Context context)
```

```
      throws IOException {
        context.getCounter(Counters.ROWS).increment(1);
        String value = null;
        try {
          Put put = new Put(row.get());
          for (KeyValue kv : columns.list()) {
            context.getCounter(Counters.COLS).increment(1);
            value = Bytes.toStringBinary(kv.getValue());
            JSONObject json = (JSONObject) parser.parse(value);
            for (Object key : json.keySet()) {
              Object val = json.get(key);
              put.add(columnFamily, Bytes.toBytes(key.toString()), ❶
                Bytes.toBytes(val.toString()));
            }
          }
          context.write(row, put);
          context.getCounter(Counters.VALID).increment(1);
        } catch (Exception e) {
          e.printStackTrace();
          System.err.println("Error: " + e.getMessage() + ", Row: " +
            Bytes.toStringBinary(row.get()) + ", JSON: " + value);
          context.getCounter(Counters.ERROR).increment(1);
        }
      }
  }

  public static void main(String[] args) throws Exception {
    ...
    Scan scan = new Scan();
    if (column != null) {
      byte[][] colkey = KeyValue.parseColumn(Bytes.toBytes(column));
      if (colkey.length > 1) {
        scan.addColumn(colkey[0], colkey[1]);
        conf.set("conf.columnfamily", Bytes.toStringBinary(colkey[0])); ❷
        conf.set("conf.columnqualifier", Bytes.toStringBinary(colkey[1]));
      } else {
        scan.addFamily(colkey[0]);
        conf.set("conf.columnfamily", Bytes.toStringBinary(colkey[0]));
      }
    }

    Job job = new Job(conf, "Parse data in " + input + ", write to " + output);
    job.setJarByClass(ParseJson.class);
    TableMapReduceUtil.initTableMapperJob(input, scan, ParseMapper.class, ❸
      ImmutableBytesWritable.class, Put.class, job);
    TableMapReduceUtil.initTableReducerJob(output, ❹
      IdentityTableReducer.class, job);

    System.exit(job.waitForCompletion(true) ? 0 : 1);
  }
```

❶ Store the top-level JSON keys as columns, with their value set as the column value.

❷ Store the column family in the configuration for later use in the mapper.

❸ Set up map phase details using the utility method.

❹ Configure an identity reducer to store the parsed data.

The example uses the utility methods to configure the map and reduce phases, specifying the `ParseMapper`, which extracts the details from the raw JSON, and an `Identity TableReducer` to store the data in the target table. Note that both—that is, the input and output table—can be the same. Launching the job from the command line can be done like this:

```
$ hadoop jar target/hbase-book-ch07-1.0-job.jar ParseJson \
-i testtable -c data:json -o testtable
11/08/08 17:44:33 INFO mapreduce.TableOutputFormat: \
 Created table instance for testtable
11/08/08 17:44:33 INFO mapred.JobClient: Running job: job_201108081021_0026
11/08/08 17:44:34 INFO mapred.JobClient:  map 0% reduce 0%
11/08/08 17:44:41 INFO mapred.JobClient:  map 100% reduce 0%
11/08/08 17:44:50 INFO mapred.JobClient:  map 100% reduce 100%
11/08/08 17:44:52 INFO mapred.JobClient: Job complete: job_201108081021_0026
...
```

The percentages show that both the map and reduce phases have been completed, and that the job overall completed subsequently. Using the `IdentityTableReducer` to store the extracted data is not necessary, and in fact the same code with one additional line turns the job into a map-only one. Example 7-4 shows the added line.

Example 7-4. MapReduce job that parses the raw data into separate columns (map phase only)

```
...
Job job = new Job(conf, "Parse data in " + input + ", write to " + output +
  "(map only)");
job.setJarByClass(ParseJson2.class);
TableMapReduceUtil.initTableMapperJob(input, scan, ParseMapper.class,
  ImmutableBytesWritable.class, Put.class, job);
TableMapReduceUtil.initTableReducerJob(output,
  IdentityTableReducer.class, job);
job.setNumReduceTasks(0);
...
```

Running the job from the command line shows that the reduce phase has been skipped:

```
$ hadoop jar target/hbase-book-ch07-1.0-job.jar ParseJson2 \
-i testtable -c data:json -o testtable
11/08/08 18:38:10 INFO mapreduce.TableOutputFormat: \
 Created table instance for testtable
11/08/08 18:38:11 INFO mapred.JobClient: Running job: job_201108081021_0029
11/08/08 18:38:12 INFO mapred.JobClient:  map 0% reduce 0%
11/08/08 18:38:20 INFO mapred.JobClient:  map 100% reduce 0%
11/08/08 18:38:22 INFO mapred.JobClient: Job complete: job_201108081021_0029
...
```

The reduce stays at 0%, even when the job has completed. You can also use the Hadoop MapReduce UI to confirm that no reduce task have been executed for this job. The advantage of bypassing the reduce phase is that the job will complete much faster, since no additional processing of the data by the framework is required.

Both variations of the ParseJson job performed the same work. The result can be seen using the HBase Shell (omitting the repetitive row key output for the sake of space):

```
hbase(main):001:0> scan 'testtable'
...
\xFB!Nn\x8F\x89}\xD8\x91+\xB9o9\xB3E\xD0
  column=data:author, timestamp=1312821497945, value=bookrdr3
  column=data:comments, timestamp=1312821497945,
    value=http://delicious.com/url/409839abddbce807e4db07bf7d9cd7ad
  column=data:guidislink, timestamp=1312821497945, value=false
  column=data:id, timestamp=1312821497945,
    value=http://delicious.com/url/409839abddbce807e4db07bf7d9cd7ad#bookrdr3
  column=data:link, timestamp=1312821497945,
    value=http://sweetsassafras.org/2008/01/27/how-to-alter-a-wool-sweater
    ...
  column=data:updated, timestamp=1312821497945,
    value=Mon, 07 Sep 2009 18:22:21 +0000
...
993 row(s) in 1.7070 seconds
```

The import makes use of the arbitrary column names supported by HBase: the JSON keys are converted into qualifiers, and form new columns on the fly.

Custom Processing

You do not have to use any classes supplied by HBase to read and/or write to a table. In fact, these classes are quite lightweight and only act as helpers to make dealing with tables easier. Example 7-5 converts the previous example code to split the parsed JSON data into two target tables. The link key and its value is stored in a separate table, named linktable, while all other fields are stored in the table named infotable.

Example 7-5. MapReduce job that parses the raw data into separate tables

```
static class ParseMapper
extends TableMapper<ImmutableBytesWritable, Writable> {

  private HTable infoTable = null;
  private HTable linkTable = null;
  private JSONParser parser = new JSONParser();
  private byte[] columnFamily = null;

  @Override
  protected void setup(Context context)
  throws IOException, InterruptedException {
    infoTable = new HTable(context.getConfiguration(),
      context.getConfiguration().get("conf.infotable")); ❶
    infoTable.setAutoFlush(false);
    linkTable = new HTable(context.getConfiguration(),
      context.getConfiguration().get("conf.linktable"));
    linkTable.setAutoFlush(false);
    columnFamily = Bytes.toBytes(
      context.getConfiguration().get("conf.columnfamily"));
  }
```

```
@Override
protected void cleanup(Context context)
throws IOException, InterruptedException {
  infoTable.flushCommits();
  linkTable.flushCommits(); ❷
}

@Override
public void map(ImmutableBytesWritable row, Result columns, Context context)
throws IOException {
  context.getCounter(Counters.ROWS).increment(1);
  String value = null;
  try {
    Put infoPut = new Put(row.get());
    Put linkPut = new Put(row.get());
    for (KeyValue kv : columns.list()) {
      context.getCounter(Counters.COLS).increment(1);
      value = Bytes.toStringBinary(kv.getValue());
      JSONObject json = (JSONObject) parser.parse(value);
      for (Object key : json.keySet()) {
        Object val = json.get(key);
        if ("link".equals(key)) {
          linkPut.add(columnFamily, Bytes.toBytes(key.toString()),
            Bytes.toBytes(val.toString()));
        } else {
          infoPut.add(columnFamily, Bytes.toBytes(key.toString()),
            Bytes.toBytes(val.toString()));
        }
      }
    }
    infoTable.put(infoPut); ❸
    linkTable.put(linkPut);
    context.getCounter(Counters.VALID).increment(1);
  } catch (Exception e) {
    e.printStackTrace();
    System.err.println("Error: " + e.getMessage() + ", Row: " +
      Bytes.toStringBinary(row.get()) + ", JSON: " + value);
    context.getCounter(Counters.ERROR).increment(1);
  }
}
}

public static void main(String[] args) throws Exception {
  ...
  conf.set("conf.infotable", cmd.getOptionValue("o")); ❹
  conf.set("conf.linktable", cmd.getOptionValue("l"));
  ...
  Job job = new Job(conf, "Parse data in " + input + ", into two tables");
  job.setJarByClass(ParseJsonMulti.class);
  TableMapReduceUtil.initTableMapperJob(input, scan, ParseMapper.class,
    ImmutableBytesWritable.class, Put.class, job);
  job.setOutputFormatClass(NullOutputFormat.class); ❺
  job.setNumReduceTasks(0);
```

```
    System.exit(job.waitForCompletion(true) ? 0 : 1);
}
```

❶ Create and configure both target tables in the **setup()** method.

❷ Flush all pending commits when the task is complete.

❸ Save parsed values into two separate tables.

❹ Store table names in configuration for later use in the mapper.

❺ Set the output format to be ignored by the framework.

 You need to create two more tables, using, for example, the HBase Shell:

```
hbase(main):001:0> create 'infotable', 'data'
hbase(main):002:0> create 'linktable', 'data'
```

These two new tables will be used as the target tables for the current example.

Executing the job is done on the command line, and emits the following output:

```
$ hadoop jar target/hbase-book-ch07-1.0-job.jar ParseJsonMulti \
-i testtable -c data:json -o infotable -l linktable
11/08/08 21:13:57 INFO mapred.JobClient: Running job: job_201108081021_0033
11/08/08 21:13:58 INFO mapred.JobClient:  map 0% reduce 0%
11/08/08 21:14:06 INFO mapred.JobClient:  map 100% reduce 0%
11/08/08 21:14:08 INFO mapred.JobClient: Job complete: job_201108081021_0033
...
```

So far, this is the same as the previous ParseJson examples. The difference is the resulting tables, and their content. You can use the HBase Shell and the *scan* command
to list the content of each table after the job has completed. You should see that the
link table contains only the links, while the *info* table contains the remaining fields of
the original JSON.

Writing your own MapReduce code allows you to perform whatever is needed during
the job execution. You can, for example, read lookup values from a different table while
storing a combined result in yet another table. There is no limit as to where you read
from, or where you write to. The supplied classes are helpers, nothing more or less,
and serve well for a large number of use cases. If you find yourself limited by their
functionality, simply extend them, or implement generic MapReduce code and use the
API to access HBase tables in any shape or form.

CHAPTER 8

Architecture

It is quite useful for advanced users (or those who are just plain adventurous) to fully comprehend how a system of their choice works *behind* the scenes. This chapter explains the various moving parts of HBase and how they work together.

Seek Versus Transfer

Before we look into the architecture itself, however, we will first address a more fundamental difference between typical RDBMS storage structures and alternative ones. Specifically, we will look briefly at B-trees, or rather *B+ trees,* as they are commonly used in relational storage engines, and *Log-Structured Merge Trees,*† which (to some extent) form the basis for Bigtable's storage architecture, as discussed in "Building Blocks" on page 16.

 Note that RDBMSes do not use B-tree-type structures exclusively, nor do all NoSQL solutions use different architectures. You will find a colorful variety of mix-and-match technologies, but with one common objective: use the best strategy for the problem at hand.

B+ Trees

B+ trees have some specific features that allow for efficient insertion, lookup, and deletion of records that are identified by keys. They represent dynamic, multilevel indexes with lower and upper bounds as far as the number of keys in each segment (also called *page*) is concerned. Using these segments, they achieve a much higher fanout compared to binary trees, resulting in a much lower number of I/O operations to find a specific key.

---

* See "B+ trees" (*http://en.wikipedia.org/wiki/B%2B_tree*) on Wikipedia.

† See "LSM-Tree" (*http://citeseerx.ist.psu.edu/viewdoc/summary?doi=10.1.1.44.2782*), O'Neil et al., 1996.

In addition, they also enable you to do range scans very efficiently, since the leaf nodes in the tree are linked and represent an in-order list of all keys, avoiding more costly tree traversals. That is one of the reasons why they are used for indexes in relational database systems.

In a B+ tree index, you get locality on a page level (where "page" is synonymous with "block" in other systems). For example, the leaf pages look something like this:

```
[link to previous page]
[link to next page]
key1 → rowid
key2 → rowid
key3 → rowid
```

In order to insert a new index entry, say `key1.5`, it will update the leaf page with a new `key1.5 → rowid` entry. That is not a problem until the page, which has a fixed size, exceeds its capacity. Then it has to split the page into two new ones, and update the parent in the tree to point to the two new half-full pages. See Figure 8-1 for an example of a page that is full and would need to be split when adding another key.

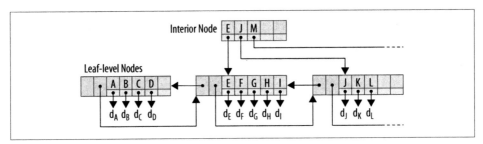

Figure 8-1. An example B+ tree with one full page

The issue here is that the new pages aren't necessarily next to each other on disk. So now if you ask to query a range from `key 1` to `key 3`, it's going to have to read two leaf pages that could be far apart from each other. That is also the reason why you will find an `OPTIMIZE TABLE` command in most layouts based on B+ trees—it basically rewrites the table in-order so that range queries become ranges on disk again.

Log-Structured Merge-Trees

Log-structured merge-trees, also known as LSM-trees, follow a different approach. Incoming data is stored in a logfile first, completely sequentially. Once the log has the modification saved, it then updates an in-memory store that holds the most recent updates for fast lookup.

When the system has accrued enough updates and starts to fill up the in-memory store, it flushes the sorted list of `key → record` pairs to disk, creating a new store file. At this point, the updates to the log can be thrown away, as all modifications have been persisted.

The store files are arranged similar to B-trees, but are optimized for sequential disk access where all nodes are completely filled and stored as either single-page or multipage blocks. Updating the store files is done in a *rolling merge* fashion, that is, the system packs existing on-disk multipage blocks together with the flushed in-memory data until the block reaches its full capacity, at which point a new one is started.

Figure 8-2 shows how a multipage block is merged from the in-memory tree into the next on-disk tree. Merging writes out a new block with the combined result. Eventually, the trees are merged into the larger blocks.

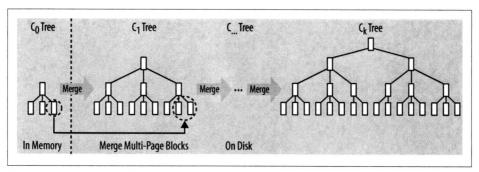

Figure 8-2. Multipage blocks iteratively merged across LSM-trees

As more flushes are taking place over time, creating many store files, a background process aggregates the files into larger ones so that disk seeks are limited to only a few store files. The on-disk tree can also be split into separate trees to spread updates across multiple store files. All of the stores are always sorted by key, so no reordering is required to fit new keys in between existing ones.

Lookups are done in a merging fashion in which the in-memory store is searched first, and then the on-disk store files are searched next. That way, all the stored data, no matter where it currently resides, forms a consistent view from a client's perspective.

Deletes are a special case of update wherein a *delete marker* is stored and is used during the lookup to skip "deleted" keys. When the pages are rewritten asynchronously, the delete markers and the key they mask are eventually dropped.

An additional feature of the background processing for housekeeping is the ability to support *predicate deletions*. These are triggered by setting a *time-to-live* (TTL) value that retires entries, for example, after 20 days. The merge processes will check the predicate and, if true, drop the record from the rewritten blocks.

The fundamental difference between B-trees and LSM-trees, though, is how their architecture is making use of modern hardware, especially disk drives.

Seek Versus Sort and Merge in Numbers[‡]

For our large-scale scenarios, computation is dominated by disk transfers. Although CPU, RAM, and disk size double every 18–24 months, seek time remains nearly constant at around a 5% increase in speed per year.

As discussed at the beginning of this chapter, there are two different database paradigms: one is *seek* and the other is *transfer*. Seek is typically found in RDBMSes and is caused by the B-tree or B+ tree structures used to store the data. It operates at the disk seek rate, resulting in `log(N)` seeks per access.

Transfer, on the other hand, as used by LSM-trees, sorts and merges files while operating at transfer rates, and takes `log(updates)` operations. This results in the following comparison given these values:

- 10 MB/second transfer bandwidth
- 10 milliseconds disk seek time
- 100 bytes per entry (10 billion entries)
- 10 KB per page (1 billion pages)

When updating 1% of entries (100,000,000), it takes:

- 1,000 days with random B-tree updates
- 100 days with batched B-tree updates
- 1 day with sort and merge

We can safely conclude that, at scale seek, is inefficient compared to transfer.

To compare B+ trees and LSM-trees you need to understand their relative strengths and weaknesses. B+ trees work well until there are too many modifications, because they force you to perform costly optimizations to retain that advantage for a limited amount of time. The more and faster you add data at random locations, the faster the pages become fragmented again. Eventually, you may take in data at a higher rate than the optimization process takes to rewrite the existing files. The updates and deletes are done at disk seek rates, rather than disk transfer rates.

LSM-trees work at disk transfer rates and scale much better to handle large amounts of data. They also guarantee a very consistent insert rate, as they transform random writes into sequential writes using the logfile plus in-memory store. The reads are independent from the writes, so you also get no contention between these two operations.

The stored data is always in an optimized layout. So, you have a predictable and consistent boundary on the number of disk seeks to access a key, and reading any number of records following that key doesn't incur any extra seeks. In general, what could be

---

[‡] From "Open Source Search" (*http://www.haifa.ibm.com/Workshops/ir2005/papers/DougCutting-Haifa05 .pdf*) by Doug Cutting, December 5, 2005.

emphasized about an LSM-tree-based system is cost transparency: you know that if you have five storage files, access will take a maximum of five disk seeks, whereas you have no way to determine the number of disk seeks an RDBMS query will take, even if it is indexed.

Finally, HBase is an LSM-tree-based system, just like Bigtable. The next sections will explain the storage architecture, while referring back to earlier sections of the book where appropriate.

Storage

One of the least-known aspects of HBase is how data is actually stored. While the majority of users may never have to bother with this, you may have to get up to speed when you want to learn the meaning of the various advanced configuration options you have at your disposal. Chapter 11 lists the more common ones and Appendix A has the full reference list.

You may also want to know more about file storage if, for whatever reason, disaster strikes and you have to recover an HBase installation. At that point, it is important to know where all the data is stored and how to access it on the HDFS level. Of course, this *shall not happen*, but who can guarantee that?

Overview

The first step in understanding the various moving parts in the storage layer of HBase is to understand the high-level picture. Figure 8-3 shows an overview of how HBase and Hadoop's filesystem are combined to store data.

The figure shows that HBase handles basically two kinds of file types: one is used for the write-ahead log and the other for the actual data storage. The files are primarily handled by the HRegionServers. In certain cases, the HMaster will also have to perform low-level file operations. You may also notice that the actual files are divided into blocks when stored within HDFS. This is also one of the areas where you can configure the system to handle larger or smaller data records better. More on that in "HFile Format" on page 329.

The general communication flow is that a new client contacts the ZooKeeper ensemble (a separate cluster of ZooKeeper nodes) first when trying to access a particular row. It does so by retrieving the server name (i.e., hostname) that hosts the -ROOT- region from ZooKeeper. With this information it can query that region server to get the server name that hosts the .META. table region containing the row key in question. Both of these details are cached and only looked up once. Lastly, it can query the reported .META. server and retrieve the server name that has the region containing the row key the client is looking for.

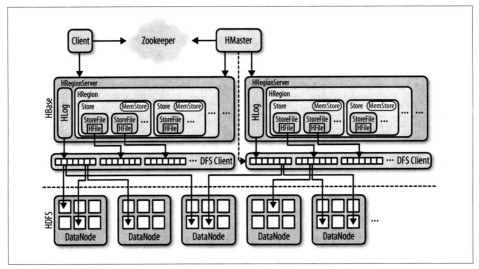

Figure 8-3. Overview of how HBase handles files in the filesystem, which stores them transparently in HDFS

Once it has been told in what region the row resides, it caches this information as well and contacts the HRegionServer hosting that region directly. So, over time, the client has a pretty complete picture of where to get rows without needing to query the .META. server again. See "Region Lookups" on page 345 for more details.

 The HMaster is responsible for assigning the regions to each HRegion Server when you start HBase. This also includes the special -ROOT- and .META. tables. See "The Region Life Cycle" on page 348 for details.

The HRegionServer opens the region and creates a corresponding HRegion object. When the HRegion is opened it sets up a Store instance for each HColumnFamily for every table as defined by the user beforehand. Each Store instance can, in turn, have one or more StoreFile instances, which are lightweight wrappers around the actual storage file called HFile. A Store also has a MemStore, and the HRegionServer a shared HLog instance (see "Write-Ahead Log" on page 333).

Write Path

The client issues an HTable.put(Put) request to the HRegionServer, which hands the details to the matching HRegion instance. The first step is to write the data to the write-ahead log (the WAL), represented by the HLog class.§ The WAL is a standard Hadoop

---

§ In extreme cases, you may turn off this step by setting a flag using the Put.setWriteToWAL(boolean) method. This is not recommended as this will disable durability.

SequenceFile and it stores HLogKey instances. These keys contain a sequential number as well as the actual data and are used to replay not-yet-persisted data after a server crash.

Once the data is written to the WAL, it is placed in the MemStore. At the same time, it is checked to see if the MemStore is full and, if so, a flush to disk is requested. The request is served by a separate thread in the HRegionServer, which writes the data to a new HFile located in HDFS. It also saves the last written sequence number so that the system knows what was persisted so far.

Preflushing on Stop

There is a second reason for memstores to be flushed: *preflushing*. When a region server is asked to stop it checks the memstores, and any that has more data than what is configured with the hbase.hregion.preclose.flush.size property (set to 5 MB by default) is first flushed to disk before blocking access to the region for a final round of flushing to close the hosted regions.

In other words, stopping the region servers forces all memstores to be written to disk, no matter how full they are compared to the configured maximum size, set with the hbase.hregion.memstore.flush.size property (the default is 64 MB), or when creating the table (see the "Maximum file size" list item in "Table Properties" on page 210). Once all memstores are flushed, the regions can be closed and no subsequent logfile replaying is needed when the regions are reopened by a different server.

Using the extra round of preflushing extends availability for the regions: during the preflush, the server and its regions are still available. This is similar to issuing a *flush* shell command or API call. Only when the remaining smaller memstores are flushed in the second round do the regions stop taking any further requests. This round also takes care of all modifications that came in to any memstore that was preflushed already. It guarantees that the server can exit cleanly.

Files

HBase has a configurable root directory in HDFS, with the default set to "/hbase". "Coexisting Clusters" on page 464 shows how to use a different root directory when sharing a central HDFS cluster. You can use the *hadoop dfs -lsr* command to look at the various files HBase stores. Before doing this, let us first create and fill a table with a handful of regions:

```
hbase(main):001:0> create 'testtable', 'colfam1', \
  { SPLITS => ['row-300', 'row-500', 'row-700' , 'row-900'] }
0 row(s) in 0.1910 seconds

hbase(main):002:0> for i in '0'..'9' do for j in '0'..'9' do \
  for k in '0'..'9' do put 'testtable', "row-#{i}#{j}#{k}", \
  "colfam1:#{j}#{k}", "#{j}#{k}" end end end
0 row(s) in 1.0710 seconds
```

```
0 row(s) in 0.0280 seconds
0 row(s) in 0.0260 seconds
...

hbase(main):003:0> flush 'testtable'
0 row(s) in 0.3310 seconds

hbase(main):004:0> for i in '0'..'9' do for j in '0'..'9' do \
  for k in '0'..'9' do put 'testtable', "row-#{i}#{j}#{k}", \
  "colfam1:#{j}#{k}", "#{j}#{k}" end end end
0 row(s) in 1.0710 seconds
0 row(s) in 0.0280 seconds
0 row(s) in 0.0260 seconds
...
```

The *flush* command writes the in-memory data to the store files; otherwise, we would have had to wait until more than the configured flush size of data was inserted into the stores. The last round of looping over the *put* command is to fill the write-ahead log again.

Here is the content of the HBase root directory afterward:

```
$ $HADOOP_HOME/bin/hadoop dfs -lsr /hbase
        ...
       0 /hbase/.logs
       0 /hbase/.logs/foo.internal,60020,1309812147645
       0 /hbase/.logs/foo.internal,60020,1309812147645/ \
foo.internal%2C60020%2C1309812147645.1309812151180
       0 /hbase/.oldlogs
      38 /hbase/hbase.id
       3 /hbase/hbase.version
       0 /hbase/testtable
     487 /hbase/testtable/.tableinfo
       0 /hbase/testtable/.tmp
       0 /hbase/testtable/1d562c9c4d3b8810b3dbeb21f5746855
       0 /hbase/testtable/1d562c9c4d3b8810b3dbeb21f5746855/.oldlogs
     124 /hbase/testtable/1d562c9c4d3b8810b3dbeb21f5746855/.oldlogs/ \
hlog.1309812163957
     282 /hbase/testtable/1d562c9c4d3b8810b3dbeb21f5746855/.regioninfo
       0 /hbase/testtable/1d562c9c4d3b8810b3dbeb21f5746855/.tmp
       0 /hbase/testtable/1d562c9c4d3b8810b3dbeb21f5746855/colfam1
   11773 /hbase/testtable/1d562c9c4d3b8810b3dbeb21f5746855/colfam1/ \
646297264540129145
       0 /hbase/testtable/66b4d2adcc25f1643da5e6260c7f7b26
     311 /hbase/testtable/66b4d2adcc25f1643da5e6260c7f7b26/.regioninfo
       0 /hbase/testtable/66b4d2adcc25f1643da5e6260c7f7b26/.tmp
       0 /hbase/testtable/66b4d2adcc25f1643da5e6260c7f7b26/colfam1
    7973 /hbase/testtable/66b4d2adcc25f1643da5e6260c7f7b26/colfam1/ \
3673316899703710654
       0 /hbase/testtable/99c0716d66e536d927b479af4502bc91
     297 /hbase/testtable/99c0716d66e536d927b479af4502bc91/.regioninfo
       0 /hbase/testtable/99c0716d66e536d927b479af4502bc91/.tmp
       0 /hbase/testtable/99c0716d66e536d927b479af4502bc91/colfam1
    4173 /hbase/testtable/99c0716d66e536d927b479af4502bc91/colfam1/ \
1337830525545548148
```

```
    0 /hbase/testtable/d240e0e57dcf4a7e11f4c0b106a33827
  311 /hbase/testtable/d240e0e57dcf4a7e11f4c0b106a33827/.regioninfo
    0 /hbase/testtable/d240e0e57dcf4a7e11f4c0b106a33827/.tmp
    0 /hbase/testtable/d240e0e57dcf4a7e11f4c0b106a33827/colfam1
 7973 /hbase/testtable/d240e0e57dcf4a7e11f4c0b106a33827/colfam1/ \
316417188262456922
    0 /hbase/testtable/d9ffc3a5cd016ae58e23d7a6cb937949
  311 /hbase/testtable/d9ffc3a5cd016ae58e23d7a6cb937949/.regioninfo
    0 /hbase/testtable/d9ffc3a5cd016ae58e23d7a6cb937949/.tmp
    0 /hbase/testtable/d9ffc3a5cd016ae58e23d7a6cb937949/colfam1
 7973 /hbase/testtable/d9ffc3a5cd016ae58e23d7a6cb937949/colfam1/ \
4238940159225512178
```

> The output was reduced to include just the file size and name to fit the
> available space. When you run the command on your cluster you will
> see more details.

The files can be divided into those that reside directly under the HBase root directory, and those that are in the *per-table* directories.

Root-level files

The first set of files are the write-ahead log files handled by the HLog instances, created in a directory called *.logs* underneath the HBase root directory. The *.logs* directory contains a subdirectory for each HRegionServer. In each subdirectory, there are several HLog files (because of log rotation). All regions from that region server share the same HLog files.

An interesting observation is that the logfile is reported to have a size of 0. This is fairly typical when the file was created recently, as HDFS is using built-in *append* support to write to this file, and only complete blocks are made available to readers—including the *hadoop dfs -lsr* command. Although the data of the put operations is safely persisted, the size of the logfile that is currently being written to is slightly off.

After, for example, waiting for an hour so that the logfile is rolled (see "LogRoller Class" on page 338 for all reasons when logfiles are rolled), you will see the existing logfile reported with its proper size, since it is closed now and HDFS can state the "correct" size. The new logfile next to it again starts at zero size:

```
249962 /hbase/.logs/foo.internal,60020,1309812147645/ \
foo.internal%2C60020%2C1309812147645.1309812151180
     0 /hbase/.logs/foo.internal,60020,1309812147645/ \
foo.internal%2C60020%2C1309812147645.1309815751223
```

When a logfile is are no longer needed because all of the contained edits have been persisted into store files, it is decommissioned into the *.oldlogs* directory under the root HBase directory. This is triggered when the logfile is rolled based on the configured thresholds.

The old logfiles are deleted by the master after 10 minutes (by default), set with the `hbase.master.logcleaner.ttl` property. The master checks every minute (by default again) for those files. This is configured with the `hbase.master.cleaner.interval` property.

 The behavior for expired logfiles is pluggable. This is used, for instance, by the replication feature (see "Replication" on page 351) to have access to persisted modifications.

The *hbase.id* and *hbase.version* files contain the unique ID of the cluster, and the file format version:

```
$ hadoop dfs -cat /hbase/hbase.id
$e627e130-0ae2-448d-8bb5-117a8af06e97
$ hadoop dfs -cat /hbase/hbase.version
7
```

They are used internally and are otherwise not very interesting. In addition, there are a few more root-level directories that appear over time. The *splitlog* and *.corrupt* folders are used by the log split process to store the intermediate split files and the corrupted logs, respectively. For example:

```
0 /hbase/.corrupt
0 /hbase/splitlog/foo.internal,60020,1309851880898_hdfs%3A%2F%2F \
localhost%2Fhbase%2F.logs%2Ffoo.internal%2C60020%2C1309850971208%2F \
foo.internal%252C60020%252C1309850971208.1309851641956/testtable/ \
d9ffc3a5cd016ae58e23d7a6cb937949/recovered.edits/0000000000000002352
```

There are no corrupt logfiles in this example, but there is one *staged* split file. The log splitting process is explained in "Replay" on page 338.

Table-level files

Every table in HBase has its own directory, located under the HBase root directory in the filesystem. Each table directory contains a top-level file named *.tableinfo*, which stores the serialized `HTableDescriptor` (see "Tables" on page 207 for details) for the table. This includes the table and column family schemas, and can be read, for example, by tools to gain insight on what the table looks like. The *.tmp* directory contains temporary data, and is used, for example, when the *.tableinfo* file is updated.

Region-level files

Inside each table directory, there is a separate directory for every region comprising the table. The names of these directories are the MD5 hash portion of a region name. For example, the following is taken from the master's web UI, after clicking on the `testta ble` link in the *User Tables* section:

```
testtable,row-500,1309812163930.d9ffc3a5cd016ae58e23d7a6cb937949.
```

The MD5 hash is d9ffc3a5cd016ae58e23d7a6cb937949 and is generated by encoding everything before the hash in the region name (minus the dividing dot), that is, testtable,row-500,1309812163930. The final dot after the hash is part of the complete region name: it indicates that this is a new style name. In previous versions of HBase, the region names did *not* include the hash.

 The -ROOT- and .META. catalog tables are still using the old style format, that is, their region names include *no* hash, and therefore end without the trailing dot:

> .META.,,1.1028785192

The encoding of the region names for the on-disk directories is also different: they use a *Jenkins* hash to encode the region name.

The hash guarantees that the directory names are always valid, in terms of filesystem rules: they do not contain any special character, such as the *slash* ("/"), which is used to divide the path. The overall layout for region files is then:

> /<hbase-root-dir>/<tablename>/<encoded-regionname>/<column-family>/<filename>

In each column-family directory, you can see the actual data files, explained in "HFile Format" on page 329. Their name is just an arbitrary number, based on the Java built-in random generator. The code is smart enough to check for collisions, that is, where a file with a newly generated number already exists. It loops until it finds an unused one and uses that instead.

The region directory also has a *.regioninfo* file, which contains the serialized information of the HRegionInfo instance for the given region. Similar to the *.tableinfo* file, it can be used by external tools to gain insight into the metadata of a region. The *hbase hbck* tool uses this to generate missing meta table entries, for example.

The optional *.tmp* directory is created on demand, and is used to hold temporary files—for example, the rewritten files from a compaction. These are usually moved out into the region directory once the process has completed. In rare circumstances, you might find leftover files, which are cleaned out when the region is reopened.

During the replay of the write-ahead log, any edit that has not been committed is written into a separate file per region. These are staged first (see the *splitlog* directory in "Root-level files" on page 323) and then—assuming the log splitting process has completed successfully—moved into the optional *recovered.edits* directory atomically. When the region is opened the region server will see the recovery file and replay the entries accordingly.

There is a clear distinction between the splitting of write-ahead logs ("Replay" on page 338) and the splitting of regions ("Region splits" on page 326). Sometimes it is difficult to distinguish the file and directory names in the filesystem, because both might refer to the term *splits*. Make sure you carefully identify their purpose to avoid confusion—or mistakes.

Once the region needs to split because it has exceeded the maximum configured region size, a matching *splits* directory is created, which is used to stage the two new daughter regions. If this process is successful—usually this happens in a few seconds or less—they are moved up into the table directory to form the two new regions, each representing one-half of the original region.

In other words, when you see a region directory that has no *.tmp* directory, no compaction has been performed for it yet. When it has no *recovered.edits* file, no write-ahead log replay has occurred for it yet.

In HBase versions before 0.90.x there were additional files, which are now obsolete. One is *oldlogfile.log*, which contained the replayed write-ahead log edits for the given region. The *oldlogfile.log.old* file (note the extra *.old* extension) indicated that there was already an existing *oldlogfile.log* file when the new one was put into place.

Another noteworthy file is the *compaction.dir* file in older versions of HBase, which is now replaced by the *.tmp* directory.

This concludes the list of what is commonly contained in the various directories inside the HBase root folder. There are more intermediate files, created by the region split process. They are discussed separately in the next section.

Region splits

When a store file within a region grows larger than the configured `hbase.hregion.max.filesize`—or what is configured at the column family level using `HColumnDescriptor`—the region is split in two. This is done initially very quickly because the system simply creates two reference files for the new regions (also called *daughters*), which each hosting half of the original region (referred to as the *parent*).

The region server accomplishes this by creating the *splits* directory in the parent region. Next, it closes the region so that it does not take on anymore requests.

The region server then prepares the new daughter regions (using multiple threads) by setting up the necessary file structures inside the *splits* directory. This includes the new region directories and the reference files. If this process completes successfully, it moves the two new region directories into the table directory. The `.META.` table is updated for the parent to state that it is now split, and what the two daughter regions are. This prevents it from being reopened by accident. Here is an example of how this looks in the .META. table:

```
row: testtable,row-500,1309812163930.d9ffc3a5cd016ae58e23d7a6cb937949.

    column=info:regioninfo, timestamp=1309872211559, value=REGION => {NAME => \
      'testtable,row-500,1309812163930.d9ffc3a5cd016ae58e23d7a6cb937949. \
      TableName => 'testtable', STARTKEY => 'row-500', ENDKEY => 'row-700', \
      ENCODED => d9ffc3a5cd016ae58e23d7a6cb937949, OFFLINE => true, \
      SPLIT => true,}

    column=info:splitA, timestamp=1309872211559, value=REGION => {NAME => \
      'testtable,row-500,1309872211320.d5a127167c6e2dc5106f066cc84506f8. \
      TableName => 'testtable', STARTKEY => 'row-500', ENDKEY => 'row-550', \
      ENCODED => d5a127167c6e2dc5106f066cc84506f8,}
    column=info:splitB, timestamp=1309872211559, value=REGION => {NAME => \
      'testtable,row-550,1309872211320.de27e14ffc1f3fff65ce424fcf14ae42. \
      TableName => [B@62892cc5', STARTKEY => 'row-550', ENDKEY => 'row-700', \
      ENCODED => de27e14ffc1f3fff65ce424fcf14ae42,}
```

You can see how the original region was split into two regions, separated at row-550. The SPLIT => true in the info:regioninfo column value also indicates that this region is now split into the regions referred to in info:splitA and info:splitB.

The name of the reference file is another random number, but with the hash of the referenced region as a postfix, for instance:

```
/hbase/testtable/d5a127167c6e2dc5106f066cc84506f8/colfam1/ \
6630747383202842155.d9ffc3a5cd016ae58e23d7a6cb937949
```

This reference file represents one-half of the original region with the hash d9ffc3a5cd016ae58e23d7a6cb937949, which is the region shown in the preceding example. The reference files only hold a little information: the key the original region was split at, and whether it is the top or bottom reference. Of note is that these references are then used by the HalfHFileReader class (which was omitted from the earlier overview as it is only used temporarily) to read the original region data files, and either the top or the bottom half of the files.

Both daughter regions are now ready and will be opened in parallel by the same server. This includes updating the .META. table to list both regions as available regions—just like any other. After that, the regions are online and start serving requests.

The opening of the daughters also schedules a compaction for both—which rewrites the store files in the background from the parent region into the two halves, while replacing the reference files. This takes place in the *.tmp* directory of the daughter regions. Once the files have been generated, they atomically replace the reference.

The parent is eventually cleaned up when there are no more references to it, which means it is removed as the parent from the .META. table, and all of its files on disk are deleted. Finally, the master is informed about the split and can schedule for the new regions to be moved off to other servers for load balancing reasons.

All of the steps involved in the split are tracked in ZooKeeper. This allows for other processes to reason about the state of a region in case of a server failure.

Compactions

The store files are monitored by a background thread to keep them under control. The flushes of memstores slowly build up an increasing number of on-disk files. If there are enough of them, the *compaction* process will combine them to a few, larger files. This goes on until the largest of these files exceeds the configured maximum store file size and triggers a region split (see "Region splits" on page 326).

Compactions come in two varieties: *minor* and *major*. Minor compactions are responsible for rewriting the last few files into one larger one. The number of files is set with the `hbase.hstore.compaction.min` property (which was previously called `hbase.hstore.compactionThreshold`, and although deprecated is still supported). It is set to 3 by default, and needs to be at least 2 or more. A number too large would delay minor compactions, but also would require more resources and take longer once the compactions start.

The maximum number of files to include in a minor compaction is set to 10, and is configured with `hbase.hstore.compaction.max`. The list is further narrowed down by the `hbase.hstore.compaction.min.size` (set to the configured memstore flush size for the region), and the `hbase.hstore.compaction.max.size` (defaults to `Long.MAX_VALUE`) configuration properties. Any file larger than the maximum compaction size is always excluded. The minimum compaction size works slightly differently: it is a threshold rather than a per-file limit. It includes all files that are under that limit, up to the total number of files per compaction allowed.

Figure 8-4 shows an example set of store files. All files that fit under the minimum compaction threshold are included in the compaction process.

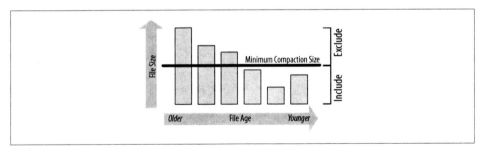

Figure 8-4. A set of store files showing the minimum compaction threshold

The algorithm uses `hbase.hstore.compaction.ratio` (defaults to 1.2, or 120%) to ensure that it does include enough files in the selection process. The ratio will also select files that are up to that size compared to the sum of the store file sizes of all newer files. The evaluation always checks the files from the oldest to the newest. This ensures that older files are compacted first. The combination of these properties allows you to fine-tune how many files are included in a minor compaction.

In contrast to minor compactions, major compactions compact all files into a single file. Which compaction type is run is automatically determined when the compaction check is executed. The check is triggered either after a memstore has been flushed to disk, after the *compact* or *major_compact* shell commands or corresponding API calls have been invoked, or by a background thread. This background thread is called the CompactionChecker and each region server runs a single instance. It runs a check on a regular basis, controlled by hbase.server.thread.wakefrequency (and multiplied by hbase.server.thread.wakefrequency.multiplier, set to 1000, to run it less often than the other thread-based tasks).

If you call the *major_compact* shell command, or the majorCompact() API call, you force the major compaction to run. Otherwise, the server checks first if the major compaction is due, based on hbase.hregion.majorcompaction (set to 24 hours) from the first time it ran. The hbase.hregion.majorcompaction.jitter (set to 0.2, in other words, 20%) causes this time to be spread out for the stores. Without the jitter, all stores would run a major compaction at the same time, every 24 hours. See "Managed Splitting" on page 429 for information on why this is a bad idea and how to manage this better.

If no major compaction is due, a minor compaction is assumed. Based on the aforementioned configuration properties, the server determines if enough files for a minor compaction are available and continues if that is the case.

Minor compactions might be promoted to major compactions when the former would include all store files, and there are less than the configured maximum files per compaction.

HFile Format

The actual storage files are implemented by the HFile class, which was specifically created to serve one purpose: store HBase's data efficiently. They are based on Hadoop's TFile class,[||] and mimic the *SSTable* format used in Google's Bigtable architecture. The previous use of Hadoop's MapFile class in HBase proved to be insufficient in terms of performance. Figure 8-5 shows the file format details.

The files contain a variable number of blocks, where the only fixed ones are the *file info* and *trailer* blocks. As Figure 8-5 shows, the trailer has the pointers to the other blocks. It is written after the data has been persisted to the file, finalizing the now immutable data store. The *index* blocks record the offsets of the *data* and *meta* blocks.

[||] See the JIRA issue HADOOP-3315 (*http://issues.apache.org/jira/browse/HADOOP-3315*) for details.

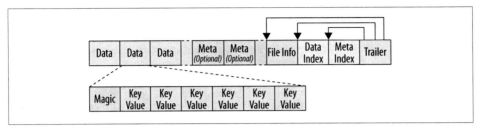

Figure 8-5. The HFile structure

Both the data and the meta blocks are actually optional. But considering how HBase uses the data files, you will almost always find at least data blocks in the store files.

The block size is configured by the `HColumnDescriptor`, which, in turn, is specified at table creation time by the user, or defaults to reasonable standard values. Here is an example as shown in the master web-based interface:

```
{NAME => 'testtable', FAMILIES => [{NAME => 'colfam1',
BLOOMFILTER => 'NONE', REPLICATION_SCOPE => '0', VERSIONS => '3',
COMPRESSION \=> 'NONE', TTL => '2147483647', BLOCKSIZE => '65536',
IN_MEMORY => 'false', BLOCKCACHE => 'true'}]}
```

The default is 64 KB (or 65,535 bytes). Here is what the `HFile` JavaDoc explains:

> Minimum block size. We recommend a setting of minimum block size between 8KB to 1MB for general usage. Larger block size is preferred if files are primarily for sequential access. However, it would lead to inefficient random access (because there are more data to decompress). Smaller blocks are good for random access, but require more memory to hold the block index, and may be slower to create (because we must flush the compressor stream at the conclusion of each data block, which leads to an FS I/O flush). Further, due to the internal caching in Compression codec, the smallest possible block size would be around 20KB-30KB.

Each block contains a *magic* header, and a number of serialized `KeyValue` instances (see "KeyValue Format" on page 333 for their format). If you are *not* using a compression algorithm, each block is about as large as the configured *block size*. This is not an exact science, as the writer has to fit whatever you give it: if you store a `KeyValue` that is larger than the block size, the writer has to accept that. But even with smaller values, the check for the block size is done after the last value was written, so in practice, the majority of blocks will be slightly larger.

When you are using a compression algorithm you will not have much control over block size. Compression codecs work best if they can decide how much data is enough to achieve an efficient compression ratio. For example, setting the block size to 256 KB and using LZO compression ensures that blocks will always be written to be less than or equal to 256 KB to suit the LZO internal buffer size.

Many compression libraries come with a set of configuration properties you can use to specify the buffer size, and other options. Refer to the source code of the JNI library to find out what is available to you.

The writer does not know if you have a compression algorithm selected or not: it follows the block size limit to write out raw data close to the configured amount. If you have compression enabled, less data will be saved less. This means the final store file will contain the same number of blocks, but the total size will be smaller since each block is smaller.

One thing you may notice is that the default block size for files in HDFS is 64 MB, which is 1,024 times the HFile default block size. As such, the HBase storage file blocks do *not* match the Hadoop blocks. In fact, there is no correlation between these two block types. HBase stores its files transparently into *a* filesystem. The fact that HDFS uses blocks is a coincidence. And HDFS also does not know what HBase stores; it only sees binary files. Figure 8-6 demonstrates how the HFile content is simply spread across HDFS blocks.

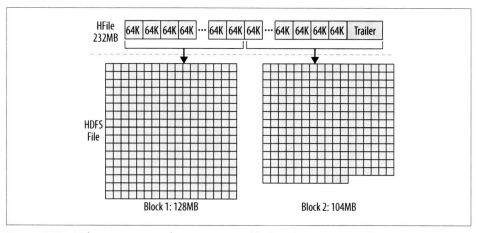

Figure 8-6. HFile content spread across HDFS blocks when many smaller HFile blocks are transparently stored in two HDFS blocks that are much larger

Sometimes it is necessary to be able to access an HFile directly, bypassing HBase, for example, to check its health, or to dump its contents. The HFile.main() method provides the tools to do that:

```
$ ./bin/hbase org.apache.hadoop.hbase.io.hfile.HFile
usage: HFile  [-a] [-b] [-e] [-f <arg>] [-k] [-m] [-p] [-r <arg>] [-v]
 -a,--checkfamily      Enable family check
 -b,--printblocks      Print block index meta data
 -e,--printkey         Print keys
 -f,--file <arg>       File to scan. Pass full-path; e.g.
                       hdfs://a:9000/hbase/.META./12/34
```

```
-k,--checkrow        Enable row order check; looks for out-of-order keys
-m,--printmeta       Print meta data of file
-p,--printkv         Print key/value pairs
-r,--region <arg>    Region to scan. Pass region name; e.g. '.META.,,1'
-v,--verbose         Verbose output; emits file and meta data delimiters
```

Here is an example of what the output will look like (shortened):

```
$ ./bin/hbase org.apache.hadoop.hbase.io.hfile.HFile -f \
/hbase/testtable/de27e14ffc1f3fff65ce424fcf14ae42/colfam1/2518469459313898451 \
-v -m -p
Scanning -> /hbase/testtable/de27e14ffc1f3fff65ce424fcf14ae42/colfam1/ \
2518469459313898451
K: row-550/colfam1:50/1309813948188/Put/vlen=2 V: 50
K: row-550/colfam1:50/1309812287166/Put/vlen=2 V: 50
K: row-551/colfam1:51/1309813948222/Put/vlen=2 V: 51
K: row-551/colfam1:51/1309812287200/Put/vlen=2 V: 51
K: row-552/colfam1:52/1309813948256/Put/vlen=2 V: 52
...
K: row-698/colfam1:98/1309813953680/Put/vlen=2 V: 98
K: row-698/colfam1:98/1309812292594/Put/vlen=2 V: 98
K: row-699/colfam1:99/1309813953720/Put/vlen=2 V: 99
K: row-699/colfam1:99/1309812292635/Put/vlen=2 V: 99
Scanned kv count -> 300
Block index size as per heapsize: 208
reader=/hbase/testtable/de27e14ffc1f3fff65ce424fcf14ae42/colfam1/ \
2518469459313898451, compression=none, inMemory=false, \
firstKey=row-550/colfam1:50/1309813948188/Put, \
lastKey=row-699/colfam1:99/1309812292635/Put, avgKeyLen=28, avgValueLen=2, \
entries=300, length=11773
fileinfoOffset=11408, dataIndexOffset=11664, dataIndexCount=1, \
metaIndexOffset=0, metaIndexCount=0, totalBytes=11408, entryCount=300, \
version=1
Fileinfo:
MAJOR_COMPACTION_KEY = \xFF
MAX_SEQ_ID_KEY = 2020
TIMERANGE = 1309812287166....1309813953720
hfile.AVG_KEY_LEN = 28
hfile.AVG_VALUE_LEN = 2
hfile.COMPARATOR = org.apache.hadoop.hbase.KeyValue$KeyComparator
hfile.LASTKEY = \x00\x07row-699\x07colfam199\x00\x00\x010\xF6\xE5|\x1B\x04
Could not get bloom data from meta block
```

The first part of the output is the actual data stored as serialized KeyValue instances. The second part dumps the internal HFile.Reader properties, as well as the trailer block details. The last part, starting with Fileinfo, is the file info block values.

The provided information is valuable to, for example, confirm whether a file is compressed or not, and with what compression type. It also shows you how many cells you have stored, as well as the average size of their keys and values. In the preceding example, the key is much larger than the value. This is caused by the overhead required by the KeyValue class to store the necessary data, explained next.

KeyValue Format

In essence, each `KeyValue` in the `HFile` is a low-level byte array that allows for *zero-copy* access to the data. Figure 8-7 shows the layout of the contained data.

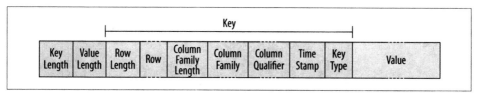

Figure 8-7. The KeyValue format

The structure starts with two fixed-length numbers indicating the size and value of the key. With that information, you can offset into the array to, for example, get direct access to the value, ignoring the key. Otherwise, you can get the required information from the key. Once the information is parsed into a `KeyValue` Java instance, you can use getters to access the details, as explained in "The KeyValue class" on page 83.

The reason the average key in the preceding example is larger than the value has to do with the fields that make up the key part of a `KeyValue`. The key holds the row key, the column family name, the column qualifier, and so on. For a small payload, this results in quite a considerable overhead. If you deal with small values, try to keep the key small as well. Choose a short row and column key (the family name with a single byte, and the qualifier equally short) to keep the ratio in check.

On the other hand, compression should help mitigate the overwhelming key size problem, as it looks at finite windows of data, and all repeating data should compress well. The sorting of all `KeyValues` in the store file helps to keep similar keys (and possibly values too, in case you are using versioning) close together.

Write-Ahead Log

The region servers keep data in-memory until enough is collected to warrant a flush to disk, avoiding the creation of too many very small files. While the data resides in memory it is volatile, meaning it could be lost if the server loses power, for example. This is a likely occurrence when operating at large scale, as explained in "Seek Versus Transfer" on page 315.

A common approach to solving this issue is *write-ahead logging*:# Each update (also called an "edit") is written to a log, and only if the update has succeeded is the client informed that the operation has succeeded. The server then has the liberty to batch or aggregate the data in memory as needed.

#For information on the term itself, read "Write-ahead logging" (*http://en.wikipedia.org/wiki/Write-ahead _logging*) on Wikipedia.

Overview

The WAL is the lifeline that is needed when disaster strikes. Similar to a *binary log* in MySQL, the WAL records all changes to the data. This is important in case something happens to the primary storage. If the server crashes, the WAL can effectively *replay* the log to get everything up to where the server should have been just before the crash. It also means that if writing the record to the WAL fails, the whole operation must be considered a failure.

"Overview" on page 319 shows how the WAL fits into the overall architecture of HBase. Since it is shared by all regions hosted by the same region server, it acts as a central logging backbone for every modification. Figure 8-8 shows how the flow of edits is split between the memstores and the WAL.

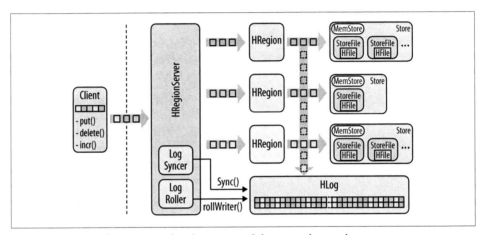

Figure 8-8. All modifications saved to the WAL, and then passed on to the memstores

The process is as follows: first the client initiates an action that modifies data. This can be, for example, a call to put(), delete(), and increment(). Each of these modifications is wrapped into a KeyValue object instance and sent over the wire using RPC calls. The calls are (ideally) batched to the HRegionServer that serves the matching regions.

Once the KeyValue instances arrive, they are routed to the HRegion instances that are responsible for the given rows. The data is written to the WAL, and then put into the MemStore of the actual Store that holds the record. This is, in essence, the *write path* of HBase.

Eventually, when the memstores get to a certain size, or after a specific time, the data is persisted in the background to the filesystem. During that time, data is stored in a volatile state in memory. The WAL guarantees that the data is never lost, even if the server fails. Keep in mind that the actual log resides on HDFS, which is a replicated filesystem. Any other server can open the log and start replaying the edits—nothing on the failed physical server is needed to effect a full recovery.

HLog Class

The class that implements the WAL is called HLog. When an HRegion is instantiated, the single HLog instance that runs inside each region server is passed on as a parameter to the constructor of HRegion. When a region receives an update operation, it can save the data directly to the shared WAL instance.

The core of the HLog functionality is the append() method. Note that for performance reasons there is an option for Put, Delete, and Increment to be called with an extra parameter set: setWriteToWAL(false). If you invoke this method while setting up, for example, a Put instance, the writing to the WAL is bypassed! That is also why the downward arrow in Figure 8-8 was created with a dashed line to indicate the optional step. By default, you certainly want the WAL, no doubt about that. But say you run a large bulk import MapReduce job that you can rerun at any time. You gain extra performance when you disable the WAL, but at the cost of having to take extra care that no data was lost during the import.

 You are strongly advised not to lightheartedly turn off writing edits to the WAL. If you do so, you will *lose data* sooner or later. And *no*, HBase cannot recover data that is lost and that has not been written to the log first.

Another important feature of HLog is the ability to keep track of changes. It does this by using a *sequence number*. It uses an AtomicLong internally to be thread-safe and starts at either zero, or the last known number persisted to the filesystem: as the region is opening its storage files, it reads the highest sequence number, which is stored as a meta field in each HFile and sets the HLog sequence number to that value if it is higher than what was recorded before. So, after it has opened all the storage files, the HLog is initialized to reflect where persisting ended and where to continue.

Figure 8-9 shows three different regions, hosted on the same region server, with each of them covering a different row key range. Each region shares the same single instance of HLog. This means the data is written to the WAL in the order it arrives. This means some extra work is needed when a log needs to be replayed (see "Replay" on page 338). But since this happens rather seldomly, the WAL is optimized to store data sequentially, giving it the best I/O performance.

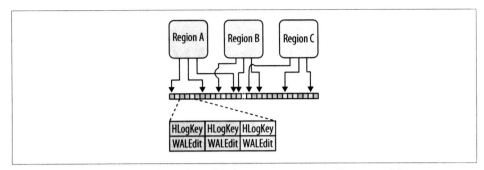

Figure 8-9. The WAL saving edits in the order they arrive, spanning all regions of the same server

HLogKey Class

Currently, the WAL uses a Hadoop `SequenceFile`, which stores records as sets of key/values. For the WAL, the value is simply the modification(s) sent from the client. The key is represented by an `HLogKey` instance: since the `KeyValue` only represents the row key, column family, column qualifier, timestamp, type, and value, there has to be a place to store what the KeyValue belongs to, in other words, the region and table name. That information is stored in the `HLogKey`. Also stored is the aforementioned sequence number. That number is incremented with each edit in order to keep a sequential order of edits.

This class also records the write time, which is a timestamp that denotes when the edit was written to the log. Finally, it stores the *cluster ID*, which is needed for replication across clusters.

WALEdit Class

Every modification sent by a client is wrapped into a `WALEdit` instance, which takes care of atomicity at the log level. Assume you update 10 columns in one row. Each column, or cell, is represented as a separate `KeyValue` instance. If the server writes five of them to the WAL and then fails, you will end up with a half-persisted row mutation.

Atomicity is guaranteed by bundling all updates that comprise multiple cells into a single `WALEdit` instance. This group of edits is then written in a single operation, ensuring that the row mutation is applied in full or not at all.

Before version 0.90.x, HBase did save the `KeyValue` instances separately.

LogSyncer Class

The table descriptor allows you to set the so-called *deferred log flush* flag, as explained in "Table Properties" on page 210. The default is `false` and it means that every time an edit is sent to the servers, it will call the log writer's `sync()` method. It is the call that forces the update to the log to be acknowledged by the filesystem so that you have durability.

Unfortunately, calling this method involves a pipelined write to *N* servers (where *N* is the replication factor set for the write-ahead log files). Since this is a rather costly operation, you have the option to slightly delay the call, and have it executed in a background process instead. Keep in mind that without the call to `sync()`, there is a chance of *data loss* in case of a server failure. Use this option carefully.

Pipeline Versus n-Way Writes

The current implementation of `sync()` is a *pipelined write*, which means when the edit is written, it is sent to the first data node to persist it. Once that has succeeded, it is sent by that data node to another data node to do the same thing, and so on. Only when all three have acknowledged the write operation is the client allowed to proceed.

Another approach to saving edits durably is the *n-way write*, where the write is sent to three machines at the same time. When all acknowledge the write, the client can continue.

The difference between pipelined and n-way writes is that a pipelined write needs time to complete, and therefore has a higher latency. But it can saturate the network bandwidth better. An n-way write has lower latency, as the client only needs to wait for the slowest data node to acknowledge (assuming the others have already reported back success). However, an n-way write needs to share the network bandwidth of the sending server, which can cause a bottleneck for heavily loaded systems.

There is work in progress to have support for both in HDFS, giving you the choice to use the one that performs best for your application.

Setting the deferred log flush flag to `true` causes the edits to be buffered on the region server, and the `LogSyncer` class, running as a background thread on the server, is responsible for calling the `sync()` method at a very short interval. The default is one second and is configured by the `hbase.regionserver.optionallogflushinterval` property.

Note that this only applies to user tables: all catalog tables are always synced right away.

LogRoller Class

There are size restrictions when it comes to the logs that are written. The `LogRoller` class runs as a background thread and takes care of rolling logfiles at certain intervals. This is controlled by the `hbase.regionserver.logroll.period` property, set by default to one hour.

Every 60 minutes the log is closed and a new one is started. Over time, the system accumulates an increasing number of logfiles that need to be managed as well. The `HLog.rollWriter()` method, which is called by the `LogRoller` to roll the current logfile, takes care of that as well by subsequently calling `HLog.cleanOldLogs()`.

It checks what the highest sequence number written to a storage file is. This is the edit sequence number of the last edit persisted out to the filesystem. It then checks if there is a log left that has edits that are all less than that number. If that is the case, it moves said logs into the *.oldlogs* directory, and leaves the remaining ones in place.

 You might see the following obscure message in your logs:

```
2011-06-15 01:45:48,427 INFO org.apache.hadoop.hbase.regionserver.HLog: \
  Too many hlogs: logs=130, maxlogs=96; forcing flush of 8 region(s):
  testtable,row-500,1309872211320.d5a127167c6e2dc5106f066cc84506f8., ...
```

This message is printed because the configured maximum number of logfiles to keep exceeds the number of logfiles that are required to be kept because they still contain outstanding edits that have not yet been persisted. This can occur when you stress out the filesystem to such an extent that it cannot persist the data at the rate at which new data is added. Otherwise, memstore flushes should take care of this.

Note, though, that when this message is printed the server goes into a special mode trying to force edits to be flushed out to reduce the number of outstanding WAL files.

The other parameters controlling log rolling are `hbase.regionserver.hlog.blocksize` (set to the filesystem default block size, or `fs.local.block.size`, defaulting to 32 MB) and `hbase.regionserver.logroll.multiplier` (set to 0.95), which will rotate logs when they are at 95% of the block size. So logs are switched out when they are considered full, or when a certain amount of time has passed—whatever comes first.

Replay

The master and region servers need to orchestrate the handling of logfiles carefully, especially when it comes to recovering from server failures. The WAL is responsible for retaining the edits safely; replaying the WAL to restore a consistent state is a much more complex exercise.

Single log

Since all edits are written to one `HLog`-based logfile per region server, you might ask: why is that the case? Why not write all edits for a specific region into its own logfile? Here is the related quote from the Bigtable paper:

> If we kept the commit log for each tablet in a separate logfile, a very large number of files would be written concurrently in GFS. Depending on the underlying file system implementation on each GFS server, these writes could cause a large number of disk seeks to write to the different physical log files.

HBase followed that principle for pretty much the same reasons: writing too many files at the same time, plus the number of rolled logs that need to be kept, does not scale well.

What is the drawback, though? If you have to split a log because of a server crash, you need to divide it into suitable pieces, as described in the next section. The master cannot redeploy any region from a crashed server until the logs for that very server have been split. This can potentially take a considerable amount of time.

Log splitting

There are two situations in which logfiles have to be replayed: when the cluster starts, or when a server fails. When the master starts—and this includes a backup master taking over duty—it checks if there are any logfiles, in the *.logs* directory under the HBase root on the filesystem, that have no region server assigned to them. The logs' names contain not just the server name, but also the *start code* of the server. This number is reset every time a region server restarts, and the master can use this number to verify whether a log has been abandoned—for example, due to a server crash.

The master is responsible for monitoring the servers using ZooKeeper, and if it detects a server failure, it immediately starts the process of recovering its logfiles, before reassigning the regions to new servers. This happens in the `ServerShutdownHandler` class.

Before the edits in the log can be replayed, they need to be separated into one logfile per region. This process is called *log splitting*: the combined log is read and all entries are grouped by the region they belong to. These grouped edits are then stored in a file next to the target region for subsequent recovery.

The actual process of splitting the logs is different in nearly every version of HBase: early versions would read the file in a single thread, directly on the master. This was improved to at least write the grouped edits per region in multiple threads. Version 0.92.0 finally introduces the concept of *distributed log splitting*, which removes the burden of doing the actual work from the master to all region servers.

Consider a larger cluster with many region servers and many (rather large) logfiles. In the past, the master had to recover each logfile separately, and—so it would not overload in terms of I/O as well as memory usage—it would do this sequentially. This meant that, for any region that had pending edits, it had to be blocked from opening until the log split and recovery had been completed.

The new distributed mode uses ZooKeeper to hand out each abandoned logfile to a region server. They monitor ZooKeeper for available work, and if the master indicates that a log is available for processing, they race to accept the task. The winning region server then proceeds to read and split the logfiles in a single thread (so as not to overload the already busy region server).

 You can turn the new distributed log splitting off by means of the `hbase.master.distributed.log.splitting` configuration property. Setting this property to `false` disables distributed splitting, and falls back to doing the work directly on the master only.

In nondistributed mode the writers are multithreaded, controlled by the `hbase.regionserver.hlog.splitlog.writer.threads` property, which is set to 3 by default. You need to be careful when increasing this number, as you are likely bound by the performance of the single log reader.

The split process writes the edits first into the *splitlog* staging directory under the HBase root folder. They are placed in the same path that is needed for the target region. For example:

```
0 /hbase/.corrupt
0 /hbase/splitlog/foo.internal,60020,1309851880898_hdfs%3A%2F%2F \
localhost%2Fhbase%2F.logs%2Ffoo.internal%2C60020%2C1309850971208%2F \
foo.internal%252C60020%252C1309850971208.1309851641956/testtable/ \
d9ffc3a5cd016ae58e23d7a6cb937949/recovered.edits/0000000000000002352
```

The path contains the logfile name itself to distinguish it from other, possibly concurrently executed, log split output. The path also contains the table name, region name (hash), and *recovered.edits* directory. Lastly, the name of the split file is the sequence ID of the first edit for the particular region.

The *.corrupt* directory contains any logfile that could not be parsed. This is influenced by the `hbase.hlog.split.skip.errors` property, which is set to `true` by default. It means that any edit that could not be read from a file causes the entire log to be moved to the *.corrupt* folder. If you set the flag to `false`, an `IOExecption` is thrown and the *entire* log splitting process is stopped.

Once a log has been split successfully, the per-region files are moved into the actual region directories. They are now ready to be recovered by the region itself. This is also why the splitting has to stall opening the affected regions, since it first has to provide the pending edits for replay.

Edits recovery

When a region is opened, either because the cluster is started or because it has been moved from one region server to another, it first checks for the presence of the *recovered.edits* directory. If it exists, it opens the contained files and starts reading the edits they contain. The files are sorted by their name, which contains the sequence ID. This allows the region to recover the edits in order.

Any edit that has a sequence ID that is less than or equal to what has been persisted in the on-disk store files is ignored, because it has already been applied. All other edits are applied to the matching memstore of the region to recover the previous state. At the end, a flush of the memstores is forced to write the current state to disk.

The files in the *recovered.edits* folder are removed once they have been read and their edits persisted to disk. If a file cannot be read, the `hbase.skip.errors` property defines what happens next: the default value is `false` and causes the entire region recovery to fail. If this property is set to `true`, the file is renamed to the original filename plus `.<currentTimeMillis>`. Either way, you need to carefully check your logfiles to determine why the recovery has had issues and fix the problem to continue.

Durability

You want to be able to rely on the system to save all your data, no matter what new-fangled algorithms are employed behind the scenes. As far as HBase and the log are concerned, you can set the log flush times to be as low as you want, or sync them for every edit—you are still dependent on the underlying filesystem as mentioned earlier; the stream used to store the data is flushed, but is it written to disk yet? We are talking about fsync (*http://en.wikipedia.org/wiki/Sync_(Unix)*) style issues. Now for HBase we are most likely dealing with Hadoop's HDFS as being the filesystem that is persisted to.

At this point, it should be abundantly clear that the log is what keeps data safe. It is being kept open for up to an hour (or more if configured to do so), and as data arrives a new key/value pair is written to the `SequenceFile`. Eventually, the log is rolled and a new one is created.

But that is not how Hadoop was designed to work. Hadoop provides an API tailored to MapReduce that allows you to open a file, write data into it (preferably a lot), and close it right away, leaving an immutable file for everyone else to read many times.

Only after a file is closed is it visible and readable to others. If a process dies while writing the data, the file is considered lost. For HBase to be able to work properly, what is required is a feature that allows you to read the log up to the point where the crashed server has written it. This was added to HDFS in later versions and is referred to as *append*.

HBase currently detects whether the underlying Hadoop library has support for `syncFs()` or `hflush()`. If a `sync()` is triggered on the log writer, it calls either method internally—or none if HBase runs in a nondurable setup. The `sync()` is using the pipe-lined write process described in "LogSyncer Class" on page 337 to guarantee the durability of the edits in the logfile. In case of a server crash, the system can safely read the abandoned logfile up to the last edits.

In summary, without Hadoop 0.21.0 and later, or a specially prepared 0.20.x with append support backported to it, you can very well face data loss. See "Hadoop" on page 46 for more information.

Read Path

HBase uses multiple store files per column family, which contain the actual cells, or `KeyValue` instances. These files are created over time as modifications aggregated in the memstores are eventually flushed as store files to disk. The background process of compactions keeps the number of files under control by rewriting smaller files into larger ones. Major compactions eventually compact the entire set of files into a single one, after which the flushes start adding smaller files again.

Since all store files are immutable, there is no way to delete a particular value out of them, nor does it make sense to keep rewriting large store files to remove the deleted cells one by one. Instead, a *tombstone marker* is written, which masks out the "deleted" information—which can be a single cell, a range of cells, or entire rows.

Consider you are writing a column in a given row today. You keep adding data in other rows over a few more days, then you write a different column in the given row. The question is, given that the original column value has been persisted as a KeyValue on disk for quite some time, while the newly written column for the same row is still in the memstore, or has been flushed to disk, where does the logical row reside?

In other words, when you are using the shell to perform a *get* command on that row, how does the system know what to return? As a client, you want to see both columns being returned—as if they were stored in a single entity. But in reality, the data lives as separate KeyValue instances, spread across any number of store files.

If you are deleting the initial column value, and you perform the *get* again, you expect the value to be gone, when in fact it still exists somewhere, but the tombstone marker is indicating that you have deleted it. But that marker is most likely stored far away from the value it "buries." A more formal explanation of the architecture behind this approach is provided in "Seek Versus Transfer" on page 315.

HBase solves the problem by using a QueryMatcher in combination with a ColumnTracker, which comes in a few variations: one for explicit matching, for when you specify a list of columns to retrieve, and another that includes all columns. Both allow you to set the maximum number of versions to match. They keep track of what needs to be included in the final result.

Why Gets Are Scans

In previous versions of HBase, the Get method was implemented as a separate code path. This was changed in recent versions and completely replaced internally by the same code that the Scan API uses.

You may wonder why that was done since a straight Get should be faster than a Scan. A separate code path could take care of some sort of special knowledge to quickly access the data the user is asking for.

That is where the architecture of HBase comes into play. There are no index files that allow such direct access of a particular row or column. The smallest unit is a block in an HFile, and to find the requested data the RegionServer code and its underlying Store instances must load a block that could potentially have that data stored and scan through it. And that is exactly what a Scan does anyway.

In other words, a Get is nothing but a scan of a single row. It is as though you have created a Scan, and set the start row to what you are looking for and the end row to start row + 1.

Before all the store files are read to find a matching entry, a quick exclusion check is conducted, which uses the timestamps and optional Bloom filter to skip files that definitely have no KeyValue belonging to the row in question. The remaining store files, including the memstore, are then scanned to find a matching key.

The scan is implemented by the RegionScanner class, which retrieves a StoreScanner for every Store instance—each representing a column family. If the read operation excludes certain column families, their stores are omitted as well.

The StoreScanner class combines the store files and memstore that the Store instance contains. It is also where the exclusion happens, based on the Bloom filter, or the timestamp. If you are asking for versions that are not more than 30 minutes old, for example, you can skip all storage files that are older than one hour: they will not contain anything of interest. See "Key Design" on page 357 for details on the exclusion, and how to make use of it.

The StoreScanner class also has the QueryMatcher (here the ScanQueryMatcher class), which will keep track of which KeyValues to include in the final result.

The RegionScanner internally is using a KeyValueHeap class to arrange all store scanners ordered by timestamps. The StoreScanner is using the same to order the stores the same way. This guarantees that you are reading KeyValues in their correct order (e.g., descending by timestamp).

When the store scanners are opened, they will position themselves at the requested row key, or—in the case of a get() call—on the next nonmatching row key. The scanner is now ready to read data. Figure 8-10 shows an example of what this looks like.

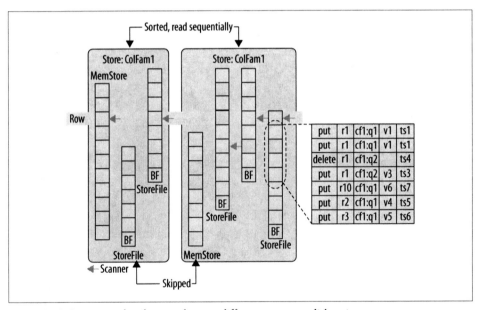

Figure 8-10. Rows stored and scanned across different stores, on disk or in memory

For a get() call, all the server has to do is to call next() on the RegionScanner. The call internally reads everything that should be part of the result. This includes all of the versions requested. Consider a column that has three versions, and you are requesting to retrieve all of them. The three KeyValue instances could be spread across any store, on disk or in memory. The next() call keeps reading from all store files until either the next row is reached, or enough versions have been found.

At the same time, it keeps track of delete markers too. As it scans through the Key Values of the current row, it will come across these delete markers and note that anything with a timestamp that is less than or equal to the marker is considered erased.

Figure 8-10 also shows the *logical* row as a list of KeyValues, some in the same store file, some on other files, spanning multiple column families. A store file and a memstore were skipped because of the timestamp and Bloom filter exclusion process. The delete marker in the last store file is masking out entries, but they are still all part of the same row. The scanners—depicted as an arrow next to the stores—are either on the first matching entry in the file, or on the one that would follow the requested key, in case the store has no direct match.

Only scanners that are on the proper row are considered during the call to next(). The internal loop would read the KeyValues from the first and last stores one after the other, in time-descending order, until they also exceed the requested row key.

For scan operations, this is repeated by calling next() on the ResultScanner until either the stop row has been found, the end of the table has been reached, or enough rows have been read for the current batch (as set via scanner caching).

The final result is a list of KeyValue instances that matched the given get or scan operation. The list is sent back to the client, which can then use the API methods to access the contained columns.

Region Lookups

For the clients to be able to find the region server hosting a specific row key range, HBase provides two special catalog tables, called -ROOT- and .META..[*]

The -ROOT- table is used to refer to all regions in the .META. table. The design considers only one root region, that is, the root region is never split to guarantee a three-level, B+ tree-like lookup scheme: the first level is a node stored in ZooKeeper that contains the location of the root table's region—in other words, the name of the region server hosting that specific region. The second level is the lookup of a matching meta region from the -ROOT- table, and the third is the retrieval of the user table region from the .META. table.

---

[*] Subsequently, they are referred to interchangeably as *root table* and *meta table*, respectively, since, for example, "-ROOT-" is how the table is actually named in HBase and calling it a root table is stating its purpose.

The row keys in the catalog tables are the region names, which are a concatenation of the region's table name, its start row, and an ID (usually the current time in milliseconds). As of HBase 0.90.0 these keys may have another hashed value attached to them. This is currently only used for user tables. See "Region-level files" on page 324 for an example.

 Avoiding any concerns about the three-level location scheme, the Bigtable paper states that with average limits on the .META. region size at 128 MB it can address 2^{34} regions, or 2^{61} bytes in 128 MB regions. Since the size of the regions can be increased without any impact on the location scheme, this is a conservative number and can be increased as needed.

Although clients cache region locations, there is an initial need to figure out where to send requests when looking for a specific row key—or when the cache is stale and a region has since been split, merged, or moved. The client library uses a recursive discovery process moving up in the hierarchy to find the current information. It asks the corresponding region server hosting the matching .META. region for the given row key and retrieves the address. If that information is invalid, it backs out, asking the root table where the .META. region is. Eventually, if all else fails, it has to do a read of the ZooKeeper node to find the root table region.

In a worst-case scenario, it would need six network round-trips to discover the user region, since stale entries in the cache are only discovered when the lookup fails, because it is assumed that assignments, especially of meta regions, do not change too often. When the cache is empty, the client needs three network round-trips to update its cache. One way to mitigate future round-trips is to prefetch location information in a single request, thus updating the client cache ahead of time. Refer to "Miscellaneous Features" on page 133 for details on how to influence this using the client-side API.

Figure 8-11 shows the mapping of user table regions, through meta, and finally to the root table information. Once the user table region is known, it can be accessed directly without any further lookups. The lookups are numbered and assume an empty cache. However, if the cache were filled with only stale details, the client would fail on all three lookups, requiring a refresh of all three and resulting in the aforementioned six network round-trips.

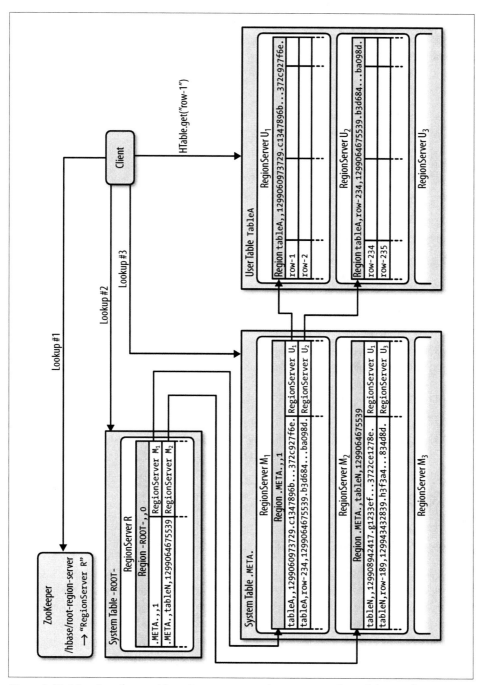

Figure 8-11. Mapping of user table regions, starting with an empty cache and then performing three lookups

The Region Life Cycle

The state of a region is tracked by the master, using the `AssignmentManager` class. It follows the region from its *offline* state, all the way through its life cycle. Table 8-1 lists the possible states of a region.

Table 8-1. Possible states of a region

State	Description
Offline	The region is offline.
Pending Open	A request to open the region was sent to the server.
Opening	The server has started opening the region.
Open	The region is open and fully operational.
Pending Close	A request to close the region has been sent to the server.
Closing	The server is in the process of closing the region.
Closed	The region is closed.
Splitting	The server started splitting the region.
Split	The region has been split by the server.

The transitions between states are commonly initiated by the master, but may also be initiated by the region server hosting the region. For example, the master assigns a region to a server, which is then opened by the assignee. On the other hand, the region server starts the split process, which in itself triggers multiple region close and open events.

Because of the distributed nature of these events, the servers are using ZooKeeper to track specific states in a dedicated znode.

ZooKeeper

Since version 0.20.x, HBase has been using ZooKeeper as its distributed coordination service. This includes tracking of region servers, where the root region is hosted, and more. Version 0.90.x introduced a new master implementation which has an even tighter integration with ZooKeeper. It enables HBase to remove critical heartbeat messages that needed to be sent between the master and the region servers. These are now moved into ZooKeeper, which informs either party of changes whenever they occur, as opposed to the fixed intervals that were used before.

HBase creates a list of znodes under its root node. The default is /hbase and is configured with the `zookeeper.znode.parent` property. Here is the list of the contained znodes and their purposes:

The examples use the ZooKeeper command-line interface (CLI) to issue the commands. You can start it with:

```
$ $ZK_HOME/bin/zkCli.sh -server <quorum-server>
```

The output of each command was shortened by the ZooKeeper internal details.

/hbase/hbaseid

Contains the cluster ID, as stored in the *hbase.id* file on HDFS. For example:

```
[zk: localhost(CONNECTED) 1] get /hbase/hbaseid
e627e130-0ae2-448d-8bb5-117a8af06e97
```

/hbase/master

Holds the server name (see "Cluster Status Information" on page 233 for details). For example:

```
[zk: localhost(CONNECTED) 2] get /hbase/master
foo.internal,60000,1309859972983
```

/hbase/replication

Contains replication details. See "Internals" on page 353 for details.

/hbase/root-region-server

Contains the server name of the region server hosting the -ROOT- regions. This is used during the region lookup (see "Region Lookups" on page 345). For instance:

```
[zk: localhost(CONNECTED) 3] get /hbase/root-region-server
rs1.internal,60000,1309859972983
```

/hbase/rs

Acts as the root node for all region servers to list themselves when they start. It is used to track server failures. Each znode inside is ephemeral and its name is the server name of the region server. For example:

```
[zk: localhost(CONNECTED) 4] ls /hbase/rs
[rs1.internal,60000,1309859972983,rs2.internal,60000,1309859345233]
```

/hbase/shutdown

Is used to track the cluster state. It contains the time when the cluster was started, and is empty when it was shut down. For example:

```
[zk: localhost(CONNECTED) 5] get /hbase/shutdown
Tue Jul 05 11:59:33 CEST 2011
```

/hbase/splitlog

The parent znode for all log-splitting-related coordination (see "Log splitting" on page 339 for details). For example:

```
[zk: localhost(CONNECTED) 6] ls /hbase/splitlog
[hdfs%3A%2F%2Flocalhost%2Fhbase%2F.logs%2Ffoo.internal%2C60020%2C \
1309850971208%2Ffoo.internal%252C60020%252C1309850971208.1309851636647,
hdfs%3A%2F%2Flocalhost%2Fhbase%2F.logs%2Ffoo.internal%2C60020%2C \
```

```
1309850971208%2Ffoo.internal%252C60020%252C1309850971208.1309851641956,
...
hdfs%3A%2F%2Flocalhost%2Fhbase%2F.logs%2Ffoo.internal%2C60020%2C \
1309850971208%2Ffoo.internal%252C60020%252C1309850971208.1309851784396]

[zk: localhost(CONNECTED) 7] get /hbase/splitlog/ \
\hdfs%3A%2F%2Flocalhost%2Fhbase%2F.logs%2Fmemcache1.internal%2C \
60020%2C1309850971208%2Fmemcache1.internal%252C60020%252C1309850971208. \
1309851784396
unassigned foo.internal,60000,1309851879862

[zk: localhost(CONNECTED) 8] get /hbase/splitlog/ \
\hdfs%3A%2F%2Flocalhost%2Fhbase%2F.logs%2Fmemcache1.internal%2C \
60020%2C1309850971208%2Fmemcache1.internal%252C60020%252C1309850971208. \
1309851784396
owned foo.internal,60000,1309851879862

[zk: localhost(CONNECTED) 9] ls /hbase/splitlog
[RESCAN0000293834, hdfs%3A%2F%2Flocalhost%2Fhbase%2F.logs%2Fmemcache1. \
internal%2C60020%2C1309850971208%2Fmemcache1.internal%252C \
60020%252C1309850971208.1309851681118, RESCAN0000293827, RESCAN0000293828, \
RESCAN0000293829, RESCAN0000293838, RESCAN0000293837]
```

These examples list various things: you can see how a log to be split was first
unassigned, and then owned by a region server. The RESCAN nodes are signifying
that the workers, that is, the region server, is supposed to check for more work, in
case a split has failed on another machine.

/hbase/table

The znode to which a disabled table is added as its parent. The name of the table
is the newly created znode, and its content is the word DISABLED. For example:

```
[zk: localhost(CONNECTED) 10] ls /hbase/table
[testtable]
[zk: localhost(CONNECTED) 11] get /hbase/table/testtable
DISABLED
```

/hbase/unassigned

Is used by the AssignmentManager to track region states across the entire cluster. It
contains znodes for those regions that are not open, but are in a transitional state.
The name of the znode is the hash of the region. For example:

```
[zk: localhost(CONNECTED) 11] ls /hbase/unassigned
[8438203023b8cbba347eb6fc118312a7]
```

Replication

HBase replication is a way to copy data between HBase deployments. It can serve as a disaster recovery solution and can contribute to provide higher availability at the HBase layer. It can also serve a more practical purpose; for example, as a way to easily copy edits from a web-facing cluster to a MapReduce cluster that will process old and new data and ship back the results automatically.

The basic architecture pattern used for HBase replication is "(HBase cluster) master-push"; this pattern makes it much easier to keep track of what is currently being replicated since each region server has its own write-ahead log (WAL or HLog), just like other well-known solutions, such as MySQL master/slave replication, where there is only one binary log to keep track of. One master cluster can replicate to any number of slave clusters, and each region server will participate to replicate its own stream of edits.

The replication is done asynchronously, meaning that the clusters can be geographically distant, the links between them can be offline for some time, and rows inserted on the master cluster will not be available at the same time on the slave clusters (eventual consistency).

Figure 8-12 shows an overview of how replication works.

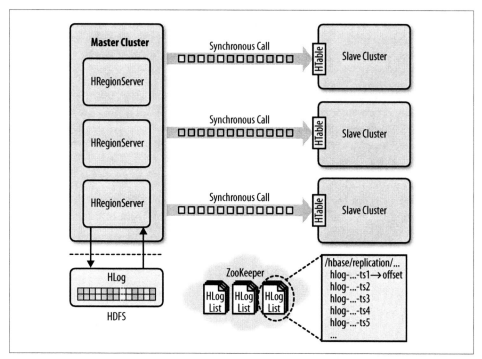

Figure 8-12. Overview of the replication architecture

The replication format used in this design is conceptually the same as MySQL's statement-based replication.[†] Instead of SQL statements, whole WALEdits (consisting of multiple cell inserts coming from the clients' Put and Delete) are replicated in order to maintain atomicity.

The HLogs from each region server are the basis of HBase replication, and must be kept in HDFS as long as they are needed to replicate data to any slave cluster. Each region server reads from the oldest log it needs to replicate and keeps the current position inside ZooKeeper to simplify failure recovery. That position can be different for every slave cluster, as can the queue of HLogs to process.

The clusters participating in replication can be of asymmetric sizes and the master cluster will do its *best effort* to balance the stream of replication on the slave clusters by relying on randomization.

Life of a Log Edit

The following sections describe the life of a single edit going from a client that communicates with a master cluster all the way to a single slave cluster.

Normal processing

The client uses an HBase API that sends a Put, Delete, or Increment to a region server. The key/values are transformed into a WALEdit by the region server and the WALEdit is inspected by the replication code that, for each family that is scoped for replication, adds the scope to the edit. The edit is appended to the current WAL and is then applied to its MemStore.

In a separate thread, the edit is read from the log (as part of a batch) and only the KeyValues that are replicable are kept (i.e., they are part of a family that is scoped as GLOBAL in the family's schema and are noncatalog so it is not .META. or -ROOT-). When the buffer is filled, or the reader hits the end of the file, the buffer is sent to a random region server on the slave cluster.

Synchronously, the region server that receives the edits reads them sequentially and separates each of them into buffers, one per table. Once all edits are read, each buffer is flushed using the normal HBase client (HTables managed by an HTablePool). This is done in order to leverage parallel insertion (MultiPut).

Back in the master cluster's region server, the offset for the current WAL that is being replicated is registered in ZooKeeper.

---

† See the online manual (*http://dev.mysql.com/doc/refman/5.1/en/replication-formats.html*) for details.

Non-Responding slave clusters

The edit is inserted in the same way. In a separate thread, the region server reads, filters, and buffers the log edits the same way as is done during normal processing. The slave region server that is contacted does not answer to the RPC, so the master region server will sleep and retry up to a configured number of times. If the slave region server still is not available, the master cluster region server will select a new subset of the region server to replicate to and will try to send the buffer of edits again.

In the meantime, the WALs will be rolled and stored in a queue in ZooKeeper. Logs that are archived by their region server (archiving is basically moving a log from the region server's logs directory to a central logs archive directory) will update their paths in the in-memory queue of the replicating thread.

When the slave cluster is finally available, the buffer will be applied the same way as during normal processing. The master cluster region server will then replicate the backlog of logs.

Internals

This section describes in depth how each of the replication's internal features operates.

Choosing region servers to replicate to

When a master cluster region server initiates a replication source to a slave cluster, it first connects to the slave's ZooKeeper ensemble using the provided cluster key (that key is composed of the value of hbase.zookeeper.quorum, zookeeper.znode.parent, and hbase.zookeeper.property.clientPort). It then scans the */hbase/rs* directory to discover all the available sinks (region servers that are accepting incoming streams of edits to replicate) and will randomly choose a subset of them using a configured ratio (which has a default value of 10%). For example, if a slave cluster has 150 machines, 15 will be chosen as potential recipients for edits that this master cluster region server will be sending. Since this is done by all master cluster region servers, the probability that all slave region servers are used is very high, and this method works for clusters of any size. For example, a master cluster of 10 machines replicating to a slave cluster of five machines with a ratio of 10% means that the master cluster region servers will choose one machine each at random; thus the chance of overlapping and full usage of the slave cluster is higher.

Keeping track of logs

Every master cluster region server has its own znode in the replication znodes hierarchy. The parent znode contains one znode per peer cluster (if there are five slave clusters, five znodes are created), and each of these contains a queue of HLogs to process. Each of these queues will track the HLogs created by that region server, but they can differ in size. For example, if one slave cluster becomes unavailable for some time, the HLogs should not be deleted, and thus they need to stay in the queue (while the others are processed). See "Region server failover" on page 355 for an example.

When a source is instantiated, it contains the current HLog that the region server is writing to. During log rolling, the new file is added to the queue of each slave cluster's znode just before it is made available. This ensures that all the sources are aware that a new log exists before HLog is able to append edits into it, but this operation is now more expensive. The queue items are discarded when the replication thread cannot read more entries from a file (because it reached the end of the last block) and that there are other files in the queue. This means that if a source is up-to-date and replicates from the log that the region server writes to, reading up to the "end" of the current file will not delete the item in the queue.

When a log is archived (because it is not used anymore or because there are too many of them per hbase.regionserver.maxlogs, typically because the insertion rate is faster than the region flushing rate), it will notify the source threads that the path for that log changed. If a particular source was already done with it, it will just ignore the message. If it is in the queue, the path will be updated in memory. If the log is currently being replicated, the change will be done atomically so that the reader does not try to open the file when it is already moved. Also, moving a file is a NameNode operation; so, if the reader is currently reading the log, it will not generate any exceptions.

Reading, filtering, and sending edits

By default, a source will try to read from a logfile and ship log entries as quickly as possible to a sink. This is first limited by the filtering of log entries; only KeyValues that are scoped GLOBAL and that do not belong to catalog tables will be retained. A second limit is imposed on the total size of the list of edits to replicate per slave, which by default is 64 MB. This means that a master cluster region server with three slaves will use, at most, 192 MB to store data to replicate. This does not take into account the data that was filtered but was not garbage-collected.

Once the maximum number of edits has been buffered or the reader has hit the end of the logfile, the source thread will stop reading and will randomly choose a sink to replicate to (from the list that was generated by keeping only a subset of slave region servers). It will directly issue an RPC to the chosen machine and will wait for the method to return. If it is successful, the source will determine if the current file is emptied or if it should continue to read from it. If the former, it will delete the znode in the queue. If the latter, it will register the new offset in the log's znode. If the RPC threw an exception, the source will retry 10 times until trying to find a different sink.

Cleaning logs

If replication is not enabled, the master's log cleaning thread will delete old logs using a configured TTL. This does not work well with replication since archived logs that are past their TTL may still be in a queue. Thus, the default behavior is augmented so that if a log is past its TTL, the cleaning thread will look up every queue until it finds the log (while caching the ones it finds). If it is not found, the log will be deleted. The next time it has to look for a log, it will first use its cache.

Region server failover

As long as region servers do not fail, keeping track of the logs in ZooKeeper does not add any value. Unfortunately, they do fail, so since ZooKeeper is highly available, we can count on it and its semantics to help us manage the transfer of the queues.

All the master cluster region servers keep a watcher on one another to be notified when one dies (just like the master does). When this happens, they all race to create a znode called `lock` inside the dead region server's znode that contains its queues. The one that creates it successfully will proceed by transferring all the queues to its own znode (one by one, since ZooKeeper does not support the rename operation) and will delete all the old ones when it is done. The recovered queues' znodes will be named with the ID of the slave cluster appended with the name of the dead server.

Once that is done, the master cluster region server will create one new source thread per copied queue, and each of them will follow the read/filter/ship pattern. The main difference is that those queues will never have new data since they do not belong to their new region server, which means that when the reader hits the end of the last log, the queue's znode will be deleted and the master cluster region server will close that replication source.

For example, consider a master cluster with three region servers that is replicating to a single slave with an ID of 2. The following hierarchy represents what the znodes' layout could be at some point in time. We can see that the region servers' znodes all contain a *peers* znode that contains a single queue. The znode names in the queues represent the actual filenames on HDFS in the form `address,port.timestamp`.

```
/hbase/replication/rs/
                    1.1.1.1,60020,123456780/
                      peers/
                           2/
                              1.1.1.1,60020.1234   (Contains a position)
                              1.1.1.1,60020.1265
                    1.1.1.2,60020,123456790/
                      peers/
                           2/
                              1.1.1.2,60020.1214   (Contains a position)
                              1.1.1.2,60020.1248
                              1.1.1.2,60020.1312
                    1.1.1.3,60020,    123456630/
                      peers/
                           2/
                              1.1.1.3,60020.1280   (Contains a position)
```

Now let's say that `1.1.1.2` loses its ZooKeeper session. The survivors will race to create a lock, and for some reason `1.1.1.3` wins. It will then start transferring all the queues to its local peers znode by appending the name of the dead server. Right before 1.1.1.3 is able to clean up the old znodes, the layout will look like the following:

```
/hbase/replication/rs/
                  1.1.1.1,60020,123456780/
                    peers/
                        2/
                            1.1.1.1,60020.1234   (Contains a position)
                            1.1.1.1,60020.1265
                  1.1.1.2,60020,123456790/
                    lock
                    peers/
                        2/
                            1.1.1.2,60020.1214   (Contains a position)
                            1.1.1.2,60020.1248
                            1.1.1.2,60020.1312
                  1.1.1.3,60020,123456630/
                    peers/
                        2/
                            1.1.1.3,60020.1280   (Contains a position)

                        2-1.1.1.2,60020,123456790/
                            1.1.1.2,60020.1214   (Contains a position)
                            1.1.1.2,60020.1248
                            1.1.1.2,60020.1312
```

Sometime later, but before 1.1.1.3 is able to finish replicating the last HLog from 1.1.1.2, let's say that it dies too (also, some new logs were created in the normal queues). The last region server will then try to lock 1.1.1.3's znode and will begin transferring all the queues. The new layout will be:

```
/hbase/replication/rs/
                  1.1.1.1,60020,123456780/
                    peers/
                        2/
                            1.1.1.1,60020.1378   (Contains a position)

                        2-1.1.1.3,60020,123456630/
                            1.1.1.3,60020.1325   (Contains a position)
                            1.1.1.3,60020.1401

                        2-1.1.1.2,60020,123456790-1.1.1.3,60020,123456630/
                            1.1.1.2,60020.1312   (Contains a position)
                  1.1.1.3,60020,123456630/
                    lock
                    peers/
                        2/
                            1.1.1.3,60020.1325   (Contains a position)
                            1.1.1.3,60020.1401

                        2-1.1.1.2,60020,123456790/
                            1.1.1.2,60020.1312   (Contains a position)
```

Replication is still considered to be an experimental feature. Carefully evaluate whether it works for your use case before you consider using it.

Advanced Usage

This chapter goes deeper into the various design implications imposed by HBase's storage architecture. It is important to have a good understanding of how to design tables, row keys, column names, and so on, to take full advantage of the architecture.

Key Design

HBase has two fundamental *key* structures: the *row key* and the *column key*. Both can be used to convey meaning, by either the data they store, or by exploiting their sorting order. In the following sections, we will use these keys to solve commonly found problems when designing storage solutions.

Concepts

The first concept to explain in more detail is the logical layout of a table, compared to on-disk storage. HBase's main unit of separation within a table is the *column family*—not the actual columns as expected from a column-oriented database in their traditional sense. Figure 9-1 shows the fact that, although you store cells in a table format logically, in reality these rows are stored as linear sets of the actual cells, which in turn contain all the vital information inside them.

The top-left part of the figure shows the logical layout of your data—you have rows and columns. The columns are the typical HBase combination of a column family name and a column qualifier, forming the *column key*. The rows also have a *row key* so that you can address all columns in one logical row.

The top-right hand side shows how the logical layout is *folded* into the actual physical storage layout. The cells of each row are stored one after the other, in a separate storage file per column family. In other words, on disk you will have all cells of one family in a *StoreFile*, and all cells of another in a different file.

Since HBase is *not* storing any unset cells (also referred to as NULL values by RDBMSes) from the table, the on-disk file only contains the data that has been explicitly set. It

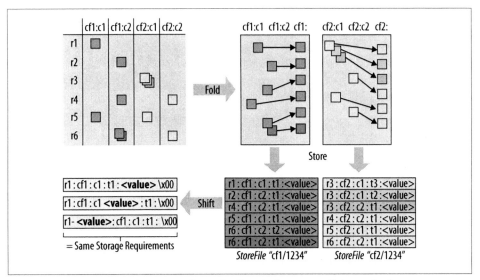

Figure 9-1. Rows stored as linear sets of actual cells, which contain all the vital information

therefore has to also store the row key *and* column key with every cell so that it can retain this vital piece of information.

In addition, multiple versions of the same cell are stored as separate, consecutive cells, adding the required *timestamp* of when the cell was stored. The cells are sorted in descending order by that timestamp so that a reader of the data will see the newest value first—which is the canonical access pattern for the data.

The entire cell, with the added structural information, is called `KeyValue` in HBase terms. It has not just the column and actual value, but also the row key and timestamp, stored for every cell for which you have set a value. The `KeyValues` are sorted by row key first, and then by column key in case you have more than one cell per row in one column family.

The lower-right part of the figure shows the resultant layout of the logical table inside the physical storage files. The HBase API has various means of querying the stored data, with decreasing granularity from left to right: you can select rows by row keys and effectively reduce the amount of data that needs to be scanned when looking for a specific row, or a range of rows. Specifying the column family as part of the query can eliminate the need to search the separate storage files. If you only need the data of one family, it is highly recommended that you specify the family for your read operation.

Although the *timestamp*—or *version*—of a cell is farther to the right, it is another important selection criterion. The store files retain the timestamp range for all stored cells, so if you are asking for a cell that was changed in the past two hours, but a particular store file only has data that is four or more hours old it can be skipped completely. See also "Read Path" on page 342 for details.

The next level of query granularity is the *column qualifier*. You can employ exact column lookups when reading data, or define filters that can include or exclude the columns you need to access. But as you will have to look at each `KeyValue` to check if it should be included, there is only a minor performance gain.

The *value* remains the last, and broadest, selection criterion, equaling the column qualifier's effectiveness: you need to look at each cell to determine if it matches the read parameters. You can only use a filter to specify a matching rule, making it the least efficient query option. Figure 9-2 summarizes the effects of using the `KeyValue` fields.

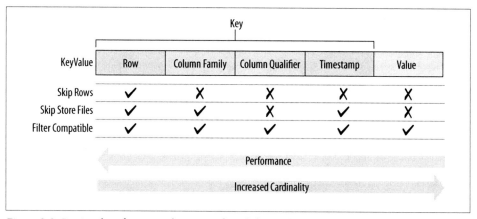

Figure 9-2. Retrieval performance decreasing from left to right

The crucial part of Figure 9-1 shows is the *shift* in the lower-lefthand side. Since the effectiveness of selection criteria greatly diminishes from left to right for a `KeyValue`, you can move all, or partial, details of the value into a more significant place—without changing how much data is stored.

Tall-Narrow Versus Flat-Wide Tables

At this time, you may be asking yourself where and how you should store your data. The two choices are *tall-narrow* and *flat-wide*. The former is a table with few columns but many rows, while the latter has fewer rows but many columns. Given the explained query granularity of the `KeyValue` information, it seems to be advisable to store parts of the cell's data—especially the parts needed to query it—in the row key, as it has the highest cardinality.

In addition, HBase can only split at row boundaries, which also enforces the recommendation to go with tall-narrow tables. Imagine you have all emails of a user in a single row. This will work for the majority of users, but there will be outliers that will have magnitudes of emails more in their inbox—so many, in fact, that a single row could outgrow the maximum file/region size and work against the region split facility.

The better approach would be to store each email of a user in a separate row, where the row key is a combination of the user ID and the message ID. Looking at Figure 9-1 you can see that, on disk, this makes no difference: if the message ID is in the column qualifier, or in the row key, each cell still contains a single email message. Here is the flat-wide layout on disk, including some examples:

```
<userId> : <colfam> : <messageId> : <timestamp> : <email-message>

12345 : data : 5fc38314-e290-ae5da5fc375d : 1307097848 : "Hi Lars, ..."
12345 : data : 725aae5f-d72e-f90f3f070419 : 1307099848 : "Welcome, and ..."
12345 : data : cc6775b3-f249-c6dd2b1a7467 : 1307101848 : "To Whom It ..."
12345 : data : dcbee495-6d5e-6ed48124632c : 1307103848 : "Hi, how are ..."
```

The same information stored as a tall-narrow table has virtually the same footprint when stored on disk:

```
<userId>-<messageId> : <colfam> : <qualifier> : <timestamp> : <email-message>

12345-5fc38314-e290-ae5da5fc375d : data : : 1307097848 : "Hi Lars, ..."
12345-725aae5f-d72e-f90f3f070419 : data : : 1307099848 : "Welcome, and ..."
12345-cc6775b3-f249-c6dd2b1a7467 : data : : 1307101848 : "To Whom It ..."
12345-dcbee495-6d5e-6ed48124632c : data : : 1307103848 : "Hi, how are ..."
```

This layout makes use of the *empty qualifier* (see "Column Families" on page 212). The message ID is simply moved to the left, making it more significant when querying the data, but also transforming each email into a separate logical row. This results in a table that is easily splittable, with the additional benefit of having a more fine-grained query granularity.

Partial Key Scans

The scan functionality of HBase, and the HTable-based client API, offers the second crucial part for transforming a table into a tall-narrow one, without losing query granularity: *partial key scans*.

In the preceding example, you have a separate row for each message, across all users. Before you had one row per user, so a particular inbox was a single row and could be accessed as a whole. Each column was an email message of the users' inbox. The exact row key would be used to match the user ID when loading the data.

With the tall-narrow layout an arbitrary message ID is now postfixed to the user ID in each row key. If you do not have an exact combination of these two IDs you cannot retrieve a particular message. The way to get around this complication is to use partial key scans: you can specify a *start* and *end* key that is set to the exact user ID only, with the stop key set to userId + 1.

The start key of a scan is inclusive, while the stop key is exclusive. Setting the start key to the user ID triggers the internal lexicographic comparison mechanism of the scan to find the exact row key, *or* the one sorting just after it. Since the table does not have an exact match for the user ID, it positions the scan at the next row, which is:

```
<userId>-<lowest-messageId>
```

In other words, it is the row key with the lowest (in terms of sorting) user ID and message ID combination. The scan will then iterate over all the messages of a user and you can parse the row key to extract the message ID.

The partial key scan mechanism is quite powerful, as you can use it as a lefthand index, with each added field adding to its cardinality. Consider the following row key structure:

```
<userId>-<date>-<messageId>-<attachmentId>
```

 Make sure that you pad the value of each field in the composite row key so that the lexicographical (binary, and ascending) sorting works as expected. You will need a fixed-length field structure to guarantee that the rows are sorted by each field, going from left to right.*

You can, with increasing precision, construct a start and stop key for the scan that selects the required rows. Usually you only create the start key and set the stop key to the same value as the start key, while increasing the least significant byte of its first field by one. For the preceding inbox example, the start key could be 12345, and the stop key 123456.

Table 9-1 shows the possible start keys and what they translate into.

Table 9-1. Possible start keys and their meaning

Command	Description
`<userId>`	Scan over all messages for a given user ID.
`<userId>-<date>`	Scan over all messages on a given date for the given user ID.
`<userId>-<date>-<messageId>`	Scan over all parts of a message for a given user ID and date.
`<userId>-<date>-<messageId>-<attachmentId>`	Scan over all attachments of a message for a given user ID and date.

---

* You could, for example, use Orderly (*http://github.com/mwdalton/orderly*) to generate the composite row keys.

These composite row keys are similar to what RDBMSes offer, yet you can control the sort order for each field separately. For example, you could do a bitwise inversion of the date expressed as a long value (the Linux epoch). This would then sort the rows in descending order by date. Another approach is to compute the following:

```
Long.MAX_VALUE - <date-as-long>
```

This will reverse the dates and guarantee that the sorting order of the date field is descending.

In the preceding example, you have the date as the second field in the composite index for the row key. This is only one way to express such a combination. If you were to never query by date, you would want to drop the date from the key—and/or possibly use another, more suitable, dimension instead.

> While it seems like a good idea to always implement a composite row key as discussed in the preceding text, there is one major drawback to doing so: *atomicity*. Since the data is now spanning many rows for a single inbox, it is not possible to modify it in one operation. If you are not concerned with updating the entire inbox with all the user messages in an atomic fashion, the aforementioned design is appropriate. But if you need to have such guarantees, you may have to go back to flat-wide table design.

Pagination

Using the partial key scan approach, it is possible to iterate over subsets of rows. The principle is the same: you have to specify an appropriate start and stop key to limit the overall number of rows scanned. Then you take an *offset* and *limit* parameter, applying them to the rows on the client side.

> You can also use the "PageFilter" on page 149, or "ColumnPagination-Filter" on page 154 to achieve pagination. The approach shown here is mainly to explain the concept of what a dedicated row key design can achieve.
>
> For pure pagination, the `ColumnPaginationFilter` is also the recommended approach, as it avoids sending unnecessary data over the network to the client.

The steps are the following:

1. Open a scanner at the start row.
2. Skip `offset` rows.
3. Read the next `limit` rows and return to the caller.
4. Close the scanner.

Applying this to the inbox example, it is possible to paginate through all of the emails of a user. Assuming an average user has a few hundred emails in his inbox, it is quite common for a web-based email client to show only the first, for example, 50 emails. The remainder of the emails are then accessed by clicking the Next button to load the next page.

The client would set the start row to the user ID, and the stop row to the user ID + 1. The remainder of the process would follow the approach we just discussed, so for the first page, where the offset is zero, you can read the next 50 emails. When the user clicks the Next button, you would set the offset to 50, therefore skipping those first 50 rows, returning row 51 to 100, and so on.

This approach works well for a low number of pages. If you were to page through thousands of pages, a different approach would be required. You could add a sequential ID into the row key to directly position the start key at the right offset. Or you could use the date field of the key—if you are using one—to remember the date of the last displayed item and add the date to the start key, but probably dropping the hour part of it. If you were using epochs, you could compute the value for midnight of the last seen date. That way you can rescan that entire day and make a more knowledgeable decision regarding what to return.

There are many ways to design the row key to allow for efficient selection of subranges and enable pagination through records, such as the emails in the user inbox example. Using the composite row key with the user ID and date gives you a natural order, displaying the newest messages first, sorting them in descending order by date. But what if you also want to offer sorting by different fields so that the user can switch at will? One way to do this is discussed in "Secondary Indexes" on page 370.

Time Series Data

When dealing with stream processing of events, the most common use case is *time series* data. Such data could be coming from a sensor in a power grid, a stock exchange, or a monitoring system for computer systems. Its salient feature is that its row key represents the event time. This imposes a problem with the way HBase is arranging its rows: they are all stored sorted in a distinct range, namely regions with specific start and stop keys.

The sequential, monotonously increasing nature of time series data causes all incoming data to be written to the same region. And since this region is hosted by a single server, all the updates will only tax this one machine. This can cause regions to really run hot with the number of accesses, and in the process slow down the perceived overall performance of the cluster, because inserting data is now bound to the performance of a single machine.

It is easy to overcome this problem by ensuring that data is spread over all region servers instead. This can be done, for example, by prefixing the row key with a nonsequential prefix. Common choices include:

Salting

You can use a *salting* prefix to the key that guarantees a spread of all rows across all region servers. For example:

```
byte prefix = (byte) (Long.hashCode(timestamp) % <number of region
servers>);
byte[] rowkey = Bytes.add(Bytes.toBytes(prefix), Bytes.toBytes(timestamp));
```

This formula will generate enough *prefix* numbers to ensure that rows are sent to all region servers. Of course, the formula assumes a specific number of servers, and if you are planning to grow your cluster you should set this number to a multiple instead. The generated row keys might look like this:

```
0myrowkey-1, 1myrowkey-2, 2myrowkey-3, 0myrowkey-4, 1myrowkey-5, \
2myrowkey-6, ...
```

When these keys are sorted and sent to the various regions the order would be:

```
0myrowkey-1
0myrowkey-4
1myrowkey-2
1myrowkey-5
...
```

In other words, the updates for row keys 0myrowkey-1 and 0myrowkey-4 would be sent to one region (assuming they do not overlap two regions, in which case there would be an even broader spread), and 1myrowkey-2 and 1myrowkey-5 are sent to another.

The drawback of this approach is that access to a range of rows must be *fanned out* in your own code and read with <number of region servers> get or scan calls. On the upside, you could use multiple threads to read this data from distinct servers, therefore parallelizing read access. This is akin to a small *map-only* MapReduce job, and should result in increased I/O performance.

Use Case: Mozilla Socorro

The Mozilla organization has built a crash reporter—named *Socorro*[†]—for Firefox and Thunderbird, which stores all the pertinent details pertaining to when a client asks its user to report a program anomaly. These reports are subsequently read and analyzed by the Mozilla development team to make their software more reliable on the vast number of machines and configurations on which it is used.

The code is open source, available online (*http://code.google.com/p/socorro/*), and contains the Python-based client code that communicates with the HBase cluster

---

† See the Mozilla wiki (*https://wiki.mozilla.org/Socorro*) page on Socorro for details.

using Thrift. Here is an example (as of the time of this writing) of how the client is merging the previously salted, sequential keys when doing a scan operation:

```
def merge_scan_with_prefix(self,table,prefix,columns):
    """
    A generator based iterator that yields totally ordered rows starting with a
    given prefix. The implementation opens up 16 scanners (one for each leading
    hex character of the salt) simultaneously and then yields the next row in
    order from the pool on each iteration.
    """

    iterators = []
    next_items_queue = []
    for salt in '0123456789abcdef':
      salted_prefix = "%s%s" % (salt,prefix)
      scanner = self.client.scannerOpenWithPrefix(table, salted_prefix, columns)
      iterators.append(salted_scanner_iterable(self.logger,self.client,
                  self._make_row_nice,salted_prefix,scanner))
    # The i below is so we can advance whichever scanner delivers us the polled
    # item.
    for i,it in enumerate(iterators):
      try:
        next = it.next
        next_items_queue.append([next(),i,next])
      except StopIteration:
        pass
    heapq.heapify(next_items_queue)

    while 1:
      try:
        while 1:
          row_tuple,iter_index,next = s = next_items_queue[0]
          #tuple[1] is the actual nice row.
          yield row_tuple[1]
          s[0] = next()
          heapq.heapreplace(next_items_queue, s)
      except StopIteration:
        heapq.heappop(next_items_queue)
      except IndexError:
        return
```

The Python code opens the required number of scanners, adding the salt prefix, which here is composed of a fixed set of single-letter prefixes—16 different ones all together. Note that an additional **heapq** object is used that manages the actual merging of the scanner results against the global sorting order.

Field swap/promotion

Using the same approach as described in "Partial Key Scans" on page 360, you can move the timestamp field of the row key or prefix it with another field. This approach uses the composite row key concept to move the sequential, monotonously increasing timestamp to a secondary position in the row key.

If you already have a row key with more than one field, you can *swap* them. If you have only the timestamp as the current row key, you need to *promote* another field from the column keys, or even the value, into the row key.

There is also a drawback to moving the time to the righthand side in the composite key: you can only access data, especially time ranges, for a given swapped or promoted field.

Use Case: OpenTSDB

The *OpenTSDB*[‡] project provides a *time series database* used to store metrics about servers and services, gathered by external collection agents. All of the data is stored in HBase, and using the supplied user interface (UI) enables users to query various metrics, combining and/or downsampling them—all in real time.

The schema promotes the *metric ID* into the row key, forming the following structure:

```
<metric-id><base-timestamp>...
```

Since a production system will have a considerable number of metrics, but their IDs will be spread across a range and all updates occurring across them, you end up with an access pattern akin to the *salted prefix*: the reads and writes are spread across the metric IDs.

This approach is ideal for a system that queries primarily by the leading field of the composite key. In the case of OpenTSDB this makes sense, since the UI asks the users to select from one or more metrics, and then displays the data points of those metrics ordered by time.

Randomization

A totally different approach is to randomize the row key using, for example:

```
byte[] rowkey = MD5(timestamp)
```

Using a hash function like MD5 will give you a random distribution of the key across all available region servers. For time series data, this approach is obviously less than ideal, since there is no way to scan entire ranges of consecutive timestamps.

On the other hand, since you can re-create the row key by hashing the timestamp requested, it still is very suitable for random lookups of single rows. When your data is not scanned in ranges but accessed randomly, you can use this strategy.

Summarizing the various approaches, you can see that it is not trivial to find the right balance between optimizing for read and write performance. It depends on your access pattern, which ultimately drives the decision on how to structure your row keys. Figure 9-3 shows the various solutions and how they affect sequential read and write performance.

---

‡ See the OpenTSDB project (*http://opentsdb.net*) website for details. In particular, the page that discusses the project's schema (*http://opentsdb.net/schema.html*) is a recommended read, as it adds advanced key design concepts for an efficient storage format that also allows for high-performance querying of the stored data.

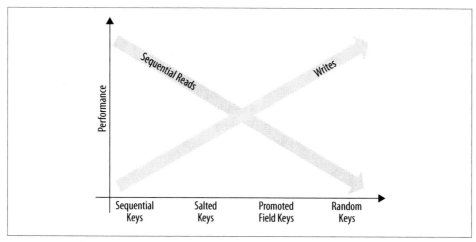

Figure 9-3. Finding the right balance between sequential read and write performance

Using the salted or promoted field keys can strike a good balance of distribution for write performance, and sequential subsets of keys for read performance. If you are only doing random reads, it makes most sense to use random keys: this will avoid creating region hot-spots.

Time-Ordered Relations

In our preceding discussion, the time series data dealt with inserting new events as separate rows. However, you can also store related, time-ordered data: using the columns of a table. Since all of the columns are sorted per column family, you can treat this sorting as a replacement for a secondary index, as available in RDBMSes. Multiple secondary indexes can be emulated by using multiple column families—although that is not the recommended way of designing a schema. But for a small number of indexes, this might be what you need.

Consider the earlier example of the user inbox, which stores all of the emails of a user in a single row. Since you want to display the emails in the order they were received, but, for example, also sorted by subject, you can make use of column-based sorting to achieve the different views of the user inbox.

 Given the advice to keep the number of column families in a table low—especially when mixing large families with small ones (in terms of stored data)—you could store the inbox inside one table, and the secondary indexes in another table. The drawback is that you cannot make use of the provided per-table row-level atomicity. Also see "Secondary Indexes" on page 370 for strategies to overcome this limitation.

The first decision to make concerns what the primary sorting order is, in other words, how the majority of users have set the view of their inbox. Assuming they have set the view in descending order by date, you can use the same approach mentioned earlier, which reverses the timestamp of the email, effectively sorting all of them in descending order by time:

```
Long.MAX_VALUE - <date-as-long>
```

The email itself is stored in the main column family, while the sort indexes are in separate column families. You can extract the subject from the email address and add it to the column key to build the secondary sorting order. If you need descending sorting as well, you would need another family.

To circumvent the proliferation of column families, you can alternatively store all secondary indexes in a single column family that is separate from the main column family. Once again, you would make use of implicit sorting by prefixing the values with an *index ID*—for example, `idx-subject-desc`, `idx-to-asc`, and so on. Next, you would have to attach the actual sort value. The actual value of the cell is the key of the main index, which also stores the message. This also implies that you need to either load the message details from the main table, display only the information stored in the secondary index, or store the display details redundantly in the index, avoiding the random lookup on the main information source. Recall that *denormalization* is quite common in HBase to reduce the required read operations in favor of vastly improved user-facing responsiveness.

Putting the aforementioned schema into action might result in something like this:

```
12345 : data : 5fc38314-e290-ae5da5fc375d : 1307097848 : "Hi Lars, ..."
12345 : data : 725aae5f-d72e-f90f3f070419 : 1307099848 : "Welcome, and ..."
12345 : data : cc6775b3-f249-c6dd2b1a7467 : 1307101848 : "To Whom It ..."
12345 : data : dcbee495-6d5e-6ed48124632c : 1307103848 : "Hi, how are ..."
...
12345 : index : idx-from-asc-mary@foobar.com : 1307099848 : 725aae5f-d72e...
12345 : index : idx-from-asc-paul@foobar.com : 1307103848 : dcbee495-6d5e...
12345 : index : idx-from-asc-pete@foobar.com : 1307097848 : 5fc38314-e290...
12345 : index : idx-from-asc-sales@ignore.me : 1307101848 : cc6775b3-f249...
...
12345 : index : idx-subject-desc-\xa8\x90\x8d\x93\x9b\xde : \
  1307103848 : dcbee495-6d5e-6ed48124632c
12345 : index : idx-subject-desc-\xb7\x9a\x93\x93\x90\xd3 : \
  1307099848 : 725aae5f-d72e-f90f3f070419
...
```

In the preceding code, one index (`idx-from-asc`) is sorting the emails in ascending order by *from address*, and another (`idx-subject-desc`) in descending order by *subject*. The subject itself is not readable anymore as it was bit-inversed to achieve the descending sorting order. For example:

```
% String s = "Hello,";
% for (int i = 0; i < s.length(); i++) {
  print(Integer.toString(s.charAt(i) ^ 0xFF, 16));
}
b7 9a 93 93 90 d3
```

All of the index values are stored in the column family index, using the prefixes mentioned earlier. A client application can read the entire column family and cache the content to let the user quickly switch the sorting order. Or, if the number of values is large, the client can read the first 10 columns starting with idx-subject-desc to show the first 10 email messages sorted in ascending order by the email subject lines. Using a scan with intra-row batching (see "Caching Versus Batching" on page 127) enables you to efficiently paginate through the subindexes. Another option is the ColumnPaginationFilter, combined with the ColumnPrefixFilter to iterate over an index page by page.

Advanced Schemas

So far we have discussed how to use the provided table schemas to map data into the column-oriented layout HBase supports. You will have to decide how to structure your row and column keys to access data in a way that is optimized for your application.

Each column value is then an actual data point, stored as an arbitrary array of bytes. While this type of schema, combined with the ability to create columns with arbitrary keys when needed, enables you to evolve with new client application releases, there are use cases that require more formal support of a more feature-rich, evolveable serialization API, where each value is a compact representation of a more complex, nestable record structure.

Possible solutions include the already discussed serialization packages—see "Introduction to REST, Thrift, and Avro" on page 241 for details—listed here as examples:

Avro
　　An exemplary project using Avro to store complex records in each column is *HAvroBase*.§ This project facilitates Avro's *interface definition language* (IDL) to define the actual schema, which is then used to store records in their serialized form within arbitrary table columns.

Protocol Buffers
　　Similar to Avro, you can use the Protocol Buffer's IDL to define an external schema, which is then used to serialize complex data structures into HBase columns.

The idea behind this approach is that you get a definition language that allows you to define an initial schema, which you can then update by adding or removing fields. The serialization API takes care of reading older schemas with newer ones. Missing fields are ignored or filled in with defaults.

---

§ See the HAvroBase GitHub (*https://github.com/spullara/havrobase*) project page.

Secondary Indexes

Although HBase has no native support for secondary indexes, there are use cases that need them. The requirements are usually that you can look up a cell with not just the primary coordinates—the row key, column family name, and qualifier—but also an alternative coordinate. In addition, you can scan a range of rows from the main table, but ordered by the secondary index.

Similar to an index in RDBMSes, secondary indexes store a mapping between the new coordinates and the existing ones. Here is a list of possible solutions:

Client-managed

Moving the responsibility completely into the application layer, this approach typically combines a data table and one (or more) lookup/mapping tables. Whenever the code writes into the data table it also updates the lookup tables. Reading data requires either a direct lookup in the main table, or, if the key is from a secondary index, a lookup of the main row key, and then retrieval of the data in a second operation.

There are advantages and disadvantages to this approach. First, since the entire logic is handled in the client code, you have all the freedom to map the keys exactly the way they are needed. The list of shortcomings is longer, though: since you have no cross-row atomicity, for example, in the form of transactions, you cannot guarantee consistency of the main and dependent tables. This can be partially overcome using regular pruning jobs, for instance, using MapReduce to scan the tables and remove obsolete—or add missing—entries.

The missing transactional support could result in data being stored in the data table, but with no mapping in the secondary index tables, because the operation failed *after* the main table was updated, but *before* the index tables were written. This can be alleviated by writing to the secondary index tables first, and to the data table at the end of the operation. Should anything fail in the process, you are left with orphaned mappings, but those are subsequently removed by the asynchronous, regular pruning jobs.

Having all the freedom to design the mapping between the primary and secondary indexes comes with the drawback of having to implement all the necessary wiring to store and look up the data. External keys need to be identified to access the correct table, for example:

```
myrowkey-1
@myrowkey-2
```

The first key denotes a direct data table lookup, while the second, using the prefix, is a mapping that has to be performed through a secondary index table. The name of the table could be also encoded as a number and added to the prefix. The flip side is this is hardcoded in your application and needs to evolve with overall schema changes, and new requirements.

Indexed-Transactional HBase

A different solution is offered by the open source *Indexed-Transactional HBase* (ITHBase) project.|| This solution extends HBase by adding special implementations of the client and server-side classes.

The core extension is the addition of *transactions*, which are used to guarantee that all secondary index updates are consistent. On top of this it adds index support, by providing a client-side `IndexedTableDescriptor`, defining how a data table is backed by a secondary index table.

Most client and server classes are replaced by ones that handle indexing support. For example, `HTable` is replaced with `IndexedTable` on the client side. It has a new method called `getIndexedScanner()`, which enables the iteration over rows in the data table using the ordering of a secondary index.

Just as with the *client-managed* index described earlier, this index stores the mappings between the primary and secondary keys in separate tables. In contrast, though, these are automatically created, and maintained, based on the descriptor. Combined with the transactional updates of these indexes, this solution provides a complete implementation of secondary indexes for HBase.

The drawback is that it may not support the latest version of HBase available, as it is not tied to its release cycle. It also adds a considerable amount of synchronization overhead that results in decreased performance, so you need to benchmark carefully.

Indexed HBase

Another solution that allows you to add secondary indexes to HBase is *Indexed HBase* (IHBase).# This solution forfeits the use of separate tables for each index but maintains them purely in memory. The indexes are generated when a region is opened for the first time, or when a memstore is flushed to disk—involving an entire region's scan to build the index. Depending on your configured region size, this can take a considerable amount of time and I/O resources.

Only the on-disk information is indexed; the in-memory data is searched as-is: it uses the memstore data directly to search for index-related details. The advantage of this solution is that the index is never out of sync, and *no* explicit transactional control is necessary.

In comparison to table-based indexing, using this approach is very fast, as it has all the required details in memory and can perform a fast binary search to find

---

|| The *ITHBase* project started as a *contrib* module for HBase. It was subsequently moved to an external repository allowing it to address different versions of HBase, and to develop at its own pace. See the GitHub project (*https://github.com/hbase-trx/hbase-transactional-tableindexed*) page for details.

#Similar to ITHBase, IHBase started as a contrib project within HBase. It was moved to an external repository for the same reasons. See the GitHub project (*http://github.com/ykulbak/ihbase*) page for details. The original documentation of the JIRA issue is online at HBASE-2037 (*https://issues.apache.org/jira/browse/HBASE -2037*).

matching rows. However, it requires a lot of extra heap to maintain the index. Depending on your requirements and the amount of data you want to index, you might run into a situation where IHBase cannot keep all the indexes you need.

The in-memory indexes are typed and allow for more fine-grained sorting, as well as more memory-efficient storage. There is support for BYTE, CHAR, SHORT, INT, LONG, FLOAT, DOUBLE, BIG_DECIMAL, BYTE_ARRAY, and CHAR_ARRAY. There is no explicit control over the sorting order; thus data is always stored in ascending order. You will need to do the bitwise inversion of the value described earlier to sort in descending order.

The definition of an index revolves around the IdxIndexDescriptor class that defines the specific column of the data table that holds the index, and the type of the values it contains, taken from the list in the preceding paragraph.

Accessing an index is handled by the client-side IdxScan class, which extends the normal Scan class by adding support to define Expressions. A scan without an explicit expression defaults to normal scan behavior. Expressions provide basic *boolean* logic with an And and Or construct. For example:

```
Expression expression = Expression
  .or(
    Expression.comparison(columnFamily1, qualifer1, operator1, value1)
  )
  .or(
    Expression.and()
      .and(Expression.comparison(columnFamily2, qualifer2, operator2, value2))
      .and(Expression.comparison(columnFamily3, qualifer3, operator3, value3))
  );
```

The preceding example uses *builder*-style helper methods to generate a complex expression that combines three separate indexes. The lowest level of an expression is the Comparison, which allows you to specify the actual index, and a filter-like syntax to select values that match a comparison value and operator. Table 9-2 list the possible operator choices.

Table 9-2. Possible values for the Comparison.Operator enumeration

Operator	Description
EQ	The *equals* operator
GT	The *greater than* operator
GTE	The *greater than or equals* operator
LT	The *less than* operator
LTE	The *less than or equals* operator
NEQ	The *not equals* operator

You have to specify a columnFamily, and a qualifier of an existing index, or else an IllegalStateException will be thrown.

The `Comparison` class has an optional `includeMissing` parameter, which works similarly to `filterIfMissing`, described in "SingleColumnValueFilter" on page 147. You can use it to fine-tune what is included in the scan depending on how the expression is evaluated.

The sorting order is defined by the first evaluated index in the expression, while the other indexes are used to *intersect* (for the *and*) or *unite* (for the *or*) the possible keys with the first index. In other words, using complex expressions is predictable only when using the same index, but with various comparisons.

The benefit of IHBase over ITHBase, for example, is that it achieves the same guarantees—namely maintaining a consistent index based on an existing column in a data table—but without the need to employ extra tables. It shares the same drawbacks, for the following reasons:

- It is quite intrusive, as its installation requires additional JAR files plus a configuration that replaces vital client- and server-side classes.

- It needs extra resources, although it trades memory for extra I/O requirements.

- It does random lookups on the data table, based on the sorting order defined by the secondary index.

- It may not be available for the latest version of HBase.*

Coprocessor

There is work being done to implement an indexing solution based on coprocessors.† Using the server-side hooks provided by the coprocessor framework, it is possible to implement indexing similar to ITHBase, as well as IHBase while not having to replace any client- and server-side classes. The coprocessor would load the indexing layer for every region, which would subsequently handle the maintenance of the indexes.

The code can make use of the scanner hooks to transparently iterate over a normal data table, or an index-backed view on the same. The definition of the index would need to go into an external schema that is read by the coprocessor-based classes, or it could make use of the generic attributes a column family can store.

Since this is in its early stages, there is not much that can be documented at this time. Watch the online issue tracking system for updates on the work if you are interested.

---

* As of this writing, IHBase only supports HBase version 0.20.5.

† See HBASE-2038 (*https://issues.apache.org/jira/browse/HBASE-2038*) in the JIRA issue tracking system for details.

Search Integration

Using indexes gives you the ability to iterate over a data table in more than the implicit row key order. You are still confined to the available keys and need to use either filters or straight iterations to find the values you are looking for. A very common use case is to combine the arbitrary nature of keys with a search-based lookup, often backed by full search engine integration.

Common choices are the *Apache Lucene*-based solutions, such as Lucene itself, or *Solr*, a high-performance enterprise search server.[‡] Similar to the indexing solutions, there are a few possible approaches:

Client-managed

These range from implementations using HBase as the data store, and using Map-Reduce jobs to build the search index, to those that use HBase as the backing store for Lucene. Another approach is to route every update of the data table to the adjacent search index. Implementing support for search indexes in combination with HBase is primarily driven by how the data is accessed, and if HBase is used as the data store, or as the index store.

A prominent implementation of a client-managed solution is the *Facebook inbox search*. The schema is built roughly like this:

- Every row is a single inbox, that is, every user has a single row in the search table.
- The columns are the terms indexed from the messages.
- The versions are the message IDs.
- The values contain additional information, such as the position of the term in the document.

With this schema it is easy to search a user's inbox for messages containing specific words. Boolean operators, such as and or or, can be implemented in the client code, merging the lists of documents found. You can also efficiently implement *type-ahead queries*: the user can start typing a word and the search finds all messages that contain words that match the user's input as a prefix.

Lucene

Using Lucene—or a derived solution—separately from HBase involves building the index using a MapReduce job. An externally hosted project[§] provides the `BuildTableIndex` class, which was formerly part of the *contrib* modules shipping with HBase. This class scans an entire table and builds the Lucene indexes, which ultimately end up as directories on HDFS—their count depends on the number of

---

‡ Solr is based on Lucene, but extends it to provide a fully featured search server. See the project's website (*http://lucene.apache.org/*) for details on either project.

§ See the GitHub project (*https://github.com/akkumar/hbasene/tree/master/src/main/java/org/hbasene/index/create/mapred*) page for details and to access the code.

---

reducers used. These indexes can be downloaded to a Lucene-based server, and accessed locally using, for example, a `MultiSearcher` class, provided by Lucene.

Another approach is to merge the index parts by either running the MapReduce job with a single reducer, or using the index merge tool that comes with Lucene. A merged index usually provides better performance, but the time required to build, merge, and eventually serve the index is longer.

In general, this approach uses HBase only to store the data. If a search is performed through Lucene, usually only the matching row keys are returned. A random lookup into the data table is required to display the document. Depending on the number of lookups, this can take a considerable amount of time. A better solution would be something that combines the search directly with the stored data, thus avoiding the additional random lookup.

HBasene

The approach chosen by *HBasene*[ll] is to build an entire search index directly inside HBase, while supporting the well-established Lucene API. The schema used stores each document field, or term, in a separate row, with the documents containing the term stored as columns inside that row.

The schema also reuses the same table to store various other details required to implement full Lucene support. It implements an `IndexWriter` that stores the documents directly into the HBase table, as they are inserted using the normal Lucene API. Searching is then done using the Lucene search API. Here is an example taken from the test class that comes with HBasene:

```
private static final String[] AIRPORTS = { "NYC", "JFK", "EWR", "SEA",
  "SFO", "OAK", "SJC" };

private final Map<String, List<Integer>> airportMap =
  new TreeMap<String, List<Integer>>();

protected HTablePool tablePool;

protected void doInitDocs() throws CorruptIndexException, IOException {
  Configuration conf = HBaseConfiguration.create();
  HBaseIndexStore.createLuceneIndexTable("idxtbl", conf, true);
  tablePool = new HTablePool(conf, 10);
  HBaseIndexStore hbaseIndex = new HBaseIndexStore(tablePool, conf,
    "idxtbl");
  HBaseIndexWriter indexWriter = new HBaseIndexWriter(hbaseIndex, "id")
  for (int i = 100; i >= 0; --i) {
    Document doc = getDocument(i);
    indexWriter.addDocument(doc, new StandardAnalyzer(Version.LUCENE_30));
  }
}

private Document getDocument(int i) {
  Document doc = new Document();
```

---

ll The GitHub page (*https://github.com/akkumar/hbasene*) has the details, and source code.

```
    doc.add(new Field("id", "doc" + i, Field.Store.YES, Field.Index.NO));
    int randomIndex = (int) (Math.random() * 7.0f);
    doc.add(new Field("airport", AIRPORTS[randomIndex], Field.Store.NO,
      Field.Index.ANALYZED_NO_NORMS));
    doc.add(new Field("searchterm", Math.random() > 0.5f ?
      "always" : "never",
      Field.Store.NO, Field.Index.ANALYZED_NO_NORMS));
    return doc;
}

public TopDocs search() throws IOException {
    HBaseIndexReader indexReader = new HBaseIndexReader(tablePool, "idxtbl",
      "id");
    HBaseIndexSearcher indexSearcher = new HBaseIndexSearcher(indexReader);
    TermQuery termQuery = new TermQuery(new Term("searchterm", "always"));
    Sort sort = new Sort(new SortField("airport", SortField.STRING));
    TopDocs docs = this.indexSearcher.search(termQuery
      .createWeight(indexSearcher), null, 25, sort, false);
    return docs;
}

public static void main(String[] args) throws IOException {
    doInitDocs();
    TopDocs docs = search();
    // use the returned documents...
}
```

The example creates a small test index and subsequently searches it. You may note that there is a lot of Lucene API usage, with small amendments to support the HBase-backed index writer.

 The project—as of this writing—is more a *proof of concept* than a production-ready implementation.

Coprocessors

Yet another approach to complement a data table with Lucene-based search functionality, and currently in development,[#] is based on coprocessors. It uses the provided hooks to maintain the index, which is stored directly on HDFS. Every region has its own index and search is distributed across them to gather the full result.

This is only one example of what is possible with coprocessors. Similar to the use of coprocessors to build secondary indexes, you have the choice of where to store the actual index: either in another table, or externally. The framework offers the enabling technology; the implementing code has the choice of how to use it.

[#]HBASE-3529 (*https://issues.apache.org/jira/browse/HBASE-3529*)

Transactions

It seems somewhat counterintuitive to talk about *transactions* in regard to HBase. However, the secondary index example showed that for some use cases it is beneficial to abandon the simplified data model HBase offers, and in fact introduce concepts that are usually seen in traditional database systems.

One of those concepts is transactions, offering ACID compliance across more than one row, and more than one table. This is necessary in lieu of a matching schema pattern in HBase. For example, updating the main data table and the secondary index table requires transactions to be reliably consistent.

Often, transactions are not needed, as normalized data schemas can be folded into a single table and row design that does not need the overhead of distributed transaction support. If you cannot do without this extra control, here are a few possible solutions:

Transactional HBase

> The *Indexed Transactional HBase* project comes with a set of extended classes that replace the default client- and server-side classes, while adding support for transactions across row and table boundaries. The region servers, and more precisely, each region, keeps a list of transactions, which are initiated with a `beginTransaction()` call, and are finalized with the matching `commit()` call. Every read and write operation then takes a transaction ID to guard the call against other transactions.

ZooKeeper

> HBase requires a ZooKeeper ensemble to be present, acting as the *seed*, or *bootstrap* mechanism, for cluster setup. There are templates, or recipes, available that show how ZooKeeper can also be used as a transaction control backend. For example, the Cages (*http://code.google.com/p/cages/*) project offers an abstraction to implement locks across multiple resources, and is scheduled to add a specialized transactions class—using ZooKeeper as the distributed coordination system.

> ZooKeeper also comes with a lock recipe that can be used to implement a *two-phase commit* protocol. It uses a specific znode representing the transaction, and a child znode for every participating client. The clients can use their znodes to flag whether their part of the transaction was successful or failed. The other clients can monitor the peer znodes and take the appropriate action.[*]

Bloom Filters

"Column Families" on page 212 introduced the syntax to declare Bloom filters at the column family level, and discussed specific use cases in which it makes sense to use them.

---

[*] More details can be found on the ZooKeeper project (*http://zookeeper.apache.org/doc/trunk/recipes.html#sc_recipes_twoPhasedCommit*) page.

The reason to use Bloom filters at all is that the default mechanisms to decide if a store file contains a specific row key are limited to the available block index, which is, in turn, fairly coarse-grained: the index stores the start row key of each contained block only. Given the default block size of 64 KB, and a store file of, for example, 1 GB, you end up with 16,384 blocks, and the same amount of indexed row keys.

If we further assume your cell size is an average of 200 bytes, you will have more than 5 million of them stored in that single file. Given a random row key you are looking for, it is very likely that this key will fall in between two block start keys. The only way for HBase to figure out if the key actually exists is by loading the block and scanning it to find the key.

This problem is compounded by the fact that, for a typical application, you will expect a certain update rate, which results in flushing in-memory data to disk, and subsequent compactions aggregating them into larger store files. Since minor compactions only combine the last few store files, and only up to a configured maximum size, you will end up with a number of store files, all acting as possible candidates to have some cells of the requested row key. Consider the example in Figure 9-4.

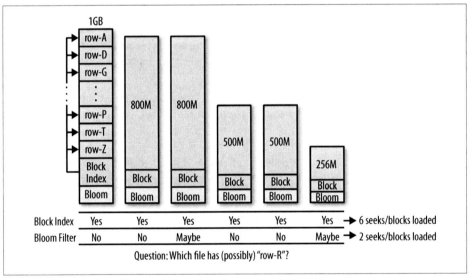

Figure 9-4. Using Bloom filters to help reduce the number of I/O operations

The files are all from one column family and have a similar spread in row keys, although only a few really hold an update to a specific row. The block index has a spread across the entire row key range, and therefore always reports positive to contain a random row. The region server would need to load every block to check if the block actually contains a cell of the row or not.

On the other hand, enabling the Bloom filter does give you the immediate advantage of knowing if a file contains a particular row key or not. The nature of the filter is that it can give you a definitive answer if the file does *not* contain the row—but might report a *false positive*, claiming the file contains the data, where in reality it does not. The number of false positives can be tuned and is usually set to 1%, meaning that in 1% of all reports by the filter that a file contains a requested row, it is wrong—and a block is loaded and checked erroneously.

 This does not translate into an immediate performance gain on individual `get` operations, since HBase does the reads in parallel, and is ultimately bound by disk read latency. Reducing the number of unnecessary block loads improves the overall throughput of the cluster.

You can see from the example, however, that the number of block loads is greatly reduced, which can make a big difference in a heavily loaded system. For this to be efficient, you must also match a specific update pattern: if you modify all of the rows on a regular basis, the majority of the store files will have a piece of the row you are looking for, and therefore would not be a good use case for Bloom filters. But if you update data in batches so that each row is written into only a few store files at a time, the filter is a great feature to reduce the overall number of I/O operations.

Another place where you will find this to be advantageous is in the *block cache*. The hit rate of the cache should improve as loading fewer blocks results in less churn. Since the server is now loading blocks that contain the requested data most of the time, related data has a greater chance to remain in the block cache and subsequent read operations can make use of it.

Besides the update pattern, another driving factor to decide if a Bloom filter makes sense for your use case is the overhead it adds. Every entry in the filter requires about *one byte* of storage. Going back to the earlier example store file that was 1 GB in size, assuming you store only counters (i.e., `long` values encoded as eight bytes), and adding the overhead of the `KeyValue` information—which is its coordinates, or, the row key, column family name, column qualifier, timestamp, and type—then every cell is about 20 bytes (further assuming you use very short keys) in size. Then the Bloom filter would be 1/20th of your file, or about 51 MB.

Now assume your cells are, on average, 1 KB in size; in this case, the filter needs only 1 MB. Taking into account further optimizations, you often end up with a row-level Bloom filter of a few hundred kilobytes for a store file of one or more gigabyte. In that case, it seems that it would always be to enable the filter.

The final question is whether to use a row or a row+column Bloom filter. The answer depends on your usage pattern. If you are doing only row scans, having the more specific row+column filter will not help at all: having a row-level Bloom filter enables you to narrow down the number of files that need to be checked, even when you do row +column read operations, but not the other way around.

The row+column Bloom filter is useful when you cannot batch updates for a specific row, and end up with store files which all contain parts of the row. The more specific row+column filter can then identify which of the files contain the data you are requesting. Obviously, if you always load the entire row, this filter is once again hardly useful, as the region server will need to load the matching block out of each file anyway.

Since the row+column filter will require more storage, you need to do the math to determine whether it is worth the extra resources. It is also interesting to know that there is a maximum number of elements a Bloom filter can hold. If you have too many cells in your store file, you might exceed that number and would need to fall back to the row-level filter.

Figure 9-5 summarizes the selection criteria for the different Bloom filter levels.

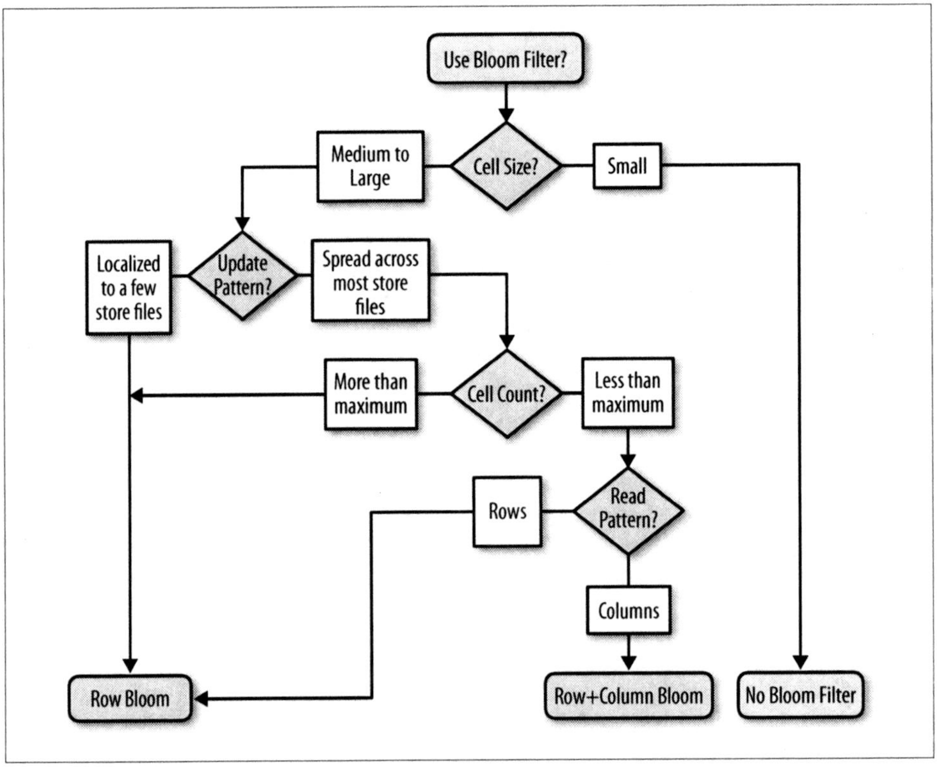

Figure 9-5. Selection criteria for deciding what Bloom filter to use

Depending on your use case, it may be useful to enable Bloom filters, to increase the overall performance of your system. If possible, you should try to use the row-level Bloom filter, as it strikes a good balance between the additional space requirements and the gain in performance coming from its store file selection filtering. Only resort to the more costly row+column Bloom filter when you would otherwise gain no advantage from using the row-level one.

Versioning

Now that we have seen how data is stored and retrieved in HBase, it is time to revisit the subject of versioning. There are a few advanced techniques when using timestamps that—given that you understand their behavior—may be an option for specific use cases. They also expose a few intricacies you should be aware of.

Implicit Versioning

I pointed out before that you should ensure that the clock on your servers is synchronized. Otherwise, when you store data in multiple rows across different servers, using the implicit timestamps, you may end up with completely different time settings.

For example, say you use the HBase URL Shortener and store three new shortened URLs for an existing user. All of the keys are considered fully distributed, so all three of the new rows end up on a different region server. Further, assuming that these servers are all one hour apart, if you were to scan from the client side to get the list of new shortened URLs within the past hour, you would miss a few, as they have been saved with a timestamp that is more than an hour different from what the client considers current.

This can be avoided by setting an agreed, or shared, timestamp when storing these values. The put operation allows you to set a client-side timestamp that is used instead, therefore overriding the server time. Obviously, the better approach is to rely on the servers doing this work for you, but you might be required to use this approach in some circumstances.[†]

Another issue with servers not being aligned by time is exposed by *region splits*. Assume you have saved a value on a server that is one hour *ahead* all other servers in the cluster, using the implicit timestamp of the server. Ten minutes later the region is split and the half with your update is moved to another server. Five minutes later you are inserting a new value for the same column, again using the automatic server time. The new value is now considered *older* than the initial one, because the first version has a timestamp one hour ahead of the current server's time. If you do a standard get call to retrieve the newest version of the value, you will get the one that was stored first.

Once you have all the servers synchronized, there are a few more interesting side effects you should know about. First, it is possible—for a specific time—to make versions of a column reappear. This happens when you store more versions than are configured at the column family level. The default is to keep the last three versions of a cell, or value.

If you insert a new value 10 times into the same column, and request a complete list of all versions retained, using the setMaxVersions() call of the Get class, you will only ever

---

† One example, although very uncommon, is based on virtualized servers. See *http://support.ntp.org/bin/view/ Support/KnownOsIssues#Section_9.2.2*, which lists an issue with NTP, the commonly used *Network Time Protocol*, on virtual machines.

receive up to what is configured in the table schema, that is, the last three versions by default.

But what would happen when you explicitly delete the last two versions? Example 9-1 demonstrates this.

Example 9-1. Application deleting with explicit timestamps

```
for (int count = 1; count <= 6; count++) { ❶
  Put put = new Put(ROW1);
  put.add(COLFAM1, QUAL1, count, Bytes.toBytes("val-" + count)); ❷
  table.put(put);
}

Delete delete = new Delete(ROW1); ❸
delete.deleteColumn(COLFAM1, QUAL1, 5);
delete.deleteColumn(COLFAM1, QUAL1, 6);
table.delete(delete);
```

❶ Store the same column six times.

❷ The version is set to a specific value, using the loop variable.

❸ Delete the newest two versions.

When you run the example, you should see the following output:

```
After put calls...
KV: row1/colfam1:qual1/6/Put/vlen=5, Value: val-6
KV: row1/colfam1:qual1/5/Put/vlen=5, Value: val-5
KV: row1/colfam1:qual1/4/Put/vlen=5, Value: val-4
After delete call...
KV: row1/colfam1:qual1/4/Put/vlen=5, Value: val-4
KV: row1/colfam1:qual1/3/Put/vlen=5, Value: val-3
KV: row1/colfam1:qual1/2/Put/vlen=5, Value: val-2
```

An interesting observation is that you have resurrected versions 2 and 3! This is caused by the fact that the servers delay the housekeeping to occur at well-defined times. The older versions of the column are still kept, so deleting newer versions makes the older versions come back.

This is only possible until a major compaction has been performed, after which the older versions are removed forever, using the predicate delete based on the configured maximum versions to retain.

 The example code has some commented-out code you can enable to enforce a flush and major compaction. If you rerun the example, you will see this result instead:

```
After put calls...
KV: row1/colfam1:qual1/6/Put/vlen=5, Value: val-6
KV: row1/colfam1:qual1/5/Put/vlen=5, Value: val-5
KV: row1/colfam1:qual1/4/Put/vlen=5, Value: val-4
```

```
      After delete call...
      KV: row1/colfam1:qual1/4/Put/vlen=5, Value: val-4
```

Since the older versions have been removed, they do not reappear anymore.

Finally, when dealing with timestamps, there is another issue to watch out for: *delete
markers*. This refers to the fact that, in HBase, a delete is actually adding a tombstone
marker into the store that has a specific timestamp. Based on that, it masks out versions
that are either a direct match, or, in the case of a column delete marker, anything that
is older than the given timestamp. Example 9-2 shows this using the shell.

Example 9-2. Deletes mask puts with explicit timestamps in the past

```
hbase(main):001:0> create 'testtable', 'colfam1'
0 row(s) in 1.1100 seconds

hbase(main):002:0> Time.now.to_i
=> 1308900346

hbase(main):003:0> put 'testtable', 'row1', 'colfam1:qual1', 'val1' ❶
0 row(s) in 0.0290 seconds

hbase(main):004:0> scan 'testtable'
ROW    COLUMN+CELL
 row1 column=colfam1:qual1, timestamp=1308900355026, value=val1
1 row(s) in 0.0360 seconds

hbase(main):005:0> delete 'testtable', 'row1', 'colfam1:qual1' ❷
0 row(s) in 0.0280 seconds

hbase(main):006:0> scan 'testtable'
ROW    COLUMN+CELL
0 row(s) in 0.0260 seconds

hbase(main):007:0> put 'testtable', 'row1', 'colfam1:qual1', 'val1', \
  Time.now.to_i - 50000 ❸
0 row(s) in 0.0260 seconds

hbase(main):008:0> scan 'testtable'
ROW    COLUMN+CELL
0 row(s) in 0.0260 seconds

hbase(main):009:0> flush 'testtable' ❹
0 row(s) in 0.2720 seconds

hbase(main):010:0> major_compact 'testtable'
0 row(s) in 0.0420 seconds

hbase(main):011:0> put 'testtable', 'row1', 'colfam1:qual1', 'val1', \
  Time.now.to_i - 50000 ❺
0 row(s) in 0.0280 seconds

hbase(main):012:0> scan 'testtable'
```

```
ROW    COLUMN+CELL
 row1 column=colfam1:qual1, timestamp=1308900423953, value=val1
1 row(s) in 0.0290 seconds
```

❶ Store a value into the column of the newly created table, and run a scan to verify.

❷ Delete all values from the column. This sets the delete marker with a timestamp of now.

❸ Store the value again into the column, but use a time in the past. The subsequent scan fails to return the masked value.

❹ Flush and conduct a major compaction of the table to remove the delete marker.

❺ Store the value with the time in the past again. The subsequent scan now shows it as expected.

The example shows that there are sometimes situations where you might see something you do not expect to see. But this behavior is explained by the architecture of HBase, and is deterministic.

Custom Versioning

Since you can specify your own timestamp values—and therefore create your own *versioning* scheme—while overriding the server-side timestamp generation based on the synchronized server time, you are free to not use epoch-based versions at all.

For example, you could use the timestamp with a global number generator[‡] that supplies you with ever increasing, sequential numbers starting at 1. Every time you insert a new value you retrieve a new number and use that when calling the put function.

You *must* do this for every put operation, or the server will insert an epoch-based timestamp instead. There is a flag in the table or column descriptors that indicates your use of custom timestamp values; in other words, your own versioning. If you fail to set the value, it is silently replaced with the server timestamp.

When using your own timestamp values, you need to test your solution thoroughly, as this approach has not been used widely in production.

Be aware that negative timestamp values are untested and, while they have been discussed a few times in HBase developer circles, they have never been confirmed to work properly.

Make sure to avoid collisions by using the same value for two separate updates to the same cell. Usually the last saved value is visible afterward.

---

‡ As an example for a number generator based on ZooKeeper, see the *zk_idgen* project (*http://sourceforge.net/projects/zkidgen/*).

With these warnings out of the way, here are a few use cases that show how a custom versioning scheme can be beneficial in the overall concept of table schema design:

Record IDs

A prominent example using this technique was discussed in "Search Integration" on page 374, that is, the *Facebook inbox search*. It uses the timestamp value to hold the message ID. Since these IDs are increasing over time, and the implicit sort order of versions in HBase is descending, you can retrieve, for example, the last 10 versions of a matching search term column to get the latest 10 messages, sorted by time, that contain said term.

Number generator

This follows on with the initially given example, making use of a distributed number generator. It may seem that a number generator would do the same thing as epoch-based timestamps do: sort all values ascending by a monotonously increasing value. The difference is subtler, because the resolution of the Java timer used is down to the millisecond, which means it is quite unlikely to store two values at the exact same time—but that can happen. If you were to require a solution in which you need an absolutely unique versioning scheme, using the number generator can solve this issue.

Using the time component of HBase is an interesting way to exploit this extra dimension offered by the architecture. You have less freedom, as it only accepts long values, as opposed to arbitrary binary keys supported by row and column keys. Nevertheless, it could solve your specific use case.

Cluster Monitoring

Once you have your HBase cluster up and running, it is essential to continuously ensure that it is operating as expected. This chapter explains how to monitor the status of the cluster with a variety of tools.

Introduction

Just as it is vital to monitor production systems, which typically expose a large number of metrics that provide details regarding their current status, it is vital that you monitor HBase.

HBase actually inherits its monitoring APIs from Hadoop. But while Hadoop is a batch-oriented system, and therefore often is not immediately user-facing, HBase is user-facing, as it serves random access requests to, for example, drive a website. The response times of these requests should stay within specific limits to guarantee a positive user experience—also commonly referred to as a service-level agreement (SLA).

With distributed systems the administrator is facing the difficult task of making sense of the overall status of the system, while looking at each server separately. And even with a single server system it is difficult to know what is going on when all you have to go by is a handful of raw logfiles. When disaster strikes it would be good to see where—and when—it all started. But digging through mega-, giga-, or even terabytes of text-based files to find the needle in the haystack, so to speak, is something only a few people have mastered. And even if you have mad log-reading skills, it will take time to draw and test hypotheses to eventually arrive at the cause of the disruption.

This is obviously not something new, and viable solutions have been around for years. These solutions fall into the groups of *graphing* and *monitoring*—with some tools covering only one of these groups, while others cover both. Graphing captures the exposed metrics of a system and displays them in visual charts, typically with a range of time filters—for example, daily, monthly, and yearly time frames. This is good, as it can quickly show you what your system has been doing lately—like they say, a picture speaks a thousand words.

The graphs are good for historical, *quantitative* data, but with a rather large time granularity it is also difficult to see what a system is doing right now. This is where *qualitative* data is needed, which is handled by the monitoring kind of support systems. They keep an ear out on your behalf to verify that each data point, or metric, exposed is within a specified range. Often, the support tools already supply a significant set of *checks*, so you only have to tweak them for your own purposes. Checks that are missing can be added in the form of plug-ins, or simple script-based extensions. You can also fine-tune how often the checks are run, which can range from seconds to days.

Whenever a check indicates a problem, or outright failure, evasive actions could be taken automatically: servers could be decommissioned, restarted, or otherwise repaired. When a problem persists there are rules to escalate the issue to, for example, the administrators to handle it manually. This could be done by sending out emails to various recipients, or SMS messages to telephones.

While there are many possible support systems you can choose from, the Java-based nature of HBase, and its affinity to Hadoop, narrow down your choices to a more limited set of systems, which also have been proven to work reliably in combination. For graphing, the system supported natively by HBase is *Ganglia*. For monitoring, you need a system that can handle the *JMX**-based metrics API as exposed by the HBase processes. A common example in this category is *Nagios*.

 You should set up the complete support system framework that you want to use in production, even when prototyping a solution, or working on a proof-of-concept study based on HBase. That way you have a head start in making sense of the numbers and configuring the system checks accordingly. Using a cluster without monitoring and metrics is the same as driving a car while blindfolded.

It is great to run load tests against your HBase cluster, but you need to correlate the cluster's performance with what the system is doing under the hood. Graphing the performance lets you line up events across machines and subsystems, which is an invaluable when it comes to understanding test results.

The Metrics Framework

Every HBase process, including the master and region servers, exposes a specific set of metrics. These are subsequently made available to the various monitoring APIs and tools, including JMX and Ganglia. For each kind of server there are multiple groups of metrics, usually pertaining to a subsystem within each server. For example, one group of metrics is provided by the Java Virtual Machine (JVM) itself, giving insight into

---

* JMX is an acronym for *Java Management Extensions*, a Java-based technology that helps in building solutions to monitor and manage applications. See the project's website (*http://www.oracle.com/technetwork/java/javase/tech/javamanagement-140525.html*) for more details, and "JMX" on page 408.—

many interesting details of the current process, such as garbage collection statistics and memory usage.

Contexts, Records, and Metrics

HBase employs the Hadoop metrics framework, inheriting all of its classes and features. This framework is based on the `MetricsContext` interface to handle the generation of data points for monitoring and graphing. Here is a list of available implementations:

GangliaContext
> Used to push metrics to Ganglia; see "Ganglia" on page 400 for details.

FileContext
> Writes the metrics to a file on disk.

TimeStampingFileContext
> Also writes the metrics to a file on disk, but adds a timestamp prefix to each metric emitted. This results in a more log-like formatting inside the file.

CompositeContext
> Allows you to emit metrics to more than one context. You can specify, for example, a Ganglia and file context at the same time.

NullContext
> The *Off* switch for the metrics framework. When using this context, nothing is emitted, nor aggregated, at all.

NullContextWithUpdateThread
> Does not emit any metrics, but starts the aggregation thread. This is needed when retrieving the metrics through JMX. See "JMX" on page 408 for details.

Each context has a unique name, specified in the external configuration file (see "HBase-related steps" on page 404), which is also used to define various properties and the actual implementing class of the `MetricsContext` interface.

> Another artifact of HBase inheriting the metrics framework from Ha-doop is that it uses the supplied `ContextFactory`, which loads the various context classes. The configuration filename is hardcoded in this class to *hadoop-metrics.properties*—which is the reason HBase uses the exact same filename as Hadoop, as opposed to the more intuitive *hbase-metrics.properties* you might have expected.

Multiple metrics are grouped into a `MetricsRecord`, which describes, for example, one specific subsystem. HBase uses these groups to keep the statistics for the master, region server, and so on. Each group also has a unique name, which is combined with the context and the actual metric name to form the fully qualified metric:

```
<context-name>.<record-name>.<metric-name>
```

The contexts have a built-in timer that triggers the push of the metrics on regular intervals to whatever the target is—which can be a file, Ganglia, or your own custom solution if you choose to build one. The configuration file enabling the context has a period property per context that is used to specify the interval period in seconds for the context to push its updates. Specific context implementations might have additional properties that control their behavior. Figure 10-1 shows a sequence diagram with all the involved classes.

The metrics are internally tracked by container classes, based on MetricsBase, which have various update and/or increment methods that are called when an event occurs. The framework, in turn, tracks the number of events for every known metric and correlates it to the time elapsed since it was last polled.

The following list summarizes the available metric types in the Hadoop and HBase metrics framework, associating abbreviations with each. These are referenced in the remainder of this chapter.

Integer value (IV)
> Tracks an integer counter. The metric is only updated when the value changes.

Long value (LV)
> Tracks a long counter. The metric is only updated when the value changes.

Rate (R)
> A float value representing a rate, that is, the number of operations/events per second. It provides an *increment* method that is called to track the number of operations. It also has a *last polled* timestamp that is used to track the elapsed time. When the metric is polled, the following happens:
>
> 1. The rate is calculated as *number of operations / elapsed time in seconds*.
> 2. The rate is stored in the *previous value* field.
> 3. The internal counter is reset to zero.
> 4. The *last polled* timestamp is set to the current time.
> 5. The computed rate is returned to the caller.

String (S)
> A metric type for static, text-based information. It is used to report the HBase version number, build date, and so on. It is never reset nor changed—once set, it remains the same while the process is running.

Time varying integer (TVI)
> A metric type in which the context keeps aggregating the value, making it a monotonously increasing counter. The metric has a simple increment method that is used by the framework to count various kinds of events. When the value is polled it returns the accrued integer value, and resets to zero, until it is polled again.

Time varying long (TVL)
> Same as TVI, but operates on a long value for faster incrementing counters, that could otherwise exceed the maximum integer value. Also resets upon its retrieval.

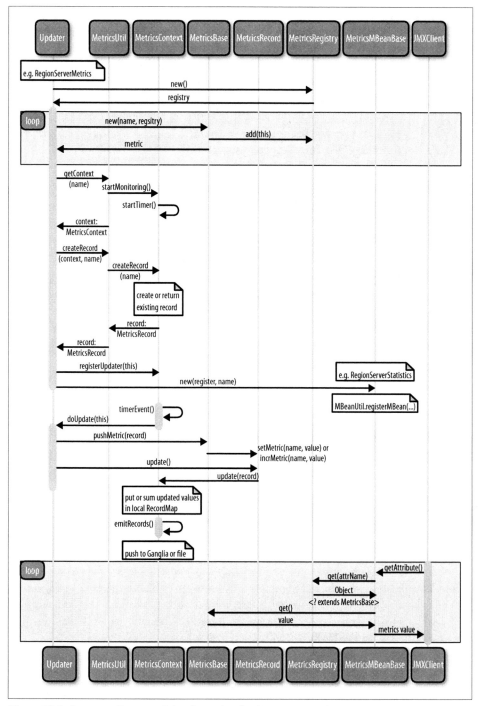

Figure 10-1. Sequence diagram of the classes involved in preparing the metrics

Time varying rate (TVR)

> Tracks the number of operations or events and the time they required to complete. This is used to compute the average time for an operation to finish. The metric also tracks the minimum and maximum *time per operation* observed. Table 10-1 shows how the values are exported under the same name, but with different postfixes.

> The values in the *Short* column are postfixes that are attached to the actual metric name. For instance, when you retrieve the metric for the `increment()` calls, as provided by `HTable`, you will see four values, named `incrementNumOps`, `incrementMinTime`, `incrementMaxTime`, and `incrementAvgTime`.

> This is not evident in all places, though. For example, the context-based metrics *only* expose the `AvgTime` and `NumOps` values, while JMX gives access to all four.

> Note that the values for operation count and time accrued are reset once the metric is polled. The number of operations is aggregated by the polling context, though, making it a monotonously increasing counter. In contrast, the average time is set as an absolute value. It is computed when the metric is retrieved at the end of a polling interval.

> The minimum and maximum observed time per operation is *not* reset and is kept until the `resetMinMax()` call is invoked. This can be done through JMX (see "JMX" on page 408), or it can be triggered for some metrics by the *extended period* property implicitly.

Persistent time varying rate (PTVR)

> An extension to the TVR. This metric adds the necessary support for the extended period metrics: since these long-running metrics are *not* reset for every poll they need to be reported differently.

Table 10-1. Values exposed by metrics based on time varying rate

Value name	Short	Description
Number Operations	NumOps	The actual number of events since the last poll.
Minimun Time	MinTime	The shortest time reported for an event to complete.
Maximum Time	MaxTime	The longest time reported for an event to complete.
Average Time	AvgTime	The average time for completing events; this is computed as the sum of the reported times per event, divided by the number of events.

When we subsequently discuss the different metrics provided by HBase you will find the type abbreviation next to it for reference, in case you are writing your own support tool. Keep in mind that these metrics behave differently when they are retrieved through a metrics context, or via JMX.

Some of the metrics—for example, the *time varying* ones—are reset once they are polled, but the containing context aggregates them as monotonously increasing counters. Accessing the same values through JMX will reveal their reset behavior, since JMX accesses the values directly, not through a metric context.

A prominent example is the NumOps component of a TVR metric. Reading it through a metric context gives you an ever increasing value, while JMX would only give you the absolute number of the last poll period.

Other metrics are only emitting data when the value has changed since the last update. Again, this is evident when using the contexts, but not when using JMX. The latter will simply retrieve the values from the last poll. If you do not set a poll period, the JMX values will never change. More on this in "JMX" on page 408. Figure 10-2 shows how, over each metric period, the different metric types are updated and emitted. JMX always accesses the raw metrics, which results in a different behavior compared to context-based aggregation.

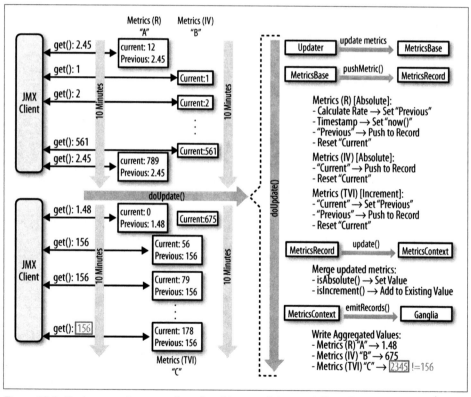

Figure 10-2. Various metric types collected and (optionally) reset differently

HBase also has some exceptional rate metrics that span across specific time frames, overriding the usual update intervals.

 There are a few long-running processes in HBase that require some metrics to be kept until the process has completed. This is controlled by the hbase.extendedperiod property, specified in seconds. The default is no expiration, but the supplied configuration sets it to a moderate 3600 seconds, or one hour.

Currently, this extended period is applied to the time and size rate metrics for compactions, flushes, and splits for the region servers and master, respectively. On the region server it also triggers a reset of all other-rate based metrics, including the read, write, and sync latencies.

Master Metrics

The master process exposes all metrics relating to its role in a cluster. Since the master is relatively lightweight and only involved in a few cluster-wide operations, it does expose only a limited set of information (in comparison to the region server, for example). Table 10-2 lists them.

Table 10-2. Metrics exposed by the master

Metric	Description
Cluster requests (R)	The total number of requests to the cluster, aggregated across all region servers
Split time (PTVR)	The time it took to split the write-ahead log files after a restart
Split size (PTVR)	The total size of the write-ahead log files that were split

Region Server Metrics

The region servers are part of the actual data read and write path, and therefore collect a substantial number of metrics. These include details about different parts of the overall architecture inside the server—for example, the block cache and in-memory store.

Instead of listing all possible metrics, we will discuss them in groups, since it is more important to understand their meaning as opposed to the separate data point. Within each group the meaning is quite obvious and needs only a few more notes, if at all.

Block cache metrics

The block cache holds the loaded storage blocks from the low-level HFiles, read from HDFS. Given that you have allowed for a block to be cached, it is kept in memory until there is no more room, at which point it is evicted.

The *count* (LV) metric reflects the number of blocks currently in the cache, while the *size* (LV) is the occupied Java heap space. The *free* (LV) metric is the remaining heap for the cache, and *evicted* (LV) counts the number of blocks that had to be removed because of heap size constraints.

The block cache keeps track of the cache *hit* (LV) and *miss* (LV) counts, as well as the *hit ratio* (IV), which is the number of cache hits in relation to the total number of requests to the cache.

Finally, the more ominous *hit caching* count is similar to the *hit ratio*, but only takes into account requests and hits of operations that had requested for the block cache to be used (see, e.g., the setCacheBlocks() method in "Single Gets" on page 95).

> All read operations will try to use the cache, regardless of whether retaining the block in the cache has been requested. Use of setCacheBlocks() only influences the retainment policy of the request.

Compaction metrics

When the region server has to perform the asynchronous (or manually invoked) housekeeping task of compacting the storage files, it reports its status in a different metric. The *compaction size* (PTVR) and *compaction time* (PTVR) give details regarding the total size (in bytes) of the storage files that have been compacted, and how long that operation took, respectively. Note that this is reported *after* a completed compaction run, because only then are both values known.

The *compaction queue size* (IV) can be used to check how many files a region server has queued up for compaction currently.

> The compaction queue size is another recommended early indicator of trouble that should be closely monitored. Usually the number is quite low, and varies between zero and somewhere in the low tens. When you have I/O issues, you usually see this number rise sharply. See Figure 10-5 on page 407 for an example.
>
> Keep in mind that *major compactions* will also cause a sharp rise as they queue up all storage files. You need to account for this when looking at the graphs.

Memstore metrics

Mutations are kept in the memstore on the region server, and will subsequently be written to disk via a *flush*. The memstore metrics expose the *memstore size MB* metric (IV), which is the total heap space occupied by all memstores for the server in megabytes. It is the sum of all memstores across all online regions.

The *flush queue size* (IV) is the number of enqueued regions that are being flushed next. The *flush size* (PTVR) and *flush time* (PTVR) give details regarding the total size (in bytes) of the memstore that has been flushed, and the time it took to do so, respectively.

Just as with the compaction metrics, these last two metrics are updated *after* the flush has completed. So the reported values slightly trail the actual value, as it is missing what is currently in progress.

 Similar to the *compaction queue* you will see a sharp rise in count for the flush queue when, for example, your servers are under I/O duress. Monitor the value to find the usual range—which should be a fairly low number as well—and set sensible limits to trigger warnings when it rises above these thresholds.

Store metrics

The *store files* (IV) metric states the total number of storage files, spread across all stores—and therefore regions—managed by the current server. The *stores* (IV) metric gives you the total number of stores for the server, across all regions it currently serves. The *store file index size MB* metric (IV) is the sum of the block index, and optional meta index, for all store files in megabytes.

I/O metrics

The region server keeps track of I/O performance with three latency metrics, all of them keeping their numbers in milliseconds. The *fs read latency* (TVR) reports the filesystem read latency—for example, the time it takes to load a block from the storage files. The *fs write latency* (TVR) is the same for write operations, but combined for all writers, including the storage files *and* write-ahead log.

Finally, the *fs sync latency* (TVR) measures the latency to sync the write-ahead log records to the filesystem. The latency metrics provide information about the low-level I/O performance and should be closely monitored.

Miscellaneous metrics

In addition to the preceding metrics, the region servers also provide global counters, exposed as metrics. The *read request count* (LV) and *write request count* (LV) report the total number of read (such as get()) and write (such as put()) operations, respectively, summed up for all online regions this server hosts.

The *requests* (R) metric is the actual request rate per second encountered since it was last polled. Finally, the *regions* (IV) metric gives the number of regions that are currently online and hosted by this region server.

RPC Metrics

Both the master and region servers also provide metrics from the RPC subsystem. The subsystem automatically tracks every operation possible between the different servers and clients. This includes the master RPCs, as well as those exposed by region servers.

The RPC metrics for the master and region servers are shared—in other words, you will see the same metrics exposed on either server type. The difference is that the servers update the metrics for the operations the process invokes. On the master, for example, you will not see updates to the metrics for `increment()` operations, since those are related to the region server. On the other hand, you do see all the metrics for all of the administrative calls, like `enableTable` or `compactRegion`.

Since the metrics relate directly to the client and administrative APIs, you can infer their meaning from the corresponding API calls. The naming is not completely consistent, though, to remove arbitration. A notable pattern is the addition of the *Region* postfix to the region-related API calls—for example, the `split()` call provided by `HBaseAdmin` maps to the `splitRegion` metric. Only a handful of metrics have no API counterpart, and these are listed in Table 10-3. These are metrics provided by the RPC subsystem itself.

Table 10-3. *Non-API metrics exposed by the RPC subsystem*

Metric	Description
RPC Processing Time	This is the time it took to process the RPCs on the server side. As this spans all possible RPC calls, it averages across them.
RPC Queue Time	Since RPC employs a queuing system that lines up calls to be processed, there might be a delay between the time the call arrived and when it is actually processed, which is the *queue time*.

Monitoring the queue time is a good idea, as it indicates the load on the server. You could use thresholds to trigger warnings if this number goes over a certain limit. These are early indicators of future problems.

The remaining metrics are from the RPC API between the master and the region servers, including `regionServerStartup()` and `regionServerReport`. They are invoked when a region server initially reports for duty at its assigned master node, and for regular status reports, respectively.

JVM Metrics

When it comes to optimizing your HBase setup, tuning the JVM settings requires expert skills. You will learn how to do this in "Garbage Collection Tuning" on page 419. This section discusses what you can retrieve from each server process using the metrics framework. Every HBase process collects and exposes JVM-related details that are helpful to correlate, for example, server performance with underlying JVM internals. This information, in turn, is used when tuning your HBase cluster setup.

The provided metrics can be grouped into related categories:

Memory usage metrics

You can retrieve the *used* memory and the *committed* memory[†] in megabytes for both *heap* and *nonheap* usage. The former is the space that is maintained by the JVM on your behalf and garbage-collected at regular intervals. The latter is memory required for JVM internal purposes.

Garbage collection metrics

The JVM is maintaining the heap on your behalf by running *garbage collections*. The *gc count* metric is the number of garbage collections, and the *gc time millis* is the accumulated time spent in garbage collection since the last poll.

> Certain steps in the garbage collection process cause so-called *stop-the-world* pauses, which are inherently difficult to handle when a system is bound by tight SLAs.
>
> Usually these pauses are only a few milliseconds in length, but sometimes they can increase to multiple seconds. Problems arise when these pauses approach the multiminute range, because this can cause a region server to miss its ZooKeeper lease renewal—forcing the master to take evasive actions.[‡]
>
> Use the garbage collection metric to track what the server is currently doing and how long the collections take. As soon as you see a sharp increase, be prepared to investigate. Any pause that is greater than the `zookeeper.session.timeout` configuration value should be considered a fault.

Thread metrics

This group of metrics reports a variety of numbers related to Java threads. You can see the count for each possible thread state, including *new*, *runnable*, *blocked*, and so on.

System event metrics

Finally, the events group contains metrics that are collected from the logging subsystem, but are subsumed under the JVM metrics category (for lack of a better place). System event metrics provide counts for various log-level events. For example, the *log error* metric provides the number of log events that occured on the

---

† See the official documentation on MemoryUsage (*http://download.oracle.com/javase/6/docs/api/java/lang/ management/MemoryUsage.html*) for details on what *used* versus *committed* memory means.

‡ "The HBase development team has affectionately dubbed this scenario a Juliet Pause—the master (Romeo) presumes the region server (Juliet) is dead when it's really just sleeping, and thus takes some drastic action (recovery). When the server wakes up, it sees that a great mistake has been made and takes its own life. Makes for a good play, but a pretty awful failure scenario!" (*http://www.cloudera.com/blog/2011/02/avoiding-full-gcs-in-hbase-with-memstore-local -allocation-buffers-part-1/*)

error level, since the last time the metric was polled. In fact, all log event counters show you the counts accumulated during the last poll period.

Using these metrics, you are able to feed support systems that either graph the values over time, or trigger warnings based on definable thresholds. It is really important to understand the values and their usual ranges so that you can make use of them in production.

Info Metrics

The HBase processes also expose a group of metrics called *info* metrics. They contain rather fixed information about the processes, and are provided so that you can check these values in an automated fashion. Table 10-4 lists these metrics and provides a description of each. Note that these metrics are only accessible through JMX.

Table 10-4. Metrics exposed by the info group

Metric	Description
date	The date HBase was built
version	The HBase version
revision	The repository revision used for the build
url	The repository URL
user	The user that built HBase
hdfsDate	The date HDFS was built
hdfsVersion	The HDFS version currently in use
hdfsRevision	The repository revision used to build HDFS
hdfsUrl	The HDFS repository URL
hdfsUser	The user that built HDFS

HDFS refers to the *hadoop-core-<X.Y-nnnn>.jar* file that is currently in use by HBase. This usually is the supplied JAR file, but it could be a custom file, depending on your installation. The values returned could look like this:

```
date:Wed May 18 15:29:52 CEST 2011
version:0.91.0-SNAPSHOT
revision:1100427
url:https://svn.apache.org/repos/asf/hbase/trunk
user:larsgeorge

hdfsDate:Wed Feb  9 22:25:52 PST 2011
hdfsVersion:0.20-append-r1057313
hdfsRevision:1057313
hdfsUrl:http://svn.apache.org/repos/asf/hadoop/common/branches/branch-0.20-append
hdfsUser:Stack
```

The values are obviously not useful for graphing, but they can be used by an administrator to verify the running configuration.

Ganglia

HBase inherits its native support for Ganglia[§] directly from Hadoop, providing a context that can push the metrics directly to it.

 As of this writing, HBase only supports the 3.0.x line of Ganglia versions. This is due to the changes in the network protocol used by the newer 3.1.x releases. The GangliaContext class is therefore not compatible with the 3.1.x Ganglia releases. This was addressed in HADOOP-4675 (*http://issues.apache.org/jira/browse/HADOOP-4675*) and committed in Hadoop 0.22.0. In other words, future versions of HBase will support the newly introduced GangliaContext31 and work with the newer Ganglia releases.

Advanced users also have the option to apply the patch themselves and replace the stock Hadoop JAR with their own. Some distributions for Hadoop—for example, CDH3 from Cloudera—have this patch already applied.

Ganglia consists of three components:

Ganglia monitoring daemon (gmond)
   The *monitoring daemon* needs to run on every machine that is monitored. It collects the local data and prepares the statistics to be polled by other systems. It actively monitors the host for changes, which it will announce using uni- or multicast network messages. If configured in multicast mode, each monitoring daemon has the complete cluster state—of all servers with the same multicast address—present.

Ganglia meta daemon (gmetad)
   The *meta daemon* is installed on a central node and acts as the federation node to the entire cluster. The meta daemon polls from one or more monitoring daemons to receive the current cluster status, and saves it in a round-robin, time-series database, using *RRDtool*.[‖] The data is made available in XML format to other clients—for example, the web frontend.

   Ganglia also supports a hierarchy of reporting daemons, where at each node of the hierarchy tree a meta daemon is aggregating the results of its assigned monitoring daemons. The meta daemons on a higher level then aggregate the statistics for multiple clusters polling the status from their assigned, lower-level meta daemons.

---

§ Ganglia is a distributed, scalable monitoring system suitable for large cluster systems. See its project website (*http://ganglia.info/*) for more details on its history and goals.

‖ See the RRDtool project website (*http://www.mrtg.org/rrdtool/*) for details.

Ganglia PHP web frontend
> The *web frontend*, supplied by Ganglia, retrieves the combined statistics from the meta daemon and presents it as HTML. It uses `RRDtool` to render the stored time-series data in graphs.

Installation

Ganglia setup requires two steps: first you need to set up and configure Ganglia itself, and then have HBase send the metrics to it.

Ganglia-related steps

You should try to install prebuilt binary packages for the operating system distribution of your choice. If this is not possible, you can download the source from the project website and build it locally. For example, on a Debian-based system you could perform the following steps.

Ganglia monitoring daemon. Perform the following on all nodes you want to monitor.

Add a dedicated user account:

```
$ sudo adduser --disabled-login --no-create-home ganglia
```

Download the source tarball from the website, and unpack it into a common location:

```
$ wget http://downloads.sourceforge.net/project/ganglia/ \
    ganglia%20monitoring%20core/3.0.7%20%28Fossett%29/ganglia-3.0.7.tar.gz
$ tar -xzvf ganglia-3.0.7.tar.gz -C /opt
$ rm ganglia-3.0.7.tar.gz
```

Install the dependencies:

```
$ sudo apt-get -y install build-essential libapr1-dev \
    libconfuse-dev libexpat1-dev python-dev
```

Now you can build and install the binaries like so:

```
$ cd /opt/ganglia-3.0.7
$ ./configure
$ make
$ sudo make install
```

The next step is to set up the configuration. This can be fast-tracked by generating a default file:

```
$ gmond --default_config > /etc/gmond.conf
```

Change the following in the */etc/gmond.conf* file:

```
globals {
  user = ganglia
}

cluster {
  name = HBase
```

```
    owner = "Foo Company"
    url = "http://foo.com/"
}
```

The *global* section defines the user account created earlier. The *cluster* section defines
details about your cluster. By default, Ganglia is configured to use multicast UDP
messages with the IP address 239.2.11.71 to communicate—which is a good for clusters
less than ~120 nodes.

Multicast Versus Unicast

While the default communication method between monitoring daemons (gmond) is
UDP multicast messages, you may encounter environments where multicast is either
not possible or a limiting factor. The former is true, for example, when using Amazon's
cloud-based server offerings, called EC2.

Another known issue is that multicast only works reliably in clusters of up to ~120
nodes. If either is true for you, you can switch from multicast to unicast messages
instead. In the */etc/gmond.conf* file, change these options:

```
udp_send_channel {
  # mcast_join = 239.2.11.71
  host = host0.foo.com
  port = 8649
  # ttl = 1
}

udp_recv_channel {
  # mcast_join = 239.2.11.71
  port = 8649
  # bind = 239.2.11.71
}
```

This example assumes you dedicate the gmond on the master node to receive the updates
from all other gmond processes running on the rest of the machines.

The host0.foo.com would need to be replaced by the hostname or IP address of the
master node. In larger clusters, you can have multiple dedicated gmond processes on
separate physical machines. That way you can avoid having only a single gmond handling
the updates.

You also need to adjust the */etc/gmetad.conf* file to point to the dedicated node. See the
note in this chapter that discusses the use of unicast mode for details.

Start the monitoring daemon with:

```
$ sudo gmond
```

Test the daemon by connecting to it locally:

```
$ nc localhost 8649
```

This should print out the raw XML based cluster status. Stopping the daemon is accomplished by using the *kill* command.

Ganglia meta daemon. Perform the following on all nodes you want to use as meta daemon servers, aggregating the downstream monitoring statistics. Usually this is only one machine for clusters less than 100 nodes. Note that the server has to create the graphs, and therefore needs some decent processing capabilities.

Add a dedicated user account:

```
$ sudo adduser --disabled-login --no-create-home ganglia
```

Download the source tarball from the website, and unpack it into a common location:

```
$ wget http://downloads.sourceforge.net/project/ganglia/ \
    ganglia%20monitoring%20core/3.0.7%20%28Fossett%29/ganglia-3.0.7.tar.gz
$ tar -xzvf ganglia-3.0.7.tar.gz -C /opt
$ rm ganglia-3.0.7.tar.gz
```

Install the dependencies:

```
$ sudo apt-get -y install build-essential libapr1-dev libconfuse-dev \
    libexpat1-dev python-dev librrd2-dev
```

Now you can build and install the binaries like so:

```
$ cd /opt/ganglia-3.0.7
$ ./configure --with-gmetad
$ make
$ sudo make install
```

Note the extra --with-gmetad, which is required to build the binary we will need. The next step is to set up the configuration, copying the supplied default *gmetad.conf* file like so:

```
$ cp /opt/ganglia-3.0.7/gmetad/gmetad.conf /etc/gmetad.conf
```

Change the following in */etc/gmetad.conf*:

```
setuid_username "ganglia"
data_source "HBase" host0.foo.com
gridname "<Your-Grid-Name>"
```

The data_source line must contain the hostname or IP address of one or more gmonds.

When you are using unicast mode you need to point your data_source to the server that acts as the dedicated gmond server. If you have more than one, you can list them all, which adds failover safety.

Now create the required directories. These are used to store the collected data in round-robin databases.

```
$ mkdir -p /var/lib/ganglia/rrds/
$ chown -R ganglia:ganglia /var/lib/ganglia/
```

Now start the daemon:

```
$ gmetad
```

Stopping the daemon requires the use of the *kill* command.

Ganglia web frontend. The last part of the setup concerns the web-based frontend. A common scenario is to install it on the same machine that runs the gmetad process. At a minimum, it needs to have access to the round-robin, time-series database created by gmetad.

First install the required libraries:

```
$ sudo apt-get -y install rrdtool apache2 php5-mysql libapache2-mod-php5 php5-gd
```

Ganglia comes fully equipped with all the required PHP files. You can copy them in place like so:

```
$ cp -r /opt/ganglia-3.0.7/web /var/www/ganglia
```

Now restart Apache:

```
$ sudo /etc/init.d/apache2 restart
```

You should now be able to browse the web frontend using http://ganglia.foo.com/ganglia—assuming you have pointed the ganglia subdomain name to the host running gmetad first. You will only see the basic graph of the servers, since you still need to set up HBase to push its metrics to Ganglia, which is discussed next.

HBase-related steps

The central part of HBase and Ganglia integration is provided by the GangliaContext class, which sends the metrics collected in each server process to the Ganglia monitoring daemons. In addition, there is the *hadoop-metrics.properties* configuration file, located in the *conf/* directory, which needs to be amended to enable the context. Edit the file like so:

```
# HBase-specific configuration to reset long-running stats
# (e.g. compactions). If this variable is left out, then the default
# is no expiration.
hbase.extendedperiod = 3600

# Configuration of the "hbase" context for ganglia
# Pick one: Ganglia 3.0 (former) or Ganglia 3.1 (latter)
hbase.class=org.apache.hadoop.metrics.ganglia.GangliaContext
#hbase.class=org.apache.hadoop.metrics.ganglia.GangliaContext31
hbase.period=10
hbase.servers=239.2.11.71:8649
```

```
jvm.class=org.apache.hadoop.metrics.ganglia.GangliaContext
#jvm.class=org.apache.hadoop.metrics.ganglia.GangliaContext31
jvm.period=10
jvm.servers=239.2.11.71:8649

rpc.class=org.apache.hadoop.metrics.ganglia.GangliaContext
#rpc.class=org.apache.hadoop.metrics.ganglia.GangliaContext31
rpc.period=10
rpc.servers=239.2.11.71:8649
```

 I mentioned that HBase currently (as of version 0.91.x) only supports Ganglia 3.0.x, so why is there a choice between `GangliaContext` and `GangliaContext31`? Some repackaged versions of HBase already include patches to support Ganglia 3.1.x. Use this context only if you are certain that your version of HBase supports it (CDH3 does, for example).

When you are using Unicast messages, the `239.2.11.71` default multicast address needs to be changed to the dedicated gmond hostname or IP address. For example:

```
...
hbase.class=org.apache.hadoop.metrics.ganglia.GangliaContext
hbase.period=10
hbase.servers=host0.yourcompany.com:8649

jvm.class=org.apache.hadoop.metrics.ganglia.GangliaContext
jvm.period=10
jvm.servers=host0.yourcompany.com:8649

rpc.class=org.apache.hadoop.metrics.ganglia.GangliaContext
rpc.period=10
rpc.servers=host0.yourcompany.com:8649
```

Once you have edited the configuration file you need to restart the HBase cluster processes. No further changes are required. Ganglia will automatically pick up all the metrics.

Usage

Once you refresh the web-based UI frontend you should see the Ganglia home page, shown in Figure 10-3.

You can change the metric, time span, and sorting on that page; it will reload automatically. On an underpowered machine, you might have to wait a little bit for all the graphs to be rendered. Figure 10-4 shows the drop-down selection for the available metrics.

Finally, Figure 10-5 shows an example of how the metrics can be correlated to find root causes of problems. The graphs show how, at around midnight, the garbage collection time sharply rose for a heavily loaded server. This caused the compaction queue to increase significantly as well.

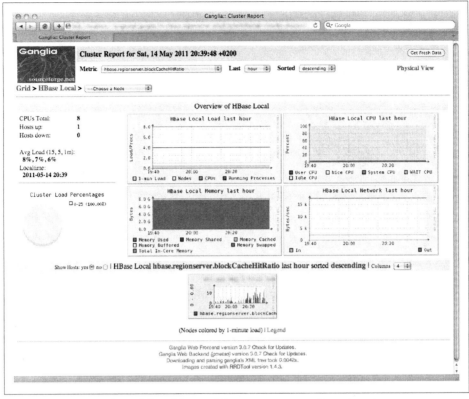

Figure 10-3. The Ganglia web-based frontend that gives access to all graphs

It seems obvious that write-heavy loads cause a lot of I/O churn, but keep in mind that you can see the same behavior (though not as often) for more read-heavy access patterns. For example, major compactions that run in the background could have accrued many storage files that all have to be rewritten. This can have an adverse effect on read latencies without an explicit write load from the clients.

Ganglia and its graphs are a great tool to go back in time and find what caused a problem. However, they are only helpful when dealing with quantitative data—for example, for performing postmortem analysis of a cluster problem. In the next section, you will see how to complement the graphing with a qualitative support system.

gexec
hbase.master.cluster_requests
hbase.master.splitSize_avg_time
hbase.master.splitSize_num_ops
hbase.master.splitTime_avg_time
hbase.master.splitTime_num_ops
hbase.regionserver.blockCacheCount
hbase.regionserver.blockCacheEvictedCount
hbase.regionserver.blockCacheFree
hbase.regionserver.blockCacheHitCachingRatio
hbase.regionserver.blockCacheHitCount
hbase.regionserver.blockCacheHitRatio
hbase.regionserver.blockCacheMissCount
hbase.regionserver.blockCacheSize
hbase.regionserver.compactionQueueSize
hbase.regionserver.compactionSize_avg_time
hbase.regionserver.compactionSize_num_ops
hbase.regionserver.compactionTime_avg_time
hbase.regionserver.compactionTime_num_ops
hbase.regionserver.flushQueueSize
hbase.regionserver.flushSize_avg_time
hbase.regionserver.flushSize_num_ops
hbase.regionserver.flushTime_avg_time
hbase.regionserver.flushTime_num_ops
hbase.regionserver.fsReadLatency_avg_time
hbase.regionserver.fsReadLatency_num_ops
hbase.regionserver.fsSyncLatency_avg_time
hbase.regionserver.fsSyncLatency_num_ops
hbase.regionserver.fsWriteLatency_avg_time
hbase.regionserver.fsWriteLatency_num_ops
hbase.regionserver.memstoreSizeMB
hbase.regionserver.readRequestsCount
✓ hbase.regionserver.regions
hbase.regionserver.requests
hbase.regionserver.storefileIndexSizeMB
hbase.regionserver.storefiles
hbase.regionserver.stores
hbase.regionserver.writeRequestsCount
jvm.metrics.gcCount
jvm.metrics.gcTimeMillis
jvm.metrics.logError
jvm.metrics.logFatal
jvm.metrics.logInfo
jvm.metrics.logWarn
jvm.metrics.memHeapCommittedM
jvm.metrics.memHeapUsedM
jvm.metrics.memNonHeapCommittedM
jvm.metrics.memNonHeapUsedM
jvm.metrics.threadsBlocked
jvm.metrics.threadsNew
jvm.metrics.threadsRunnable
jvm.metrics.threadsTerminated
jvm.metrics.threadsTimedWaiting
jvm.metrics.threadsWaiting
load_fifteen

Figure 10-4. The drop-down box that provides access to the list of metrics

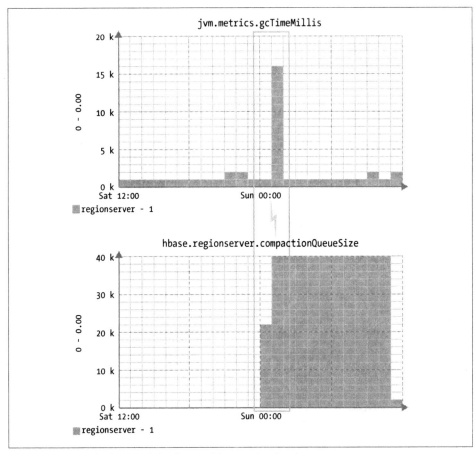

Figure 10-5. Graphs that can help align problems with related events

JMX

The *Java Management Extensions* technology is *the* standard for Java applications to export their status. In addition to what we have discussed so far regarding Ganglia and the metrics context, JMX also has the ability to provide operations. These allow you to remotely trigger functionality on any JMX-enabled Java process.

Before you can access HBase processes using JMX, you need to enable it. This is accomplished in the *$HABASE_HOME/conf/hbase-env.sh* configuration file by un-commenting—and amending—the following lines:

```
# Uncomment and adjust to enable JMX exporting
# See jmxremote.password and jmxremote.access in $JRE_HOME/lib/management to
# configure remote password access. More details at:
# http://java.sun.com/javase/6/docs/technotes/guides/management/agent.html
#
export HBASE_JMX_BASE="-Dcom.sun.management.jmxremote.ssl=false \
  -Dcom.sun.management.jmxremote.authenticate=false"
export HBASE_MASTER_OPTS="$HBASE_JMX_BASE \
  -Dcom.sun.management.jmxremote.port=10101"
export HBASE_REGIONSERVER_OPTS="$HBASE_JMX_BASE \
  -Dcom.sun.management.jmxremote.port=10102"
export HBASE_THRIFT_OPTS="$HBASE_JMX_BASE \
  -Dcom.sun.management.jmxremote.port=10103"
export HBASE_ZOOKEEPER_OPTS="$HBASE_JMX_BASE \
  -Dcom.sun.management.jmxremote.port=10104"
```

This enables JMX with remote access support, but with no security credentials. It is assumed that, in most cases, the HBase cluster servers are not accessible outside a firewall anyway, and therefore no authentication is needed. You can enable authentication if you want to, which makes the setup only slightly more complex.# You also need to restart HBase for these changes to become active.

When a server starts, it not only registers its metrics with the appropriate context, it also exports them as so-called JMX attributes. I mentioned already that when you want to use JMX to access the metrics, you need to at least enable the NullContext WithUpdateThread with an appropriate value for period—for example, a minimal *hadoop-metrics.properties* file could contain:

```
hbase.class=org.apache.hadoop.metrics.spi.NullContextWithUpdateThread
hbase.period=60

jvm.class=org.apache.hadoop.metrics.spi.NullContextWithUpdateThread
jvm.period=60

rpc.class=org.apache.hadoop.metrics.spi.NullContextWithUpdateThread
rpc.period=60
```

This would ensure that all metrics are updated every 10 seconds, and therefore would be retrievable as JMX attributes. Failing to do so would yield all JMX attributes useless. You could still use the JMX operations, though. Obviously, if you already have another context enabled—for example, the GangliaContext—this is adequate.

JMX uses the notion of *managed beans*, or *MBeans*, which expose a specific set of attributes and operations. There is a loose overlap between the metric context, as provided by the metrics framework, and the MBeans exposed over JMX. These MBeans are addressed in the form:

```
hadoop:service=<service-name>,name=<mbean-name>
```

#The HBase page metrics (*http://hbase.apache.org/metrics.html*) has information on how to add the password and access credentials files.

The following MBeans are provided by the various HBase processes:

`hadoop:service=Master,name=MasterStatistics`
Provides access to the master metrics, as described in "Master Metrics" on page 394.

`hadoop:service=RegionServer,name=RegionServerStatistics`
Provides access to the region metrics, as described in "Region Server Metrics".

`hadoop:service=HBase,name=RPCStatistics-` *<port>*
Provides access to the RPC metrics, as described in "RPC Metrics" on page 396. Note that the *port* in the name is dynamic and may change when you reconfigure where the master, or region server, binds to.

`hadoop:service=HBase,name=Info`
Provides access to the info metrics, as described in "Info Metrics" on page 399.

The `MasterStatistics`, `RegionServerStatistics`, and `RPCStatistics` MBeans also provide one operation: `resetAllMinMax`. Use this operation to reset the minimal and maximal observed completion times to time varying rate (TVR) metrics.

You have a few options to access the JMX attributes and operations, two of which are described next.

JConsole

Java ships with a helper application called *JConsole*, which can be used to connect to local and remote Java processes. Given that you have the `$JAVA_HOME` directory in your search path, you can start it like so:

```
$ jconsole
```

Once the application opens, it shows you a dialog that lets you choose whether to connect to a local or a remote process. Figure 10-6 shows the dialog.

Since you have configured all HBase processes to listen to specific ports, it is advisable to use those and treat them as remote processes—one advantage is that you can reconnect to a server, even when the process ID has changed. With the local connection method this is not possible, as it is ultimately bound to said ID.

Figure 10-6. Connecting to local or remote processes when JConsole starts

Connecting to a remote HBase process is accomplished by using *JMX Service URLs*, which follow this format:

```
service:jmx:rmi:///jndi/rmi://<server-address>:<port>/jmxrmi
```

This uses the *Java Naming and Directory Interface* (JNDI) registry to look up the required details. Adjust the `<port>` to the process you want to connect to. In some cases, you may have multiple Java processes running on the same physical machine—for example, the Hadoop name node and the HBase Master—so that each of them requires a unique port assignment. See the *hbase-env.sh* file contents shown earlier, which sets a port for every process. The master, for example, listens on port `10101`, the region server on port `10102`, and so on. Since you can only run one region server per physical machine, it is valid to use the same port for all of them, as in this case, the `<server-address>`— which is the hostname or IP address—changes to form a unique *address:port* pair.

Once you connect to the process, you will see a tabbed window with various details in it. Figure 10-7 shows the initial screen after you have connected to a process. The constantly updated graphs are especially useful for seeing what a server is currently up to.

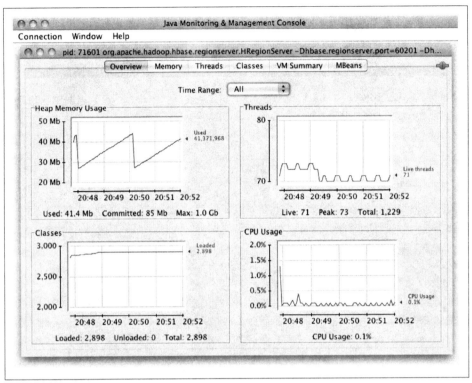

Figure 10-7. The JConsole application, which provides insight into a running Java process

Figure 10-8 is a screenshot of the *MBeans* tab that allows you to access the attributes and operations exposed by the registered managed beans. Here you see the `compaction QueueSize` metric.

See the official documentation (*http://download.oracle.com/javase/6/docs/technotes/guides/management/jconsole.html*) for all the possible options, and an explanation of each tab with its content.

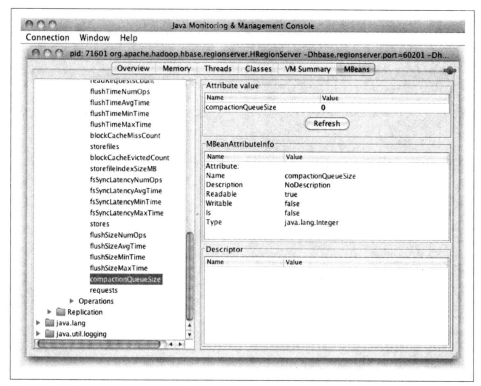

Figure 10-8. The MBeans tab, from which you can access any HBase process metric.

JMX Remote API

Another way to get the same information is the *JMX Remote API*, using *remote method invocation* or RMI.[*] Many tools are available that implement a client to access the remote managed Java processes. Even the Hadoop project is working on adding some basic support for it.[†]

As an example, we are going to use the *JMXToolkit*, also available in source code online (*https://github.com/larsgeorge/jmxtoolkit*). You will need the *git* command-line tools, and Apache Ant. Clone the repository and build the tool:

```
$ git clone git://github.com/larsgeorge/jmxtoolkit.git
Initialized empty Git repository in jmxtoolkit/.git/
...
$ cd jmxtoolkit
$ ant
```

---

[*] See the official documentation (*http://www.oracle.com/technetwork/java/javase/tech/index-jsp-136424.html*) for details.

[†] See HADOOP-4756 (*http://issues.apache.org/jira/browse/HADOOP-4756*) for details.

```
Buildfile: jmxtoolkit/build.xml
...
jar:
      [jar] Building jar: /private/tmp/jmxtoolkit/build/hbase-jmxtoolkit.jar

BUILD SUCCESSFUL
Total time: 2 seconds
```

After the building process is complete (and successful), you can see the provided options by invoking the -h switch like so:

```
$ java -cp build/hbase-jmxtoolkit.jar \
  org.apache.hadoop.hbase.jmxtoolkit.JMXToolkit -h

Usage: JMXToolkit [-a <action>] [-c <user>] [-p <password>]
  [-u url] [-f <config>] [-o <object>] [-e regexp]
  [-i <extends>] [-q <attr-oper>] [-w <check>]
  [-m <message>] [-x] [-l] [-v] [-h]

  -a <action>    Action to perform, can be one of the following
                         (default: query)

        create  Scan a JMX object for available attributes
        query   Query a set of attributes from the given objects
        check   Checks a given value to be in a valid range (see -w below)
        encode  Helps creating the encoded messages (see -m and -w below)
        walk    Walk the entire remote object list
...
  -h             Prints this help
```

You can use the JMXToolkit to *walk*, or print, the entire collection of available attributes and operations. You do have to know the exact names of the MBean and the attribute or operation you want to get. Since this is not an easy task, because you do not have this list yet, it makes sense to set up a basic configuration file that will help in subsequently retrieving the full list. Create a properties file with the following content:

```
$ vim hbase.properties
$ cat hbase.properties
; HBase Master
[hbaseMasterStatistics]
@object=hadoop:name=MasterStatistics,service=Master
@url=service:jmx:rmi:///jndi/rmi://${HOSTNAME1|localhost}:10101/jmxrmi
@user=${USER|controlRole}
@password=${PASSWORD|password}
[hbaseRPCMaster]
@object=hadoop:name=RPCStatistics-60000,service=HBase
@url=service:jmx:rmi:///jndi/rmi://${HOSTNAME1|localhost}:10101/jmxrmi
@user=${USER|controlRole}
@password=${PASSWORD|password}

; HBase RegionServer
[hbaseRegionServerStatistics]
@object=hadoop:name=RegionServerStatistics,service=RegionServer
@url=service:jmx:rmi:///jndi/rmi://${HOSTNAME2|localhost}:10102/jmxrmi
@user=${USER|controlRole}
```

```
@password=${PASSWORD|password}
[hbaseRPCRegionServer]
@object=hadoop:name=RPCStatistics-60020,service=HBase
@url=service:jmx:rmi:///jndi/rmi://${HOSTNAME2|localhost}:10102/jmxrmi
@user=${USER|controlRole}
@password=${PASSWORD|password}

; HBase Info
[hbaseInfo]
@object=hadoop:name=Info,service=HBase
@url=service:jmx:rmi:///jndi/rmi://${HOSTNAME1|localhost}:10101/jmxrmi
@user=${USER|controlRole}
@password=${PASSWORD|password}

; EOF
```

This configuration can be fed into the tool to retrieve all the attributes and operations of the listed MBeans. The result is saved in *myjmx.properties*:

```
$ java -cp build/hbase-jmxtoolkit.jar \
  org.apache.hadoop.hbase.jmxtoolkit.JMXToolkit \
  -f hbase.properties -a create -x > myjmx.properties

$ cat myjmx.properties
[hbaseMasterStatistics]
@object=hadoop:name=MasterStatistics,service=Master
@url=service:jmx:rmi:///jndi/rmi://${HOSTNAME1|localhost}:10101/jmxrmi
@user=${USER|controlRole}
@password=${PASSWORD|password}
splitTimeNumOps=INTEGER
splitTimeAvgTime=LONG
splitTimeMinTime=LONG
splitTimeMaxTime=LONG
splitSizeNumOps=INTEGER
splitSizeAvgTime=LONG
splitSizeMinTime=LONG
splitSizeMaxTime=LONG
cluster_requests=FLOAT
*resetAllMinMax=VOID
...
```

 These commands assume you are running them against a pseuodistrib-uted, local HBase instance. When you need to run them against a remote set of servers, simply set the variables included in the template properties file. For example, adding the following lines to the earlier command will specify the hostnames (or IP addresses) for the master and a slave node:

```
-DHOSTNAME1=master.foo.com -DHOSTNAME2=slave1.foo.com
```

When you look into the newly created *myjmx.properties* file you will see all the metrics you have seen already. The operations are prefixed with a * (i.e., the star charater).

You can now start requesting metric values on the command line using the toolkit and the populated properties file. The first query is for an attribute value, while the second is triggering an operation (which in this case does not return a value):

```
$ java -cp build/hbase-jmxtoolkit.jar \
    org.apache.hadoop.hbase.jmxtoolkit.JMXToolkit \
    -f myjmx.properties -o hbaseRegionServerStatistics -q compactionQueueSize
compactionQueueSize:0

$ java -cp build/hbase-jmxtoolkit.jar \
    org.apache.hadoop.hbase.jmxtoolkit.JMXToolkit \
    -f myjmx.properties -o hbaseRegionServerStatistics -q *resetAllMinMax
```

Once you have created the properties files, you can retrieve a single value, all values of an entire MBean, trigger operations, and so on. The toolkit is great for quickly scanning a managed process and documenting all the available information, thereby taking the guesswork out of querying JMX MBeans.

JMXToolkit and Cacti

Once the JMXToolkit JAR is built, it can be used on a Cacti server. The first step is to copy the JAR into the Cacti *scripts* directory (which can vary between installs, so make sure you know what you are doing). Next, extract the scripts:

```
$ cd $CACTI_HOME/scripts
$ unzip hbase-jmxtoolkit.jar bin/*
$ chmod +x bin/*
```

Once the scripts are in place, you can test the basic functionality:

```
$ bin/jmxtkcacti-hbase.sh host0.foo.com hbaseMasterStatistics

splitTimeNumOps:0 splitTimeAvgTime:0 splitTimeMinTime:-1 splitTimeMaxTime:0 \
splitSizeNumOps:0 splitSizeAvgTime:0 splitSizeMinTime:-1 splitSizeMaxTime:0 \
cluster_requests:0.0
```

The JAR also includes a set of Cacti templates[‡] that you can import into it, and use as a starting point to graph various values exposed by Hadoop's and HBase's JMX MBeans. Note that these templates use the preceding script to get the metrics via JMX.

Setting up the graphs in Cacti is much more involved compared to Ganglia, which dynamically adds the pushed metrics from the monitoring daemons. Cacti comes with a set of PHP scripts that can be used to script the addition (and updates) of cluster servers as a bulk operation.

---

‡ As of this writing, the templates are slightly outdated, but should work for newer versions of HBase.

Nagios

Nagios is a very commonly used support tool for gaining qualitative data regarding cluster status. It polls current metrics on a regular basis and compares them with given thresholds. Once the thresholds are exceededing it will start evasive actions, ranging from sending out emails, or SMS messages to telephones, all the way to triggering scripts, or even physically rebooting the server when necessary.

Typical checks in Nagios are either the supplied ones, those added as plug-ins, or custom scripts that have to return a specific exit code and print the outcome to the standard output. Integrating Nagios with HBase is typically done using JMX. There are many choices for doing so, including the already discussed JMXToolkit.

The advantage of JMXToolkit is that once you have built your properties file with all the attributes and operations in it, you can add Nagios thresholds to it. (You can also use a different monitoring tool if you'd like, so long as it uses the same exit code and/or standard output message approach as Nagios.) These are subsequently executed, and changing the check to, for example, different values is just a matter of editing the properties file. For example:

```
attributeXYZ=INTEGER|0:OK%3A%20%7B0%7D|2:WARN%3A%20%7B0%7D:80:<| \
1:FAILED%3A%20%7B0%7D:95:<
*operationABC=FLOAT|0|2::0.1:>=|1::0.5:>
```

You can follow the same steps described earlier in the Cacti install. You can then wire the Nagios checks to the supplied JMXToolkit script. If you have checks defined in the properties file, you only specify the object and attribute or operation to query. If not, you can specify the check within Nagios like so:

```
$ bin/jmxtknagios-hbase.sh host0.foo.com hbaseRegionServerStatistics \
   compactionQueueSize "0:OK%3A%20%7B0%7D|2:WARN%3A%20%7B0%7D:10:>=| \
   1:FAIL%3A%20%7B0%7D:100:>"
OK: 0
```

Note that JMXToolkit also comes with an *action* to encode text into the appropriate format.

Obviously, using JMXToolkit is only one of many choices. The crucial point, though, is that monitoring and graphing are essential to not only maintain a cluster, but also be able to track down issues much more easily. It is highly recommended that you implement both monitoring and graphing early in your project. It is also vital that you test your system with a load that reflects your real workload, because then you can become familiar with the graphs, and how to read them. Set thresholds and find sensible upper and lower limits—it may save you a lot of grief when going into production later on.

Performance Tuning

Thus far, you have seen how to set up a cluster and make use of it. Using HBase in production often requires that you turn many knobs to make it hum as expected. This chapter covers various advanced techniques for tuning a cluster and testing it repeatedly to verify its performance.

Garbage Collection Tuning

One of the lower-level settings you need to adjust is the garbage collection parameters for the region server processes. Note that the master is not a problem here as it does not handle any heavy loads, and data does not pass through it. These parameters only need to be added to the region servers.

You might wonder why you have to tune the garbage collection parameters to run HBase efficiently. The problem is that the Java Runtime Environment comes with basic assumptions regarding what your programs are doing, how they create objects, how they allocate the heap to handle data, and so on. These assumptions work well in a lot of cases. In addition, the JRE has heuristic algorithms that adjust these assumptions as your process is running. Even with those in place, the JRE is limited to the implementation of such heuristics and can handle some use cases better than others.

The bottom line is that the JRE does *not* handle region servers very well. This is caused by certain workloads, especially write-heavy ones, stressing the memory allocation mechanisms to a degree that it cannot safely rely on the JRE assumptions alone: you need to use the provided JRE options to tweak the garbage collection strategies to suit the workload.

For write-heavy use cases, the memstores are creating and discarding objects at various times, and in varying sizes. As the data is collected in the in-memory buffers, it needs to remain there until it has outgrown the configured minimum flush size, set with `hbase.hregion.memstore.flush.size` or at the table level.

Once the data is greater than that number, it is flushed to disk, creating a new store file. Since the data that is written to disk mostly resides in different locations in the Java heap—assuming it was written by the client at different times—it leaves *holes* in the heap.

Depending on how long the data was in memory, it resided in different locations in the generational architecture of the Java heap: data that was inserted rapidly and is flushed equally fast is often still in the so-called *young generation* (also called *new generation*) of the heap. The space can be reclaimed quickly and no harm is done.

However, if the data stays in memory for a longer period of time—for example, within a column family that is less rapidly inserted into—it is *promoted* to the *old generation* (or *tenured generation*). The difference between the young and old generations is primarily size: the young generation is between 128 MB and 512 MB, while the old generation holds the remaining available heap, which is usually many gigabytes of memory.

> You can set the following garbage collection-related options by adding them in the *hbase-env.sh* configuration file to the `HBASE_OPTS` or the `HBASE_REGIONSERVER_OPTS` variable. The latter only affects the region server process (as opposed to the master, for example), and is the recommended way to set these options.

You can specify the young generation size like so:

```
-XX:MaxNewSize=128m -XX:NewSize=128m
```

Or you can use the newer and shorter specification which combines the preceding code into one convenient option:

```
-Xmn128m
```

> Using 128 MB is a good starting point, and further observation of the JVM metrics should be conducted to confirm satisfactory use of the new generation of the heap.
>
> Note that the default value is *too low* for any serious region server load and *must* be increased. If you do not do this, you might notice a steep increase in CPU load on your servers, as they spend most of their time collecting objects from the new generation space.

Both generations need to be maintained by the JRE, to reuse the holes created by data that has been written to disk (and obviously any other object that was created and discarded subsequently). If the application ever requests a size of heap that does *not* fit into one of those holes, the JRE needs to compact the *fragmented* heap. This includes implicit requests, such as the promotion of longer-living objects from the young to the old generation. If this fails, you will see a *promotion failure* in your garbage collection logs.

It is highly recommended that you enable the JRE's log output for garbage collection details. This is done by adding the following JRE options:

```
-verbose:gc -XX:+PrintGCDetails -XX:+PrintGCTimeStamps \
  -Xloggc:$HBASE_HOME/logs/gc-$(hostname)-hbase.log"
```

Once the log is enabled, you can monitor it for occurrences of "concurrent mode failure" or "promotion failed" messages, which oftentimes precede long pauses.

Note that the logfile is not rolled like the other files are; you need to take care of this manually (e.g., by using a *cron*-based daily log roll task).

The process to rewrite the heap generation in question is called a *garbage collection*, and there are parameters for the JRE that you can use to specify different garbage collection implementations. The recommended values are:

```
-XX:+UseParNewGC and -XX:+UseConcMarkSweepGC
```

The first option is setting the garbage collection strategy for the young generation to use the *Parallel New Collector*: it stops the entire Java process to clean up the young generation heap. Since its size is small in comparison, this process does not take a long time, usually less than a few hundred milliseconds.

This is acceptable for the smaller young generation, but *not* for the old generation: in a worst-case scenario this can result in processes being stopped for seconds, if not minutes. Once you reach the configured ZooKeeper session timeout, this server is considered lost by the master and it is abandoned. Once it comes back from the garbage collection-induced stop, it is notified that it is abandoned and shuts itself down.

This is mitigated by using the *Concurrent Mark-Sweep Collector* (CMS), enabled with the latter option shown earlier. It works differently in that it tries to do as much work concurrently as possible, without stopping the Java process. This takes extra effort and an increased CPU load, but avoids the required stops to rewrite a fragmented old generation heap—until you hit the promotion error, which forces the garbage collector to stop everything and clean up the mess.

The CMS has an additional switch, which controls when it starts doing its concurrent mark and sweep check. This value can be set with this option:

```
-XX:CMSInitiatingOccupancyFraction=70
```

The value is a percentage that specifies when the background process starts, and it needs to be set to a level that avoids another issue: the *concurrent mode failure*. This occurs when the background process to mark and sweep the heap for collection is still running when the heap runs out of usable space (recall the holes analogy). In this case, the JRE *must* stop the Java process and free the space by forcefully removing discarded objects, or tenuring those that are old enough.

Setting the initiating occupancy fraction to 70% means that it is slightly larger than the configured 60% of heap usage by the region servers, which is the combination of the default 20% block cache and 40% memstore limits. It will start the concurrent collection process early enough before the heap runs out of space, but also not too early for it to run too often.

Putting the preceding settings together, you can use the following as a starting point for your configuration:

```
export HBASE_REGIONSERVER_OPTS="-Xmx8g -Xms8g -Xmn128m -XX:+UseParNewGC \
  -XX:+UseConcMarkSweepGC -XX:CMSInitiatingOccupancyFraction=70 -verbose:gc \
  -XX:+PrintGCDetails -XX:+PrintGCTimeStamps \
  -Xloggc:$HBASE_HOME/logs/gc-$(hostname)-hbase.log"
```

 Note that -XX:+CMSIncrementalMode is *not* recommended on actual server hardware.

These settings combine the current best practices at the time of this writing. If you use a newer version than Java 6, make sure you carefully evaluate the new garbage collection implementations and choose one that fits your use case.

It is important to size the young generation space so that the tenuring of longer-living objects is not causing the older generation heap to fragment too quickly. On the other hand, it should not be too large either, as this might cause too many short pauses. Although this will not cause your region servers to be abandoned, it does affect the latency of your servers, as they frequently stop for a few hundred milliseconds.

Also, when tuning the block cache and memstore size, make sure you set the initiating occupancy fraction value to something slightly larger. In addition, you *must not* specify these two values to go over a reasonable value, but definitely make sure they are less than 100%. You need to account for general Java class management overhead, so the default total of 60% is reasonable. More on this in "Configuration" on page 436.

Memstore-Local Allocation Buffer

Version 0.90 of HBase introduced an advanced mechanism to mitigate the issue of heap fragmentation due to too much churn on the memstore instances of a region server: the *memstore-local allocation buffers*, or *MSLAB* for short.

The preceding section explained how tenured KeyValue instances, once they are flushed to disk, cause holes in the old generation heap. Once there is no longer enough space for a new allocation caused by the fragmentation, the JRE falls back to the *stop-the-world* garbage collector, which rewrites the entire heap space and compacts it to the remaining active objects.

The key to reducing these *compacting collections* is to reduce fragmentation, and the MSLABs were built to help with that. The idea behind them is that only objects of exactly the same size should be allocated from the heap. Once these objects tenure and eventually get collected, they leave holes in the heap of a specific size. Subsequent allocations of new objects of the exact same size will always reuse these holes: there is no promotion error, and therefore no stop-the-world compacting collection is required.

The MSLABs are buffers of fixed sizes containing `KeyValue` instances of varying sizes. Whenever a buffer cannot completely fit a newly added `KeyValue`, it is considered full and a new buffer is created, once again of the given fixed size.

The feature is *enabled* by default in version 0.92, and *disabled* in version 0.90 of HBase. You can use the `hbase.hregion.memstore.mslab.enabled` configuration property to override it either way. It is recommended that you thoroughly test your setup with this new feature, as it might delay the inevitable only longer—which is a good thing—and therefore you still have to deal with long garbage collection pauses. If you are still experiencing these pauses, you could plan to restart the servers every few days, or weeks, before the pause happens.

 As of this writing, this feature is not yet widely tested in long-running production environments. Due diligence is advised.

The size of each allocated, fixed-sized buffer is controlled by the `hbase.hregion.mem store.mslab.chunksize` property. The default is 2 MB and is a sensible starting point. Based on your `KeyValue` instances, you may have to adjust this value: if you store larger cells, for example, 100 KB in size, you need to increase the MSLAB size to fit more than just a few cells.

There is also an upper boundary of what is stored in the buffers. It is set by the `hbase.hregion.memstore.mslab.max.allocation` property and defaults to 256 KB. Any cell that is larger will be directly allocated in the Java heap. If you are storing a lot of `KeyValue` instances that are larger than this upper limit, you will run into fragmentation-related pauses earlier.

The MSLABs do not come without a cost: they are more wasteful in regard to heap usage, as you will most likely not fill every buffer to the last byte. The remaining unused capacity of the buffer is wasted. Once again, it's about striking a balance: you need to decide if you should use MSLABs and benefit from better garbage collection but incur the extra space that is required, or not use MSLABs and benefit from better memory efficiency but deal with the problem caused by garbage collection pauses.

Finally, because the buffers require an additional byte array copy operation, they are also slightly slower, compared to directly using the `KeyValue` instances. Measure the impact on your workload and see if it has no adverse effect.

Compression

HBase comes with support for a number of compression algorithms that can be enabled at the column family level. It is recommended that you enable compression unless you have a reason not to do so—for example, when using already compressed content, such as JPEG images. For every other use case, compression usually will yield overall better performance, because the overhead of the CPU performing the compression and decompression is less than what is required to read more data from disk.

Available Codecs

You can choose from a fixed list of supported compression algorithms. They have different qualities when it comes to compression ratio, as well as CPU and installation requirements.

 Currently there is no support for pluggable compression algorithms. The provided ones either are part of Java itself or are added on the operating-system level. They require support libraries which are either built or shipped with HBase.

Before looking into each available compression algorithm, refer to Table 11-1 to see the compression algorithm comparison Google published in 2005.[*] While the numbers are old, they still can be used to compare the qualities of the algorithms.

Table 11-1. Comparison of compression algorithms

Algorithm	% remaining	Encoding	Decoding
GZIP	13.4%	21 MB/s	118 MB/s
LZO	20.5%	135 MB/s	410 MB/s
Zippy/Snappy	22.2%	172 MB/s	409 MB/s

Note that some of the algorithms have a better compression ratio while others are faster during encoding, and a lot faster during decoding. Depending on your use case, you can choose one that suits you best.

---

[*] The video of the presentation is available online (*http://norfolk.cs.washington.edu/htbin-post/unrestricted/colloq/details.cgi?id=437*).

Before Snappy was made available in 2011, the recommended algorithm was LZO, even if it did not have the best compression ratio. GZIP is very CPU-intensive and its slight advantage in storage savings is usually not worth the slower performance and CPU usage it exposes.

Snappy has similar qualities as LZO, it comes with a compatible license, and first tests have shown that it slightly outperforms LZO when used with Hadoop and HBase. Thus, as of this writing, you should consider Snappy over LZO.

Snappy

With *Snappy*, released by Google under the BSD License, you have access to the same compression used by Bigtable (where it is called *Zippy*). It is optimized to provide high speeds and reasonable compression, as opposed to being compatible with other compression libraries.

The code is written in C++, and HBase—as of version 0.92—ships with the required JNI[†] libraries to be able to use it. It requires that you first install the native executable binaries, by either using a packet manager, such as *apt*, *rpm*, or *yum*, or building them from the source code and installing them so that the JNI library can find them.

When setting up support for Snappy, you *must* install the native binary library on *all* region servers. Only then are they usable by the libraries.

LZO

Lempel-Ziv-Oberhumer (LZO) is a lossless data compression algorithm that is focused on decompression speed, and written in ANSI C. Similar to Snappy, it requires a JNI library for HBase to be able to use it.

Unfortunately, HBase cannot ship with LZO because of licensing issues: HBase uses the Apache License, while LZO is using the incompatible GNU General Public License (GPL). This means that the LZO installation needs to be performed separately, *after* HBase has been installed.[‡]

GZIP

The *GZIP* compression algorithm will generally compress better than Snappy or LZO, but is slower in comparison. While this seems like a disadvantage, it comes with an additional savings in storage space.

The performance issue can be mitigated to some degree by using the native GZIP libraries that are available on your operating system. The libraries used by HBase (which

---

† Java uses the *Java Native Interface* (JNI) to integrate native libraries and applications.

‡ See the wiki page "Using LZO Compression" (*http://wiki.apache.org/hadoop/UsingLzoCompression*) for information on how to make LZO work with HBase.

are provided by Hadoop) automatically check if the native libraries are available[§] and will make use of them. If not, you will see this message in your logfiles: "Got brand-new compressor". This indicates a failure to load the native version while falling back to the Java code implementation instead. The compression will still work, but is slightly slower.

An additional disadvantage is that GZIP needs a considerable amount of CPU resources. This can put unwanted load on your servers and needs to be carefully monitored.

Verifying Installation

Once you have installed a supported compression algorithm, it is highly recommended that you check if the installation was successful. There are a few mechanisms in HBase to do that.

Compression test tool

HBase includes a tool to test if compression is set up properly. To run it, type `./bin/hbase org.apache.hadoop.hbase.util.CompressionTest`. This will return information on how to run the tool:

```
$ ./bin/hbase org.apache.hadoop.hbase.util.CompressionTest
Usage: CompressionTest <path> none|gz|lzo|snappy

For example:
  hbase class org.apache.hadoop.hbase.util.CompressionTest file:///tmp/testfile gz
```

You need to specify a file that the tool will create and test in combination with the selected compression algorithm. For example, using a test file in HDFS and checking if GZIP is installed, you can run:

```
$ ./bin/hbase org.apache.hadoop.hbase.util.CompressionTest \
/user/larsgeorge/test.gz gz
11/07/01 20:27:43 WARN util.NativeCodeLoader: Unable to load native-hadoop \
  library for your platform... using builtin-java classes where applicable
11/07/01 20:27:43 INFO compress.CodecPool: Got brand-new compressor
11/07/01 20:27:43 INFO compress.CodecPool: Got brand-new compressor
SUCCESS
```

The tool reports SUCCESS, and therefore confirms that you can use this compression type for a column family definition. Note how it also prints the "Got brand-new compressor" message explained earlier: the server did not find the native GZIP libraries, but it can fall back to the Java code-based library.

Trying the same tool with a compression type that is not properly installed will raise an exception:

[§] The Hadoop project has a page (*http://hadoop.apache.org/common/docs/current/native_libraries.html*) describing the required steps to build and/or install the native libraries, which includes the GZIP support.

```
$ ./bin/hbase org.apache.hadoop.hbase.util.CompressionTest \
  file:///tmp/test.lzo lzo
Exception in thread "main" java.lang.RuntimeException: \
 java.lang.ClassNotFoundException: com.hadoop.compression.lzo.LzoCodec
     at org.apache.hadoop.hbase.io.hfile.Compression$Algorithm$1.getCodec)
     at org.apache.hadoop.hbase.io.hfile.Compression$Algorithm.getCompressor
```

If this happens, you need to go back and check the installation again. You also may have to restart the servers after you installed the JNI and/or native compression libraries.

Startup check

Even if the compression test tool reports success and confirms the proper installation of a compression library, you can still run into problems later on: since JNI requires that you first install the native libraries, it can happen that while you provision a new machine you miss this step. Subsequently, the server fails to open regions that contain column families using the native libraries (see "Basic setup checklist" on page 471).

This can be mitigated by specifying the (by default unset) hbase.regionserver.codecs property to list all of the required JNI libraries. Should one of them fail to find its native counterpart, it will prevent the entire region server from starting up. This way you get a fast failing setup where you notice the missing libraries, instead of running into issues later.

For example, this will check that the Snappy and LZO compression libraries are properly installed when the region server starts:

```
<property>
  <name>hbase.regionserver.codecs</name>
  <value>snappy,lzo</value>
</property>
```

If, for any reason, the JNI libraries fail to load the matching native ones, the server will abort at startup with an IOException stating "Compression codec <codec-name> not sup ported, aborting RS construction". Repair the setup and try to start the region server daemon again.

You can conduct this test for every compression algorithm supported by HBase. Do not forget to copy the changed configuration file to all region servers and to restart them afterward.

Enabling Compression

Enabling compression requires installation of the JNI and native compression libraries (unless you only want to use the Java code-based GZIP compression), as described earlier, and specifying the chosen algorithm in the column family schema.

One way to accomplish this is during table creation. The possible values are listed in "Column Families" on page 212.

```
hbase(main):001:0> create 'testtable', { NAME => 'colfam1', COMPRESSION => 'GZ' }
0 row(s) in 1.1920 seconds

hbase(main):012:0> describe 'testtable'
DESCRIPTION                                                  ENABLED
{NAME => 'testtable', FAMILIES => [{NAME => 'colfam1',        true
BLOOMFILTER => 'NONE', REPLICATION_SCOPE => '0', VERSIONS
=> '3', COMPRESSION => 'GZ', TTL => '2147483647', BLOCKSIZE
=> '65536', IN_MEMORY => 'false', BLOCKCACHE => 'true'}]}
1 row(s) in 0.0400 seconds
```

The *describe* shell command is used to read back the schema of the newly created table. You can see the compression is set to GZIP (using the shorter GZ value as required). Another option to enable—or change, or disable—the compression algorithm is to use the *alter* command for existing tables:

```
hbase(main):013:0> create 'testtable2', 'colfam1'
0 row(s) in 1.1920 seconds

hbase(main):014:0> disable 'testtable2'
0 row(s) in 2.0650 seconds

hbase(main):016:0> alter 'testtable2', { NAME => 'colfam1', COMPRESSION => 'GZ' }
0 row(s) in 0.2190 seconds

hbase(main):017:0> enable 'testtable2'
0 row(s) in 2.0410 seconds
```

Note how the table was first disabled. This is necessary to perform the alteration of the column family definition. The final *enable* command brings the table back online.

Changing the compression format to NONE will disable the compression for the given column family.

Delayed Action

Note that although you enable, disable, or change the compression algorithm, nothing happens right away. All the store files are still compressed with the previously used algorithm—or not compressed at all. All newly flushed store files *after* the change will use the new compression format.

If you want to force that all existing files are rewritten with the newly selected format, issue a *major_compact '<tablename>'* in the shell to start a major compaction process in the background. It will rewrite all files, and therefore use the new settings. Keep in mind that this might be very resource-intensive, and therefore should only be forcefully done when you are sure that you have the required resources available. Also note that the major compaction will run for a while, depending on the number and size of the store files. Be patient!

Optimizing Splits and Compactions

The built-in mechanisms of HBase to handle splits and compactions have sensible defaults and perform their duty as expected. Sometimes, though, it is useful to change their behavior to gain additional performance.

Managed Splitting

Usually HBase handles the splitting of regions automatically: once the regions reach the configured maximum size, they are split into two halves, which then can start taking on more data and grow from there. This is the default behavior and is sufficient for the majority of use cases.

There is one known problematic scenario, though, that can cause what is called *split/ compaction storms*: when you grow your regions roughly at the same rate, eventually they all need to be split at about the same time, causing a large spike in disk I/O because of the required compactions to rewrite the split regions.

Rather than relying on HBase to handle the splitting, you can turn it off and manually invoke the *split* and *major_compact* commands. This is accomplished by setting the `hbase.hregion.max.filesize` for the entire cluster, or when defining your table schema at the column family level, to a very high number. Setting it to `Long.MAX_VALUE` is not recommended in case the manual splits fail to run. It is better to set this value to a reasonable upper boundary, such as 100 GB (which would result in a one-hour major compaction if triggered).

The advantage of running the commands to split and compact your regions manually is that you can time-control them. Running them staggered across all regions spreads the I/O load as much as possible, avoiding any split/compaction storm. You will need to implement a client that uses the administrative API to call the `split()` and `majorCom pact()` methods. Alternatively, you can use the shell to invoke the commands interactively, or script their call using *cron*, for instance. Also see the `RegionSplitter` (added in version 0.90.2), discussed shortly, for another way to split existing regions: it has a *rolling split* feature you can use to carefully split the existing regions while waiting long enough for the involved compactions to complete (see the `-r` and `-o` command-line options).

An additional advantage to managing the splits manually is that you have better control over which regions are available at any time. This is good in the rare case that you have to do very low-level debugging, to, for example, see why a certain region had problems. With automated splits it might happen that by the time you want to check into a specific region, it has already been replaced with two *daughter* regions. These regions have new names and tracing the evolution of the original region over longer periods of time makes it much more difficult to find the information you require.

Region Hotspotting

Using the metrics discussed in "Region Server Metrics" on page 394,[||] you can determine if you are dealing with a write pattern that is causing a specific region to run hot.

If this is the case, refer to the approaches discussed in Chapter 9, especially those discussed in "Key Design" on page 357: you may need to *salt* the keys, or use *random* keys to distribute the load across all servers evenly.

The only way to alleviate the situation is to manually split a hot region into one or more new regions, at exact boundaries. This will divide the region's load over multiple region servers. As you split a region you can specify a split key, that is, the row key where you can split the given region into two. You can specify any row key within that region so that you are also able to generate halves that are completely different in size.

This might help only when you are not dealing with completely sequential key ranges, because those are always going to hit one region for a considerable amount of time.

Table Hotspotting

Sometimes an existing table with many regions is not distributed well—in other words, most of its regions are located on the same region server.[#] This means that, although you insert data with random keys, you still load one region server much more often than the others. You can use the move() function, as explained in "Cluster Operations" on page 230, from the HBase Shell, or use the HBaseAdmin class to explicitly move the server's table regions to other servers. Alternatively, you can use the unassign() method or shell command to simply remove a region of the affected table from the current server. The master will immediately deploy it on another available server.

Presplitting Regions

Managing the splits is useful to tightly control when load is going to increase on your cluster. You still face the problem that when initially loading a table, you need to split the regions rather often, since you usually start out with a single region per table. Growing this single region to a very large size is not recommended; therefore, it is better to start with a larger number of regions right from the start. This is done by *presplitting* the regions of an existing table, or by creating a table with the required number of regions.

The createTable() method of the administrative API, as well as the shell's *create* command, both take a list of *split keys*, which can be used to presplit a table when it is

---

[||] As an alternative, you can also look at the *number of requests* values reported on the master UI page; see "Main page" on page 277.

[#] Work has been done to improve this situation in HBase 0.92.0.

created. HBase also ships with a utility called `RegionSplitter`, which you can use to create a presplit table. Starting it without a parameter will show usage information:

```
$ ./bin/hbase org.apache.hadoop.hbase.util.RegionSplitter
usage: RegionSplitter <TABLE>
 -c <region count>       Create a new table with a pre-split number of
                         regions
 -D <property=value>     Override HBase Configuration Settings
 -f <family:family:...>  Column Families to create with new table.
                         Required with -c
 -h                      Print this usage help
 -o <count>              Max outstanding splits that have unfinished
                         major compactions
 -r                      Perform a rolling split of an existing region
    --risky              Skip verification steps to complete
                         quickly.STRONGLY DISCOURAGED for production
                         systems.
```

By default, it used the `MD5StringSplit` class to partition the row keys into ranges. You can define your own algorithm by implementing the `SplitAlgorithm` interface provided, and handing it into the utility using the `-D split.algorithm=<your-algorithm-class>` parameter. An example of using the supplied split algorithm class and creating a presplit table is:

```
$ ./bin/hbase org.apache.hadoop.hbase.util.RegionSplitter \
  -c 10 testtable -f colfam1
```

In the web UI of the master, you can click on the link with the newly created table name to see the generated regions:

```
testtable,,1309766006467.c0937d09f1da31f2a6c2950537a61093.
testtable,0ccccccc,1309766006467.83a0a6a949a6150c5680f39695450d8a.
testtable,19999998,1309766006467.1eba79c27eb9d5c2f89c3571f0d87a92.
testtable,26666664,1309766006467.7882cd50eb22652849491c08a6180258.
testtable,33333330,1309766006467.cef2853e36bd250c1b9324bac03e4bc9.
testtable,3ffffffc,1309766006467.00365940761359fee14d41db6a73ffc5.
testtable,4ccccccc8,1309766006467.f0c5045c304c2ff5338be27e81ae698e.
testtable,59999994,1309766006467.2d854f337aa6c09232409f0ba1d4964b.
testtable,66666660,1309766006467.b1ec9df9fd90d91f54cb18da5edc2581.
testtable,7333332c,1309766006468.42e179b78663b64401079a8601d9bd06.
```

Or you can use the shell's *create* command:

```
hbase(main):001:0> create 'testtable', 'colfam1', \
  { SPLITS => ['row-100', 'row-200', 'row-300', 'row-400'] }
0 row(s) in 1.1670 seconds
```

This generates the following regions:

```
testtable,,1309768272330.37377c4ab0a944a326ba8b6596a29396.
testtable,row-100,1309768272331.e6092cc777f58a08c61bf081aba14916.
testtable,row-200,1309768272331.63c9630a79b37ebce7b58cde0235dfe5.
testtable,row-300,1309768272331.eead6ad2ff3303ffe6a3126e0df3ff7a.
testtable,row-400,1309768272331.2bee7417fa67e4ac8c7210ce7325708e.
```

As for the number of presplit regions to use, you can start low with 10 presplit regions per server and watch as data grows over time. It is better to err on the side of too few regions and using a rolling split later, as having too many regions is usually not ideal in regard to overall cluster performance.

Alternatively, you can determine how many presplit regions to use based on the largest store file in your region: with a growing data size, this will get larger over time, and you want the largest region to be just big enough so that is not selected for major compaction—or you might face the mentioned compaction storms.

If you presplit your regions too thin, you can increase the major compaction interval by increasing the value for the `hbase.hregion.majorcompaction` configuration property. If your data size grows too large, use the `RegionSplitter` utility to perform a network I/O safe rolling split of all regions.

Use of manual splits and presplit regions is an advanced concept that requires a lot of planning and careful monitoring. On the other hand, it can help you to avoid the compaction storms that can happen for uniform data growth, or to shed load of hot regions by splitting them manually.

Load Balancing

The master has a built-in feature, called the *balancer*. By default, the balancer runs every five minutes, and it is configured by the `hbase.balancer.period` property. Once the balancer is started, it will attempt to equal out the number of assigned regions per region server so that they are within one region of the average number per server. The call first determines a new *assignment plan*, which describes which regions should be moved where. Then it starts the process of moving the regions by calling the `unassign()` method of the administrative API iteratively.

The balancer has an upper limit on how long it is allowed to run, which is configured using the `hbase.balancer.max.balancing` property and defaults to half of the balancer period value, or two and a half minutes.

You can control the balancer by means of the *balancer switch*: either use the shell's *balance_switch* command to toggle the balancer status between enabled and disabled, or use the `balanceSwitch()` API method to do the same. When you disable the balancer, it no longer runs as expected.

The balancer can be explicitly started using the shell's *balancer* command, or using the `balancer()` API method. The time-controlled invocation mentioned previously calls this method implicitly. It will determine if there is any work to be done and return `true` if that is the case. The return value of `false` means that it was not able to run the balancer, because either it was switched off, there was no work to be done (all is balanced), or something else was prohibiting the process. One example for this is the *region in transition* list (see "Main page" on page 277): if there is a region currently in transition, the balancer will be skipped.

Instead of relying on the balancer to do its work properly, you can use the *move* command and API method to assign regions to other servers. This is useful when you want to control where the regions of a particular table are assigned. See "Region Hotspotting" on page 430 for an example.

Merging Regions

While it is much more common for regions to split automatically over time as you are adding data to the corresponding table, sometimes you may need to merge regions— for example, after you have removed a large amount of data and you want to reduce the number of regions hosted by each server.

HBase ships with a tool that allows you to merge two adjacent regions as long as the cluster is not online. You can use the command-line tool to get the usage details:

```
$ ./bin/hbase org.apache.hadoop.hbase.util.Merge
Usage: bin/hbase merge <table-name> <region-1> <region-2>
```

Here is an example of a table that has more than one region, all of which are subsequently merged:

```
$ ./bin/hbase shell

hbase(main):001:0> create 'testtable', 'colfam1', \
 {SPLITS => ['row-10','row-20','row-30','row-40','row-50']}
0 row(s) in 0.2640 seconds

hbase(main):002:0> for i in '0'..'9' do for j in '0'..'9' do \
 put 'testtable', "row-#{i}#{j}", "colfam1:#{j}", "#{j}" end end
0 row(s) in 1.0450 seconds

hbase(main):003:0> flush 'testtable'
0 row(s) in 0.2000 seconds

hbase(main):004:0> scan '.META.', { COLUMNS => ['info:regioninfo']}
ROW                           COLUMN+CELL
 testtable,,1309614509037.612d1e0112 column=info:regioninfo, timestamp=130...
 406e6c2bb482eeaec57322.       STARTKEY => '', ENDKEY => 'row-10'
 testtable,row-10,1309614509040.2fba column=info:regioninfo, timestamp=130...
 fcc9bc6afac94c465ce5dcabc5d1. STARTKEY => 'row-10', ENDKEY => 'row-20'
 testtable,row-20,1309614509041.e7c1 column=info:regioninfo, timestamp=130...
 6267eb30e147e5d988c63d40f982. STARTKEY => 'row-20', ENDKEY => 'row-30'
 testtable,row-30,1309614509041.a9cd column=info:regioninfo, timestamp=130...
 e1cbc7d1a21b1aca2ac7fda30ad8. STARTKEY => 'row-30', ENDKEY => 'row-40'
 testtable,row-40,1309614509041.d458 column=info:regioninfo, timestamp=130...
 236feae097efcf33477e7acc51d4. STARTKEY => 'row-40', ENDKEY => 'row-50'
 testtable,row-50,1309614509041.74a5 column=info:regioninfo, timestamp=130...
 7dc7e3e9602d9229b15d4c0357d1. STARTKEY => 'row-50', ENDKEY => ''
6 row(s) in 0.0440 seconds
```

```
hbase(main):005:0> exit
```

```
$ ./bin/stop-hbase.sh
```

```
$ ./bin/hbase org.apache.hadoop.hbase.util.Merge testtable \
  testtable,row-20,1309614509041.e7c16267eb30e147e5d988c63d40f982. \
  testtable,row-30,1309614509041.a9cde1cbc7d1a21b1aca2ac7fda30ad8.
```

The example creates a table with five split points, resulting in six regions. It then inserts some rows and flushes the data to ensure that there are store files for the subsequent merge. The scan is used to get the names of the regions, but you can also use the web UI of the master: click on the table name in the *User Tables* section to get the same list of regions.

 Note how the shell wraps the values in each column. The region name is split over two lines, which you need to copy and paste separately. The web UI is easier to use in that respect, as it has the names in one column and in a single line.

The content of the column values is abbreviated to the start and end keys. You can see how the *create* command using the split keys has created the regions. The example goes on to exit the shell, and stop the HBase cluster. Note that HDFS still needs to run for the merge to work, as it needs to read the store files of each region and merge them into a new, combined one.

Client API: Best Practices

When reading or writing data from a client using the API, there are a handful of optimizations you should consider to gain the best performance. Here is a list of the *best practice* options:

Disable auto-flush

When performing a lot of put operations, make sure the auto-flush feature of HTable is set to false, using the setAutoFlush(false) method. Otherwise, the Put instances will be sent one at a time to the region server. Puts added via HTable.add(Put) and HTable.add(<List> Put) wind up in the same write buffer. If auto-flushing is disabled, these operations are not sent until the write buffer is filled. To explicitly flush the messages, call flushCommits(). Calling close on the HTable instance will implicitly invoke flushCommits().

Use scanner-caching

If HBase is used as an input source for a MapReduce job, for example, make sure the input Scan instance to the MapReduce job has setCaching() set to something greater than the default of 1. Using the default value means that the map task will make callbacks to the region server for every record processed. Setting this value to 500, for example, will transfer 500 rows at a time to the client to be processed.

There is a cost to having the cache value be large because it costs more in memory for both the client and region servers, so bigger is *not* always better.

Limit scan scope

Whenever a Scan is used to process large numbers of rows (and especially when used as a MapReduce source), be aware of which attributes are selected. If Scan.add Family() is called, *all* of the columns in the specified column family will be returned to the client. If only a small number of the available columns are to be processed, only those should be specified in the input scan because column overselection incurs a nontrivial performance penalty over large data sets.

Close ResultScanners

This isn't so much about improving performance, but rather *avoiding* performance problems. If you forget to close ResultScanner instances, as returned by HTable.getScanner(), you can cause problems on the region servers.

Always have ResultScanner processing enclosed in try/catch blocks, for example:

```
Scan scan = new Scan();
// configure scan instance
ResultScanner scanner = table.getScanner(scan);
try {
  for (Result result : scanner) {
  // process result...
} finally {
  scanner.close();  // always close the scanner!
}
table.close();
```

Block cache usage

Scan instances can be set to use the block cache in the region server via the setCacheBlocks() method. For scans used with MapReduce jobs, this should be false. For frequently accessed rows, it is advisable to use the block cache.

Optimal loading of row keys

When performing a table scan where only the row keys are needed (no families, qualifiers, values, or timestamps), add a FilterList with a MUST_PASS_ALL operator to the scanner using setFilter(). The filter list should include both a First KeyOnlyFilter and a KeyOnlyFilter instance, as explained in "Dedicated Filters" on page 147. Using this filter combination will cause the region server to only load the row key of the first KeyValue (i.e., from the first column) found and return it to the client, resulting in minimized network traffic.

Turn off WAL on Puts

A frequently discussed option for increasing throughput on Puts is to call write ToWAL(false). Turning this off means that the region server will *not* write the Put to the write-ahead log, but rather only into the memstore. *However*, the consequence is that if there is a region server failure *there will be data loss*. If you use writeToWAL(false), do so with extreme caution. You may find that it actually makes little difference if your load is well distributed across the cluster.

In general, it is best to use the WAL for Puts, and where loading throughput is a concern to use the bulk loading techniques instead, as explained in "Bulk Import" on page 459.

Configuration

Many configuration properties are available for you to use to fine-tune your cluster setup. "Configuration" on page 63 listed the ones you need to change or set to get your cluster up and running. There are advanced options you can consider adjusting based on your use case. Here is a list of the more commonly changed ones, and how to adjust them.

> The majority of the settings are properties in the *hbase-site.xml* configuration file. Edit the file, copy it to all servers in the cluster, and restart the servers to effect the changes.

Decrease ZooKeeper timeout

The default timeout between a region server and the ZooKeeper quorum is three minutes (specified in milliseconds), and is configured with the `zookeeper.session.timeout` property. This means that if a server crashes, it will be three minutes before the master notices this fact and starts recovery. You can tune the timeout down to a minute, or even less, so the master notices failures sooner.

Before changing this value, be sure you have your JVM garbage collection configuration under control, because otherwise, a long garbage collection that lasts beyond the ZooKeeper session timeout will take out your region server. You might be fine with this: you probably want recovery to start if a region server has been in a garbage collection-induced pause for a long period of time.

The reason for the default value being rather high is that it avoids problems during very large imports: such imports put a lot of stress on the servers, thereby increasing the likelihood that they will run into the garbage collection pause problem. Also see "Stability issues" on page 472 for information on how to detect such pauses.

Increase handlers

The `hbase.regionserver.handler.count` configuration property defines the number of threads that are kept open to answer incoming requests to user tables. The default of 10 is rather low in order to prevent users from overloading their region servers when using large write buffers with a high number of concurrent clients. The rule of thumb is to keep this number low when the payload per request approaches megabytes (e.g., big puts, scans using a large cache) and high when the payload is small (e.g., gets, small puts, increments, deletes).

It is safe to set that number to the maximum number of incoming clients if their payloads are small, the typical example being a cluster that serves a website, since puts are typically not buffered, and most of the operations are gets.

The reason why it is dangerous to keep this setting high is that the aggregate size of all the puts that are currently happening in a region server may impose too much pressure on the server's memory, or even trigger an `OutOfMemoryError` exception. A region server running on low memory will trigger its JVM's garbage collector to run more frequently up to a point where pauses become noticeable (the reason being that all the memory used to keep all the requests' payloads cannot be collected, no matter how hard the garbage collector tries). After some time, the overall cluster throughput is affected since every request that hits that region server will take longer, which exacerbates the problem.

Increase heap settings

HBase ships with a reasonable, conservative configuration that will work on nearly all machine types that people might want to test with. If you have larger machines—for example, where you can assign 8 GB or more to HBase—you should adjust the `HBASE_HEAPSIZE` setting in your *hbase-env.sh* file.

Consider using `HBASE_REGIONSERVER_OPTS` instead of changing the global `HBASE_HEAP SIZE`: this way the master will run with the default 1 GB heap, while you can increase the region server heap as needed independently.

This option is set in *hbase-env.sh*, as opposed to the *hbase-site.xml* file used for most of the other options.

Enable data compression

You should enable compression for the storage files—in particular, Snappy or LZO. It's near-frictionless and, in most cases, boosts performance. See "Compression" on page 424 for information on all the compression algorithms.

Increase region size

Consider going to larger regions to cut down on the total number of regions on your cluster. Generally, fewer regions to manage makes for a smoother-running cluster. You can always manually split the big regions later should one prove hot and you want to spread the request load over the cluster. "Optimizing Splits and Compactions" on page 429 has the details.

By default, regions are 256 MB in size. You could run with 1 GB, or even larger regions. Keep in mind that this needs to be carefully assessed, since a large region also can mean longer pauses under high pressure, due to compactions.

Adjust `hbase.hregion.max.filesize` in your *hbase-site.xml* configuration file.

Adjust block cache size

The amount of heap used for the block cache is specified as a percentage, expressed as a float value, and defaults to 20% (set as `0.2`). The property to change this percentage is `perf.hfile.block.cache.size`. Carefully monitor your block cache usage (see "Region Server Metrics" on page 394) to see if you are encountering many block evictions. In this case, you could increase the cache to fit more blocks.

Another reason to increase the block cache size is if you have mainly reading workloads. Then the block cache is what is needed most, and increasing it will help to cache more data.

 The total value of the block cache percentage and the upper limit of the memstore should not be 100%. You need to leave room for other purposes, or you will cause the server to run out of memory. The default total percentage is 60%, which is a reasonable value. Only go above that percentage when you are absolutely sure it will help you—and that it will have no adverse effect later on.

Adjust memstore limits

Memstore heap usage is set with the `hbase.regionserver.global.memstore.upper Limit` property, and it defaults to 40% (set to `0.4`). In addition, the `hbase.region server.global.memstore.lowerLimit` property (set to 35%, or `0.35`) is used to control the amount of flushing that will take place once the server is required to free heap space. Keep the upper and lower limits close to each other to avoid excessive flushing.

When you are dealing with mainly read-oriented workloads, you can consider reducing both limits to make more room for the block cache. On the other hand, when you are handling many writes, you should check the logfiles (or use the region server metrics as explained in "Region Server Metrics" on page 394) if the flushes are mostly done at a very small size—for example, 5 MB—and increase the memstore limits to reduce the excessive amount of I/O this causes.

Increase blocking store files

This value, set with the `hbase.hstore.blockingStoreFiles` property, defines when the region servers block further updates from clients to give compactions time to reduce the number of files. When you have a workload that sometimes spikes in regard to inserts, you should increase this value slightly—the default is seven files—to account for these spikes.

Use monitoring to graph the number of store files maintained by the region servers. If this number is consistently high, you might not want to increase this value, as you are only delaying the inevitable problems of overloading your servers.

Increase block multiplier

The property `hbase.hregion.memstore.block.multiplier`, set by default to `2`, is a safety latch that blocks any further updates from clients when the memstores exceed the *multiplier * flush size* limit.

When you have enough memory at your disposal, you can increase this value to handle spikes more gracefully: instead of blocking updates to wait for the flush to complete, you can temporarily accept more data.

Decrease maximum logfiles

Setting the `hbase.regionserver.maxlogs` property allows you to control how often flushes occur based on the number of WAL files on disk. The default is 32, which can be high in a write-heavy use case. Lower it to force the servers to flush data more often to disk so that these logs can be subsequently discarded.

Load Tests

After installing your cluster, it is advisable to run performance tests to verify its functionality. These tests give you a baseline which you can refer to after making changes to the configuration of the cluster, or the schemas of your tables. Doing a *burn-in* of your cluster will show you how much you can gain from it, but this does not replace a test with the load as expected from your use case.

Performance Evaluation

HBase ships with its own tool to execute a performance evaluation. It is aptly named *Performance Evaluation* (PE) and its usage details can be gained from using it with no command-line parameters:

```
$ ./bin/hbase org.apache.hadoop.hbase.PerformanceEvaluation
Usage: java org.apache.hadoop.hbase.PerformanceEvaluation \
  [--miniCluster] [--nomapred] [--rows=ROWS] <command> <nclients>

Options:
 miniCluster    Run the test on an HBaseMiniCluster
 nomapred       Run multiple clients using threads (rather than use mapreduce)
 rows           Rows each client runs. Default: One million
 flushCommits   Used to determine if the test should flush the table.
                Default: false
 writeToWAL     Set writeToWAL on puts. Default: True

Command:
 filterScan     Run scan test using a filter to find a specific row based
                on it's value (make sure to use --rows=20)
 randomRead     Run random read test
 randomSeekScan Run random seek and scan 100 test
 randomWrite    Run random write test
 scan           Run scan test (read every row)
 scanRange10    Run random seek scan with both start and stop row (max 10 rows)
 scanRange100   Run random seek scan with both start and stop row (max 100 rows)
 scanRange1000  Run random seek scan with both start and stop row (max 1000 rows)
 scanRange10000 Run random seek scan with both start and stop row (max 10000 rows)
 sequentialRead Run sequential read test
 sequentialWrite Run sequential write test

Args:
 nclients       Integer. Required. Total number of clients (and HRegionServers)
                running: 1 <= value <= 500
Examples:
```

To run a single evaluation client:
```
$ bin/hbase org.apache.hadoop.hbase.PerformanceEvaluation sequentialWrite 1
```

By default, the PE is executed as a MapReduce job—unless you specify for it to use 1 client, or because you used the `--nomapred` parameter. You can see the default values from the usage information in the preceding code sample, which are reasonable starting points, and the command to run a test is given as well:

```
$ ./bin/hbase org.apache.hadoop.hbase.PerformanceEvaluation sequentialWrite 1
11/07/03 13:18:34 INFO hbase.PerformanceEvaluation: Start class \
  org.apache.hadoop.hbase.PerformanceEvaluation$SequentialWriteTest at \
  offset 0 for 1048576 rows
...
11/07/03 13:18:41 INFO hbase.PerformanceEvaluation: 0/104857/1048576
...
11/07/03 13:18:45 INFO hbase.PerformanceEvaluation: 0/209714/1048576
...
11/07/03 13:20:03 INFO hbase.PerformanceEvaluation: 0/1048570/1048576
11/07/03 13:20:03 INFO hbase.PerformanceEvaluation: Finished class \
  org.apache.hadoop.hbase.PerformanceEvaluation$SequentialWriteTest \
  in 89062ms at offset 0 for 1048576 rows
```

The command starts a single client and performs a *sequential write* test. The output of the command shows the progress, until the final results are printed. You need to increase the number of clients (i.e., *threads* or MapReduce tasks) to a reasonable number, while making sure you are not overloading the client machine.

There is no need to specify a table name, nor a column family, as the PE code is generating its own schema: a table named `TestTable` with a family called `info`.

 The read tests require that you have previously executed the write tests. This will generate the table and insert the data to read subsequently.

Using the random or sequential read and write tests allows you to emulate these specific workloads. You cannot mix them, though, which means you must execute each test separately.

YCSB

The *Yahoo! Cloud Serving Benchmark*[*] (YCSB) is a suite of tools that can be used to run comparable workloads against different storage systems. While primarily built to compare various systems, it is also a reasonable tool for performing an HBase cluster *burn-in*—or performance test.

---

* See the project's GitHub repository (*https://github.com/brianfrankcooper/YCSB*) for details.

Before you can use YCSB you need to create the required test table, named `usertable`. While the name of the table is hardcoded, you are free to create a column family with a name of your choice. For example:

```
$ ./bin/hbase shell

hbase(main):001:0> create 'usertable', 'family'
0 row(s) in 0.3420 seconds
```

Starting YCSB without any options gives you its usage information:

```
$ java -cp build/ycsb.jar:db/hbase/lib/* com.yahoo.ycsb.Client
Usage: java com.yahoo.ycsb.Client [options]
Options:
  -threads n: execute using n threads (default: 1) - can also be specified as the
              "threadcount" property using -p
  -target n: attempt to do n operations per second (default: unlimited) - can also
             be specified as the "target" property using -p
  -load: run the loading phase of the workload
  -t: run the transactions phase of the workload (default)
  -db dbname: specify the name of the DB to use (default: com.yahoo.ycsb.BasicDB) -
              can also be specified as the "db" property using -p
```

```
        -P propertyfile: load properties from the given file. Multiple files can
                         be specified, and will be processed in the order specified
        -p name=value:  specify a property to be passed to the DB and workloads;
                         multiple properties can be specified, and override any
                         values in the propertyfile
        -s:  show status during run (default: no status)
        -l label:  use label for status (e.g. to label one experiment out of a whole
                   batch)

    Required properties:
        workload: the name of the workload class to use
                  (e.g. com.yahoo.ycsb.workloads.CoreWorkload)

    To run the transaction phase from multiple servers, start a separate client
    on each. To run the load phase from multiple servers, start a separate client
    on each; additionally, use the "insertcount" and "insertstart" properties to
    divide up the records to be inserted
```

The first step to test a running HBase cluster is to load it with a number of rows, which are subsequently used to modify the same rows, or to add new rows to the existing table:

```
$ java -cp $HBASE_HOME/conf:build/ycsb.jar:db/hbase/lib/* \
com.yahoo.ycsb.Client -load -db com.yahoo.ycsb.db.HBaseClient \
-P workloads/workloada -p columnfamily=family -p recordcount=100000000 \
-s > ycsb-load.log
```

This will run for a while and create the rows. The layout of the row is controlled by the given workload file, here *workloada*, containing these settings:

```
$ cat workloads/workloada
# Yahoo! Cloud System Benchmark
# Workload A: Update heavy workload
#   Application example: Session store recording recent actions
#
#   Read/update ratio: 50/50
#   Default data size: 1 KB records (10 fields, 100 bytes each, plus key)
#   Request distribution: zipfian

recordcount=1000
operationcount=1000
workload=com.yahoo.ycsb.workloads.CoreWorkload

readallfields=true

readproportion=0.5
updateproportion=0.5
scanproportion=0
insertproportion=0

requestdistribution=zipfian
```

Refer to the online documentation of the YCSB project for details on how to modify, or set up your own, workloads. The description specifies the data size and number of columns that are created during the load phase. The output of the tool is redirected into a logfile, which will contain lines like these:

```
YCSB Client 0.1
Command line: -load -db com.yahoo.ycsb.db.HBaseClient -P workloads/workloada \
-p columnfamily=family -p recordcount=100000000 -s
[OVERALL], RunTime(ms), 915.0
[OVERALL], Throughput(ops/sec), 1092.896174863388
[INSERT], Operations, 1000
[INSERT], AverageLatency(ms), 0.457
[INSERT], MinLatency(ms), 0
[INSERT], MaxLatency(ms), 314
[INSERT], 95thPercentileLatency(ms), 1
[INSERT], 99thPercentileLatency(ms), 1
[INSERT], Return=0, 1000
[INSERT], 0, 856
[INSERT], 1, 143
[INSERT], 2, 0
[INSERT], 3, 0
[INSERT], 4, 0
...
```

This is useful to keep, as it states the observed write performance for the initial set of rows. The default record count of 1000 was increased to reflect a more real-world number. You can override any of the workload configuration options on the command line. If you are running the same workloads more often, create your own and refer to it on the command line using the -P parameter.

The second step for a YCSB performance test is to execute the workload on the prepared table. For example:

```
$ java -cp $HBASE_HOME:build/ycsb.jar:db/hbase/lib/* \
com.yahoo.ycsb.Client -t -db com.yahoo.ycsb.db.HBaseClient \
-P workloads/workloada -p columnfamily=family -p operationcount=1000000 -s \
-threads 10 > ycsb-test.log
```

As with the loading step shown earlier, you need to override a few values to make this test useful: increase (or use your own modified workload file) the number of operations to test, and set the number of concurrent threads that should perform them to something reasonable. If you use too many threads you may overload the test machine (the one you run YCSB on). In this case, it is more useful to run the same test at the same time from different physical machines.

The output is also redirected into a logfile so that you can evaluate the test run afterward. The output will contain lines like these:

```
]$ cat transactions.dat
YCSB Client 0.1
Command line: -t -db com.yahoo.ycsb.db.HBaseClient -P workloads/workloada -p \
columnfamily=family -p operationcount=1000 -s -threads 10
[OVERALL], RunTime(ms), 575.0
[OVERALL], Throughput(ops/sec), 1739.1304347826087
[UPDATE], Operations, 507
[UPDATE], AverageLatency(ms), 2.546351084812623
[UPDATE], MinLatency(ms), 0
[UPDATE], MaxLatency(ms), 414
[UPDATE], 95thPercentileLatency(ms), 1
```

```
[UPDATE], 99thPercentileLatency(ms), 1
[UPDATE], Return=0, 507
[UPDATE], 0, 455
[UPDATE], 1, 49
[UPDATE], 2, 0
[UPDATE], 3, 0
...
[UPDATE], 997, 0
[UPDATE], 998, 0
[UPDATE], 999, 0
[UPDATE], >1000, 0
[READ], Operations, 493
[READ], AverageLatency(ms), 7.711967545638945
[READ], MinLatency(ms), 0
[READ], MaxLatency(ms), 417
[READ], 95thPercentileLatency(ms), 3
[READ], 99thPercentileLatency(ms), 416
[READ], Return=0, 493
[READ], 0, 1
[READ], 1, 165
[READ], 2, 257
[READ], 3, 48
[READ], 4, 11
[READ], 5, 4
[READ], 6, 0
...
[READ], 998, 0
[READ], 999, 0
[READ], >1000, 0
```

Note that YCSB can hardly emulate the workload you will see in your use case, but it can still be useful to test a varying set of loads on your cluster. Use the supplied workloads, or create your own, to emulate cases that are bound to read, write, or both kinds of operations.

Also consider running YCSB while you are running batch jobs, such as a MapReduce process that scans subsets, or entire tables. This will allow you to measure the impact of either on the other.

 As of this writing, using YCSB is preferred over the HBase-supplied Performance Evaluation. It offers more options, and can combine read and write workloads.

Cluster Administration

Once a cluster is in operation, it may become necessary to change its size or add extra measures for failover scenarios, all while the cluster is in use. Data should be backed up and/or moved between distinct clusters. In this chapter, we will look how this can be done with minimal to no interruption.

Operational Tasks

This section introduces the various tasks necessary while operating a cluster, including adding and removing nodes.

Node Decommissioning

You can stop an individual region server by running the following script in the HBase directory on the particular server:

```
$ ./bin/hbase-daemon.sh stop regionserver
```

The region server will first close all regions and then shut itself down. On shutdown, its ephemeral node in ZooKeeper will expire. The master will notice that the region server is gone and will treat it as a *crashed* server: it will reassign the regions the server was carrying.

Disabling the Load Balancer Before Decommissioning a Node

If the *load balancer* runs while a node is shutting down, there could be contention between the load balancer and the master's recovery of the just-decommissioned region server. Avoid any problems by disabling the balancer first: use the shell to disable the balancer like so:

```
hbase(main):001:0> balance_switch false
true
0 row(s) in 0.3590 seconds
```

This turns the balancer off. To reenable it, enter the following:

```
hbase(main):002:0> balance_switch true
false
0 row(s) in 0.3590 seconds
```

A downside to this method of stopping a region server is that regions could be offline for a good period of time—up to the configured ZooKeeper timeout period. Regions are closed in order: if there are many regions on the server, the first region to close may not be back online until all regions close and after the master notices the region server's ZooKeeper *znode* being removed.

HBase 0.90.2 introduced the ability for a node to gradually shed its load and then shut itself down. This is accomplished with the *graceful_stop.sh* script. When you invoke this script without any parameters, you are presented with an explanation of its usage:

```
$ ./bin/graceful_stop.sh
Usage: graceful_stop.sh [--config &conf-dir>] [--restart] [--reload] \
                        [--thrift] [--rest] &hostname>
   thrift      If we should stop/start thrift before/after the hbase stop/start
   rest        If we should stop/start rest before/after the hbase stop/start
   restart     If we should restart after graceful stop
   reload      Move offloaded regions back on to the stopped server
   debug       Move offloaded regions back on to the stopped server
   hostname    Hostname of server we are to stop
```

When you want to decommission a loaded region server, run the following:

```
$ ./bin/graceful_stop.sh HOSTNAME
```

where HOSTNAME is the host carrying the region server you want to decommission.

> The HOSTNAME passed to *graceful_stop.sh* must match the hostname that HBase is using to identify region servers. Check the list of region servers in the master UI for how HBase is referring to each server. It is usually hostname, but it can also be an FQDN, such as hostname.foobar.com. Whatever HBase is using, this is what you should pass the *graceful_stop.sh* decommission script.
>
> If you pass IP addresses, the script is not (yet) smart enough to make a hostname (or FQDN) out of it and will fail when it checks if the server is currently running: the graceful unloading of regions will not run.

The *graceful_stop.sh* script will move the regions off the decommissioned region server one at a time to minimize region churn. It will verify the region deployed in the new location before it moves the next region, and so on, until the decommissioned server is carrying no more regions.

At this point, the *graceful_stop.sh* script tells the region server to *stop*. The master will notice the region server gone but all regions will have already been redeployed, and because the region server went down cleanly, there will be no WALs to split.

Rolling Restarts

You can also use the *graceful_stop.sh* script to restart a region server after the shutdown *and* move its old regions back into place. (You might do the latter to retain data locality.) A primitive rolling restart might be effected by running something like the following:

```
$ for i in `cat conf/regionservers|sort`; do ./bin/graceful_stop.sh \
    --restart --reload --debug $i; done &> /tmp/log.txt &
```

Tail the output of */tmp/log.txt* to follow the script's progress. The preceding code pertains to region servers only. Be sure to disable the load balancer before using this code.

You will need to perform the master update separately, and it is recommended that you do the rolling restart of the region servers. Here are some steps you can follow to accomplish a rolling restart:

1. Unpack your release, make sure of its configuration, and then rsync it across the cluster. If you are using version 0.90.2, patch it with HBASE-3744 and HBASE-3756.

2. Run *hbck* to ensure the cluster is consistent:

   ```
   $ ./bin/hbase hbck
   ```

   Effect repairs if inconsistent.

3. Restart the master:

   ```
   $ ./bin/hbase-daemon.sh stop master; ./bin/hbase-daemon.sh start master
   ```

4. Disable the region balancer:

   ```
   $ echo "balance_switch false" | ./bin/hbase shell
   ```

5. Run the *graceful_stop.sh* script per region server. For example:

   ```
   $ for i in `cat conf/regionservers|sort`; do ./bin/graceful_stop.sh \
       --restart --reload --debug $i; done &> /tmp/log.txt &
   ```

   If you are running Thrift or REST servers on the region server, pass the `--thrift` or `--rest` option, as per the script's usage instructions, shown earlier (i.e., run it without any commandline options to get the instructions).

6. Restart the master again. This will clear out the dead servers list and reenable the balancer.

7. Run *hbck* to ensure the cluster is consistent.

Adding Servers

One of the major features HBase offers is built-in scalability. As the load on your cluster increases, you need to be able to add new servers to compensate for the new requirements. Adding new servers is a straightforward process and can be done for clusters running in any of the distribution modes, as explained in "Distributed Mode" on page 59.

Pseudodistributed mode

It seems paradoxical to scale an HBase cluster in an all-local mode, even when all daemons are run in separate processes. However, pseudodistributed mode is the closest you can get to a real cluster setup, and during development or prototyping it is advantageous to be able to replicate a fully distributed setup on a single machine.

Since the processes have to share all the local resources, adding more processes obviously will not make your test cluster perform any better. In fact, pseudodistributed mode is really suitable only for a very small amount of data. However, it allows you to test most of the architectural features HBase has to offer.

For example, you can experiment with master failover scenarios, or regions being moved from one server to another. Obviously, this does *not* replace testing at scale on the real cluster hardware, with the load expected during production. However, it does help you to come to terms with the administrative functionality offered by the HBase Shell, for example.

Or you can use the *administrative API* as discussed in Chapter 5. Use it to develop tools that maintain schemas, or to handle shifting server loads. There are many applications for this in a production environment, and being able to develop and test a tool locally first is tremendously helpful.

> You need to have set up a pseudodistributed installation before you can add any servers in psuedodistributed mode, and it must be running to use the following commands. They add to the existing processes, but do not take care of spinning up the local cluster itself.

Adding a local backup master. Starting a local backup master process is accomplished by using the *local-master-backup.sh* script in the *bin* directory, like so:

```
$ ./bin/local-master-backup.sh start 1
```

The number at the end of the command signifies an offset that is added to the default ports of 60000 for RPC and 60010 for the web-based UI. In this example, a new master process would be started that reads the same configuration files as usual, but would listen on ports 60001 and 60011, respectively.

In other words, the parameter is required and does not represent a number of servers to start, but where their ports are bound to. Starting more than one is also possible:

```
$./bin/local-master-backup.sh start 1 3 5
```

This starts three backup masters on ports 60001, 60003, and 60005 for RPC, plus 60011, 60013, and 60015 for the web UIs.

Make sure you do not specify an offset that could collide with a port that is already in use by another process. For example, it is a bad idea to use 30 for the offset, since this would result in a master RPC port on 60030—which is usually already assigned to the first region server as its UI port.

The start script also adds the offset to the name of the logfile the process is using, thus differentiating it from the logfiles used by the other local processes. For an offset of 1, it would set the logfile name to be:

```
logs/hbase-${USER}-1-master-${HOSTNAME}.log
```

Note the added 1 in the name. Using an offset of, for instance, 10 would add that number into the logfile name.

Stopping the backup master(s) involves the same command, but replacing the start command with the aptly named stop, like so:

```
$ ./bin/local-master-backup.sh stop 1
```

You need to specify the offsets of those backup masters you want to stop, and you have the option to stop only one, or any other number, up to all of the ones you started: whatever offset you specify is used to stop the master matching that number.

Adding a local region server. In a similar vein, you are allowed to start additional local region servers. The script provided is called *local-regionservers.sh*, and it takes the same parameters as the related *local-master-backup.sh* script: you specify the command, that is, if you want to start or stop the server, and a list of offsets.

The difference is that these offsets are added to 60200 for RPC, and 60300 for the web UIs. For example:

```
$ ./bin/local-regionservers.sh start 1
```

This command will start an additional region server using port 60201 for RPC, and 60301 for the web UI. The logfile name has the offset added to it, and would result in:

```
logs/hbase-${USER}-1-regionserver-${HOSTNAME}.log
```

The same concerns apply: you need to ensure that you are specifying an offset that results in a port that is not already in use by another process, or you will receive a java.net.BindException: Address already in use exception—as expected.

Starting more than one region server is accomplished by adding more offsets:

```
$ ./bin/local-regionservers.sh start 1 2 3
```

You do not have to start with an offset of 1. Since these are added to the base port numbers, you are free to specify any offset you prefer.

Stopping any additional region server involves replacing the `start` command with the `stop` command:

```
$ ./bin/local-regionservers.sh stop 1
```

This would stop the region server using offset 1, or ports 60201 and 60301. If you specify the offsets of all previously started region servers, they will all be stopped.

Fully distributed cluster

Operating an HBase cluster typically involves adding new servers over time. This is more common for the region servers, as they are doing all the heavy lifting. For the master, you have the option to start backup instances.

Adding a backup master. To prevent an HBase cluster master server from being the single point of failure, you can add backup masters. These are typically located on separate physical machines so that in a worst-case scenario, where the machine currently hosting the active master is failing, the system can fall back to a backup master.

The master process uses ZooKeeper to negotiate which is the currently active master: there is a dedicated ZooKeeper znode that all master processes race to create, and the first one to create it wins. This happens at startup and the winning process moves on to become the current master. All other machines simply loop around the znode check and wait for it to disappear—triggering the race again.

The */hbase/master* znode is ephemeral, and is the same kind the region servers use to report their presence. When the master process that created the znode fails, ZooKeeper will notice the end of the session with that server and remove the znode accordingly, triggering the election process.

Starting a server on multiple machines requires that it is configured just like the rest of the HBase cluster (see "Configuration" on page 63 for details). The master servers usually share the same configuration with the other servers in the cluster. Once you have confirmed that this is set up appropriately, you can run the following command on a server that is supposed to host the backup master:

```
$ ./bin/hbase-daemon.sh start master
```

Assuming you already had a master running, this command will bring up the new master to the point where it waits for the znode to be removed.[*] If you want to start many masters in an automated fashion and dedicate a specific server to host the current one, while all the others are considered backup masters, you can add the `--backup` switch like so:

```
$ ./bin/hbase-daemon.sh start master --backup
```

---

[*] As of this writing, the newly started master also has no web-based UI available. In other words, accessing the master info port on that server will not yield any results.

This forces the newly started master to wait for the dedicated one—which is the one that was started using the normal *start-hbase.sh* script, or by the previous command but *without* the --backup parameter—to create the */hbase/master* znode in ZooKeeper. Once this has happened, they move on to the master election loop. Since now there is already a master present, they go into idle mode as explained.

> If you started more than one master, and you experienced failovers, there is no easy way to tell which master is currently active. This causes a slight problem in that there is no way for you to know where the master's web-based UI is located. You will need to try the http://host name:60010 URL on all possible master servers to find the active one.[†]

Since HBase 0.90.x, there is also the option of creating a *backup-masters* file in the *conf* directory. This is akin to the *regionservers* file, listing one hostname per line that is supposed to start a backup master. For the example in "Example Configuration" on page 65, we could assume that we have three backup masters running on the ZooKeeper servers. In that case, the *conf/backup-masters*, would contain these entries:

```
zk1.foo.com
zk2.foo.com
zk3.foo.com
```

Adding these processes to the ZooKeeper machines is useful in a small cluster, as the master is more a *coordinator* in the overall design, and therefore does not need a lot of resources.

> You should start as many backup masters as you feel satisfies your requirements to handle machine failures. There is no harm in starting too many, but having too few might leave you with a weak spot in the setup. This is mitigated by the use of monitoring solutions that report the first master to fail. You can take action by repairing the server and adding it back to the cluster. Overall, having two or three backup masters seems a reasonable number.

Note that the servers listed in *backup-masters* are what the backup master processes are started on, while using the --backup switch. This happens as the *start-hbase.sh* script starts the primary master, the region servers, and eventually the backup masters. Alternatively, you can invoke the *hbase-backup.sh* script to initiate the start of the backup masters.

[†] There is an entry in the issue tracking system to rectify this inconvenience, which means it will improve over time. For now, you could use a script that reads the current master's hostname from ZooKeeper and updates a DNS entry pointing a generic hostname to it.

Adding a region server. Adding a new region server is one of the more common procedures you will perform on a cluster. The first thing you should do is to edit the *regionservers* file in the *conf* directory, to enable the launcher scripts to automat the server start and stop procedure.‡ Simply add a new line to the file specifying the hostname to add.

Once you have updated the file, you need to copy it across all machines in the cluster. You also need to ensure that the newly added machine has HBase installed, and that the configuration is current.

Then you have a few choices to start the new region server process. One option is to run the *start-hbase.sh* script on the master machine. It will skip all machines that have a process already running. Since the new machine fails this check, it will appropriately start the region server daemon.

Another option is to use the launcher script directly on the new server. This is done like so:

```
$ ./bin/hbase-daemon.sh start regionserver
```

 This *must* be run on the server on which you want to start the new region server process.

The region server process will start and register itself by creating a znode with its hostname in ZooKeeper. It subsequently joins the *collective* and is assigned regions.

Data Tasks

When dealing with an HBase cluster, you also will deal with a lot of data, spread over one or more tables. Sometimes you may be required to move the data as a whole—or in parts—to either archive data for backup purposes or to bootstrap another cluster. The following describes the possible ways in which you can accomplish this task.

Import and Export Tools

HBase ships with a handful of useful tools, two of which are the *Import* and *Export* MapReduce jobs. They can be used to write subsets, or an entire table, to files in HDFS, and subsequently load them again. They are contained in the HBase JAR file and you need the *hadoop jar* command to get a list of the tools:

```
$ hadoop jar $HBASE_HOME/hbase-0.91.0-SNAPSHOT.jar
An example program must be given as the first argument.
```

‡ Note that some distributions for HBase do not require this, since they do not make use of the supplied *start-hbase.sh* script.

```
Valid program names are:
  CellCounter: Count cells in HBase table
  completebulkload: Complete a bulk data load.
  copytable: Export a table from local cluster to peer cluster
  export: Write table data to HDFS.
  import: Import data written by Export.
  importtsv: Import data in TSV format.
  rowcounter: Count rows in HBase table
  verifyrep: Compare the data from tables in two different clusters.
    WARNING: It doesn't work for incrementColumnValues'd cells since the
      timestamp is changed after being appended to the log.
```

Adding the export program name then displays the options for its usage:

```
$ hadoop jar $HBASE_HOME/hbase-0.91.0-SNAPSHOT.jar export
ERROR: Wrong number of arguments: 0
Usage: Export [-D <property=value>]* <tablename> <outputdir> \
  [<versions> [<starttime> [<endtime>]] \
  [^[regex pattern] or [Prefix] to filter]]

  Note: -D properties will be applied to the conf used.
  For example:
   -D mapred.output.compress=true
   -D mapred.output.compression.codec=org.apache.hadoop.io.compress.GzipCodec
   -D mapred.output.compression.type=BLOCK
  Additionally, the following SCAN properties can be specified
  to control/limit what is exported..
   -D hbase.mapreduce.scan.column.family=<familyName>
```

You can see how you can supply various options. The only two required parameters are tablename and outputdir. The others are optional and can be added as required. §
Table 12-1 lists the possible options.

Table 12-1. Parameters for the Export tool

Name	Description
tablename	The name of the table to export.
outputdir	The location in HDFS to store the exported data.
versions	The number of versions per column to store. Default is 1.
starttime	The start time, further limiting the versions saved. See "Introduction" on page 122 for details on the setTimeRange() method that is used.
endtime	The matching end time for the time range of the scan used.
regexp/prefix	When starting with ^ it is treated as a regular expression pattern, matching row keys; otherwise, it is treated as a row key prefix.

§ There is an entry open in the issue tracking system to replace the parameter parsing with a more modern command-line parser. This will change the how the job is parameterized in the future.

The `regexp` parameter makes use of the `RowFilter` and `RegexStringCom` parator, as explained in "RowFilter" on page 141, and the `prefix` version uses the `PrefixFilter`, discussed in "PrefixFilter" on page 149.

You do need to specify the parameters from left to right, and you cannot omit any inbetween. In other words, if you want to specify a row key filter, you *must* specify the versions, as well as the start and end times. If you do not need them, set them to their minimum and maximum values—for example, 0 for the start and 9223372036854775807 (since the time is given as a `long` value) for the end timestamp. This will ensure that the time range is not taken into consideration.

Although you are supplying the HBase JAR file, there are a few extra dependencies that need to be satisfied before you can run this MapReduce job successfully. MapReduce requires access to the following JAR files: *zookeeper-xyz.jar*, *guava-xyz.jar*, and *google-collec tions-xyz.jar*. You need to make them available in such a way that the MapReduce task attempt has access to them. One way is to add them to `HADOOP_CLASSPATH` variable in the *$HADOOP_HOME/conf/hadoop-env.sh*.

Running the command will start the MapReduce job and print out the progress:

```
$ hadoop jar $HBASE_HOME/hbase-0.91.0-SNAPSHOT.jar export \
  testtable /user/larsgeorge/backup-testtable
11/06/25 15:58:29 INFO mapred.JobClient: Running job: job_201106251558_0001
11/06/25 15:58:30 INFO mapred.JobClient:  map 0% reduce 0%
11/06/25 15:58:52 INFO mapred.JobClient:  map 6% reduce 0%
11/06/25 15:58:55 INFO mapred.JobClient:  map 9% reduce 0%
11/06/25 15:58:58 INFO mapred.JobClient:  map 15% reduce 0%
11/06/25 15:59:01 INFO mapred.JobClient:  map 21% reduce 0%
11/06/25 15:59:04 INFO mapred.JobClient:  map 28% reduce 0%
11/06/25 15:59:07 INFO mapred.JobClient:  map 34% reduce 0%
11/06/25 15:59:10 INFO mapred.JobClient:  map 40% reduce 0%
11/06/25 15:59:13 INFO mapred.JobClient:  map 46% reduce 0%
11/06/25 15:59:16 INFO mapred.JobClient:  map 53% reduce 0%
11/06/25 15:59:19 INFO mapred.JobClient:  map 59% reduce 0%
11/06/25 15:59:22 INFO mapred.JobClient:  map 65% reduce 0%
11/06/25 15:59:25 INFO mapred.JobClient:  map 71% reduce 0%
11/06/25 15:59:28 INFO mapred.JobClient:  map 78% reduce 0%
11/06/25 15:59:31 INFO mapred.JobClient:  map 84% reduce 0%
11/06/25 15:59:34 INFO mapred.JobClient:  map 90% reduce 0%
11/06/25 15:59:37 INFO mapred.JobClient:  map 96% reduce 0%
11/06/25 15:59:40 INFO mapred.JobClient:  map 100% reduce 0%
11/06/25 15:59:42 INFO mapred.JobClient: Job complete: job_201106251558_0001
11/06/25 15:59:42 INFO mapred.JobClient: Counters: 6
11/06/25 15:59:42 INFO mapred.JobClient:   Job Counters
11/06/25 15:59:42 INFO mapred.JobClient:     Rack-local map tasks=32
11/06/25 15:59:42 INFO mapred.JobClient:     Launched map tasks=32
```

```
11/06/25 15:59:42 INFO mapred.JobClient:     FileSystemCounters
11/06/25 15:59:42 INFO mapred.JobClient:       HDFS_BYTES_WRITTEN=3648
11/06/25 15:59:42 INFO mapred.JobClient:     Map-Reduce Framework
11/06/25 15:59:42 INFO mapred.JobClient:       Map input records=0
11/06/25 15:59:42 INFO mapred.JobClient:       Spilled Records=0
11/06/25 15:59:42 INFO mapred.JobClient:       Map output records=0
```

Once the job is complete, you can check the filesystem for the exported data. Use the *hadoop dfs* command (the lines have been shortened to fit horizontally):

```
$ hadoop dfs -lsr /user/larsgeorge/backup-testtable
drwxr-xr-x   - ...       0 2011-06-25 15:58 _logs
-rw-r--r--   1 ...     114 2011-06-25 15:58 part-m-00000
-rw-r--r--   1 ...     114 2011-06-25 15:58 part-m-00001
-rw-r--r--   1 ...     114 2011-06-25 15:58 part-m-00002
-rw-r--r--   1 ...     114 2011-06-25 15:58 part-m-00003
-rw-r--r--   1 ...     114 2011-06-25 15:58 part-m-00004
-rw-r--r--   1 ...     114 2011-06-25 15:58 part-m-00005
-rw-r--r--   1 ...     114 2011-06-25 15:58 part-m-00006
-rw-r--r--   1 ...     114 2011-06-25 15:58 part-m-00007
-rw-r--r--   1 ...     114 2011-06-25 15:58 part-m-00008
-rw-r--r--   1 ...     114 2011-06-25 15:59 part-m-00009
-rw-r--r--   1 ...     114 2011-06-25 15:59 part-m-00010
-rw-r--r--   1 ...     114 2011-06-25 15:59 part-m-00011
-rw-r--r--   1 ...     114 2011-06-25 15:59 part-m-00012
-rw-r--r--   1 ...     114 2011-06-25 15:59 part-m-00013
-rw-r--r--   1 ...     114 2011-06-25 15:59 part-m-00014
-rw-r--r--   1 ...     114 2011-06-25 15:59 part-m-00015
-rw-r--r--   1 ...     114 2011-06-25 15:59 part-m-00016
-rw-r--r--   1 ...     114 2011-06-25 15:59 part-m-00017
-rw-r--r--   1 ...     114 2011-06-25 15:59 part-m-00018
-rw-r--r--   1 ...     114 2011-06-25 15:59 part-m-00019
-rw-r--r--   1 ...     114 2011-06-25 15:59 part-m-00020
-rw-r--r--   1 ...     114 2011-06-25 15:59 part-m-00021
-rw-r--r--   1 ...     114 2011-06-25 15:59 part-m-00022
-rw-r--r--   1 ...     114 2011-06-25 15:59 part-m-00023
-rw-r--r--   1 ...     114 2011-06-25 15:59 part-m-00024
-rw-r--r--   1 ...     114 2011-06-25 15:59 part-m-00025
-rw-r--r--   1 ...     114 2011-06-25 15:59 part-m-00026
-rw-r--r--   1 ...     114 2011-06-25 15:59 part-m-00027
-rw-r--r--   1 ...     114 2011-06-25 15:59 part-m-00028
-rw-r--r--   1 ...     114 2011-06-25 15:59 part-m-00029
-rw-r--r--   1 ...     114 2011-06-25 15:59 part-m-00030
-rw-r--r--   1 ...     114 2011-06-25 15:59 part-m-00031
```

Each *part-m-nnnnn* file contains a piece of the exported data, and together they form the full backup of the table. You can now, for example, use the *hadoop distcp* command to move the directory from one cluster to another, and perform the import there.

Also, using the optional parameters, you can implement an *incremental* backup process: set the start time to the value of the last backup. The job will still scan the entire table, but only export what has been modified since.

It is usually OK to only export the last version of a column value, but if you want a complete table backup, set the number of versions to 2147483647, which means all of them.

Importing the data is the reverse operation. First we can get the usage details by invoking the command without any parameters, and then we can start the job with the table name and inputdir (the directory containing the exported files):

```
$ hadoop jar $HBASE_HOME/hbase-0.91.0-SNAPSHOT.jar import
ERROR: Wrong number of arguments: 0
Usage: Import <tablename> <inputdir>

$ hadoop jar $HBASE_HOME/hbase-0.91.0-SNAPSHOT.jar import \
  testtable /user/larsgeorge/backup-testtable
11/06/25 17:09:48 INFO mapreduce.TableOutputFormat: Created table instance \
  for testtable
11/06/25 17:09:48 INFO input.FileInputFormat: Total input paths to process : 32
11/06/25 17:09:49 INFO mapred.JobClient: Running job: job_201106251558_0003
11/06/25 17:09:50 INFO mapred.JobClient:  map 0% reduce 0%
11/06/25 17:10:04 INFO mapred.JobClient:  map 6% reduce 0%
11/06/25 17:10:07 INFO mapred.JobClient:  map 12% reduce 0%
11/06/25 17:10:10 INFO mapred.JobClient:  map 18% reduce 0%
11/06/25 17:10:13 INFO mapred.JobClient:  map 25% reduce 0%
11/06/25 17:10:16 INFO mapred.JobClient:  map 31% reduce 0%
11/06/25 17:10:19 INFO mapred.JobClient:  map 37% reduce 0%
11/06/25 17:10:22 INFO mapred.JobClient:  map 43% reduce 0%
11/06/25 17:10:25 INFO mapred.JobClient:  map 50% reduce 0%
11/06/25 17:10:28 INFO mapred.JobClient:  map 56% reduce 0%
11/06/25 17:10:31 INFO mapred.JobClient:  map 62% reduce 0%
11/06/25 17:10:34 INFO mapred.JobClient:  map 68% reduce 0%
11/06/25 17:10:37 INFO mapred.JobClient:  map 75% reduce 0%
11/06/25 17:10:40 INFO mapred.JobClient:  map 81% reduce 0%
11/06/25 17:10:43 INFO mapred.JobClient:  map 87% reduce 0%
11/06/25 17:10:46 INFO mapred.JobClient:  map 93% reduce 0%
11/06/25 17:10:49 INFO mapred.JobClient:  map 100% reduce 0%
11/06/25 17:10:51 INFO mapred.JobClient: Job complete: job_201106251558_0003
11/06/25 17:10:51 INFO mapred.JobClient: Counters: 6
11/06/25 17:10:51 INFO mapred.JobClient:   Job Counters
11/06/25 17:10:51 INFO mapred.JobClient:     Launched map tasks=32
11/06/25 17:10:51 INFO mapred.JobClient:     Data-local map tasks=32
11/06/25 17:10:51 INFO mapred.JobClient:   FileSystemCounters
11/06/25 17:10:51 INFO mapred.JobClient:     HDFS_BYTES_READ=3648
11/06/25 17:10:51 INFO mapred.JobClient:   Map-Reduce Framework
11/06/25 17:10:51 INFO mapred.JobClient:     Map input records=0
11/06/25 17:10:51 INFO mapred.JobClient:     Spilled Records=0
11/06/25 17:10:51 INFO mapred.JobClient:     Map output records=0
```

 You can also use the Import job to store the data in a different table. As long as it has the same schema, you are free to specify a different table name on the command line.

The data from the exported files was read by the MapReduce job and stored in the specified table. Finally, this Export/Import combination is per-table only. If you have more than one table, you need to run them separately.

> ## Using DistCp
>
> You need to use a tool supplied by HBase to operate on a table. It seems tempting to use the *hadoop distcp* command to copy the entire */hbase* directory in HDFS. This is *not* a recommended procedure—in fact, it copies files without regard for their state: you may copy store files that are halfway through a memstore flush operation, leaving you with a mix of new and old files.
>
> You also ignore the in-memory data that has not been flushed yet. The low-level copy operation only sees the persisted data. One way to overcome this is to disallow write operations to a table, flush its memstores explicitly, and then copy the HDFS files.
>
> Even with this approach, you would need to carefully monitor how far the flush operation has proceeded, which is questionable, to say the least. Be warned!

CopyTable Tool

Another supplied tool is *CopyTable*, which is primarily designed to bootstrap cluster replication. You can use is it to make a copy of an existing table from the master cluster to the slave cluster. Here are its command-line options:

```
$ hadoop jar $HBASE_HOME/hbase-0.91.0-SNAPSHOT.jar copytable
Usage: CopyTable [--rs.class=CLASS] [--rs.impl=IMPL] [--starttime=X]
       [--endtime=Y] [--new.name=NEW] [--peer.adr=ADR] <tablename>

Options:
 rs.class      hbase.regionserver.class of the peer cluster
               specify if different from current cluster
 rs.impl       hbase.regionserver.impl of the peer cluster
 starttime     beginning of the time range
               without endtime means from starttime to forever
 endtime       end of the time range
 new.name      new table's name
 peer.adr      Address of the peer cluster given in the format
   hbase.zookeeer.quorum:hbase.zookeeper.client.port:zookeeper.znode.parent
 families      comma-seperated list of families to copy

Args:
 tablename     Name of the table to copy

Examples:
 To copy 'TestTable' to a cluster that uses replication for a 1 hour window:
 $ bin/hbase org.apache.hadoop.hbase.mapreduce.CopyTable \
   --rs.class=org.apache.hadoop.hbase.ipc.ReplicationRegionInterface
   --rs.impl=org.apache.hadoop.hbase.regionserver.replication.ReplicationRegionServer
   --starttime=1265875194289 --endtime=1265878794289
   --peer.adr=server1,server2,server3:2181:/hbase TestTable
```

CopyTable comes with an example command at the end of the usage output, which you can use to set up your own copy process. The parameters are all documented in the output too, and you may notice that you also have the start and end time options, which you can use the same way as explained earlier for the Export/Import tool.

In addition, you can use the `families` parameter to limit the number of column families that are included in the copy. The copy only considers the latest version of a column value. Here is an example of copying a table within the same cluster:

```
$ hadoop jar $HBASE_HOME/hbase-0.91.0-SNAPSHOT.jar copytable \
  --new.name=testtable3 testtable
11/06/26 15:20:07 INFO mapreduce.TableOutputFormat: Created table instance for \
testtable3
11/06/26 15:20:07 INFO mapred.JobClient: Running job: job_201106261454_0003
11/06/26 15:20:08 INFO mapred.JobClient:  map 0% reduce 0%
11/06/26 15:20:19 INFO mapred.JobClient:  map 6% reduce 0%
11/06/26 15:20:22 INFO mapred.JobClient:  map 12% reduce 0%
11/06/26 15:20:25 INFO mapred.JobClient:  map 18% reduce 0%
11/06/26 15:20:28 INFO mapred.JobClient:  map 25% reduce 0%
11/06/26 15:20:31 INFO mapred.JobClient:  map 31% reduce 0%
11/06/26 15:20:34 INFO mapred.JobClient:  map 37% reduce 0%
11/06/26 15:20:37 INFO mapred.JobClient:  map 43% reduce 0%
11/06/26 15:20:40 INFO mapred.JobClient:  map 50% reduce 0%
11/06/26 15:20:43 INFO mapred.JobClient:  map 56% reduce 0%
11/06/26 15:20:46 INFO mapred.JobClient:  map 62% reduce 0%
11/06/26 15:20:49 INFO mapred.JobClient:  map 68% reduce 0%
11/06/26 15:20:52 INFO mapred.JobClient:  map 75% reduce 0%
11/06/26 15:20:55 INFO mapred.JobClient:  map 81% reduce 0%
11/06/26 15:20:58 INFO mapred.JobClient:  map 87% reduce 0%
11/06/26 15:21:01 INFO mapred.JobClient:  map 93% reduce 0%
11/06/26 15:21:04 INFO mapred.JobClient:  map 100% reduce 0%
11/06/26 15:21:06 INFO mapred.JobClient: Job complete: job_201106261454_0003
11/06/26 15:21:06 INFO mapred.JobClient: Counters: 5
11/06/26 15:21:06 INFO mapred.JobClient:   Job Counters
11/06/26 15:21:06 INFO mapred.JobClient:     Launched map tasks=32
11/06/26 15:21:06 INFO mapred.JobClient:     Data-local map tasks=32
11/06/26 15:21:06 INFO mapred.JobClient:   Map-Reduce Framework
11/06/26 15:21:06 INFO mapred.JobClient:     Map input records=0
11/06/26 15:21:06 INFO mapred.JobClient:     Spilled Records=0
11/06/26 15:21:06 INFO mapred.JobClient:     Map output records=0
```

The copy process *requires* for the target table to exist: use the shell to get the definition of the source table, and create the target table using the same. You can omit the families you do not include in the copy command.

The example also uses the optional `new.name` parameter, which allows you to specify a table name that is different from the original. The copy of the table is stored on the same cluster, since the `peer.adr` parameter was not used.

Note that for both the CopyTable and Export/Import tools you can only rely on row-level atomicity. In other words, if you *export* or *copy* a table while it is being modified by other clients, you may not be able to tell exactly what has been copied to the new location.

Especially when dealing with more than one table, such as the secondary indexes, you need to ensure from the client side that you have copied a consistent view of all tables. One way to handle this is to use the start and end time parameters. This will allow you to run a second update job that only addresses the recently updated data.

Bulk Import

HBase includes several methods of loading data into tables. The most straightforward method is to either use the `TableOutputFormat` class from a MapReduce job (see Chapter 7), or use the normal client APIs; however, these are not always the most efficient methods.

Another way to efficiently load large amounts of data is via a *bulkimport*. The bulk load feature uses a MapReduce job to output table data in HBase's internal data format, and then directly loads the data files into a running cluster. This feature uses less CPU and network resources than simply using the HBase API.

A problem with loading data into HBase is that often this must be done in short bursts, but with those bursts being potentially very large. This will put additional stress on your cluster, and might overload it subsequently. Bulk imports are a way to alleviate this problem by not causing unnecessary churn on region servers.

Bulk load procedure

The HBase bulk load process consists of two main steps:

Preparation of data

The first step of a bulk load is to generate HBase data files from a MapReduce job using `HFileOutputFormat`. This output format writes out data in HBase's internal storage format so that it can be later loaded very efficiently into the cluster.

In order to function efficiently, `HFileOutputFormat` must be configured such that each output HFile fits within a single region: jobs whose output will be bulk-loaded into HBase use Hadoop's `TotalOrderPartitioner` class to partition the map output into disjoint ranges of the key space, corresponding to the key ranges of the regions in the table.

`HFileOutputFormat` includes a convenience function, `configureIncrementalLoad()`, which automatically sets up a `TotalOrderPartitioner` based on the current region boundaries of a table.

Load data

> After the data has been prepared using `HFileOutputFormat`, it is loaded into the cluster using the `completebulkload` tool. This tool iterates through the prepared data files, and for each one it determines the region the file belongs to. It then contacts the appropriate region server which adopts the HFile, moving it into its storage directory and making the data available to clients.
>
> If the region boundaries have changed during the course of bulk load preparation, or between the preparation and completion steps, the `completebulkload` tool will automatically split the data files into pieces corresponding to the new boundaries. This process is not optimally efficient, so you should take care to minimize the delay between preparing a bulk load and importing it into the cluster, especially if other clients are simultaneously loading data through other means.

This mechanism makes use of the *merge read* already in place on the servers to scan memstores and on-disk file stores for `KeyValue` entries of a row. Adding the newly generated files from the bulk import adds an additional file to handle—similar to new store files generated by a memstore flush.

What is even more important is that all of these files are sorted by the timestamps the matching `KeyValue` instances have (see "Read Path" on page 342). In other words, you can bulk-import *newer* and *older* versions of a column value, while the region servers sort them appropriately. The end result is that you immediately have a consistent and coherent view of the stored rows.

Using the importtsv tool

HBase ships with a command-line tool called `importtsv` which, when given files containing data in *tab-separated value* (TSV) format, can prepare this data for bulk import into HBase. This tool uses the HBase `put()` API by default to insert data into HBase one row at a time.

Alternatively, you can use the `importtsv.bulk.output` option so that `importtsv` will instead generate files using `HFileOutputFormat`. These can subsequently be bulk-loaded into HBase. Running the tool with no arguments prints brief usage information:

```
$ hadoop jar $HBASE_HOME/hbase-0.91.0-SNAPSHOT.jar importtsv
Usage: importtsv -Dimporttsv.columns=a,b,c <tablename> <inputdir>

Imports the given input directory of TSV data into the specified table.

The column names of the TSV data must be specified using the -Dimporttsv.columns
option. This option takes the form of comma-separated column names, where each
column name is either a simple column family, or a columnfamily:qualifier. The
special column name HBASE_ROW_KEY is used to designate that this column should
be used as the row key for each imported record. You must specify exactly one
column to be the row key, and you must specify a column name for every column
that exists in the input data.

By default importtsv will load data directly into HBase. To instead generate
```

```
HFiles of data to prepare for a bulk data load, pass the option:
  -Dimporttsv.bulk.output=/path/for/output
  Note: if you do not use this option, then the target table must already
    exist in HBase

Other options that may be specified with -D include:
  -Dimporttsv.skip.bad.lines=false - fail if encountering an invalid line
  '-Dimporttsv.separator=|' - eg separate on pipes instead of tabs
  -Dimporttsv.timestamp=currentTimeAsLong - use the specified timestamp for the import
  -Dimporttsv.mapper.class=my.Mapper - A user-defined Mapper to use instead \
    of org.apache.hadoop.hbase.mapreduce.TsvImporterMapper
```

The usage information is self-explanatory, so you simply need to run the tool, while specifying the option it requires. It will start a job that reads the files from HDFS and prepare the bulk import store files.

Using the completebulkload Tool

After a data import has been prepared, either by using the `importtsv` tool with the `importtsv.bulk.output` option, or by some other MapReduce job using the `HFileOutputFormat`, the `completebulkload` tool is used to import the data into the running cluster.

The `completebulkload` tool simply takes the output path where `importtsv` or your Map-Reduce job put its results, and the table name to import into. For example:

```
$ hadoop jar $HBASE_HOME/hbase-0.91.0-SNAPSHOT.jar completebulkload \
-conf ~/my-hbase-site.xml /user/larsgeorge/myoutput mytable
```

The optional `-conf config-file` parameter can be used to specify a file containing the appropriate HBase parameters, if not supplied already on the CLASSPATH. In addition, the CLASSPATH must contain the directory that has the ZooKeeper configuration file, if ZooKeeper is *not* managed by HBase.

> If the target table does not already exist in HBase, this tool will create it for you.

The `completebulkload` tool completes quickly, after which point the new data will be visible in the cluster.

Advanced usage

Although the `importtsv` tool is useful in many cases, advanced users may want to generate data programatically, or import data from other formats. To get started doing so, peruse the `ImportTsv.java` class, and check the JavaDoc for `HFileOutputFormat`.

The import step of the bulk load can also be done from within your code: see the `LoadIncrementalHFiles` class for more information.

Replication

The architecture of the HBase *replication* feature was discussed in "Replication" on page 351. Here we will look at what is required to enable replication of a table between two clusters.

The first step is to edit the *hbase-site.xml* configuration file in the *conf* directory to turn the feature on for the entire cluster:

```
<configuration>
  <property>
    <name>hbase.zookeeper.quorum</name>
    <value>zk1.foo.com,zk2.foo.com,zk3.foo.com</value>
  </property>
  <property>
    <name>hbase.rootdir</name>
    <value>hdfs://master.foo.com:8020/hbase</value>
  </property>
  <property>
    <name>hbase.cluster.distributed</name>
    <value>true</value>
  </property>
  <property>
    <name>hbase.replication</name>
    <value>true</value>
  </property>
</configuration>
```

This example adds the new hbase.replication property, where setting it to true enables replication support. This puts certain low-level features into place that are required. Otherwise, you will not see any changes to your cluster setup and functionality. Do not forget to copy the changed configuration file to all machines in your cluster, and to restart the servers.

Now you can either alter an existing table—you need to disable it before you can do that—or create a new one with the *replication scope* set to 1 (also see "Column Families" on page 212 for its value range):

```
hbase(main):001:0> create 'testtable1', 'colfam1'
hbase(main):002:0> disable 'testtable1'
hbase(main):003:0> alter 'testtable1', NAME => 'colfam1', \
  REPLICATION_SCOPE => '1'
hbase(main):004:0> enable 'testtable1'

hbase(main):005:0> create 'testtable2', { NAME => 'colfam1', \
  REPLICATION_SCOPE => 1}
```

Setting the scope further prepares the master cluster for its role as the replication source. Now it is time to add a slave—here also called a *peer*—cluster and start the replication:

```
hbase(main):006:0> add_peer '1', 'slave-zk1:2181:/hbase'
hbase(main):007:0> start_replication
```

The first command adds the ZooKeeper quorum details for the peer cluster so that modifications can be shipped to it subsequently. The second command starts the actual shipping of modification records to the peer cluster. For this to work as expected, you need to make sure that you have already created an identical copy of the table on the peer cluster: it can be empty, but it needs to have the same schema definition and table name.

 For development and prototyping, you can use the approach of running two local clusters, described in "Coexisting Clusters" on page 464, and configure the peer address to point to the second local cluster:

```
hbase(main):006:0> add_peer '1', 'localhost:2181:/hbase-2'
```

There is one more change you need to apply to the *hbase-site.xml* file in the *conf.2* directory on the secondary cluster:

```
<property>
    <name>hbase.replication</name>
    <value>true</value>
</property>
```

Adding this flag will allow for it to act as a peer for the master replication cluster.

Since replication is now enabled, you can add data into the master cluster, and within a few moments see the data appear in the peer cluster table with the same name.

No further changes need to be applied to the peer cluster. The replication feature uses the normal client API on the peer cluster to apply the changes locally. Removing a peer and stopping the translation is equally done, using the reverse commands:

```
hbase(main):008:0> stop_replication
hbase(main):009:0> remove_peer '1'
```

Note that stopping the replication will still complete the shipping of all queued modifications to the peer, but all further processing is ended.

Finally, verifying the replicated data on two clusters is easy to do in the shell when looking only at a few rows, but doing a systematic comparison requires more computing power. This is why the *Verify Replication* tool is provided; it is available as `verifyrep` using the *hadoop jar* command once more:

```
$ hadoop jar $HBASE_HOME/hbase-0.91.0-SNAPSHOT.jar verifyrep
Usage: verifyrep [--starttime=X] [--stoptime=Y] [--families=A] <peerid>
       <tablename>

Options:
  starttime     beginning of the time range
                without endtime means from starttime to forever
  stoptime      end of the time range
  families      comma-separated list of families to copy
```

```
Args:
 peerid      Id of the peer used for verification, must match the one given
             for replication
 tablename   Name of the table to verify

Examples:
 To verify the data replicated from TestTable for a 1 hour window with peer #5
 $ bin/hbase org.apache.hadoop.hbase.mapreduce.replication.VerifyReplication \
   --starttime=1265875194289 --stoptime=1265878794289 5 TestTable
```

T has to be run on the master cluster and needs to be provided with a peer ID (the one provided when establishing a replication stream) and a table name. Other options let you specify a time range and specific families.

Additional Tasks

On top of the operational and data tasks, there are additional tasks you may need to perform when setting up or running a test or production HBase cluster. We will discuss these tasks in the following subsections.

Coexisting Clusters

For testing purposes, it is useful to be able to run HBase in two separate instances, but on the same physical machine. This can be helpful, for example, when you want to prototype replication on your development machine.

 Running multiple instances of HBase, including any of its daemons, on a distributed cluster is *not* recommended, and is not tested at all. None of HBase's processes is designed to share the same server in production, nor is doing so part of its design. Be warned!

Presuming you have set up a local installation of HBase, as described in Chapter 2, and configured it to run in standalone mode, you can first make a copy of the configuration directory like so:

```
$ cd $HBASE_HOME
$ cp -pR conf conf.2
```

The next step is to edit the *hbase-env.sh* file in the new *conf.2* directory:

```
# Where log files are stored.  $HBASE_HOME/logs by default.
export HBASE_LOG_DIR=${HBASE_HOME}/logs.2

# A string representing this instance of hbase. $USER by default.
export HBASE_IDENT_STRING=${USER}.2
```

This is required to have no overlap in local filenames. Lastly, you need to adjust the *hbase-site.xml* file:

```xml
<configuration>
  <property>
    <name>hbase.zookeeper.quorum</name>
    <value>localhost</value>
  </property>
  <property>
    <name>hbase.rootdir</name>
    <value>hdfs://localhost:8020/hbase-2</value>
  </property>
  <property>
    <name>hbase.tmp.dir</name>
    <value>/tmp/hbase-2-${user.name}</value>
  </property>
  <property>
    <name>hbase.cluster.distributed</name>
    <value>true</value>
  </property>
  <property>
    <name>zookeeper.znode.parent</name>
    <value>/hbase-2</value>
  </property>
  <property>
    <name>hbase.master.port</name>
    <value>60100</value>
  </property>
  <property>
    <name>hbase.master.info.port</name>
    <value>60110</value>
  </property>
  <property>
    <name>hbase.regionserver.port</name>
    <value>60120</value>
  </property>
  <property>
    <name>hbase.regionserver.info.port</name>
    <value>60130</value>
  </property>
</configuration>
```

The highlighted properties contain the required changes. You need to assign all ports differently so that you have a clear distinction between the two cluster instances. Operating the secondary cluster requires specification of the new configuration directory:

```
$ HBASE_CONF_DIR=conf.2 bin/start-hbase.sh
$ HBASE_CONF_DIR=conf.2 ./bin/hbase shell
$ HBASE_CONF_DIR=conf.2 ./bin/stop-hbase.sh
```

The first command starts the secondary local cluster, the middle one starts a shell connecting to it, and the last command stops the cluster.

Required Ports

The HBase processes, when started, bind to two separate ports: one for the RPCs, and another for the web-based UI. This applies to both the master and each region server. Since you are running each process type on one machine only, you need to consider two ports per server type—unless you run in a nondistributed setup. Table 12-2 lists the default ports.

Table 12-2. Default ports used by the HBase daemons

Node type	Port	Description
Master	60000	The RPC port the master listens on for client requests. Can be configured with the hbase.master.port configuration property.
Master	60010	The web-based UI port the master process listens on. Can be configured with the hbase.master.info.port configuration property.
Region server	60020	The RPC port the region server listens on for client requests. Can be configured with the hbase.regionserver.port configuration property.
Region server	60030	The web-based UI port the region server listens on. Can be configured with the hbase.regionserver.info.port configuration property.

In addition, if you want to configure a firewall, for example, you also have to ensure that the ports for the Hadoop subsystems, that is, MapReduce and HDFS, are configured so that the HBase daemons have access to them.[||]

Changing Logging Levels

By default, HBase ships with a configuration which sets the log level of its processes to DEBUG, which is useful if you are in the installation and prototyping phase. It allows you to search through the files in case something goes wrong, as discussed in "Analyzing the Logs" on page 469.

For a production environment, you can switch to a less verbose level, such as INFO, or even WARN. This is accomplished by editing the *log4j.properties* file in the *conf* directory. Here is an example with the modified level for the HBase classes:

```
...
# Custom Logging levels

log4j.logger.org.apache.zookeeper=INFO
#log4j.logger.org.apache.hadoop.fs.FSNamesystem=DEBUG
log4j.logger.org.apache.hadoop.hbase=INFO
# Make these two classes INFO-level. Make them DEBUG to see more zk debug.
log4j.logger.org.apache.hadoop.hbase.zookeeper.ZKUtil=INFO
```

[||] Hadoop uses a similar layout for the port assignments, but since it has more process types it also has additional ports. See this blog post (*http://www.cloudera.com/blog/2009/08/hadoop-default-ports-quick-reference/*) for more information.

```
log4j.logger.org.apache.hadoop.hbase.zookeeper.ZooKeeperWatcher=INFO
#log4j.logger.org.apache.hadoop.dfs=DEBUG
# Set this class to log INFO only otherwise its OTT
...
```

This file needs to be copied to all servers, which need to be restarted subsequently for the changes to take effect.

Another option to either temporarily change the level, or when you have made changes to the properties file and want to delay the restart, use the web-based UIs and their log-level page. This is discussed and shown in "Shared Pages" on page 283. Since the UI log-level change is only affecting the server it is loaded from, you will need to adjust the level separately for every server in your cluster.

Troubleshooting

This section deals with the things you can do to heal a cluster that does not work as expected.

HBase Fsck

HBase comes with a tool called *hbck* which is implemented by the HBaseFsck class. It provides various command-line switches that influence its behavior. You can get a full list of its usage information by running it with -h:

```
$ ./bin/hbase hbck -h
Unknown command line option : -h
Usage: fsck [opts]
 where [opts] are:
   -details Display full report of all regions.
   -timelag {timeInSeconds}  Process only regions that  have not experienced
           any metadata updates in the last  {{timeInSeconds} seconds.
   -fix Try to fix some of the errors.
   -sleepBeforeRerun {timeInSeconds} Sleep this many seconds before checking
           if the fix worked if run with -fix
   -summary Print only summary of the tables and status.
```

The details switch prints out the most information when running *hbck*, while summary prints out the least. No option at all invokes the normal output detail, for example:

```
$ ./bin/hbase hbck
Number of Tables: 40
Number of live region servers: 19
Number of dead region servers: 0
Number of empty REGIONINFO_QUALIFIER rows in .META.: 0
Summary:
  -ROOT- is okay.
    Number of regions: 1
    Deployed on:  host1.foo.com:60020
  .META. is okay.
    Number of regions: 1
    Deployed on:  host4.foo.com:60020
```

```
    testtable is okay.
      Number of regions: 15
      Deployed on:  host7.foo.com:60020 host14.foo.com:60020
...
    testtable2 is okay.
      Number of regions: 1
      Deployed on:  host11.foo.com:60020
0 inconsistencies detected.
Status: OK
```

The extra parameters, such as `timelag` and `sleepBeforeRerun`, are explained in the usage details in the preceding code. They allow you to check subsets of data, as well as delay the eventual re-check run, to report any remaining issues.

Once started, the *hbck* tool will scan the `.META.` table to gather all the pertinent information it holds. It also scans the HDFS root directory HBase is configured to use. It then proceeds to compare the collected details to report on inconsistencies and integrity issues.

Consistency check

This check applies to a region on its own. It is checked whether the region is listed in `.META.` and exists in HDFS, as well as if it is assigned to exactly one region server.

Integrity check

This concerns a table as a whole. It compares the regions with the table details to find missing regions, or those that have holes or overlaps in their row key ranges.

The `fix` option allows you to repair a list of these issues. Over time, this feature is going to be enhanced so that more problems can be fixed. As of this writing, the `fix` option can handle the following problems:

- Assign `.META.` to a single new server *if* it is unassigned.
- Reassign `.META.` to a single new server *if* it is assigned to multiple servers.
- Assign a user table region to a new server *if* it is unassigned.
- Reassign a user table region to a single new server *if* it is assigned to multiple servers.
- Reassign a user table region to a new server if the current server does not match what the `.META.` table refers to.

> Be aware that sometimes *hbck* reports inconsistencies which are temporal, or transitional only. For example, when regions are unavailable for short periods of time during the internal housekeeping process, *hbck* will report those as inconsistencies too. Add the `details` switch to get more information on what is going on and rerun the tool a few times to confirm a permanent problem.

Analyzing the Logs

In rare cases it is necessary to directly access the logfiles created by the various HBase processes. They contain a mix of messages, some of which are printed for informational purposes and others representing internal warnings or error messages. While some of these messages are temporary, and do not mean that there is a permanent issue with the cluster, others state a system failure and are printed just before the process is forcefully ended.

Table 12-3 lists the various default HBase, ZooKeeper, and Hadoop logfiles. user is replaced with the user ID the process is started by, and hostname is the name of the machine the process is running on.

Table 12-3. The various server types and the logfiles they create

Server type	Logfile
HBase Master	$HBASE_HOME/logs/hbase-<user>-master-<hostname>.log
HBase RegionServer	$HBASE_HOME/logs/hbase-<user>-regionserver-<hostname>.log
ZooKeeper	Console log output only
NameNode	$HADOOP_HOME/logs/hadoop-<user>-namenode-<hostname>.log
DataNode	$HADOOP_HOME/logs/hadoop-<user>-datanode-<hostname>.log
JobTracker	$HADOOP_HOME/logs/hadoop-<user>-jobtracker-<hostname>.log
TaskTracker	$HADOOP_HOME/logs/hadoop-<user>-jobtracker-<hostname>.log

Obviously, this can be modified by editing the configuration files for either of these systems.

When you start analyzing the logfiles, it is useful to begin with the master logfile first, as it acts as the coordinator service of the entire cluster. It contains informational messages, such as the balancer printing out its background processing:

```
2011-06-03 09:12:55,448 INFO org.apache.hadoop.hbase.master.HMaster: balance \
hri=testtable,mykey1,1308610119005.dbccd6310dd7326f28ac09b60170a84c., \
src=host1.foo.com,60020,1308239280769, dest=host3.foo.com,60020,1308239274789
```

or when a region is split on a region server, duly reporting back the event:

```
2011-06-03 09:12:55,344 INFO org.apache.hadoop.hbase.master.ServerManager: \
Received REGION_SPLIT:
testtable,myrowkey5,1308647333895.0b8eeffeba8e2168dc7c06148d93dfcf.:
Daughters; testtable,myrowkey5,1308647572030.bc7cc0055a3a4fd7a5f56df6f27a696b.,
testtable,myrowkey9,1308647572030.87882799b2d58020990041f588b6b31c.
from host5.foo.com,60020,1308239280769
```

Many of these messages at the INFO level show you how your cluster evolved over time. You can use them to go back in time and see what happened earlier on. Typically the master is simply printing these messages on a regular basis, so when you look at specific time ranges you will see the common patterns.

If something fails, though, these patterns will change: the log messages are interrupted by others at the WARN (short for warning) or even ERROR level. You should find those patterns and reset just before the common pattern was disturbed.

 An interesting metric you can use as a gauge for where to start is discussed in "JVM Metrics" on page 397, under *System Event Metrics*: the error log event metric. It gives you a graph showing you where the server(s) started logging an increasing number of error messages in the logfiles. Find the time before this graph started rising and use it as the entry point into your logs.

Once you have found where the processes began logging ERROR level messages, you should be able to identify the root cause. A lot of subsequent messages are often collateral damage: they are a side effect of the original problem.

Not all of the logged messages that indicate a pattern change are using an elevated log level. Here is an example of a region that has been in the *transition* table for too long:

```
2011-06-21 09:19:20,218 INFO org.apache.hadoop.hbase.master.AssignmentManager:
Regions in transition timed out:
testtable,myrowkey123,1308610119005.dbccd6310dd7326f28ac09b60170a84c.
state=CLOSING, ts=1308647575449

2011-06-21 09:19:20,218 INFO org.apache.hadoop.hbase.master.AssignmentManager:
Region has been CLOSING for too long, this should eventually complete or the
server will expire, doing nothing
```

The message is logged on the info level because the system will eventually recover from it. But it could indicate the beginning of larger problems—for example, when the servers start to get overloaded. Make sure you reset your log analysis to where the *normal* patterns are disrupted.

Once you have investigated the master logs, move on to the region server logs. Use the monitoring metrics to see if any of them shows an increase in log messages, and scrutinize that server first.

If you find an error message, use the online resources to search#for the message in the public mailing lists (see *http://hbase.apache.org/mail-lists.html*). There is a good chance that this has been reported or discussed before, especially with recurring issues, such as the mentioned server overload scenarios: even errors follow a pattern at times.

Here is an example error message, caused by session loss between the region server and the ZooKeeper quorum:

```
2011-06-09 15:28:34,836 ERROR
org.apache.hadoop.hbase.regionserver.HRegionServer:
ZooKeeper session expired
2011-06-09 15:28:34,837 ERROR
```

#A dedicated service you can use is Search Hadoop (*http://search-hadoop.com/*).

```
org.apache.hadoop.hbase.regionserver.HRegionServer:
java.io.IOException: Server not running, aborting
...
```

You can search in the logfiles for occurrences of "ERROR" and "aborting" to find clues about the reasons the server in question stopped working.

Common Issues

The following gives you a list to run through when you encounter problems with your cluster setup.

Basic setup checklist

This section provides a checklist of things you should confirm for your cluster, before going into a deeper analysis in case of problems or performance issues.

File handles. The *ulimit -n* for the DataNode processes and the HBase processes should be set high. To verify the current ulimit setting you can also run the following:

```
$ cat /proc/<PID of JVM>/limits
```

You should see that the limit on the number of files is set reasonably high—it is safest to just bump this up to 32000, or even more. "File handles and process limits" on page 49 has the full details on how to configure this value.

DataNode connections. The DataNodes should be configured with a large number of transceivers—at least 4,096, but potentially more. There's no particular harm in setting it up to as high as 16,000 or so. See "Datanode handlers" on page 51 for more information.

Compression. Compression should almost always be on, unless you are storing precompressed data. "Compression" on page 424 discusses the details. Make sure that you have verified the installation so that all region servers can load the required compression libraries. If not, you will see errors like this:

```
hbase(main):007:0> create 'testtable', { NAME => 'colfam1', COMPRESSION => 'LZO' }
ERROR: org.apache.hadoop.hbase.client.NoServerForRegionException: \
  No server address listed in .META. for region \
  testtable2,,1309713043529.8ec02f811f75d2178ad098dc40b4efcf.
```

In the logfiles of the servers, you will see the root cause for this problem (abbreviated and line-wrapped to fit the available width):

```
2011-07-03 19:10:43,725 INFO org.apache.hadoop.hbase.regionserver.HRegion: \
  Setting up tabledescriptor config now ...
2011-07-03 19:10:43,725 DEBUG org.apache.hadoop.hbase.regionserver.HRegion: \
  Instantiated testtable,,1309713043529.8ec02f811f75d2178ad098dc40b4efcf.
2011-07-03 19:10:43,839 ERROR org.apache.hadoop.hbase.regionserver.handler. \
OpenRegionHandler: Failed open of region=testtable,,1309713043529. \
8ec02f811f75d2178ad098dc40b4efcf.
java.io.IOException: java.lang.RuntimeException: \
  java.lang.ClassNotFoundException: com.hadoop.compression.lzo.LzoCodec
```

```
at org.apache.hadoop.hbase.util.CompressionTest.testCompression
at org.apache.hadoop.hbase.regionserver.HRegion.checkCompressionCodecs
...
```

The missing compression library triggers an error when the region server tries to open the region with the column family configured to use LZO compression.

Garbage collection/memory tuning. We discussed the common Java garbage collector settings in "Garbage Collection Tuning" on page 419. If enough memory is available, you should increase the region server heap up to at least 4 GB, preferably more like 8 GB. The recommended garbage collection settings ought to work for any heap size.

Also, if you are colocating the region server and MapReduce task tracker, be mindful of resource contention on the shared system. Edit the *mapred-site.xml* file to reduce the number of slots for nodes running with ZooKeeper, so you can allocate a good share of memory to the region server. Do the math on memory allocation, accounting for memory allocated to the task tracker and region server, as well as memory allocated for each child task (from *mapred-site.xml* and *hadoop-env.sh*) to make sure you are leaving enough memory for the region server but you're not oversubscribing the system. Refer to the discussion in "Requirements" on page 34. You might want to consider separating MapReduce and HBase functionality if you are otherwise strapped for resources.

Lastly, HBase is also CPU-intensive. So even if you have enough memory, check your CPU utilization to determine if slots need to be reduced, using a simple Unix command such as *top*, or the monitoring described in Chapter 10.

Stability issues

In rare cases, a region server may shut itself down, or its process may be terminated unexpectedly. You can check the following:

- Double-check that the JVM version is not 1.6.0u18 (which is known to have detrimental effects on running HBase processes).
- Check the last lines of the region server logs—they probably have a message containing the word "aborting" (or "abort"), hopefully with a reason.

The latter is often an issue when the server is losing its ZooKeeper session. If that is the case, you can look into the following:

ZooKeeper problems. It is vital to ensure that ZooKeeper can perform its tasks as the coordination service for HBase. It is also important for the HBase processes to be able to communicate with ZooKeeper on a regular basis. Here is a checklist you can use to ensure that your do not run into commonly known problems with ZooKeeper:

Check that the region server and ZooKeeper machines do not swap
    If machines start swapping, certain resources start to time out and the region servers will lose their ZooKeeper session, causing them to abort themselves. You can use Ganglia, for example, to graph the machines' swap usage, or execute

```
$ vmstat 20
```

on the server(s) while running load against the cluster (e.g., a MapReduce job): make sure the "si" and "so" columns stay at 0. These columns show the amount of data swapped in or out. Also execute

```
$ free -m
```

to make sure that no swap space is used (the swap column should state 0). Also consider tuning the kernel's swappiness value (/proc/sys/vm/swappiness) down to 5 or 10. This should help if the total memory allocation adds up to less than the box's available memory, yet swap is happening anyway.

Check network issues

If the network is flaky, region servers will lose their connections to ZooKeeper and abort.

Check ZooKeeper machine deployment

ZooKeeper should never be codeployed with task trackers or data nodes. It is permissible to deploy ZooKeeper with the name node, secondary name node, and job tracker on small clusters (e.g., fewer than 40 nodes).

It is preferable to deploy just one ZooKeeper peer shared with the name node/job tracker than to deploy three that are collocated with other processes: the other processes will stress the machine and ZooKeeper will start timing out.

Check pauses related to garbage collection

Check the region server's logfiles for a message containing "slept"; for example, you might see something like "We slept 65000ms instead of 10000ms". If you see this, it is probably due to either garbage collection pauses or heavy swapping. If they are garbage collection pauses, refer to the tuning options mentioned in "Basic setup checklist" on page 471.

Monitor slow disks

HBase does not degrade well when reading or writing a block on a data node with a slow disk. This problem can affect the entire cluster if the block holds data from the META region, causing compactions to slow and back up. Again, use monitoring to carefully keep these vital metrics under control.

"Could not obtain block" errors. Often, this is the xceiver problem, discussed in "Basic setup checklist". Double-check the configured xceivers value. Also check the data node for log messages containing "exceeds the limit", which would indicate the xceiver issue. Check both the data node and region server log for "Too many open files" errors.

HBase Configuration Properties

This appendix lists all configuration properties HBase supports with their default values and a description of how they are used. Use it to reference what you need to put into the *hbase-site.xml* file. The following list is sorted alphabetically for easier lookup. See "Configuration" on page 436 for details on how to tune the more important properties.

 The description for each property is taken *as-is* from the *hbase-default.xml* file. The *Type*, *Default*, and *Unit* fields were added for your convenience.

`hbase.balancer.period`

Period at which the region balancer runs in the master.

Type: `int`

Default: `300000 (5 mins)`

Unit: `milliseconds`

`hbase.client.keyvalue.maxsize`

Specifies the combined maximum allowed size of a `KeyValue` instance. This is to set an upper boundary for a single entry saved in a storage file. Since they cannot be split, it helps avoiding that a region cannot be split any further because the data is too large. It seems wise to set this to a fraction of the maximum region size. Setting it to zero or less disables the check.

Type: `int`

Default: `10485760`

Unit: bytes

`hbase.client.pause`

General client pause value. Used mostly as value to wait before running a retry of a failed get, region lookup, etc.

Type: long

Default: 1000 (1 sec)

Unit: milliseconds

hbase.client.retries.number

Maximum retries. Used as maximum for all retryable operations such as fetching of the root region from root region server, getting a cell's value, starting a row update, etc.

Type: int

Default: 10

Unit: number

hbase.client.scanner.caching

Number of rows that will be fetched when calling next on a scanner if it is not served from (local, client) memory. Higher caching values will enable faster scanners but will eat up more memory and some calls of next may take longer and longer time when the cache is empty. Do not set this value such that the time between invocations is greater than the scanner timeout; i.e. hbase.region server.lease.period.

Type: int

Default: 1

Unit: number

hbase.client.write.buffer

Default size of the HTable client write buffer in bytes. A bigger buffer takes more memory—on both the client and server side since server instantiates the passed write buffer to process it—but a larger buffer size reduces the number of RPCs made. For an estimate of server-side memory-used, evaluate hbase.cli ent.write.buffer * hbase.regionserver.handler.count.

Type: long

Default: 2097152

Unit: bytes

hbase.cluster.distributed

The mode the cluster will be in. Possible values are false for standalone mode and true for distributed mode. If false, startup will run all HBase and ZooKeeper daemons together in the one JVM.

Type: boolean

Default: false

hbase.coprocessor.master.classes

A comma-separated list of org.apache.hadoop.hbase.coprocessor.MasterObserver coprocessors that are loaded by default on the active HMaster process. For any implemented coprocessor methods, the listed classes will be called in order. After implementing your own `MasterObserver`, just put it in HBase's classpath and add the fully qualified class name here.

Type: class names

Default: `<empty>`

`hbase.coprocessor.region.classes`

A comma-separated list of Coprocessors that are loaded by default on all tables. For any override coprocessor method, these classes will be called in order. After implementing your own Coprocessor, just put it in HBase's classpath and add the fully qualified class name here. A coprocessor can also be loaded on demand by setting `HTableDescriptor`.

Type: class names

Default: `<empty>`

`hbase.defaults.for.version.skip`

Set to `true` to skip the `hbase.defaults.for.version` check. Setting this to `true` can be useful in contexts other than the other side of a maven generation; i.e., running in an IDE. You'll want to set this boolean to `true` to avoid seeing the RuntimeException complaint `"hbase-default.xml file seems to be for an old version of HBase (@@@VERSION@@@), this version is X.X.X-SNAPSHOT"`.

Type: `boolean`

Default: `false`

`hbase.hash.type`

The hashing algorithm for use in `HashFunction`. Two values are supported now: `murmur` (MurmurHash) and `jenkins` (JenkinsHash). Used by Bloom filters.

Type: `string`

Default: `murmur`

`hbase.hregion.majorcompaction`

The time (in milliseconds) between major compactions of all `HStoreFiles` in a region. Default: 1 day. Set to 0 to disable automated major compactions.

Type: `long`

Default: `86400000 (1 day)`

Unit: `milliseconds`

`hbase.hregion.max.filesize`

Maximum `HStoreFile` size. If any one of a column families' `HStoreFiles` has grown to exceed this value, the hosting `HRegion` is split in two.

Type: `long`

Default: `268435456 (256 * 1024 * 1024)`

Unit: `bytes`

hbase.hregion.memstore.block.multiplier

Block updates if memstore has hbase.hregion.block.memstore time hbase.hregion.flush.size bytes. Useful for preventing runaway memstore during spikes in update traffic. Without an upper bound, the memstore fills such that when it flushes, the resultant flush files take a long time to compact or split, or worse, we OOME.

Type: int

Default: 2

Unit: number

hbase.hregion.memstore.flush.size

Memstore will be flushed to disk if size of the memstore exceeds this number of bytes. Value is checked by a thread that runs every hbase.server.thread.wakefre quency.

Type: long

Default: 67108864 (1024*1024*64L)

Unit: bytes

hbase.hregion.memstore.mslab.enabled

Enables the MemStore-Local Allocation Buffer, a feature which works to prevent heap fragmentation under heavy write loads. This can reduce the frequency of stop-the-world GC pauses on large heaps.

Type: boolean

Default: true

hbase.hregion.preclose.flush.size

If the memstores in a region are this size or larger when we go to close, run a "pre-flush" to clear out memstores before we put up the region closed flag and take the region offline. On close, a flush is run under the close flag to empty memory. During this time the region is offline and we are not taking on any writes. If the memstore content is large, this flush could take a long time to complete. The preflush is meant to clean out the bulk of the memstore before putting up the close flag and taking the region offline so the flush that runs under the close flag has little to do.

Type: long

Default: 5242880 (1024 * 1024 * 5)

Unit: bytes

hbase.hstore.blockingStoreFiles

If more than this number of StoreFiles in any one Store (one StoreFile is written per flush of MemStore) then updates are blocked for this HRegion until a compaction is completed, or until hbase.hstore.blockingWaitTime has been exceeded.

Type: int

Default: 7, hardcoded: -1

Unit: number

hbase.hstore.blockingWaitTime

The time an HRegion will block updates for after hitting the StoreFile limit defined by hbase.hstore.blockingStoreFiles. After this time has elapsed, the HRegion will stop blocking updates even if a compaction has not been completed.

Type: int

Default: 90000

Unit: milliseconds

hbase.hstore.compaction.max

Max number of HStoreFiles to compact per minor compaction.

Type: int

Default: 10

Unit: number

hbase.hstore.compactionThreshold

If more than this number of HStoreFiles in any one HStore (one HStoreFile is written per flush of memstore) then a compaction is run to rewrite all HStoreFiles files as one. Larger numbers put off compaction, but when it runs, it takes longer to complete.

Type: int

Default: 3, hardcoded: 2

Unit: number

hbase.mapreduce.hfileoutputformat.blocksize

The mapreduce HFileOutputFormat writes store files/HFiles. This is the minimum HFile blocksize to emit. Usually in HBase, when writing HFiles, the blocksize is gotten from the table schema (HColumnDescriptor) but in the MapReduce output format context, we don't have access to the schema, so we get the blocksize from the configuration. The smaller you make the blocksize, the bigger your index will be and the less you will fetch on a random access. Set the blocksize down if you have small cells and want faster random access of individual cells.

Type: int

Default: 65536

Unit: bytes

hbase.master.dns.interface

The name of the network interface from which a master should report its IP address.

Type: string

Default: "default"

hbase.master.dns.nameserver

The hostname or IP address of the name server (DNS) which a master should use to determine the hostname used for communication and display purposes.

Type: string

Default: "default"

hbase.master.info.bindAddress

The bind address for the HBase Master web UI.

Type: String

Default: 0.0.0.0

hbase.master.info.port

The port for the HBase Master web UI. Set to -1 if you do not want a UI instance run.

Type: int

Default: 60010

Unit: number

hbase.master.kerberos.principal

Example: "hbase/_HOST@EXAMPLE.COM". The Kerberos principal name that should be used to run the HMaster process. The principal name should be in the form: user/hostname@DOMAIN. If "_HOST" is used as the hostname portion, it will be replaced with the actual hostname of the running instance.

Type: string

Default:

hbase.master.keytab.file

Full path to the Kerberos keytab file to use for logging in the configured HMaster server principal.

Type: string

Default:

hbase.master.logcleaner.plugins

A comma-separated list of LogCleanerDelegates invoked by the LogsCleaner service. These WAL/HLog cleaners are called in order, so put the HLog cleaner that prunes the most HLog files in front. To implement your own LogCleanerDele gate, just put it in HBase's classpath and add the fully qualified class name here. Always add the above default log cleaners in the list.

Type: string

Default: org.apache.hadoop.hbase.master.TimeToLiveLogCleaner

hbase.master.logcleaner.ttl

Maximum time an HLog can stay in the *.oldlogdir* directory, after which it will be cleaned by a master thread.

Type: long

Default: 600000

Unit: milliseconds

hbase.master.port

The port the HBase Master should bind to.

Type: int

Default: 60000

Unit: number

hbase.regions.slop

Rebalance if any region server has average + (average * slop) regions. Default is 20% slop.

Type:

Default: 0.2

Unit: float (percent)

hbase.regionserver.class

The RegionServer interface to use. Used by the client opening proxy to remote region server.

Type: class name

Default: org.apache.hadoop.hbase.ipc.HRegionInterface

hbase.regionserver.dns.interface

The name of the network interface from which a region server should report its IP address.

Type: string

Default: "default"

hbase.regionserver.dns.nameserver

The hostname or IP address of the name server (DNS) which a region server should use to determine the hostname used by the master for communication and display purposes.

Type: string

Default: "default"

hbase.regionserver.global.memstore.lowerLimit

When memstores are being forced to flush to make room in memory, keep flushing until we hit this mark. Defaults to 35% of heap. This value equal to hbase.region server.global.memstore.upperLimit causes the minimum possible flushing to occur when updates are blocked due to memstore limiting.

Type: float

Default: 0.35, hardcoded: 0.25

Unit: float (percent)

`hbase.regionserver.global.memstore.upperLimit`

Maximum size of all memstores in a region server before new updates are blocked and flushes are forced. Defaults to 40% of heap.

Type: `float`

Default: `0.4`

Unit: `float (percent)`

`hbase.regionserver.handler.count`

Count of RPC Listener instances spun up on RegionServers. The same property is used by the master for count of master handlers.

Type: `int`

Default: `10`

Unit: `number`

`hbase.regionserver.hlog.reader.impl`

The HLog file reader implementation.

Type: `class name`

Default: `org.apache.hadoop.hbase.regionserver.wal.SequenceFileLogReader`

`hbase.regionserver.hlog.writer.impl`

The HLog file writer implementation.

Type: `class name`

Default: `org.apache.hadoop.hbase.regionserver.wal.SequenceFileLogWriter`

`hbase.regionserver.info.bindAddress`

The address for the HBase RegionServer web UI.

Type: `string`

Default: `0.0.0.0`

`hbase.regionserver.info.port`

The port for the HBase RegionServer web UI. Set to -1 if you do not want the RegionServer UI to run.

Type: `int`

Default: `60030`

Unit: `number`

`hbase.regionserver.info.port.auto`

Whether or not the Master or RegionServer UI should search for a port to bind to. Enables automatic port search if `hbase.regionserver.info.port` is already in use. Useful for testing; turned off by default.

Type: `boolean`

Default: `false`

`hbase.regionserver.kerberos.principal`

Example: "hbase/_HOST@EXAMPLE.COM". The Kerberos principal name that should be used to run the HRegionServer process. The principal name should be in the form user/hostname@DOMAIN. If "_HOST" is used as the hostname portion, it will be replaced with the actual hostname of the running instance. An entry for this principal must exist in the file specified in `hbase.regionserver.keytab.file`.

Type: `string`

Default: `<empty>`

`hbase.regionserver.keytab.file`

Full path to the Kerberos keytab file to use for logging in the configured HRegion-Server server principal.

Type: `string`

Default: `<empty>`

`hbase.regionserver.lease.period`

HRegion server lease period in milliseconds. Default is 60 seconds. Clients must report in within this period else they are considered dead.

Type: `long`

Default: `60000 (1 min)`

Unit: `milliseconds`

`hbase.regionserver.logroll.period`

Period at which we will roll the commit log regardless of how many edits it has.

Type: `long`

Default: `3600000`

Unit: `milliseconds`

`hbase.regionserver.msginterval`

Interval between messages from the RegionServer to the HBase Master in milliseconds.

Type: `int`

Default: `3000 (3 secs)`

Unit: `milliseconds`

`hbase.regionserver.nbreservationblocks`

The number of reservoir blocks of memory released on OOME so we can clean up properly before server shutdown.

Type: `int`

Default: `4`

Unit: `number`

hbase.regionserver.optionallogflushinterval

Sync the HLog to the HDFS after this interval if it has not accumulated enough entries to trigger a sync.

Type: long

Default: 1000 (1 sec)

Unit: milliseconds

hbase.regionserver.port

The port the HBase RegionServer binds to.

Type: int

Default: 60020

Unit: number

hbase.regionserver.regionSplitLimit

Limit for the number of regions after which no more region splitting should take place. This is not a hard limit for the number of regions, but acts as a guideline for the RegionServer to stop splitting after a certain limit. Default is set to MAX_INT; that is, do not block splitting.

Type: int

Default: 2147483647

Unit: number

hbase.rest.port

The port for the HBase REST server.

Type: int

Default: 8080, hardcoded: 9090

Unit: number

hbase.rest.readonly

Defines the mode the REST server will be started in. Possible values are false, which means all HTTP methods are permitted (GET, PUT, POST, and DELETE); and true, which means only the GET method is permitted.

Type: boolean

Default: false

hbase.rootdir

The directory shared by region servers and into which HBase persists. The URL should be fully qualified to include the filesystem scheme. For example, to specify the HDFS directory */hbase* where the HDFS instance's namenode is running at namenode.example.org on port 9000, set this value to hdfs://namenode.exam ple.org:9000/hbase. By default, HBase writes into */tmp*. Change this configuration else all data will be lost on machine restart.

Type: string

Default: `file:///tmp/hbase-${user.name}/hbase`

`hbase.rpc.engine`

Implementation of `org.apache.hadoop.hbase.ipc.RpcEngine` to be used for client/server RPC call marshaling.

Type: class name

Default: `org.apache.hadoop.hbase.ipc.WritableRpcEngine`

`hbase.server.thread.wakefrequency`

Time to sleep in between searches for work (in milliseconds). Used as sleep interval by service threads such as log roller.

Type: `int`

Default: `10000 (10 secs)`

Unit: `milliseconds`

`hbase.tmp.dir`

Temporary directory on the local filesystem. Change this setting to point to a location more permanent than */tmp* (the */tmp* directory is often cleared on machine restart).

Type: `string`

Default: `/tmp/hbase-${user.name}`

`hbase.zookeeper.dns.interface`

The name of the network interface from which a ZooKeeper server should report its IP address.

Type: `string`

Default: "default"

`hbase.zookeeper.dns.nameserver`

The hostname or IP address of the name server (DNS) which a ZooKeeper server should use to determine the hostname used by the master for communication and display purposes.

Type: `string`

Default: "default"

`hbase.zookeeper.leaderport`

Port used by ZooKeeper for leader election. See *http://hadoop.apache.org/zookeeper/docs/r3.1.1/zookeeperStarted.html#sc_RunningReplicatedZooKeeper* for more information.

Type: `int`

Default: `3888`

Unit: `number`

`hbase.zookeeper.peerport`

> Port used by ZooKeeper peers to talk to each other. See *http://hadoop.apache.org/zookeeper/docs/r3.1.1/zookeeperStarted.html#sc_RunningReplicatedZooKeeper* for more information.
>
> *Type:* int
>
> *Default:* 2888
>
> *Unit:* number

`hbase.zookeeper.property.clientPort`

> Property from ZooKeeper's *zoo.cfg* configuration file. The port at which the clients will connect.
>
> *Type:* int
>
> *Default:* 2181
>
> *Unit:* number

`hbase.zookeeper.property.dataDir`

> Property from ZooKeeper's *zoo.cfg* configuration file. The directory where the snapshot is stored.
>
> *Type:* string
>
> *Default:* ${hbase.tmp.dir}/zookeeper

`hbase.zookeeper.property.initLimit`

> Property from ZooKeeper's *zoo.cfg* configuration file. The number of ticks that the initial synchronization phase can take.
>
> *Type:* int
>
> *Default:* 10
>
> *Unit:* number

`hbase.zookeeper.property.maxClientCnxns`

> Property from ZooKeeper's *zoo.cfg* configuration file. Limit on number of concurrent connections (at the socket level) that a single client, identified by IP address, may make to a single member of the ZooKeeper ensemble. Set high to avoid ZooKeeper connection issues running standalone and pseudodistributed.
>
> *Type:* int
>
> *Default:* 30
>
> *Unit:* number

`hbase.zookeeper.property.syncLimit`

> Property from ZooKeeper's *zoo.cfg* configuration file. The number of ticks that can pass between sending a request and getting an acknowledgment.
>
> *Type:* int
>
> *Default:* 5
>
> *Unit:* number

`hbase.zookeeper.quorum`

Comma-separated list of servers in the ZooKeeper Quorum. For example, by default, "host1.mydomain.com,host2.mydomain.com,host3.mydomain.com" is set to localhost for local and pseudodistributed modes of operation. For a fully distributed setup, this should be set to a full list of ZooKeeper quorum servers. If `HBASE_MANAGES_ZK` is set in *hbase-env.sh*, this is the list of servers on which we will start/stop ZooKeeper.

Type: `string`

Default: `localhost`

`hfile.block.cache.size`

Percentage of maximum heap (`-Xmx` setting) to allocate to block cache used by `HFile/StoreFile`. Default of 0.2 means allocate 20%. Set to 0 to disable.

Type: `float`

Default: `0.2`

Unit: `float (percent)`

`zookeeper.session.timeout`

ZooKeeper session timeout. HBase passes this to the ZooKeeper quorum as the suggested maximum time for a session (this setting becomes ZooKeeper's `maxSessionTimeout`). See *http://hadoop.apache.org/zookeeper/docs/current/zookeeperProgrammers.html#ch_zkSessions*. "The client sends a requested timeout, the server responds with the timeout that it can give the client."

Type: `int`

Default: `180000`

Unit: `milliseconds`

`zookeeper.znode.parent`

Root znode for HBase in ZooKeeper. All of HBase's ZooKeeper files that are configured with a relative path will go under this node. By default, all of HBase's ZooKeeper file paths are configured with a relative path, so they will all go under this directory unless changed.

Type: `string`

Default: `/hbase`

`zookeeper.znode.rootserver`

Path to znode holding root region location. This is written by the master and read by clients and region servers. If a relative path is given, the parent folder will be *${zookeeper.znode.parent}*. By default, this means the root location is stored at */hbase/root-region-server*.

Type: `string`

Default: `root-region-server`

Road Map

HBase is still being heavily developed. Here is a road map of what is planned in the next releases.

HBase 0.92.0

This upcoming version is being called the *Coprocessor Release*. The planned availability date is Q3 2011. It adds the following major features:

Coprocessors
> Coprocessors represent a major new feature in HBase. Coprocessors enable users to write code that runs within each region, accessing data directly where it resides. See "Coprocessors" on page 175 for details.

Distributed log splitting
> The write-ahead log (WAL) is now split completely distributed on all region servers in parallel. This brings HBase on a par with Bigtable.

Running tasks in the UI
> Previously it was difficult to know what the servers were working on in the background, such as compactions or splits. This is now visualized in the web-based UIs that the master and region servers provide. See "Web-based UI" on page 277 for details.

Performance improvements
> Many miscellaneous performance enhancements were added to this release to make it the best performing HBase ever. More than 260 fixes went into 0.92.0 (see *https://issues.apache.org/jira/browse/HBASE/fixforversion/12314223* for the full list).

Development for 0.92.0 is still ongoing, even while this book is going into print. Check with the aforementioned link online to see the complete list of features once this version is released.

HBase 0.94.0

Current plans for this version, which is preliminarily being called the *Security Release*, call for an early 2012 release date. This version is scheduled to include the following new features. See *https://issues.apache.org/jira/browse/HBASE/fixforversion/12316419* for more information.

Security
> This release will add Kerberos integration to HBase.

Secondary indexes
> This coprocessor-backed extension allows you to create and maintain secondary indexes based on columns of tables.

Search integration
> This feature lets you create and maintain a search index, for example, based on Apache Lucene, per region, so that you can perform searches on rows and columns.

HFile v2
> This introduces a new storage format to overcome current limitations with the existing file format.

Other interesting issues are also being worked on and may find their way into this release. One of them is the *pluggable block cache* feature: it allows you to facilitate a memory manager outside the Java JRE heap. This will reduce the amount of garbage collection churn a large heap causes—which is one of the concerns when running a large-scale HBase cluster with heavy read and write loads.

Upgrade from Previous Releases

Upgrading HBase involves careful planning, especially when the cluster is currently in production. With the addition of *rolling restarts* (see "Rolling Restarts" on page 447), it has become much easier to update HBase with no downtime.

 Depending on the version of HBase you are using or upgrading to, you may need to upgrade the underlying Hadoop version first so that it matches the required version for the new version of HBase you are installing. Follow the upgrade guide found on the Hadoop website.

Upgrading to HBase 0.90.x

Depending on the versions you are upgrading from, a different set of steps might be necessary to update your existing cluster to a newer version. The following subsections address the more common update scenarios.

From 0.20.x or 0.89.x

This version of 0.90.x HBase can be started on data written by HBase 0.20.x or HBase 0.89.x, and there is no need for a migration step. HBase 0.89.x and 0.90.x do write out the names of region directories differently—they name them with an MD5 hash of the region name rather than a Jenkins hash, which means that once you have started, there is no going back to HBase 0.20.x.

Be sure to remove the *hbase-default.xml* file from your *conf* directory when you upgrade. A 0.20.x version of this file will have suboptimal configurations for HBase 0.90.x. The *hbase-default.xml* file is now bundled into the HBase JAR and read from there. If you would like to review the content of this file, you can find it in the *src* directory at *$HBASE_HOME/src/main/resources/hbase-default.xml* or see Appendix A.

Finally, if upgrading from 0.20.x, check your `.META.` schema in the shell. In the past, it was recommended that users run with a 16 KB `MEMSTORE_FLUSHSIZE`. Execute

```
hbase(main):001:0> scan '-ROOT-'
```

in the shell. This will output the current `.META.` schema. Check if the `MEMSTORE_FLUSH SIZE` size is set to 16 KB (`16384`). If that is the case, you will need to change this. The new default value is 64 MB (`67108864`). Run the script *$HBASE_HOME/bin/set_meta_memstore_size.rb*. This will make the necessary changes to your `.META.` schema. Failure to run this change will cause your cluster to run more slowly.[*]

Within 0.90.x

You can use a rolling restart during any of the minor upgrades. Simply install the new version and restart the region servers using the procedure described in "Rolling Restarts" on page 447.

Upgrading to HBase 0.92.0

No rolling restart is possible, as the wire protocol has changed between versions. You need to prepare the installation in parallel, then shut down the cluster and start the new version of HBase. No migration is needed otherwise.

[*] See "HBASE-3499 Users upgrading to 0.90.0 need to have their .META. table updated with the right MEMSTORE_SIZE" (*http://issues.apache.org/jira/browse/HBASE-3499*) for details.

Distributions

There are more choices to install HBase than using the Apache releases. Here we list what is available alternatively.

Cloudera's Distribution Including Apache Hadoop

Cloudera's Distribution including Apache Hadoop (hereafter CDH) is based on the most recent stable version of Apache Hadoop with numerous patches, backports, and updates. Cloudera makes the distribution available in a number of different formats: source and binary tar files, RPMs, Debian packages, VMware images, and scripts for running CDH in the cloud. CDH is free, released under the Apache 2.0 license and available at *http://www.cloudera.com/hadoop/*.

To simplify deployment, Cloudera hosts packages on public *yum* and *apt* repositories. CDH enables you to install and configure Hadoop, and HBase, on each machine using a single command. Kickstart users can commission entire Hadoop clusters without manual intervention.

CDH manages cross-component versions and provides a stable platform with a compatible set of packages that work together. As of CDH3, the following packages are included, many of which are covered elsewhere in this book:

HDFS	Self-healing distributed filesystem
MapReduce	Powerful, parallel data processing framework
Hadoop Common	A set of utilities that support the Hadoop subprojects
HBase	Hadoop database for random read/write access
Hive	SQL-like queries and tables on large data sets
Pig	Dataflow language and compiler
Oozie	Workflow for interdependent Hadoop jobs
Sqoop	Integrates databases and data warehouses with Hadoop

Flume	Highly reliable, configurable streaming data collection
ZooKeeper	Coordination service for distributed applications
Hue	User interface framework and SDK for visual Hadoop applications
Whirr	Library for running Hadoop, and HBase, in the cloud

In regard to HBase, CDH solves the issue of running a truly reliable cluster setup, as it has all the required HDFS patches to enable durability. The Hadoop project itself has no officially supported release in the 0.20.x family that has the required additions to guarantee that no data is lost in case of a server crash.

To download CDH, visit *http://www.cloudera.com/downloads/*.

Hush SQL Schema

Here is the *HBase URL Shortener*, or *Hush*, schema expressed in SQL:

```
CREATE TABLE user (
  id INTEGER UNSIGNED NOT NULL AUTO_INCREMENT,
  username CHAR(20) NOT NULL,
  credentials CHAR(12) NOT NULL,
  roles CHAR(10) NOT NULL, // could be a separate table "userroles", but \
    for the sake of brevity it is folded in here, eg. "AU" == "Admin,User"
  firstname CHAR(20),
  lastname CHAR(30),
  email VARCHAR(60),
  CONSTRAINT pk_user PRIMARY KEY (id),
  CONSTRAINT idx_user_username UNIQUE INDEX (username)
);

CREATE TABLE url (
  id INTEGER UNSIGNED NOT NULL AUTO_INCREMENT,
  url VARCHAR(4096) NOT NULL,
  refShortId CHAR(8),
  title VARCHAR(200),
  description VARCHAR(400),
  content TEXT,
  CONSTRAINT pk_url (id),
)

CREATE TABLE shorturl (
  id INTEGER UNSIGNED NOT NULL AUTO_INCREMENT,
  userId INTEGER,
  urlId INTEGER,
  shortId CHAR(8) NOT NULL,
  refShortId CHAR(8),
  description VARCHAR(400),
  CONSTRAINT pk_shorturl (id),
  CONSTRAINT idx_shorturl_shortid UNIQUE INDEX (shortId),
  FOREIGN KEY fk_user (userId) REFERENCES user (id),
  FOREIGN KEY fk_url (urlId) REFERENCES url (id)
)

CREATE TABLE click (
```

```
    id INTEGER UNSIGNED NOT NULL AUTO_INCREMENT,
    datestamp DATETIME,
    shortId CHAR(8) NOT NULL,
    category CHAR(2),
    dimension CHAR(4),
    counter INTEGER UNSIGNED,
    CONSTRAINT pk_clicks (id),
    FOREIGN KEY fk_shortid (shortId) REFERENCES shortid (id);
)
```

HBase Versus Bigtable

Overall, HBase implements close to all of the features described in Chapter 1. Where it differs, it may have to because either the Bigtable paper was not very clear to begin with, or it relies on other open source projects to provide various services and those simply work differently.

HBase stores timestamps in milliseconds—as opposed to Bigtable, which uses microseconds. This is not much of an issue and can possibly be attributed to C and Java having different preferred timer resolutions.

While we have not yet addressed the specific details, it should be pointed out that both also use different compression algorithms. HBase uses those supplied in Java, but can also use LZO (with a bit of work; we will look into this later).[*] Bigtable has a two-phase compression using BMDiff and Zippy.

HBase has *coprocessors* that are different from what Sawzall, the scripting language used in Bigtable to filter or aggregate data, or the Bigtable Coprocessor framework,[†] provides. The details on Google's coprocessor implementation are rather sketchy, so if there are more differences, they are unknown. On the other hand, HBase has support for server-side filters that help reduce the amount of data being moved from the server to the client.

HBase does primarily work with the *Hadoop Distributed File System* (HDFS), while Bigtable uses GFS. But HBase can also work on other filesystems thanks to the pluggable FileSystem class provided by Hadoop. There are implementations for Amazon S3 (raw or emulated HDFS), as well as EBS.

HBase cannot map storage files into memory, something that is available in Bigtable. There is ongoing work in HBase to optimize I/O performance, and with the addition

---

[*] While writing this book, Google made Zippy available under the Apache license and the name *Snappy*. The work to integrate it with HBase is still in progress. See the project's online repository (*http://code.google.com/p/snappy/*) for details.

[†] Jeff Dean gave a talk at LADIS '09 (*http://www.scribd.com/doc/21631448/Dean-Keynote-Ladis2009*) (pages 66-67) mentioning coprocessors.

of more widespread use of Java's *New I/O* (NIO), it may be something that could be enhanced.

Bigtable has a concept called *locality groups*, which allow the client to group specific column families together and apply shared features, such as compression. This is also useful when the contained columns are accessed together, as all the data is stored in the same storage files. Column families in Bigtable are used for accounting and access control. In HBase, on the other hand, there is only the concept of column families, combining the features that Bigtable has in two distinct concepts.

Apart from the block cache that both systems have, Bigtable also implements a *key/value cache*, probably for cells that are accessed a lot.

The handling and implementation of the commit log also differs slightly. Bigtable has two commit logs to handle slow writes and is able to switch between them to compensate for that. This could be implemented in HBase, but it does not seem to be a topic for discussion, and therefore is omitted for the time being.

In contrast, HBase has an option to skip the commit log completely on writes for performance reasons and when the possibility of not being able to replay those logs after a server crash is acceptable.

The METADATA table in Bigtable is also used to store secondary information such as log events related to each tablet. This historical data can be used to analyze tablet transitions, splits, and/or merges. HBase had the notion of a *historian* in earlier versions that implemented the same concept, but its performance was not good enough and it has been removed.

While splitting regions/tablets is the same for both, merging is handled differently. HBase has a tool that helps you to merge regions manually, while in Bigtable this is handled automatically by the master. Merging in HBase is a delicate operation and currently is left to the operator to decide what is best.

Another very minor difference is that the master in Bigtable is doing the garbage collection of obsolete storage files. One reason for this could be the fact that, in Bigtable, the storage files are tracked in the METADATA table. For HBase, the cleanup is done by the region server that has done the split and no file location is recorded explicitly.

Bigtable can memory-map entire storage files and use them to perform lookups without a single disk seek. HBase has an in-memory option per column family and uses its LRU cache[‡] to retain blocks for subsequent use.

There are also some differences in the compaction algorithms. For example, a merging compaction also includes a memtable flush. Mostly, though, they are the same and simply use different names.

[‡] See Cache algorithms (*http://en.wikipedia.org/wiki/LRU_cache*) on Wikipedia.

Region names, as stored in the meta table in HBase, are a combination of the table name, the start row key, and an ID. In Bigtable, the corresponding tablet names consist of the table identifier and the end row. This has a few implications when it comes to locating data in the storage files (see "Read Path" on page 342).

Finally, it can be noted that HBase has two separate catalog tables, -ROOT- and .META., while in Bigtable the root table, since in both systems it only ever consists of one single region/tablet, is stored as part of the meta table. The first tablet in the METADATA table is the root tablet, and all subsequent ones are the meta tablets. This is just an implementation detail.

Index

We'd like to hear your suggestions for improving our indexes. Send email to *index@oreilly.com*.

balance_switch command, HBase Shell, 274, 432, 445
base64 command, 248
Base64 encoding, with REST, 247, 248
BaseEndpointCoprocessor class, 195–199
BaseMasterObserver class, 192–193
BaseRegionObserver class, 187–189
Batch class, 194, 197
batch clients, 257
batch operations
    for scans, 129–132, 162
    on tables, 114–118
batch() method, HTable class, 114–118, 168
Bigtable storage architecture, 17, 27, 29, 497–499
"Bigtable: A Distributed Storage System for Structured Data" (paper, by Google), xix, 17
bin directory, 57
BinaryComparator class, 139
BinaryPrefixComparator class, 139
binarySearch() method, Bytes class, 135
bioinformatics, data requirements of, 5
BitComparator class, 139
block cache, 216
    Bloom filters affecting, 379
    controlling use of, 96, 124, 435
    enabling and disabling, 216
    metrics for, 394
    settings for, 437
block replication, 293–294
blocks, 329–332
    compressing, 330
    size of, 215, 330
Bloom filters, 217, 377–380
bypass() method, ObserverContext class, 187
Bytes class, 77, 97, 134–135

C

caching, 127
    (see also block cache; Memcached)
    regions, 134
    for scan operations, 127–132, 434, 476
Cacti server, JMXToolkit on, 416
call() method, Batch class, 194
CAP (consistency, availability, and partition tolerance) theorem, 9
CAS (compare-and-set)
    for delete operations, 112

for put operations, 93–95
CaS (core aggregation switch), 40
Cascading, 267–268
causal consistency, 9
CDH3 Hadoop distribution, 47, 493–494
cells, 17–21
    timestamp for (see versioning)
cellular services, data requirements of, 5
CentOS, 41
checkAndDelete() method, HTable class, 112–114
checkAndPut() method, HTable class, 93–95
checkHBaseAvailable() method, HBaseAdmin class, 230
checkTableModifiable() method, MasterServices class, 191
Chef, deployment using, 70
CLASSPATH variable, 67
clearRegionCache() method, HTable class, 134
client API, 23–24, 75
    batch operations, 114–118
    byte conversion operations, 134–135
    connection handling, 203–205
    coprocessors, 175–199
    counters, 168–174
    delete method, 105–114
    filters, 137–167
    get method, 95–105
    HTablePool class, 199–202
    put method, 76–95
    row locks, 118–122
    scan operations, 122–132
    utility methods, 133–134
client library, 26
client-managed search integration, 374
client-managed secondary indexes, 370
client-side write buffer (see write buffer)
clients, 241–244
    (see also HBase Shell; web-based UI for HBase)
    batch, 257–268
    configuration for, 67
    interactive, 244–257
Clojure-based MapReduce API, 258
close() method, HBaseAdmin class, 220
close() method, HTable class, 133
close() method, ResultScanner class, 124

preCheckAndDelete() method,
    RegionObserver class, 185
preCheckAndPut() method, RegionObserver
    class, 185
preClose() method, RegionObserver class, 184
preCompact() method, RegionObserver class,
    184
preCreateTable() method, MasterObserver
    class, 190
preDelete() method, RegionObserver class,
    184
preDeleteColumn() method, MasterObserver
    class, 190
preDeleteTable() method, MasterObserver
    class, 190
predicate deletions, 19, 317
predicate pushdown, 137
preDisableTable() method, MasterObserver
    class, 190
preEnableTable() method, MasterObserver
    class, 190
preExists() method, RegionObserver class,
    185
PrefixFilter class, 149, 167
preFlush() method, RegionObserver class, 184
preGet() method, RegionObserver class, 184
preGetClosestRowBefore() method,
    RegionObserver class, 185
preIncrement() method, RegionObserver class,
    185
preIncrementColumnValue() method,
    RegionObserver class, 185
preModifyColumn() method, MasterObserver
    class, 190
preModifyTable() method, MasterObserver
    class, 190
preMove() method, MasterObserver class, 190
preOpen() method, RegionObserver class, 183
prepare() method, ObserverContext class, 187
prePut() method, RegionObserver class, 184
preScannerClose() method, RegionObserver
    class, 185
preScannerNext() method, RegionObserver
    class, 185
preScannerOpen() method, RegionObserver
    class, 185
preShutdown() method, MasterObserver class,
    190
preSplit() method, RegionObserver class, 184

preStopMaster() method, MasterObserver
    class, 190
preUnassign() method, MasterObserver class,
    190
preWALRestore() method, RegionObserver
    class, 184
prewarmRegionCache() method, HTable class,
    134
process limits, 49–51
processors (see CPU)
profiles, Maven, 297–298
Project Object Model (see POM)
properties, for configuration, 475–487
Protocol Buffers, 242
    encoding for REST, 249
    schema used by, 369
pseudodistributed mode, 59, 448–450
PSU (power supply unit), requirements for, 39
PTVR (Persistent time varying rate), 392
Puppet, deployment using, 70
Put class, 77–80
put command, HBase Shell, 33, 273
Put type, KeyValue class, 85
put() method, HTable class, 76–95
    (see also checkAndPut() method, HTable
    class)
    list-based, 90–93
    for multiple operations, 86–93
    for single operations, 77–83
putLong() method, Bytes class, 134
putTable() method, HTablePool class, 201
PyHBase client, 257

Q

QualifierFilter class, 144, 167
quit command, HBase Shell, 270
quotes, in HBase Shell, 271

R

RAID, 38
RAM (see memory)
RandomRowFilter class, 155, 167
range partitions, 22
Rate (R) metric type, 390
raw() method, Result class, 98
RDBMS (Relational Database Management
    System)
    converting to HBase, 13–16

limitations of, 2–3, 5–8
read-only tables, 211
read/write performance, 11
readFields() method, Writable interface, 208
record IDs, custom versioning for, 385
RecordReader class, 290
recovered.edits directory, 325, 340, 341
Red Hat Enterprise Linux (see RHEL)
Red Hat Package Manager (see RPM)
Reducer class, 292
referential integrity, 6
RegexStringComparator class, 139
region hotspotting, 430
region servers, 22, 26
    adding, 452
    for fully distributed mode, 60
    heap for, 472
    local, adding, 449
    logfiles created by, 469
    metrics exposed by, 394–396
    ports for, 466
    properties for, 481–484
    rolling restart for, 447
    shutting down, troubleshooting, 472–473
    startup check for, 427
    status information for, 72, 233, 279, 283
    stopping, 232, 445–446
    workloads of, handling, 419
RegionCoprocessorEnvironment class, 185
.regioninfo file, 325
RegionLoad class, 235
RegionObserver class, 182–189
regions, 22–23, 209
    assigning to a server, 274
    cache for, 134
    closing, 230, 274
    compacting, 231, 274, 281, 328–329
    deploying or undeploying, 232
    files for, 324–326
    flushing, 231, 274
    life-cycle state changes, 183–184, 348
    listing, 280, 281
    lookups for, 345
    map of, 134
    merging, 433–434
    moving to a different server, 232, 274
    presplitting, 430–432
    reassigning to a new server, 468
    size of, increasing, 437

splitting, 22, 231, 274, 281, 326–328, 429
    status information for, 233, 235
    in transition, map of, 233, 279
    unassigning, 274
RegionScanner class, 344
regionservers file, 60, 65, 66, 68
    (see also configuration)
RegionSplitter utility, 431
Relational Database Management System (see RDBMS)
remote method invocation (RMI), 413
remote procedure call (see RPC)
RemoteAdmin class, 250
RemoteHTable class, 250–251
remove() method, HTableDescriptor class, 212
removeFamily() method, HTableDescriptor class, 210
remove_peer command, HBase Shell, 274
replication, 351–356, 462–464
    for column families, 218
    in HBase Shell, 274
Representational State Transfer (see REST)
requests, current number of, 233
reset() method, Filter interface, 162
REST (Representational State Transfer), 241–244–251, 484
    Base64 encoding used in, 247, 248
    documentation for, 245
    formats supported by, 246–249
    Java client for, 250–251
    JSON format for, 248–249
    plain text format for, 246–247
    port for, 245
    Protocol Buffer format for, 249
    raw binary format for, 249
    starting gateway server for, 244
    stopping, 245
    verifying operation of, 245
    XML format for, 247–248
Result class, 98–100
ResultScanner class, 124–127, 435
RHEL (Red Hat Enterprise Linux), 42
RMI (remote method invocation), 413
rolling restarts, 447
-ROOT- table, 345
RootComparator class, 84
RootKeyComparator class, 84
round-trip time, 86

About the Author

Lars George has been involved with HBase since 2007, and became a full HBase committer in 2009. He has spoken at various Hadoop User Group meetings, as well as large conferences such as FOSDEM in Brussels. He also started the Munich OpenHUG meetings. He now works for Cloudera as a Solutions Architect to support Hadoop and HBase in and around Europe through technical support, consulting work, and training.

Colophon

The animal on the cover of *HBase: The Definitive Guide* is a Clydesdale horse. Named for the district in Scotland where it originates, the breed dates back to the early nineteenth century, when local mares were crossed with imported Flemish stallions. The horse was bred to fulfill the needs of farmers within the district, as well as to carry coal and other heavy haulage throughout the country. Due to its reliability as a heavy draft horse, by the early twentieth century, the Clydesdale was exported to many countries, including Australia, New Zealand, Canada, and the United States. The mechanical age brought a decline in the breed, and although the late twentieth century saw a slight rise in popularity and numbers, the horse is still considered vulnerable to extinction.

The modern Clydesdale is slightly larger than the original Scottish horse, with breed standards dictating that the height should range between 16 and 18 hands (about 64 to 72 inches) and the weight between 1,600 and 2,200 pounds. However, the appearance of the horse has mostly remained the same throughout its history. Especially compared to other draft breeds, the Clydesdale has very distinctive characteristics, marked particularly by its feathered legs and high-stepping gait. It is usually bay, brown, or black in color, and often roan, or white hair scattered throughout the coat, is also seen. Its darkly colored body stands in contrast to its bright white face and legs, though it is not uncommon for the legs to be black. The horse is also well known for the size of its feet, which are fitted into horseshoes comparable in size to dinner plates.

Although largely replaced by the tractor, Clydesdales remain an indispensable asset for some agricultural work, and are also ridden and shown, used for carriage services, and kept for pleasure in many places. In the United States, the best-known ambassadors for the breed are perhaps the horses that make up the team used in marketing campaigns for the Anheuser-Busch Brewing Company.

The cover image is from *Wood's Animate Creation*. The cover font is Adobe ITC Garamond. The text font is Linotype Birka; the heading font is Adobe Myriad Condensed; and the code font is LucasFont's TheSansMonoCondensed.

Get even more for your money.

Join the O'Reilly Community, and register the O'Reilly books you own. It's free, and you'll get:

- $4.99 ebook upgrade offer
- 40% upgrade offer on O'Reilly print books
- Membership discounts on books and events
- Free lifetime updates to ebooks and videos
- Multiple ebook formats, DRM FREE
- Participation in the O'Reilly community
- Newsletters
- Account management
- 100% Satisfaction Guarantee

Signing up is easy:

1. Go to: oreilly.com/go/register
2. Create an O'Reilly login.
3. Provide your address.
4. Register your books.

Note: English-language books only

To order books online:
oreilly.com/store

For questions about products or an order:
orders@oreilly.com

To sign up to get topic-specific email announcements and/or news about upcoming books, conferences, special offers, and new technologies:
elists@oreilly.com

For technical questions about book content:
booktech@oreilly.com

To submit new book proposals to our editors:
proposals@oreilly.com

O'Reilly books are available in multiple DRM-free ebook formats. For more information:
oreilly.com/ebooks

Spreading the knowledge of innovators   oreilly.com

Have it your way.

CPSIA information can be obtained at www.ICGtesting.com
Printed in the USA
LVOW051452290911

248438LV00003B/42/P